Social Psychology

To Pam and Maddie

Social Psychology

Core Concepts and Emerging Trends

Daniel W. Barrett

Western Connecticut State University

Los Angeles | London | New Delhi
Singapore | Washington DC

Los Angeles | London | New Delhi
Singapore | Washington DC

FOR INFORMATION:

SAGE Publications, Inc.
2455 Teller Road
Thousand Oaks, California 91320
E-mail: order@sagepub.com

SAGE Publications Ltd.
1 Oliver's Yard
55 City Road
London EC1Y 1SP
United Kingdom

SAGE Publications India Pvt. Ltd.
B 1/I 1 Mohan Cooperative Industrial Area
Mathura Road, New Delhi 110 044
India

SAGE Publications Asia-Pacific Pte. Ltd.
3 Church Street
#10-04 Samsung Hub
Singapore 049483

Printed in the United States of America

Library of Congress Cataloging-in-Publication Data

Names: Barrett, Daniel W., author.

Title: Social psychology : core concepts and emerging trends / Daniel W. Barrett.

Description: Los Angeles : SAGE, [2017] | Includes bibliographical references and index.

Identifiers: LCCN 2015038684

ISBN 978-1-5063-1060-2 (pbk. : alk. paper)

Subjects: LCSH: Social psychology.

Classification: LCC HM1033 .B36 2017 | DDC 302—dc23 LC record available at http://lccn.loc .gov/2015038684

This book is printed on acid-free paper.

Acquisitions Editor: Reid Hester
Development Editor: Nathan Davidson
Editorial Assistant: Morgan McCardell
Production Editor: Veronica Stapleton Hooper
Copy Editor: Karin Rathert
Typesetter: C&M Digitals (P) Ltd.
Proofreader: Dennis W. Webb
Indexer: Judy Hunt
Cover Designer: Glenn Vogel
Marketing Manager: Katherine Hepburn

SUSTAINABLE FORESTRY INITIATIVE
Certified Chain of Custody
Promoting Sustainable Forestry
www.sfiprogram.org
SFI-01268
SFI label applies to text stock

16 17 18 19 20 10 9 8 7 6 5 4 3 2 1

Brief Contents

Part V Affiliative Behavior / 347

Part VI Emerging Topics in Social Psychology / 475

Detailed Contents

4 | What Is the Self?   110

5 | Social Perception

Part IV Moral Behavior 271

8 | Helping 272

9 | Aggression 308

Part VI Emerging Topics in Social Psychology 475

13 | Three Emerging Trends: The Social Psychology of Happiness, Religion, and Sustainability 476

Preface

WHY ANOTHER SOCIAL PSYCHOLOGY TEXTBOOK?

Social Psychology: Core Concepts and Emerging Trends provides a focused survey of social psychology's essential theories, principles, concepts, and research, and limits attention given to those at the margins. This tailored approach reflects my philosophy of teaching, which emphasizes deep, meaningful learning. Over the years I have developed my version of the so-called *inverted or flipped* classroom, in which students are exposed to the primary content outside of class via readings and videos and engage in what has traditionally been homework—solving problems, applying concepts, and so forth—during class. The overwhelming majority of class time is devoted to discussion, critical inquiry, application, and related class activities. I have been able to cut my lectures down to no more than 20% of class time for any given section and often even less. My students appreciate my strategy and commonly tell me that they have learned *more* and remembered *better* the material from my class than from most of their college courses and, at the same time, have greatly *enjoyed* the classroom experience. Perhaps more importantly, they really seem to "get" the core concepts in social psychology as well as key emerging trends. *Core Concepts* is designed for introductory courses in social psychology offered at institutions of higher education across the nation, from large universities to small liberal arts schools to community colleges.

I have written this text in part to share my teaching philosophy and pedagogy with other social psychology instructors. *Core Concepts* is intentionally moderate in length in order to facilitate this focused approach for both faculty and students. To accomplish this, I needed to separate the proverbial wheat from the chaff in the ever-expanding field of social psychology and, consequently, omit some theory and research coverage that you would expect to find in a more comprehensive text. Although instructors may not concur with all of my choices, I hope that they will agree that I have captured the essence of social psychology. Moreover, *Core Concepts*—like my social psychology class—is friendly, accessible, and application focused yet rigorous and challenging.

A second motive for writing *Core Concepts* was to address what I saw as a lack of a substantive unifying framework in most modern textbooks. The unfortunate by-product is that students come to understand social psychology as an assortment of loosely related theories, concepts, and studies that resembles a random list of "must see" historical sites rather than a carefully planned, thematic tour of the landscape. *Core Concepts* presents a thematic, principle-based framework that thoughtfully guides students on their journey through the topography of social psychology. Please see below for a detailed accounting of the themes that will serve as a guide for students throughout this text.

The third major impetus for *Core Concepts* was to address what I saw as the failure of other texts to present the true nature of science. Most traditional texts paint an incomplete picture of the scientific enterprise, tending to portray science as a set of outcomes and static "facts." Science, however, is more appropriately characterized as a self-correcting *process* of asking questions, developing hypotheses, and designing research in an attempt to answer these questions.

This misunderstanding of science seems to be partially the result of the relegation of the scientific method to a free standing, often ponderously boring chapter, as if methodology were not integral to the science of social psychology. Chapters and large sections devoted to research methods are probably the most poorly received and misunderstood parts of social psychology textbooks. The impression that students are left with is that research methods are just one more set of "facts" to be memorized for an exam and then forgotten.

In contrast, *Core Concepts* offers a more dynamic depiction of the scientific method and distributes discussion of research methods across all of the chapters. My text incorporates methods *in situ* and, by doing so, both increases their perceived relevance to a thorough understanding of the field and enhances their interest value. After reading *Core Concepts*, students should be able to demonstrate meaningful advances in their overall scientific literacy, a skill that is becoming increasingly critical in college and in the life beyond.

THEMATIC HIGHLIGHTS

Grounding in Life's Fundamental Questions. *Core Concepts* casts social psychology in terms of fundamental questions about human existence that both perplex and fascinate college students. In my experience, undergraduates are intrigued by deep questions—such as whether or not they have free will or how independent or conforming they are—and enjoy thinking about and discussing them. These expansive questions will be tied to specific bodies of research and particular outcomes that will provide arguments and empirical evidence to further student thinking on these topics—even if social psychology is unable to definitively answer them.

These fundamental issues cut across the major topics and are the following:

- Free will. Are we free to make our own decisions and choices? Are we in conscious control of our actions?
- Independence. Are we conformists or individuals following our own paths? How and when do others influence us?
- Rationality. Are we capable of truly objective or unbiased thinking? Can we separate our emotional and cognitive processes?
- Sociality. Do we need other people and, if so, why?
- The Self. Who am I? What is the nature of the self?
- Morality. Are humans intrinsically prone to and/or capable of truly prosocial/ selfless behavior or are we naturally aggressive/selfish?

Basic Principles of Social Psychology. Core Concepts articulates four fundamental principles of social psychology that are critical for understanding the field's approach to the explanation of social behavior. The principles are that social behavior is purposive, stems from both dispositional and situational influences, is affected by how people construe the social world, and is cultural. The principles are useful because they serve as general guides to our thinking and as starting points for our empirical investigations into the causes of social behavior.

Social Neuroscience and the Social Brain. *Core Concepts* is the only social psychology textbook that devotes a chapter to the origin and nature of the social brain and the methods of social neuroscience. The role of the brain in social behavior is increasingly studied, and understanding how the brain works is becoming essential to understanding social psychology. This chapter provides an accessible overview of brain biology and the primary tools of social neuroscience.

Emerging Trends. *Core Concepts* is the only textbook that provides significant coverage to the relatively new fields of the social psychology of happiness, religion, and sustainability. Research on the first trend—happiness—has grown tremendously over the last decade and has yet to reach its apex. After decades under the radar, religion has caught the interest of social psychologists and is slowly emerging as a topic worthy of theoretical and empirical work and publishable in our major journals. I expect that we will see the study of religion moving closer to the mainstream of social psychology in the coming decade. The importance of understanding the social psychology of sustainability—our third trend—needs little explanation. We should—indeed we must—adopt more sustainable lifestyles if we are to prevent or at least slow catastrophic climate change. Social psychology has demonstrated its ability to tackle other difficult problems, and I am confident that it can help us here too. My hope is that students use what they learn in this section to begin changing the world.

PEDAGOGICAL HIGHLIGHTS

As a professor genuinely interested in meaningful learning and as the former director of Western's Center for Excellence in Learning and Teaching, I have delved deeply into the scholarship of learning and teaching. My overall approach to this course—focusing on depth rather than breadth—and my inclusion of the pedagogical components described below—are in large part a result of what I have learned about the science of learning. Getting students to think about what they will read, are reading, and have read are crucial, as is learning how to apply material so that it becomes both meaningful and memorable.

Each chapter includes the following:

- An introductory story, topic, or question relevant to the chapter content
- *Think Ahead!* questions designed to spur thinking at the beginning of the chapter

- *Think Again!* questions peppered throughout the text that are intended to provoke critical thinking, review key ideas, and encourage students to transfer knowledge to new applications. These questions could easily be deployed to stimulate small group, full class, or online discussion, and could serve as written assignments to be handed in or posted to a discussion board.
- Applying Social Psychology sections highlighting applications of social psychology to health, work, and the law
- Self-reflection exercises that allow students to respond to pertinent questions and then turn the page to learn more
- Presentation of research methods relevant to the chapter content
- Research boxes that illustrate hypotheses, methods, results, and conclusions of relevant studies
- Listing of Core Concepts at the end of each chapter
- *Think Further!* questions and applications at the end of each chapter to stimulate deeper thinking
- Suggested classic and recent readings at the end of each chapter
- Online student resources

  - Direct links and access to relevant articles published by the Association for Psychological Science and the Society for Personality and Social Psychology provided at no cost to the student as well as links to scholarly videos, such as TED Talks and YouTube clips
  - Recent linked articles focused on key issues from the chapters
  - Flashcards for each glossary term
  - 15 practice questions for each chapter

- Online instructor manual with complete PowerPoint slides, lecture outlines, learning objectives, suggestions for in-class discussion and individual and small group activities, and downloadable graphics.

So there you have it. I hope you find this textbook to be relevant, concise, accurate, and readable. I also hope that it will stimulate your interest and spur you to further explore the nature, causes, and consequences of social behavior. If you have questions, comments, and/or suggestions for improvement, I hope that you will contact me.

ACKNOWLEDGMENTS

First, I'd like to thank the people at Sage: Executive Editor Reid Hester for helping to finalize the text and see it through to publication; Michael Carmichael and Luke Block at Sage U.K. for their guidance and patience and for keeping the book on track; Michele Sordi, vice president, for bringing me to SAGE, embracing my vision for the book, and believing in me as an author; Nathan Davidson and Lucy Berbeo, for helping to strengthen the text and online materials; and Morgan McCardell, Keri Dickens, Monira Begum, and Allana Clogan, who provided valuable editorial assistance at various stages along the way. Second, I'd like to acknowledge Wendy Nelson who, as a publisher's textbook representative, listened to my frustration with existing textbooks and encouraged me to write my own. Third, I want to express my gratitude to the former students who assisted me with literature searches, locating online resources, and other tasks: Jessica Richards, Catherine Di Leo, Adrienne Ostrove, Shannon Engel, Michele Liscio, Mike Dellagoia, Harrison Duncan, Matt Korduner, and Hannah Grassie. Fourth, I want to state my appreciation for the Society for Personality and Social Psychology (SPSP) and the Association for Psychological Science (APS) for allowing us to provide students with free access to key published articles. Fifth, I'd like thank the individuals who reviewed my book at various stages along the way, including Amy E. Sickel (Walden University), Anila Bhagavatula (California State University, Long Beach), Laura N. May (South University), Pamela Lemons (Salt Lake Community College), John Skowronski (Northern Illinois University), Warren Reich (Hunter College, City University of New York), Courtney Mozo (Old Dominion University), Jamie Loran Franco-Zamudio (Spring Hill College), and Melissa Streeter (University of North Carolina, Wilmington). Finally, and most importantly, I'd like to thank my family: my wonderful wife Pam—for her unwavering emotional support and her invaluable help with editing and preparing the text and ancillary materials—and my daughter Maddie—for putting up with my (occasional) grumpiness and intense focus on the book.

ⓢSAGE edge™

SAGE edge offers a robust online environment you can access anytime, anywhere, and features an impressive array of free tools and resources to keep you on the cutting edge of your learning experience. Go to **edge.sagepub.com/barrett** to access the SAGE edge companion website.

SAGE edge for Students provides a personalized approach to help you accomplish your coursework goals in an easy-to-use learning environment.

- Mobile-friendly **eFlashcards** strengthen your understanding of key terms and concepts.
- Mobile-friendly **practice quizzes** allow you to independently assess your mastery of course material.
- A complete **online action plan** includes tips and feedback on your progress and allows you to individualize your learning experience.
- **Chapter summaries** with **learning objectives** reinforce the most important material.

- **Interactive exercises** and meaningful web links make it easy to mine internet resources, further explore topics, and answer critical thinking questions.
- EXCLUSIVE! Access to full-text **SAGE journal articles** that have been carefully chosen to support and expand on the concepts presented in each chapter.

SAGE edge for Instructors supports your teaching by making it easy to integrate quality content and create a rich learning environment for students.

- An **author-created test bank** with 125 questions per chapter, including multiple choice, short answer and essay, provides a diverse range of pre-written options as well as the opportunity to edit any question and/or insert personalized questions to effectively assess students' progress and understanding.
- Editable, chapter-specific and **author-created PowerPoint® slides** offer complete flexibility for creating a multimedia presentation for the course.
- **Sample course syllabi** for semester and quarter courses provide suggested models for structuring one's course.
- An **Instructor's Manual** provides chapter-by-chapter lecture notes, discussion questions, class activities, and more to ease preparation for lectures and class discussions.
- A robust set of **Web Exercises** hones in on three key areas (Applications, Social Media and Technology, and In the News), connecting chapter coverage with current web resources and related, carefully crafted follow-up exercises to help students master key concepts.
- **Multimedia content** includes videos that appeal to students with different learning styles.

About the Author

Daniel W. Barrett is a professor in the Department of Psychology at Western Connecticut State University, Danbury, Connecticut. He received his PhD in Social Psychology from Arizona State University, Tempe, Arizona, and his BA from the College of Social Studies, Wesleyan University, Middletown, Connecticut. Prior to joining WCSU, Dr. Barrett served as a postdoctoral research fellow in Health Communication at the Annenberg School for Communication, University of Pennsylvania. At WCSU, he has served as the director of the Center for Excellence in Learning and Teaching and the director of Faculty Advising. He is currently the president of the University Senate. His research interests include persuasion, social influence, and cross-cultural psychology.

FOUNDATIONS OF SOCIAL PSYCHOLOGY

1

Introducing Social Psychology

A married couple in West Hollywood, CA, celebrate the June 2015 Supreme Court ruling legalizing same-sex marriage.

David McNew/Stringer/Getty Images News/Getty Images.

LEARNING OBJECTIVES

1.1 Define social psychology and contrast it with the other social sciences and psychology subdisciplines.

1.2 Identify the six fundamental questions of human existence and explain their relevance to social psychology.

1.3 Outline how social psychology has evolved since the early 20th century; explain how the first textbooks contributed to the development of social psychology; describe Kurt Lewin's contribution to understanding social behavior; discuss the three levels of explanation and illustrate how they can help us understand social behavior.

1.4 Identify the four principles of social psychology and provide an example to illustrate each.

1.5 Discuss the hindsight bias and its relevance to the study of social psychology; describe the four essential characteristics of science as a process; identify the three goals of science.

1.6 Explain what hypotheses and theories are and show their role in scientific research; contrast correlational and causal relationships; define experiment, independent variable, dependent variable, experimental group, control group, and confound, and discuss what is meant by experimental control and why it is important.

⑤SAGE edge™

Get the edge on your studies.
edge.sagepub.com/barrett

Take a quiz to find out what you've learned.
Watch videos that enhance chapter content.
Explore related web and social media activities.

THE MYSTERY OF ROMANTIC ATTRACTION

On June 26, 2013, the U.S. Supreme Court struck down the federal Defense of Marriage Act (DOMA), which had denied federal medical and other job-related benefits to spouses in same-sex marriages. This decision, along with recent related efforts in many states to allow same-sex couples to marry, form civil unions, and obtain other privileges accorded to heterosexual couples across the nation, reignited longstanding debates in the United States about same-sex attraction. President Barack Obama extended health and other benefits to gay partners of federal employees one year later, in June 2014. Following the U.S. Supreme Court's decision in *Obergefell v. Hodges* issued on June 26, 2015, gay marriage is now allowed throughout the United States. People in the United States and around the globe—including both those who embrace and those who object to same-sex relations—have struggled to understand it. Is same-sex attraction "normal"? Or is it deviant, perhaps the product of character, spiritual, or genetic defects? The way a given culture explains the origins of social behavior impacts how it is handled in the media, by its government, and by its religious institutions. Are same-sex relations encouraged, tolerated, or outlawed? Are homosexuals persecuted, prosecuted, institutionalized, or just left alone? If it is a mental illness, can it be cured?

Like many laypeople, social psychologists have wondered about the nature and origins of sexual attraction, including between individuals of the same sex. However, social psychologists are different than laypeople because we examine such social behaviors more systematically and bring to the table a wealth of theories and research in our efforts to explain them. For instance, we may ask whether the principles underlying opposite-sex attraction and relationships apply to all people, regardless of their sexual preferences. In addition, social psychologists would consider a wide range of possible explanatory factors, including variation across cultures, social influences, genetic factors, and a person's learning history. In fact, these types of factors are the same ones that we'll look to when we try to understand other social behavior. We will return more specifically to the topic of sexual attraction later in this chapter and again in Chapter 11 on affiliation and love.

More broadly, social psychologists utilize a multilevel approach that incorporates several types of explanatory mechanisms as we try to understand human social behavior. This book provides a wide-ranging survey of the most important social psychological theories, approaches, and research findings in an effort to show you, the reader, how social psychologists have sought and continue to seek answers to fundamental questions of human existence, such as free will, human sociality, independence, and moral behavior. Rather than provide an overly detailed and exhaustive coverage of social psychology, I focus on the core of our field: delivering only the most important and useful concepts, theories, and research. I do not want readers to get lost in the forest by focusing too much on the trees! Along our path to achieving that goal, we'll touch on many fascinating topics and themes, including how we think about ourselves and other people, the roles of biology and culture in shaping human thought and behavior, attitudes and attitude change, aggression, romantic love, and prejudice, among others. Hold on for an exciting tour of the social psychology of human behavior!

Think Ahead!

1. *What is social psychology and why should you study it?*
2. *How can social psychology help to understand human nature?*
3. *What makes social psychology unique among the other sciences?*

THE PERSON IN THE CROWD In the modern world, it can be difficult to develop a sense of individuality and self-determination in the midst of social pressures to conform.

Geoff Tompkinson / Science Source.

SOCIAL PSYCHOLOGY MATTERS: DEFINING THE FIELD

What is social psychology? Before offering a definition, let's briefly discuss the nature of definitions. Definitions can be tricky, because they are immensely important yet at the same time exceedingly trivial. They are important because they provide a mini snapshot of the field, a first exposure for the new student. Definitions matter because we need to be able to agree on what we are talking about—we need a common language so that we can understand each other. Yet definitions are trivial as well (this is heresy coming from an academic), because there are often many ways to define a single word, concept, or scientific discipline. Definitions are not set in stone but instead evolve over time. Moreover, definitions are somewhat independent from actual work in a field: The science, teaching, and practice of social psychology will continue to take place in thousands of laboratories, classrooms, and applied settings around the globe regardless of how a particular person or book defines social psychology. In the end to be useful, definitions must provide *clarity,* be *generally agreed upon,* and serve as a *launching point* for further investigation. Now let's move onto our definition of social psychology.

Social psychologists seek to understand how other people affect the behavior, thoughts, and feelings of individuals. We might examine, for instance, how a person's Facebook friends affect what she posts online or how being the lone minority member of a group affects that member's thoughts about himself. In both of these cases we ask about social aspects of human existence: people influencing individuals. The emphasis on *social* distinguishes our discipline from other domains of psychology, and *social* is of course the core concept in our field: **Social psychology** *is the scientific study of the social experiences and behaviors of individuals.* Let's examine each element of this definition.

First, social psychology is a *science:* It relies on the rigorous application of scientific methods in the same way that physics or biology does. Like these other sciences, social psychology is not a collection of commonsense, simple observations and intuitive ideas. Rather, it is a systematic examination of social phenomena that utilizes both traditional and novel scientific methods involving careful experimentation, advanced technology, and sophisticated statistical analyses (and sometimes develops new ones). For example, we investigate the sexual orientation of many people using rigorous research, as opposed to merely asking opinions from a few individuals.

Second, social psychology focuses on *individuals* rather than groups. For instance, we are interested in how a crowd affects its members but not in how one crowd influences another crowd. Third, we'd like to understand the ways in which individual social *behavior* is affected by others. Social behaviors are observable actions that stem from the direct or indirect influence of others. With regards to sexual attraction, one question social psychologists would try to answer is how other people impact who we are attracted to.

Finally, social psychologists study the individual's social *experiences.* The term *experience* encompasses conscious thoughts and feelings as well as nonconscious processes, brain activation, and hormone regulation. Thus, neurophysiological changes that are neither self-reportable nor obvious to an independent observer—say, activation of the amygdala—are included in this definition. We'll have much more to say about nonconscious processes later, but for now, suffice it to say that we are not always aware of how others affect our thoughts, feelings, and behavior. Again returning to our opening vignette, social psychologists are likely to examine how both conscious and nonconscious processes affect to whom we are attracted.

In sum, social psychologists investigate how people influence the social experiences and behaviors of other humans. For the sake of simplicity, I will often shorten "social

Social Psychology: Scientific study of the social experiences and behaviors of individuals

experiences and behaviors" to "social behaviors" and will make it clear when I am referring only to observable actions. What social psychology is and is not will be further clarified below when we contrast it with other branches of the social sciences and of psychology.

[Dear Student: I have placed Think Again! questions throughout the text in order to help you gauge your comprehension of and memory for what you have just read. I urge you to try to answer each question you encounter right away—preferably by writing it down—and, if needed, to look back at the chapter to solidify your understanding.]

Think Again!

1. *In your own words, what is social psychology?*

2. *Name three social behaviors that you would like to understand better and hope to learn more about in this text.*

Why Social Psychology?

If you are reading this book, then you are likely already enrolled in a social psychology course. Why should you stay in it or sign up if you haven't already? Well, consider that social behavior is virtually everywhere around (and inside) us all of the time. To social psychologists, the world is our proverbial oyster. Many of the same behaviors that fascinate you, as a student, captivate our imagination and literally call out for investigation. There are four compelling reasons to study social psychology. First, social psychology investigates the most fascinating topic in the universe: us. Second, social psychology provides tremendous insight into *what people do* and *why people do it*. You'll undoubtedly come to a much deeper understanding of yourself and others by the time you finish reading this text. Students invariably tell me how much they have learned about why they and others do what they do and how they excitedly share what they learn with partners, family, and friends. For instance, they'll tell a friend that they observed a car salesperson appeal to the consistency principle and now understand why it worked (more on this later). Or they realized that others did not in fact notice their "bad hair" day as much as they had expected. You too will be applying the lessons from social psychology almost immediately—and doing so is one effective way to learn them.

Third, social psychology is *useful*: It helps us to solve serious real-world problems in ways that other sciences cannot. It aids us in improving schools, increasing helping behavior, reducing violence, and overcoming prejudice. Many of our central research streams originate in our desire to change the world for the better and are often rooted in our personal experiences and observations. For instance, Muzafer Sherif began to study social psychology after having narrowly escaped death in a violent ethnic dispute and sought to comprehend, among other things, the nature and causes of intergroup conflict

FIGURE 1.1   Muzafer Sherif on Why He Studied Social Psychology

> "THEY CAME . . . AND THEY STARTED KILLING PEOPLE RIGHT AND LEFT . . .
>
> the immediate thing that concerned me was that somebody else beside me was killed . . . I thought . . . that I'd be killed too that day. Then the soldier . . . looked at me for a few minutes. He was ready to stab me. Then he walked away . . . There and then I became interested in understanding why these things were happening among human beings"

Source: Aron & Aron (1989). The Heart of Social Psychology).

(reported in Trotter, 1985) (see Figure 1.1). On a less serious note, I may be walking across campus and notice a staff person throwing an empty glass bottle into a trash bin rather than the adjacent bright blue bin clearly displaying a recycling symbol and ask myself, "Hmm, why didn't she recycle that bottle?" I could choose to conduct a study to figure out why (I have in fact studied recycling behavior).

Fourth, social psychology is *fun*. Not only do we learn the sometimes-surprising reasons people do what they do, but also we often get to concoct funny experiments to figure out why. For instance, one prominent social psychologist convinced research participants to suck on a pacifier while waiting to begin an experiment on Freud (Sarnoff & Zimbardo, 1961). I surely wish I had seen that one!

Social Psychology Is Unique

Social psychology is a diverse, dynamic discipline that investigates a wide range of topics, issues, and aspects of human social behavior. Although all of the social sciences study people, social psychology stands apart in the way that we examine the person in the group, take into account multiple levels of analysis, and focus primarily on laboratory research. Let's briefly contrast social psychology with several other social sciences and psychology subdisciplines.

Sociology overlaps with social psychology, because it also emphasizes social aspects of human existence. However, sociology examines group-level phenomena—such as societal trends, cultural norms, the effects of race or social class, and so forth—without examining the internal processes occurring at the individual level that are affected by those phenomena. **Anthropology** is similar to social psychology in that both examine the relationship between culture and social behavior. Anthropology seeks culture-level explanations for human behavior by exploring a specific culture in-depth utilizing observational research, whereas social psychologists study cultural and noncultural explanations, primarily using laboratory experimentation, and also typically compare social behavior in multiple cultures.

Sociology:
Examines group-level phenomena—such as societal trends, cultural norms, the effects of race or social class, and so forth

Anthropology:
Seeks culture-level explanations for human behavior by exploring a specific culture in depth, utilizing primarily observational research

Biological/Physiological Psychology inquires about the influence of genes, hormones, brain functioning and structure, and other elements of the nervous system on all kinds of human behavior. As we've seen, social psychology takes biology into account, but it focuses exclusively on social behavior and considers other, nonbiological levels of explanation for it.

Cognitive psychology seeks to explain mental processes such as memory, problem solving, decision-making, language, and the nature of consciousness. Although social psychologists examine some of these same processes, we limit ourselves to their *social* aspects, such as *person* memory, judgments of *persons,* and so forth.

Clinical psychology examines the nature, causes, and consequences of mental disorders and dysfunction of individuals who deviate from the norm and seeks ways to treat them. Social psychology emphasizes normal psychological functioning; how *most people* act, feel, or think.

Personality psychologists investigate the development and nature of personality traits over the lifespan. Social psychologists often examine personality characteristics but are more interested in how social situations affect most people, regardless of their personalities. Both clinical and personality psychologists are primarily concerned with individual-level causes, whereas social psychologists balance individual- and group-level explanations for social behavior.

> ## *Think Again!*
>
> 1. *Take a social behavior—say helping others—and imagine how social psychologists might study it. Then contrast that with the way other kinds of psychologists and social scientists might examine it.*

SOCIAL PSYCHOLOGY AND THE QUEST FOR HUMAN NATURE

What is human nature? If you had to list the fundamental topics that get to the very heart of what it means to be human, what would they be? When I ask my students, friends, or dead philosophers, several common themes emerge: Do humans have free will? Are people mostly independent or conformist? Are we rational? What is the self? Do we really need other people? Are people inherently good? These issues go a long way toward capturing the essence of humanity. (See Table 1.1.) Questions like these often come to the fore during late adolescence and early adulthood and are most salient during our college years (Hofer & Pintrich, 1997). They have been pondered across thousands of years of human history and in cultures all around the globe, in part because their answers have profound implications for how we understand ourselves. The fact

---

Biological/ Physiological Psychology: Examines the influence of genes, hormones, brain functioning and structure and other elements of the nervous system on all kinds of human behavior

Cognitive Psychology: Seeks to explain mental processes such as memory, problem solving, decision-making, language, and the nature of consciousness

Clinical Psychology: Examines the nature, causes, and consequences of mental disorders and dysfunction of individuals who deviate from the norm and seeks ways to treat them

Personality Psychology: Investigates the development and nature of personality traits over the lifespan

that we *can* and *do* contemplate these questions in part defines the very essence of who we—as intelligent, self-aware beings—are as well as how we are different from other animals. The French sculptor Auguste Rodin captured the human propensity for wonder in his famous work, *The Thinker* (see photo).

These six enduring questions will serve as continuing themes throughout this book, providing reminders about the relevance of social psychological research to the core of human nature and to our everyday lives. One appealing aspect of social psychology is that it can shed light on these questions. Social psychology cannot give life meaning or determine what is good or evil, but it can inform our thinking about these topics by scientifically studying what we do and why we do it. Although these questions are both philosophical and psychological, we'll leave the philosophy to the philosophers and in this text focus on only their psychological, scientific aspects. Let's elaborate on these questions.

Auguste Rodin's
The Thinker

Getty—516604053.

TABLE 1.1   Life's Fundamental Questions

Question	Example
Do we have free will?	Are we in conscious control of our actions or are they determined by forces over which we have no control?
Are we independent or conformist?	How much do other people influence what you do and what you say? Are you relatively independent from others or mostly conformist?
Are we rational beings?	Can we engage in cold, rational thinking that is not affected by our feelings and motivations?
What is the self?	Who am I? What is my psychological core?
Do we need other people and, if so, why?	Why are our relationships so important, and what goals do they help us meet? Why do we need friends or lovers?
Are we inherently altruistic or selfish?	Is it possible to help another person for purely selfless reasons, with no material or psychological benefit to the helper?

Free Will

If you raise your hand to ask a question in class or choose to eat chocolate cheesecake rather than artichoke salad, are you making your decisions consciously? That is, do you do them out of your own free will? When I ask my students this, the overwhelming majority believe that yes, we have free will, and *of course* humans can consciously control what we do or think (Sharif et al., 2014). But psychologists are not so sure (Baer, Kaufman, & Baumeister, 2008; Hassin, Uleman, & Bargh, 2005). There is ample evidence that nonconscious processes—those we are *not* aware of—significantly affect what we think, feel, and do (Andersen, Moskowitz, Blair, & Nosek, 2007; Bar-Anan, Wilson, & Hassin, 2010; Evans & Frankish, 2009). For example, would you believe that exposure to words that relate to being elderly can make you act as if you were much older? In a fascinating study of nonconscious influences on behavior, participants were asked to unscramble sentences containing words suggestive of being older—like *lonely, grey, wrinkled, forgetful*—and this activity caused them to walk more slowly in comparison to a control group (Bargh, Chen, & Burrows, 1996). Since this behavior change occurred below the level of awareness, it could be argued that it undermined the free will of the participants. What do you think? More broadly, in what ways do think you exercise your free will? (To gauge your own beliefs about free will, see Self-Reflection Box 1.1.)

Independence

A second important question has to do with how independent we are from outside influences. How much do other people affect what you do and what you say? Are you relatively independent from others or mostly conformist? What about obedience to authority—would you be able to resist authority when it matters most, like if someone's well being depended on it? Whereas the free will question probes the effects of internal, nonconscious processes on social thinking, feeling, and behavior, the independence question asks how external pressures—namely, people—around us can affect those same things. It is obvious that humans can sometimes change other humans. Social psychologists investigate *when* and *how* those social influences occur (Bocchiaro & Zimbardo, 2010; Cialdini, 2008; Kim & Hommel, 2015; Pratkanis, 2007a). The subject of social influence is integral to the science of social psychology and, in fact, several of the field's best-known studies deal with this very topic. In one, individuals were asked—actually, told—by an experimenter to continue giving another person severe electric shocks, even after that person had stopped responding and may have been unconscious or worse (more on this in Chapter 6) (Milgram, 1965). If you were in that situation, what would you do—go along and administer more shocks or rebel against the experimenter and refuse to follow his request?

Rationality

We are often encouraged by friends, family, and even professors to be "objective" and not allow personal feelings and motivations to interfere with judgments and decisions. Put aside your biases and look at this issue from the perspective of a disinterested third party!

SELF-REFLECTION 1.1
Do You Think You Have Free Will? (Part 1)

Do you believe that you have the free will to choose what to do or not to do? In your opinion, is your fate in your own hands? In one 36-nation study, over 70% of respondents think that it is (International Social Survey Programme, 1998). One measure of belief in free will is the Free Will and Determinism Scale (FAD-Plus, Paulhus & Carey, 2011), which can be found in Table 1.2. Take a minute and complete the questions below and then turn the page to learn more about your beliefs about free will.

TABLE 1.2   Free Will and Determinism Scale

For each statement, choose a number from 1 to 5 to indicate how much you agree or disagree and then turn the page to better understand your score.

Item	Response options				
	Strongly disagree	Disagree	Undecided	Agree	Strongly agree
1. People have complete control over the decisions they make.	1	2	3	4	5
2. People must take full responsibility for any bad choices they make.	1	2	3	4	5
3. People can overcome any obstacles if they truly want to.	1	2	3	4	5
4. Criminals are totally responsible for the bad things they do.	1	2	3	4	5
5. People have complete free will.	1	2	3	4	5
6. People are always at fault for their bad behavior.	1	2	3	4	5
7. Strength of mind can always overcome the body's desires.	1	2	3	4	5

Source: Paulhus, D. L., & Carey, J. M. (2011). The FAD-Plus: Measuring lay beliefs regarding free will and related constructs. *Journal of Personality Assessment, 93*, 96–104.

TURN THE PAGE TO FIND OUR ANSWERS.

SELF-REFLECTION 1.2
Do You Think You Have Free Will? (Part 2)

Add up your answers for all 7 items and then divide by 7 to get your average or mean score. Paulhus and Carey (2011) found that the average female college student scored a 3.31 and the average male college student 3.47. How do you compare? If your total is less than these, then your belief in free will is weaker than average; If it is greater, then your belief is stronger than average. Fun fact: According to one study, students who have stronger beliefs in free will were *less* likely to cheat on an experimental math task than those who have weaker beliefs (Vohs & Schooler, 2008). It seems that when people feel less responsible for their behavior, their behavior becomes less moral (Carey & Paulhus, 2013).

Often we try, but can we really do it? Do you think that it is possible to truly separate our thinking from our feeling?

Social psychologists used to assume that we could engage in rational, dispassionate, unbiased thinking—what we call "cold cognition"—but research in the past couple of decades has undermined that assumption (Gladwin & Figner, 2015; Kahneman, 2011). We now recognize that cognition is very often "hot," which is to say that it is affected by our emotions and motivations. This is the case even when we try to be unbiased. For example, in one study participants were more likely to judge information as valid when they were in a good mood versus a neutral mood (Garcia-Marques, Mackie, Claypool, & Garcia-Marques, 2004). This demonstrates how feeling can alter thinking. Have you ever wondered whether someone who claims to be unbiased is letting his feelings affect his judgment without realizing it?

The Self

Virtually all of us, at one time or another, have asked "Who am I?" The answer to this question is called our self-concept or identity: It is the set of beliefs we have about the characteristics we possess. The self-concept is at the core of everything we think, feel, or do. It is our anchor and the filter through which we perceive ourselves and the world. Because the self lies at the center of our being, social psychologists have exerted tremendous effort to better understand how social experiences affect and are affected by it (Baumeister, 2010; Leary & Toner, 2015; Sedikides & Spencer, 2007).

One of the key influences on the self-concept is the culture that we grow up in. For instance, persons from **individualistic cultures** tend to define themselves as separate from other people, whereas those from **collectivistic cultures** are more likely to define themselves *in terms of* their relationships to others (Chua, Carbonneau, Milyavskaya, & Koestner, 2015; Markus & Kitayama, 1991). Our conception of the self is closely connected to the culture in which we reside. We will have much more to say about the cultural dimension of social behavior later. For now, be aware that whether we think of ourselves as fundamentally separate from or connected to others has implications for many other

Individualistic Culture: Type of society in which people's self-concepts tend to be stable, not tied to particular groups, and people place their personal preferences and goals above those of the group and value individual choice

Collectivistic Culture: Type of society in which people's self-concepts tend to be intimately tied to and defined by their group memberships, people subordinate personal preferences and goals to the group's, and where individual choice is not highly valued

aspects of our lives, such as our motivations to perform well and the kinds of choices that we make. What is your self-concept, and how do you think it is affected by culture?

Sociality

One of the most fascinating and complex aspects of human nature is our *sociality,* which is our tendency to develop and maintain relationships with others (Crosier, Webster, & Dillon, 2012; Gifford, 2013; Leary, 2010; Semin & Echterhoff, 2011). Humans, like other primates, are fundamentally social creatures (Gamble, Gowlett, & Dunbar, 2014). In this text, we'll examine why our relationships are so important and what sorts of goals they help us meet. Why do you think we need friends or lovers? Each semester I ask my students to think about one of their stronger platonic (nonromantic) friendships and to write down the reasons the friendship developed and why they maintained it. Students frequently mention similarity of attitudes and interests, that they can have fun together, or the ability to depend on each other in times of need, which are all of course important. However, one factor that they often neglect is physical proximity—who they live near, work with, or sit next to in class. As we will discuss in Chapter 11, proximity is one of the strongest influences on who we befriend. In fact, a study of police cadets—who were both seated in class and assigned rooms in a residence hall alphabetically—showed that last name was a strong predictor of who became friends with whom (Segal, 1974). Cadets with last names that begin with the same or nearby letter were more likely to become friends than other pairs of cadets. Why do you think that you have the romantic and nonromantic relationships that you have? What role might proximity have played?

People are inherently social creatures.

Will & Deni McIntyre / Science Source.

Morality

One of the questions that my students love to discuss (but have a difficult time resolving) is whether or not *pure* altruism exists. Pure altruism occurs when a person helps another in a completely selfless way and derives absolutely no benefit from helping (Batson, Ahmad, & Stocks, 2011; Newman & Cain, 2014). Students offer compelling arguments on both sides of the issue. One student may say, for instance, that altruism must exist, because how else can we explain the actions of a firefighter who loses her life while heroically trying to save an unknown child? Typically, another responds that the firefighter did not expect to die and, had she lived, would have benefited, because helping makes us feel good. At the same time, still others wonder how we can even speak of human goodness when there have been so many instances of mass killing and senseless violence in our history. Some people argue that not only are humans selfish, but we can be downright evil (Miller, 2004a)!

Social psychologists have extensively studied moral behavior in order to understand the factors that lead people to engage in helpful, prosocial behavior versus undesirable, antisocial behavior. In one study, researchers gave young children a chance to "steal" extra candy during Halloween trick-or-treating. How they behaved depended on whether or not they could be personally identified (Diener, Fraser, Beaman, & Kelem, 1976). The kids were much more likely to steal when they thought they were anonymous. As you will see, whether or not a person behaves morally depends on a number of personal and situational factors. Think about a time when you helped someone else. What motivated you? Did you gain some benefit, even a small one?

These six topics—free will, independence, rationality, the self, sociality, and morality—together get at the essence of human nature. Each has served as a launching pad for some of the most exciting and thought-provoking research in social psychology. Although the questions have spurred separate research streams, it is critical to note that these seemingly disparate topics are interconnected in important ways. For instance, the extent to which we believe we have free will is closely tied to our identity or self-concept. Identity, in turn, is connected to our sociality through the groups to which we belong and the people with whom we associate. Furthermore, the types of groups that we join and the strength of our bonds with those groups impact the extent to which we are independent or conforming. Moreover, our ability to develop and maintain friendships is partially dependent on

Think Again!

1. *What are the six enduring questions about human nature?*
2. *Which one(s) do you find most interesting? Which do you find most difficult to wrap your head around?*
3. *Can you think of examples in your own life or the lives of people around you that illustrate each of them?*

how we treat others, either morally or immorally. These examples illustrate the myriad of interrelationships among the six questions. It is easy to see, then, how social psychological science is grounded in fundamental questions about human nature. Let's turn our attention to the historical development of social psychology.

THE EVOLVING NATURE OF SOCIAL PSYCHOLOGY: YESTERDAY, TODAY, AND TOMORROW

Early Social Psychological Studies

Several of our fundamental questions about human nature can be traced back to the ancient Greeks more than 2,000 years ago. For instance, Plato examined the nature of nonromantic (now often referred to as platonic) friendship in *The Symposium* and other dialogues. The pioneering social psychologist Gordon Allport (1985) was right when he argued that the questions that form the core of current social psychological thinking were precisely those asked by its intellectual predecessors.

The most important difference between the philosophical musings of the ancient Greeks and today's social psychology is the application of the scientific method. Unlike social psychologists, both ancient and contemporary philosophers base their theories primarily on intuition and logic and generally are not interested in collecting data to test them (Jackson, 1988). The modern origins of social psychology stem from the fertile intellectual milieu of the late 19th century, when psychology—originally viewed as a branch of philosophy—became an independent discipline (G. W. Allport, 1985). Around the turn of the century, psychologists began running experiments and collecting data to see if their hypotheses about human behavior reflected what actually happened in the real world!

One of the earliest studies was conducted by the French agricultural engineer Ringelmann in the 1880s (published in 1913) after he noted that men who participated in a rope pulling task exerted *less* effort when working in tandem with other rope pullers than when pulling alone. Ringelmann found a way to measure how much effort each person exerted on the task and concluded that individuals worked harder when alone than when in a group. Several years later Triplett (1897) observed that bicyclists rode faster when racing against others versus against a clock and developed a relatively simple laboratory study to explore the notion that people exert more effort on a task in the presence of others. He asked 40 adolescents to turn a fishing reel either alone or in the presence of another child doing the same task. Half of the children worked faster when paired with another child versus when reeling alone, one-quarter worked at a slower speed, and the remaining one-quarter neither increased nor decreased their solitary speed. Although Triplett concluded from his study that the mere presence of other individuals led to *greater* effort by facilitating the production of what he called "nervous energy" (Triplett, 1897), later analysis revealed that the differences were not statistically significant (Stroebe, 2012; Strube, 2005).

Okay, so Ringelmann found that group activities can reduce individual effort, yet Triplett came to an apparently opposite conclusion. Does the presence of others make us lazier or harder working? The simple answer is that both tendencies occur—sometimes being in a group leads to more effort, sometimes less (Zajonc, 1965). We discuss why in Chapter 12 on group behavior. Puzzles like this are the bread and butter of social psychologists and have spurred countless creative experiments and clever theories in social psychology.

The First Textbooks

Another milestone in the history of our field was the publication of the first social psychology textbooks. In 1908 William McDougall (1908/1960) and Edward Ross (1908) separately published books titled *Social Psychology*. Why is the publication of a textbook (which seems commonplace enough) significant? Textbooks indicate that a field of inquiry has come into its own and help it to establish an identity separate from competing fields. Textbooks (like the one you are reading now) serve at least two purposes. One is a pedagogical one: They are designed to facilitate learning a particular field of knowledge. A second function is to define the focus and scope of the field of knowledge. Both of these early textbooks helped to launch social psychology as an independent discipline.

Although each of these was important and helped to publicize social psychology, neither identified many of the core concepts that are critical to contemporary social psychology. This was particularly true in McDougall's case, in which the primary emphasis was on the role of instincts in producing human social behavior. Like McDougall, contemporary social psychologists acknowledge the important role that evolutionary pressures and prewired tendencies play in the generation of social behavior (Neuberg, Kenrick, & Schaller, 2010). However, as discussed below, there are many other important influences on social behavior that McDougall provided little or no treatment of. In contrast, Ross's (1908) text was much closer to the heart of what we now recognize as social psychology: Social psychology, according to Ross, "deals with the uniformities due to social causes, *i.e.*, to *mental contacts* or *mental interactions*" (p. 3). According to Jones (1985), despite the early experimental findings by Ringelmann and Triplett, social psychology remained largely nonexperimental until the 1930s. It is unfortunate that the experimental gains initiated by Ringelmann and Triplett were not followed by controlled research in social psychology until decades later. Instead of empirical research, social psychologists like McDougall and Ross were primarily occupied by the "big questions" of human existence, such as the nature versus nurture controversy and whether social behavior was a product of an individual's personality or of social pressures (Jackson, 1988).

About a generation after those first texts, Floyd Allport (1924) published a textbook that helped to redefine social psychology, an event that has been called the beginning of experimental social psychology (Stroebe, 2012). Allport was very critical of existing conceptualizations of social psychology and sought to place the field on a firm scientific footing. He argued that many key concepts, such as the "group mind," were pseudoscientific; they were vague notions that were resistant to truly scientific examination and missed the critical role of the individual (Collier, Minton, & Reynolds, 1991). According to Allport, the causes of social behavior can be uncovered not through the investigation of large-scale phenomena but rather via analysis of the psychology of the individual. Allport initiated a shift in focus from the *group* to the *individual* and from *nonscientific* to *scientific* investigations.

A Creative Synthesis: The Mutual Influences of the Person and the Situation

During its formative years in the early 20th century, social psychology was heavily influenced by B. F. Skinner's behaviorism—which focused solely on external causes—and Sigmund Freud's psychoanalysis—which emphasized internal factors. These two perspectives on the causes of social behavior were seemingly incompatible. Resolution of this disagreement between advocates of the externalist versus internalist positions was achieved by Kurt Lewin, a Jewish émigré who fled Germany to escape persecution by the Nazis. Lewin theorized that human behavior was a product of *both* the person and the situation. That is, human social behavior can only be understood when both characteristics of the person and features of the environment are considered. For instance, understanding why a young mother yelled at her son at the local grocery store requires knowledge of her internal states (thoughts, emotions, personality traits, etc.) and of the context (what the child had done, the number and nature of bystanders, etc.).

Lewin (1946) called his formulation "field theory" in order to signify the need to examine the person in the context. Let's take a person walking through a crowd as an example. Any explanation of the path she takes is incomplete unless we consider how assertively she walks, her goals in passing through, and so forth, as well as aspects of the crowd, such as its density, whether or not people are moving, and so forth (see Figure 1.2). Lewin (1946) offered a simple yet elegant representation of this formulation: $B = F(P,E)$. Behavior (B), Lewin argued, was a function (F) or product of both the person (P) and the environment (E).

Will Joanna walk around the crowd, through the crowd, or to her friends en route to her destination? This figure illustrates Lewin's formulation of behavior as the product of the person and the environment ($B = F(P,E)$). Joanna's behavior (B) depends on person (P) and environment (E) factors such as (a) her internal traits (e.g., assertive and willing to push through the crowd, conscientious about getting to her job on time, etc.), (b) who she encounters (how many people, density, etc.), (c) how important her friends are; and (d) what her goals are (going to work or the art museum).

During the 1940s, 1950s, and 1960s, social psychology was strongly influenced by the atrocities of World War II and other historical events and, especially in the United States, developed an increasingly experimental focus as it examined their psychological underpinning (Moscovici & Markova, 2006). For instance, the unimaginable horror of the Holocaust led Stanley Milgram (1963) to investigate why people obey authority, even when ordered to harm innocent victims. In Chapter 6 we will examine Stanley Milgram's research on obedience, along with other forms of social influence.

One major theoretical advance that occurred during these years was prompted by Leon Festinger's desire to understand why people sometimes say one thing but do the opposite and/or simultaneously hold two attitudes that conflict with one another. Festinger (1957)

FIGURE 1.2   Lewin's Field Theory

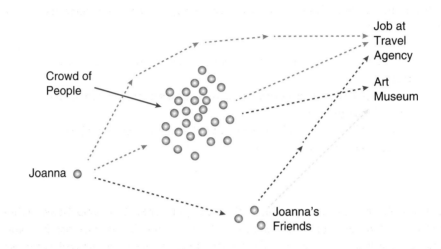

created the *theory of cognitive dissonance* to help explain these inconsistencies, arguing that the existence of these inconsistencies sometimes produces discomfort or dissonance in people. Festinger postulated that, in general, people will strive to overcome this dissonance by changing an attitude, belief, or behavior accordingly and thereby removing the inconsistency. Festinger's theory was enormously influential and will be discussed in much greater detail in Chapter 7 on persuasion.

Further Developments: The Multiple Causes of Social Behavior

Although the basic groundwork for social psychological science was laid out by these earlier thinkers, social psychology matured throughout the remainder of the 20th century. During those years—and continuing into the 21st century—social psychologists have expanded our theory and research to incorporate additional influences on social behavior. When you think about why people do what they do, what kinds of explanations come to mind? Consider the reasons we are romantically attracted to particular others of the same or opposite sex. Is romantic attraction based in our genes? Personality? Family background? Cultural and media influences? If you were asked to choose one of these explanations, which would it be?

I suspect that you found it hard to select just one. Social psychologists are with you, and one of social psychology's most appealing and important features is that it considers multiple explanations for any given behavior. Social phenomena are not so simple that they can be fully explained by any single factor, and consequently, social psychology has incorporated a number of approaches to understanding them.

In fact, several of the most important developments in social psychology since the middle of last century reflect these different approaches to explaining social behavior.

These different perspectives or levels of analysis complement each other, allowing us to develop a more holistic understanding of social phenomena (Bruner, 1990; De Houwer & Moors, 2015). These three levels of explanation vary in scope and method and are the (see Figure 1.3)

- evolutionary level, which emphasizes the genetic history of the human race;
- contextual level, which looks at group pressures, societal influences, and cultural background;
- individual level, which asks about a person's own learning history, experiences, and cognitive processes.

Evolutionary Factors

The early American social psychologist McDougall, influenced by Charles Darwin's theory of evolution, placed natural instincts at the forefront of his explanations for social behavior. McDougall's instinct-based approach quickly fell out of favor as a primary cause of human behavior and was replaced with a more externally focused, behaviorist perspective (Jackson, 1988). As a result, for several decades little attention was devoted to evolutionary or biological influences on social behavior. However, since the 1990s social psychologists have come a long way toward remedying this oversight, and today the study of biological influences on social psychological processes has been integrated into the mainstream of our science (Duntley & Buss, 2008; Kenrick & Cohen, 2012).

FIGURE 1.3   Different Levels of Explanation for Social Behavior

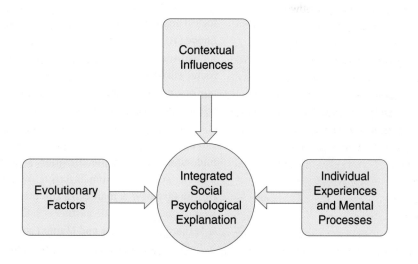

Natural Selection:
Genes that tend to
increase the chances
of survival of their
carrier are more
likely to be passed on
to a new generation

Social psychologists have recognized how traits handed down to us by our ancestors continue to influence social functioning. This evolutionary perspective derives from Darwin's theory of **natural selection**, which, in a nutshell, states that genes that tend to increase the chances of survival of their carrier are more likely to be passed on to a new generation (Darwin, 1859/1994). In other words, these genes—what are called adaptive genes—endow their animal or plant carrier with advantages that make them more likely to survive and reproduce in comparison to those that do not have them. Darwin recognized that there is natural variation in the genes of the members of a species, and that as a result, some members are better adapted to their environments than are others (see photo). The fortunate members have a higher probability of producing healthy offspring and, over time, their adaptive genes and corresponding traits become more common in the population. Eventually, virtually all members of the species carry the adaptive traits. For example, all humans (and all primates) have opposable thumbs, a feature that we now take for granted but that evolved over the course of millions of years.

One of the implications of natural selection is that characteristics—whether physiological or psychological—that are universally shared in a species are very likely the result of evolution. If similar psychological tendencies are found in humans regardless of culture, then there is a high probability that evolutionary pressures are responsible. For instance, individuals in all cultures share a taboo against incest. Whenever I talk to my students about incest, they shake their heads and show expressions of disgust. Yes, it is disgusting to think about—but why? Once we get past the mere disgust factor, students correctly point out that inbreeding increases the chances that offspring will have characteristics—genetic defects—that decrease the probability of survival. Evolutionary pressures have led to universal incest avoidance, and the disgust that we feel about incest is a psychological adaptation that has minimized its likelihood (HBO's fantasy series *Game of Thrones* notwithstanding!). Biology clearly has a profound effect on social behavior. Returning to our opening example, how might our biology affect our sexual orientation?

A recent study nicely illustrates how the evolutionary perspective can be applied to understanding romantic attraction. Consider that the scent of a woman during ovulation can impact how a man rates the attractiveness of potential female partners (S. L. Miller & Maner, 2011). Miller and Maner (2011) had individual males work on a puzzle involving

Charles Darwin

Darwin

©iStockphoto.com/stockcam.

building blocks with a young female who was secretly working with the experimenter and was trained to refrain from flirtatious behavior. After the task the men were asked to rate her attractiveness, and how highly they rated her depended on two factors: whether or not they were in a romantic relationship and, believe it or not, whether or not she was ovulating. Single males rated her as more attractive when she was fertile versus when she was not, but men with partners showed the opposite tendency. Committed men downgraded her attractiveness, as if they were trying to avoid the temptation of an attractive woman! This is just one recent example of how biological factors can influence social behavior.

Moreover, advances in technology have ushered in the new subfield of social neuroscience that studies the relationships between social psychology and the brain (see Figure 1.4) (Todorov, Fiske, & Prentice, 2011). Social neuroscience applies sophisticated technology to investigating the complex interrelationships between social psychological phenomena—thoughts, feelings, and behavior—and the human nervous system (Ochsner, 2007). Chapter 2 provides a detailed explication of the logic and methods of social neuroscience, and we will discuss it throughout the text to show how it can complement existing approaches to a wide variety of topics.

FIGURE 1.4   Social Neuroscience: Connecting Brain and Social Behavior

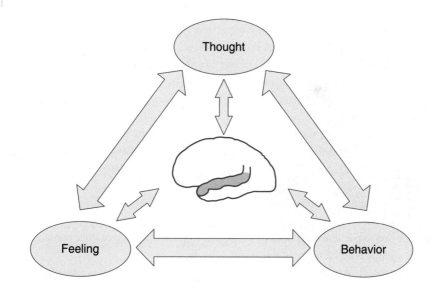

Social neuroscience—sometimes called social cognitive neuroscience—uses advanced technology to examine the interrelationships among the brain and social experiences, including thoughts, feelings, and behaviors.

Sometimes called social cognitive neuroscience—social neuroscience uses advanced technology to examine the interrelationships among the brain and social experiences, including thoughts, feelings, and behaviors.

Contextual Influences

This second level of analysis focuses on group-level explanations for social behavior and compliments insights gleaned from the evolutionary approach. Here we focus on broad influences such as culture, social class, race, and religion. For example, Leon Mann (1981) adopted this approach when he investigated how crowd size impacts the likelihood that onlookers encourage—or bait—a would-be suicide jumper into actually leaping from a bridge or building. Interestingly, he found that baiting was more prevalent in larger groups! We discuss additional ways in which group size affects social behavior in the chapters on social influence, persuasion, and group processes (Chapters 6, 7, and 12, respectively).

For much of the 20th century, psychologists mostly studied wealthy white North American male college students and assumed that the findings were universal and therefore as valid in Cairo or Rio de Janeiro as in Boston (Heine, 2010a). In other words, culture's effects on social behavior were not widely recognized by psychologists. However, in recent years there has been an increasing recognition of the profound effects of culture on our social behavior, including phenomena as varied as self-concept, self-esteem, perceptions of time, attitudes toward marriage, and beliefs about mental illness (Gelfand, Chiu, & Hong, 2011; Valsiner, 2012; Vauclair et al., 2015). **Culture** can be defined as a system of enduring meanings, perceptions, attitudes, beliefs, and practices shared by a large group of people. It is important to note that, although nations may be dominated by a particular culture, cultures are not necessarily nations. For instance, scholars have described cross-cultural differences that extend across nations, such as those between Western and Eastern cultures (Hofstede, Hofstede, & Minkov, 2010; Triandis, 1993), as well as within-culture differences, like those distinguishing the American South from the North (Nisbett & Cohen, 1996).

The most widely studied cross-cultural variable is individualism-collectivism (IC), which was initially conceptualized as broadly distinguishing the Western cultures of North America and parts of Europe from Eastern ones in South and East Asia, including China and Japan (Hofstede, 1986; Triandis, 1993; van Hoorn, 2015). However, more recently researchers have discovered that the IC dimension is more complex, varying within cultures and extending to cultures on other continents, including South America. Succinctly put, individualists are self-focused: They define themselves as containing stable, internal traits not tied to particular groups, value individual choice, and place their personal preferences and goals above those of the group.

In contrast, collectivists tend to be other-focused: Their self-concept is intimately tied to and defined by their group memberships, individual choice is not highly valued, and personal preferences and goals are subordinated to those of the group (Triandis, 1993). It is important to note that, although we often talk about individualist and collectivistic cultures as if they were completely different, there is in fact considerable overlap: People in one type of culture

Culture: System of enduring meanings, perceptions, attitudes, beliefs, and practices shared by a large group of people

can and do exhibit characteristics common in people from the other type (Cialdini, Wosinska, Barrett, Butner, & Gornik-Durose, 1999; Hofstede, de Hilal, Malvezzi, Tanure, & Vinken, 2010; Triandis & Gelfand, 2012; Triandis & Singelis, 1998). We will return again and again to culture's prominent role in explaining elements of social behavior throughout this text.

Individual Factors

The third level of analysis seeks to explain social behavior by examining a particular person's experiences, learning history, and mental processes. What have you learned and how does that affect your social experiences? Psychologists speak of three learning processes (that you undoubtedly were exposed to in your introductory psychology course): classical, instrumental, and social. **Classical conditioning** was accidentally discovered by the Russian physiologist Pavlov (1906) during his famous dog salivation research. As you may recall, Pavlov observed that dogs associated a neutral stimulus—the sound of a tone—with meat powder and began salivating in anticipation of receiving it. The dogs learned that the tone signalled the impending release of the meat powder. Thereafter, a sound that had nothing to do with food became a proxy for food and created the salivation response. Okay, so that is all fine and good when it comes to dogs, but how does that apply to people? Well, let's say that McDonald's is your favorite fast food restaurant. You are driving down Main Street and spot a McDonald's. You may begin feeling hungry, and perhaps *you* will salivate a little. Why? Because McDonald's golden arches act like the tone for the dogs and signals to you that food may be on the way (it is unlikely that you were born with this association already in mind!).

Instrumental conditioning was pioneered by John Watson and B. F. Skinner and occurs when a person becomes more likely to engage in a behavior after being rewarded for doing it (reinforcement) or less likely after being penalized for it (punishment) (Watson, 1925/1998; Weiss, 2014). Instrumental conditioning helps to explain why people bring coupons to the grocery store (reward: saving money) and students try to get their papers in on time (punishment for failing to do so: F). A final type of learning that gained prominence in the latter half of the 20th century, **social learning**, takes place when a person observes or hears that someone else was reinforced or punished for engaging in a particular behavior (like robbing a bank) and then behaves accordingly either to gain a reward (free money) or avoid a penalty (going to prison) (Bandura, 2012; Bandura & Walters, 1963). The contemporary debate about whether exposure to violence on TV and in films leads to real-world aggression centers around whether these media exhibit a social learning effect on viewers (Anderson et al., 2004).

One major type of individual-level explanation focuses on the social cognitive processes occurring in the individual just prior to or during the phenomenon under study. In the 1970s, social psychology experienced a "cognitive revolution" (North & Fiske, 2012). Psychologists rejected simplistic behavioral and psychoanalytic explanations and discovered the role of conscious mental processes, such as a person's stated attitudes and beliefs, in generating social behavior. Social psychologists acknowledged how individual interpretations—called construals—of social situations affect social behavior (Kruglanski, 1989; L. Ross, 1977). For

Classical Conditioning: Form of learning in which a previously neutral stimulus becomes a conditioned stimulus after being paired with an unconditioned stimulus

Instrumental Conditioning: Form of learning in which reinforcement is given or punishment is administered in order to increase or decrease a specific behavior

Social Learning: Learning by observing or hearing that someone else was reinforced or punished for engaging in a particular behavior

Sovfoto Universal Images Group/Newscom.

Pavlov discovered the power of classical conditioning during research on the salivary responses in dogs.

instance, whether failing your first exam in social psychology leads you to work harder or simply give up on the class can depend upon how you interpret that failure. If, on the one hand, you believe that your poor grade was a result of not studying and that if you study for the next one you will do better, then you are more likely to increase your effort. If, on the other hand, you think that the professor is unfair, her tests are too difficult, and that no amount of studying will pay off, then you may withdraw from the class.

Social cognition can be defined as the "mental processes involved in perceiving, attending to, remembering, thinking about, and making sense of" oneself and others (Moskowitz, 2005, p. 3). As you read these words, your mind is switching among the multiple mental processes required to focus on and comprehend them, interpret their meaning, glance at the time, remember you have a lunch date, make a quick decision about whether to answer the text message you just received, and choose between continuing to read or getting your third cup of coffee.

Social Cognition:
Mental processes involved in perceiving, attending to, remembering, thinking about, and making sense of oneself and others

Although each of these activities is conscious, social cognitive processes often take place beneath the surface, nonconsciously (Carlston, 2013). Recall the research mentioned earlier that involved unscrambling sentences: Participants exposed to elderly related words walked more slowly (Bargh et al., 1996). Were they aware of this? Certainly not. Even when specifically asked if they thought that the task affected their behavior in any way, they denied it. It is not that the students were lying about the influence of the elderly related words. Rather, they were simply unaware of that influence.

Let's say your lunch date is with your new boss who you have only seen in passing. One of your coworkers told you that the boss is usually late, wears shabby clothes, has terrible body odor, and talks with her mouth full. What kind of expectations would you hold of your boss? Imagine, instead, that the boss has a reputation for being timely, generous, well groomed, and polite. Would your expectations change? Regardless of which expectations you held, your behavior during lunch is likely to be affected by them. In the one case, you might not worry about being a few minutes late, you may dress casually, decide not to eat at all (so you don't get grossed out), and wear extra cologne to mask undesirable smells. In the other, you'd be on time, dress well, plan to eat, and wear the usual amount of cologne (or none at all). This simple example demonstrates how expectations—another component of social cognition—can affect behavior. Chapter 3 is devoted in its entirety to explaining the centrality of social cognitive processes to virtually everything that we do. What we have learned and how we think about ourselves and others have repercussions for the kinds of romantic relationships that we seek, as we will see in Chapter 11.

Social Psychology in Europe

As mentioned above, the bulk of the empirical research in social psychology has focused on North American, white, educated males, and was conducted by North American scholars (Henrich, Heine, & Norenzayan, 2010). Nevertheless, social psychologists from Europe and elsewhere have had and continue to have a very important impact on the theory and research. From a historical perspective, two of social psychology's founding "fathers"—Sherif and Lewin—in addition to many other, lesser-known scholars, were immigrants to the United States. Moreover, European social psychologists have made significant contributions to our understanding of social identity, intergroup relations, minority influence in groups, and many other topics discussed later in this text (Jahoda, 2007; Moscovici & Markova, 2006).

Emerging Trends

Social psychology is a dynamic and exciting field that continues to move in new directions. The final chapter of this book highlights three of these emerging topics and offers insights into where the field may be heading in the next 10 to 20 years. First we'll describe the rise of positive psychology and incorporation of "happiness studies" into social psychology. Second, we'll explore the renewed interest in the study of religion and will explain how we can scientifically investigate religious phenomena. Finally, we'll discuss the emergence of the social psychological study of environmental sustainability—how social psychological insights can help us create a greener, cleaner, future.

Integrating Explanations

As you can see, there are many approaches to understanding the causes of social behavior. Which one is correct? The answer is that, on its own, none is: Social behavior cannot be reduced to a single cause. Not only is every social phenomenon a product of both personal and situational factors—which right away suggests more than a single cause—but virtually any behavior can be examined from each of these three levels of analysis. A complete understanding of a particular behavior will involve utilizing multiple explanations (see Figure 1.3). Let's take obedience to authority as an illustration. From an evolutionary perspective, we could ask whether it was adaptive for our ancestors to have been, at least some of the time, obedient to the authority in their group, family network, tribe, or community. The answer would be yes, because too much disobedience would likely have led to expulsion from the group, and that would have placed the rebel at a distinct disadvantage when it comes to mating, finding food, and protection from dangerous animals and humans.

Yet group-level influences are also evident when we consider how obedience can differ across cultures. Obedience and respect for authority are much more important in collectivistic than individualistic cultures (Blass, 2012; Bond & Smith, 1996b). Individual experiences and learning history play a role in that from a very early age we are rewarded for doing what our parents or other authorities tell us to do and punished when we disobey. Moreover, social cognitive processes are also crucial to obedience: We must attend to the authority, interpret what she says as a command that applies to us, and so on. As you can see, these approaches are complementary and together provide a more complete understanding of social phenomena.

One quick qualification is necessary: Often one of these three perspectives provides more insight or explanatory power for a specific social behavior than the others, and for the purposes of this text, we may focus only on that primary explanation. For instance, certain characteristics that men prefer in potential female mates are considered to be universal and therefore apply to all cultures. In this case, we'll emphasize the evolutionary perspective. In contrast, if we focus instead on ways that marital arrangements vary across cultures, then we'll emphasize culture-based explanations. Let's take a look at the guiding principles that guide social psychology's investigation of human behavior.

Think Again!

1. _What are the two elements of Lewin's field theory, and why are they important?_

2. _Can you briefly describe the three levels of understanding and apply them to explain one of your behaviors?_

PRINCIPLE MATTERS: SOCIAL PSYCHOLOGY'S GUIDING PRINCIPLES

We stated above that one impetus for social psychological theory and research stems from life's enduring questions. As important and fascinating as these questions are, they reveal more about the possibilities and complexities of human nature than they do about how humans actually behave. What we need is a general framework for understanding the actual causes of social behavior. Fortunately, social psychology has such a framework. From the vast array of research findings, we can derive a set of four guiding principles about the causes of human social behavior that together reflect the collective wisdom of generations of social psychologists. The principles are useful because they serve as general guides to our thinking and as starting points for our empirical investigations into the causes of social behavior. Together these four principles form the core lessons gleaned from over 100 years of research in social psychology.

TABLE 1.3   Four Guiding Principles of Social Psychology

Social Behavior is			
Purposive	Caused by dispositional and situational influences	Influenced by how people construe or interpret situations	Cultural

The four fundamental principles of social psychology are that social behavior is (1) purposive; (2) stems from both dispositional and situational influences; (3) is affected by how people construe the social world; and (4) is cultural (see Table 1.3) (Kenrick, Neuberg, & Cialdini, 2006). Each of these is described more fully below and is further developed over the course of this text. We will demonstrate their validity again and again as we venture through the exciting terrain of social psychology.

Principle 1: Social Behavior Is Purposive

Social psychologists assume that social behavior is purposive, which is to say that it is intended to achieve specific goals (Fishbach & Ferguson, 2007). We don't initiate a romantic relationship or insult a competitor or protect our young child from a vicious dog just for the heck of it. Rather, each of these behaviors is goal oriented (Elliot & Fryer, 2008). The potential romantic partner may have qualities that suggest he'll be a good provider. Derogating a member of the opposing team may make us feel better about ourselves, especially when our team is losing badly. Rescuing our child helps to ensure that our gene pool will persist a little longer. As you can see, none of these behaviors is accidental or random. The assumption that social behavior is purposive is what drives social psychologists to find causes. What would be the point of investigating completely random behavior?

Principle 2: Social Behavior Stems From Both Dispositional and Situational Influences

Why did Adam Lanza kill 26 children and staff at Sandy Hook Elementary School in 2012? Was it because he was a mean nasty young adult with an inborn propensity for violence? Did he have a serious mental disorder? Neglectful parents? Was he bullied by other kids while growing up? Or was it because he had easy access to weapons? What we are asking here is whether Lanza was entirely to blame for his actions or were outside factors the cause of his behavior? Stated differently, was his violent behavior a product of just his internal characteristics—such as his personality—or was it the result of external, situational features—such as violence in the media (Aronson, 2001)? More generally, is social behavior a result of *only* internal characteristics or *only* external conditions? The answers are "no" and "no."

As Lewin argued many years ago, explaining behavior as because of only one or the other is overly simplistic. Social psychologists believe in interactionism—that all social behavior is a result of *both* the person and the situation (L. Ross & Nisbett, 1991). In the

Gordon M. Grant / Splash News/Newscom.

Scene from the site of the Sandy Hook Elementary School Shooting, Newtown, Connecticut. A memorial site has been made to remember the victims of the school shooting.

case of the Sandy Hook shooting, if personality were the sole explanation, why didn't Lanza act violently in other contexts? If situational pressures were the only cause, why don't we see more mass killings? Clearly, both characteristics of the person—what we call the person's disposition—and features of the situation *together* produce social behavior. In other words, social behavior is a product of both dispositional and situational influences. Apply this to one of your behaviors—say going to college—and try to identify the internal and external factors that led you to do so.

Principle 3: Social Behavior Is Influenced by How People Construe Situations

It almost goes without saying that people differ in how they construe or interpret situations. One student may construe an upcoming oral presentation as terribly threatening, whereas another could view it as a chance to show off her oratorical skills. Our construal of situations affects many aspects of our social experiences, including how we judge others and explain their behavior (Fujita & Carnevale, 2012; L. Ross & Nisbett, 1991; Trope & Liberman, 2012). A study of how football fans perceived the events in a contentious 1951 football game between Princeton University and Dartmouth College nicely illustrates this (Hastorf & Cantril, 1954). Hastorf and Cantril queried both Princeton and Dartmouth fans about their perceptions of how fairly and cleanly the game was played. Not surprisingly, the way the fans interpreted the behavior of the players on the two teams depended on which team they favored. For instance, the Princeton fans claimed that the Dartmouth players committed more than twice as many rule violations as the Dartmouth fans thought they did (Hastorf & Cantril, 1954). According to Hastorf and Cantril, the motivations of the Princeton and Dartmouth fans—with each preferring to see their team as fairer than the opponents—led to divergent interpretations of the game. In fact, these researchers argued that the fans essentially watched *different* football games! Throughout this text we will examine the myriad ways in which our thoughts, feelings, and behavior are often profoundly influenced by our construal of social situations. Have you and one of your friends ever construed the same situation in very different ways?

Principle 4: Social Behavior Is Cultural

The notion that social behavior is affected by culture may strike you as exceedingly obvious. Yet, for much of the 20th century, as mentioned earlier, psychologists of all stripes believed that human psychology was essentially the same everywhere on the planet. It is now widely recognized that humans are, in fact, a cultural species, and that human behavior cannot be adequately understood without consideration of its sociocultural context (Baumeister, 2005; Heine, 2010a; Segall, Dasen, Berry, & Poortinga, 1999). Earlier we touched on how self-concepts can differ between individualistic and collectivistic cultures. There are countless other ways that culture can affect social behavior. For instance, Robert Levine and his colleagues studied perceptions of time in Brazil and the United States (Levine, 2015; Levine, West, & Reis, 1980). They found that Brazilians tend to view time as continuous and unlimited, whereas Americans see it as separable into discrete units and treat it as if it were quickly running out! One of the consequences of these different time perspectives is that, in Brazil, being "on time" for appointments and completing tasks "on time" are not nearly as important as they are in the United States. What elements of your culture have had major impacts on how you see yourself and the world?

These four fundamental principles—that social behavior is purposive, caused by both dispositional and situational factors, affected by construals, and cultural—provide the grounding from which we launch our social psychological project. They are assumptions upon which we can build our explanatory models, theories, and concepts, and help guide our investigation of social psychological phenomena. These principles will serve as unifying themes in the chapters that follow as we look for the causes of social behavior.

Think Again!

1. *What are the four principles of social psychology?*
2. *Think about the night you graduated from high school. How would each of the principles apply to your feelings and behavior that night?*

SCIENCE MATTERS: SOCIAL PSYCHOLOGY IS A SCIENCE

Each of us has theories about why people (including ourselves) do what they do. As meaning-seeking creatures, we have a propensity for generating explanations for thoughts, feelings, and behavior (Malle, 2011; Weiner, 1995). Typically we conceive these explanations based on observation of only limited aspects of a person's life—perhaps we only see her at work or in class—or on what someone else reports about what he has seen (probably also based on scant evidence). These explanations for behavior are called **lay theories,** because they are created by ordinary people without advanced training in psychology and without using scientific methods (Beruchashvili, Moisio, & Heisley, 2014; Kruglanski, 1989; L. Ross, 1977). Lay theories seem like common sense, such as when we say "opposites attract." But don't "birds of a feather flock together?" Are "two heads better than one," or do "too many cooks spoil the broth?" Lay theories like these are often contradictory and overly simplistic. Perhaps more importantly, the validity of lay theories is frequently undermined by the scientific evidence. As we discussed at the beginning of this chapter, social psychology is a science that carefully applies scientific methods in order to develop a thorough understanding of social phenomena. Social psychology provides evidence-based explanations that may contradict commonsense psychology.

Hindsight Bias

One common mistake that you need to be aware of—and avoid—is that, if a social psychological explanation seems obvious, you may be tempted to think "I knew it all along." This "knew it all along" tendency is called the **hindsight bias,** and it is demonstrated when people believe, after they have already learned the outcome of a particular event, that they would have correctly predicted it had they been given the chance (Arkes, 2013; Fischhoff, 1975; Roese & Vohs, 2012; Slovic & Fischhoff, 1977). Let's say that social psychologists found that people who have very low self-esteem are more aggressive than people who have very high self-esteem. Does this seem obvious? Well, if you said yes, then you would be incorrect. Very high, not very low, self-esteem is associated with more aggression (Bushman & Baumeister, 1998; Bushman et al., 2009). As you will see, social psychology usually isn't obvious, but when it seems to be don't assume that you already knew it.

It is worth noting that this hindsight bias is *not* one of these "obvious" findings. Let me explain. Fischhoff (1975) provided randomly assigned experimental participants with one of several possible outcomes of an historical event, such as who won a military battle. He asked them to estimate the likelihood that the outcome that they read had occurred. Participants were informed that the event and the outcome they read about had in fact happened. Other participants who were not told the outcome read the same passage but were presented with four possible outcomes and predicted how likely each outcome was. Participants who knew the actual outcome rated the likelihood of that outcome as much greater than did participants who did not know the outcome (see Figure 1.5). In other words, participants believed that they were more likely to have predicted the correct outcome than they actually were. They thought they knew it all along (Adapted from Fischhoff, B., 1975).

Lay Theory:
Explanation for social behavior that is possessed by an ordinary (lay) person without advanced training in psychology and without using scientific methods

Hindsight Bias:
Incorrect belief that, after a person has already learned the outcome of a particular event, he or she would have accurately predicted the outcome before it occurred

FIGURE 1.5   Hindsight Bias: Did You Really "Know It All Along"?

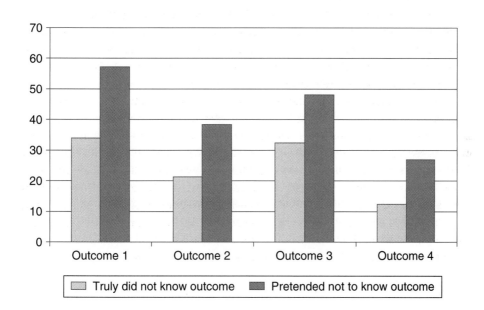

Experimental participants were provided with one of several possible outcomes of an actual military battle. They were asked to estimate the likelihood that the outcome that they were given had in fact occurred but to do so imagining that they did not already know that outcome. Participants who knew the actual outcome rated the likelihood of that outcome as much greater than did participants who did not know the outcome. They exhibited the hindsight bias: They thought they knew it all along.

Source: Adapted from Fischhoff, B. (1975). Hindsight is not equal to foresight: The effect of outcome knowledge on judgment under uncertainty. *Journal of Experimental Psychology: Human Perception and Performance, 1*(3), 288–299.

The general idea is that people often believe that they could have accurately predicted the occurrence of an actual event if they had been asked to predict it before it occurred: The outcome is seen as obvious or inevitable (Hoffrage, Hertwig, & Gigerenzer, 2011). Similarly, students often (erroneously) believe that they *already knew* the results of a given social psychological study and could have correctly predicted it. However, they fail to realize that their knowledge of the actual outcome has biased their belief that they would have known the outcome before being told. In short, once we know the answer, it suddenly seems obvious! The hindsight bias may lead you to study less than you should because you "knew it all" ahead of time: Don't wait until your first disappointing test to find out that you didn't. Many a student has come to me after receiving a low grade on an exam with a distraught look muttering something like "I thought I understood everything—it all seemed so straightforward." So watch out and study well!

Science Is Not What You Think

In my high school science classes I was taught that science was comprised of universal truths uncovered by people with advanced degrees. For instance, I had the impression that my chemistry book was filled with unassailable scientific facts about the composition and properties of matter and that if I successfully committed them to memory, then I would understand the science of chemistry. However, the idea that science is just a collection of unchanging facts constitutes a fundamental misunderstanding of the nature of science.

One of the most important lessons that I want you to take away from this text is that science is not a *collection of facts*; rather, it is *a process of discovery*. It is true that the body of social psychological knowledge that we call "facts" constitutes the overwhelming bulk of the information in this book and, no doubt, much of what your professor will test you on. However, it is critical that you also understand the nature of science and especially of good psychological science. Science is a process of asking questions, developing hypotheses, and designing research in order to answer these questions (Hull, 1988). Briefly, four key characteristics of science as a process are

- Creative: Researchers need to be inventive and flexible when developing ways to explore social phenomena and test ideas;
- Dynamic: It is progressive and forward looking, continually asking new questions while building upon what has been learned;
- Honest: Scientists share what we know and how we know it, allowing others to understand the methods and techniques used to make our discoveries; and
- Self-correcting: Scientists sometimes make mistakes and, through rigorous investigation, research replication, and with a fervent desire to find the truth, we and/or other scientists will uncover and correct those mistakes.

In the pages of this text, you will encounter many rich and varied examples of scientists at work. Not only will you learn about the results of their research, but you'll also get to witness how they discovered them as well as some of the mistakes made along the way. So rid yourself of the notion that science is always correct or that "facts" never change. Having said that, virtually all of the findings that will be presented in this text are based on rigorous, peer-reviewed research in which we can have confidence. Results that are controversial or tenuous or theories that are highly speculative will be identified as such.

Social psychological science—like any science—has three goals: *description, explanation,* and *prediction.* First we describe social behavior. Social psychologists are natural born people watchers, sometimes obsessively so. We record what we see, whether it be in a coffee shop, a parking lot, a classroom, or a laboratory. But observing *what* they did is simply a starting point for tackling the more interesting question of *why.* Social psychologists conduct research to understand *why* people thought, felt, or behaved as they did, including what characteristics of the person and the situation produced what we have observed. Good explanations are the crux of good science. Finally, social psychologists try to predict what will happen in the future, both in subsequent studies and, perhaps more importantly, in the real world. This chapter's *Doing Research* section introduces you to how social psychologists perform these.

DOING RESEARCH: AN INTRODUCTION TO RESEARCH METHODS

Research Matters: Beyond Lay Theories

As noted in the main text, all individuals create what may be called lay theories about why people do what they do. Like scientists, laypersons often informally "test" their theories while acting on and in the world (Kelly, 1963). For instance, a college male may believe that pointing out how beautiful his potential boss's legs are beneath her short skirt is a good strategy for securing an offer during a job interview and may act on this. Once he recognizes the indignant facial expression and her finger pointing toward the door, he will likely reconsider his strategy and revise his lay theory of interpersonal influence. Scientists too test our theories about human behavior, but we do so in a much more systematic fashion (and with more tact!). We don't rely on one or even a handful of cases but instead gather large amounts of data from many people in carefully selected circumstances before drawing conclusions (Sansone, Morf, & Panter, 2004).

Okay, social psychologists like to observe, explain, and predict human social behavior, and we do so by moving past lay theories and into the realm of rigorous research. How do we do it? What methods do we use? Throughout this text I will describe the most commonly used research methods, from the tried-and-true paper-and-pencil laboratory experiments to cutting edge, high tech procedures like functional magnetic resonance imagery (fMRI; see Chapter 2). Rather than trying to cover the huge range of research terms, methods, and challenges in one chapter (which may seem a bit arduous or tedious), I will instead spread them across chapters, introducing these in the context of actual social psychological research. For now, let us look at the importance of well-crafted questions, the need for testable hypotheses, and the role of theory in science.

Questions Matter: Good Questions and Good Hypotheses

What makes for a good social psychological question? The primary criterion is the extent to which the question is answerable using social psychological methods. In other words, a good question is an empirical question—one that can be tackled by systematically collecting and analyzing data. Take a question commonly asked in philosophy classes: "Are humans inherently evil or good?" While a profound and intriguing question, it is not one that can be answered by studying people and gathering data about their thoughts, feelings, or behavior. However, by narrowing it down we can transform it into a question worthy of social psychology. First, pick a behavior that you would say that, when people enact it, they are doing "good" (go ahead and choose one). Perhaps you consider recycling to be a good behavior and want to know why more people don't recycle. Next you need to identify something about the recycling process that may be a factor in whether or not people recycle. For instance, you could ask what kinds of message appeals are effective in increasing recycling.

Hypothesis:
Prediction about the nature of social phenomena, oftentimes in the form of a proposition about how two factors are related to one another

The next step is to turn your question into a scientific **hypothesis** or a prediction about the nature of social phenomena. Oftentimes hypotheses take the form of propositions about how two factors are related to one another. In this case, you might hypothesize that messages that tell people what they should do (which is to recycle) will work better than messages that tell people what they shouldn't do (which is to stop throwing recyclable materials into trash cans). Once a testable hypothesis has been formed, the study can be designed and conducted. In the next section, we move to the important role of theories in social psychology.

Theory Matters: What Are Theories For?

Theory: Set of interrelated statements that explain and predict patterns of observable events

Specific, testable, hypotheses are crucial to the collection of meaningful data. However, their very applicability to a small set of related experiments limits our ability to understand patterns of data that extend to other experiments and observations. Social psychologists seek broader explanations that allow us to connect and make sense of a number of isolated experiments and observations. A **theory** is a set of interrelated statements that explains and predicts patterns of observable events (Crano & Brewer, 1973) (see Figure 1.6). For instance, evolutionary theory does not explain why a particular woman is attracted to a particular man but rather why women in general tend to prefer certain characteristics in male partners. In our recycling example, a hypothesis would be used to predict the outcome of an experiment using a specific set of messages, but a theory would link this experiment with other experiments that used different yet related sets of messages, thereby facilitating a more general understanding of the kinds of messages that are likely to be effective. By providing a general framework for understanding and integrating known facts, a theory helps guide future research.

Social psychologists utilize many different research methods to test our hypotheses (yet another advantage to working in our field!). Which one we choose depends on the phenomena we want to study and what hypotheses we wish to test. For instance, Bargh et al. (1996) hypothesized that exposure to certain words would lead people to walk slowly. Another example is a researcher who hypothesized that the amount of time teens

FIGURE **1.6**   The Role of Theory in Social Psychology

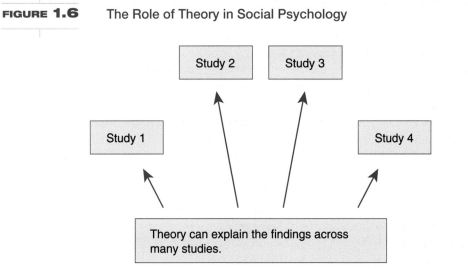

spend playing violent video games is associated with aggressive behavior (Anderson & Dill, 2000; Anderson et al., 2010). These two variables—game playing and aggression— are postulated to be related to each other in some way.

Two kinds of relationships between variables are possible. The first type of relationship exists when the variables change at the same time but may not cause each other to change. For instance, as the average temperature decreases in North America during fall, it increases in South America. This relationship is called a **correlation**. Two variables are correlated when a change in one variable is associated with a change in the other variable. Simply because two variables change at the same time does *not* mean that they are causally related. Without further evidence, we cannot assume that one *causes* the other. Since there is no meteorological theory that would predict that seasonal changes in one hemisphere cause the seasonal changes in the other, the most we can say is that the two are correlated.

Similarly, if all that we know is that teens who play more violent video games also tend to be more aggressive (but we can't say which causes the other), then we call the relationship correlational. It is possible that excessive playing of violent video games causes teens to become aggressive, or it may be that aggressive teens are more likely to play violent video games. As with the weather example, merely knowing that they covary—or change together—does not tell us whether one causes the other. All we can say is that the relationship is correlational. This is an illustration of a scientific mantra that you will often hear as you learn more about psychological science: *correlation does not mean causation.* Simply because two variables are correlated does not imply that one causes the other (see Figure 1.7).

Correlation:
Two variables are correlated when a change in one variable is associated with a change in the other variable

FIGURE 1.7   Aggression and Violent Video Games: Correlation Is Not Causation

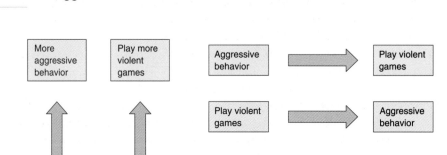

Causal Relationship: Relationship that exists when a change in one variable can be shown to produce a change in another one

Experiment: Study in which one or more variables are systematically varied in order to examine the effects on one or more other variables

Independent Variable: Manipulated variable that is expected to change the dependent variable

Dependent Variable: Measured variable that is expected to be affected by manipulation of the independent variable

The second type of relationship between two variables is called a **causal relationship**, and it exists when a change in one of the variables can be shown to produce a change in the other one. The study design used by Bargh et al. (1996) allowed them to infer that a causal connection existed between priming and walking. Another example is research that demonstrated that thinking about death caused people to express more support for then-President George W. Bush than they otherwise would have (Landau et al., 2004).

The best strategy for discerning whether there is a causal relationship between two variables is to carefully control the context in which we examine them by utilizing the experimental method. An **experiment** can be defined as research in which one or more variables are systematically varied in order to examine the effects on one or more other variables. The experimenter manipulates or changes the **independent variable** (IV) to determine whether or not it causes a change in a different one, the **dependent variable** (DV). The IV is the purported cause, and the DV the predicted effect.

To learn about the effects of playing violent video games on aggression, we can easily perform an experiment in which we manipulate game playing and then measure resulting aggression. We manipulate the independent variable—type of game played—by giving participants different levels or versions of it; some play a violent game and others play a nonviolent one. The IV is the potential cause, and the DV the expected effect. We could recruit teens from a local high school and randomly assign half to play *Wulfenstein* (a shoot'em up game) and half to play *Tetris* (a nonviolent game). After they played their respective games, we could have all the participants play a second game in which they have the opportunity to be aggressive toward an opponent. This is just what Anderson et al. (2004) did, and they found that the *Wulfenstein* players acted more aggressively in the second game than did the *Tetris* players. At least within the context of this experiment, playing a violent game (IV) caused participants to be more aggressive (DV). Similarly, the content of the unscrambled sentences differentially affected walking speed.

One of the key features of experiments is that they have two or more conditions that participants can be assigned to. The manipulation of the IV produces at least two levels of that variable, each representing a different condition. The aggression experiment had two groups or conditions corresponding to the two games. One group is called the **treatment group**, because the participants assigned to it receive the treatment (in this case they played *Wulfenstein*). The treatment is the variable being tested and thus is the primary interest of the experimenter. The other group is called the control group, because its participants did not receive the treatment (they played a nonviolent game). A **control group** serves as a comparison group against which we may measure the effects of the treatment. In the video game study, if we find that there is no difference in aggression between the groups in the second game, then the treatment had no effect. In the priming study, the elderly-related word condition was the treatment condition, and the unrelated word condition was the control. Similarly, in cancer research, for instance, the treatment group receives the drug being tested, whereas the control group is given a placebo. If the cancer treatment and the control groups recover at the same rate, then there was no treatment effect.

A second key feature of experiments is control: The experimenter needs to be certain that the only variable that could cause the DV to change is the IV. The potential influence of outside variables, called extraneous variables, must be eliminated. Researchers do this by preventing variables other than the IV from changing during the experiment. Let's say that in the aggression study the experimenters allowed *participants* to pick which game to play, and the more aggressive ones played *Wulfenstein* and less aggressive ones chose *Tetris*. If a difference were found in aggressive behavior between the two groups in the second game, can we say what caused it? Think about it. The answer is no: With this design, we would not know if prior aggressive tendencies or playing the violent game caused the *Wulfenstein* group to act more aggressively. By allowing the participants to choose their condition, we have introduced a confound or confusion variable. **Confound** variables are factors that change along with the independent variable and can complicate a clear assessment of the effects of the IV on the DV. Confound variables are extraneous and undesirable. If we can eliminate them, then we can have more confidence in our results. There are many possible sources of confounds, including some based on participant characteristics and others on features of the situation.

How do we rule out the participant-based confounds? We do this by ensuring, as much as possible, that the participants in the groups are similar in all relevant ways. In the aggression study, we would want the participants at the beginning of the experiment in the treatment group to be no more or less aggressive than those in the control group. In the priming study, the experimenter has to maximize the likelihood that

Treatment Group: Group of participants assigned to receive the treatment

Control Group: Group of participants that did not receive the treatment and serves as a comparison to assess the effects of the treatment

Confound: In an experiment, a factor that changes along with the independent variable and can prevent a clear assessment of the effects of the IV on the DV

Random Assignment: Each participant in a study has an equal chance of being assigned to any condition

there were as many "slow" walkers as "fast" walkers in each group. To ensure parity between the groups, the experimenter assigns participants to the groups in a random fashion. **Random assignment** means that each participant has an equal chance of being assigned to any condition. Random assignment can be done by flipping a coin, pulling numbers out of a hat, or in countless other ways. By randomly placing participants in the two game conditions, the number of previously aggressive participants should be about the same in each. Furthermore, the two groups should have about the same proportion of extroverts, artists, fast walkers, and chemistry majors. With random assignment, we can be reasonably confident that differences on the dependent variable between the groups could only have been caused by the independent variable. In all relevant ways, the groups are otherwise essentially the same.

Although random assignment can minimize the likelihood of participant-based undesirable effects, it may not prevent situational factors from inadvertently influencing experimental outcomes and confounding the research. What if, say, all participants who played *Wulfenstein* did so in a very hot, humid room, whereas those playing *Tetris* sat in a cool, dry room? Since research has shown that heat can increase aggression (Anderson, 2001), we would be unable to determine whether increased aggression in the *Wulfenstein* condition was because of the game or room temperature. Therefore, we must carefully design our experiments to prevent the unwanted influence of such situational variables.

In summary, all of us create informal or lay theories about the causes of social behavior that are usually based on casual observations and/or anecdotes. Although occasionally accurate, these lay theories must be scientifically tested. Correlational studies can show that two variables are related to one another, but controlled, randomized experiments are necessary to demonstrate cause and effect. Researchers design experiments that manipulate at least one variable, called the IV, and measure its potential influence on at least one other variable, called the DV. In order to help prevent confounds, experimenters randomly assign participants to condition. In addition, researchers control situational features so that all participants are tested in nearly identical circumstances, with the only differences being the level of the IV as determined by the experimenter.

Think Again!

1. *What are the two key features of an experiment?*

2. *What is the difference between an independent variable and a dependent one?*

3. *What is a confound, and how do researchers minimize the likelihood of confounds?*

FINAL THOUGHTS: SOCIAL PSYCHOLOGY AND HUMAN NATURE REVISITED

After reading this opening chapter, you should have a pretty good feel for social psychology as the scientific study of the social experiences and behaviors of individuals. I hope you share my fascination for learning what people do and understanding why they do it, and for how social psychology is particularly suited for investigating these topics. Note that social psychology is more than simply a sum of its individual research findings; rather, it is a theoretically driven, empirically based process for pursuing answers to fundamental questions of human nature. The six questions that we'll return to again and again are:

Do we have free will? Are we independent or conformist? Are we rational beings? What is the self? Do we need other people and, if so, why? Are we inherently altruistic or selfish? Returning to our opening story, consider how the various perspectives incorporated into social psychology help us explore such topics as same and opposite sex romantic attraction, how we think about ourselves and other people, the roles of biology and culture in shaping human thought and behavior, attitudes and attitude change, the formation and maintenance of prejudice, stereotypes, and altruism, among many others.

CORE CONCEPTS

- Social psychology is the scientific study of the social experiences and behaviors of individuals. Social psychology is different from other disciplines because it examines the relationships between individuals and groups, considers multiple levels of explanation, and focuses primarily on laboratory research.

- Social psychology is driven by the desire to examine the fundamental questions of human nature having to do with free will, independence, rationality, the self, sociality, and morality.

- During the early 20th century, social psychology grew from a nonexperimental to an experimental science. Two early textbooks helped to define social psychology and differentiate it from other social scientific approaches.

- Kurt Lewin's field theory articulated how social behavior is a product of the interactions between dispositional and situational influences on social behavior.

- Social psychologists acknowledge that social behavior has many causes and integrate them to develop more complete understandings of social behavior. These three levels of explanation are (1) evolutionary forces, (2) contextual influences, and (3) individual experiences.

- The four principles of social psychology are that social behavior is purposive; stems from both dispositional and situational influences; is affected by how people construe the social world; is cultural.

- The hindsight bias is demonstrated when people believe that they could have accurately predicted the occurrence of an actual event if they had been asked to predict it before it occurred. Students of social psychology need to be aware of this so that they don't mistakenly think that some research findings are "obvious" and, consequently, not fully appreciate them.

- Social psychological science is a process of discovery that is creative, dynamic, honest, and self-correcting, and is not merely a body of facts. Social psychology seeks to describe, explain, and predict social behavior.

- Social psychologists generate hypotheses— or predictions about the nature of social phenomena—to direct their research and develop theories—sets of interrelated statements that explain and predict patterns of observable events—derived from their research. These theories help guide future research.

- Correlations exist when two variables change (either up or down) at the same time. However, they do not demonstrate that the variables have a causal relationship (where changes in one variable cause changes in the other).

- An experiment is research in which one or more variables are systematically varied in order to examine the effects on one or more other variables. The experimenter manipulates or changes the independent variable (IV) to determine whether or not it causes a change in a different one, the dependent variable (DV). The IV is the purported cause, and the DV the predicted effect.

- Treatment groups receive the treatment or variable being tested, whereas control groups do not receive the treatment and serve as comparison groups against which we may measure the effects of the treatment. Confound variables are factors that change along with the independent variable and can complicate a clear assessment of the effects of the IV on the DV.

- Random assignment occurs when each participant has an equal chance of being assigned to any condition in an experiment and helps to prevent confounds and ensure parity between the groups.

- Controlled, randomized experiments are important, because they can demonstrate cause and effect. Experiments manipulate the IV and measure its potential influence on the DV. In addition, researchers control situational features so that all participants are tested in nearly identical circumstances, with the only differences being the level of the IV as determined by the experimenter.

▶ **⑤SAGE** edge™ Test your understanding of chapter content. Take the practice quiz. edge.sagepub.com/barrett

KEY TERMS

Anthropology, 7

Biological/Physiological Psychology, 8

Causal Relationship, 36

Classical, Conditioning, 23

Clinical Psychology, 8

Cognitive Psychology, 8

Collectivistic Culture, 12

Control Group, 37

Confound, 37

Correlation, 35

Culture, 22

Dependent Variable, 36

Experiment, 36

Hindsight Bias, 30

Hypothesis, 34

Independent Variable, 36

Individualistic Culture, 12

Instrumental Conditioning, 23

Lay Theory, 29

Natural Selection, 20

Personality Psychology, 8

Random Assignment, 38

Social Cognition, 24

Social Learning, 23

Social Psychology, 5

Sociology, 7

Theory, 34

Treatment Group, 37

▶ $SAGE edge™ Review key terms with eFlashcards.
edge.sagepub.com/barrett

THINK FURTHER!

- What is particularly *social* about social psychology?

- How can social psychology help us understand human nature?

- Take a social behavior that interests you and think through how the three levels of explanation might help explain it.

- Which of the guiding principles of social psychology do you think is the most important, and why?

- How might you see if your friends fall victim to the hindsight bias regarding an upcoming election or sporting event?

- What separates social psychology from lay thinking about social behavior (in other words, how is science different from ordinary experience)?

SUGGESTED READINGS

Aron, A., & Aron, E. N. (1989). *The heart of social psychology: A backstage view of a passionate science* (2nd ed.). Lexington, MA: Lexington Books.

Fujita, K., & Carnevale, J. J. (2012). Transcending temptation through abstraction: The role of construal level in self-control. *Current Directions in Psychological Science, 21,* 248–252.

Jones, E. E. (1985). Major developments in social psychology during the past five decades. In G. Lindzey & E. Aronson (Ed.), *Handbook of social psychology* (3rd ed., Vol. 1, pp. 47–107). New York, NY: Random House.

Lewin, K. (1946). Behavior and development as a function of the total situation. In L. Carmichael (Ed.), *Manual of child psychology.* (pp. 791–844). Hoboken, NJ: John Wiley & Son.

Roese, N. J., & Vohs, K. D. (2012). Hindsight bias. *Perspectives on Psychological Science, 7,* 411–426.

WANT A BETTER GRADE?

Get the tools you need to sharpen your study skills. Access practice quizzes, eFlashcards, web exercises, and multimedia at edge.sagepub.com/barrett

$SAGE edge™

2

The Social Brain

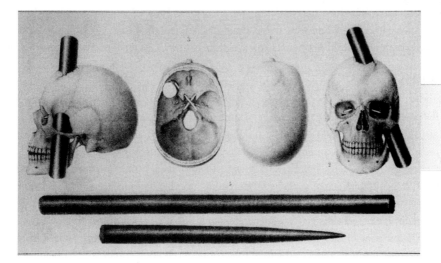

Various views of the famous wound made by an iron rod in the skull of Phineas Gage as well as the rod itself.

Everett Collection/Newscom.

LEARNING OBJECTIVES

2.1 Discuss dualism and the mind/body problem and explain how they relate to the concept of embodied cognition.

2.2 Compare the components of the tripartite structure of the brain, define the neocortex ratio, and evaluate the ecological and social theories of brain evolution.

2.3 Describe the functions of: neuron, dendrite, soma, axon, synaptic gap.

2.4 List and describe the roles of the five key neurotransmitters.

2.5 Describe the functions of the brain lobes and the prefrontal cortex, limbic system, insula, thalamus, hypothalamus, chromosomes, DNA, genes, and alleles, and explain how gene variation occurs.

2.6 Define social neuroscience and discuss its major methods: GSR, EMG, EEG, MEG, fMRI.

THE CASE OF PHINEAS GAGE

The case of American Phineas Gage is one of the most famous in the history of psychology. In 1848, the 25-year-old construction worker was the victim of a most unfortunate accident that occurred during construction of a railroad in Vermont. On this fateful day, Gage dropped a 13 pound, three-foot iron tamping rod into a hole lined with blasting powder before the necessary preparation for a controlled blast was finished. The rod inadvertently triggered a spark that caused an explosion that launched the rod into Gage's left cheek, through the frontal lobe, and out of the top of his head (Macmillan, 2008). Given the state of medical knowledge and care at that time, it is amazing that Gage not only survived this brain trauma but lived another 11 years with many of his psychological capacities intact. Contemporary observers noted that the incident transformed him from a competent, well-liked, rational man into an irresponsible, difficult, and impatient one (Macmillan, 2008). Since shortly after the accident, the precise location of the brain injury as well as his post-injury mental health have been controversial and oft debated (Macmillan & Lena, 2010). Over the last two decades a number of researchers, using modern brain imaging techniques, have attempted to specify which brain regions were damaged when the rod passed through Gage's head (H. Damasio, Grabowski, Frank, Galaburda, & Damasio, 2005; Macmillan & Lena, 2010; van Horn et al., 2012). The exact nature of the trauma is not important for our purposes, but the case provides a nice backdrop for our discussion of the neurobiological substrate of social behavior.

The purpose of this chapter is to provide a brief introduction to the social brain and social neuroscience. I am well aware that some psychology students (and faculty!) shy away from learning about the brain. However, social neuroscientific research is an emerging trend in the study of social behavior, and consequently students should be exposed to its core concepts. In this chapter I provide an overview of the topics, brain structures and physiology, and the methodologies most commonly used by social neuroscientists. Many of the later chapters include social neuroscientific research, and comprehension of those segments will be greatly strengthened by a careful reading of the current chapter.

Think Ahead!

1. *Why is studying the brain important to social psychology?*
2. *What is the relationship between mind and body?*
3. *How did the brains of primates become so large?*

WHAT IS THE BRAIN?

Today, asking *what is the brain?* seems almost laughable. We read or hear about the brain nearly every time we turn around, including on television, in newspaper articles, and across a wide variety of online sites. Almost everyone "knows" that the brain is the seat of thinking. However, what the brain is and what it does has not always been so clear. In fact, beginning with the ancient Greeks, through the Enlightenment and well into the 20th century, there was considerable confusion about the location of thinking in the body and even about the nature of thinking itself. For example, Plato accurately believed that reason resides in the brain but incorrectly believed that mental processes are unaffected by bodily ones (Hunt, 2007). The perspective that the mind operates independently of the body and is not constrained by it is called **dualism**, a term that suggests that the mind and body are two distinct things. Plato's pupil Aristotle contradicted him, claiming (inaccurately) that the heart hosted the mind. To Aristotle's credit, however, he proposed that mind and body were intimately interconnected. Understanding the exact nature of the relationship between the two has proven to be quite challenging, and it is commonly referred to as the **mind/body problem** (A. R. Damasio, 2010; Dennett & Weiner, 1991; Hergenhahn & Henley, 2014; Hunt, 2007).

Let's fast forward to the 17th century and another of the most influential philosophers in the Western tradition, the Frenchman René Descartes. Descartes sided with Plato and famously argued that the mind is indeed separate from the body. According to Descartes, the mind is made up of "nonphysical" stuff—what he called animal spirits—and, despite its attachment to the body, it is fundamentally independent of it (Descartes, 1641/1960). He proposed that the mind had no need of the physical body and was unaffected by the fact that it was trapped within it. Descartes further argued that he could understand the workings of this disembodied mind—literally, the mind separated from the body—simply through introspection or looking inward (introspection is discussed in more detail in Chapter 4). It is difficult to overestimate the enormous influence of Cartesian dualism on Western culture: Much of contemporary philosophy and psychology as well as conventional Western approaches to medicine continue to be haunted by Descartes' ghost (Churchland, 1988; A. R. Damasio, 2010).

For the past several decades, Cartesian dualism has been under fire from psychologists, neuroscientists, and others who have proposed that the mind can only be understood with reference to the fact that it resides within a body (Keefer, Landau, Sullivan, & Rothschild, 2014; Lakoff & Johnson, 1999). This means that reasoning and other mental processes arise from and/or are influenced by the sensory experiences of the body (Varela, Thompson, & Rosch, 1991). In other words, what we think about and how we think about it are affected by our physical location and the physiological limitations of our bodies (Cacioppo & Berntson, 2005; Rotella & Richeson, 2013). For example, humans cannot avoid categorizing everything that we experience, and the categories that we use—such as girl, poodle, or iPhone—come from our experience of the world (Lakoff & Johnson, 1999).

A classic study by Wells and Petty (1980) found that U.S. participants were more likely to agree with a persuasive message if they nodded their heads—a physical movement that

Dualism: The philosophical position that the mind and body are separate

Mind/Body Problem: Challenge of determining how the mind and the body are related

generally means *yes*—than if they shook their heads—a gesture that generally means *no*. Thinking must have been influenced by what the body was doing; otherwise, agreement would have been the same in both conditions. Do you find this to be strange? Surely one would expect that whether or not an advertisement or other persuasive message is convincing would have nothing to do with what our body was doing when we heard it. But let me give you two more examples.

In another study, participants were asked to list as many possible alternate uses for everyday things, like tires or buttons, a task intended to assess creative thinking (Oppezzo & Schwartz, 2014). They completed this task twice, the first time when either sitting or walking, and the second also when sitting or walking. As you can see in Figure 2.1, those who generated ideas while walking were much more creative than those who sat. So, the next time you struggle to come up with a new idea for a paper or project, try taking a walk!

Finally, would you believe that you may be more likely to seek the company of a socially warm friend when you are physically feeling cold versus when you are feeling warm? Researchers in Zhang and Risen's (2014) study randomly approached students who were outdoors in fairly cold weather (less than 44°F) or indoors in a heated building (72°F). While either cold or warm, participants reported how much they were interested in experiencing 10 different activities. Some of activities were socially warm ones, such as visiting their parents or having dinner with their "loved one," whereas others were positive but not warm, such as having their plane arrive early on a flight or getting a great haircut. The cold participants were significantly more likely to prefer the socially warm activities than the positive but socially neutral ones.

Clearly, mental processes do not take place in a vacuum-like state that is isolated or disconnected from the body or the environment. These and other studies convincingly demonstrate the embodied nature of cognition: Where you are and how you feel influence how you think and what you think about (Adam, Obodaru, & Galinsky, 2015; Beilock, 2015; Keefer et al., 2014).

Thinking—as we will see later in this book—is also linked to and influenced by our motivation and our emotional states (A. R. Damasio, 1994). Psychologists recognize that cognition that appears to be objective, rational, or culturally universal is vulnerable to many biases and shortcomings, some of which will be discussed in later chapters. The hindsight bias discussed in Chapter 1 is but one example of this. Moreover, as we'll see in Chapter 4, introspection does not provide us with the accurate insight into our mental processes that Descartes believed it did, in part because much of our thinking occurs at a nonconscious level that our conscious mind cannot access.

Social psychology has made a critical contribution to this reorientation toward embodied cognition: Not only must we take into account the physiological foundation of mental processes, but we need to further consider both their *social context* and *content* (Semin & Echterhoff, 2011).

As I discuss in Chapter 3, social cognition is not a subset of nonsocial cognition but is fundamentally different from it. Briefly, how we think about people diverges in important ways

FIGURE 2.1   Embodied Cognition: To Think Better, Take a Walk!

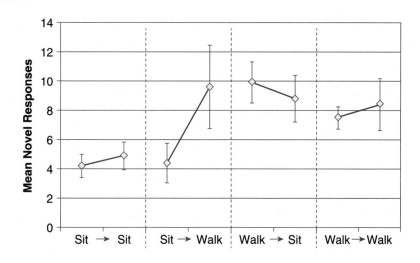

Students were asked to generate alternate uses of everyday things such as a tire or button. They completed the task twice, while sitting or walking. As you can see, walking produced more creativity than sitting. The next time you are struggling to come up with a new idea for a paper or project, take a walk!

Source: Study 3 in Oppezzo, M., & Schwartz, D. L. (2014). Give your ideas some legs: The positive effect of walking on creative thinking. *Journal of Experimental Psychology: Learning, Memory, and Cognition, 40*, 1142–1152.

from how we think about objects, although of course their reliance on common brain structures and processes ensures that there is also much overlap (Cacioppo & Berntson, 2005; Mitchell, Heatherton, & Macrae, 2002). Lieberman (2010, 2013; Spunt, Meyer, & Lieberman, 2015) puts forth the somewhat radical argument that social thinking is the *default* state of our mental processing, which is to say that our mind naturally focuses on people whenever it is at rest. For instance, if you take a break from madly typing your social psychology paper, the chances are you will begin thinking about people or people-related things. In a sense, social thinking is more fundamental than nonsocial thinking (Spunt et al., 2015).

So what does all of this have to do with social neuroscience? Let me address that question by defining our topic. The term **social neuroscience** was proposed by Cacioppo and Bernston (1992) in a paper describing the importance of studying the brain in order to more fully understand social behavior. Cacioppo and Bernston (2005) state that social neuroscience focuses on the dynamic interactions of the mind "with the biological systems of the brain and body and the social world in which it resides" (p. xiii). More specifically, Cacioppo and Decety (2011) define social neuroscience as the "interdisciplinary field devoted to the study of neural, hormonal, cellular, and genetic mechanisms, and to the study of the associations and influences between social and biological levels of organization" (p. 3). In short,

Social Neuroscience: Interdisciplinary field devoted to the study of neural, hormonal, cellular, and genetic mechanisms, and to the study of the associations and influences between social and biological levels of organization

social neuroscience examines the reciprocal or two-way relationship between physiology and social behavior (Matusall, Kaufmann, & Christen, 2011). Social neuroscience's ability to map social behavior onto specific regions of the brain permits inferences about the functions of those regions in the enactment of social behavior (Ochsner, 2007). Such mapping allows researchers to deepen their understanding of how the brain creates social behavior (Ochsner, 2007). Given the special status that social behavior has in the brain, one can argue that the brain is fundamentally a *social* brain that has evolved at least partially in response to specifically social pressures and affordances (Grossmann, 2015; Lieberman, 2010, 2013). Let's now turn to a brief discussion of the origins of the social brain.

Think Again!

1. *What is the mind/body problem?*
2. *How does the notion of the embodied mind resolve the mind/body problem?*
3. *What is social neuroscience?*

ORIGINS OF THE SOCIAL BRAIN

Our brain can be seen as possessing a tripartite structure that consists of the reptilian, mammalian, and neomammalian or higher brains (Hirth, 2010; MacLean, 1973). The reptilian brain is, in evolutionary terms, the most ancient part of the brain and one that we largely share with lizards and similar species. The mammalian brain refers to structures of the brain, such as the amygdala, hippocampus, and thalamus, that play a central role in fear, aggression, hunger, thirst, and sex. The core functions of the mammalian brain revolve around basic physiological survival needs. Finally, the higher brain consists of the neocortex or outer layer of the cortex that we commonly associate with our most advanced brain functions, including reasoning, planning, personality, and language. The neocortex comprises a much larger portion of the brain in humans than in other species. Although this tripartite model is overly simplistic, it is useful as a quick sketch of the evolutionary origins and structure of the brain.

One of the most interesting questions regarding the human brain is how it evolved to its current size and complexity. In order to answer this, scientists have tried to identify the conditions and pressures that led to the appearance of the larger brain in our primate ancestors. A number of theories have been offered to explain this evolutionary advance, but I'll discuss two types of explanations: ecological and social (R. Dunbar, 1998; Gamble, Gowlett, & Dunbar, 2014). Ecological theories hold that the larger, more intelligent brain is a consequence of features of the nonsocial environment, such as climate or geography. One theory is that as primates increasingly relied on fruit for sustenance, they needed to be able to maintain mental maps of the locations of various fruits and keep track of when they were likely to ripen (R. Dunbar, 2011; Harvey, Clutton-Brock, & Mace, 1980). Such detailed and extensive mapping would have required considerable cognitive ability, and those who were better able to remember where food was located—presumably those with slightly larger brains—would have been more likely to survive and reproduce.

An alternative ecological hypothesis states that greater intellectual capacities were necessary to be able to extract the most nutritious components from food sources, such as nuts and seeds (Parker & Gibson, 1977; Walker, Burger, Wagner, & Von Rueden, 2006). Thus the more intelligent individuals would able to maintain their own health and strength as well as those of their mates and offspring, and consequently, their gene pool was more likely to be passed along. The premise of both these theories is that nonsocial pressures were the primarily drivers of the increase in brain size.

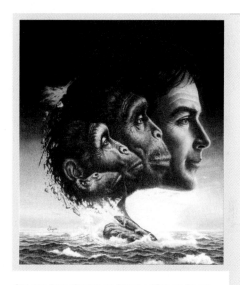

Christian Jegou Publiphoto Diffusion / Science Source.

In contrast, the social brain hypothesis holds that greater intelligence was required to monitor increasingly complex social networks (R. Dunbar, 1998, 2011; Humphrey, 1976; Stevens & King, 2013). That is, with larger communities comes more frequent interaction with greater numbers of people, and in order to successfully negotiate all of the social relationships among members of a community, an individual needed to be able to predict the consequences of his or her behavior and the behavior of others. Furthermore, larger communities required more hierarchy, alliances, and cooperation and the need to keep track of them all. In other words, successful navigation of these complex social networks required greater social intelligence (Humphrey, 1976).

Dunbar (1993, 1998; R. I. M. Dunbar, 2014) provided an empirical test of these competing models by seeing how well variations in diet or community size predicted social intelligence. As an index of social intelligence, Dunbar used what he called the **neocortex ratio**, which is the quotient of the neocortex volume divided by the volume of the rest of the brain. Higher neocortex ratios reflect enhanced ability for complex reasoning, planning, and greater social intelligence. By plotting the neocortex ratios of various nonhuman primate groups against appropriate comparison measures—percent of fruit in the diet or group size—it became clear that trends in group size fit much better with the data and therefore more adequately explained the origin of our sophisticated brains (see Figure 2.2). In other words, there is a positive correlation between neocortex ratio and group size, but no correlation between the ratio and fruit consumption. The human brain, as you can see, is truly *social*, both in terms of how it processes information and in the way that it evolved (Mercer, 2013; Vugt & Kameda, 2014).

Neocortex Ratio: Quotient of the neocortex volume divided by the volume of the rest of the brain

Think Again!

1. *What is the tripartite brain?*

2. *What is the ecological perspective on the origins of the big brain?*

3. *What is the social brain hypothesis?*

FIGURE 2.2   Origin of the Social Brain

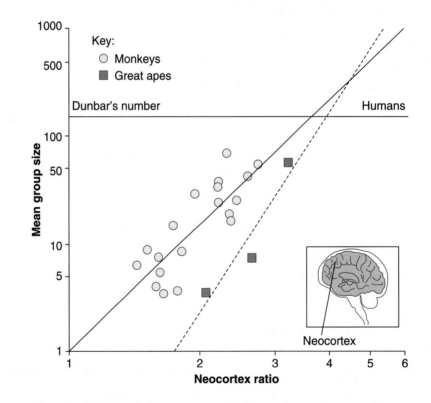

Neocortex ratio plotted against mean group size for monkey and ape species demonstrates the positive correlation between them. Notice the lack of correlation between neocortex ratio and % of fruit in the diet.

Source: Gamble, C., Gowlett, J., & Dunbar, R. (2014). *Thinking big: How the evolution of social life shaped the human mind.* London: Thames & Hudson.

SELF-REFLECTION 2.1
When a Picture IS Worth 1,000 Words (Part 1)

Is a picture really worth 1,000 words? When it comes to fact-based news articles, how much do they add to the credibility of the articles? Researchers interested in the power of images to persuade readers have examined this issue in a number of studies. Imagine you read a brief article titled "Watching TV Is Related to Math Ability," which claimed that watching television, because it activates the temporal lobe in the same way doing math problems does, can increase a person's math ability. Imagine further that text was accompanied either by no image, a bar graph, or a brain image (Figure 2.3). Take a minute and complete the questions below and then turn the page to learn more.

How much would you likely agree with each of the following (response options: strongly disagree, disagree, agree, strongly agree)?

1. The article was well written.

2. The title was a good description of the results.

3. The scientific reasoning in the article made sense.

Now turn the page to see what they found.

TABLE 2.1   When a Picture IS Worth a Thousand Words

Item	Response options			
	Strongly disagree	Disagree	Agree	Strongly agree
1. The article was well written.	1	2	3	4
2. The title was a good description of the results.	1	2	3	4
3. The scientific reasoning in the article made sense.	1	2	3	4

Source: McCabe, D. P., & Castel, A. D. (2008). Seeing is believing: The effect of brain images on judgments of scientific reasoning. *Cognition, 107*, 343–352.

TURN THE PAGE TO FIND OUR ANSWERS.

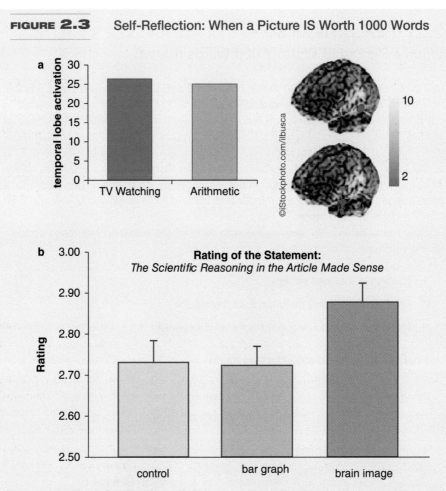

FIGURE 2.3   Self-Reflection: When a Picture IS Worth 1000 Words

Source: From McCabe, D. P., & Castel, A. D. (2008). Seeing is believing: The effect of brain images on judgments of scientific reasoning. *Cognition, 107,* 343–352.

SELF-REFLECTION 2.2
When a Picture IS Worth 1,000 Words (Part 2)

McCabe and Castel (2008) investigated the effects of including a photo of a brain image in a news article on believability. Although there were no differences in how much respondents agreed that the title was a good description, presence of the brain image led to greater endorsement of the quality of the writing and the scientific reasoning, in comparison with the other conditions. That is, respondents generally thought that the article with the brain image was more credible, when compared to articles with a bar graph or no image. It is important to note that the basic reasoning in the article was flawed and consequently should not have "made sense" to any of the respondents. This should be a warning to you, the student, when you are reading about science (even in textbooks!). Unfortunately, it could allow disreputable sources to persuade naïve consumers into having more faith in supposedly factual articles than they should have. Similarly, inserting scientific formulas and trivial graphs can also increase believability (Tal & Wansink, 2014). Perhaps more important, though, is that photos of brain scans and even testimony or textual evidence that make claims based on neuroscience can sway juries toward particular verdicts (McCabe & Castel, 2008; Weisberg, Keil, Goodstein, Rawson, & Gray, 2008). We will return to the nature of source credibility in persuasion in Chapter 7.

ANATOMY OF THE BRAIN

What Is a Neuron?

In order to fully appreciate social neuroscience, you need an understanding of the core components of the brain and nervous system. Let's start at the neuronal level. A neuron is the basic building block of the brain and nervous system. Although some variation exists in the structure of neurons, they typically have three major sections: the soma, dendrites, and the axon (see Figure 2.4). Within the soma or cell body is the nucleus, which houses DNA, mitochondria, and other elements that are heavily involved in the production of electricity and various metabolic processes. Dendrites are branching structures that extend from the soma and receive messages or information from adjacent axons. Finally, axons are relatively long and narrow structures that transmit the messages or information to the dendrites of other neurons via the terminals located at their ends.

Neurons generally do not touch one another; rather, information that is communicated between them must pass through the fluid in the synapse or synaptic gap. The messages themselves are specialized chemicals or neurotransmitters that are released by axon terminals and are, to varying degrees, "taken up" by the receiving dendrites. Neurotransmitters typically either excite (turn on) or inhibit (turn off) other neurons, and many of them are particularly critical to normal mental functioning. You have no doubt heard of neurotransmitters such as dopamine and serotonin, and perhaps norepinephrine, GABA, and acetylcholine (see Table 2.2). Dopamine, for instance, is released when we engage in enjoyable activities, such as eating chocolate, or receiving social rewards, such as a compliment. Serotonin, as you may know, helps in the regulation of emotion: Low levels of serotonin have been associated with social isolation and depression.

Neurons come in many shapes and sizes and serve a variety of functions in the nervous system. For our purposes, the most important ones are motor, sensory, interneurons, and mirror neurons. Motor neurons send information to the muscles to create movement, whereas sensory neurons transmit sensations received at various points of the body to the central nervous system. Interneurons connect motor and sensory neurons. Mirror neurons, only recently discovered in 1990s, have a very specific function: to allow one organism to imitate the actions—and perhaps emotions—of another organism (Iacoboni, 2008). These neurons are activated when we observe the actions of another person and essentially "mirror" that action. For instance, seeing the angry face of another person activates the muscles in your own face that are involved in displaying anger, and consequently, you are better able to put yourself in that person's shoes (Pfeifer & Dapretto, 2009). Similarly, your cringe reaction to watching a girl stub her toe suggests you come close to feeling her pain. More generally, researchers have argued that this mirror system provides the physiological basis for empathy (Iacoboni, 2009).

TABLE 2.2   Selected Neurotransmitters

Name	Effect	Inhibitory/Excitatory
Dopamine	Attention, learning, reward, and motivation	Can be either
Serotonin	Eating, aggression, sleep/wake, mood (especially depression)	Inhibitory
Norepinephrine	Mood, arousal, memory	Excitatory
GABA (Gamma aminobutyric acid)	General nervous system inhibitory	Inhibitory
Acetylcholine	Motor activity, arousal, attention, memory	Mostly excitatory

FIGURE 2.4   The Parts of a Neuron

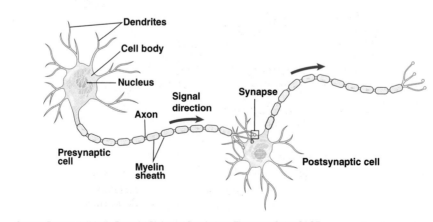

Source: Barnes, J. (2013). *Essential Biological Psychology.* Thousand Oaks, SAGE.

Structures of the Brain

The brain has two hemispheres that largely mirror each other in structure and function but also demonstrate some specialization or lateralization (Hugdahl & Westerhausen, 2010). For instance, language functions are located in the left hemisphere for most people, whereas complex visual processing tends to occur in the right one. The hemispheres are separated by the corpus callosum, which is a dense network of fibers that allows for communication between the hemispheres. When scientists have separated the hemispheres of certain patients with epilepsy by cutting the corpus callosum, the patients' left hands literally did not know what their right hands were doing (Sperry, 1961)!

Each of the hemispheres is composed of four lobes: frontal, temporal, parietal, and occipital (see Figure 2.5). The frontal lobes—considered the seat of planning and rationality as well as being critical to gross and fine motor functioning—are, well, where you'd

FIGURE 2.5   The Four Brain Lobes

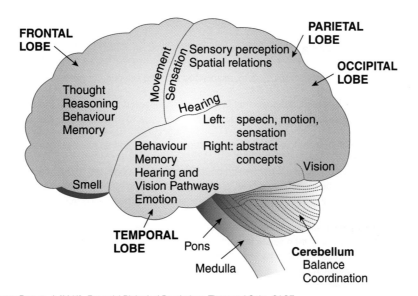

Source: Barnes, J. (2013). *Essential Biological Psychology.* Thousand Oaks, SAGE.

expect them to be, in the front part of the brain. It makes sense, then, that Gage's ability to manage projects and to control his impulses would be compromised by the damage that his frontal lobe sustained in the explosion. The temporal lobes lie roughly behind the temples and play a central role in auditory processing, including comprehension of speech.

The parietal lobes, heavily involved in the sensation of touch, sit atop the temporal lobes, extending to the top of the brain. Social neuroscientists have been particularly interested in the junction between the temporal and parietal lobes (the temporal-parietal junction or TPJ), because it is activated when a person is induced to adopt another person's perspective (see Chapter 8) (Ruby & Decety, 2004; St. Jacques, Conway, Lowder, & Cabeza, 2011). Finally, the occipital lobes—most closely associated with vision, constitute the rear of the brain. One critical stage in the perception of faces is located here, and hence facial recognition can be hampered when it is damaged (Haxby, Hoffman, & Gobbini, 2000, 2002). Imagine how different your social interactions would be if you were unable to recognize the faces of your friends and family. Trauma to the occipital lobe can also cause what is known as blindsight, wherein your eyes register sensory input and you may be able to spatially locate objects, but you experience blindness.

Although identifying the lobes associated with certain functions can be useful at a gross level, mental processes correspond more closely with specific structures and/or regions within the lobes rather than with the lobes in their entirety. Here we will focus on a subset of brain structures that have been more heavily researched in social neuroscience and figure prominently in the explanation of social behavior (see Table 2.3). These are the prefrontal cortex, the limbic system, the insula, and thalamus and hypothalamus.

TABLE 2.3   Key Internal Brain Structures

Name	Function
Prefrontal cortex	Executive of the nervous system, associated with the selection of behaviors to enact
Amygdala	An almond-shaped structure that is physically connected to the ends of the basal ganglia and is closely associated with the detection of and response to threat, such as fear and avoidance
Hippocampus	Plays an important role in memory formation and recall and spatial awareness and navigation
Insula	Has a central role in the perception of taste and pain. Connected to the olfactory bulbs and is involved in the reaction to smells, such as the disgusting smell of spoiled meat and unpleasant odors stemming from other people. Also associated with moral disgust
Thalamus and hypothalamus	Sensory information (with the exception of olfactory) is transmitted to the thalamus, which processes it and then sends it to other parts of the brain, including the amygdala. The hypothalamus—through its effects on the release of hormones by the pituitary gland—seems to have a role in virtually all aspects of behavior, such as sexuality, sleeping, and feeding, and is also involved in the regulation of bodily temperature. These structures are associated with the experience and expression of emotion.

Prefrontal Cortex

Sometimes called the executive of the nervous system, the prefrontal cortex is associated with selecting and guiding behavior. It receives information from many parts of the brain and integrates these when setting goals, planning, and directing behavior (Miller & Cohen, 2001). Remember how the injury to Gage's prefrontal cortex prevented him from setting goals and controlling his behavior. Our ability to take environmental cues and conditions into account when deciding how to behave is dependent on the prefrontal cortex (Miller & Cohen, 2001). For instance, when do you decide to scratch or ignore an itch in a private part of your body? Obviously, context matters. Hopefully, you will ignore it when you are speaking in public, but you may deal with it immediately when you are home alone in your living room. This sensitivity to external cues is particularly important for social behavior because it so often is (or should be!) responsive to context.

Limbic System

The limbic system is a set of connected structures that are central to the experience and regulation of emotions, motivation (including eating, drinking, and sex), and memory. The limbic structures most relevant to social psychology are the amygdala and hippocampus. (See Figure 2.6.)

- Amygdala. An almond-shaped structure that is physically connected to the ends of the basal ganglia and is closely associated with the detection of and response to threat. Damage to the amygdala appears to inhibit people from experiencing an appropriate fear response to potentially threatening stimuli—such as a receiving a painful shock (Olsson & Phelps, 2004). For example, if a person is unable to feel fear when he notices that another man is becoming very angry at him, then he is much more likely to be vulnerable to potential aggression.

FIGURE 2.6   The Limbic System

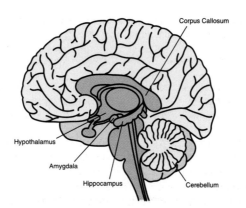

Source: Kuther, T. L. (2017). *Lifespan Development: Lives in Context.* Thousand Oaks, CA: SAGE.

- Hippocampus. This structure plays a crucial role in memory formation and recall and, together with the amygdala, creates emotional memories. The hippocampus is a key component of the controlled processing system that we discuss in detail in Chapter 3 (Lieberman, 2007b). The hippocampus is also key to spatial awareness and navigation, as demonstrated by the fact that the right side is enlarged in the brains of London taxi drivers (Maguire & Gadian, 2000). However, the hippocampus-taxi driver relationship is correlational, and therefore it is unclear how the two are causally connected, if at all. Individuals who are unable to create long-term memories often have damage to the hippocampus.

Insula

The insula is connected to the olfactory bulbs and is involved in the reaction to smells, such as the disgusting aroma of spoiled meat and unpleasant odors stemming from other people. The olfactory bulbs are part of the only sensory system in which stimuli from the external world are piped directly to the brain (including the amygdala) without first passing through the thalamus. As a result, smells such as those indicating spoiled meat and the presence of predators or other people have a particularly powerful influence on behavior. The insula has also been associated with moral disgust, and there is evidence that the brain responds to moral and physical disgust in similar ways (see Research Box 2.1) (Tybur, Lieberman, Kurzban, & DeScioli, 2013).

Thalamus and Hypothalamus

Sensory information (with the exception of smell) is transmitted to the thalamus, which processes it and then sends to other parts of the brain, including the amygdala. The hypothalamus—through its effects on the release of hormones by the pituitary gland—seems to have a role in virtually all aspects of behavior, such as sexuality, sleeping, and feeding, and is also involved in the regulation of bodily temperature. These structures are associated with the experience and expression of emotion and with the fight-or-flight response.

Think Again!

1. *How does injury to the prefrontal cortex affect behavior?*
2. *What is the function of the amygdala?*
3. *Imagine a person's insula were severely damaged and she could no longer experience disgust. What would the consequences be?*

RESEARCH BOX 2.1
MORAL DISGUST AND THE INSULA HYPOTHESIS: THE PERCEPTION OF DISGUST

Hypothesis: The perception of disgust responses in the facial expressions of others would be associated with activation of the insula but not the amygdala.

Research Method: Across four experiments, seven participants viewed photos of male and female facial expressions reflecting disgust, fear, or no emotion. They believed that the purpose of the study was to identify the sex of the person in the photo, when in fact the researchers were interested in their perception of and response to facial expressions. The experiments were completed while the participants were undergoing fMRI scanning.

Results: As expected, perception of disgust expressions led to greater activation of the insula (but not the amygdala), whereas exposure to fear expressions activated the amygdala (but not the insula).

Conclusion: This study demonstrated that there are specific and distinct neural bases for the perception of disgust and of fear. Prior research found that the insula was activated in the experience of food-related disgust. Importantly, this study showed that the neural substrate for nonmoral disgust (associated with foul odors) is similar to that for moral disgust.

Source: Adapted from Phillips, M. L., Young, A. W., Senior, C., Brammer, M., Andrew, C., Clader, E. T., . . . David, A. S. (1997). A specific neural substrate for perceiving facial expressions of disgust. *Nature, 389*, 495–498.

CHROMOSOMES, GENES, AND DNA

The tiniest physiological aspects of the brain that are most relevant to our discussion of the biological basis of social behavior are chromosomes, genes, and DNA. A typical human cell body contains 46 chromosomes, consisting of 23 chromosomal pairs. The only exceptions to the 23-pair rule are sex cells, which contain just one-half of a pair (the missing half is supplied by the other parent at fertilization). Chromosomes are composed of both DNA molecules and proteins. DNA or deoxyribonucleic acid consists of two strands of genes arranged in the familiar ascending staircase structure of a double helix. Chromosomes can also be considered strands of genes, because each gene is a segment of DNA. Chromosomes provide the blueprint for thousands of proteins, whereas a gene directs the synthesis of a particular protein. Finally, variants of genes are called **alleles**. People often refer to genes as units of heredity; although that

Alleles: Gene variants that carry the information essential for the expression of traits

is not incorrect, it is more accurate to say that alleles carry the information essential for the expression of traits. Psychologists who study the effects these traits have on social behavior focus primarily on alleles.

As we've noted, gene variants or alleles are the basic unit of heritability. That is to say that evolutionary processes are thought to work at the level of genes, not individuals, groups, or species (Keller, Howrigan, & Simonson, 2011). Although I may at times refer to the natural selection of individuals, it is simply a manner of speaking. I do so because genes cannot be passed down and cannot survive except by residing in human vehicles. Evolutionary theorists have largely agreed that genes are selected for, not individuals. In recent years, several experts have argued that natural selection does in fact work at the level of groups, although this issue remains quite controversial (Boyd & Richerson, 2007; Wilson, 2007).

Exactly how does gene-level natural selection occur? As mentioned in Chapter 1, genes that are adaptive are selected for, which is to say that individuals carrying those genes have an evolutionary advantage over those who do not. As a result of that advantage, those adaptive genes may spread throughout a population over time via sexual reproduction. This of course begs the question of how the "new" adaptive genes appear in the first place. There are two ways that gene variation can occur. One is through recombination: The fertilization of the egg by the sperm results in the combination of one-half of the female's chromosomes with one-half of the male's. Thus, reproduction can produce novel combinations of alleles and, by extension, traits and individuals.

The second source of variation is mutation, which is the result of random errors in the duplication of genes within a given individual. Mutations typically produce recessive alleles, are "invisible," and are generally not adaptive. These mutations will only "appear" if the carrier reproduces with another carrier of the same gene (such as a close relative). However, mutations occasionally create both dominant and adaptive genes and, if the carrier successfully passes them down to the offspring, then they may eventually become present in the entire population. Dominant genes (such as for brown eyes) are expressed if the parts of a pair of genes are different, but the expression of recessive genes (such as for blue eyes) only occurs when both halves of a pair are identical. Psychological tendencies and personality traits, such as extraversion or conscientiousness, are partially inherited in much the same way.

Although we tend to think about the evolution of genes in terms of natural selection, recent research suggests that advances in culture have also affected the evolution of genes. In other words, genes and culture have coevolved and together have produced the human mind as we know it today (Chiao, 2011; Richerson, Boyd, & Henrich, 2010). Cultural variation in diet and disease exposure have affected specific alleles, such that these alleles differ in prevalence across cultures. For instance, differences in the desirability and frequency of culture-related traits like individualism-collectivism may be correlated with genetic variation (Fincher, Thornhill, Murray, & Schaller, 2008). Later we discuss the role that disease may have played in the historic development of collectivistic cultures (see Chapter 6). The takeaway message here is that not only can genes affect social behavior, but also that social behavior can impact genes.

> ### *Think Again!*
>
> 1. *What is a gene? An allele?*
> 2. *What is a chromosome?*
> 3. *How can a single gene mutation affect evolution?*

DOING RESEARCH: METHODS OF SOCIAL NEUROSCIENCE

Not that many years ago scientists had only relatively primitive tools available to study the brain and consequently could only guess at the physiological processes that underlie social behavior. Fortunately, technologies developed in recent decades have led to exponential growth in our understanding of how the brain works. Today, social neuroscientists employ a range of methods and technologies that vary in cost, accessibility, complexity, frequency of use, invasiveness, and what they measure. In this section I will touch on a few that are the most useful for introductory social psychology students.

Galvanic Skin Response

When you are nervous or anxious, does your heart beat a little faster and do you sweat a bit more? Well, early research in physiological psychology focused primarily on measuring relatively obvious overt bodily responses to situations and stimuli. One of the most researched psychophysiological constructs targeted by social neuroscience was arousal (Cacioppo, Berntson, & Crites, 1996). When we are physiologically aroused, we typically experience increased heart rate, blood pressure, pupil dilation, and sweating. The primary method for assessing arousal was the measurement of skin conductance or galvanic skin response (GSR). GSR—more recently labeled electrodermal activity or EDA—is used as a measure of arousal, because arousal induces the individual to produce a small amount of sweat, even if that person cannot detect it (Mendes, 2009).

Typically, two electrodes are placed on the hand, a weak electrical current is applied, and the time it takes for the electricity to pass from one electrode to the other is measured. An increase in skin conductance (faster transmission of current across the skin) occurs when a person sweats and suggests that the person is aroused (unless her hand is moist for some other reason). The polygraph or lie detector measures GSR and other indices of arousal but is famously unreliable as way to determine the veracity of a person's testimony or answers. The primary reason for this is that a person's arousal could be caused by any number of factors, only one of which is lying (see Chapter 5 for more on lie detection). For instance, a person may become aroused simply because he is being asked about whether he is lying.

Electromyography

Electromyography (EMG) also measures electrical activity but does so by detecting muscle movements instead of surface skin conductance. Social psychologists have employed

EMG to measure muscle movements in the face that are thought to reflect emotional and/ or attitudinal states, and self-reports of depth of message processing (Cacioppo & Petty, 1981). The underlying rationale is that the activity of specific muscles is correlated with verbal self-reports and behavioral measures, and thus the EMG can provide additional evidence of cognitive and affective processes (Blascovich, 2000; Blascovich & Seery, 2007). For instance, Cacioppo and Petty (1981) describe how increased movement (and electrical activity) of facial muscles associated with speech parallel other measures of deeper processing of persuasive messages. As we'll discuss in Chapter 7, how carefully we examine the arguments in a message impacts how much we are persuaded by them. It is fascinating that our facial muscles can reflect whether or not we are thinking deeply or superficially! Facial EMG can also detect the positivity or negativity of emotional reactions and the intensity of those reactions among message recipients during message exposure (Cacioppo, Petty, Losch, & Kim, 1986). Social psychologists have utilized facial EMG in research on the mere exposure effect (see Chapter 11) (Harmon-Jones & Allen, 2001), stereotyping (see Chapter 10) (Vanman, Saltz, Nathan, & Warren, 2004), and other topics in social psychology (Bartholow & Dickter, 2007; Hess, 2009).

Electroencephalography (EEG) and Magnetoencephalography (MEG)

An EEG measures electrical activity generated by the brain, whereas an MEG targets the magnetic signals associated with electrical output. You have most likely read about EEG in

your introduction to psychology course in the context of measuring brain wave patterns as a way to identify and track the stages of sleep. EEGs are also used to record abnormal electrical activity associated with epilepsy. Regardless of its purpose, an EEG is conducted by placing electrodes at numerous places on the scalp in order to detect brain wave patterns. Social psychologists are specifically interested in how the brain responds to particular social stimuli and therefore focus on changes in the

A patient undergoes an electroencephalography (EEG). EEG examines the electric activity of the brain using electrodes placed at key places on the skull.

C3336 Klaus Rose Deutsch Presse Agentur/Newscom.

electrical activity, called **event-related potentials** (ERPs), during and immediately after stimulus presentation. These stimuli can be visual, auditory, olfactory, or tactile (Cacioppo, Lorig, Nusbaum, & Berntson, 2004).

Given that ERPs are fairly weak and can easily be drowned out by baseline electrical activity, researchers enhance signal detection by gathering data over many trials and averaging the data from multiple electrodes. MEGs typically utilize form-fitting caps with multiple electrodes that, like EEGs, examine how the brain responds to various stimuli. Both technologies are useful for examining these responses over time. For instance,

Event-Related Potentials (ERPs):
Changes in electrical activity in the brain that reflect how it responds to particular stimuli

researchers interested in person perception have measured differences in ERPs with an EEG immediately after a person's exposure to body movements (Puce & Perrett, 2005) or to faces from blacks and whites (Ito, 2011). The magnitude of the ERP should increase when a person is exposed to stimuli she perceives as very different from one another (such as when viewing a black and then a white face). Similarly, ERPs associated with the categorization of faces have been studied using MEG (Bartholow & Dickter, 2007; Liu, Harris, & Kanwisher, 2002). Figure 2.7 shows how the amplitude of the ERP response at particular brain sites is greater after exposure to human faces than to other objects (Liu et al., 2002). This difference in activation provides further evidence that the brain processes social and nonsocial information in different ways.

FIGURE 2.7   Strength of ERP Response to People Versus Other Objects

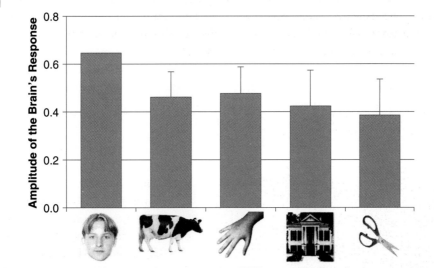

The presentation of faces produces a stronger ERP response than the presentation of other objects.

Source: Liu, J., Harris, A., & Kanwisher, N. (2002). Stages of processing in face perception: An MEG study. *Nature Neuroscience, 5*(9), 911.

Functional Magnetic Resonance Imaging (*f*MRI)

The techniques discussed so far—GSR, EMG, EEG, MEG—are all considered *noninvasive* because they do not have any effects on the body or brain but merely record electrical activity in a passive manner. In contrast, functional magnetic resonance imaging (*f*MRI) is categorized as *invasive* because it temporarily changes the brain. *f*MRI is a technique for examining the soft structures or tissues of the brain that Xrays cannot capture because they pass right through. The *f*MRI was a considerable advance over the MRI, because the MRI provides only static images of the brain, akin to a still shot of a running dog. Although static images are useful, tracking changes in the brain over time allows us to better examine brain processes, which is more like watching a video recording of the dog in motion. Ogawa, Lee, Kay, and Tank (1990) were the first to observe that the MRI could be used to examine dynamic processes.

Briefly, a relatively strong magnetic field—one thousand times stronger than the Earth's—is uniformly applied to the brain, and this field forces randomly oriented hydrogen atoms to change their spatial orientation and become aligned with one another. Next, a radio pulse is sent into the brain that pushes the hydrogen atoms into a position that is at a 90-degree angle from that new alignment. The shift in position of the atoms produces a tiny fluctuation in their magnetic properties. As the brain performs various tasks and functions, oxygenated blood is dispersed to active areas, and this changes the oxygen content of the blood. The magnetic properties of oxygenated and deoxygenated blood diverge slightly, and this difference is what the *f*MRI actually detects. This is referred to as the blood oxygen level dependent (BOLD) response: Heightened activity of the neurons leads to an increase in both blood flow and the ratio of oxygenated to deoxygenated hemoglobin (which carries the oxygen in the blood) (Cacioppo & Berntson, 2005). Why is this ratio important? The reason is that it shows how the brain changes over time, such as when a person is reading a passage or engaged in social interaction. The *f*MRI tracks changes in these magnetic properties of the blood to create a series of three-dimensional images that reflect dynamic brain activity.

There are several distinct advantages of *f*MRI versus other physiological approaches for social psychologists (Cacioppo et al., 2004; Wager & Lindquist, 2011). First, as previously stated, it provides dynamic measurement and thus allows for the observation of changes in the brain over time. Second, it has high temporal resolution, which means

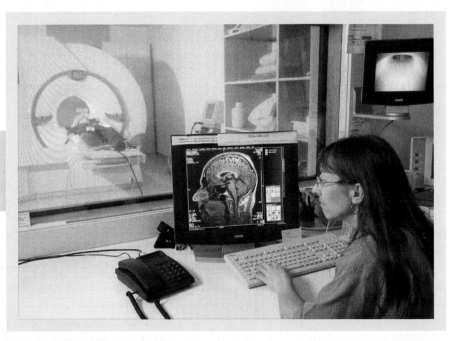

Brain researcher in the control room of a functional magnetic resonance imaging (fMRI) scanner.

Philippe Psaila / Science Source.

that it can capture changes that occur over very short time periods, such as a few seconds. Third, *f*MRI has very good spatial resolution, and consequently, researchers are able to pinpoint specifically where in the brain the focal activity is located. It is important to note that, unlike the EEG, which directly measures neuronal electrical activity, *f*MRI measures a consequence of neuronal activity (i.e., magnetic properties associated with BOLD changes) and not the activity itself. Thus it is a little bit like tracking how a tennis ball moves after being hit without recording the action of the racket hitting the ball.

*f*MRI has helped social psychologists understand the physiological basis for a wide variety of social behaviors. Particularly interesting examples are activation of various brain regions in interactive games with other people (Rilling, 2011), differentiating between person and object knowledge (Mitchell et al., 2002), the dehumanization of undesirable others (Harris & Fiske, 2009), and social pain associated with rejection by others (DeWall et al., 2012). Figure 2.8 includes *f*MRI images obtained in an investigation of brain activity during exposure to social versus nonsocial objects. Later on we will highlight additional *f*MRI studies that have identified neural correlates to key social behaviors.

FIGURE 2.8   Social Versus Nonsocial Brain Activation

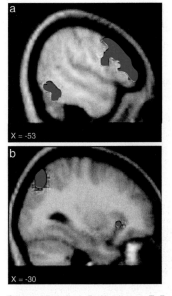

Differential activation of the brain when thinking about a person versus an object. Here, activation of particular regions of the brain is greater when thinking about an object.

Source: Mitchell, J. P., Heatherton, T. F., & Macrae, C. N. Distinct neural systems subserve person and object knowledge. *Proceedings of the National Academy of Sciences of the United States of America, 99*(23), 15238-15243. Copyright © 2002 National Academy of Sciences, U.S.A.. Reprinted with permission.

Other Methods

GSR, EEG, MEG, MRI, and *f*MRI have been among the most popular approaches to understanding the physiological bases of social behavior. However, researchers have also used positron emission tomography (PET), the physical induction of lesions directly on the brain, transcranial magnetic stimulation (TMS), and other methods (Beadle & Tranel, 2011; Decety & Cacioppo, 2011; Todorov, Fiske, & Prentice, 2011). PET provides an alternative way of imaging the brain that, like *f*MRI, examines blood flow. However, PET is a more invasive approach in that it utilizes injected radioactive or other substances and consequently makes it somewhat less appealing to social psychologists. Both lesion induction and TMS are disruptive techniques in that they impair normal functioning of the brain in order to see the effects of psychological processes. Lesioning involves causing irreversible damage to the brain, raising obvious ethical concerns. For this reason, lesion studies are usually conducted on animals or on humans who have already experienced brain trauma outside the laboratory (Beadle & Tranel, 2011). Had Gage's severe brain injury occurred today, he would have been a prime candidate for one of these studies!

TMS uses a magnetic field to create an electric current that stimulates targeted areas of the brain and temporarily prevents normal functioning. For example, one study used TMS to briefly shut down the mirror neuron system in order to verify its role in imitating others (described earlier and again in Chapter 8). Researchers found that people's ability to imitate others was significantly hampered, thus providing additional evidence of the function of mirror neurons (Heiser, Iacoboni, Maeda, Marcus, & Mazziotta, 2003).

Multimethods

Each of these techniques—like all research methods—has its strengths and weaknesses. Therefore, social psychologists prefer to use more than one method to investigate social behavior. As a result, our understanding of the neuroscience of social behavior is more comprehensive and sophisticated (Ochsner, 2007; Wager & Lindquist, 2011). As we will see later, the principle of combining multiple research methods to examine a common phenomenon in order to strengthen our knowledge of social behavior applies more broadly to all methods of inquiry.

Think Again!

1. *What is a galvanic skin response?*
2. *What are the advantages of fMRI?*
3. *Why is it important to use multiple methods for studying the brain?*

SOCIAL NEUROSCIENCE AND THE FUNDAMENTAL QUESTIONS

By now the importance of the studying the brain for understanding social behavior should be clear. As appealing and important as social neuroscience is, one can, however, be easily seduced by the *ahhh!* factor and captivated by the beauty and power of these powerful technologies (Satel & Lilienfeld, 2013). In fact, we may even be tempted to reduce social behavior to its brain biology and point to a particularly vivid region on a multicolored,

APPLYING SOCIAL NEUROSCIENCE TO LAW
CAN fMRI DETECT LIES?

As you'll see in the remainder of this text, social neuroscience has wide applications in social psychology and beyond. Recently, researchers have been studying whether or not fMRI can be used in law enforcement and the courts, specifically to detect deception in suspects and witnesses (Langleben & Moriarty, 2013). Given the challenges people face in detecting lies on their own (which are discussed in Chapter 5), law enforcement has sought a foolproof, technological solution. How might an fMRI identify lies? Briefly, it has been proposed that there are discernable differences in brain processes when people tell the truth versus when they do not (Bizzi et al., 2009). The short answer is that neuroscientists largely agree, at least at this time, the fMRI is unable to identify such differences (Bizzi et al., 2009; Ganis, Kosslyn, Stose, Thompson, & Yurgelun-Todd, 2003; Langleben & Moriarty, 2013). Some of the criticisms include the following:

FIGURE 2.9 fMRI as a Lie Detector

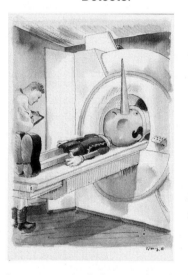

In theory, a markedly improved method of lie detection could have as profound an impact as DNA evidence.

Source: Barry Blitt, *The New Yorker* (July 2, 2007).

- Different types of lies may show different brain activation patterns, and therefore no single brain "signature" for deception exists.
- Existing research has involved only very small samples.
- Lying in a laboratory setting is artificial and not reflective of real-world conditions, and consequently, generalizability to non-experimental situations is low.
- In addition to the scientific concerns, questions have been raised regarding the ethics of using an fMRI for lie detection: Would it violate the Fifth Amendment prohibition of forced self-incriminating testimony? Would it violate the Fourth Amendment protection from warrantless search?

three-dimensional brain image and claim *there it is, the root of prejudice* (or some other social behavior)! However, the brain processes that occur during social behavior are just one component of a much larger social psychological explanatory framework with multiple levels of analysis. In other words, we cannot even come close to an adequate understanding of social behavior if we engage in such **reductivism**—which is the assumption that we need only study the brain to understand the causes of social behavior. Many prominent social neuroscientists have argued instead the importance of examining social behavior from multiple perspectives (Decety & Cacioppo, 2011; Lieberman, 2010). The unique contributions of social neuroscience to our understanding of specific social behaviors are important, but they are only part of the story. Indeed, social neuroscience, in addition to deepening our understanding of social behaviors, is highly relevant to the six fundamental questions of human existence.

Reductivism: Idea that we need only study the brain to fully understand the causes of social behavior

Free Will

Research in social neuroscience is probably most relevant for the question of free will. In fact, a number of prominent research programs have challenged the notion that humans are in conscious control of our mental and behavioral processes (Baer, Kaufman, & Baumeister, 2008; Gazzaniga, 2011). If scientists can pinpoint the biology of nonconscious processes, and if these processes can predict social behavior without needing to factor in the conscious mind, then does it make any sense for us to talk about free will (Bargh, 2008; Baumeister, 2008)? For many social psychologists, the answer is yes: Even if we do not actually have free will, both the *experience* of free will and the reasons people believe in it are important for understanding social behavior (Baumeister, 2008). For example, a person who believes that he has the free will to shape his future is more likely to persist in the face of failure than is someone who thinks that he is powerless and that his fate has already been decided (Dweck, 1999).

Independence

As of this writing, social neuroscience has not really focused on the physiological bases of independent versus conformist or obedient behavior (but see Berns et al., 2005). As more research is conducted and we learn about the direct effects that outside pressures (e.g., from peers or authorities) can have on our biological states, our understanding of independent versus conformist responding will surely deepen.

Rationality

The explosion of social neuroscience has provided ample empirical evidence of the ways that emotion and motivation impact so-called rational thinking. We will devote more time to the emotion-reason connection in Chapter 3 on social cognition.

Self

Social neuroscientific research, by demonstrating patterns of brain activation when we think about the self or engage in behaviors that are closely tied to our sense of self, can lead to improved understanding. Moreover, such research shows the fallacy of Cartesian dualism—thinking that the mind is separate from the body. However, a critical aspect of the self is our *experience* of the self, and it seems to me that, as I suggested with regard to the experience of free will, social neuroscience will likely have less to say about this.

Sociality

The human need for sociality is fundamental to our emotional and physical health and, of course, essential for the propagation of our species. Social neuroscience has already provided substantial research supporting the biological underpinnings of our mental health, and it is worth noting that one of our most prominent social neuroscientists, John Cacioppo, is also one of our leading researchers in the psychology of affiliation and loneliness (Cacioppo & Patrick, 2008). Among the many insights that this body of research has provided is the way in which brain activation associated with the pain of social rejection resembles that related to physical pain (see Chapter 9).

Morality

One of the core components of moral behavior is the extent to which we help or harm others. Empathic feelings play a key role in decisions to help others. As mentioned earlier, social neuroscience has shown how the mirror neuron system is central to empathy and has opened up an entirely new way of thinking about altruistic behavior (Decety & Ickes, 2009). The neural basis for empathy and altruism will be discussed at greater length in Chapter 8.

Think Again!

1. *What is reductivism?*

2. *How might social neuroscience illuminate the free will debate?*

FINAL THOUGHTS: EVOLUTION, BRAIN PLASTICITY, AND CULTURE

One of the threads woven throughout this text is the evolutionary basis of social behavior. According to evolutionary theory, universal social behavior either is or must have been adaptive; otherwise, it would likely have been dropped from our behavioral repertoire by virtue of selection pressures on the gene pool. Social neuroscience—based in biology—falls under the evolutionary approach. Yet, as discussed in Chapter 1, social behavior is influenced by a number of other factors, such as culture, individual learning, and how people construe their world. Researchers used to think that the brain stopped developing relatively early in life and that the organization of neurons and the brain regions involved in specific activities were largely fixed. However, we know now that many neurons can regenerate and reorganize throughout the life cycle. Moreover, some changes in the brain (and even the genes) occur as a result of a person's experience (Francis, 2011). That is, the brain exhibits plasticity or flexibility, which means that it is sensitive to external social, cultural, and environmental influences (Duffy & Kitayama, 2010). Evidence has been accumulating with regard to the coevolution of genes and culture, demonstrating that culture and genes have affected each other over the course of human evolution (Chiao, 2011; Donald, 2000; Richerson & Boyd, 2005). These and related findings bring home the lesson that a comprehensive understanding of social behavior requires examining it from multiple levels of explanation, including but not limited to social neuroscience.

CORE CONCEPTS

- Dualism is the perspective that the mind operates independently of the body and is not constrained by it. Understanding the exact nature of the relationship between the two is called the mind/body problem.

- Contemporary social psychologists view the mind as embodied or inextricably bound up with the body; the social brain is now seen as the default state of mind and mental processing.

- The tripartite brain is composed of the reptilian, mammalian, and higher brains. The social brain hypothesis holds that increasingly large social networks produced pressures that selected for more sophisticated thinking and larger brains. The ecological hypotheses explain the larger brains as caused by nonsocial factors, but they have less empirical support than does the social brain hypothesis.

- Neurons are the basic units of the brain and nervous system and have three major sections: soma, dendrites, and axons. Neurons communicate via neurotransmitter messages that are released across the synaptic gap, from the axon from one neuron to the dendrites of others.

- The roles of five key neurotransmitters are discussed in the chapter: dopamine, serotonin, norepinephrine, GABA, and acetylcholine.

- Structures of the brain that are key to understanding social behavior include the prefrontal cortex, limbic system, thalamus and hypothalamus, and insula.

- Social neuroscience is the interdisciplinary field devoted to the study of neural, hormonal, cellular, and genetic mechanisms and to the study of the associations and influences between social and biological levels of organization.

- Social neuroscience uses a variety of methods to investigate the neurobiology of social behavior, and since each has its strengths and weaknesses, multiple methods are often used.

- *f*MRI has been proposed as a method for detecting deception, but research has not supported its use.

- The brain is clearly hardwired as a result of evolutionary processes; nevertheless, it is also surprisingly flexible or plastic, as it is capable of being rewired throughout the life cycle.

▶ $SAGE edge™ Test your understanding of chapter content. Take the practice quiz. edge.sagepub.com/barrett

KEY TERMS

Alleles, 59
Dualism, 45
Event-Related
    Potentials (ERPs), 63
Mind/Body Problem, 45

Neocortex Ratio, 48
Reductivism, 66

▶ $SAGE edge™ Review key terms with eFlashcards. edge.sagepub.com/barrett

Social Neuroscience, 47

THINK FURTHER!

- Why is the brain considered to be inherently *social?*

- Why is studying the brain crucial to understanding the foundations of social behavior?

- If you could choose one structure of the brain to research in depth and learn more about its role in social behavior, which would it be and why?

- In your opinion, which of the methods of social neuroscience represents the most

significant advance in understanding the social brain?

- If the *f*MRI were shown to be a valid and reliable way to detect deception, do you think it would be ethical to use it this way? Why or why not?

- What is brain plasticity and why is this important for understanding the relationships among genes, evolution, and culture?

SUGGESTED READINGS

Baer, J., Kaufman, J. C., & Baumeister, R. F. (2008). *Are we free? Psychology and free will.* New York, NY: Oxford University Press.

Cacioppo, J. T., & Berntson, G. G. (2005). *Social neuroscience: Key readings.* New York, NY: Psychology Press.

Ito, T. A., Thompson, E., & Cacioppo, J. T. (2004). Tracking the timecourse of social perception: The effects of racial cues on event-related brain potentials. *Personality and Social Psychology Bulletin, 30,* 1267–1280.

Richerson, P. J., & Boyd, R. (2005). *Not by genes alone: How culture transformed human evolution.* Chicago, IL: University of Chicago Press.

Vanman, E. J., Saltz, J. L., Nathan, L. R., & Warren, J. A. (2004). Racial discrimination by low-prejudiced Whites facial movements as implicit measures of attitudes related to behavior. *Psychological Science, 15,* 711–714.

II

THINKING ABOUT THE SELF AND OTHERS

3

Social Cognition

Figure skating pairs silver medal winners Jamie Sale and David Pelletier of Canada, left, look toward Russians figure skating pairs and gold medal winners Yelena Berezhnaya and Anton Sikharulidze during and awards ceremony at the Winter Olympics in Salt Lake City, Monday, February 11, 2002. Canadian outrage forced figure skating's ruling body to launch an inquiry into judging at the Olympics following Russia's controversial victory over the Canadians in the event.

AP Photo/Doug Mills.

LEARNING OBJECTIVES

3.1 Identify the five ways in which social cognition is different from nonsocial cognition and explain why people cannot NOT believe whatever they hear.

3.2 Define and compare and contrast the two types of processing; identify the four criteria for automaticity and list the three types of automatic processes; describe priming and spreading activation and illustrate them with an example.

3.3 Explain heuristics and describe availability, representativeness, base rate fallacy, base rate, and anchoring and adjustment.

3.4 Define reliability, validity, internal validity, and external validity and illustrate each with an example.

3.5 Explain what is meant by motivated reasoning and how it is illustrated by belief perseverance, confirmation bias, and biased assimilation.

3.6 Summarize the basic differences between cognition in the East and in the West.

BELIEVING IS SEEING

Do you see what I see? This seems like a simple question, but is it? A recent analysis of international media reporting of a 2002 Olympic skating scandal provides a nice illustration of how people can see the same thing differently and specifically the influence of preexisting loyalties on the perception of a single event (Stepanova, Strube, & Hetts, 2009). In the 2002 winter Olympics, the Russian skaters Yelena Berezhnaya and Anton Sikharulidze were awarded the gold medal in the figure skating pairs competition, and the Canadians Jamie Salé and David Pelletier received the silver. However, shortly after the event, reports of "vote trading" among the judges led to an investigation and additional scrutiny of the performances of the skating pairs. In the tradition of Hastorf and Cantril's (1954) examination of the Princeton-Dartmouth football game, Stepanova, Strube, and Hetts (2009) analyzed 425 newspaper reports of the controversy from Russia and the United States to determine what, if any, biases might have been present. Recall that Hastorf and Cantril (1954) found that both media reports and observations by fans of the Princeton-Dartmouth game demonstrated clear differences in perceptions of the fairness of the game that aligned with fan loyalties. Stepanova et al. (2009) analyzed 169 Russian and 256 U.S. articles using native-speaking Russian and American coders. They found that media reports in the two nations were consistent with East West loyalties: That is, the Russian reports construed both the skating event and the overall scandal in a pro-Russian, anti-West manner, whereas the U.S. stories reflected a pro-Canadian, anti-East interpretation. Of additional interest is that the U.S. media often acknowledged the bias (but demonstrated it nonetheless), but the Russian news outlets did not. The Stepanova et al. (2009) research is notable for two reasons: It updated and replicated the Hastorf and Cantril study, and it examined how construal can vary across cultures.

As mentioned in Chapter 1, prior to the 1950s psychologists and laypeople alike thought that there was one "reality" that all of us see and understand in essentially the same manner. However, research starting in the 1950s punctured this somewhat naïve perspective, leading to a new appreciation for the role of individual construal in social perception (Freeman & Ambady, 2014). The broader point here is that the ways in which individuals come to know and understand the world are affected by a multitude of forces, including desires, feelings, and goals, which can constrain and alter our seemingly unbiased perceptions (Bruner, 1957; Hahn & Harris, 2014; Ross, Lepper, & Ward, 2010). In this chapter we will survey research on social cognition—a topic discussed in both Chapters 1 and 2—and will place special emphasis on how our thinking processes are biased in both obvious and subtle ways.

Think Ahead!

1. *How might social cognition be different from nonsocial cognition?*

2. *To what extent are your thoughts, feelings, and behaviors influenced by non-conscious processes?*

3. *Do people reason differently across cultures?*

THE PSYCHOLOGY OF SOCIAL THINKING

In order to successfully navigate our complex social world, we must be able to make sense out of it. For most people, sense making has been seen as relatively uncontroversial, and the world was an objective reality that people could largely agree on. In other words, people generally believed that we "saw" objects, people, and events as they "really were." However, with the advent of the "New Look" in cognitive psychology around the middle of the 20th century, psychologists began to explore ways in which our minds go "beyond the information given" and actually *construct* the world as we process it (Bruner, 1957). They recognized that our sensory processes do not passively funnel information to our mental systems but instead actively work on and change that information, in effect *re*presenting it in an altered form. As we further explore our mental processes in this chapter, we will highlight two of our four core assumptions of social psychology. One is the role of individual *construal* in perceiving and making sense of our social worlds. The second is the principle of the *cultural* embeddedness of social cognition—that is, how cultural background can influence basic reasoning processes.

As defined in Chapter 1, social cognition is the study of mental processes associated with making sense of oneself and others (Fiske & Taylor, 2013). These processes include both conscious and nonconscious thinking as well as perception, attention, and remembering (Moskowitz, 2005). These social cognitive processes are particularly relevant to three of our enduring questions of human nature: free will, rationality, and

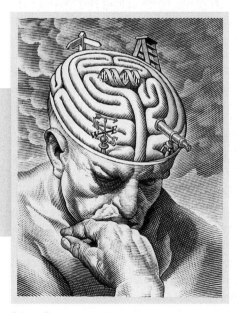

The gyri of the thinker's brain as a maze of choices. A gyrus is a ridge on the cerebral cortex. It is generally surrounded by one or more sulci (depressions or furrows).

Science Source.

the self. For instance, we'll discuss how apparently voluntary behaviors are affected by nonconscious, involuntary processes that may undermine our exercise of free will. We will also describe some of the biases in social cognition that lead us to question our ability to engage in rational or objective thought. In addition, we'll describe some mental shortcuts that people take to save time and energy and how they can reduce judgmental accuracy. Not surprisingly, the self plays a central role in social cognition, in part because our interpretations frequently reflect our need to bolster the self, as we will discuss more in Chapter 4. As you would expect, this chapter focuses primarily on the individual level of explanation, although both evolutionary and contextual influences will be incorporated.

©iStockphoto.com/laflor.

Are People Different Than Things? The "Social" in Social Cognition

©iStockphoto.com/PeopleImages.

Is thinking about people the same as thinking about nonpeople (such as objects, plants, animals, etc.)? In other words, is *social* cognition simply a subset of general cognition, or is it significantly different? People are obviously not things, but does it matter when it comes to mental processing? Social psychologists agree that people differ from things in several ways that have important implications for those processes (Jenkins & Mitchell, 2011; Mitchell, Heatherton, & Macrae, 2005; Moskowitz, 2005). Consider the following:

- **People think back** (and we think about their thinking). Probably the biggest difference between social and nonsocial cognition is that the object of our thoughts—people—are also social thinkers. Consequently, while we are thinking about them, they are thinking about us (Fiske & Taylor, 1991, 2013; Moskowitz, 2005). Since we are aware of their thinking, we begin thinking about their thinking, and so on. For instance, say you are strolling along the sidewalk and eye a stranger walking toward you. As you are looking at him, he glances at you. You can't help but wonder: *Does he notice my wrinkled shirt? My bad hair?* Your thoughts are affected by what you think his thoughts are, and his thoughts are in turn influenced by his judgments about you. In this way, our beliefs about others' perceptions of us affect our beliefs and perceptions about ourselves. Cooley (1902) called this phenomenon the **looking-glass self**, by which he meant that we see ourselves in other people because they are reflections of ourselves; we imagine how others imagine us, and this in turn affects how we think about ourselves.

Looking-Glass Self: Imagining how other people perceive and judge one's self, which in turn can affect that sense of self

- **People have special relevance for our goals.** Let's say that, as the stranger approaches, you recognize him as the husband of your boss, whom you met at a recent work party. Since you are due for your annual job performance evaluation and you hope for a raise, you worry just a little more about his impression of you and what he may say to your boss. How he thinks about you is particularly important to you and will change how you think about and handle your interaction. More generally, encounters with other people have a special relevance for us, in part because they can affect whether or not we achieve our goals, such as getting a raise or doing well on a group project in class (Fiske & Taylor, 1991, 2013; Moskowitz, 2005). Not all people are equally relevant for us, of course; the greater their potential impact on our goals, the more likely we are to devote our mental resources to thinking about them.

- **Thinking about people almost always involves social explanation.** Virtually every time we think about other people we engage in some type of social explanation (Fiske & Taylor, 1991, 2013; Malle, 2011; Moskowitz, 2005). Perhaps you notice that your social psychology professor has not called on you for the past couple of classes despite the fact that you have repeatedly raised your hand and that she has called on you in the past. You may wonder whether she dislikes you or is not interested in what you have to say. This is natural, as all of us seek to understand *why* others behave as they do. We more commonly look for the meaning behind the behavior of other people than of nonhuman events, such as a flat tire or snow storm.

- **We think more about people than about nonpeople.** There are clearly important qualitative differences—differences in *how* we process social versus nonsocial information. In addition, there is a quantitative one: People think *more* about people than about objects, animals, and plants (Lieberman, 2013). Consider your typical day. How much time do you spend thinking about your friends, family, and other people? About things like your car, home, or textbook? Most of us devote much more effort to pondering the intentions, motivations, and behavior of other people, including partners, friends, coworkers, and even complete strangers (such as celebrities, athletes, politicians, etc.). Thoughts about people (including ourselves) dominate our consciousness and consequently impact our social experiences more than thoughts about nonpeople.

- **Brains process people differently from nonpeople.** The burgeoning field of social neuroscience has amply demonstrated important differences in brain activation between social and nonsocial cognition (Todorov, Fiske, & Prentice, 2011). As we discussed in Chapter 2, social thinking relies on neural regions that are not typically involved when we are engaging in nonsocial thinking (Lieberman, 2013; Mitchell et al., 2005; Parkinson & Wheatley, 2015).

Think Again!

1. _What are five ways in which thinking about people is different from thinking about things?_

2. _What does it mean when we say that thinking about people almost always involves social explanation?_

3. _Can you imagine what a person's life would be like if he was not aware that other people think back at him?_

THE NATURE OF SOCIAL COGNITION

As we've said, social cognition is a set of interrelated processes that includes perceiving, attending to, remembering, thinking about, and making sense of ourselves and other people (see Figure 3.1). Each of these processes uniquely affects social cognition and has implications for the others. First, human perception actively works on stimuli by filtering and organizing information. Perception automatically categorizes what is perceived by placing it into groups or assigning an identity to it (Bruner, 1957). Second, our attention further screens information and, in general, the greater attention we devote to particular information—that is, the longer the information is held in short-term memory—the greater the likelihood that it will enter long-term memory. Although the layperson typically uses the word "attention" to refer to a conscious process, attention can also be non-conscious and automatic. For instance, if you are sitting on a park bench and a crow flies just overhead, the chances are you will reflexively look at it without making a conscious decision to do so. In addition, there may be stimuli in the environment that are subliminal in that they appear and disappear too quickly for your conscious mind to process them, but they nevertheless are attended to by your nonconscious mind and may affect your thoughts, feelings, and behavior.

FIGURE 3.1   Dynamic Processes of Social Cognition

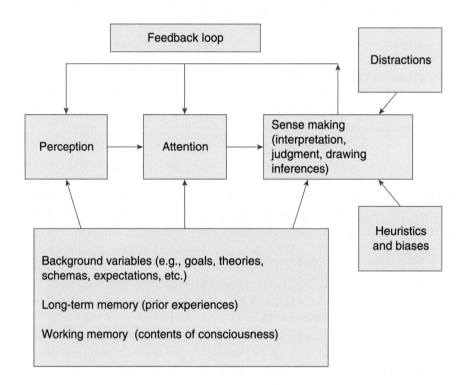

Clearly, we are able to attend to only a subset of what we perceive. Memory further narrows the social world, because only a small portion of what we perceive can be stored. Stimuli that are remembered—even temporarily—become the "stuff" of thinking. How we make sense of ourselves and others is in turn affected by all of these processes: what we perceive, attend to, what is stored in long-term memory, and what occupies our working memory at that moment. Making sense of ourselves or others involves integrating the information available to us, such as relevant external aspects of the person (such as gender, race, age, etc.) as well as inferences about internal aspects (such as motivations, desires, traits, intentions, etc.) (Freeman & Ambady, 2014). We use this personal information and features of the situation to understand, explain, and potentially, to predict how people will respond in the future.

Some examples of social cognition include

- noticing that a professor has his pants on backwards,
- construing or interpreting that professor's aberrant dressing habits as reflective of shocking absentmindedness,

- drawing a conclusion about the motivation of a potential date who just cancelled dinner plans with you, and
- trying to understand why a woman would kill herself and her three children by driving her car into a lake.

Social cognition may seem simple, because so much of it is automatic and effortless. In reality, it is a complex process and one that, due to resource and time constraints, can tax our mental system. Note too, that, like social experience itself, social cognition is *dynamic* (Freeman & Ambady, 2014; Moskowitz, 2005). Our thoughts are in perpetual flux as our perception, attention, and memory rapidly move from one focus or stimulus to another. Moreover, the social world is itself continuously changing as people adjust to their environment, move across contexts, and alter their situations, and as our relationships with the social world are modified. Partly as a result of the limits to what we can perceive, attend to, think about, and remember, social cognition is not a perfectly accurate process and is susceptible to a number of errors and mistakes, some of which we'll describe in the next section. Figure 3.1 illustrates the complexity of social cognition, its primary components, and some of the factors that influence it. Later in this text, we will focus on how social cognitive processes impact social perception (Chapter 5) and the evaluation of individuals in the context of stereotyping and prejudice (Chapter 10).

As you know, one of our four principles of social psychology is that social behavior is purposive or goal driven. What, then, are its goals? For one thing, as Darwin has taught us, the overarching goals of any living organism are its survival and reproduction. However, since all normal human activity is ultimately intended to continue our gene pool, our discussion of the purposes of social behavior will generally focus on more immediate goals that themselves help to ensure survival and reproduction.

Humans need to successfully navigate the physical and social worlds in order to attain the means to survive and reproduce. Such navigation requires the capacity to accurately assess the opportunities and risks that we may encounter. However, although it is important, striving to be accurate comes with a price: the expending of our cognitive resources. Deep, careful processing designed to maximize accuracy requires more mental energy than does shallow, rapid processing (Kunimi & Kojima, 2014; Petty, Cacioppo, Strathman, & Priester, 2005). Given that our mental resources are limited (Mandler, 2013), we must conserve them so that they are available for the tasks where they are needed most. Hence social cognition has the two interrelated goals of accuracy and the conservation of mental resources, and there is often a trade-off between these two goals (Andersen, Moskowitz, Blair, & Nosek, 2007). That is, accurate processing tends to be resource-intensive, whereas rapid processing requires fewer resources and may be less accurate (Andersen et al., 2007). We only want to devote as much mental energy as is necessary to be as accurate as we need to be, but no more (Chaiken, Liberman, & Eagly, 1989). For instance, the amount of mental energy you decide to allocate to studying for your next social psychology exam will partially depend on the extent to which being accurate (getting a good grade) or conserving cognitive resources (to spend on other activities) is important to you (Petersen, Skov, Serritzlew, & Ramsøy, 2013).

In addition to the goals of accurate processing and conserving cognitive resources, social cognition serves the goal of self-enhancement or of helping a person maintain a positive self-image (Andersen et al., 2007; Fiske & Taylor, 1991; Kruglanski, 1989). People want to feel good about themselves and consequently may interpret information in ways that can enhance their self-image. For example, people often blame other people or events for their own failures, thereby preserving a positive view of the self. This third goal can affect how we search for and process information, as we'll see later in this chapter and again in Chapter 4. The next section introduces one fascinating feature of our mental systems: that we must believe information before we can even understand it.

Understanding Is Believing: How You Cannot NOT Believe

Have you ever sat in class and thought to yourself "I understand what my professor is saying, but I just don't believe her"? Would you believe me, your textbook author, if I argued that in order to understand a statement you *must* first believe it to be true? If accurate, this would imply that you "can't NOT believe everything you read" (Gilbert, Tafarodi, & Malone, 1993). Furthermore, if this tendency is real, it suggests another obstacle to separating truth from lies.

In a set of clever studies, social psychologist Dan Gilbert and his colleagues have garnered substantial evidence for this rather surprising claim. In one study, Gilbert et al. (1993) provided participants with both true and false statements about two local crimes. Participants were informed as to which statements were true and which false, and half of the participants read these statements under conditions of divided attention, which required that they work on a different task at the same time. The crucial question was whether the false statements would influence the assignment of prison sentences. If the participants were able to identify and reject the false statements, then the false statements should not have affected the lengths of the prison sentences. However, when asked to assign prison sentences for the suspects, false statements that made the crime appear more severe led to much longer prison sentences, but only for the divided attention participants. The reason is that the divided attention participants were not able to ignore statements that they knew to be false. What this and related research has shown is that the mere act of comprehension—simply understanding a statement—requires believing, at least for a moment.

According to Gilbert (1991), the decision to reject a claim by decertifying its validity and thereby declaring it false happens in a second step, following the initial comprehension and acceptance. The divided attention participants lacked the cognitive resources to "unbelieve" the false statements and were unable to move onto the second step and reject the false arguments. Therefore, only in retrospect can one decide that a statement is false.

More broadly, Gilbert has argued that our mental systems must believe that a statement is true in order to comprehend it—to understand what it means. We can't NOT believe it is true before deciding it is false. Believing is the default or automatic process that occurs upon comprehension. The controlled process—rejecting the claim—only becomes operative if the available mental resources are sufficient to make the extra effort. A good everyday example of this is a person—we'll him call Steve—who always sets his watch ten minutes early. One morning at the coffee shop Steve glances at his watch and panics—swearing profusely about being late for class—but almost immediately realizes that he actually has ten minutes to spare, which is plenty of time to walk across campus. Steve initially "believed" his watch before he unbelieved it! The same is true when you hear your professor say that people automatically believe everything they hear—you have to believe the claim before you can reject it!

Think Again!

1. *What does it mean to say that social cognition narrows or filters the world?*

2. *As you sit in class or a coffee shop, take a minute and write down examples of each of the core components that you are engaging in.*

3. *Think about what you did yesterday. What trade-offs did you make between accuracy and mental resource conservation?*

4. *Why do people believe what they hear before disbelieving it?*

THE DUAL MIND: AUTOMATIC AND CONTROLLED PROCESSING

How many minds do you have? You probably think this a silly question and answer "One, of course!" Well, many psychologists claim that humans possess a *dual* mind—two minds in one. Evolution has given us two minds—one that we share with many other species and one that, by and large, we do not (Sherman, Gawronski, & Trope, 2014; Stanovich & West, 2002). These two minds or processing systems, called the automatic and consciously controlled systems, coexist in one brain yet seem to compete for control of our mental system (Evans, 2010; Evans & Stanovich, 2013). The primary distinction between them is that the former involves relatively little or no conscious awareness to operate, whereas the latter is largely conscious. The automatic system is, from an evolutionary point of view, both ancient and widespread, shared by many other animals. The conscious or controlled system, in contrast, is a relatively recent adaptation that is largely confined to the human species and, perhaps to a lesser extent, other primates (Corr, 2010; Lieberman, 2007b).

TABLE 3.1   Automatic and Controlled Processes

Automatic—the X-system	Controlled—the C-system
Unintentional	Intentional
Rapid	Slow
Capable of parallel processing	Serial processing
Intuitive	Logical
Real-time experiences	Reactions to those experiences
Narrowly defined problems	Abstract or general problems
Implicit memory	Concrete working memory
Context dependent	Can dissociate from context
Efficient	Effortful
Nonconscious	Consciously controlled

A simple way to understand the differences between the two systems is to contrast sitting at your computer in your room typing a class paper with reflexively ducking to avoid being hit by an errant Frisbee on the college green. Completing the class paper requires considerable deliberation and planning and relies on the higher brain. Getting out of the way of the Frisbee occurs without forethought, is essentially an automatic response to an environmental stimulus, and is performed by the lower brain. There are several other features that distinguish the two systems (see Table 3.1). The controlled system is relatively slow and sequential (i.e., it performs one task at a time), rational (although not necessarily unbiased), capable of abstract thinking, able to tackle complex problems and future planning, and relies on the working memory system (Evans, 2010; Sloman, 2014). In contrast, the automatic system is quick, engages in parallel processing (simultaneously accomplishing multiple tasks), is intuitive, includes instinctive behaviors, is limited to narrowly defined problems and processes, and relies on implicit learning and memory. The automatic system is also more context dependent, which is to say that, as in the Frisbee example, it responds to and can be automatically triggered by environmental stimuli.

Another distinction between the two systems is evident in the domain of emotions. For instance, if you were asked to eat a cockroach, you'd most likely experience an instant gut-level disgust reaction, especially because we associate cockroaches with dirt and garbage. This response is automatic, difficult to suppress, and a product of the automatic mind. However, after further consideration of the pros and cons of ingesting one—let's say after it was properly sterilized, maybe even covered in chocolate, and you are offered a decent sum of money to do it—you might choose to override the initial disgust reaction and eat the cockroach (Rozin & Fallon, 1987). In this case the two systems initiated responses that were incompatible with one another, and the conscious one held sway. This example illustrates another feature of the automatic/controlled duality: Sometimes the controlled system can overrule the automatic one.

These two components of the dual mind are sometimes called the X- and C-systems (Lieberman, 2010). The **X-system** is primarily reflexive, implicit, or automatic (the "X" stems from the "x" in reflexive), responding without conscious thought. In contrast, the **C-system** is largely reflective, explicit, and deliberative (the "C" refers to the "c" in reflective) and

X-system: Primarily reflexive, nonconscious, or automatic parallel processing system

C-system: Largely reflective, sequential, conscious, or deliberative mental processing system involves conscious thought (Lieberman,2007a; Lieberman, Gaunt, Gilbert, & Trope, 2002). These two systems rely on somewhat distinct brain regions. According to Lieberman et al. (2002), the X-system (also referred to as System 1) engages in parallel processing and consists of the amygdala, the basil ganglia, and the lateral temporal, ventromedial prefrontal, and dorsal anterior cingulate cortexes. Involved primarily with conscious processes, the C-system (also referred to as System 2) is composed mostly of the lateral prefrontal and posterior parietal cortexes, along with the hippocampus and medial temporal lobe region.

On the one hand, the X-system furnishes us with our ongoing immediate experience with reality and its associated cognitive processes. On the other hand, the C-system reflects on those experiences and responds to X-system processes and outputs. As suggested above, the systems are not completely independent; although the two systems work together much of the time, there are times when the C-system appears to react to, suppress, and/or overrule the X-system. For instance, a habit that is sustained by the X-system—such as swearing profusely at every red light while driving—may need to be occasionally suppressed—such as when your boyfriend's or girlfriend's parents are in the car.

The conceptual distinction between automatic and controlled processes is a useful one that nicely maps onto our social experiences. However, the difference is really more of matter of gray than of black and white. It is more accurate to ask how *much* of a given behavior is automatic versus controlled rather than whether it is one or the other. There are actually four components of **automaticity**, and a given event will be considered more automatic to the extent that it is (1) unintentional, (2) occurs without conscious awareness, (3) is accomplished efficiently, and (4), once begun, cannot be controlled (Andersen et al., 2007; Bargh, 1994; Fiedler & Hütter, 2014; Spunt & Lieberman, 2013). Take for example the experience of a song that keeps "playing" in your mind after you hear it blasting down the hallway in your residence. As you walk away and are no longer within earshot of the music, you find that the tune continues to cycle in your mind. This experience meets three of the four criteria for automaticity. First, note that this happens without intention: You did not consciously begin to mentally replay the song. Second, the song streams effortlessly and generally does not detract you from performing other tasks and is therefore efficient. Often, the song plays over and over with no conscious control required.

Third, to the extent that you cannot stop "playing" this song, the more automatic it is. However, because you are clearly conscious of the song, it is not an example of pure automaticity. In contrast, take the example of the Bargh scrambled sentence study described in Chapter 1 where participants walked more slowly after being exposed to elderly related words. This behavior is purely automatic, because it occurred without conscious intent and outside of awareness (participants did not know how the words changed their behavior), was efficiently performed (little effort was required), and could not be controlled (because the participants were not aware of it).

There are several types of automatic processes. The first consists of processes that were initially explicitly learned and later became automatic (Dijksterhuis, 2010). Take for instance learning to tie our shoes, which requires that we initially slow our thinking and

Automaticity: Extent to which a given event is unintentional, occurs without conscious awareness, is accomplished efficiently, and once begun, cannot be controlled

SELF-REFLECTION 3.1
How Do You *Feel* About Robots? (Part 1)

The 2014 Hollywood movie *The Imitation Game* relays the story of Alan Turing, a British computer scientist who was instrumental in decoding secret German military communications and, consequently, helping to defeat the Nazis in World War II. Turing worked in the area of artificial intelligence and was fascinated with whether or not a computer would ever be able to think as well as a human. Indeed, one of his lasting legacies is what is called the Turing Test: A computer could be said to think like a human if, when verbally interacting with a human, the human could not distinguish it from an actual human conversation partner. The fact that artificially intelligent machines are already assuming many complex tasks that previously only humans could accomplish is scary for many people. What are your attitudes toward intelligent robots? Take a minute and answer the following questions and then turn the page to see what others think.

TABLE 3.2　　How Do You *Feel* About Robots?

Item	Response options				
	Strongly disagree	Disagree	Undecided	Agree	Strongly agree
1. I would feel uneasy if I was given a job where I had to use robots.	1	2	3	4	5
2. The word "robot" means nothing to me.	1	2	3	4	5
3. I would feel nervous operating a robot in front of other people.	1	2	3	4	5
4. I would hate the idea that robots or artificial intelligences were making judgments about things.	1	2	3	4	5
5. I would feel very nervous just standing in front of a robot.	1	2	3	4	5

TURN THE PAGE TO FIND OUR ANSWERS.

SELF-REFLECTION 3.1
(Continued)

Item	Response options				
	Strongly disagree	**Disagree**	**Undecided**	**Agree**	**Strongly agree**
6. I would feel paranoid talking with a robot.	1	2	3	4	5
7. I would feel uneasy if robots really had emotions.	1	2	3	4	5
8. Something bad might happen if robots developed into living beings.	1	2	3	4	5
9. I feel that if I depend on robots too much, something bad might happen.	1	2	3	4	5
10. I am concerned that robots would be a bad influence on children.	1	2	3	4	5
11. I feel that, in the future, society will be dominated by robots.	1	2	3	4	5
12. I would feel relaxed talking with robots.	1	2	3	4	5
13. If robots had emotions, I would be able to make friends with them.	1	2	3	4	5
14. I feel comforted being with robots that have emotions.	1	2	3	4	5

Source: Tsui, K. M., Desai, M., Yanco, H. A., Cramer, H., & Kemper, N. (2010). Measuring attitudes toward telepresence robots. *International Journal of Intelligent Control and Systems*, 1–11.

SELF-REFLECTION 3.2
How Do You *Feel* About Robots? (Part 2)

These questions are drawn from an online study of Americans and Asian Indians conducted by Tsui, Desai, Yanco, Cramer, and Kemper (2010) into people's attitudes toward telepresence robots. Robots are telepresence when they cannot be moved around without direct human control. To obtain your results, first reverse the scoring for the final three items (1 = 5, 2 = 4, 3 = 3, 4 = 2, 5 = 1) and then total Items 1 through 6, 7 through 11, and 12 through 14 to get three totals. Finally, divide each by the number of questions to obtain your average response. Your average for Items 1 through 6 reflects your attitude towards interacting with robots, your average for Items 7 through 11 indicates how you would feel about the future ability of robots to socially influence people, and the average for Items 12 through 14 indicates how you think you'd feel if robots could experience emotions. See how your attitudes compare to those of your classmates. Higher numbers mean more positive views of telepresence robots.

movements down and watch our fingers make the proper motions. Once we have mastered the skill, we perform it without thinking. A second type of automatic process occurs when concepts that have been learned implicitly affect subsequent behavior (Andersen et al., 2007; Dijksterhuis, 2010). For instance, we can develop certain attitudes, called implicit attitudes, without conscious intent, and these attitudes may alter how we evaluate and interact with people (Dovidio, Pagotto, & Hebl, 2011; Greenwald & Banaji, 1995). Many Americans harbor implicit negative prejudices toward the elderly that they probably "picked up" without conscious thought (Nelson, 2009). The third category of automatic processes is priming, which was demonstrated in the scrambled sentence study mentioned in Chapter 1; here, an environmental stimulus temporarily and nonconsciously guided behavior.

Priming: When a concept or other knowledge structure is automatically triggered or activated by an environmental stimulus, thereby becoming more likely to affect subsequent related thoughts, feelings, and behaviors

Spreading Activation: Activation of one node in the mental system leads to the activation of other concepts that are closely associated with it in memory

Priming: Thinking and Doing Without Knowing

One of the ways in which social behavior can be affected outside of conscious awareness is through a process called priming. **Priming** occurs when a concept or other knowledge structure is automatically triggered or activated by an environmental stimulus, thereby becoming more likely to affect subsequent thoughts, feelings, and behaviors (Förster & Liberman, 2007; Higgins, 1989; Welsh & Ordóñez, 2014). When you read the word *gun,* what other concepts or words come to mind? Perhaps *bullet, violence,* and *soldier* (see Figure 3.2 on page 90)? The activation of *fire engine* led to the activation of other concepts that are closely associated with it in your memory, a process called **spreading activation** (Collins & Loftus, 1975; Newell & Shanks, 2014; Sansom-Daly & Forgas, 2010). In Bargh's scrambled sentence task described earlier, words related to *elderly* were consciously processed and activated, and this in turn triggered the nonconscious activation of the actual concept, *elderly* (Bargh, Chen, & Burrows, 1996). Bargh et al. (1996) similarly nonconsciously primed participants with neutral, rude, or polite words, and they subsequently acted consistently with that prime (see Figure 3.3 on page 90). In addition to concepts, other knowledge structures that can be automatically activated by stimuli in the environment include goals, motivations, and evaluations (Bargh, Gollwitzer, Lee-Chai, Barndollar, & Tröschel, 2001; Hassin, Bargh, & Zimerman, 2009; Sansom-Daly & Forgas, 2010). For instance, nonconsciously activating the goal of impression formation can lead people to form more coherent impressions of a target person (Chartrand & Bargh, 1996) than control individuals do.

Recently, research on priming has come under intensive scrutiny after a number of failures to replicate what had been considered to be solid, reliable findings (Molden, 2014; Pashler, Coburn, & Harris, 2012; Pashler, Rohrer, & Harris, 2013). Concerns about the replicability of priming effects has led to a wider debate about what constitutes a true replication and to what extent we can expect highly context-sensitive effects to replicate across settings (Cesario, 2014). Currently the debate rages on, and it will be fascinating to watch in the coming years as researchers closely examine when and why nonconscious activation of concepts, feelings, and goals may occur.

Think Again!

1. *What is the dual mind?*

2. *List four of the differences between the two components of the dual mind.*

3. *Can you think of a task you do that once required controlled processing but is now automatic? How about one that you wish were automatic?*

4. *What is priming? If you wanted to prime someone to act in a very helpful way, how might you do it?*

Free Will and the Dual Mind

The fact that humans possess these dual-processing systems has implications for one of our fundamental questions about human nature: whether or not humans have free will. The existence of free will hinges upon the relative roles of controlled and automatic processing in determining human behavior. If virtually everything that we do is a product of mostly nonconscious processes, then there is little free will. If, however, we have conscious control of most of what we do, then this suggests a greater degree of free will. As you learn more about social psychology, you will likely be amazed—and perhaps shocked—at the many ways that nonconscious processes seem to dominate conscious ones (Baer,

FIGURE 3.2   Spreading Activation

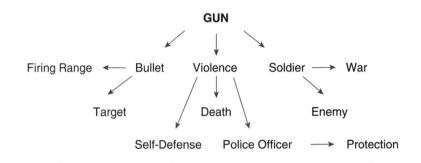

Hearing the word *gun* can activate associated concepts in your mind.

FIGURE 3.3   Nonconscious Priming Can Make You Rude

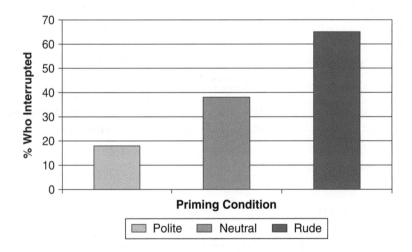

In one study, participants were by primed by exposure to words related to being polite or rude or unrelated neutral words. In a subsequent encounter in which the participants needed to gain the attention of an experimenter engaged in a conversation, the percentage of those who interrupted within a 10-minute time limit varied consistently with the prime.

Source: Adapted from Figure 1, Bargh, J. A., Chen, M., & Burrows, L. (1996). Automaticity of social behavior: Direct effects of trait construct and stereotype activation on action. *Journal of Personality and Social Psychology, 71*(2), 230–244.

Kaufman, & Baumeister, 2008; Baumeister & Bargh, 2014; Dijksterhuis, Strick, Bos, & Nordgren, 2014; Hassin, Uleman, & Bargh, 2005). In fact, one prominent social psychologist has argued that conscious control is largely an illusion and that humans have little free will (Nahmias, Shepard, & Reuter, 2014; Wegner, 2002). After reviewing several common mental shortcuts, we'll take a look at a number of ways in which humans *seem* to engage in willful behavior, such as deciding not to believe a claim we previously accepted, engaging in counterfactual thinking, and some types of reasoning.

HEURISTICS: MENTAL SHORTCUTS

In an ideal world, beliefs would be based on careful assessment of relevant evidence. However, we inhabit a world in which we are faced with information overload, continuous, competing distractions, and frequent pressure to multitask. These factors minimize our ability to engage in the controlled processing needed for a thorough review of the information and consequently we make many judgments in a quick and cursory fashion (Goldstein & Gigerenzer, 2011; Hertwig & Hoffrage, 2013; Kahneman, 2011). Given the trade-off between accurate processing and conserving mental resources, we sometimes forego accuracy for expediency, and this can lead to mistaken beliefs or inferences. That is, we often take mental shortcuts so that we can make rapid decisions either because we are not motivated to think carefully or we do not have the ability to do so. When either or both are the case, we may utilize intuitive strategies that will quickly lead us to a conclusion. These strategies are called **heuristics** or mental shortcuts, and they facilitate rapid inferences without much thought (Gilovich & Griffin, 2010; Tversky & Kahneman, 1974). Oftentimes these heuristics or rules of thumb produce successful or accurate judgments, and therefore, it makes sense for us to save time and mental energy and rely on them (see Table 3.3). However, they are easy to use, and this increases the likelihood that we will resort to them when we should not, which can lead to incorrect conclusions.

> **Heuristic:** Mental shortcut that facilitates rapid inferences without much thought

Availability

Quick, do more Americans die in homicides or suicides each year? I imagine that your first response was homicides. After all, it is pretty easy to think of the many homicides regularly reported in the press. However, according to the U.S. government, there were over 16,000 homicides and over 41,000 suicides in 2013 (Centers for Disease Control and Prevention, n.d.). Another question: Are there more words in the English language that begin with the letter *r* or that have *r* as the third letter? Although you, like most people, may have guessed that there are more that begin with *r*, you would be incorrect. There are actually far more English words with *r* as the third letter (Tversky & Kahneman, 1974). What led you to an incorrect inference? Well, it was probably easier for you to rapidly think of more words beginning with *r,* and you relied on this shortcut in providing your answer.

TABLE 3.3   Some Cognitive Heuristics and Biases

Name	Description	Example
Availability	Make a judgment about the frequency or likelihood of an event based on how easily it comes to mind.	Thinking there are more homicides than suicides each year in the United States because examples of homicides are easier to think of
Representativeness	When we categorize a particular instance based on how similar the instance is to a typical member of that category	Assuming that Jose is a wrestler and not a debater because he looks more like a stereotypical wrestler
Base rate fallacy	Occurs when we ignore underlying probabilities—the base rate or frequency of an event—and instead focus on unusual or atypical instances	Claiming that a scientific finding is inaccurate, because you can think of an exception, and ignoring what is most frequently accurate
Anchoring and adjustment	To rely on readily available information on which to base estimation	Guessing that the Mississippi River is close to 750 miles because that number was made available to you

Availability Heuristic: Mental shortcut in which people judge the frequency or likelihood of an event based on how easily relevant examples come to mind

Psychologists call this shortcut the **availability heuristic**; we make a judgment about the frequency or likelihood of an event based on how easily examples come to mind. Information is said to be available when it comes to mind easily (Braga, Ferreira, & Sherman, 2014; Förster & Liberman, 2007; Tversky & Kahneman, 1973). Rather than carefully scanning our internal dictionary for the two categories of words, we base our answer on the availability of relevant information. Judgments based on the availability heuristic often have significant real-world consequences. For instance, financial decisions by investors are often made prematurely (and unwisely) when they rely too much on information that is immediately available—such as how a given stock performed in the prior year—rather than on all relevant information (Kliger & Kudryavtsev, 2010). As we will discuss later in Chapter 10, ease of recall can affect a wide variety of judgments, including how we evaluate strangers in ways that conform to available stereotypes, even if we consciously reject those stereotypes.

Representativeness

Is it true that if it looks like a duck and quacks like a duck, it is a duck? Say your university has a 32-member debate team and a three-member wrestling team. You see Jose, a tall, muscular male student walking across campus dressed in athletic gear, and a friend asks you if Jose is a wrestler or a debater. At first glance and without much thought you respond "wrestler." Why? Because Jose resembles your image of a stereotypical wrestler, you may immediately assume that he is one. However, upon further reflection, you'd realize that not only is the debate team larger than the wrestling team (which means that he is automatically more likely to debate than to wrestle) but also that debaters come in all shapes and sizes, as do wrestlers. Therefore, the student is much more likely to be a debater than a wrestler—he just happens not to represent your vision of the typical debater. This illustrates the **representativeness heuristic**, another shortcut that we often rely on to conserve mental resources and make rapid decisions. The representativeness heuristic is used when we categorize a particular instance based on how similar the instance is to a typical member of that category (Kahneman & Frederick, 2002; Tversky & Kahneman, 1974).

In one study, participants were presented with a personality profile of Steve, whose name was randomly pulled out of a set of 100 profiles, 70 of whom were engineers and 30 of whom were librarians. Steve was described as "very shy and withdrawn, invariably helpful, but with little interest in people, or in the world of reality. A meek and tidy soul, he has a need for order and structure, and a passion for detail." Is Steve an engineer or a librarian? Because Steve resembles the stereotypical librarian, most people would guess librarian. However, in doing so they would be ignoring the base rate probabilities that Steve is one or the other (Jasper & Ortner, 2014; Tversky & Kahneman, 1974). Note that a name randomly pulled out of that set is much more likely to be an engineer, based solely on probabilities. In the Steve example, we fail to take into account the base rate at which the phenomenon occurs.

A second common mistake has to do with the way people appeal to personal anecdotes or limited observation to reject the findings of a particular social psychological study. On many occasions, I have presented research results in class and a student raised his hand and said something to the effect that "I was in a situation like that and I (or someone I know) didn't act the way the people in the study did, and therefore the study isn't valid." For instance, we may be discussing how people tend to affiliate with winning teams—often by donning that team's shirts and caps—and dissociate from losers (Cialdini et al., 1976), a trend that this is very noticeable after a major sporting event like the Super Bowl or World Cup. A student may say that she wore her Denver Broncos T-shirt the day after they lost to the Seattle Seahawks in the 2014 Super Bowl and consequently conclude that the study is incorrect. However, both she and you need to be cognizant of the fact that social psychology is not able to predict the behavior of any particular person or of every person—nor does it attempt to. Rather, we describe, explain, and predict what *most* people are likely to think, feel, and do in specific situations. Very rarely—if ever—does each and every one of the participants in a study behave in exactly the same way. Therefore, identifying an apparent exception or counterexample for a given phenomenon and arguing that this *dis*proves the finding represents an overreliance on anecdotal information and a neglect of base rate information.

This **base rate fallacy** occurs when we ignore underlying probabilities—the base rate or frequency of an event—and instead focus on unusual or atypical instances

---

Representativeness Heuristic: Mental shortcut in which people categorize a particular instance based on how similar the instance is to a typical member of that category

---

Base Rate Fallacy: Judging how likely an event is to occur, based on unusual or atypical instances, while ignoring its actual base rate or probability of occurrence

(Bar-Hillel, 1980). We are particularly likely to do this when we reject the validity of abstract information in favor of concrete, vivid examples, such as anecdotes (Schwarz, Strack, Hilton, & Naderer, 1991; Taylor & Thompson, 1982). In our football example, the fact that most people behave in a specific way (an abstract statement) is not undermined by an instance of one person acting differently (a concrete example). The **base rate** is how frequent members of various categories occur in the corresponding population (Bar-Hillel, 1990; Kahneman & Tversky, 1972). Given that there are more debaters than wrestlers in the university population, there is a much greater likelihood that Jose is a debater. Likewise, for Steve being an engineer versus librarian.

Relying on the base rate can clearly lead to incorrect decisions. But is it ever useful? Of course it is. We categorize people (and things) for a reason: Categories allow us to simplify our world and make it cognitively manageable. Category members, by definition, share particular traits or characteristics. The traits that make up a category are different from those that make up another category, although some of these characteristics may overlap. Therefore, it is not only natural but also desirable that we use similarity as a basis for categorizing people. The underlying problem with doing so occurs when we ignore other relevant information (like base rates) and use *only* representativeness (Fiedler, Brinkmann, Betsch, & Wild, 2000).

Anchoring and Adjustment

Before reading further, write down whether the Mississippi River is longer or shorter than 800 miles. How many miles long is it? Did you guess 775 or 900 or another number in the rough vicinity of 800? What if I were to instead ask if the Mississippi River is longer or shorter than 2100 miles, and then you were to estimate its length? Would you have given a different estimate? If you are like most of my social psychology students, then you would have guessed a much larger number after being asked the latter question. Why? The reason is that you assume that the number that I inserted into the question—either 800 or 2100—is relevant to the answer and reasonably close to the river's actual length. You expect that the number was presented for a reason and therefore that you should use it as an informational guide for your answer (Chapman & Johnson, 2002; Morrow, 2002). You start with the given number—you anchor your estimate on it—and then adjust it either up or down (Tversky & Kahneman, 1974). The human tendency to rely on readily available information on which to base estimation and then to adjust that estimate up or down is another mental shortcut, called the **anchoring and adjustment heuristic** (Tversky & Kahneman, 1974). We use this heuristic in order to simplify the estimation process and conserve our mental resources. It often serves us well, providing a generally correct answer that can then be tweaked to produce an even better one. Interestingly, people adjust the anchor less if that anchor is more precise rather than rounded. For instance, participants in one study made smaller adjustments to the precise anchor of $4,998 versus the rounded anchor of $5,000 (see Research Box 3.1) (Janiszewski & Uy, 2008).

Base Rate: Frequency at which a given phenomenon occurs

Anchoring and Adjustment Heuristic: Mental shortcut in which people use readily available information on which to base estimation and then adjust that estimate up or down to arrive at a final judgment

RESEARCH BOX 3.1
ANCHORING AND ADJUSTMENT

Hypothesis: Estimates of the value of goods would diverge more from the anchor if given imprecise or rounded anchors versus more precise anchors.

Research Method: Participants were randomly assigned to receive either imprecise or precise anchor values for a variety of consumer goods, including a plasma TV, beverage, or a chunk of cheese. For example, some participants were given the estimates $5,000, $10, and $5, respectively, whereas others were given $4,998, $9.80, and $4.85. Participants were asked to estimate the actual costs of these items.

Results: Estimates in the imprecise condition diverged significantly more from their respective anchors than did estimates in the precise condition.

Conclusion: People seem to have greater confidence in the validity of precise values than rounded values and consequently make smaller adjustments to them. This finding has real-world implications. For example, people who are negotiating the price of a home or the amount of a legal settlement may gain a more favorable outcome if they initially offer a specific price or settlement amount.

Source: Janiszewski, C., & Uy, D. (2008). Precision of the anchor influences the amount of adjustment. *Psychological Science, 19*, 121–127.

Why do we make this error? We do so because we assume that the information that we are provided is relevant to the answer requested (Chapman & Johnson, 2002). The assumption makes perfect sense—much of the time. Typically when we are faced with a problem or puzzle, whatever information is provided is relevant to the problem being solved. Again, this heuristic often works, but like availability and representativeness, it can sometimes lead us into error. A real-world illustration of anchoring and adjustment can be seen in the way that juries determine awards in liability cases based on whatever numbers are presented to them, regardless of the origin of or justification for those numbers (Chapman & Bornstein, 1996). This is the reason attorneys for the plaintiff often initially ask for unreasonable large dollar amounts in a legal settlement. Similar findings have been found with regard to the valuation of homes in real estate (Northcraft & Neale, 1987), estimating how long Gandhi lived (F. Strack & Mussweiler, 1997), and guessing the year in which George Washington was elected U.S. president (Epley & Gilovich, 2001).

> ### *Think Again!*
>
> 1. *What are heuristics and why do we rely on them?*
>
> 2. *Give an explanation and your own example of the availability, representativeness, and anchoring and adjustment heuristics.*

DOING RESEARCH: RELIABILITY AND VALIDITY

In Chapter 1 we discussed how experiments can help determine whether one variable is causally related to another. Specifically, we saw how using multiple conditions (typically at least one experimental and one control) and random assignment to condition can enhance our confidence in the experimental results. Now let's turn to a couple of other features of experiments—and other types of studies—that can similarly impact our confidence in social psychological research: reliability and validity.

Say you jumped on the scale to weigh yourself one morning and the digital readout displayed 142 pounds, which is a bit more than you hoped for. So you step off and then on again and are surprised to see that *now* the scale shows 133, which is closer to, perhaps a little lower than, what you'd be happy with. But just to be sure you reweigh yourself, and this time the scale reads 148! Confused, you try a few more times, with results of 146, 136, 142, 139, and 137 pounds. *Okay, so what do I really weigh?* you wonder. Using that scale and those results, it is impossible to answer that question with much confidence. Given how the results of your measurement attempts fluctuate so widely, you cannot determine your true weight. In order to feel more certain that your measurement tool—your scale—is reasonably accurate, it first needs to be reliable.

Reliability of a given measurement method is how consistently each measurement of the same phenomenon produces approximately the same result under the same conditions. In other words, a reliable measure should provide the same result across multiple measurement occasions of the same phenomenon. This of course assumes that the thing being measured has not changed between measurement attempts. If your scale gave you the same or close to the same weight—such as 138 pounds—each time you stepped on it, then it would be reliable.

Note, however, that simply because the scale gives the same result each time it does not necessarily mean that that weight is the correct one. That is, the scale might indicate that you weigh 142 pounds on four consecutive measurements, but your actual weight may be 138. The scale could be systematically providing results that are too high (or too low) every time it is used: Perhaps it is not properly calibrated, and the "0" is in fact "4" pounds. In addition to being reliable, then, the ideal measurement tool is also valid: It indicates your true weight. **Validity** is the extent to which a particular measurement tool provides accurate results. If you actually weigh 138, then a valid scale would report this.

Reliability: How consistently each measurement of the same phenomenon using the same measurement tool produces approximately the same result under the same conditions

Validity: Extent to which a particular measurement tool provides accurate results

Social psychologists seek to develop methods of measurement that are both reliable and valid. If we would like to measure attitudes toward, say, the environment, then we want to construct the scale so that it is reliable. For instance, if the wording of the questions were ambiguous—and could be interpreted in different ways—then it is unlikely to be reliable because it might give different results at different times. Say we want to assess a person's need for cognition or the extent to which she tends to enjoy and engage in careful thinking (Cacioppo & Petty, 1982; Cacioppo, Petty, & Kao, 1984). To do so we administer the 18-item Need for Cognition Scale (NCS), in which responses are recorded on nine-point scale (−4 to 4+). Let's say that Gisele completes the scale with a mean response of 3.2, suggesting a high need for cognition. A couple of weeks later, Gisele completes the scale again, and this time the mean response is −1.4. With two widely divergent results, it is impossible to know what Gisele's "true" score is, and as a result, the scale would be considered unreliable. Valid methods provide accurate or correct results—in the case of NCS, the mean response for a given person would be fairly close to her "true" need for cognition.

Social psychologists are most concerned with two types of validity. One type, called **internal validity**, refers to the extent to which we can be sure that the purported cause—the IV—is the only factor influencing the purported effect—the DV (Campbell & Stanley, 1963). If, as we described in Chapter 1, the researcher successfully controlled all extraneous variables and confounds and used random assignment, then the experiment can be said to have internal validity. In our earlier example of the effects of playing a violent video game on aggression, if we are confident that only the manipulation of the video game led to the different amounts of aggression in the subsequent game, then the study has good internal validity.

The second type, **external validity**, indicates how well the results of the study can be generalized or applied to other settings and populations (Campbell & Stanley, 1963). For instance, a laboratory study is said to have external validity if the effects can be generalized to real-life situations. In the video game example, if real-world aggression increased as a result of playing violent games, then we can say that the study has external validly. In Chapter 8 on prosocial behavior, we'll elaborate on external validity and generalizability.

MOTIVATED REASONING

The errors that we have discussed so far are rooted in "cold" mental processes that reflect simple overreliance on shortcuts and misperceptions of reality. That is, the perceiver has no particular stake in the answer and is not interpreting available information in order to achieve a certain goal or outcome. In contrast, other cognitive errors can result from "hot" cognition: the perceiver's reasoning is motivated or intended to reach a desired conclusion, solution, or outcome. **Motivated reasoning**—hot cognition—occurs when a person's mental processing is influenced by that person's desires, feelings, or goals (Hahn & Harris, 2014; Kunda, 1990). Here again we see the principle of construal at work: how individual interpretation of the social environment affects our social behavior. The basic idea here is that we first decide what the answer is and then gather data or

Internal Validity: Extent to which an experimenter can be sure that the purported cause—the IV—is the only factor influencing the purported effect—the DV

External Validity: Extent to which the results of a study can be generalized or applied to other settings and populations (also called generalizability)

Motivated Reasoning: Person's mental processing is influenced by her or his desires, feelings, or goals

evaluate the available information to justify or support that answer. The case for motivated reasoning was most cogently laid out in a famous paper by Ziva Kunda (1990) and has been well-substantiated across many domains of social behavior, including how people evaluate new technologies (Druckman & Bolsen, 2011), count ballots in disputed elections (Kopko, Bryner, Budziak, Devine, & Nawara, 2011), understand important political issues (Slothuus & de Vreese, 2010), interpret consumer brand information (Jain & Maheswaran, 2000), and apply stereotypes (Kunda & Sinclair, 1999). This section introduces a couple of biases that, as you will see, may prevent relatively unbiased thinking and instead lead the perceiver to a preferred conclusion.

Belief Perseverance: Believing When There Is No Evidence

A belief is a conviction we hold about whether something is true or false and is often formed on the basis of evidence or information that we accept as true. Sometimes we have a belief that, when originally formed, was based on reasonably good evidence. Take for instance belief in the existence of weapons of mass destruction (WMDs) in Iraq before the 2002 multinational invasion. U.S. political leaders—including President Bush and Secretary of State Colin Powell—argued that Iraq was an imminent and significant threat to Americans because it had substantial stockpiles of WMDs that could be used against the United States or its allies. At the time, ordinary Americans, U.S. Senators and Representatives, and the leaders of the United Nations and many allied nations accepted the data supplied by the U.S. government as valid evidence for this claim. However, after the invasion and intensive efforts to locate material traces of WMDs, it became clear that there were in fact none to be found. Nevertheless, many people—even those who acknowledged the fact that the initial evidence that led them to believe Iraq had WMDs was false—continued to believe that Iraq had them (Lewandowsky, Stritzke, Oberauer, & Morales, 2005).

Belief Perseverance: Phenomenon of holding onto a belief when its validity has been undermined by the facts

In the Iraq case, beliefs about WMDs that were formed on the basis of specific evidence persisted despite the fact that all of the evidence was later demonstrated to be false. This phenomenon of holding onto a belief that been undermined by the facts is called unwarranted **belief perseverance** (Bui, 2014; Ross, Lepper, & Hubbard, 1975). Belief perseverance occurs when the evidence for a particular belief has been completely discredited, yet the belief continues.

In one laboratory study, Craig Anderson (1983) provided data to some participants that demonstrated that risk takers made more successful fire fighters than risk avoiders, whereas participants in another condition were supplied with data stating the opposite (that risk takers were less successful fire fighters than risk avoiders). After all participants wrote a short paragraph justifying their beliefs, Anderson told them that the data that they were provided had been completely falsified, and that there was no evidence that risk taking and fire fighting success were in any way correlated. After the evidence for their beliefs had been undermined, participants stated what their true beliefs were about this relationship, as if they had not been exposed to the evidence in this experiment at all. Despite this clear and total undermining of the supposed evidence, participants typically believed that a relationship existed between risk taking and fire fighting success. In other words, their beliefs persevered despite the fact that there was no longer any evidence to support them. These participants seemed to think that their beliefs about this relationship predated the experiment, although this was highly unlikely. Control group participants not exposed to any evidence about this relationship tended to have no strong belief about the relationship between risk taking and success as a firefighter (see Figure 3.4).

Why do false beliefs persist? In part because we feel pressure to stick with our commitments, including commitments to beliefs, and therefore find it surprisingly difficult to give them up (Cialdini, 2008; Ross et al., 1975). Second, the explanations that the participants had created to justify their belief—perhaps based on a story of a firefighter who took a risk and saved a life that they had learned about in another context—continued to support the participants' initial beliefs and remained available to the participant after the given explanation was undermined (Anderson, 1983; Anderson, Lepper, & Ross, 1980; Davies, 1997; Nestler, 2010). It did not seem to matter that their self-generated explanations were not based on evidence.

Can you think of a way to overcome this problem? Take a minute . . . if thinking about an event makes it seem more likely to be true, then is there something else one can think about that might counter it? What about carefully considering how the exact opposite of what you initially believed could instead be true?

FIGURE 3.4   Debiasing in the Perseverance of Social Theories

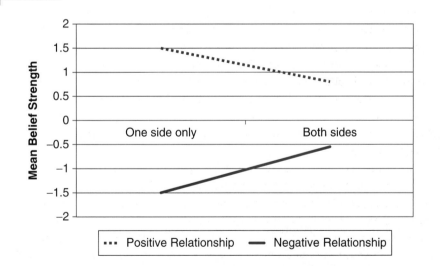

Values that are farther from zero indicate greater perseverance. Note how thinking about both sides of an argument reduced unwarranted belief perseverance.

Source: Adapted from Figure 1, Anderson, C. A. (1982). Inoculation and counterexplanation: Debiasing techniques in the perseverance of social theories. *Social Cognition, 1*(2), 126–139.

Considering the Opposite

If a complete undermining of the evidence used to create and support a belief failed to shake many participants of their patently false beliefs, then what more can be done to convince them to reject those beliefs? One strategy was examined by Anderson (1982). As described above, Anderson provided participants with evidence about the relationship between taking or avoiding risks and success as a firefighter. Participants exposed to evidence that risk takers were more successful wrote explanations arguing both for and against this claim, and those exposed to the opposite evidence did the same. All were forced to consider how the *opposite* of what they read could be true. Next they were given a chance to report what their true beliefs about the relationship were before the experiment began. Unlike in the case of simply being told that the evidence for their belief was fabricated, those participants who engaged in **considering the opposite** did in fact overcome their unsupported beliefs. Imagining how their beliefs could be false largely wiped out the belief perseverance effect described above (Anderson, 1982; Nestler, 2010).

In sum, sometimes our beliefs are mistaken: They simply are not true. As we've seen, there are a number of reasons that we nevertheless hold onto them. One reason is that we may have clung to a belief despite the fact that its evidence is undermined, because we created new reasons for maintaining it (Anderson et al., 1980). A second reason is that we may not have seriously considered alternative beliefs (Anderson, 1982).

Considering the Opposite: Imagining how one's beliefs could be false

Think Again!

1. *What is a belief?*

2. *What is belief perseverance, and how can "considering the opposite" overcome it?*

Confirmation Bias

Imagine you are about to interview another student to determine if she is extraverted. You are given a set of questions to select from, some of which focus on behaviors and experiences indicative of extraversion (such as how would you liven up a party?) and others of introversion (such as in what situations would you like to be more outgoing?). Would you choose questions the answers to which are more likely to produce evidence consistent or inconsistent with the answer you are seeking? Well if you are like the students in Snyder and Swann's (1978b) study, you'll favor the consistent items that focus on extraversion. If, on the other hand, you are trying to learn whether she is introverted, you'll prefer the introversion items. Why?

In Chapter 1, we described how people are natural hypothesis testers; we develop ideas about how the world works and test our ideas in relevant situations (remember the interviewee's comment about the interviewer's legs?) (Ross & Nisbett, 1991). Such hypothesis testing can be influenced by the motivations that are active at the time, thereby enhancing the likelihood that we will reach a desired conclusion (Mullen & Skitka, 2006). When gathering evidence to evaluate the validity of a belief, we tend to look primarily at instances that confirm that belief and to ignore or discount those that do not (Traut-Mattausch, Jonas, Frey, & Zanna, 2011; Trope & Liberman, 1996). For instance, if you are testing the proposition that Norwegian men are handsome, then you are likely to look primarily for cases that could support it (finding Norwegian men who are attractive) rather than those that might undermine it (searching for less attractive Norwegian men) (Snyder & Swann, 1978b). We call this tendency to search only for evidence that supports our beliefs and to ignore information that disagrees with them the **confirmation bias** (Gilbey & Hill, 2012; Nickerson, 1998; Snyder & Swann, 1978a). Evidence for the confirmation bias has been found in how people assess the accuracy of sex role stereotypes (Marks & Fraley, 2006), assignment of diagnoses by psychiatrists (Mendel et al., 2011), and how people gather evidence about a suspect in criminal investigations (Kukucka & Kassin, 2014; Rassin, Eerland, & Kuijpers, 2010).

Confirmation Bias: Tendency to search only for evidence that supports one's beliefs and to ignore information that disagrees with them

Biased Evaluation of Information

People's motivations can influence not only searches for new information but also the evaluation of existing information. Vallone, Ross, and Lepper (1985) exposed research participants to news videos reporting the killing of civilians by Israeli soldiers in a refugee camp in the Middle Eastern nation of Lebanon in 1982. Students who were already pro-Arab perceived the news reports to be biased against Arabs, whereas pro-Israeli students interpreted the reports as biased against Israelis. In each case, participants held preexisting beliefs that the media were biased against their own opinions and perceived the news stories as confirming that media bias. Of course, sometimes the media really are biased in its reports of world events, such as in the case of the 2002 Olympic skating controversy, discussed above (Stepanova et al., 2009). More generally, sometimes people will interpret information in ways that make that information appear to support their own perspectives (Greitemeyer, Fischer, Frey, & Schulz-Hardt, 2009; Mojzisch, Grouneva, & Schulz-Hardt, 2010). For instance, viewers of presidential debates overwhelmingly believe that their favored candidate "won" against an opponent (Kinder & Sears, 1985).

Such **biased assimilation**—the interpretation of information so that it seems similar to or consistent with one's preferred perspective—occurs even when people are evaluating purportedly scientific evidence. Lord, Ross, and Lepper (1979) provided pro- and anti-capital punishment participants with two studies, one which supported the deterrent effects of capital punishment and one that demonstrated the opposite. The "pro" individuals assessed the "pro" study as more valid than the "anti" study, whereas

Biased Assimilation: Construing information so that it seems similar to or consistent with one's preferred perspective

the "anti" students evaluated them in the opposite way. This occurred despite the fact that the researchers controlled for differences in the methodologies between the studies: Whichever study participants disagreed with was more strongly criticized. Even psychologists are not immune to such biased thinking, at times evaluating the validity of research results in a manner consistent with their own preferred explanations (Hergovich, Schott, & Burger, 2010). Think about the ongoing debate about whether the death penalty reduces crime rates . . . how do you suppose advocates on each side evaluate evidence that contradicts their perspectives?

As you can see, people often engage in motivated reasoning that results in the gathering and/or evaluation of evidence so that it appears consistent with what they want to believe. In later chapters, we'll extend our discussion of the effects that motivations, feelings, and goals have on many other social psychological processes, including how we determine the causes of social behavior, susceptibility to social influence, and perceptions of other groups. For now, let's turn our attention to another key influence on our reasoning processes: culture.

Think Again!

1. _What are the implications of motivated reasoning for your own thinking?_

2. _Define and give your own example of the confirmation bias._

3. _What does it mean to engage in biased assimilation?_

CULTURE AND COGNITION

Which is true? (a) Cigarette smoking is correlated with being skinny; (b) heavy doses of nicotine often result in becoming overweight. Although I cannot predict which one you chose, I am betting that you selected _only one_. People from Western cultures, such as those in Western Europe and North America, tend to believe that only one of the statements is true because they appear to contradict one another. East Asians, in contrast, would be less likely to view them in an either/or fashion and would instead try to identify a third way, one in which _both_ can be correct or partially correct (Peng & Nisbett, 1999). This example, adapted from research by Peng and Nisbett (1999), illustrates how tolerance for contradiction in particular and fundamental reasoning processes more generally vary across cultures.

That humans must categorize information, store information in memory, and solve social and other problems is universally true; however, the way we accomplish these tasks can depend on our cultural background (Berry, 2015; Chiu & Hong, 2007; Segall, Dasen, Berry, & Poortinga, 1999). Some of the most important cultural variations in cognitive

SOCIAL PSYCHOLOGY APPLIED TO HEALTH
STRESS AND COPING

You don't need me to tell you that college can be very stressful, especially if you live away from home for the first time and are juggling work and/or time with a partner and other friends. What are your biggest stressors? Some of the stressors most common among college students relate to time management in a less structured setting, navigating social relationships, isolation/separation from family and friends, and use of drugs and/or alcohol (Baghurst & Kelley, 2014; O'Hara, Armeli, Boynton, & Tennen, 2014; Stoliker & Lafreniere, 2015). Why, do you suppose, do those events or situations cause you to feel stress? Well, some obviously involve change, and changes—even those we embrace enthusiastically—can lead to stress. Clearly, people vary in what we find stressful. Psychologists argue that stress has more to do with how we subjectively construe and respond to life situations than with the "objective" events themselves (Lazarus, 2012; Lazarus & Folkman, 1984).

According to the **appraisal model of stress**, we engage in two appraisal processes regarding a potential stressor that impact how we emotionally respond to it (see Figure 3.5) (Folkman & Lazarus, 1988; Folkman, Lazarus, Gruen, & DeLongis, 1986; Lazarus, 2006). The primary appraisal process involves interpreting the event or situation as a negative threat, a positive opportunity, or simply irrelevant to us. The secondary appraisal process is an assessment of what the person can do to respond to the event or situation in order to minimize or avoid the harm or maximize the benefit. For instance, how are you likely to think about an upcoming social psychology exam? Do you see it as an opportunity to demonstrate what you have learned or as a threat to your self-esteem and/or grade? After this primary appraisal, you would secondarily consider whether you have the ability to adequately handle this exam. These appraisals will partially determine whether you look forward to or dread the exam.

There is one more crucial stage in the Lazarus and Folkman's (1984) model: coping. Once you have evaluated the upcoming exam as, say, a threat, you then need to decide what to do about it.

Emotion-focused coping seeks to manage the emotions associated with the event or situation. For instance, a person may deal with the anxiety by using alcohol or drugs. However, this is a short-term, ill-advised strategy because it fails to deal with the underlying cause of the stress. Instead,

(Continued)

Appraisal Model of Stress: States that people engage in two appraisal processes—primary and secondary—of a potential stressor that impact how they emotionally respond to it

(Continued)

FIGURE **3.5**   Appraisal Model of Stress

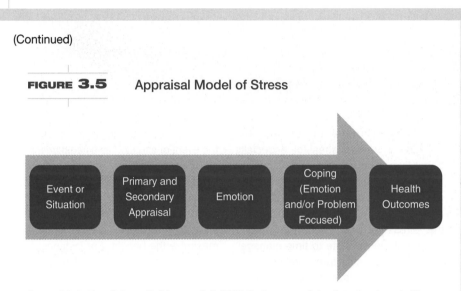

Source: Adapted from Folkman, S., & Lazarus, R. S. (1988). Coping as a mediator of emotion. *Journal of Personality and Social Psychology, 54,* 466–475.

problem-focused coping leads a person to develop solutions that are not mere window dressing. For instance, after construing an exam as a threat, you could create a study guide, alter plans to allow for adequate study time, find a tutor, and so forth. Focusing on solving the problem can help deal with its emotional aspects as well as (we hope) appropriately handling the problem. Research has shown that problem-focused coping can lead to better outcomes in many domains of life (Baghurst & Kelley, 2014; J. Strack & Esteves, 2015; Wemm et al., 2013). I encourage you to reflect on your own methods of dealing with stress and whether they are working for you.

processes roughly occur along an East-West division, with the East referring to East Asia and the West to North America and Western Europe (Zaroff, D'Amato, & Bender, 2014). These cultural distinctions can be traced back at least 2,000 years to the Chinese scholar Confucius, on the one hand, and the Greek philosopher Socrates, on the other (Nisbett, Peng, Choi, & Norenzayan, 2001).

The core distinction is nicely summarized by a statement made by a Chinese student to Richard Nisbett, an American social psychologist: "The difference between you and me is that I think the world is a circle, and you think it is a line" (Nisbett, 2003, p. xiii). What this short sentence refers to is the fundamentally divergent ways that reality is perceived by Easterners versus Westerners (Medin & Atran, 2004; Norenzayan, Choi, & Peng, 2007). A Westerner may zoom in on a circle and see only

By Poemandpainting (Own work) [CC BY-SA 3.0 (http://creativecommons.org/licenses/by-sa/3.0)], via Wikimedia Commons. Author: Mr. Chen Minglou.

Heritage Images/Corbis. Author: George Orleans De La Motte.

one segment, which would resemble a line. An Easterner would stand back and see the entire circle. The Westerner sees change as linear and one directional, as if a person were traveling along a one-way road leading into the future. In contrast, the Easterner sees change as cyclical, as if a person were traversing a path that repeatedly folds back onto itself.

Another East-West difference is illustrated by prototypical paintings from each cultural group. Masuda, Gonzalez, Kwan, and Nisbett (2008) examined the content and perspective in paintings of people by Chinese and Western artists. They found that, in general, Chinese paintings depicted people as relatively small in relationship to their environment, whereas the Western paintings place people at the forefront of the painting, generally overshadowing the background. The difference in perspective further exemplifies how East Asians tend to step back and look at the big picture, whereas North Americans hone in on close-ups of particular elements. Hence, we generally find that landscape paintings from the East have higher horizons, in contrast to paintings from the West. Moreover, Westerners tend to view persons and objects as separate from their environments rather than as parts of larger sets of relationships among people or things (Norenzayan, Choi, & Nisbett, 2002). In general, Easterners see the world as much more complex than do Westerners. This broader view taken by Easterners is *holistic,* in contrast to Westerners' more *analytic* approach. The former considers the whole picture or situation, whereas the latter analyzes or breaks it down into its parts.

These differences even extend to how these two cultural groups solve problems. In one study, participants were asked to evaluate the usefulness of various clues in solving a hypothetical murder mystery (Choi, Dalal, Kim-Prieto, & Park, 2003). Korean participants viewed far more details of the circumstances surrounding the crime as relevant to solving it, whereas Americans quickly eliminated less important details and focused on only a few clues. In other words, the Koreans took into account many more factors than did the Americans.

In sum, East-West differences extend well beyond language and custom to such phenomena as fundamental reasoning processes (Norenzayan, Smith, Kim, & Nisbett, 2002), susceptibility to cognitive illusions (Segall, Campbell, & Herskovits, 1963), how people explain social behavior (see Chapter 5) (Morris & Peng, 1994), and laypeople's understanding of biology (Medin, Unsworth, & Hirschfeld, 2007).

Think Again!

1. *How are holistic and analytic thinking different?*

2. *What did the Chinese student mean when he suggested that Westerners conceptualize the world as a line, but Easterners do so as a circle?*

FINAL THOUGHTS: FREE WILL AND RATIONALITY REVISITED

Studying social cognition provides insight into the questions of free will and rationality by demonstrating two important phenomena: the powerful role that nonconscious processes play in the determination of thought, feeling, and behavior, and showing us how seemingly objective, rational processes are affected by motivations, desires, and goals. If one defines free will as the execution of conscious decision-making, then one can't help but conclude that much human behavior is not the product of free will. Rather, automatic processes—unintentional, occurring without conscious awareness, efficient, and uncontrollable—play a much greater role in social behavior than most people realize, undermining romantic notions of free will. Moreover, when we add in the overwhelming evidence that apparently objective, rational, cognition is often biased and subject to various shortcomings, we begin to build a new model of human nature. This is not a bad thing. These corrections to the naïve understanding do not downgrade the value of human life but instead provide us with the knowledge we need to improve our decision-making and enrich our lives.

CORE CONCEPTS

- We think about people differently than we think about things because people think back, people have special relevance for our goals, thinking about people involves social explanation, and we just think more about people than nonpeople and our brains process people differently from nonpeople. Our mental systems first believe information provided to them in order to understand it; subsequently, that information may be rejected as false.

- People have a dual mind that consists of the C-system or controlled system that is a slow and sequential processor that can engage in abstract thinking and the X-system or automatic system that is a rapid and parallel processor characterized by intuitive thinking.

- The four components of automaticity are the following: it is unintentional, occurs without conscious awareness, is accomplished efficiently, and once begun, cannot be controlled.

- Priming occurs when a concept or other knowledge structure is automatically triggered or activated by an environmental stimulus, thereby becoming more likely to affect subsequent thoughts, feelings, and behaviors; spreading activation is the process by which associated concepts are activated.

- People often rely on heuristics when making judgments (such as availability, representativeness, and anchoring and adjustment heuristics, along with ignoring the base rate).

- Social psychologists seek to create surveys, studies, and scales that are both reliable (how consistently each measurement of the same phenomenon produces approximately the same result under the same conditions) and valid (the extent to which a particular measurement tool provides accurate results). Internal validity refers to the extent to which we can be sure that the purported cause—the IV—is the only factor influencing the purported effect—the DV. External validity indicates how well the results of the study can be generalized or applied to other settings and populations.

- People engage in motivated reasoning, such as belief perseverance, confirmation bias, and biased assimilation.

- Reasoning is subject to cultural influences. Some characteristics of East Asian thinking is that it is a holistic approach, tolerant of contradictions, focuses on the big picture; characteristics of North Americans thinking include the following: It is analytic, avoids contradictions, and has a relatively narrow focus.

➤ **⑤SAGE edge™** Test your understanding of chapter content. Take the practice quiz. edge.sagepub.com/barrett

KEY TERMS

Anchoring and Adjustment Heuristic, 94
Appraisal Model of Stress, 102
Automaticity, 85
Availability Heuristic, 92
Base Rate, 94
Base Rate Fallacy, 93
Belief Perseverance, 98
Biased Assimilation, 101
C-system, 84

Causal Relationship, 00
Confirmation Bias, 101
Considering the Opposite, 99
External Validity, 97
Heuristic, 91
Internal Validity, 97
Looking-Glass Self, 78

Motivated Reasoning, 97
Priming, 86
Reliability, 96
Representativeness Heuristic, 93
Spreading Activation, 86
Validity, 96
X-system, 84

➤ **⑤SAGE edge™** Review key terms with eFlashcards. edge.sagepub.com/barrett

THINK FURTHER!

- As you sit at the library or coffee shop chatting or doing school work, become aware of the differences between social and nonsocial thinking that are occurring in your mind.

- How does social cognition "funnel" information into our mental systems?

- Try testing the anchoring and adjustment bias on your friends. Look up a fact that is numerically based and create a couple of false anchors. Then provide them (separately) with the anchors and ask them to estimate the number. What happens?

- If you could create a human-like robot companion that engaged in only controlled or automatic processing, which would you prefer and why?

SUGGESTED READINGS

Bargh, J. A. (1994). The four horsemen of automaticity: Awareness, intention, efficiency, and control in social cognition. In R. S. Wyer & T. K. Srull (Eds.), *Handbook of social cognition, Vol. 1: Basic processes; Vol. 2: Applications* (2nd ed., pp. 1–40). Hillsdale, NJ: Lawrence Erlbaum.

Evans, J. S. B. T., & Stanovich, K. E. (2013). Dual-process theories of higher cognition: Advancing the debate. *Perspectives on Psychological Science, 8*, 223–241.

Janiszewski, C., & Uy, D. (2008). Precision of the anchor influences the amount of adjustment. *Psychological Science, 19*, 121–127.

Kunda, Z. (1990). The case for motivated reasoning. *Psychological Bulletin, 108*(3), 480–498.

Tversky, A., & Kahneman, D. (1974). Judgment under uncertainty: Heuristics and biases. *Science, 185*, 1124–1131.

4

What Is the Self?

Depiction of Anger, Disgust, Joy, Fear and Sadness from the animated movie *Inside Out*.

Pictorial Press/Alamy.

LEARNING OBJECTIVES

4.1 Define the self, self-concept, schema, and self-schema; describe self-discrepancy theory and the actual, ideal, and ought selves.

4.2 Contrast introspection and self-perception and explain the limits to learning about the self via each process; describe how the facial feedback hypothesis relates to self-perception.

4.3 Describe the strengths and weaknesses of surveys and self-report methods and the following biases: response effects, acquiescence, extremity, and context effects.

4.4 Define intrinsic motivation, extrinsic motivation, and overjustification, and illustrate each with examples; define global and specific self-esteem and interpret them in terms of the sociometer hypothesis.

4.5 Explain each of the following and state how they are related to the goal of self-enhancement: social comparison theory, self-evaluation maintenance, downward and upward social comparison, better-than-average effect, self-serving judgments, the bias blind spot.

4.6 Define impression management, contrast high and low self-monitoring, and explain the spotlight effect, the illusion of transparency, ingratiation, and self-handicapping.

4.7 Define self-regulation and its relation to willpower and ironic processes; explain self-verification.

⑤SAGE edge™

Get the edge on your studies.
edge.sagepub.com/barrett

Take a quiz to find out what you've learned.
Watch videos that enhance chapter content.
Explore related web and social media activities.

THE MANY "ME'S" OF THE SELF

What is "your" self? Pause for 60 seconds and write down the first six to ten thoughts that come to mind. . . . Most likely you wrote down external features of your self, such as your gender, race, university affiliation, family status, and so forth. Although these are undoubtedly important aspects of who you are, social psychologists would urge you to delve more deeply into the mystery of the self and to consider less obvious attributes of the self, to even go as far as to ask if you possess just a single self. Over 100 years ago the famous American poet Walt Whitman (1892) wrote "I am large. I contain multitudes." Whitman felt that he had multiple selves that, together, constituted "Walt Whitman." Social psychologists follow Whitman in viewing the self in a more abstract sense that cannot be narrowed down to one noun or adjective. Recently, in the 2015 animated movie *Inside Out*, the mental life of the main character, Riley, is portrayed as a struggle among her various emotions (anger, disgust, joy, fear, and sadness), each presented as a different self. Although this fictional movie does not reflect how social psychologists view the self, it is consistent with the general idea of multiple selves. As you will see, the self may be more accurately construed as a multiplicity of properties and psychological processes that interrelate in complex and fascinating ways (Sedikides & Gregg, 2003).

One compelling perspective defines the self as that *something* that allows us to even ask the question, "what is the self?" According to this view, the **self** is the *psychological apparatus that gives a person the capacity to consciously think about him or herself* (Leary & Tangney, 2003; MacDonald, 2007). The self is defined as the ability to think about the self! It is almost impossible to imagine that a being can be said to have a self if it lacks the capacity for self-reflection. If a creature can't ask, "what is the self?" then it doesn't have one! Because the self lies at the center of our very being, as you'll see in this chapter, social psychologists have exerted enormous effort toward developing a better understanding of its nature.

Self: The psychological apparatus that gives a person the capacity to consciously think about him or herself

TABLE 4.1   The Many Selves

Name	Description	Illustration
Self-concept	Beliefs about yourself, who you are	Student, brother, athlete
Self-esteem	Feelings about yourself, your self-evaluation	Good student, trustworthy brother, skilled athlete
Interpersonal self	Who you present to other people	Friendly, caring, selfless
Executive self	Engages in self-regulation, exercises willpower	Impulse control, delayed gratification

The self, then, is your experience of who you are. This encompasses your *beliefs* about yourself, what you *present* to other people, and how you *regulate* your self (see Table 4.1). These three components of the self are called the self-concept, the interpersonal self, and the executive self (Baumeister, 1987, 2011; Baumeister, Schmeichel, & Vohs, 2007; Cavallo, Holmes, Fitzsimons, Murray, & Wood, 2012). An additional component is self-esteem or how you *feel* about yourself. In this chapter we will review each of these aspects. We will also revisit several of the core themes of social psychology introduced in Chapter 1, including free will, rationality, sociality, and of course, the self. The self is the place where all of these themes intersect: Each is a constituent of the self, and together they comprise the fundamental dimensions of the self.

Think Ahead!

1. *What is the purpose of the self?*
2. *How do you come to know yourself?*
3. *What influences your self-esteem?*

WHAT IS THE SELF: THE SELF AS THINKER AND THE THOUGHT

Knowing Oneself: The Self-Concept

Over 2,000 years ago the Greek philosopher Socrates encouraged people to "know thyself," important advice that on its face seems pretty straightforward (although we'll see later it may not be). As we've said, the very fact that we have a self means that we engage in some level of self-reflection. Thus the self is both the thinker and the thought: It is that which ponders the self—the thinker—and that which is pondered by the self—the thought. The self begins to emerge at a very young age, and as we transition through adolescence and into young adulthood, we tend to be much more preoccupied with knowing ourselves (Erickson, 1950). Unfortunately, although the desire to know ourselves is strong, there are limits to our ability to uncover certain aspects of the self, such as our motivations, desires, preferences, and behavioral tendencies, as well as the reasons for our behavior (Nisbett & Wilson,

©iStockphoto.com/GeorgiosArt.

Over 2000 years ago Socrates encouraged people to "know thyself."

1977; T. D. Wilson, 2002). Before we discuss these, let's investigate several key features of the self, including our self-concept and possible selves.

The answer to the question "Who am I" is called our **self-concept**: the set of beliefs we have about the characteristics we possess (Amiot, de la Sablonniere, Smith, & Smith, 2015; Burkley, Curtis, Burkley, & Hatvany, 2015). The self-concept is at the core of everything we think, feel, or do, and it serves as a framework for understanding the social world (Slotter, Winger, & Soto, 2015). For instance, my self-concept includes such elements as father, psychology professor, textbook author, husband, and so on. The set of all of my beliefs about myself is my self-concept, and each of these beliefs is known as a self-schema. **Schemas** are cognitive structures that serve to organize knowledge about particular objects of thought, such as concepts, experiences, or roles (Brannon, Markus, & Taylor, 2015; H. Markus, 1977). We have schemas for people, things, places, and events that are automatically activated when we think about each of these (H. Markus & Wurf, 1987). For instance, what is your schema for a library? I expect that when you think of a college library you likely imagine the presence of books, computers, students working quietly, and so forth. What is your schema for a grocery store?

Self-schemas are one kind of schema that organize information about yourself with respect to specific domains of your life (such as work, school, family, a sport, etc.) and are particularly important when they are clear and unambiguous (H. Markus, 1977). Self-schemas affect how you process information relevant to you and often guide your behavior. Go back and look at what you wrote down about your self. Did you list any roles that you play? Perhaps a student, store clerk, or restaurant worker? Or a son, daughter, or uncle? Each of these roles serves as a self-schema and, when activated, affects how you think, feel, and act.

Self-Concept: Set of beliefs a person has about the characteristics she or he possesses

Schemas: Cognitive structures that organize knowledge about particular objects of thought, such as concepts, experiences, or roles

Self-Schema: Schema that organizes information about oneself with respect to specific domains of one's life

Who you are in one domain of your life will in some ways be different from and in others the same as who you are in another domain. In my case, who I am varies depending on whether I am leading discussion in a social psychology class, at home playing games with my daughter, or at a pub playing pool with a friend. These selves are of course interrelated and have much in common (McConnell & Strain, 2007). Many of my "professor" traits—such as the tendency to be responsible, take initiative, and provide sound guidance—will mirror my "father" traits. Yet there are other traits that would be manifest in one self but not another. For instance, I can get pretty silly when goofing off with my daughter, and although I try to inject humor into the classroom (albeit, with mixed success), it is not generally of the silly variety. Because we hold many self-schemas, it makes sense for us to think about the self not as a single unit but rather as multiple distinct yet overlapping elements (Swann & Bosson, 2010).

Another crucial feature of the self is its cultural embeddedness (Lee, Leung, & Kim, 2014). In Chapter 1 we discussed the individualism-collectivism (IC) dimension that, in a nutshell, reflects the extent to which individuals and cultures view the self as separate from others or closely tied to them. In relatively individualistic cultures, the self is seen as *independent*: as defined by its inner attributes, traits, and characteristics, and as stable over time and place (H. R. Markus & Kitayama, 1991). In contrast, people in collectivistic cultures understand the self as interdependent: It is largely derived from its connections to others and the groups to which it belongs. The independent self is considered to be unique, and in fact individualists seek to affirm its separate identity. The interdependent self overlaps with the selves of others and prefers to blend in rather than stand out. Although psychologists commonly refer to these two types of self-construal as distinct, in reality people are more flexible and fall somewhere in between. Moreover, situations may prime one or the other self-construal and hence lead people to think more about their own needs and goals or those of others, and this in turn can affect social behavior (Trafimow & Clayton, 2006). We will return to this fundamental dimension at various places in this text.

Self-Discrepancy Theory and Possible Selves

When you reflect on who you are, do you ever think about your *possible* selves, such as who you would *like* to be or what kind of a person you *ought* to be? **Self-discrepancy theory** postulates that each of us has an actual self, an ideal self, and an ought self (Hardin & Larsen, 2014; Higgins, 1989b, 1997; Stanley & Burrow, 2015). Our understanding of who we are is called our **actual self** and is closely tied to our self-concept. In addition, we can imagine the person we would like to be—called the **ideal self**—that consists of the qualities and features that we wish we had (Hardin & Larsen, 2014). Perhaps you work at Starbucks but would rather be interning at a local mental health center. When we feel a discrepancy such as this between our actual and ideal selves, we tend to feel frustrated, dissatisfied, or disappointed (Higgins, 1989).

People also have thoughts about who they think others think they *should* be—what is called the **ought self**. Your ought self comes into play, say, if your parents own the

Self-Discrepancy Theory: Idea that each person has an actual, ideal, and ought self

Actual Self: Who one is

Ideal Self: Image of a hypothetical self that possesses the qualities and features that a person's wishes he had

Ought Self: Image of a hypothetical self who a person believes important others think he or she should be

©iStockphoto.com/sturti.

©iStockphoto.com/annebaek.

IS, OUGHT, AND
IDEAL SELVES

Are you who your
parents want you to
be? Who you want
to be? Perhaps you
work in package
delivery (is self), yet
you want to be a
basketball player
(ideal self), and your
parents want you to
be a doctor (ought
self).

©iStockphoto.com/Aksonov.

local hardware store and have been pressuring you to work there and eventually be the owner. You think that you *ought* to be following the career that your parents prefer, but you have elected to choose your own career path (see photos). Here you would experience an actual-ought discrepancy and may feel guilty, ashamed, or anxious (Higgins, 1989b). As you can see, discrepancies between the actual, ideal, and ought selves have important implications for how we evaluate or feel about ourselves, a theme we will return to later in this chapter in the context of self-esteem.

Think Again!

1. *What is your self-concept? A schema?*

2. *What are your actual, ideal, and ought selves?*

KNOWING WHO WE ARE: INTROSPECTION AND SELF-PERCEPTION

How do you know who you are? Sounds like an odd question, right? You are probably thinking something like "I know who I am because I can look inside and see myself." Unfortunately, looking internally at the self to examine who we are, how we feel, and so forth—a process we call **introspection**—may not be as straightforward as it seems (Corallo, Sackur, Dehaene, & Sigman, 2008). As we'll discuss in a moment, there is no guarantee that mere reflection will uncover important aspects of the self. When introspection falls short, we can engage in a second process called self-perception, during which we essentially examine ourselves from the outside, similarly to what others may do. A third method for learning about the self involves focusing on the responses that other people have to us. In these different ways, others can serve as mirrors that help us better understand who we are.

Cooley (1902) called this aspect of the self the looking-glass self, because we see ourselves partially through the eyes of others or, rather, how we *think* they perceive us (see Chapter 3). Not only can we gain self-knowledge by taking the perspectives of others, but we may also derive an element of our self-esteem from how we believe they appraise us, what are called reflected self-appraisals (Asencio, 2013; Carlson, Vazire, & Furr, 2011). The interdependence between our self-understanding and our relationships with others further demonstrates once again the close connection between two of our fundamental questions: the nature of the self and of our sociality.

Introspection

Who was your third-grade teacher? It probably took you a moment, but eventually the name popped into your mind. How did you produce this answer? Easily, you respond—*I just thought about it!* Or maybe—*I just knew it!* But if I were to press you further and ask you to explain how you retrieved this from your memory, you'd likely hesitate before offering an answer. This is because you typically do not have access to the "how" you generated your response but only the response itself. Let's look at another scenario. Suppose I were to place four blue sweaters side-by-side on a shelf. I inform you that the sweaters are of differing quality and ask you and nineteen others to individually select your preferred sweater. Unbeknownst to all of you, the sweaters are identical. Judging by the results of

Introspection:
Looking internally at the self to examine who one is, how one feels, and so forth

a similar study by Nisbett and Wilson (1977), the vast majority would pick the sweater farthest to the right. When asked to explain why, most would likely state that the one on the right was of better quality than the other three. You would be unaware that the physical placement of the sweaters had an impact on your choice. Why? Because humans often have little access to and knowledge of our internal processes. Nisbett and Wilson (1977) have pro-

David Grossman / Science Source.

All of us engage in introspection in our efforts to better understand ourselves.

vocatively argued that, although we know the result of our thought processes (e.g., what our third-grade teacher's name was), we often do not know *how* we arrived at that result.

In the fascinating book *Strangers to Ourselves,* Timothy Wilson (2002) reviews the vast research literature on this topic that provides convincing evidence regarding the limits of introspection. Wilson shows that not only are we unaware of how are thoughts are produced, we often don't know who we are, what we feel, or why we do what we do! In another study, participants watched a film either while a very loud power saw was operated just outside of the room or with no distracting noise (Nisbett & Wilson, 1977). Respondents were asked to rate the film on a number of dimensions, and the distraction participants also indicated whether or not the noise affected their evaluations. A majority of the distraction participants reported, erroneously, that the noise had in fact lowered their evaluation of the film. Here, participants believed a stimulus affected them when in fact it did not, and again, introspection failed to uncover the truth.

There is another way in which introspection can fail us: The process of thinking about how we feel can itself change the way we feel (T. D. Wilson et al., 1993). In one study, participants evaluated two artistic and three humorous posters and later had the opportunity to bring one of them home after the experiment. Participants in the *reasons* condition described why they liked each of the posters, whereas those in the *control* condition did not. Wilson et al. predicted and found that participants in the reasons condition were more likely to bring home a humorous poster than were control participants, most likely because it was easier to provide a rationale for preferring the humorous poster to the art poster: it was funny. When all participants were asked at the end of the semester how happy they were with their poster choice, those who had earlier listed reasons were less satisfied than the control participants, especially when they had chosen and justified selection of a humorous poster. The amusing effects of the comical poster—although humor was the initial reason for choosing it—seem to have worn off during the semester. Think about it—how many times can you laugh at the same joke?! Wilson et al.'s (1993) study demonstrates that analyzing reasons for preferences can undermine the pleasure produced by those preferences: Introspection can reduce satisfaction with one's decisions.

FIGURE 4.1   Introspecting About Reasons Can Undermine Satisfaction

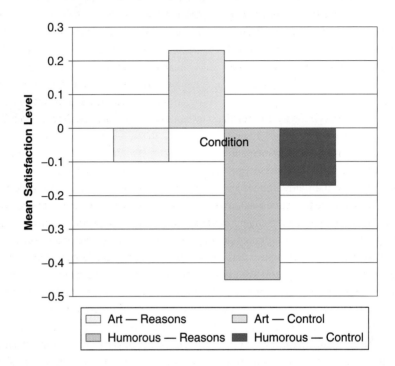

Participants who provided reasons for their choice of poster were less satisfied several weeks after making their choice than control participants, especially if they selected the humorous poster.

Source: Adapted from Wilson, T. D., Lisle, D. J., Schooler, J. W., Hodges, S. D., Klaaren, K. J., & LaFleur, S. J. (1993). Introspecting about reasons can reduce post-choice satisfaction. *Personality and Social Psychology Bulletin, 19*, 331–339.

Similarly, another study found that analyzing reasons for liking one's romantic partner decreased satisfaction with that partner (T. D. Wilson & Kraft, 1993).

Clearly, using introspection as a way to understand our thoughts, feelings, and behaviors has its limits (Corallo et al., 2008; E. A. Locke, 2009). Not only might we fail to understand why we act as we do, even thinking about the reasons for liking something can reduce that liking. And here we see that how our understanding of the self is inextricably tied to the limits of our reasoning and the nature of rationality itself. Attempting to achieve rationality can have interesting, if unintended, consequences for the self.

Self-Perception

As we've seen, introspection is an imperfect way to gain knowledge about who we are. What other means are at our disposal for gaining self-understanding? Well, how do you get to know other people when you don't have direct access to their inner processes? One way is to simply ask them, but then of course you are relying on the questionable veracity of their introspection. Another strategy is to observe their behavior to see how they act in a variety of situations and under various conditions and use this as a guide to determine their attitudes and beliefs. Although not a perfect method, merely watching them could give us insights that asking them could not. The social psychologist Daryl Bem suggested that we can use the same method for gaining insight into our own selves: observe our own behavior. According to Bem's (1967) **self-perception theory,** you can infer your attitude in this same way that a third party might do so: by watching your own behavior (Olson & Stone, 2005; Yee & Bailenson, 2009). Let me say that again: Bem argues that there are times when we rely on observations of our own behavior to figure out what our attitude, emotions, and personality traits are. This is particularly true when our attitudes are weak or ambiguous (Bem, 1967).

Take for example the results of a study of environmental attitudes by Chaiken and Baldwin (1981). Based on their responses to a survey completed earlier in the semester, participants were classified as either holding well-defined or poorly defined attitudes toward protecting the environment. During the subsequent experimental session, participants were led to focus either on their past pro-ecology behaviors or their past anti-ecology behaviors. Finally, they again responded to several questions in which they indicated the extent to which they consider themselves environmentalists. Chaiken and Baldwin predicted that individuals with weak attitudes would, when completing the final attitude measure, infer their attitude toward the environment from the behaviors that they focused on. In this way people with weak attitudes would "observe" their own behavior to determine their attitude. Consequently, those focused on pro-ecology behaviors should identify themselves as pro-ecology, whereas those focused on anti-ecology behaviors should lean toward the anti-ecology attitudes. In contrast, individuals with strong pre-existing attitudes would not need to resort to self-perception to infer their attitudes and therefore would not show any effects of the experimental manipulation.

The findings were as predicted: Self-reported attitudes corresponded to whichever type of behavior participants with weakly defined attitudes concentrated on but not for those with previously well-defined attitudes. In short, consistent with self-perception theory, participants with weak attitudes relied on their own behavior to infer their attitudes (Chaiken & Baldwin, 1981). Two recent extensions of self-perception theory have shown that people's perception of their own avatars—their virtual selves inserted into computer games or online social media—can affect their self-concept as well as their behavior (Yee & Bailenson, 2009) and that people may use their observation of the *behavior* of others to learn about themselves (see Figure 4.2).

Other research has demonstrated that people may also infer their motivation from their behavior, which in turn has implications for whether they will engage in subsequent related behavior. Before discussing this research in class, I present my students with the following scenario: Say my daughter loves to read and does so with great frequency on her own (which is true). Now say I decide to reward her for reading over the summer by giving her

Self-Perception Theory: Idea that peoples sometimes infer their own attitudes in the same way that a third party might infer their attitudes: by watching their behavior

FIGURE **4.2**   Vicarious Self-Perception

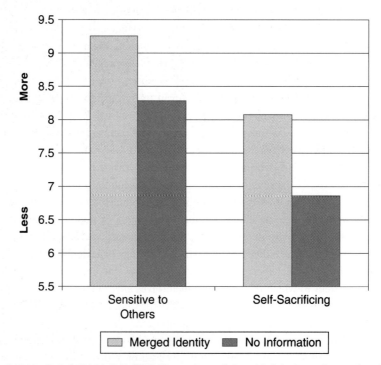

Source: Goldstein, N. J., & Cialdini, R. B. (2007). The spyglass self: A model of vicarious self-perception. *Journal of Personality and Social Psychology, 92*, 402–417.

All participants listened to an interview in which the interviewee ultimately decided to provide additional, unexpected help to the interviewer/experimenter. Participants were either led to believe that they were very similar to the interviewee (merged identity condition) or were given no information about similarity (no information condition). Merged-identity participants saw themselves as more sensitive to others and more self-sacrificing versus the no-information participants (higher numbers reflect greater self-rating of sensitivity or self-sacrificing). That is, their self-perceptions changed as a result of witnessing the behavior of a similar other. In addition, as a result of the similarity manipulation, the merged-identity participants were more likely to help the experimenter than were the no-information participants.

Source: Adapted from Study 2, Goldstein, N. J., & Cialdini, R. B. (2007). The spyglass self: A model of vicarious self-perception. *Journal of Personality and Social Psychology, 92*, 402–417.

$4 for every book she reads (which I don't). By the end of the summer, I am deeply in debt to her and give her the money she earned. When school starts and I stop rewarding her for reading, is she likely to freely read even more, read about the same, or read less than she did before being offered the money? Most students believe that she will read more because she has been rewarded. In all likelihood, however, my daughter's reading frequency would likely *decrease,* because she has now associated reading with money, and when the money stops, so too will the reading. As a consequence of my paying her to read, her **intrinsic motivation**—the desire to engage in a behavior simply because it is interesting or enjoyable—would be undermined by an **extrinsic motivation**—the desire to perform the behavior as a result of external rewards or pressures (Cerasoli, Nicklin, & Ford, 2014; Durik & Harackiewicz, 2007; Harackiewicz, Durik, & Barron, 2005). My daughter may reconstrue reading as something that she does for money rather than for sheer enjoyment. Hence she will infer that she must only be reading for money and may stop reading in the absence of this external reinforcement.

This anecdote illustrates the **overjustification effect**, which occurs when one's intrinsic motivation—such as enjoyment experienced by simply enacting the behavior—is weakened by the presence of extrinsic motivation (Forehand, 2000; Lepper, Greene, & Nisbett, 1973; Lepper, Henderlong, & Gingras, 1999). In one study, giving small children a reward for playing with special, colorful felt-tipped markers made them less likely to voluntarily choose to play with those same markers later (Lepper et al., 1973). Although external rewards may sometimes deter desirable behavior, they are often useful. For instance, rewarding children by praising them for working hard rather than being smart can increase self-motivation and school achievement (Henderlong & Lepper, 2002).

There is another arena where Bem's self-perception theory offers a useful way of understanding oneself: emotion. Earlier we described how people may not always know how they feel, especially when introspection can itself change one's feelings. Is it possible that, like with attitudes and motivation, observing our behavior may help us determine what we are feeling? According to the **facial feedback hypothesis**, the answer is yes, at least under certain circumstances (Dzokoto, Wallace, Peters, & Bentsi-Enchill, 2014). For instance, Strack, Martin, and Stepper (1988) showed cartoons to participants who evaluated their funniness while holding a pen either between their teeth or in their lips. Participants with the pen

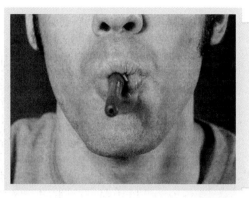

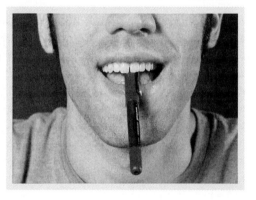

HOW FACIAL EXPRESSIONS CAN AFFECT YOUR EMOTIONS

Participants who held a pen in their lips rated a comic as less humorous than those who held a pen in their teeth.

Intrinsic Motivation: Desire to engage in a behavior simply because it is interesting or enjoyable

Extrinsic Motivation: Desire to perform a behavior as a result of external rewards or pressures

Overjustification Effect: When one's intrinsic motivation—such as enjoyment experienced by simply enacting the behavior—is weakened by the presence of extrinsic motivation

Facial Feedback Hypothesis: Idea that people infer their feelings from their facial expressions

A Chinese census taker collecting personal information. Self-reports are often accurate and can be very useful, particularly when the information sought is noncontroversial and the respondent is unlikely to wish to hide his answers from the researcher.

AP Photo/Liu mingxiang - Imaginechina.

between their teeth—which just happens to produce a facial expression that mimics a smile—rated the comics as more humorous than did those with it in their lips—a pose that causes a frown-like expression. Similarly, Kleinke, Peterson, and Rutledge (1998) found that simply watching oneself in the mirror intentionally posing angry or happy facial expressions led people to feel angrier or happier than others who made the expressions but did not see themselves in the mirror. Here again we see how people infer their inner states by observing their own behavior.

As surprising and counterintuitive as self-perception theory may be, it has wide-ranging application and has received a great deal of empirical support. Note though that Bem (1967) did not argue that we rely exclusively on observing our own behavior when determining our attitudes, feelings, and personality traits, but that we do so only when are uncertain about them. Earlier in this chapter, we asked how it is that we come to know ourselves. So far we have discussed two ways in which people can learn about their self-concept: introspection and self-perception. But there is alternative approach: looking to other people for feedback about how we are doing. We will elaborate on this method in the section on self-evaluation and self-enhancement below.

Think Again!

1. *What are the limits to introspection?*

2. *What does self-perception theory say about how we learn about the self?*

3. *Try listing a couple of activities that you are intrinsically and a couple that you are extrinsically motivated to do.*

DOING RESEARCH: QUESTIONING SELF-REPORTS AND SURVEYS

Self-Report:
Individual's conscious response to a question or situation

The most commonly used method for obtaining data in social psychology is the **self-report**, which is an individual's conscious response to a question or situation. A direct question asking about your attitude toward your college is a self-report. Self-reports are often accurate and can be very useful, particularly when the information sought is noncontroversial and the respondent is unlikely to wish to hide his answers from the researcher. For example, self-reported gender is likely to be accurate, whereas attitudes toward members of another race is less likely to be. Researchers use self-reports to obtain a variety of data, including people's opinions, feelings, behaviors, and physiological experiences (e.g., hunger or pain). Three advantages of self-report measures are that they are relatively easy to construct, are inexpensive, and can be utilized in a variety of research methods, including surveys, interviews, and many experiments.

There are also several disadvantages to using self-reports, whether in surveys, interviews, or experiments. One is that self-reports may not always provide accurate information, either as a result of participant psychology or the construction of the questions (Krosnick, Lavarakas, & Kim, 2014; Schwarz, 2007b). Researchers have extensively investigated the psychology of self-reports and have identified a number of undesirable response effects that can undermine the accuracy of the answers. **Response effects** are unintended variations in question responses that stem from procedural aspects or features of the survey instrument, such as the wording of a question or the order of the questions (Heintzelman, Trent, & King, 2015; Helmes, Holden, & Ziegler, 2015; Schwarz, 1999; Tourangeau, Rips, & Rasinski, 2000). These survey features may affect how participants understand questions, the role of memory and judgment in generating potential responses, and how participants report their answers (Schwarz, 1999, 2007a; Tourangeau et al., 2000).

One response effect is the **acquiescence bias**, which is the tendency to agree with or say "yes" to questions (Savalei & Falk, 2014). This is of particular concern when conducting cross-cultural research, because clear culture-based differences have been found (Riemer & Shavitt, 2011). For instance, East Asians are more likely to agree with questions than are certain other groups (Grimm & Church, 1999). Another type of response effect is the **extremity bias**, wherein respondents provide answers that are at the extremes of the response options (Levashina, Weekley, Roulin, & Hauck, 2014). For instance, on a scale ranging from "very unlikely" to "very likely," a person exhibiting this bias will tend to chose one of the endpoints of the scale rather than the more moderate options, such as "likely" or "unlikely." As with the acquiescence bias, the extremity bias varies across cultures: African Americans and Hispanics are more likely to demonstrate extreme responding than European Americans, whereas East Asians are less likely (Bachman & O'Malley, 1984; Chen, Lee, & Stevenson, 1995; Hui & Triandis, 1989). Question wording can also bias or distort the answers (Schwarz, 2007a). A recent example is a survey reported in the *New York Times* in which 20% of respondents said that the U.S. government spent too little on "welfare," but 65% indicated that it spent too little on "assistance to the poor" (See Figure 4.3) (Schneiderman, 2008).

Another response bias may result from the context in which the question is asked. For instance, participants in one study provided different explanations for a mass murder depending on whether the letterhead at the top of the survey was a fictional "Institute for Social Research" or "Institute for Personality Research." In the "social" condition

Response Effects: Unintended variations in question responses that stem from procedural aspects or features of the survey instrument, such as the wording of a question or the order of the questions

Acquiescence Bias: Tendency to agree with or say "yes" to questions

Extremity Bias: Tendency to provide answers that are at the extremes of the response options

FIGURE 4.3   Do Americans Still Hate Welfare? Depends on How You Ask

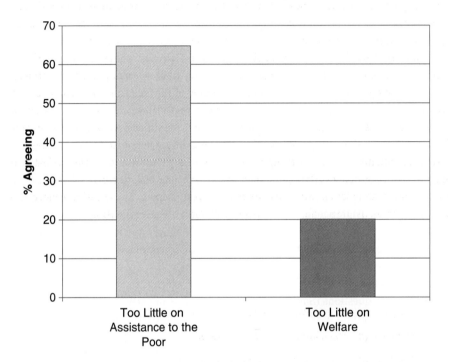

The U.S. Government Spends...

Source: Based on Schneiderman, R. M. (2008, October 30). Do Americans Still Hate Welfare? *The New York Times*.

Often different data can be obtained by asking the same question in varying ways. A recent example is a 2006 survey by the National Opinion Research Center reported in the *New York Times* in which 20% of respondents said that the U.S. government spent too little money on "welfare," but 65% indicated that it spent too little on "assistance to the poor."

Source: Reported in Schneiderman, R. M. (2008, October 30). Do Americans still hate welfare. *The New York Times*.

respondents tended to focus on external or environmental causes, in contrast to the internal or personality factors emphasized in the "personality" condition (Norenzayan & Schwarz, 1999). Such **context effects**—variations in responding because of survey features encountered prior to answering a question—are also seen when the presence or wording of earlier questions alters responses to later ones (Schwarz, 1999; Toepoel & Couper, 2011; Weijters, Geuens, & Baumgartner, 2013). Researchers need to consider these biases when designing surveys and other self-reports (Schwarz, 1999, 2007a). One additional weakness in self-reports was discussed above: We often do not know how we

Context Effects:
Variations in responding because of survey features encountered prior to answering a question

know what we know; that is, we cannot report on many of our mental processes, even if we can report on the outcome (Nisbett & Wilson, 1977).

Surveys are questionnaires that consist entirely of self-report items that can be administered on paper, computer, online, or during interviews. Survey research has several advantages over other strategies: It is relatively inexpensive, questionnaires are fairly easy to construct and implement, and they can be administered to large numbers of people quickly. As a result, surveys are widely used in social psychological research.

Unfortunately, there are several disadvantages that may outweigh the benefits of doing survey research. The first is that it does not allow for the manipulation of variables that is at the core of experimental research (discussed in Chapter 1). As a consequence, survey findings are only correlational and cannot be used to establish causal relations among variables. Second, there are many social psychological phenomena that cannot be studied using the survey method. For instance, asking people to imagine being in a particular situation—say, in a group of people of a different race—may not replicate the effects of actually being in that group. Finally, the utility of survey research depends upon the sample of individuals who participate in it—responses from Caucasian college students in Boston may not reflect those from Argentinians in Buenos Aires.

Think Again!

1. *What are the advantages of self-reports?*
2. *What are the disadvantages of self-reports?*
3. *What are the three types of response biases?*

EVALUATING HOW WE ARE DOING

Self-Esteem

Let's say that you have a pretty good grasp of your self-concept—who you are as a person. How do you feel about the person you are? Do you like your personality, your social skills, your competencies, your relationships? Are there qualities or characteristics that you'd like to change? Your positive or negative evaluation of yourself as a whole is called your **self-esteem** (MacDonald, 2007; Rosenberg, 1965, 1989). In contrast to self-concept, which is who you are, self-esteem reflects how you *feel* about who you are (Carmichael, Tsai, Smith, Caprariello, & Reis, 2007; Sharma & Agarwala, 2014). If you have a generally positive view of yourself, then you have relatively high self-esteem. If instead you generally feel bad about yourself, your self-esteem is relatively low.

Surveys:
Questionnaires that consist entirely of self-report items that can be administered on paper, computer, online, or in interviews

Self-Esteem:
Overall positive or negative evaluation of oneself

When laypeople talk about self-esteem, they typically mean *global* self-esteem, which is an overall evaluation of your whole self that encompasses many narrower self-evaluations confined to particular domains (Crocker & Wolfe, 2001; Schmitt & Allik, 2005). Self-esteem is a multifaceted construct, as you may have different evaluations of yourself regarding various elements of your personality, social skills, and competencies, with more weight given to those that are important to you (Crocker, Luhtanen, Blaine, & Broadnax, 1994; Wagner, Hoppmann, Ram, & Gerstorf, 2015). Perhaps you consider yourself to be a pretty good student, a reliable friend, an unusually skilled musician, and a poor public speaker. If most of your self-concept is associated with how you perform as a musician, for instance, your self-esteem is heavily dependent on how you do in just that one domain. A failure or setback in that domain—such as blowing an audition for a band—can be quite devastating. In contrast, a person whose self-esteem is drawn from many domains—musician, student, long distance runner, parent, and so forth—tends to be more resilient, because any one setback is not as important. Self-esteem based on performance in multiple domains tends to be more stable. Self-esteem stability, in turn, helps predict how we will feel from day to day, as stable self-esteem means that a person's self-image will not bounce around in response to everyday pleasures and pains, setbacks, and successes.

Not surprisingly, people with high self-esteem also exhibit more self-esteem stability (Seery, Blascovich, Weisbuch, & Vick, 2004; Wagner et al., 2015). Crocker and Wolfe (2001) call the way in which self-esteem draws from multiple domains the contingencies of self-worth (L. E. Park & Maner, 2009). College students tend to derive most of their self-esteem from their academic performance, moral behavior, identity, approval from others, appearance, and religion (Crocker, Luhtanen, Cooper, & Bouvrette, 2003). There may also be genetic influences on both the level and stability of self-esteem (Neiss, Sedikides, & Stevenson, 2006).

Why do people want high self-esteem? One explanation is that high self-esteem feels better than low self-esteem, and people obviously prefer the former. In this sense one can argue that people want a positive self-image or high self-esteem because it feels good. That is of course accurate, but it may only be part of the story. According to the **sociometer hypothesis**, self-esteem is closely linked to the quality of the relationships we have with other people (Kavanagh, Robins, & Ellis, 2010; Leary, 1999, 2005). Given the enormous importance of our memberships in groups for survival and reproduction, people are particularly sensitive to social inclusion and exclusion. As a consequence of evolutionary pressures, humans have developed a psychological mechanism—the sociometer—that assesses the strength and importance of those relationships—what Leary (2005) calls their relational value. Self-esteem, then, is essentially an index of that relational value: how much you think important others value their relationships with you or accept you (MacDonald, 2007). In other words, how you feel about yourself is closely tied to how you feel others evaluate you. The sociometer hypothesis has been empirically supported both by cross-cultural research (MacDonald, 2007) and studies of brain functioning, in which a specific part of the brain—called the ventral anterior cingulate cortex (vACC)—is uniquely

Sociometer Hypothesis: Idea that people have a psychological mechanism—the sociometer—that assesses the strength and importance of social relationships and that these relationships strongly influence self-esteem

responsive to feedback regarding one's acceptance or rejection by others (Heatherton, Krendl, Macrae, & Kelley, 2007).

Self-esteem has important implications for how we view and respond to the world—we often see the world through a lens of self-protective mechanisms designed to shield self-esteem from bumps and bruises (more on this later) (Carmichael et al., 2007). In general, people strive to have high self-esteem and to instill it in their children (Crocker & Park, 2004). People assume that high self-esteem a good thing—but is it? Well, it depends on how high. Reasonably—but not excessively—high self-esteem is clearly adaptive and is positively cor-related with overall physical and psychological health, especially if it is also stable (Kernis, 2005). People who have high self-esteem tend to demonstrate greater self-reported well-being, life satisfaction, better coping, and more positive affect, and persist longer at complet-ing tasks, including difficult ones (Sedikides & Gregg, 2003). Furthermore, low self-esteem is related to poor health outcomes, signs of psychological distress (including hopelessness, anx-iety, and depression), and increased vulnerability to personal failures and setbacks. However, excessively high self-esteem is associated with more aggression, bullying, and exhibitionism (Baumeister, Campbell, Krueger, & Vohs, 2003). Despite the central role of self-esteem in psy-chological functioning and the enormous quantity of research focused on it, questions remain about how best to measure self-esteem (see Self-Reflection 4.1) (Falk & Heine, 2015; Koole, Dijksterhuis, & van Knippenberg, 2001; Kwan & Mandisodza, 2007; Pelham et al., 2005).

What about gender and ethnic differences in self-esteem? We often hear that men generally have higher self-esteem than women (Williams & Best, 1990). By and large, that is correct, although the difference is not great. Interestingly, the disparities between the sexes tend to be found only for women in the middle and lower classes. This is likely due to the fact that women in these circumstances are less able to obtain desirable occupational positions than men: They are excluded to a greater extent from important domains of life (Major, Barr, Zubek, & Babey, 1999). These gender differences emerge during adoles-cence and adulthood, after females have been subjected to devaluation and discrimination (Kling, Hyde, Showers, & Buswell, 1999). Moreover, the differences are found primarily between Caucasian men and women: Women and men minorities generally don't differ in their levels of self-esteem. Lastly, although there is a perception that minorities have lower self-esteem than Caucasians, the picture is more complex. African Americans tend to have higher self-esteem than do Caucasians, but the self-esteem of members of Asian, Hispanic, and Native American groups tends to be lower (Twenge & Crocker, 2002).

What influences our self-esteem? For one thing, individuals with a clearer self-concept—what is called self-concept clarity—have higher self-esteem than those with more ambiguous self-concepts (Campbell, 1990; Usborne & Taylor, 2010). Being more certain about who you are appears to help buffer your self-esteem from the ups and downs of everyday life. In the remainder of the chapter we'll discuss several other important influences on self-esteem: how we cope with successes and failures, comparisons we make, and how we perceive the way others evaluate us. We will also review some of the strategies that people use to promote and protect their self-esteem.

Self-Enhancement

Given how important it is to feel good about ourselves, it is not surprising that we expend tremendous effort engaging in a variety of self-evaluation and self-enhancement strategies. We continuously monitor how we are doing and adjust our behavior accordingly in an effort to be liked by others, particularly those who are important to us (Church et al., 2014). How do we do this? According to Leon Festinger's **theory of social comparison processes** (1954), we first look to unambiguous, objective standards to help determine how we are doing; when such objective measures are unavailable, we resort to subjective social comparison. For instance, if you regularly jog three miles, you can time yourself and track whether or not you are getting faster (or slower!). However, in many important competencies, attributes, and opinions, no objective standards are available. Instead, says Festinger (1954), we will look to others to help with our self-evaluation. Festinger assumed that people are motivated to be accurate in their beliefs and opinions and that **social comparison** can provide us with critical feedback (Wood, 1996). For example, how do you know what to wear when meeting your partner's parents for the first time? You ask your partner. Do you think that President Obama is doing a good job? You may have your own thoughts, but it is quite likely that you'll check around to see what others think—perhaps people in the media, the professor in your history class, your friends—and their opinions will inform your own. You want to hold correct opinions, and social comparison can provide us with important information concerning their accuracy (Mussweiler, Rüter, & Epstude, 2006; Vogel, Rose, Roberts, & Eckles, 2014).

Who are you most likely to compare yourself to? Our general tendency is to compare ourselves with similar others, such as peers or siblings. But if that comparison results in a lowered self-evaluation—like if your little brother is a superior piano player—then you may avoid comparing yourself to him (Lockwood & Matthews, 2007; Nicholls & Stukas, 2011). According to Tesser's **self-evaluation maintenance model** (SEM), you'll typically only make comparisons when they will improve your self-evaluation; if they will make you look or feel good (Nicholls & Stukas, 2011; Tesser, 1988; Wood, Michela, & Giordano, 2000). SEM theory assumes that (a) people are motivated to maintain or enhance positive self-evaluation, and (b) there are two primary ways that people do this: social comparison and reflection (Tesser, 1988).

In the piano player example, if a close friend outperforms us on a dimension that is relevant to our self-concept, then we may attempt to distance ourselves from the friend and not engage in social comparison (Lockwood & Matthews, 2007). Alternatively, we could practice even more to improve our performance, simply avoid the comparison altogether, or give up the piano. To the extent that piano playing is no longer relevant to the self-concept, the reflection process becomes more important than the comparison process. By reflection, Tesser means that we allow the successes of others to reflect on us, thereby helping us to maintain a positive self-image. If your brother is an outstanding piano player, then by more closely associating with him you can enhance your self-esteem, because his success reflects well on you (Tesser, 1988, 2003).

Theory of Social Comparison Processes: Idea that people will evaluate how they are doing using subjective standards when objective standards are not available

Social Comparison: Monitoring how one is doing and adjusting one's behavior accordingly in an effort to be liked by important others

Self-Evaluation Maintenance Model (SEM): Postulates that a person typically only makes social comparisons when this will improve her or his self-evaluation

SELF-REFLECTION 4.1
Measuring Your Self-Esteem (Part 1)

As you see in the main text, self-esteem is how we feel about or evaluate our self. One of the most frequently used self-esteem measures is the 10-item scale published by Morris Rosenberg (1965). This scale is primarily used to measure global, as opposed to specific, self-esteem (see text). To get a rough idea as to your self-esteem, take a minute and answer the following questions, and then turn the page to interpret your score.

TABLE 4.2   Measuring Your Self-Esteem

Item	Response options			
	Strongly disagree	Disagree	Agree	Strongly agree
1. On the whole, I am satisfied with myself.	1	2	3	4
2. At times, I think I am no good at all.	1	2	3	4
3. I feel that I have a number of good qualities.	1	2	3	4
4. I am able to do things as well as most other people.	1	2	3	4
5. I feel I do not have much to be proud of.	1	2	3	4
6. I certainly feel useless at times.	1	2	3	4
7. I feel that I am a person of worth, at or on an equal plane with others.	1	2	3	4
8. I wish I could have more respect for myself.	1	2	3	4
9. All in all, I am inclined to feel that I am a failure.	1	2	3	4
10. I take a positive attitude toward myself.	1	2	3	4

Source: Adapted from Rosenberg, M. (1989). *Society and the adolescent self-image* (Rev. ed.). Middletown, CT England: Wesleyan University Press.

TURN THE PAGE TO FIND OUR ANSWERS.

SELF-REFLECTION 4.2
Measuring Your Self-Esteem (Part 2)

Scoring key: for items 1, 3, 4, 7, and 10, SA = 3, A = 2, D = 1, SD = 0; for items 2, 5, 6, 8 and 9: SA = 0, A = 2, D = 2, SD = 3. To calculate your score, write the number corresponding to your answer to the right of each item. Next add up all of the scores to obtain your total score. The higher the score, the higher you self-esteem is. Your score should fall between 0 and 30. The average score for an adult is about 22, and the majority of people score between 15 and 25. (*Please note that your score is simply a rough estimate and does not constitute a clinical diagnosis.*)

The social comparison and reflection processes are but two of the many strategies people use to manage their self-esteem via self-protection or self-promotion (Hepper, Gramzow, & Sedikides, 2010). **Self-protection** refers to efforts to maintain or defend one's positive self-image, whereas **self-promotion** is focused on enhancing one's self-image (Alicke & Sedikides, 2009; Higgins, 1997). In the next couple of sections we'll review some common strategies people use in the service of self-protection and/or self-promotion.

Social Comparison: Looking Up and Looking Down

An important postulate of SEM is that people manage their social comparisons in order to maintain a positive self-image (Strickhouser & Zell, 2015; Tesser, 2003). We decide who to compare ourselves to based on whether or not the comparison will enhance our self-worth. When people engage in **downward social comparison,** they contrast their own performance, ability, or situation with individuals who did less well, have weaker abilities, or are in worse situations (Johnson & Knobloch-Westerwick, 2014; Ross & Bowen, 2010). Say you drive a rusty 1988 Volkswagen with numerous dings, scratches, dents, and malfunctioning controls, and occasionally think "I drive such a crappy, ugly car." But then you may remember that your best friend has no car at all, and as a result, you feel a bit better (Buunk & Oldersma, 2001). Even cancer patients may contrast the severity of their disease with that of others who are worse off as a way of feeling better about their own situation (Wood, Taylor, & Lichtman, 1985). Another self-enhancing comparison people often make is with their former selves, typically believing that they have improved over the years (Kanten & Teigen, 2008).

In contrast to downward comparison, you may instead engage in **upward social comparison,** in which you evaluate your performance, ability, or situation with a superior person's (Crusius & Mussweiler, 2012; Tesser, 1988). Perhaps you look at the "A" a classmate received on an exam and compare it to your "B." Or maybe you notice how

Self-Protection: Efforts intended to maintain or defend one's positive self-image

Self-Promotion: Efforts designed to enhance one's self-image

Downward Social Comparison: Contrasting one's own performance, ability, or situation with individuals who did less well, have weaker abilities, or are in worse situations

Upward Social Comparison: Contrasting one's performance, ability, or situation with individuals who performed better, have stronger abilities, or are in better situations

an acquaintance keeps beating you at Wii tennis. Using these comparisons to motivate yourself to work hard and perform better would be a beneficial result of upward comparison (Blanton, Buunk, Gibbons, & Kuyper, 1999). In this case, your motive is neither accurate self-evaluation nor self-enhancement but rather self-improvement. In contrast, a negative result of such upward comparison occurs when you allow the comparison to demoralize you by focusing your thoughts on what you haven't achieved (Dunn, Ruedy, & Schweitzer, 2012). Both upward and downward social comparisons are most useful when you compare yourself to people who are similar to you on relevant characteristics (Tiggemann & Polivy, 2010). For instance, you may be better off contrasting your cycling prowess with your brother's rather than Lance Armstrong's.

A related tactic people can use to improve their self-esteem is to engage in **counterfactual thinking** or imagining what *could* have happened (Medvec, Madey, & Gilovich, 1995; Petrocelli, Percy, Sherman, & Tormala, 2011). Victoria Medvec and her colleagues studied silver and bronze medalists' reactions to their event placements in the 1992 Summer Olympic games and the 1994 Empire State Games. Who do you think would feel better after completing an important competition, the bronze medal winners who placed third or silver medal winners who placed second? Using videotapes of the award ceremonies and interviews with winners, they found that bronze medalists were *more* satisfied with their medals than were silver medalists, despite the fact that silver medalists had obviously performed better than their counterparts. Why? Well, bronze medalists primarily focused on the counterfactual that they *almost* received no medal at all (almost came in fourth), and that increased their satisfaction with their achievement. In contrast, silver medalists thought more about a different alternative outcome—that they *almost* won the gold medal—and as result were more disappointed (Medvec et al., 1995).

> **Counterfactual Thinking:** Imagining what *could* have happened (but did not)

False Consensus and False Uniqueness

Would you prefer to be like most other people or different from them? It probably depends on what aspects of yourself you are thinking about. In some domains—such as opinions and behaviors—people would rather that others see the world in the same way that they do, but in others—such as personal abilities—we prefer to stand out. Oftentimes people believe that their opinions or behaviors are more common than they actually are, and thus exhibit the **false consensus effect** (Mullen, 1985; H. S. Park, 2012; L. Ross, Greene, & House, 1977). In one study, students were asked to wear a sandwich board sign displaying either "Repent" or "Eat at Joe's" for 30 minutes. Whether they said yes or no, each estimated how many other students were likely to agree to the same request. Most of the participants *over*estimated the number of students who would make the same decision that they did. This was especially true for those who agreed to wear the "Eat at Joe's" sign: Only 30% of the students actually agreed to carry it, but they predicted that 57% of other students would (L. Ross et al., 1977).

> **False Consensus Effect:** Believing that one's opinions or behaviors are more common than they actually are

People demonstrate the false consensus effect in many arenas of life, including adolescents' predictions of peer substance use and adults' estimates of how others will respond to particular behavioral experiences or how many showers others will take during a shower ban (Henry, Kobus, & Schoeny, 2011; Kammrath, 2011; Monin & Norton, 2003), and are especially likely to do so when in an opinion minority (Marks & Miller, 1987). For instance, Whitley (1998) found that sexually active college women overestimated the level of sexual activity of other college women, as compared to the estimates of nonsexually active women. Believing that other people hold the same opinions or engage in the same behaviors can maintain our self-esteem (Marks & Miller, 1987), and avoiding discussion of topics on which there is potential disagreement may help us maintain this belief (Goel, Mason, & Watts, 2010).

Although we often find comfort when we think others are similar to us, there are times when we'd prefer to stand out from the crowd. This primarily occurs with respect to one's abilities or competencies, because we'd like to think that we are uncommonly talented. As in the case with false consensus, we are often mistaken about how we compare to others, except that here we inaccurately believe that we are *different* from them. For instance, people who engage in socially desirable behaviors, like giving blood, may underestimate how many others would do the same (Goethals, 1986). When we hold incorrect beliefs about how different we are, we demonstrate the **false uniqueness effect**, and as with the false consensus effect, this tendency serves to enhance our self-esteem (Goethals, 1986; Monin & Norton, 2003; H. S. Park, 2012). Both the false consensus and false uniqueness effects stem in part from our lack of knowledge of the true attitudes or attributes of others.

Are you more or less socially skilled than the average person? More ethical? A better driver? Well, most people believe that they are more ethical and are better-than-average drivers, even if they have a history of auto accidents (Guerin, 1994; Lovett, 1997). In fact, you probably think that you are better-than-average on most desirable characteristics, which is called the **better-than-average effect** (see Research box 4.1) (Gilovich, 1991; Guenther & Alicke, 2010). This effect is also known in the United States as the Lake Wobegon effect, because in Lake Wobegon, the fictional community invented by Garrison Keilor, "the women are strong and the men are good-looking and all the children are above average." When do people prefer to see themselves as distinct versus similar to others? It depends on the desirability of the behavior in question. If the behavior is seen as positive, then people overestimate their uniqueness; however, for our negative behaviors, we'd rather believe that many others do them as well (Marks, 1984).

Self-Serving Judgments

When you do well on a psychology exam, what is the reason? Did you work hard? Or are you simply smart? What if you fail? Were the professor's questions incomprehensible? Or were you deathly sick the night before? People often answer questions like these with judgments that enhance their self-esteem (Gilovich, 1991; Mezulis, Abramson, Hyde, & Hankin, 2004). If, like many of us, you take credit for your successes but blame outside

False Uniqueness Effect: Holding incorrect beliefs about how different one is from others

Better-Than-Average Effect: Judging that one is above average on most desirable characteristics

RESEARCH BOX 4.1
THE BETTER-THAN-AVERAGE EFFECT

Hypothesis: Participants will rate themselves as better or higher than their college peers across a range of personality traits.

Research Method: As part of a larger testing situation, participants rated themselves or their average college peer on twenty-three traits, including cooperativeness, intelligence, truthfulness, kindness, attractiveness, and athleticism. Participants in a control condition did not complete these ratings. Eight weeks later, participants who initially rated themselves now rated the average peer, and those who initially rated their average peer now rated themselves. Control participants rated both themselves and their average peer.

Results: The results confirmed the hypothesis. Regardless of whether participants rated themselves before, after, or simultaneously with the ratings of their peers, their self-ratings were typically higher than their peer ratings.

Conclusion: College students continue to believe that they are better than the average college student.

Source: Adapted from Guenther, C. L., & Alicke, M. D. (2010). Deconstructing the better-than-average effect. *Journal of Personality and Social Psychology, 99,* 755–770.

factors for your failures, you are demonstrating one type of self-serving belief known as the **self-serving attributional bias** or, more simply, the self-serving bias (Shepperd, Malone, & Sweeny, 2008). Attributions are explanations that people give for their own or others' behavior; when you attribute your high grade to hard work, you are claiming that your grade was a result of your personal effort. The self-serving bias helps us maintain our self-esteem by bolstering us when things go well and buffering us against negative events by blaming outside factors. Basically, you feel good when you succeed, *and* you feel good when you fail (because it wasn't your fault).

The Bias Blind Spot: Being Biased About Being Biased

One of the most interesting self-serving biases is the bias people have about being biased. While acknowledging that the average American exhibits many of the biases described in this section, people tend to believe *they* and they alone are somehow immune to those very same biases, including the self-serving bias! Pronin, Lin, and Ross (2002) found

Self-Serving Attributional Bias: Taking credit for one's successes but blaming outside factors for one's failures

that people exhibit this **bias blind spot** for several different types of cognitive biases. Instances of this blindness often occur in the context of negotiations, wherein the conflicting parties are unable to identify their own biases but are quick to do so in their adversaries (Frantz, 2006). Even when people admit to having biases in theory, they tend to deny them in specific situations (West, Meserve, & Stanovich, 2012).

Think Again!

1. *How is self-esteem different from self-concept?*
2. *What are two ways do you enhance your self-esteem?*
3. *What is the bias blind spot? Do you think you have this bias?*

SELF-PRESENTATION: DISPLAYING ONESELF

We've already seen that the self-concept is the sum total of what you believe about yourself—your attributes, qualities, competencies, and so forth—and how self-esteem represents your evaluation of your self-concept. There is a third aspect to the self that is also important in building and shaping who we are: our **interpersonal self**, which is the self we present to others (Burusic & Ribar, 2014). We manage our self-image and protect our self-esteem through tactical self-presentation or impression management. **Impression management** represents our efforts to project the image that we wish others to have of us (Bourdage, Wiltshire, & Lee, 2015; Ogunfowora, Bourdage, & Nguyen, 2013; Schlenker, 2000). The specific tactics that we choose will partially depend on how we imagine other people perceive and judge us, which in turn can affect our sense of self. We engage in self-presentational strategies so that others will see us as we see ourselves, which of course requires that we attempt to take the perspective of others to gain insight into our self-presentation (Leary & Allen, 2011). There are several goals of self-presentation: We want others to like us, to see us as competent, and to verify or affirm the self (Jones, 1990; Swann, 1990; Uziel, 2010).

Self-Monitoring

When you walk into class or a party, how much do you think about the impressions you are making on others? Do you wonder how others perceive your actions and appearance? If you do this a lot, then you are probably high in **self-monitoring**. Self-monitoring is the extent to which people chronically think about how they appear to others and, as a consequence, change their appearance and behavior to fit the circumstances (Abell & Brewer, 2014; Choi, Moon, & Chun, 2015; Gangestad & Snyder, 2000). People who are

Bias Blind Spot: Believing that one is immune to cognitive biases that affect others

Interpersonal Self: Way we present ourselves to other people

Impression Management: Efforts to project the image of the self that a person wants others to have

Self-Monitoring: Extent to which people chronically think about how they appear to others and, as a consequence, change their appearance and behavior to fit the circumstances

low in self-monitoring tend to be less concerned about others' perceptions of them and usually act in similar ways across situations (Kurt, Inman, & Argo, 2011). For instance, do you know someone who behaves in pretty much the same way no matter what setting she is in—perhaps is loud, profane, unkempt, and dressed in a baseball cap, T-shirt, and jeans regardless of the situation? She would be a low self-monitor. Compare her with a high self-monitor, who carefully selects his clothing and hairstyle to match social situations and tries hard to fit in with whomever he is with.

A high self-monitor tends to express different attitudes to different audiences—even if it entails endorsing attitudes that he doesn't hold—and is more likely to mimic the behavior of others (Estow, Jamieson, & Yates, 2007; Leary & Allen, 2011). In contrast to low self-monitors, high self-monitors are more likely to act in accordance with social norms and are better able to read and respond to the interpersonal cues and emotions of others (Fuglestad & Snyder, 2010; Snyder, 1974). Differences between high and low self-monitors extend to romantic relationships—where the former focus more on surface characteristics such as physical attractiveness—and advertising—where image-oriented ads appeal to those at the high end of the scale (Snyder & DeBono, 1985). Some of my students have argued that self-monitoring is undesirable because it is overly conformist. However, they backpedal a bit when they realize how frequently they self-monitor and how important matching the behavior of others and fitting in are.

The Spotlight Effect and the Illusion of Transparency

How would you feel if you were asked, while wearing a T-shirt with a large headshot of Justin Bieber, to enter a room with 6 college students, all of whom could potentially notice your shirt (and are unlikely to be Bieber fans)? Perhaps a bit embarrassed? How many of them would likely remember who was on your shirt? Well, if you were like the participants in a set of studies by Gilovich, Medvec, and Savitsky (2000), you'd think that more people took note of it than actually did. Irrespective of our dispositional self-monitoring level, many of us overestimate the extent to which other people are observing and noticing us—something called the **spotlight effect** (Gilovich et al., 2000; Lawson, 2010). In one study, participants wore a T-shirt displaying the somewhat embarrassing image of Barry Manilow when they entered a room of college students (See Figure 4.4). Participants later estimated that 46% of observers would remember the celebrity on the T-shirt, when in fact only 23% did. People similarly exaggerate how many others notice when they wear a nonembarrassing shirt or make positive or negative contributions to a group discussion or engage in another social blunder (Epley, Savitsky, & Gilovich, 2002; Gilovich et al., 2000). In effect, people tend to think they are in a veritable social spotlight.

A related phenomenon occurs with respect to how strongly we believe that others can "read" our emotions or detect lies that we utter merely by looking at our facial expressions. Social psychologists call this the **illusion of transparency** (Gilovich, Savitsky, & Medvec, 1998; Holder & Hawkins, 2007). For example, participants in one study were asked to hide

Spotlight Effect:
Overestimation of the extent to which other people are observing and noticing one

Illusion of Transparency:
Incorrect belief that others can "read" our emotions or detect our lies merely by looking at our facial expressions

FIGURE 4.4   The Spotlight Effect

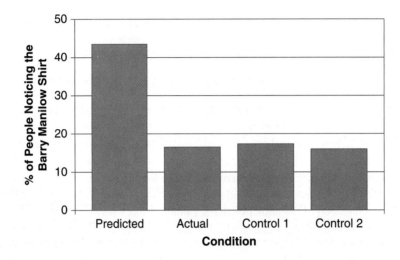

Source: Adapted from Gilovich, T., Medvec, V. H., & Savitsky, K. (2000). The spotlight effect in social judgment: An egocentric bias in estimates of the salience of one's own actions and appearance. *Journal of Personality and Social Psychology, 78*, 211–222.

their expressions of disgust while drinking unpleasant fluids and subsequently overestimated how many observers accurately perceived their true reaction (Brown & Stopa, 2007; Gilovich et al., 1998; MacInnis, Mackinnon, & MacIntyre, 2010). Both the spotlight effect and the illusion of transparency illustrate the fact that accurately understanding how other people perceive us can be challenging (Gilovich & Savitsky, 1999).

Getting Them to Like Me: Ingratiation

People often say "flattery will get you nowhere." However, contrary to this common cliché, flattery will get you everywhere, unless it is too obvious (Westphal & Stern, 2007)! One of the best ways to get people to like you is to make them believe that you like them, and flattery is one strategy for accomplishing that (see Table 4.3) (Seiter, 2007). **Ingratiation** refers to attempts to get particular persons to like us, and ingratiation tactics include flattery, providing favors and gifts, agreeing with them, emphasizing that person's positive qualities, and acting modestly (Jones, 1990; Romero-Canyas et al., 2010). As Jones (1990) noted, we like people who like us. At times we may we even go as far as to change our reported attitudes so that we appear to agree with those of an attractive member of the opposite sex who we expect to meet shortly (Rowatt, Cunningham, & Druen, 1998; Zanna & Pack, 1975).

Ingratiation:
Attempts to get particular persons to like us

TABLE 4.3   Strategies of Self-Presentation

Name	Examples
Self-monitoring	Changing one's behavior and attitudes to fit in
Ingratiation	Flattery, giving gifts, doing favors, opinion agreement
Self-promotion	Demonstrating competence, claiming competence
Self-handicapping	Creating obstacles to provide excuses for failure

Ingratiation techniques can backfire, however, if they are seen as blatant attempts to gain favor (Brodsky & Cannon, 2006). Therefore, in order to be successful, ingratiation has to be conducted illicitly, so as not to be too obvious (Tal-Or, 2010b). There is a paradoxical aspect to ingratiation: Sometimes the very people we want to impress are high status individuals who are particularly attuned to attempts to garner favor (Jones, 1990). They are particularly skilled at recognizing when others try to ingratiate themselves. Fortunately, the target of ingratiation is more likely to believe that ingratiation tactics—such as compliments—are authentic or accurate than are neutral third parties (Varma, Toh, & Pichler, 2006). As you can see, ingratiation tactics are especially suited to obtaining the first self-presentational goal: to be seen as likable.

Getting Them to Appreciate Me: Self-Promotion

Although it is important to be liked, there are times when we prefer to be seen as competent—as a capable student, barista, professor, and so forth (Proost, Schreurs, De Witte, & Derous, 2010). Self-promotion refers to efforts designed to convince others of one's competence (Cialdini et al., 1976; Jones, 1990). As with ingratiation, there are a number of self-promotional tactics that may be employed. One is to demonstrate competence by performing the requisite behavior in front of those we want to impress (e.g., come watch me teach!). For example, study participants expecting to be contestants on a *Jeopardy* game show chose to sit in a more visible, prominent seat when they believed they would perform well—that they would know the answers—as compared to those who were less confident (Akimoto, Sanbonmatsu, & Ho, 2000). Another is simply by stating it: "I am a good teacher"—of course, be sure that you can back up your claim to competence! A third is by referring to other sources of objective information ("just look at my teaching evaluations and my teaching award!") (Cialdini et al., 1976; Pfeffer, Fong, Cialdini, & Portnoy, 2006; Tal-Or, 2010a).

Self-promotion becomes particularly important when you are trying to obtain a job, a raise, or entry into college or graduate school (See the Social Psychology Applied to

Work: Managing Impressions text box). Obviously, it is important to convince a potential employer that you are competent, and self-promotional strategies have been shown to accomplish that (Stevens & Kristof, 1995). As with ingratiation, there is a paradox of self-promotion: Truly competent people don't need to claim it, because their performance should be sufficient to demonstrate their competence (Jones, 1990). In fact, self-promotion can sometimes backfire, especially for women, for whom norms of modesty are more salient (Moss-Racusin & Rudman, 2010; Rudman, 1998). Earlier we mentioned that people can use modesty as an ingratiation tactic ("I owe all of my teaching proficiency to my graduate mentors and colleagues!"). However, too much modesty might actually mask your competence—and if the modesty is seen as false, then liking may decrease along with perceived competence.

SOCIAL PSYCHOLOGY APPLIED TO WORK
MANAGING IMPRESSIONS

As you know, people strive to ensure that others have favorable opinions of them. One domain of life in which positive impressions are particularly important is work—otherwise we wouldn't be able to obtain, keep, or advance in our jobs. Social psychologists and others have extensively investigated how people attempt to manage the impressions they make during interviews as well as on the job (Barrick, Shaffer, & DeGrassi, 2009; Bourdage et al., 2015; Cialdini, Petrova, & Goldstein, 2004; Ingold, Kleinmann, König, & Melchers, 2015; Jones & Pittman, 1982). There are many strategies people may use to manage impressions, including providing answers that are more socially desirable than their true answers (e.g., stating that they like working in teams even if

they don't because they think the interviewer wants to hear this) or claiming skills and/or experiences that they do not have (Levashina & Campion, 2007; Roulin, Bangerter, & Levashina, 2015; Tsai, Huang, Wu, & Lo, 2010; Weiss & Feldman, 2006).

For instance, using three measures of faking, O'Connell, Kung, and Tristan (2011) found that job applicants were more deceptive than existing employees and that they also gave significantly more positive self-reports than did employees (see this chapter's *Doing Research* text box). Levashina and Campion (2007) developed an Interview Faking Behavior Scale that could accurately reveal when individuals were faking answers during interviews. They learned that more deception occurs when people are asked about hypothetical situations (e.g., "Suppose you have a great idea, but there is opposition to it among your colleagues. What would you do to persuade your colleagues to 'see things your way'?") than past behavior (e.g., "Describe a time when you had a great idea, but there was opposition to it. How did you do persuade your colleagues to 'see things your way'?"). Moreover, participants tended to fake their answers more when the interviewers did not engage in follow-up questioning after receiving the initial answers.

People of course differ in the extent to which they actively manage impressions. For example, it won't surprise you that individuals who are relatively high on an honesty-humility personality dimension are less likely to engage in impression management (Bourdage et al., 2015). Extraverts have a greater tendency to self-promote and attempt to ingratiate themselves than do introverts, and more agreeable individuals also engage in ingratiation. Other research has shown that people who are actively managing impressions are also more prone to misrepresenting themselves on personality scales (Ingold et al., 2015). Guadagno and Cialdini (2007) conducted a qualitative review of the literature and concluded that men and women seem to manage their self-presentations generally in line with traditional gender roles. Hogue, Levashina, and Hang (2013) provide empirical evidence that men and women who are high in Machiavellianism (the desire to further self-interest regardless of the cost) more intensively attempt to ingratiate themselves than women low in it. Individuals who are concerned that their group membership may lead to negative impressions, such as gays and lesbians (Jones & King, 2014) and Asian Americans (Roberts, Cha, & Kim, 2014), often actively seek to manage their self-presentations.

I Failed But I Am Still Competent! Self-Handicapping

Most of us are concerned that a personal failure will be perceived as lack of competence, which can in turn damage self-esteem. One common way to ward off such threats to self-esteem is to have excuses ready to be rolled out. However, simply making excuses itself can be damaging, especially if used too often. Some people go one step further than making excuses, and that is to actually create obstacles to success so that, if failure occurs, they can protect their self by attributing the failure to something other than their own ability or competence (Jones & Berglas, 1978). This tactic, called **self-handicapping**, involves arranging events that may in fact reduce the likelihood of success but also serve to protect one's self-esteem by deflecting responsibility

Self-Handicapping:
Arranging events that may reduce one's likelihood of success but also protect one's self-esteem by serving as excuses for possible failure

(Gadbois & Sturgeon, 2011; Jones & Berglas, 1978; Park & Brown, 2014). For instance, partying the night before an exam gives a person an excuse for failing to perform well. Essentially one can say—both to oneself and others—that "I could have done better if I had stayed home and studied."

Self-handicapping provides automatic cover for possible failure and the appearance of incompetence (Rhodewalt, 1990). Several years ago during a discussion of self-handicapping, one of my students (I'll call her Julie) described how, as an outstanding clarinet player about to compete in the finals of a state competition, she decided not to practice the entire week before the event! Julie explained that she was worried that she would lose the competition and that she couldn't cope with that failure. By not practicing, she would have a good way to explain her poor performance that wouldn't challenge her competence. The key component of effective self-handicapping is that it essentially prevents attributions of incompetence by providing an external reason for the failure (Gadbois & Sturgeon, 2011).

There are many ways people self-handicap, including not studying, not preparing for competition or not practicing a task, using alcohol or drugs, or giving an opponent a head start in a race or some other advantage (Higgins & Harris, 1988; Rhodewalt, Saltzman, & Wittmer, 1984). There is an obvious downside to self-handicapping: Performance may in fact worsen and failure may become more likely. That is, by engaging in self-handicapping people may prevent the very success they hope for (McCrea & Hirt, 2001). Having an excuse for failure may protect self-esteem, but it is unlikely to boost it the way that success could.

In sum, an important aspect of the self is the interpersonal self—the one we present to others (Baumeister et al., 2007). Self-presentational concerns influence many of our social interactions: We strategically manage our impressions so that others will like us and think we are competent. We engage in a variety of tactics to do this, including self-monitoring, ingratiation, self-promotion, and self-handicapping. However, our impression management must be done in ways that are not too transparent, or they may backfire. In the next section we'll elaborate on another important aspect of the self: how we control our thoughts, feelings, and behaviors.

Think Again!

1. _What are high and low self-monitoring? Are you high or low? Why do you think that?_

2. _What is the illusion of transparency?_

3. _When have you self-handicapped? Why did you do it?_

SELF-REGULATION: CONTROLLING ONESELF

Have you ever made a New Year's resolution to start a new, good habit (such as exercising) or stopping an old, bad habit (like eating fast food) that you have been unable to maintain? If so, you are not unusual, and you are likely to do it again! According to one study, some 60% of people who failed to achieve their New Year's goal will try again the following year (Prochaska, DiClemente, & Norcross, 1992). Initiating and maintaining self-related goals can indeed be challenging.

So far in this chapter we have described the self-concept as the set of beliefs about the self, self-esteem as the evaluation of the self-concept, and self-presentation as those efforts to project a particular image of the self to others. There is one more key aspect of the self that binds the first two together and impacts the third: self-regulation. **Self-regulation** is the capacity of the self to control our internal states and responses, including thoughts, feelings, and behavior (Bartels & Magun-Jackson, 2009; Baumeister et al., 2007; Blair, Ursache, Vernon-Feagans, & Greenberg, 2015; Vohs & Schmeichel, 2007). Successful self-regulation is under the purview of the executive self and requires the ability to think about and plan the future, which may be one of the characteristics that separates humans from other animals (Baumeister et al., 2007). Failure of self-regulation is implicated in many important social ills, including alcoholism, drug dependence, smoking cigarettes, obesity, personal financial problems, procrastination, low achievement in school, and much criminal behavior (Baumeister et al., 2007; de Ridder, Kuijer, & Ouwehand, 2007; Ferrari, 2001; Gottfredson & Hirschi, 1990; Wilson, Petaja, Stevens, Mitchell, & Peterson, 2011). For example, inability to curb one's alcohol consumption can result in addiction, and difficulty avoiding spending money can lead to insufficient saving, excessive credit card debt, and even bankruptcy (D'Lima, Pearson, & Kelley, 2012; Tangney, Baumeister, & Boone, 2004).

One prominent model postulates that successful self-regulation depends on the availability of **willpower** or mental energy needed to change the activities of the self to meet desired standards (Baumeister, Bratslavsky, Muraven, & Tice, 1998). Resisting temptation, curbing impulses, and other forms of self-regulation tap this limited mental energy or resource pool, in effect depleting it and preventing it from being used for other purposes (Hung & Labroo, 2011; Job, Walton, Bernecker, & Dweck, 2015). The notion that willpower can be used up or depleted was tested in a study in which participants who had skipped a meal were seated at a table that contained freshly baked chocolate chip cookies and other chocolates as well as a plate of radishes (Baumeister et al., 1998). They were instructed to eat either the chocolates or the radishes. After five minutes had elapsed, the participants were asked to solve a challenging puzzle (that was actually unsolvable, although they did not know this). The researchers wanted to see how long participants would persist at solving the puzzle, and compared the length of time they worked before giving up to a control group that had skipped the eating stage and immediately proceeded to the puzzle task. Baumeister et al. (1998) expected that participants who had resisted the chocolate would give up on the puzzle more quickly than the other participants.

Self-Regulation: The capacity to control one's thoughts, feelings, and behavior

Willpower: Mental energy needed to change the activities of the self to meet the desired standards

Consistent with the willpower-as-resource model, the chocolate resisters worked only about half as long as the radish resisters or the control group (See Figure 4.5). Essentially, the chocolate resisters depleted their store of willpower while controlling the urge to eat the chocolate, and therefore had less mental energy to devote to solving the impossible puzzle (Baumeister et al., 1998). Baumeister and others have conducted a large number of studies encompassing many different behaviors and have consistently found that willpower functions very much like a limited resource (Ciarocco, Echevarria, & Lewandowski, 2012; Muraven & Baumeister, 2000).

Another important feature of willpower is that it seems to function like a muscle in the sense that it can be strengthened with practice (Baumeister et al., 2007; Hung & Labroo, 2011). In fact, like physical strength, willpower is more likely to be depleted at night following a busy day versus the morning after a restful night's sleep. Finally, people differ in their capacity for self-control, and persons who are have greater self-control tend to earn higher grades in school, reported better mental health, higher self-esteem, better interpersonal relationships, fewer impulse control problems, and better job performance (Hennecke & Freund, 2010; Porath & Bateman, 2006; Tangney et al., 2004).

FIGURE 4.5   The Limits of Willpower

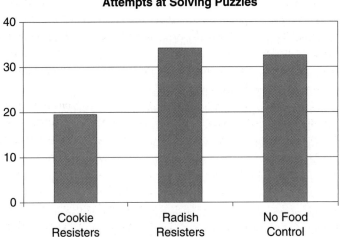

Consistent with the willpower as resource model, participants who were asked to resist eating chocolate worked only about half as hard at solving problems than did the radish resisters or the control group. Essentially, the chocolate resisters depleted their store of willpower while controlling the urge to eat the chocolate, and therefore had less mental energy to devote to solving the impossible puzzle.

Source: Adapted from Study 1, Baumeister, R. F., Bratslavsky, E., Muraven, M., & Tice, D. M. (1998). Ego depletion: Is the active self a limited resource? *Journal of Personality and Social Psychology, 74*, 1252–1265.

Effective self-regulation is viewed as an important ingredient to successfully nego-tiating the journey from childhood to stable, healthy adulthood. This intuitive notion is supported by extensive research by the personality psychologist Walter Mischel and his collaborators (Mischel & Ayduk, 2011). Mischel assessed the self-regulatory capacities of about 500 four- and five-year olds by offering them the opportunity to either imme-diately eat one treat, such as a cookie or marshmallow, or waiting—and delaying their gratification—until a short while later and receiving two treats instead. Mischel followed these children into adulthood and found that the effective self-regulators had higher SAT scores, were better able to deal with a variety of stressors, more likely to plan and to set personal goals, and were rated as higher in rationality and social competence than the less effective ones (Mischel & Ayduk, 2011).

Self-Control Failure and Ironic Processes

Imagine a white bear. Think about what it would look like, what it eats, how its fur would feel, its weight, its sharp teeth, and so forth. Now set the timer on your cell phone for one minute and try to stop thinking about that white bear until the alarm sounds. Can you do it? Well, if you are like the participants in a study by Wegner and colleagues, trying NOT to think of the white bear will result in more thoughts of a white bear when compared to a control group that was not asked to stop thinking about it (Koster, Soetens, Braet, & De Raedt, 2008; Wegner, Schneider, Carter, & White, 1987). The upshot of this is that conscious attempts to control one's thoughts by avoiding a given topic can lead, ironically, to increased thoughts about that topic. That is, intended thought *suppression* can lead to apparent thought *production*. This **ironic process of mental control** produces the very thoughts or behavior that you are trying not to produce (Miklowitz, Alatiq, Geddes, Goodwin, & Williams, 2010; Wegner et al., 1987).

Try not to think of a gray elephant, and you are more likely to think about a gray elephant. Why? The reason is that two tasks must be performed to effectively suppress a thought or behavior. One is an automatic process that monitors whatever it is that has been deliberately banished from consciousness—the monitoring occurs so that it can warn consciousness that the thought is emerging. The second process is more controlled and involves attempts to distract thoughts away from the undesirable topic toward some competing topic, such as a vision of a bright green parrot. The reason this happens is that the monitoring process requires that you think about the green parrot to be certain that you are not thinking about it. In order to be certain that you are not thinking about something, you need to "check" up on that very thing—to monitor it—to be sure that you are not thinking about it! In a sense these two systems are competing, and the automatic process sometimes will "win" by facil-itating the intrusion of the unwanted thoughts into consciousness. Difficulty with thought suppression is particularly likely under conditions of cognitive load, when consciousness is attempting to multitask, such as when you are trying to recite the alphabet backwards or memorize a twelve-digit number (see Figure 4.6) (Miklowitz et al., 2010).

Ironic Process of Mental Control: Trying to control one's thoughts or behavior in a way that produces the very thoughts or behavior that one is trying to avoid

FIGURE **4.6** Processes of Ironic Control

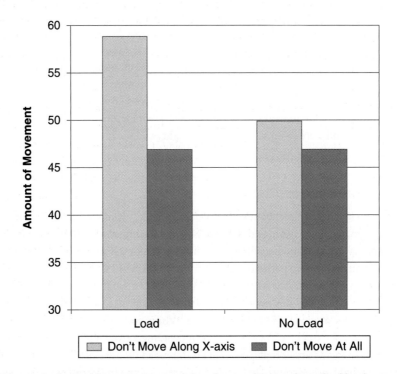

Participants instructed to prevent a pendulum from swinging along the X-axis were less successful in holding it still then were participants simply asked to hold it steady, especially under cognitive load—again, demonstrating that initiating a particular goal consciously may generate the opposite behavior than what was intended.

Source: Adapted from Study 2, Wegner, D. M., Ansfield, M., & Pilloff, D. (1998). The putt and the pendulum: Ironic effects of the mental control of action. *Psychological Science, 9,* 196–199.

Think Again!

1. *What are self-regulation and willpower?*

2. *What is an ironic process? What are its two components?*

3. *The next time you have a song "stuck" in your head, try to suppress it. Describe the experience.*

Confirming the Self: Self-Verification

The final "self" concept that we will discuss in this chapter is based in a motive related to self-regulation and self-concept: what is called the need for self-consistency or self-verification. In the chapter on persuasion we'll describe consistency theory in more detail; for now suffice it to say that people often seek feedback from others that is consistent with their self-concept. That is, they wish to confirm or verify what they believe is true about themselves, a tendency called **self-verification** (North & Swann, 2009a; Swann, 1990; Valentiner, Hiraoka, & Skowronski, 2014). According to Swann (1990), people want to maximize their perceptions of control and predictability with respect to themselves and their situation, and doing so involves confirming one's beliefs about the self. Perhaps, paradoxically, people don't just want others to verify their positive attributes, but they also seek feedback consistent with their self-identified negative attributes (Swann, 1990; Valentiner, Skowronski, McGrath, Smith, & Renner, 2011). For instance, in one study participants who held negative self-views chose to interact with individuals who had negatively evaluated them rather than others who had given them a positive evaluation (Swann, Pelham, & Krull, 1989). Note how this motivation differs from that for accurate self-knowledge and for self-enhancing information: Seeking true accuracy would require soliciting and being open to feedback that may not be consistent with one's self-view, whereas self-enhancing implies searching for and/or attending to only positive feedback (Sedikides & Gregg, 2003). In contrast, self-verification invokes strategies designed to reinforce one's self-concept, whether or not it results in accurate self-knowledge or unflattering evaluation (Swann, 1990; Swann, Chang-Schneider, & Angulo, 2008). Despite the fact that self-verification can provide individuals with negative feedback, this and other drawbacks are often outweighed by the benefits of self-verification (North & Swann, 2009b). By way of example, people tend to seek romantic partners who help verify their self-concepts, including their less desirable features (Swann et al., 2008).

> **Self-Verification:** Seeking information that will confirm one's self-concept

A Clash of Motives?

As you can see from the preceding paragraph, the motives of accuracy, enhancement, and verification may be at loggerheads: Efforts to satisfy one of them may prevent the satisfaction of the others (Kwang & Swann, 2010). For instance, in one study, when given the option of choosing what feedback to receive, participants preferred self-enhancing to self-verifying feedback and were least interested in obtaining self-evaluative information (Sedikides, 1993). In other words, feeling good about oneself was more important than confirming the self, and obtaining accurate feedback was least important. Although direct research examining conflicts among these three motives is sparse, what is available suggests that self-enhancement may be one of the most fundamental of all motives (Anseel & Lievens, 2006).

FINAL THOUGHTS: THE PARADOX OF THE SELF

As you can see from reading this chapter, the seemingly simple question, "what is the self?" is actually quite complex. The self is not one "thing." Instead it is a nexus of motives, cognitions, and other features that intersect, overlap, and interact in complicated and fascinating ways. We learn about our selves in several ways, including introspection and by the self-perception process of observing how we behave. The self presents a bit of a paradox: It is defined as the experience of the self, suggesting that it is independent, stable, and coherent. However, research shows that it is also dependent on and tied closely to other people— at least how we perceive our relationships with others and how we think they view us—and other people play a particularly large role in self-evaluation. Moreover, our many selves differ from each other and may vary across situations as we engage in self-monitoring and impression management. The self is the product of all of these activities and is continually evolving even as we try to hold it steady. Finally, the self lies at the core of several of the fundamental issues of social psychology, including the extent to which we have free will and the rationality of our thought processes.

CORE CONCEPTS

- The self is the psychological apparatus that gives a person the capacity to consciously think about him or herself and includes self-concept, self-esteem, the interpersonal self, and the executive self. The self-concept is composed of the characteristics that we believe we possess. Schemas are cognitive structures that organize knowledge about the world, including ourselves. Self-discrepancy theory states that we possess actual, ideal, and ought selves that vary in how different they are from each other.

- Introspection or looking within is limited because we often are unaware of our mental processes, even if we know their outcomes, and also because it can change how we feel. Self-perception involves looking at ourselves the way someone else might but applies primarily to when we are uncertain about how we feel. The facial feedback hypothesis states that facial expressions and movements can alter rather than merely reflect what we feel.

- Self-reports are commonly used in social psychology research but may be biased, because some people tend toward extreme responding, are more likely to agree than disagree, and/or are affected by other factors like context and question wording. Surveys are advantageous because they are relatively cheap, easy to construct, and facilitate gathering large quantities of data quickly. However, if researchers are interested uncovering cause and effect, then they should opt for controlled experimentation.

- People are intrinsically motivated when they engage in the activity for its own sake but are extrinsically motivated when they do so for reasons other than for its own sake. Overjustification occurs when external rewards undermine our intrinsic motivation. Self-esteem or our evaluation of how we are doing is closely linked to the quality of our relationships with other people or the extent to which they like and accept us—which is called the sociometer hypothesis.

- Strategic self-presentation can serve self-enhancement, and people differ in the extent to which they self-monitor or carefully regulate the impressions they make. Self-evaluation maintenance explains how we make comparisons only when those comparisons are likely to boost our self-esteem. Strategies that we use to self-enhance include comparing ourselves to people who are doing better or worse, making self-serving judgments, ingratiating ourselves to others, self-promotion, and self-handicapping. People often feel like others are paying more attention to them than they in fact are, that others can "see" how they feel and that they are unbiased and better than most people: They may self-handicap by creating obstacles to performing well on task.

- Self-regulation is another key component of the self and may be compromised because our willpower is a limited resource and may be thwarted when people ironically end up doing the opposite of what they intended.

➤ **⑤SAGE edge™** Test your understanding of chapter content. Take the practice quiz. edge.sagepub.com/barrett

KEY TERMS

▶ **ⓈSAGE edge™**   Review key terms with eFlashcards.
edge.sagepub.com/barrett

THINK FURTHER!

- What is the self? Does the definition in this chapter make sense to you? Are there any problems or disadvantages to defining it this way?

- Define and give examples of self-concept, self-esteem, the interpersonal self, and the executive self.

- Define and then sketch out your actual, ideal, and ought selves. What feelings are typically triggered by wide discrepancies between the selves? Do you experience any of these feelings?

- Compare and contrast introspection and self-perception as ways of learning about the self. If you could only use one strategy to understand who you are, which would you choose and why?

- What are the advantages and disadvantages to using self-reports to investigate social psychological phenomena? If you decided to use self-reports for a research project, how would you determine whether or not your participants were demonstrating response effects?

- Willpower is often described as analogous to a muscle that can be strengthened with practice. Explain what this means. Pick an activity over which you wish you had more control. How might you practice to strengthen your willpower here?

SUGGESTED READINGS

Baumeister, R. F. (1987). How the self became a problem: A psychological review of historical research. *Journal of Personality and Social Psychology, 51,* 163–176.

Bem, D. J. (1967). Self-perception: An alternative interpretation of cognitive dissonance phenomena. *Psychological Review, 74,* 183–200.

Dweck, C. S. (1999). *Self-theories: Their role in motivation, personality, and development.* New York, NY: Psychology Press.

Kwang, T., & Swann, W. B. (2010). Do people embrace praise even when they feel unworthy? A review of critical tests of self-enhancement versus self-verification. *Personality and Social Psychology Review, 14,* 263–280.

Lee, H. I., Leung, A. K. y., & Kim, Y. H. (2014). Unpacking East–West differences in the extent of self-enhancement from the perspective of face versus dignity culture. *Social and Personality Psychology Compass, 8,* 314–327.

5

Social Perception

Speed interviewing is used by a wide range of companies. Here, an applicant for job in petroleum engineering strives to leave a favorable impression.

AP Photo/Tim Johnson.

LEARNING OBJECTIVES

5.1 Explain the additive and configural models of impression formation and illustrate each with an example.

5.2 Describe what is meant by a "thin slice" and the research that has supported its predictive value; describe implicit personality theories; explain how expectations or prophecies can be self-fulfilling.

5.3 Name and define Ekman's five categories of nonverbal behavior; identify the six universal facial expressions; explain blended emotions and display rules.

5.4 Identify and explain the major challenges of cross-cultural research.

5.5 Summarize the research on conscious and nonconscious deception detection and on the four cognitive illusions.

5.6 Define attribution and explain the fundamental attribution error, correspondence bias, actor/observer effect, and Kelley's covariation matrix.

"NICE TO MEET YOU. YOU'RE HIRED!" JOB INTERVIEWS IN SECONDS

You have probably heard of speed dating, where singles gather in a large room and rapidly move from table to table, person to person, quickly evaluating others who are also searching for a romantic partner. Many employers have applied this notion to the hiring process to increase administrative efficiency. The basic setup is similar: a large job fair with multiple employers seated at various tables and job applicants—often including college students—who bounce from table to table in hopes of making a splash in their brief time before the interviewer. Interactions typically last between five and fifteen minutes, forcing interviewers to rapidly "size up" job candidates. Speed interviewing is becoming increasingly popular among U.S. corporations (Needleman, 2007; Ramsey, 2006) and has been utilized by companies ranging from IBM, Texas Instruments, Abbott Labs, to Travelodge. But can employers make good decisions based on a such brief exposure to candidates? Quite possibly. Research on "thin slices" suggests that humans are capable of making remarkably accurate impressions of strangers within a few minutes and sometimes less.

Psychologist John Gottman has demonstrated a similar phenomenon with respect to marital longevity (Gottman & Levenson, 1999). Gottman's research team examined videotapes of fifteen-minute discussions of marital conflict between one hundred twenty-four newlywed couples. His researchers coded each second of the interview with an emotion word based on facial expressions and then used these ratings to form an overall impression of the relationship. Gottman found that his interviewers were able to accurately predict whether or not the couple was still married *six years* later based on just the first three minutes of the marital interaction! This is the same basic logic behind speed interviewing: Ask a few targeted questions, monitor nonverbal behavior (e.g., eye contact) and verbal responses, and decide who to immediately reject and who to invite back for an extended interview. As we'll see in this chapter, forming impressions of others can occur in a remarkably brief period of time, often quite accurately. Sometimes, though, rapid first impressions rely too heavily on shortcuts, leading to imperfect assessments. Here again we see the trade-off between rapid, efficient processing (the X-system) and more deliberate, resource-intensive processing (the C-system) discussed previously; the trade-off is the hinge pin for claiming that we have free will. We'll describe the key components of social perception, discussing evolutionary, contextual, and individual-level influences on this very important dimension of human social behavior. In addition, social perception is a key element in our sociality because our construals of the actions and motives of others affects not only how we treat them but also how they treat us.

Think Ahead!

1. *How do people form impressions of others?*

2. *To what extent are facial expressions of emotion similar across cultures?*

3. *How good are people at using nonverbal cues to detect lies?*

4. *How do we try to explain the behavior of others?*

IMPRESSION FORMATION

Early Research

One of the early pioneers of research on social perception was Solomon Asch, who sought to determine how people form initial impressions of others. Asch (1946) suggested two possible processes by which first impressions are created. The first is an *additive* process, in which, upon encountering a person for the first time, the perceiver observes particular personality traits and combines them to produce an overall impression of the target. For instance, during your initial encounter with a person—we'll call her Maria—you may notice that she is intelligent. You may also realize that Maria is funny, unfriendly, and belligerent. According to the additive model, your impression of Maria would essentially be a sum of each of these traits (as well as any others) that you think she possesses (impression = intelligent + funny + unfriendly + belligerent). This is an algebraic model because the individual traits are added together to form the whole (see Figure 5.1). The alternative hypothesis postulates that the perceivers form an overall impression (the "sum") first and only later individualize that impression by isolating specific composite traits. This is the *configural* model, which means that we perceive the person as a psychological unity or configuration of characteristics and that this unity affects how we construe individual elements (see Figure 5.1).

Asch (1946) tested these two models in a series of twelve studies in which participants were exposed to varying sets of personal adjectives and subsequently asked to form overall impressions of the targets described by those adjectives. In the primary experiment, participants heard one of the two following lists, which differed only in their fourth term: (a) *intelligent-skillful-industrious-warm-determined-practical-cautious,* (b) *intelligent-skillful-industrious-cold-determined-practical-cautious.* Asch (1946) found that the overall person descriptions differed remarkably between the two groups. Simply substituting one word—cold for warm—significantly changed the general impression. For instance, a "warm" target person was likely to be seen as *generous* and *wise,* whereas a "cold" person was instead described as *ungenerous* and *shrewd.* Remember, only one adjective differed between the groups. Asch ran several variants on this study in which he examined how other combinations of adjectives affected overall impressions. In one version he substituted *polite-blunt* for *warm-cold,* and found much weaker effects on the overall impression than for *warm-cold.* From this and his remaining studies Asch derived two primary conclusions. First, impression formation seemed more in line with the configural, as opposed to algebraic, model. Second, certain traits—including *warm-cold,* appear to be more influential in the impression formation process. Variations in these *central* traits affected the overall impressions more than did variations in such *peripheral* traits, such as *polite-blunt* (Asch, 1946).

Several years later Harold Kelley (1950) conducted an interesting follow-up study in which he provided student participants with a written description of a guest lecturer in their economics class. The lecturer, previously unknown to the participants, was introduced as a "rather cold person, industrious, critical, practical, and determined" to about half of the participants and as a "very warm person, industrious, critical, practical, and determined" to the remaining participants. Participants were not aware of the fact that not all students received the same descriptions. After the guest delivered his lecture, participants were asked to evaluate him. Kelley (1950) wanted to determine how *expectations* of what a target would be like could affect the interpretation and evaluation of that target. Kelley found that participants given the expectation that the lecturer was warm evaluated the lecturer's performance much more positively than did the participants in the cold condition, even though they witnessed the exact same lecture. Furthermore, the

FIGURE **5.1**   How We Form Impressions

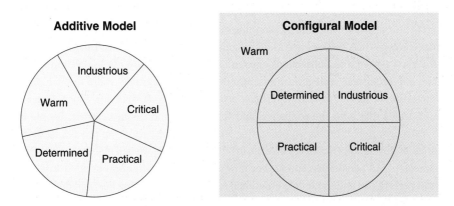

Asch (1946) tested two models of impression formation. The figure at the left illustrates the additive model in which the total of the individual traits produces the impression. In contrast, the configural model at the right shows how one trait, in this case warm, envelopes the other traits and affects how they are construed.

Source: Based on Asch, S. E. (1946). Forming impressions of personality. *The Journal of Abnormal and Social Psychology, 41*(3), 258–290.

behavior of the students toward the lecturer depended on which descriptor was used: Participants in the *warm* condition were more likely to initiate interactions with him. Kelley's research provided an important supplement to Asch's, paving the way for subsequent, more fine-grained research on impression formation (Widmeyer & Loy, 1988).

Think Again!

1. *What are the additive and configural models of impression formation?*

2. *How can initial impressions people form affect their subsequent behavior?*

Forming First Impressions

How do we form first impressions? Person perception begins with the initial exposure to information about a target, such as observation of or contact with the person herself, second-hand exposure (e.g., a rumor, a third party, etc.), or some other source, such as the web. Let's take the case of Emil's first encounter with Sandra, a fellow college student enrolled in his psychology course. Emil notices Sandra, who is sitting three rows in front of him, on the first day of class. He immediately forms an overall impression of Sandra based on various aspects of her physical appearance (e.g., her skin tone, facial features, style of dress, age, etc.) and her behavior (raising her hand, talking to other students, checking text messages, etc.). Each characteristic facilitates Emil's effortless categorization of Sandra along a number of dimensions, including what are called the "Big Three" characteristics: race/ethnicity, age, and sex (Fiske, 1998; Zarate & Smith, 1990). Emil will likely begin to interpret her behaviors by ascribing meaning and explanations to them, and relevant stereotypes may be activated and may guide these interpretations. During the course of the class period and subsequent encounters, he may modify his initial impressions of her, add or subtract categorizations, and develop an integrated, more individualized, nuanced, impression (Bos & Dijksterhuis, 2011; Fiske, Lin, & Neuberg, 1999). Research demonstrates that both the configural and the additive models are correct: People use both categorization or top-down processing and additive or bottom-up processing during impression formation (North & Fiske, 2012). In Chapter 10, we will elaborate on the role of stereotypes in person perception. For now we'll turn our attention to other aspects of person perception: understanding emotional expressions, detecting lies, and determining the causes of social behavior.

Thin Slices

As mentioned above, people are remarkably skilled at forming impressions based on exposure to "thin slices" of a target person's overall features, behaviors, and personality (Ambady, 2010; Ambady & Rosenthal, 1993). In a fascinating study, Todorov and his colleagues asked participants to rate photos of U.S. Senate candidates on attractiveness, likeability, trustworthiness, and competence after only one second of exposure (Todorov, Mandisodza, Goren, & Hall, 2005). Todorov then compared these evaluations to the outcomes of the actual elections and found that ratings of competence were positively and significantly correlated with the voting results: Candidates judged as relatively more competent were more likely to win their respective elections. A later study demonstrated that impressions formed in even *less* than a second—in fact in as little as one-tenth of a second—closely matched ratings by participants who had as much time as they needed to provide the evaluations on traits such as likeability, aggressiveness, attractiveness, competence, and trustworthiness (Willis & Todorov, 2006).

Ambady and Rosenthal (1992) found that ratings of graduate teaching fellows based on thirty seconds of muted videotape were very good predictors of the evaluations provided by students who spent the entire semester in their classes. Similarly, people can accurately determine male sexual orientation by looking at faces for as little as 50 milliseconds, providing additional evidence of the validity of rapid impressions (Rule & Ambady, 2008). Ambady and Rosenthal (1993) suggest that the ability to make these rapid inferences stems from older, more primitive areas of the brain, associated primarily with the X-system (Lieberman, 2007a). Accurate, rapid inferences about personality traits are formed not only from photos or brief physical encounters but also from other sources of information, including email, dormitory rooms, personal offices, and iPod music lists (see box on page 56) (Back et al., 2010; Gosling, Augustine, Vazire, Holtzman, & Gaddis, 2011; McAndrew & De Jonge, 2011; Wang, Moon, Kwon, Evans, & Stefanone, 2010).

In sum, humans are both extraordinarily fast and surprisingly adept at forming reasonably accurate impressions of others. Not only would this ability have provided our ancestors with adaptive advantages, but it likely helps facilitate successful navigation of our increasingly complex and relationship-dense social world. Humans rely on rapid processing in the person perception process but can and will be more deliberative when needed (Brewer, 1988; Fiske et al., 1999; Todorov & Porter, 2014).

BIASES IN SOCIAL PERCEPTION

In Chapter 3, we described some biases in human cognition, including the availability and representativeness heuristics. Here we'll revisit the topic of cognitive biases in the context of person perception. One set of biases are called **implicit personality theories** or lay theories about the kinds of person characteristics that are typically found together (Asch, 1946; Bruner & Taiguri, 1954; Christensen, Drewsen, & Maaløe, 2014; Sedikides & Anderson, 1994). Implicit personality theories are, like schemas, knowledge structures that influence how we construe our social world (Dunning, 2003; Yeager et al., 2014). One of the most prevalent implicit personality theories in the United States is "what is beautiful is good," which suggests that people who are physically attractive also possess a number of other positive characteristics, including higher intelligence,

Implicit Personality Theory: Lay or unscientific theory about the kinds of person characteristics that are typically found together

Electronic Person Perception: What Your Online Presentation Says About You

If we were to strip a sample of your email messages of your name and other personally identifying information, what could others infer from just your writing style? Recently, McAndrew & De Jonge (2011) provided fabricated, unsigned messages to undergraduate participants that were written either in the first or third person, and either included or excluded

©iStockphoto.com/ psphotograph.

typographical errors and expressive punctuation (question marks and exclamation points). One hundred sixty-six participants rated the message authors on a number of dimensions and perceived the authors of third person messages and those lacking expressive punctuation as angrier and more likely to be supervisors (versus subordinates). In addition, messages without the question marks and exclamation points were seen as more likely to be written by males. Research on electronic person perception has been exploding, and social psychologists are delving deeper into the inferences people make based on even brief online cyber encounters and Facebook profiles.

happier marriages, more occupational success, and overall happiness (Dion, Berscheid, & Walster, 1972; Wheeler & Kim, 1997). Recent research demonstrates that a person's implicit theories about the covariation of particular pairs of traits in other people is partly a function of whether the perceiver believes he or she possesses the paired traits. People project patterns of traits that they detect in themselves onto other people (See Research Box 5.1) (Critcher & Dunning, 2009; Mehl, Gosling, & Pennebaker, 2006). For instance, if you see yourself as idealistic and confident that you can control your future, then you'll likely think that, in general, people who are idealistic also believe they control their future (Critcher & Dunning, 2009).

Schemas, such as implicit personality theories, are learned and, like many other aspects of our psychology, are culture-based (Hoffman, Lau, & Johnson, 1986). Evidence for this stems from a study of memory for culture-based implicit personality theories embedded in the English and Chinese languages. Hoffman and colleagues (1986) provided participants with four personality sketches reflecting distinct character types. Two of the character types—*artistic* and *liberal*—were rooted in the English language, whereas the other two—*shi gu* and *shen cang bu lou*—were Chinese-based. Each

RESEARCH BOX 5.1
IMPLICIT PERSONALITY THEORIES

Hypothesis: Participants will project their beliefs about how their own personality traits covary onto other persons. They would assume that if their own traits—say creativity and extraversion—were positively correlated, then they would project that same correlation onto the social targets.

Research Method: College freshmen rated both themselves and their roommates on 11 personality traits and also reported their beliefs about how likely it was that, if a person possessed one trait, that that person also possessed the other.

Results: The results confirmed the hypothesis: Participants' implicit personality theories predicted their assessment of the qualities of their roommates.

Conclusion: People use their beliefs about their own personalities as anchors from which to understand or predict the personalities of others.

Source: Adapted from Critcher, C. R., & Dunning, D. (2009). Egocentric pattern projection: How implicit personality theories recapitulate the geography of the self. *Journal of Personality and Social Psychology, 97,* 1–16.

character was given a name, but the personality type label was not provided to respondents. There were three groups of participants: One group spoke only English, a second group was English Chinese bilingual and read and responded to the materials in English, and the third group was also English Chinese bilingual but read and responded in Chinese. Five days after reading the four personality sketches, participants returned to the lab and wrote down their impressions of the four characters in either English or Chinese. One of the critical dependent measures was the number of character traits that respondents listed in their free responses that were not included in the original descriptions but were consistent with the corresponding character type and the description originally provided.

The researchers expected that individuals who completed the study in English would "fill in" more descriptors that were consistent with the two English labels—*artistic* and *liberal*—than they would for the Chinese ones—*shi gu* and *shen cang bu lou*—whereas the Chinese-language respondents would do the opposite. This is in fact what happened. English-language respondents clearly relied on implicit personality theories of artists and liberals and embellished those in stereotype-consistent ways. However,

©iStockphoto.com/Iculig.

Self-Fulfilling Prophecy: When an initially inaccurate expectation leads to behaviors that cause that expectation to come true

given that they were unaware of the two Chinese personality types, they did not embellish those in stereotype-consistent ways. The Chinese language respondents showed the opposite pattern. The bottom line here is that implicit personality theories are at least partially culture-based (Chiu, Hong, & Dweck, 1997; Chiu, Morris, Hong, & Menon, 2000; Hoffman et al., 1986).

Why do implicit theories matter? Well, they, along with other schemas, act as expectations that people have about particular persons or situations and affect how we think about, plan for, and behave around those persons or in those situations. If, for example, you expect a professor to have specific personality characteristics or tendencies, then you are likely to act accordingly. Remember Kelley's (1950) study of the warm-cold variable? There, expectations about what the guest lecturer was like significantly impacted how the students responded to him. But expectations may do more than simply alter the behavior of the perceiver—they can, as a result, also shape the behavior of the target. When a perceiver has inaccurate expectations about a target but acts *as if* they were true, he can shape the target's behavior to be consistent with those expectations (See Figure 5.2). Essentially, behavior that the target persons would otherwise *not* have engaged in is produced by the perceiver, thereby fulfilling or realizing those inaccurate expectations. Such a **self-fulfilling prophecy** occurs when an initially inaccurate expectation leads to behaviors that cause that expectation to come true (Jussim & Harber, 2005; Madon, Willard, Guyll, & Scherr, 2011; Merton, 1948; Wurm, Warner, Ziegelmann, Wolff, & Schüz, 2013). The sociologist Robert K. Merton (1948) first described this phenomenon with reference to runs on U.S. banks in the 1930s, during which thousands of customers decided to withdraw their bank savings because they believed that their banks would be closing. In reality, the banks were not endangered, but many were forced to close *because* of the actions of the customers. A false construal of a situation led to behavior that changed reality and thereby confirmed that construal.

One of the most famous demonstrations of the self-fulfilling prophecy was conducted by the social psychologist Robert Rosenthal in 1964 in a San Francisco elementary school. Rosenthal administered an intelligence test to all of the students in 18 classrooms and told the teachers that the test predicted which students would show "intellectual blooming" during the following academic year (Rosenthal & Jacobson, 1968). Rosenthal randomly designated 20% of the students as very likely to go through an intellectual growth spurt and indicated to the teachers (but not the students or their parents) which ones fell into

FIGURE 5.2   Self-Fulfilling Prophecy: Making Your Misperceptions Come True

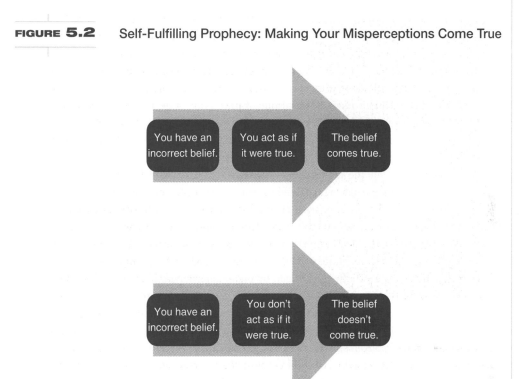

Imagine that you are about to start a group project with another student who you heard was selfish, arrogant, and difficult to work with. Since you have not met him, you don't really know what kind of a person he is. How would you behave during your first interactions with him? If you started off by being on your guard and treated him as if he were selfish, arrogant, and difficult, is it possible that you could, by your own actions, cause him to act that way? Sometimes people begin with misperceptions of another person or situation, and they behave in such a way as to produce the very behavior that they think would happen in the absence of their own behavior.

this category. At the end of the school year, the students took the test again; remarkably, those students "predicted" to intellectually improve did so rather significantly in comparison to the remaining 80%. Given that the designation was done randomly, the *only* difference between the experimental and control groups was in the minds of the teachers. The inference is clear: False teacher expectations led teachers to treat the experimental students in ways that made those expectations come true—such as giving them more attention and individual feedback (Jussim & Harber, 2005; Rosenthal & Jacobson, 1968).

Self-fulfilling prophecies have been found in many other contexts, including in a study of maze learning in rats (Rosenthal & Fode, 1963), where naïve experimenters were told that certain randomly designated rats should learn mazes faster than others. Although there were in fact no pre-treatment differences between the groups, the experimental rats did in fact learn faster, presumably because they were treated differently by the lab assistants. Rosenthal's startling findings led to research that has shown similar effects both in and outside the laboratory (Jussim, Robustelli, & Cain, 2009; Madon et al., 2011). One particularly disconcerting study found that mothers who hold false beliefs—in this case, overestimates—about the likelihood that their adolescent children will drink alcohol, behaved in such a way so as to actually *increase* the alcohol consumption of those children (Madon et al., 2008). Fortunately, field research has shown that self-fulfilling prophecies can be used to improve substance abuse treatment. For instance, parental positive predictions about the effectiveness of treatment of adolescent drug abuse that involved parents were more likely to be fulfilled when the adolescents were assigned to parent-involved treatment versus when they were assigned to a no parental-involvement treatment (Madon et al., 2013).

Self-fulfilling prophecies have been shown to be operative in the realm of physical attraction; people not only interact differently with targets they deem attractive, but they can also elicit relevant behaviors from those targets, which can then affect how other individuals perceive the targets. For example, in one study, male undergraduates engaged in a get-acquainted conversation with women by phone after having seen a photo of their conversational partner (Snyder, Tanke, & Berscheid, 1977). One group of men talked with someone they believed was attractive, whereas the other group believed their partner was unattractive. The photos were of course randomly assigned, and the men never saw a photo of their actual conversational partner. The conversations were recorded, and later, when a different group of people who did not see photos of the women listened to just the women's end of the conversation, they rated the attractive women as warmer and more socially adept than the women previously deemed unattractive. Thus, the initial male discussion partners who thought their female partner was attractive behaved in ways that elicited more socially desirable behavior from those female partners than did the males who believed that their partner was unattractive. The upshot is that even false expectations about the attractiveness of another person can produce behavior consistent with those expectations! Later, in Chapter 10 on stereotypes, we will encounter related research on the effects of stereotype-based expectations on the behavior of stereotyped persons.

NONVERBAL COMMUNICATION AND EMOTIONAL EXPRESSIONS

Words exchanged between people are tremendously influential in the kinds of relationships they develop and the impressions they form of each other. Another very important element of interpersonal perception is the behavior that accompanies our communication (Hall, Coats, & LeBeau, 2005; Weisbuch, Seery, Ambady, & Blascovich, 2009). Nonverbal behavior and communication form the foundation of human social behavior (Ambady & Weisbuch, 2010) and are essential to the smooth functioning of nonhuman primate societies, such as chimpanzee groups (Preston & de Waal, 2002). In this section we'll talk about two categories of nonverbal communication: body language and emotional expression, both of which provide information to other people about what we are thinking, feeling, and intending.

Nonverbal behavior includes any perceptible social behavior that is extra linguistic and not primarily intended to manipulate the physical world (Ambady & Weisbuch, 2010; Depaulo & Friedman, 1998). Paul Ekman broke down nonverbal communicative behaviors into five categories, each with a different communicative function: emblems, illustrators, manipulators, regulators, and emotional expressions (Ekman, 2004). *Emblems* are gestures that have a direct linguistic translation into one or two words or a phrase. A great example of an emblem is the fist pump, which many athletes, like golfer Tiger Woods, display to convey a celebratory *Yeah!* Other examples include elements of sign language and gestures such as the "OK" signal or the Y-shaped peace sign. *Illustrators* are gestures that help to illustrate what is being said, and they typically accompany rather than replace words. Pointing to an object or holding one's hands a certain distance apart to convey a particular size are illustrators.

The third type of nonverbal behavior consists of *regulators,* which help to guide interactions between people. For instance, nodding one's head can represent "mm-hmm," and turning one's head and body away from one conversation partner to signal that it is time for him to stop talking and to yield the floor to another conversation partner. Ekman calls his fourth category *adaptors* and describes them as behaviors that, while they may have once been performed to fulfill a bodily need or to manage emotions or interpersonal contacts, have evolved to serve a communicative function. For instance, children may learn to self-groom in order to improve their appearance, but as adults may engage in the same behavior even when grooming is not intended. Thus scratching one's head may become a symbol for deep thinking, whereas wiping the forehead can suggest a tiring thought or situation (Ekman, 2004). The final category is affective displays or emotional expressions and is the subject of the next section.

Emotional Expressions: Universal or Culturally Specific?

How skilled are you at accurately detecting a person's mood with just a quick glance at her face? You are probably pretty good: The perception of faces may be our most developed perceptual skill (Haxby, Hoffman, & Gobbini, 2000), and research has shown that faces are processed by the brain differently than are other stimuli (Viggiano & Marzi, 2010). This is not surprising, given that emotional expressions are almost entirely contained in the face (Ekman, 1999). One of the primary research questions related to emotional expressions has to do with their universality or cultural specificity. Do you think that other people—including those from cultures different from you own—interpret facial expressions the way that you do? Some of the most important early thinking about the evolutionary basis of emotional expressions was by Charles Darwin in his seminal 1872 book *The Emotional Expression of Emotions in Man and Animals.*

During his world travels, Darwin (1872) observed numerous similarities in the facial expressions of humans across different cultures and between humans and some nonhuman animals. Darwin obtained data from several sources, including his own observations of infants and of animals, responses to facial photos of expressions from a small sample of adults, and a survey of missionaries and others who had contact with isolated cultures. Darwin (1872) argued that the primary function of facial expressions

Nonverbal Behavior:
Perceptible social behavior that is extra linguistic and not primarily intended to manipulate the physical world

was communication between individuals and that the ability to recognize the emotions reflected in many expressions had great survival value to our ancestors (Matsumoto, Keltner, Shiota, O'Sullivan, & Frank, 2008).

The evolutionary perspective on emotional expression makes five basic claims, each of which has received considered empirical support: specific facial expressions of emotion (1) are universally found in appropriate, emotionally arousing situations; (2) are correlated with self-reports of emotional experiences; (3) are embedded in broader sets of emotional responses; (4) are universally recognized as distinct; and, (5) serve important functions in interpersonal relationships and social situations (Matsumoto et al., 2008). For instance, research conducted over the last few decades has supported Darwin's claims about both the universality of some expressions and the cultural specificity of others. Take a look at the photo below. Can you name each of the emotions conveyed in the six facial expressions? The chances are that you have little difficulty in doing so. These six expressions—anger, surprise, fear, happiness, sadness, and disgust—are held to be universally recognized across cultures (Ekman, 2007; Ekman & Friesen, 1971; Ekman et al., 1987).

UNIVERSAL
RECOGNITION
OF FACIAL
EXPRESSIONS

Can you name these
six expressions?
Happiness, Sadness,
Surprise, Anger,
Disgust, Fear

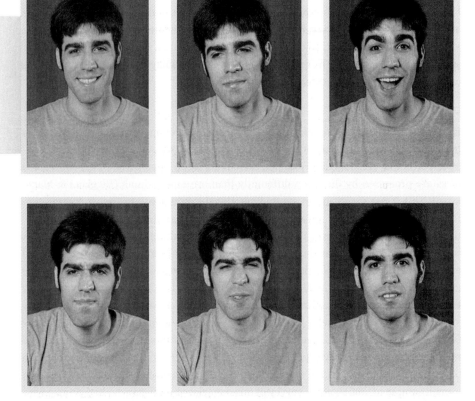

WCSU, Peggy Stewart.

Paul Ekman, who conducted much of the cross-cultural research on expressions, makes the fascinating admission that when he began studying facial expressions, he was firmly convinced that Darwin was *wrong* and that facial expressions were socially learned and entirely culture dependent (Ekman, 2007). In his very readable book on emotions, Ekman relays how, after being initially convinced of the contrary, his own research proved that *he* was incorrect and that, in fact, the six expressions listed above were cross-culturally universal. Ekman's story demonstrates the self-correcting nature of science: Careful scientific research can help scientists resist the confirmation bias and throw out incorrect hypotheses. In addition, a review of Ekman's progression of studies shows how persistence and the use of multiple research methods in the pursuit of truth can allow science to continually improve its validity.

Ekman and his colleagues conducted three types of studies over the course of several decades. In one type, individuals from various cultures (including an isolated group of New Guineans) posed expressions corresponding to these six emotions, and to the extent that expressions from one culture were correctly labeled by members of other cultures, universality was demonstrated (Ekman & Friesen, 1971). Although individuals made correct identifications most of the time, not all emotions were accurately labeled. In addition, the fact that the expressions were posed rather than spontaneous limited the scope of these findings (Ekman et al., 1987).

In a second type of study, American and Japanese men were secretly filmed while watching either an emotionally neutral nature video or one depicting bodily mutilation (Ekman, 1972). The men viewed the films either alone or with an experimenter present. Researchers predicted that Japanese men would show a disgust reaction to the mutilation film when alone but would suppress it when another person was present. In contrast, the Americans were expected to express their emotions whether or not they were alone. The findings supported the hypothesis and demonstrated that the two cultures have different **display rules** dictating when it is appropriate to show certain facial expressions (C. M. Moran, Diefendorff, & Greguras, 2013). The Japanese participants clearly felt disgust, as shown in the "alone" condition, but chose not to show this when an observer was present. The cultural boundedness of the display rule was demonstrated by the fact that the Americans made no such attempt to hide their disgust. This study was important because it was the first to empirically show differences in display rules; however, its generalizability is limited because only two cultures and two expressions were investigated (Ekman et al., 1987).

In the third and most important type of study, Ekman and other researchers exposed individuals from 12 cultures to photographs of facial expressions (Ekman, Sorenson, & Friesen, 1969; Izard, 1971) and found high levels of agreement across the six major emotions. In a follow-up study, Ekman found agreement in 10 cultures—including the United States, Japan, Sumatra, Estonia, and Turkey—on the same six primary emotions.

More recently Elfenbein and Ambady (2002) conducted a meta-analysis of 97 studies encompassing 42 cultures and over 20,000 participants. A **meta-analysis** combines multiple studies—usually conducted by different researchers—into one analysis that allows the researcher to look at larger sets of data than are included in any single study. The researcher can have greater confidence in the validity of conclusions drawn from this analysis of

Display Rules:
Rules indicating which facial expressions are appropriate in a given context

Meta-analysis:
Combines multiple studies, usually by different researchers, into one analysis that allows the researcher to draw conclusions about the set of studies as a whole

analyses that considers all of the data than from just one of these studies. Elfenbein and Ambady's findings validated earlier research with regard to the six core emotions—anger, surprise, fear, happiness, sadness, and disgust. Interestingly, they also found that individuals were generally better at correctly recognizing expressions from individuals who were in their same region, ethnic, or national group versus those in different groups (Elfenbein & Ambady, 2002). Overall, while there is some universality in the expression of emotions, much cultural variability also exists (Haidt & Keltner, 1999; Izard, 1994; Perrett, 2012).

Cross-cultural similarities in emotional expressions, including groups with no previous contact with the outside world, provide strong evidence for Darwin's claim about the innateness of emotional expressions. Other research has extended the findings described above. For instance, Tracy and Robins (2007) found many commonalities among pride displays in the United States, Italy, and in an isolated, preliterate West African tribe. Pride is associated with meaningful achievements and is often displayed with a low-intensity smile, head tilt, expanded posture, and hands either raised above the head or resting on the hips (Tracy & Robins, 2007; Tracy, Shariff, Zhao, & Henrich, 2013). Furthermore, one analysis revealed that sighted, blind, and congenitally blind athletes from over 30 countries demonstrated many similarities in their pride expressions following Olympic or Paralympic success (Matsumoto & Willingham, 2009; Tracy & Matsumoto, 2008). Tracy and Matsumoto (2008) also found that shame—in this case resulting from athletic failure—was displayed in similar ways among all of the groups, although the displays were moderated (weaker) in persons from more individualistic cultures.

Finally, Keltner and Buswell (1997) noted a number of cross-species commonalities in expressions of embarrassment or what they call appeasement behavior, such as gazing down, covering the face, and contraction or shrinkage of posture (Keltner, 1995). According to these theorists, appeasement follows the violation of a social norm and is essentially a display of submissive and affiliative behaviors designed to solidify social relations. In sum, the fact that the primary emotions are similar across cultures supports evolutionary theory, but the existence of some cross-cultural variability reinforces the notion that evolution is not the whole story.

One potentially significant qualification is in order here. Although the cultural universality of the six basic emotions has been widely recognized and generally assumed, very recent research has called this into question. Several researchers have argued that the few studies that have included truly remote cultures—previously without contact with the West—have a flawed methodology (Jack, 2013; Jack, Blais, Scheepers, Schyns, & Caldara, 2009). For instance, studies by Ekman and others typically supplied emotion words along with the facial expressions and asked participants to match them up. It is possible that, by providing the emotion words, the researchers shaped the responses of non-Western participants in a way that made them appear to be consistent with the Western participants. However, recent studies of remote, non-Western cultures without previous contact with the West in which emotion words were withheld found important differences in emotion recognition (Barrett, Mesquita, & Gendron, 2011; Gendron, Roberson, van der Vyver, & Barrett, 2014). If this research is replicated and holds up to scrutiny, then psychologists will have to rethink this claim to universality. The fact that psychologists continue to examine and reexamine the assumptions and findings of prior research reflects one of my favorite things about science: its self-corrective nature.

Recognizing Happiness

Would you predict that humans are faster at identifying a happy face or an angry face when the face is embedded in a crowd of non-happy or non-angry faces? Recall that Darwin argued that the ability to both read and signal emotions via facial expressions provide an adaptive advantage. It would seem, then, that individuals who quickly read and appropriately respond to facial expressions could more successfully navigate the social landscape. Therefore, you might expect that we would be adept at noticing expressions suggestive of potential threats to our well-being, such as angry faces (Reed, DeScioli, & Pinker, 2014). Several years ago, when I began writing this textbook, psychological research on facial recognition supported this notion. For instance, Hansen and Hansen (1988) asked participants to identify, as quickly as possible, a single divergent expression from a sea of faces. In some cases a happy face was hidden in a sea of neutral or angry faces, whereas in others an angry face was placed with neutral or happy faces. Almost invariably, angry faces were identified much more rapidly than happy or neutral faces. Hansen and Hansen (1988) dubbed this the *face-in-the-crowd effect* and found it whether the crowd faces were all of the same or different persons (Schmidt-Daffy, 2011).

However, relatively recent research has not only called this effect into question but has demonstrated the opposite one: People are actually faster at finding happy faces! Becker and Wright (2011) ran seven studies that reversed the way psychologists view facial recognition. Since the details about how they did this are too complicated to delve into here, I will give you the short version. Becker and Wright identified and eliminated a number of confounds with the earlier face-in-the-crowd studies that led the earlier researchers to mistakenly believe that the differences in their dependent variables were caused by the manipulations of their independent variables. Once Becker and Wright altered the experimental procedures, they found that smiling, happy faces were easier to spot. This was true even if they used closed-mouth smiles in which teeth were hidden. These researchers hypothesize that people are better at detecting happy faces because they are far more prevalent than are angry expressions and that happy faces have evolved to be more easily recognizable.

Emotion Blends and Dialects

Given that facial expressions and other nonverbal behavior play a key role in the development and maintenance of social relations (Ambady & Weisbuch, 2010; Keltner & Kring, 1998), we would expect to find both cross-cultural and cross-species similarities in emotional expressions. As noted above, for at least six primary expressions, humans are consistently able to accurately identify the underlying emotion. However, there are several situations in which people are less consistent in correctly reading facial expressions. One is the case of **blended emotions**, wherein an expression reflects more than one emotion (Ekman et al., 1987; Ekman et al., 1969), such as fear and surprise or disgust and

Blended Emotions: Wherein an expression reflects more than one emotion

contempt. Although researchers have discovered cross-cultural agreement in the identification of secondary emotions, these rates are somewhat lower than for primary emotions (Ekman et al., 1987). Second, the presence of emotion dialects—slight variations in specific displays of emotion between cultures—can reduce accuracy in emotion recognition across cultures (Elfenbein & Ambady, 2002). For instance, a tongue-bite is indicative of embarrassment in India but not in the United States (Haidt & Keltner, 1999).

A third limitation of human facial perception is in the difficulty people have in unmasking feelings and thoughts that the target seeks to hide. As Ekman and Friesen's (1971) study of disgust expressions among Japanese and American men demonstrated, cultures vary in their display rules, thereby interfering with the **decoding** or interpretation of facial expressions and other nonverbal behavior (Kafetsios, Andriopoulos, & Papachiou, 2014). Differences in the display of negative emotions have been also found between Costa Ricans and Americans (Stephan, Stephan, & de Vargas, 1996) and in the expression of contempt, disgust, fear, and sadness among whites, African Americans, Asian Americans, and Latinos in the United States (Matsumoto, 1993).

Decoding:
Interpretation of facial expressions and other nonverbal behaviour

Think Again!

1. *What are the six universal emotional expressions?*

2. *What are cultural display rules?*

3. *How does the series of studies by Ekman illustrate the self-correcting nature of science?*

DOING RESEARCH: THE CHALLENGES OF CROSS-CULTURAL STUDIES

Social psychologists' primary aim in studying human social behavior can be boiled down to our wish to understand human nature. The evolutionary approach is particularly pertinent because it can help identify aspects of human social behavior that are universal. Yet, as we have said, social behavior is inherently *cultural* (Leung & Cohen, 2011). It has been argued that one of the universal aspects of human nature is that it is molded by culture and that humans are "beasts for culture" (Baumeister, 2005; Heine, 2010b). Given the potential for variability in social behavior across the globe, then, it is critical that we examine humans from a wide variety of cultures and in a large sample of contexts. Until recently, most psychological research has focused on individuals from WEIRD (Western, educated, industrialized, rich, and democratic) cultures (Henrich, Heine, & Norenzayan, 2010). You are no doubt aware that WEIRD cultures represent only a small percentage of the world's population, and therefore our ability to draw broad inferences from such research findings is severely limited. Unfortunately, cross-cultural research is not simply a matter of transplanting an experiment or a survey originally completed in, say, London, to Tokyo or

Istanbul. Rather, cross-cultural studies present several significant challenges that must be met in order to create valid and reliable studies, including those pertaining to language, situational equivalence, response styles, and sampling (Cohen, 2007; Heine, 2010a).

Language. One of the most obvious yet profound differences between cultures is language (Chiu, Leung, & Kwan, 2007). As anyone who has learned a second or third language knows, finding close or even reasonably accurate translations can sometimes be difficult. If you know a second language, then try translating "when it is your turn, please turn to the left and then turn over the green sheet." My guess is that the use of the word "turn" to signify three different activities complicates your task! Imagine trying to translate entire paragraphs, surveys, or complex, detailed experimental instructions in other languages. To illustrate, take a look at the problems with the translations and back translations of several phrases in Table 5.1. Humans could of course do a much better translation job than computer algorithms, but you get the idea.

In addition to the need to produce adequate translations of everyday words and phrases, psychologists sometimes wish to examine more abstract or nuanced ones, many of which have no direct translation in other languages. For instance, the English term "self-esteem" has no direct equivalent in Chinese, and therefore an investigator can't simply ask a Chinese respondent whether or not she has low self-esteem (Miller, Wang, Sandel, & Cho, 2002). Another concern with cross-cultural translations is related to the Sapir-Whorf linguistic relativity hypothesis (Whorf, 1956), which, in its strong form, states that people who speak different languages

One of the challenges of cross-cultural research is accurately translating questions, instructions, and responses from one language to another.

REUTERS/Albert Gea.

think about the world in fundamentally divergent ways, with the implication that accurate translation is extremely difficult, if not impossible (Tohidian, 2009). However, most psychologists subscribe to a weaker version of the hypothesis, believing that, although language does impact thinking, cross-cultural communication and reasonably good translations are possible, even if not always perfect (Chiu et al., 2007; Matsumoto & Juang, 2004; Pinker, 2007).

The most common method for overcoming this problem in psychological research is via back translation (Heine, Lehman, Peng, & Greenholtz, 2002). Back translation involves at least two translators, both of whom are fluent in the two languages (Brislin, 1970). Ideally, there is at least one native speaker of each of the languages. One person translates from, say, English to Spanish, and the other translates the Spanish version back into English. The two English versions are then compared by the translators and discrepancies are resolved (Heine, 2010a).

Experimental equivalence. Most citizens of the world have not been exposed to many of the conditions and situations and formats that Western psychologists incorporate into our experiments (Berry, Poortinga, Segall, & Dasen, 2002; Heine, 2010a). For instance, Americans are very familiar with surveys, being asked personal and occasionally intimate questions, people in lab coats (as may be seen in an experiment), and with computers and other forms of technology that may be used to conduct a study. However, much of the rest of the world has had little or no exposure to these and other features of psycho-

TABLE 5.1   Translate This!

Take a phrase in one language and, using an online tool (such as Google Translate at http://translate .google.com), translate it into another language. Next, copy and paste the new text into a second online translation tool (such as Yahoo Babelfish at https://www.babelfish.com/ and translate it back into the original language. How good was the translation? The table below provides several examples and demonstrates one challenge associated of cross-cultural research.

Original English Text	Translation (http://translate.google.com)	Back Translation (https://www.babelfish.com/)
When it is your turn, please turn to the left and then turn over the green sheet.	Cuando es su turno, por favor, gire a la izquierda y luego a su vez sobre la hoja verde.	When it is its turn, please, it turns soon to the left and as well on the green leaf.
Please fill in the circle corresponding to your response, and be sure not to make any stray pencil marks on the page.	Por favor, rellene el círculo correspondiente a su respuesta, y estar seguro de no hacer las marcas de lápiz callejeros en la página.	Please, it fills up the circle corresponding to its answer, and to be safe of not making the street marks of pencil in the page.
Proceed quickly but carefully through the program.	Actuar rápidamente pero con cuidado a través del programa.	To act quickly but with well-taken care of through program.

logical studies, and their lack of familiarity may have significant consequences for how participants interpret the wishes of the researcher and the demands of the experiment (J. G. Miller, 2004). Consequently, key elements of psychological studies may not be construed in the same way across cultures, and this can potentially undermine the validity of their findings (Berry et al., 2002; Cohen, 2007). In other words, members of different cultures may understand the instructions in divergent ways, and determining whether discrepancies in responses to the experimental manipulations are caused by true cultural differences or a result of poor translations or misconstruals can be tricky. Two options for addressing this problem are ensuring that researchers have a good understanding of the cultures being studied and/or involving representatives from each of the cultures being studied in research design and implementation (Heine, 2010a; J. G. Miller, 2004).

Response styles. In Chapter 3 we discussed how response biases can influence participant answers to surveys and questionnaires. Although response biases can be a challenge within a culture, they can also pose a problem when surveying individuals from different cultures (Berry et al., 2002; Grimm & Church, 1999). For instance, the extremity bias described earlier is more common among some groups, such as African Americans, than others, such as East Asians (Chen, Lee, & Stevenson, 1995; Hui & Triandis, 1989). Culture-based response biases can be challenging to overcome, and perhaps the best way to prevent them from confounding psychological studies is to gather data from individuals using several different methods in hopes of finding convergent or consistent results (Cohen, 2007). In this way, possible biases in any one method can be revealed and corrected via other methods.

Sampling. An additional problem that can arise when conducting cross-cultural research is determining how to sample across cultures or persons within cultures (Berry et al., 2002; Matsumoto & Juang, 2004). How does the researcher decide which cultures to choose? Sometimes this can be a matter of convenience, such as when the researchers have direct contacts in more than one culture. Other times psychologists select cultures that are likely to be or have been previously shown to be different on a key variable, such as individualism/collectivism. Both researchers and students must remember the fact that there is great variation between nations despite the fact that these nations may be similar in their overall levels of individualism/collectivism. Once the cultures have been chosen, researchers then must determine which samples in the cultures to include in the research. Given the enormous variability within cultures, care must be taken when selecting samples to ensure that they are as equivalent as possible (J. G. Miller, 2004). White participants from, say, working class Manchester, UK, may be very different from White participants living in a wealthy suburb of London. Moreover, a mostly White sample drawn from an elite U.S. educational institution may be different in terms of socioeconomic variables from a sample drawn from an elite university in, say, Kenya. As a result, researchers should be cautious in their interpretation of results from cross-cultural studies. Potential confounds related to differences in samples that cannot be avoided need to be considered, and generalizations to other cultures should be made judiciously (Cohen, 2007).

SELF-REFLECTION 5.1
Measuring Individualism/Collectivism (Part 1)

As we have discussed, the individualism/collectivism dimension is one of the most widely researched cross-cultural variables (Na, Kosinski, & Stillwell, 2015; Taras et al., 2014). Although researchers have often placed nations and cultures in either the individualism or collectivism category, this variable is truly dimensional—there are many points along a continuum that reflect varying degrees—and there is a fair amount of intranational or intracultural variation. In other words, not all people in individualistic nations (like the United States) are individualistic, and not all people in collectivistic nations (e.g., China) are collectivistic (Ralston et al., 2014). For research purposes, we need to know where each participant in a study falls on this dimension. In this chapter, we describe some of the challenges to cross-cultural research, and there are many ways to measure this or related dimensions. To get a rough idea as to your IC level, take a minute and answer the following questions from a brand new scale and then turn the page to interpret your score. For "class," simply think about students in your grade/year of college (e.g., freshmen, sophomore, etc.).

TABLE 5.2   Measuring Individualism/Collectivism

Item	Response options				
	Very good	Rather good	Neither good nor bad	Rather bad	Very bad
In this section, we want to know what your class thinks about various topics. Please think about the general opinion in your class.					
What does your class think . . .					
1. Of classmates asking for advice when they have a problem	1	2	3	4	5
2. Of solving tasks in groups	1	2	3	4	5
3. Of classmates holding a different opinion than the teacher does	1	2	3	4	5
4. Of classmates, who do not want to participate in group activity	1	2	3	4	5

SELF-REFLECTION 5.1

Item	Response options				
	Very good	Rather good	Neither good nor bad	Rather bad	Very bad
5. Of other classmates, who want to push through their own opinion	1	2	3	4	5
6. Of classmates solving a difficult task completely on their own	1	2	3	4	5
7. Of a classmate refusing to change his or her opinion, even though all the others think differently than he or she does	1	2	3	4	5

In this section, we want to know what you think about various topics. Please think about the general opinion in your class.

What do you think . . .

Item					
8. Of classmates asking for advice when they have a problem	1	2	3	4	5
9. Of solving tasks in groups	1	2	3	4	5
10. Of classmates holding a different opinion than the teacher does	1	2	3	4	5
11. Of classmates, who do not want to participate in group activity	1	2	3	4	5
12. Of other classmates, who want to push through their own opinion	1	2	3	4	5
13. Of classmates solving a difficult task completely on their own	1	2	3	4	5
14. Of a classmate refusing to change his or her opinion, even though all the others think differently than he or she does	1	2	3	4	5

Source: Yanagida, T., Strohmeier, D., Toda, Y., & Spiel, C. (2014). The Self Group Distinction Scale: A new approach to measure individualism and collectivism in adolescents. *Psychological Test and Assessment Modeling, 56*, 304–313.

TURN THE PAGE TO FIND OUR ANSWERS.

SELF-REFLECTION 5.2
Measuring Individualism/Collectivism (Part 2)

To determine your score, add up your responses to Questions 1 through 7 and for Questions 8 through 14. Then subtract the total of the "you" questions from the total of the "class" questions. If the number is negative, simply drop the negative sign. Next divide your answer by 7 to obtain a mean. These items are from the Self Group Distinction Scale (SGD) that was developed for adolescents, but of course, the underlying dimension is not limited to that age group (Yanagida, Strohmeier, Toda, & Spiel, 2014). The means for the Japanese (mostly collectivistic) and Austrian (mostly individualistic) participants were .33 and .72. The higher the number, the more a person separates her or himself from the group, and therefore the more individualistic that person appears to be.

Robert DeNiro administers a lie detector to Ben Stiller in *Meet the Parents.*

© AF archive / Alamy Stock Photo.

DETECTING DECEPTION

How good are you at determining when someone is lying? What signs do you look for? Lying is quite prevalent: Most of us lie at least once or twice per day (DePaulo, Kashy, Kirkendol, Wyer, & Epstein, 1996). One diary study suggests that college students lie in one out of every three social interactions, whereas nonstudents do so in about one in five of their interactions (DePaulo et al., 1996). We also tend to engage in more deception with those with whom we are less familiar than those we are closer to (DePaulo & Kashy, 1998). You may be surprised to learn that our ability to detect lies from facial expressions and other nonverbal behavior is surprisingly weak, despite what we see in popular television dramas (Ambady & Weisbuch, 2010; Bond & DePaulo, 2006). A recent meta-analysis of over 200 studies, most of which involved detecting lies from audiovisual materials, found that people successfully distinguish truth from lies at barely above chance rates, around 54% (See Table 5.3) (Bond & DePaulo, 2006). This detection rate drops to 51% if observers are given only visual information (i.e., the sound is muted) (Bond & DePaulo, 2006).

In a large meta-analysis that examined 142 studies, no evidence was found for any individual systematic differences in lie detection accuracy; in other words, personality, education, gender, and other characteristics were not significantly correlated with accuracy (Bond, Jr. & DePaulo, 2008).

Despite the frequency of lying, we are not particularly good at differentiating truths from lies when given only nonverbal cues. Why aren't we better? One reason is that we tend to assume that people are telling the truth and therefore are not generally on the lookout for lies (Bond & DePaulo, 2006). A second reason is that people hold inaccurate beliefs about which nonverbal cues might reveal that a person is lying. Research shows that, in general, nonverbal cues to deceit are more difficult to detect than verbal ones (DePaulo et al., 2003). Despite common preconceptions, there is no evidence of differences in eye contact, eye shifting, or gaze aversion between liars and truth tellers (DePaulo et al., 2003). Although some research suggests that there may be some other behavioral differences between liars and truth tellers (Vrij, Edward, Roberts, & Bull, 2000), DePaulo et al. (2003) found no evidence of differences in posture shifts or movements of the foot, leg, or hand. Overall, while reliable cues to deception are generally weak, they may be more pronounced when the liar is very motivated to deceive and the lie involves a moral transgression (DePaulo et al., 2003). Be sure to remember this before inferring that a friend, partner, or politician is lying based solely on his facial or body movements! In contrast, research supports the notion that there are a few *verbal* cues to deception, such as that liars provide fewer details about events, lies tend to make less sense and contain more contradictory statements than truths, and lies often include fewer ordinary imperfections and unusual details (DePaulo et al., 2003).

So far we have focused primarily on conscious or C-system processing in lie detection—which, as we know, is not particularly adept. But what about the nonconscious, X-system? Can it do any better? Recent research suggests that it can. In one study, Reinhard, Greifeneder, and Scharmach (2013) exposed participants to video recordings of individuals who made both true and false statements. After viewing the clips, some participants

TABLE 5.3   Conscious Detection of Deception

Population	Detection Accuracy	Source
All	54%	Bond & DePaulo (2006)
All	51% (if given only visual information)	Bond & DePaulo (2006)
Professional lie catchers	54%	Aamodt & Custer (2006)
Criminals	65%	Aamodt & Custer (2006)
Parole officers	40%	Aamodt & Custer (2006)

Criminals are the only group who can detect lies significantly above chance levels.

were given three minutes of distraction-free time to reflect on the statements and distinguish truths from lies, whereas others did so only after spending those three minutes engaged in a mentally taxing activity. The purpose of the distracting task was to prevent participants from consciously analyzing the behavior of the individuals in the video recordings and focusing on inaccurate or unreliable deception cues, forcing them to rely only on nonconscious processing when distinguishing truth from falsity. In this and subsequent studies Reinhard et al. found that participants in the nonconscious processing conditions were significantly better at identifying true versus false statements than were those able to consciously examine the evidence (See Figure 5.3). At least in these studies, the automatic system performed better than the controlled one.

HOW OBSERVATIONS CAN FAIL US: FOUR COGNITIVE ILLUSIONS: CONTROL, GAMBLING, SHOOTING STREAKS, AND IMAGINED ASSOCIATIONS

The difficulty in detecting lies from nonverbal cues reveals one limitation in our perceptual toolkit. In addition to errors related to the inappropriate use of the mental shortcuts mentioned above, humans are vulnerable to a number of other perceptual or judgmental

FIGURE 5.3   Detecting Deception Nonconsciously

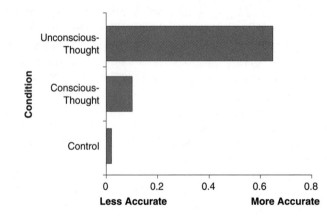

Participants more accurately detected deception in the nonconscious thought condition as compared to conscious thought or a control.

Source: Adapted Study 1, from Reinhard, M. -A., Greifeneder, R., & Scharmach, M. (2013). Unconscious processes improve lie detection. *Journal of Personality and Social Psychology, 105*, 721–739.

SOCIAL PSYCHOLOGY APPLIED TO LAW
CATCHING LIARS

If naive individuals are unable to accurately detect deception, then what about professionals? In most cases, training of law enforcement officers is based on the classic book on criminal interrogations by Inbau and his colleagues (Inbau, Reid, Buckley, & Jayne, 2013). Inbau et al. developed the Behavioral Analysis Interview that recommends asking questions that are likely to produce a behavioral response in the suspect, such as nervous movements or changes in eye contact. However, careful research has failed to support Inbau et al.'s claims. Not only do liars fail to demonstrate the expected behaviors (e.g., less eye contact, more fidgeting), they may actually be less likely to show them (Vrij, Fisher, Mann, & Leal, 2010). Even professional lie catchers hold incorrect beliefs (e.g., avoidance of eye contact), which is why they are no more successful than nonprofessionals (Vrij et al., 2000). In fact, even professional lie catchers—individuals trained in the detection of deception—only succeed at about the same rate as students, about 54% of the time (Aamodt & Custer, 2006). Interestingly, criminals outperform most other groups, with an average accuracy rate around 65%, whereas parole officers are accurate only 40% of the time (Aamodt & Custer, 2006).

SNAP/REX/Newscom.

Even trained lie catchers often mistakenly assume that a suspect's behavior—such as eye contact or leg movement—can reveal lying.

If law enforcement can't detect lies using the Inbau et al. techniques and/or simply by monitoring a person's overt behavior, what can they do? There are a number of possibilities. First, they can focus more on the words suspects use and the stories they tell, as there is some evidence that liars tend to relay less detail than do truth tellers (Vrij, Mann, Jundi, Hillman, & Hope, 2014). The reason for this is that liars are afraid that they may make a mistake if they provide too many details, especially if there were witnesses to the event in question (Granhag & Hartwig, 2008; Vrij et al., 2014). Liars are also

(Continued)

(Continued)

more likely to make contradictory or inconsistent statements because they have to remember what they previously invented in response to questions.

Second, they can adopt a different approach to interviewing suspects, one that does not make the same assumptions as the Inbau technique. For instance, Vrij et al. (Vrij, Granhag, Mann, & Leal, 2011) developed the Cognitive Lie Detection Approach based on the idea that lying requires more mental effort than truth telling. If that is correct, then increasing the cognitive load of the suspect during interviewing should reduce the interviewees ability to suppress signs of deceit. For instance, the interviewer can ask the suspect to tell the story backwards, a task that is difficult for anyone but is expected to be a little easier for the truth teller. In addition, the interviewer should ask unanticipated questions that the suspect would not have previously rehearsed or prepared for. For example, the suspect could be asked to draw a layout of a place where she said she had been and then later asked to give a verbal description of that place. According to Vrij et al. (2009), there should be greater discrepancies between the verbal and pictorial depictions from liars (because they are making details up as they go) than from truth tellers. Although this approach is relatively new, it seems to hold some promise.

Perhaps one more option for distinguishing liars from truth tellers has come to your mind: the polygraph or lie detector. In Chapter 2, I suggested that the polygraph was not a reliable way of unmasking liars. The reason is relatively straightforward. The polygraph measures skin conductance and other physiological symptoms of arousal, and its proponents argue that spikes in arousal are likely to occur while suspects are asked about difficult or unpleasant details related to the crime. The problem is that arousal is nonspecific, which is to say that it can be caused by many factors. Thus a truth teller might become aroused out of fear, disgust, anger, or anxiety, and that arousal could be (mis)construed by the interviewer as signs of a lie. Given its lack of reliability, the polygraph is not admissible in U.S. courts.

mistakes. For instance, sometimes we base our beliefs on evidence that we think unambiguously provides justification for those beliefs. The reality, however, can be different, and upon closer inspection we may find that our shortcuts have betrayed us, and that the evidence is more imaginary than real. In this section we'll describe four cognitive illusions that can lead us astray (See Table 5.4).

Illusion of Control

Say you bought a lottery ticket for a $1, and on the day of the lottery are given a chance to sell that ticket. How much would you sell it for? Since it is only worth $1, shouldn't that be your asking price? Well, according to a study by Ellen Langer (1975), it depends on whether or not you personally chose your lottery ticket. Langer found that individuals who had picked their own ticket requested four times as much money as did others who had not selected their own ticket. Individuals in this and other studies exhibited what Langer termed an **illusion of control**, which is a false belief that one can control or influence random or chance events (Langer, 1975, 1977; Thompson, Armstrong, & Thomas, 1998; Thompson & Schlehofer, 2008; Yarritu, Matute, & Vadillo, 2014). Here they believed that they were more likely to win the lottery because they had selected their ticket versus if the ticket had been randomly selected for them. The idea that they can somehow beat the odds and win more than they lose keeps casino slot machine players returning again and again, despite the fact that slot machines keep about 90% of the money put into them (which means that they rake in nine times more money than they return to customers) (Witts, Loudermilk, & Kosel, 2014).

Illusion of Control: False belief that one can control or influence random or chance events

Gambler's Fallacy and the Hot Hand Illusion

Say you are playing roulette and the ball has landed on an even number on the last seven throws. Given that there is the same number of odd and even numbers on a roulette wheel, is the next throw more likely to land on an odd or an even number? Many people believe that the chances of the ball landing on an odd number are greater because the last seven throws were even. But no, the chances are precisely the same for either result. People often fail to recognize that the odds of landing on an odd number are 50–50, regardless of what the last seven or 20 or 100 results were. Each throw of the ball is independent of prior throws, and therefore the odds never change. This is a similar to a situation when a person who believes that the odds of a coin coming up heads are greater after having just come up tails rather than heads in the last flip. Although all of us are vulnerable to this misunderstanding of the nature of random events, gamblers and financial investors seem particularly susceptible, and this cognitive illusion is often referred to as the **gambler's fallacy:** a false belief that the outcome of a random event is dependent on previous outcomes of the same event (Huber, Kirchler, & Stuckl, 2010; Sundali & Croson, 2006).

Gambler's Fallacy: Believing that the odds of a coin coming up heads are greater after having just come up tails rather than heads in the last flip

Have you ever watched a basketball game in which, as time is running out, the point guard failed to give the ball to the shooting guard who made her last five shots and instead passed it to the center, who missed and, as a consequence, the team lost? Did you swear at the point guard and wonder why she didn't give the ball to the player with the "hot hand"? Well, many of us have felt the same way. Unfortunately, research has clearly demonstrated that the **hot hand illusion**—a belief that identical random outcomes are "streaks"—is a myth, rendering our ire at the point guard unjustified. Gilovich, Vallone,

Hot Hand Illusion: Incorrectly thinking that identical random outcomes are "streaks"

and Tversky (1985) examined shooting trends during the 1980 through 1981 season of the National Basketball Association's (NBA) Philadelphia 76ers. The researchers statistically evaluated whether players were more likely to make a basket following one or more successful shots as opposed to missed shots. If so-called shooting streaks really exist, then there should be more "clustering" of made shots than would be expected by chance. However, the evidence directly contradicted the notion of the hot hand: Players made 54% of their shots following a *missed* shot, but only 51% after a made shot. Similarly, 53% were made following two misses and 56% following three misses, in contrast to 50% and 46%, after making the last two or three shots, respectively (Gilovich et al., 1985). This and other evidence has led Gilovich et al. to declare that the hot hand is an illusion (Alter & Oppenheimer, 2006; Sundali & Croson, 2006). Interestingly, recent evidence suggests that there may in fact be a "hot hand" in volleyball (Raab, Gula, & Gigerenzer, 2011), and that belief in the existence of such nonrandom streaks can be adaptive (Scheibehenne, Wilke, & Todd, 2011). Nevertheless, as with illusions of control, what people believe to be true and what is actually true are frequently not the same.

Illusory Correlation

There is another way in which people can misperceive reality and hold unsupported beliefs: Sometimes they see correlations that do not exist. As a parent I have often been told by another parent or a teacher that children are harder to control when they have had a lot of sugar, even though there is no evidence for such a relationship (Kunda, 1999). To take another example, have you heard your grandmother or someone else (perhaps on television) complain that hot, humid weather worsens her arthritis pain? Redelmeier and Tversky (2004) investigated this purported correlation and collected patient self-reports, physician examinations, and barometric information from a set of arthritis sufferers over a 15-month span. Despite common perceptions, no such relationship between arthritis pain and the weather was found (Redelmeier & Tversky, 2004). Each of these two false beliefs represents an **illusory correlation**: an overestimation about the extent to which two variables are related to one another (Chapman, 1967; Hamilton & Gifford, 1976; Kutzner & Fiedler, 2015).

Illusory Correlation: Overestimation of the extent to which two variables are correlated

Think Again!

1. *Define and give your own examples of the illusion of control, gambler's fallacy, and illusory correlation.*

2. *Why is the "hot hand" really a myth?*

3. *Can you think of a correlation that you have previously believed existed but may in fact be illusory?*

TABLE 5.4   Errors in Social Perception

Name	Description	Source
Illusion of Control	A false belief that one can control or influence random or chance events	A person believing that, because he chose his own lottery ticket, he has a better chance of winning versus if it were selected randomly for him
Gambler's Fallacy	A false belief that the outcome of a random event is dependent on previous outcomes of the same event	A roulette player thinking that the next throw is more likely to be an odd number, because the previous four throws were even numbers
Hot Hand Illusion	A belief that identical random outcomes are "streaks"	A basketball player expecting that, because she made her last four shots, she is more likely to make the next shot
Illusory Correlation	An overestimation about the extent to which two variables are related to one another	A person mistakenly perceiving two unrelated events as correlated

In another study, participants were exposed to a series of pairs of words that were either related (bacon-eggs or lion-tiger) or unrelated (bacon-tiger or lion-eggs) (Chapman, 1967). Although all word pairs were presented at the same frequency, respondents believed that the related pairs were shown more times than the unrelated ones. Like the arthritis patients, these participants perceived a correlation that did not exist. Examples of illusory correlations abound. For instance, people who are politically conservative are more likely to believe that negative behaviors are correlated with minority groups (Carraro, Negri, Castelli, & Pastore, 2014; Castelli & Carraro, 2011). So, the next time you hear someone claim that two things are related yet offers no evidence in support, ask yourself whether the correlation is merely illusory.

ATTRIBUTIONS: DETERMINING THE CAUSES OF BEHAVIOR

Humans are meaning-seeking creatures, and determining the causes of social behavior (including our own) is crucial to understanding why the social world is as it is (Bruner, 1990; Malle, 2004). We have already discussed how introspection and self-perception are used in identifying the reasons for our own thoughts, feelings, and behaviors. Let's turn now to how people explain the social behavior of others. When people make a judgment about the cause of a social behavior, they are making an **attribution** (Crandall, Silvia, N'Gbala, Tsang, & Dawson, 2007; Hewstone, 1989; Weiner, 2010). Stating that a shooting rampage on a school campus was entirely the result of the culprit's mental disorder is an example of a dispositional attribution. Saying instead that exposure to media violence

Attribution: Judgment about the cause of behavior

and access to weapons are entirely to blame is a situational attribution (Malle, 2011). As discussed in Chapter 1, social psychologists always consider both the person and the situation when seeking to understand the causes of behavior.

Earlier we discussed the two mental systems—one fast, one slow—that describe how people process information about the world (Lieberman, 2007b). These two systems can be usefully applied in the context of explaining behavior. Sometimes we make rapid inferences with little thought, whereas at other times we use more deliberative reasoning. Although in an ideal world lay thinkers would be cognizant of the social psychological principle that social behavior is a function of both the person and the situation (Ross & Nisbett, 1991), the fact is that people commonly rely on shortcuts and/or incomplete reasoning that result in the neglect of possible alternative explanations (Gilbert, 1998; Trope & Liberman, 1993). In this section, we'll review evidence for two attributional biases: fundamental attribution error and the actor/observer bias.

In the 1970s, social psychologist Lee Ross argued that people typically focus on dispositional factors and ignore situational ones, thus committing what he called the **fundamental attribution error** (FAE; Maruna & Mann, 2006; Moran, Jolly, & Mitchell, 2014; Ross, 1977; Tal-Or & Papirman, 2007). Ross called this an error because it violated the assumption that both personal and situational factors are implicated in the production of social behavior and described it as fundamental, because he believed it was a universal tendency (Ross, 1977; Ross & Nisbett, 1991). Stating that if a man trips, then he is clumsy, or if a woman loses her cell phone, then she is careless, are examples of the FAE: possible situation-based causes of the behavior are ignored. Edward Jones calls this attributional process the "rocky road from acts to dispositions," because it is fraught with obstacles and pitfalls that can lead one away from the correct attributional path that would take both personal and situational factors into account (Jones, 1979).

One classic experiment asked participants to report the true attitudes of students who had written essays espousing either pro-Fidel Castro (the former Communist leader of Cuba) or anti-Fidel Castro sentiments, and either had choice or no choice as to which side to argue for (Jones & Harris, 1967). Not surprisingly, participants assumed that the students who chose which position to take held the attitudes expressed in their essays: That the authors of the pro-Castro essays actually supported Castro and those of the anti-Castro essays did not (see Figure 5.4). Perhaps more counterintuitive, when predicting the true attitudes of the authors who were assigned which position to take, the participants similarly believed that the essays reflected the authors' actual sentiments, despite the fact that they had no choice in which side to argue for! In other words, the participants assumed that outward *behavior* corresponded to inward *attitudes,* thereby ignoring obvious situational pressures. Social psychologists call this tendency the **correspondence bias**, and it is closely related to the fundamental attribution error (Gawronski, 2004; Gilbert & Malone, 1995). The correspondence bias is fairly prevalent among U.S. adults; using an essay evaluation paradigm similar to the Jones and Harris (1967) study, Bauman and Skitka (2010) found that 53% of adults in a nationally representative sample exhibited the bias.

Fundamental Attribution Error: Attributing behavior to dispositional factors, while ignoring situational ones

Correspondence Bias: Tendency to assume that outward *behavior* corresponds to inward *attitudes* and to ignore situational influences

Although Ross (1977) conceptualized the FAE as a psychological universal, subsequent research in nonWEIRD populations has demonstrated its cultural boundedness (Choi, Nisbett, & Norenzayan, 1999; Miller, 1984; Morris & Peng, 1994). For instance, Morris and Peng (1994) found greater evidence of the FAE among Chinese college students than European American ones for social but not physical explanations. They also found that attributions for murder in a U.S.-based, English-language newspaper emphasized dispositional causes, whereas a U.S.-based, Chinese-language newspaper focused on situational causes (Morris & Peng, 1994). Although the evidence is mixed (Krull et al., 1999), it turns out that the fundamental attribution error may not be so fundamental after all! Research on attributional biases lends further support for one of the principles of social psychology: that social behavior is culturally situated (Li et al., 2012).

Another well-researched attributional bias is the **actor/observer effect** (Dong, Dai, & Wyer, 2015; Gioia & Sims, 1985; Jones & Nisbett, 1971), which occurs when behavioral attributions vary according to whether one is the actor (doing the behavior) or an observer (watching the behavior). Actors are more likely to focus on situational explanations for their own behavior, whereas observers' tend to emphasize dispositional ones (Jones & Nisbett,

Actor/Observer Effect: When the attributions for a person's behavior vary according to whether one is the actor (doing the behavior) or an observer (of the behavior)

FIGURE 5.4   The Correspondence Bias in Attributions

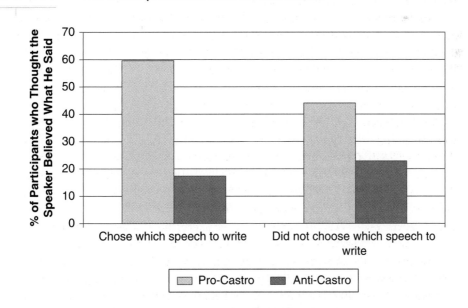

Even when observers are told that a person had *no choice* regarding whether to write a pro- or anti-Castro speech, they assumed that the speech reflected the true attitudes of the speechwriter. The higher values indicate greater pro-Castro attitudes.

Source: Adapted from Study 1, Jones, E. E., & Harris, V. A. (1967). The attribution of attitudes. *Journal of Experimental Social Psychology, 3*, 1–24.

1971). For example, a study by Gioia and Sims (1985) in an organizational context demonstrated that subordinates tend to blame external factors for their work-related failures, but their supervising managers attributed those failures to internal features of the subordinates. Or take an instance of a basketball player who is kicked out of a game because he has committed too many fouls. The player/actor will likely blame situational factors—referees, opposing players, and so forth—for his ejection. However, observers may believe the fouls to be a direct result of his aggressive or reckless playing style—thereby making a dispositional attribution.

Social psychologists have offered two primary explanations for the actor/observer bias. One reason is perceptual: The actor does not "see" his behavior but rather focuses primarily on other events. As we've said, people find causes where they look for them, and the actors "look" primarily at the behavior of others. In contrast, observers focus their attention primarily on the actor and may neglect surrounding events. A second reason for the actor/observer difference has to do with the amount of knowledge available to each. Actors have insight into their own behavior, motives, and so forth, which observers do not share, and this knowledge will affect the attributions they make (Jones & Nisbett, 1971).

In the true spirit of science as a self-correcting mechanism, more recent research has cast doubt on the existence of the actor/observer bias. Malle (2006) conducted a meta-analysis of 173 published studies of this effect and found no evidence for a widespread tendency for actors and observers to make systematically divergent attributions. Malle did uncover specific factors that heightened the likelihood that individuals would demonstrate the actor/observer difference, such as for negative events that might cast aspersion on the actor (Malle, 2006; Malle, Knobe, & Nelson, 2007). For instance, a politician embroiled in a corruption scandal that could destroy her career may show an exaggerated actor bias as compared with a news outlet reporting that scandal.

One of the more interesting approaches to dissecting the causes of behavior was developed by the social psychologist Harold Kelley, who we discussed earlier in the context of first impressions. Kelley's (1967) covariation matrix provides a useful way of distinguishing among various possible causes of a particular event or behavior (Hewstone & Jaspars, 1987). Kelley suggested that we commonly seek three types of information about a social behavior when trying to identify its cause: consensus, distinctiveness, and consistency (see Figure 5.5). For instance, say you are a teacher in a fourth-grade classroom and you see 10-year-old Sally tell another student, Rosa, to "shut up." In addition to helping Sally to improve her social skills, you may want to know why she acted that way; you'll want to know the source of the apparent problem between the two girls. Is there something about Sally, something about Rosa, or some aspect of their particular interactions that led to this outburst? One question that you may want to ask is whether other kids tend to respond to Rosa in a similar way—that is, does *consensus* exist in the way students respond to Rosa. If others are engaging in the same or similar behavior, you'll wonder whether Rosa has some characteristic or behavioral tendency that makes it more likely that kids will yell at her to be quiet. In contrast, if there is no behavioral consensus, if others do not do this, then you'd be more likely to identify Sally as the cause.

A second important piece of information has to do with whether this particular incident is unique or occurs frequently: Does Sally tend to yell at kids other than Rosa, telling them to "shut up"? If she does, then this particular incident is not *distinctive*—Sally does this all of the time. Therefore you can focus even more closely on Sally and wonder if she has a characteristic or behavioral tendency to treat others this way. On the one hand, you might infer that Sally is the primary source of the problem: She may be ill-tempered and impatient and prone to angry outbursts. If on the other hand, Sally rarely or never yells at other students, how then do you explain this incident? Well, there is a third piece of information that could further aid you in identifying the primary cause of her outburst: Does Sally *consistently* respond in a hostile way only to Rosa? In other words, is there something about the interactions between Sally and Rosa (but not between Sally and other kids or Rosa and other kids) that leads to this type of behavior? It may be that Rosa frequently teases Sally because of the glasses she wears, and consequently, Sally yells at her. Or perhaps there is something else specific to Rosa that uniquely sets Sally off (but not other kids). To summarize: If other kids also tell Rosa to shut up, then there is consensus and an attribution to Rosa is more likely.

FIGURE 5.5   Why Did She Do That?! Kelley's Covariation Matrix

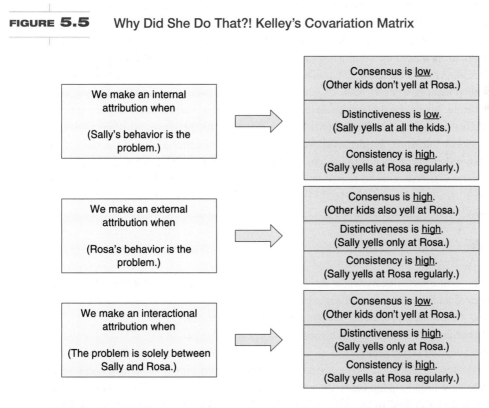

Source: Adapted from Kelley, H. H. (1967). Attribution theory in social psychology. *Nebraska Symposium on Motivation, 15*, 192–238.

If Sally's behavior is not distinctive—she tells other kids to shut up also—then an attribution to Sally is more appropriate. Finally, if Sally consistently tells Rosa—but not other kids—to shut up, then an attribution to both Sally and Rosa is more likely to be made.

FINAL THOUGHTS: SEX CATEGORIZATION AND FREE WILL

Humans like to know why the world is as it is. We devote considerable mental resources to attempting to comprehend and explain social events and the behavior of individuals. Humans are amazingly good at social perception: We often "read" people's emotions and personality rather quickly and with little thought and oftentimes can gain impressively accurate information. Social perception is a complex process that, as we have seen, is influenced by a number of factors, including individual construal, implicit personality theories and, at least in some cases, culture. Before concluding our discussion of social perception, let's briefly consider an additional influence: gender. Although the ability to categorize accurately people as male or female is essential to reproductive success, the process is not as straightforward as you may think. For instance, females are faster, more accurate, and more efficient at categorizing males (but not females) during ovulation—their peak fertility—than at other points in the menstrual cycle (Johnston, Miles, & Macrae, 2010). However, sexual motivation also plays a role, given that females taking oral contraception show an enhanced ability and greater sexual desire throughout their cycle and that lesbians are better able to categorize *female* faces when ovulating. Findings such as these, along with others in this chapter reflecting the role of nonconscious processes, further illustrate the apparent undermining of the claim that we have free will by social psychological research.

CORE CONCEPTS

- People form impressions using a combination of additive (bottom-up) and configural (top-down) processes, and these impressions can be based on "thin slices" or brief exposures to a person.

- People hold implicit personality theories about what traits tend to "go with" other traits; incorrect prophecies that people make about the behavior of others can come true because of the way the perceiver behaves.

- Nonverbal behavior is fundamental to the smooth functioning of human social relationships and emotional expressions—many of which are cultural—play a particularly important role. The five categories of nonverbal behavior are emblems, illustrators, manipulators, regulators, and emotional expressions. The six universal expressions are anger, happiness, sadness, surprise, disgust, and fear. Blended emotions are combinations of emotions. Display rules determine the contexts in which emotions are typically expressed or suppressed.

- Researchers examining social behavior in multiple cultures face particular methodological challenges related to language differences, creating situational equivalences, understanding and dealing with possible response styles, and in utilizing equivalent samples across cultures.

- Research suggests that people are generally not skillful in detecting deception based on nonverbal behavior, whereas there is some evidence that nonconscious detection may be more successful;

- When making attributions or explanations for social behavior, people sometimes focus on internal causes and ignore external ones, thereby committing the fundamental attribution error; similarly, people often assume that external behavior corresponds to internal dispositions; actors tend to make different attributions for their behavior than do observers; when making attributions, people consider the extent to which the behavior is common, distinctive, and consistent.

▶ ⑤SAGE edge™ Test your understanding of chapter content. Take the practice quiz. edge.sagepub.com/barrett

KEY TERMS

Actor/Observer Effect, 181
Attribution, 179
Blended Emotions, 166
Correspondence
    Bias, 180
Decoding, 166
Display Rules, 163
Fundamental
    Attribution Error, 180

Gambler's Fallacy, 177
Hot Hand Illusion, 177
Illusion of Control, 177
Illusory Correlation, 178
Implicit Personality
    Theory, 155

Meta-analysis, 164
Nonverbal Behavior, 161
Self-Fulfilling
    Prophecy, 158

▶ ⑤SAGE edge™   Review key terms with eFlashcards. edge.sagepub.com/barrett

THINK FURTHER!

- What are the two models of impression formation? Can you give an example of each? If you had to use just one word to describe yourself holistically, what would it be? What if you could list six words?

- What are implicit personality theories and how can they affect behavior? How might you prevent them from inappropriately affecting social perception?

- How can you explain the fact that some emotional expressions are universally recognized, whereas others are more culturally bounded? Does this make sense to you?

- Describe the four challenges of cross-cultural research defined in this chapter. How can they be overcome?

- According to Kelley's attribution matrix, when are people more likely to make dispositional, situational, or interactional attributions? Try applying the three components to a behavior of your choosing.

SUGGESTED READINGS

Asch, S. E. (1946). Forming impressions of personality. *The Journal of Abnormal and Social Psychology, 41*(3), 258–290.

Back, M. D., Stopfer, J. M., Vazire, S., Gaddis, S., Schmukle, S. C., Egloff, B., & Gosling, S. D. (2010). Facebook profiles reflect actual personality, not self-idealization. *Psychological Science, 21,* 372–374.

Ekman, P. (2007). *Emotions revealed: Recognizing faces and feelings to improve communication and emotional life.* New York, NY: Henry Holton.

Malle, B. F. (2006). The actor-observer asymmetry in attribution: A (surprising) meta-analysis. *Psychological Bulletin, 132,* 895–919.

McAndrew, F. T., & De Jonge, C. R. (2011). Electronic person perception: What do we infer about people from the style of their e-mail messages? *Social Psychological and Personality Science, 2*(4), 403–407.

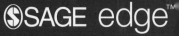

INTERPERSONAL
INFLUENCE

6

Social Influence

U.S. Pfc. Lynndie England holding a leash attached to a detainee in late 2003 at the Abu Ghraib prison in Baghdad, Iraq.

AP Photo/ Photos of the Decade.

LEARNING OBJECTIVES

6.1 Define social influence, explain why we succumb to it, and compare/contrast it with persuasion, compliance, conformity, and obedience.

6.2 Identify and describe the six principles of social influence and give examples of each.

6.3 Describe the limited-quantity and deadline techniques and discuss the role of reactance in each.

6.4 Describe the labeling and bait-and-switch techniques and how they rely on the need for consistency; compare FITD (foot-in-the-door) and DITF (door-in-the-face) and explain the social influence principles that undergird each.

6.5 Define social norm, focus theory of normative conduct, descriptive norm, injunctive norm; describe Sherif's autokinetic research and Asch's line judgment research.

6.6 Summarize Milgram's obedience studies; explain the controversy surrounding them and the purpose of Burger's replication.

6.7 Examine the ethical dilemma faced by social psychologists when using deception in research and the justification often used to defend deception.

⑤SAGE edge™

Get the edge on your studies.
edge.sagepub.com/barrett

Take a quiz to find out what you've learned.
Watch videos that enhance chapter content.
Explore related web and social media activities.

GOOD PEOPLE TURNING BAD

In 2004 news media around the world lit up with disturbing words and images from the American-run Abu Ghraib prison in Iraq. U.S. soldiers had brutalized dozens of Iraqi prisoners—including beating them, forcing them into humiliating, often naked, poses and formations, sodomizing at least one detainee with a hard object, terrifying them with trained military dogs, and more—and there were photos to prove it (Hersh, 2004b). By the time the press became aware of this dehumanizing treatment, the military had begun an investigation that eventually led to the prosecution and punishment of several members of a military police unit. Although some governmental and military officials justified the harsh treatment on the grounds that the prisoners posed a threat to U.S. forces, virtually all of the several thousand prisoners at Abu Ghraib were civilians—including women, children, and old men—who had been rounded up and detained without justification. Some commentators tried to explain away these events by claiming that the abusive behavior was the result of a few bad apples and did not represent the directives or intentions of their military superiors.

Other observers, including Major General Anthony Taguba, the author of the official, damning report of the incidents, concluded that the conditions for such behavior were created as a result of official policies designed to remake the prison into an interrogation center—one that would operate according to its own set of rules, not bound by the U.S. military code or the Geneva Convention governing treatment of prisoners (Hersh, 2004b). In fact, several of the accused claimed that they were simply doing what they were told by their superiors and did not question the legitimacy of the treatment of the detainees. One of the burning questions raised by this pattern of behavior is *how could decent human beings with no history of abusive behavior engage in such reprehensible activities?* The answer can be found in the surprising power of a situation to influence human behavior (Zimbardo, 2007).

This chapter focuses primarily on how particular types of social influences—such as direct requests and unspoken social pressures—affect social behavior. We'll describe six influence principles that appear across a wide variety of situations and serve as psychological triggers for behavior change. Over the course of the chapter, you'll see four of our fundamental questions of human existence popping up: independence, sociality, free will, and morality. The ways in which our own thoughts, behaviors, and feelings are *independent* from or are reactions to others—the heart of social influence itself—constitute the central theme in this chapter. Our *sociality* is key to understanding succumbing to social pressures, particularly when it involves seeking the approval of others in order to create and/or maintain social ties. The question of *free will* arises in the context of the nonconscious shaping of our behavior. Finally, the problem of *morality* is highly relevant to our discussion of obedience to unethical authority as well as of the ethics of potentially harmful psychological research in social influence.

Think Ahead!

1. *Why do people—even those who think of themselves as individualists—often follow the crowd?*

2. *What are some of the reasons people succumb to social influence?*

3. *Why might a person agree to hurt an innocent person just because she is told to?*

TYPES OF SOCIAL INFLUENCE

The events at Abu Ghraib demonstrate how situational influences can seemingly overwhelm personal ones. However, as we have discussed and as one of our guiding principles indicates, social behavior is the result of both personal and situational factors; understanding it requires the analysis of sources of influence stemming from both. Even within Abu Ghraib, individuals such as Master-at-Arms William J. Kimbro rejected attempts by others to involve him in the abusive treatment of the detainees because he knew that it was inappropriate (Hersh, 2004a). Lewin's (1946) field theory is useful in its conceptualization of the person-situation relationship as an individual moving across a field of influences that shape and are shaped by actions of the individual (see Chapter 1).

As you have learned, a person's metaphorical movement across the Lewinian social field is partially directed by her goals. What are the goals of social influence? We discussed two of these in the context of social cognition—the need to be correct and the need to be accepted—and here we'll add a third: the desire to be consistent with our prior commitments and past behavior (Festinger, 1962). The current chapter describes several types of **social influence**, which is broadly defined as an internal or external change in a person caused by *real* or *imagined* pressure from others (See Table 6.1; Dolinski, 2016; Pratkanis, 2007a). Here we'll focus primarily on observable behavior, whereas Chapter 7 examines **persuasion**, by which we mean changes in attitudes or beliefs. Keep in mind, given that alterations in

Social Influence: An internal or external change in a person caused by the real or imagined pressure from others

Persuasion: Change in attitudes or beliefs

TABLE 6.1   Varieties of Social Influence

Name	Definition	Example
Social Influence	An internal or external change in a person caused by the real or imagined pressure from others	Joseph decides to wear jeans instead of khakis after imagining that that is what his girlfriend would want.
Persuasion	A change in attitudes or beliefs	Serena begins liking jazz after a friend tells her how great it is.
Informational Influence	The adoption of others' behaviors, attitudes, and/or beliefs because those individuals are perceived as sources of valid information about objective reality	Vera begins to believe in the efficacy of capitol punishment after her friends give her evidence supporting this position.
Normative Influence	The alteration of one's behavior, attitude, or belief in order to be accepted by another person or group.	Gino starts cheering for a different basketball team in order to be accepted by others who like that team.
Compliance	A behavioral response to a request	Dr. Nichols writes a prescription after her patient asks her to.
Conformity	A change in one's behavior in order to fit in	Leo buys a new style of jeans after noticing that his friends wore them, although they never asked him to do so.
Obedience	A behavioral response to a request from an authority	Michael sits down after his father told him to.

external behaviors may or may not be associated with internal ones, social influence can occur without persuasion, but when persuasion occurs so to does social influence.

Real pressure in the context of social influence refers to overt requests that are given in order to change the message recipient's behavior, attitudes, or beliefs. For instance, if your boss asks you to work an extra shift this week, then real or actual pressure is present. In contrast, *imagined* pressure is at work when a person believes—correctly or incorrectly—that others want or expect her to engage in a particular behavior or adopt an attitude or belief. For example, if you are pondering what to wear to an upcoming party and choose clothes based on what you think your date would like, then you are bowing to imagined pressure.

People like to be correct in their behaviors, beliefs, and attitudes. When we change our behavior in order to align it with what we believe is the correct behavior, we are succumbing to one type of social influence called informational influence. **Informational influence** can be defined as the adoption of other's behaviors, attitudes, and/or beliefs because those individuals are perceived as sources of valid information about objective reality (Barrett, 2007; Cialdini & Goldstein, 2004; Deutsch & Gerard, 1955; Skewes, Skewes, Roepstorff, & Frith, 2013; Williamson, Weber, & Robertson, 2013). This type of influence is operational when one or more individuals communicate new information or arguments to the target person, resulting in the target's adoption of a novel position. Informational influence is obvious in ordinary face-to-face encounters or telephone conversations. Recent research has shown how informational influence can also occur via computer-mediated communication, such as Facebook and Twitter, affecting such phenomena as attitudes toward and participation in online auctions (Chen, 2011; Egermann, Kopiez, & Altenmüller, 2013; M. K. O. Lee, Shi, Cheung, Lim, & Sia, 2011; Shedlosky-Shoemaker, Costabile, DeLuca, & Arkin, 2011).

Informational influence may be contrasted with **normative influence**, which is the alteration of one's behaviors, attitudes, or beliefs in order to be accepted by another person or group (Cialdini & Goldstein, 2004; Deutsch & Gerard, 1955; Egermann et al., 2013; Monin, 2007). Normative influence stems from people's tendency to seek approval from others for their own decisions without regard to being objectively correct (Huang, Kendrick, & Yu, 2014; Schultz, Tabanico, & Rendón, 2008). For example, encouraging people to engage in environmentally conscientious behavior such as recycling can be accomplished by exposing them to evidence that many relevant others are enacting that same behavior (Schultz et al., 2008). Deutsch and Gerard (1955) originally conceptualized these two types of influence in the context of research into why minorities in groups yield to pressures from the majority; in Chapter 12 we'll also explore how minorities affect majorities.

SIX PRINCIPLES OF INTERPERSONAL INFLUENCE

The noted social psychologist Robert Cialdini (2008) created a taxonomy of principles that he argues underlie most attempts at interpersonal influence. Unlike most academics, Cialdini pursued his social psychological interests beyond the laboratory, conducting participant field research by joining the world of influence professionals. With his identity as a psychological researcher safely hidden, Cialdini received training in a variety of influence-related industries, including both sales and advertising. Drawing from both his own hands-on experiences and laboratory research, Cialdini distilled countless social influence processes down to six fundamental principles: scarcity, liking/friendship, commitment/consistency, reciprocity, social validation, and authority (Cialdini, 2008; Cialdini & Goldstein, 2004). Several of these principles are integral to the achievement of **compliance**, by which we mean a behavioral response to a request. Agreeing to have lunch when asked by a friend or to wash dishes when requested to by a spouse are examples of compliance.

Informational Influence: Adoption of other's behaviors, attitudes, and/or beliefs because those individuals are perceived as sources of valid information about objective reality

Normative Influence: Alteration of one's behaviors, attitudes, or beliefs in order to be accepted by another person or group

Compliance: Behavioral response to a request

The **scarcity principle** suggests that people are more likely to value options and items when they are difficult to find or otherwise limited in their availability (Cialdini, 2008; S. Y. Lee, Oh, & Jung, 2014; Lynn, 1992). Consequently, compliance with behavioral requests that highlight the limited opportunities to obtain an item or take a certain course of action tends to be enhanced. For instance, some advertisements describe items as restricted in quantity—such as *only three cars left at this price!*—informally known as the **limited-quantity technique** (See Table 6.2). Others offer sale prices that are applicable for a only a short time or coupons that will soon expire—only three days left of a sale!—informally called the **deadline technique**. If you shop online at Amazon.com or similar retailers, you have probably seen how it informs you about how many items are left, in part to take advantage of this scarcity principle (Cialdini & Trost, 1998; DeVoe & Pfeffer, 2011; Howard, Shu, & Kerin, 2007).

Actual or perceived scarcity often leads to people to engage in activities that they were not likely to have done otherwise. One explanation for this result is that people perceive their freedom or independence to be threatened by the loss of opportunity, and they may, consequently, act to preserve that freedom (Cialdini, 2008; Pratkanis, 2007b). This restriction of freedom can cause an unpleasant or negative arousal, called **reactance**, which may in turn lead them to enact behavior intended to protect or reinstate their freedom (Brehm, 1966). Psychological reactance may motivate people to purchase a scarce item in order to avoid losing their freedom or ability to obtain it (Cialdini, 2008; Highhouse, Beadle, Gallo, & Miller, 1998). Furthermore, people's awareness of the limited availability of an item triggers what Mittone and Savadori (2009) call the *scarcity bias:* the automatic increase in the value ascribed to the item because of its lack of abundance. In other words, we think scarce items are more valuable simply because they are scarce.

Another of Cialdini's principles—**liking/friendship**—refers to increased adherence to a request from a positively evaluated other, such as a friend or an admired person. Cialdini (2008) reviews in detail how we like others more because they are physically attractive, similar, or familiar, and consequently, comply more frequently to their requests. The power that liking has to increase compliance is clearly demonstrated by the frequency with which advertisers and social marketers incorporate well-known, liked celebrities such as David Beckham or Lebron James into their campaigns (Burger, Soroka, Gonzago, Murphy, & Somervell, 2001). Connecting one's product or company with a liked

TABLE 6.2 Social Influence Principles and Tactics

Underlying Principle	Tactic
Scarcity	Setting a deadline
	Limiting quantity
Commitment/consistency	Foot-in-the-door
	Labeling
	Low-ball
	Bait-and-switch
Reciprocity	Door-in-the-face
	That's-not-all

Scarcity Principle: People are more likely to value options and items when they are difficult to obtain or otherwise limited in their availability

Limited-Quantity Technique: Restricting the quantity of a product, service, or opportunity in order to increase its desirability

Deadline Technique: Setting a specific end date for an opportunity, such as a sale or service, in order to increase its desirability

Reactance: Unpleasant arousal that triggers behavior intended to protect or reinstate freedoms that are restricted or threatened

Liking/Friendship Principle: People are more likely to adhere to a request from a positively evaluated other, such as a friend or an admired person

celebrity can of course backfire if that person's reputation suffers a blow, such as when Tiger Woods's marital problems drew international attention, resulting in decreased revenue for his sponsors and the loss of lucrative contracts by the celebrity.

Cialdini's third social influence principle—**commitment/consistency**—is based on the fact that people often prefer to be consistent with their own past behavior and to follow through on commitments to specific courses of action (Festinger, 1962). Thus, when a person is a habitual recycler, then an appeal that reminds that person of her "green" past is more likely to be successful. Similarly, inducing a target to make a commitment—especially a public one—takes advantage of our need for consistency and will typically increase compliance. Cialdini and others have empirically demonstrated the role that consistency pressures play in a variety of social influence strategies (Burger & Caldwell, 2003; Demarque, Apostolidis, & Joule, 2013; Guadagno & Cialdini, 2010; Stone, 2012). In Chapter 7, we will focus in greater detail on the psychological underpinnings of consistency pressures and cognitive dissonance theory; for now, let's review some social influence strategies that rely on such pressures.

Imagine that you are sitting at home and you receive a phone call from an unknown organization asking permission for five or six men to visit your home to spend a couple of hours looking through your cupboards and storage spaces. The caller claims to be interested in recording the cleaning products that are stored in your home and plans to incorporate the information into a consumer product guide. What are the chances that you would agree? Would it matter if, three days prior to the request, that caller had first asked you to answer, over the phone, a few questions about your household cleaning products?

Well, if you are like many of the participants in Freedman and Fraser's (1966) study, receiving the earlier phone call would significantly increase the likelihood that you would agree. These researchers contacted 156 housewives near Stanford University by phone, utilizing one of the scripts corresponding to each of four conditions. Participants in the *performance condition* were asked to answer eight survey questions about household products. Those in the *agree-only* condition were informed of the survey and their participation was elicited, but they were not asked the survey questions during that phone call. In the *familiarization* condition, participants were engaged in a several-minute discussion about the sponsoring organization and the survey, but their willingness to complete the survey was not assessed.

Three days later, all of these participants were called a second time and asked to consent to the larger request (the home visit). Finally, a fifth group was called once, the *one-contact* condition, with that calling involving an appeal for the home visit only, with no mention of the survey. Compliance with the larger request depended on whether or not the initial call was made and what was asked during that call. Thus, whereas only 22.2% of the *one-contact* participants agreed to the visit, 52.8% of those in the performance condition did. Agreement in the remaining conditions fell somewhere between these rates (see Figure 6.1). Here's why. Compliance with the larger request is enhanced because people have already agreed to the smaller one. This initial compliance matters,

---

Commitment/ Consistency Principle: Increased likelihood that people will enact a behavior that is consistent with their own past behavior and allows them to follow through on prior commitments

FIGURE **6.1**   Foot-in-the-Door

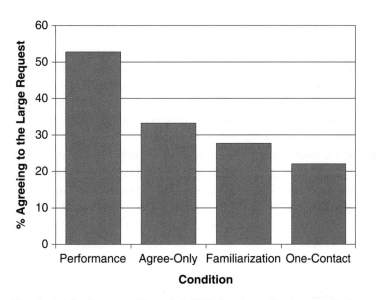

Source: Adapted from Study 1, Freedman, J. L., & Fraser, S. C. (1966). Compliance without pressure: The foot-in-the-door technique. *Journal of Personality and Social Psychology, 4*, 195–202.

because it leads to a change in the person's self-perception (Bem & McConnell, 1970); performing the smaller request led participants to begin seeing themselves as the type of person who agrees to favors from strangers (Freedman & Fraser, 1966). As a result of this *commitment* to their new self-image, participants felt internal pressure to behave *consistently* with that image, and therefore were more likely to agree to the larger request. This approach is sometimes dubbed the **foot-in-the-door** technique (FITD).

Since Freedman and Fraser's (1966) original research, over 50 studies have explored the nature and limits of the FITD. For instance, agreeing to address envelopes for an environmental advocacy organization produced greater compliance with a subsequent larger request to help construct a hiking trail (Burger & Guadagno, 2003; Dillard, 1990). A meta-analysis of this research concluded that the FITD is moderately effective in increasing compliance, especially when the requests are prosocial or beneficial and there is a delay between the two requests (Chartrand, Pinckert, & Burger, 1999; Dillard, Hunter, & Burgoon, 1984; Souchet & Girandola, 2013). Even people who try but fail to fulfill the initial request—such as when they are asked to give directions to a nonexistent address—are more likely to agree to a subsequent larger request (Dolinski, 2000).

Foot-in-the-Door Technique (FITD): Sequential procedure in which (a) a small request is made and, following compliance, (b) a larger request is made

Labeling Technique:
Bestowing a positive label on a person in order to gain compliance to a request

Three other commonly used social influence techniques similarly take advantage of people's preference for consistency. The **labeling technique** builds on people's need to live up to a positive label bestowed upon them from outside (Pratkanis, 2007b). Cialdini (2008) describes how former Egyptian President Anwar Sadat flattered counterparts from other nations with whom he was about to negotiate by stating that they were noted for being fair and cooperative. By doing so, these leaders felt compelled to act in a fair and cooperative manner, thereby unknowingly smoothing negotiations. Labeling has proven to be effective in increasing blood donations (Sénémeaud et al., 2014), producing voter turnout after adults were called "above average citizens" (Tybout & Talch, 1980), and in encouraging children to work on their penmanship (Cialdini, Eisenberg, Green, Rhoads, & Bator, 1998).

Low-Ball Tactic:
Enticing consumers to agree to purchase something and then subsequently inform them that the price is higher than initially promised

The remaining consistency-based tactics induce customers to commit to a given product at a given price, and then either (a) increase that price or (b) replace the product with a more costly one. Salespersons utilizing the **low-ball tactic** entice consumers to agree to purchase something and then subsequently inform them that the price is higher than initially promised (Burger & Petty, 1981; Cialdini, Cacioppo, Bassett, & Miller, 1978; Guéguen, Pascual, & Dagot, 2002). Some years ago, I encountered this strategy firsthand while I was considering the purchase of a late-model used Toyota pickup. After I verbally agreed to buy the truck at a particular price, the sales manager informed me that the price was considerably higher than what I had been told. He apologized and said that his salesman had made a simple math mistake (I did not believe him). After telling them both that I had been low-balled, I walked away, empty-handed but relieved that I had seen through their deception. Controlled investigation of the low-ball tactic nicely backs up my unscientific anecdote (Cialdini et al., 1978; Guéguen & Pascual, 2014; Joule, 1987). For example, Burger and Cornelius (2003) found college students, induced to commit to donating to a scholarship fund after being promised a coupon for a free smoothie, followed through on their initial commitment even after being informed that the coupon was, unfortunately, no longer available.

Bait-and-Switch:
Social influence tactic in which a person psychologically commits to a product and then, suddenly, the product is replaced with a related product that is more expensive

One final tactic, known as **bait-and-switch**, elicits a psychological commitment to a product and then replaces the product with a related one that *just happens to be more expensive* (Breen, 2014; Cialdini, 2008; Enos, 2014). An example of this would be a store that proudly advertises a high-end stereo, for, say, $1,200, but has only one or two in stock. Consumers—who probably made a psychological commitment to purchase the stereo prior to arriving at the store—are justifiably disappointed upon learning that the stereo they pined for is no longer available. Instead they are offered a more expensive alternative, say for $1,400. The customer then faces a choice: either follow through on the commitment to obtaining a stereo that day at that location or make the psychologically difficult decision to abandon the commitment and return home, empty-handed. Many an unwary customer has fallen for this trick and, quite literally, paid the price (Hess & Gerstner, 1998; Wilkie, Mela, & Gundlach, 1998).

Think Again!

1. *What are the two kinds of social influence?*

2. *What is the foot-in-the-door technique, and why does it work?*

3. *Define the scarcity, liking, and commitment/consistency principles.*

THE PRINCIPLE OF RECIPROCITY

In addition to outlining the ways the scarcity, liking/friendship, and commitment/ consistency principles facilitated social influence, Cialdini (2008) described the wide-ranging power of reciprocity. The **reciprocity** (or reciprocation) **principle** refers to the increased likelihood that an individual will comply with a request from a person or an entity who has previously done a favor for that individual (Bowles & Gintis, 2011; Forgas, 2011). Noted sociologist Alvin Gouldner (1960) has argued that the general rule of reciprocation is a universal glue that binds people and groups together and has existed in all known societies and cultures (Axelrod, 2006; Sober & Wilson, 1998). That is, the sense of obligation embedded in reciprocity is essential to our sociality. Cialdini (2008) reviews many of the contexts and domains in which the reciprocity norm regulates our behavior. For instance, charitable organizations will often provide free gifts—books, address stickers, even flowers—in an attempt to harness the power of social obligation to elicit a donation. Researchers have investigated a number of social influence tactics that are based on the obligation a person feels to return a favor, gift, or service (Burger, 1986; Burger, Sanchez, Imberi, & Grande, 2009; O'Keefe & Figgé, 1999; Roberts, 2015).

One such influence strategy, called **door-in-the-face** (DITF) **technique**, involves (a) making a relatively large request, (b) waiting until the request has been refused, and (c) subsequently scaling back to a smaller request (Cialdini et al., 1975; Ebster & Neumayr, 2008; Henderson & Burgoon, 2014; Lecat, Hilton, & Crano, 2009). DITF has been demonstrated to be an effective compliance strategy in numerous studies across a variety of conditions (Feeley, Anker, & Aloe, 2012). For instance, in one study, college students were contacted and asked if they would be willing to devote 15 hours per week tutoring children at a boys and girls club (O'Keefe & Figgé, 1999). Predictably, most students refused this request. The caller then asked them to take just one afternoon to chaperone kids to a movie or museum.

How would you have responded? Importantly, what would you have felt? Most of us would have been simultaneously relieved that the requestor reduced his large request yet compelled to respond favorably the smaller request (Burger, Horita, Kinoshita, &

Reciprocity Principle: Increased likelihood that an individual will comply with a request from a person or an entity who has previously done a favor to that individual

Door-in-the-Face Technique: Sequential procedure of (a) making a relatively large request, (b) waiting until the request has been refused, and (c) subsequently scaling back to a smaller request

Roberts, 1997; Cialdini & Ascani, 1976). This is in fact what happened: Compared to the number of students who were only asked the smaller favor, many more agreed after the concession (See Figure 6.2) (O'Keefe & Figgé, 1999). Successful application of the DITF is particularly promising when there is only a short delay between the requests (Burger et al., 1997), the same individual makes them both, the stated reason for the request is prosocial, and when the persuader and target are members of the same ingroup (Lecat et al., 2009; M. M. Turner, Tamborini, Limon, & Zuckerman-Hyman, 2007).

Another tactic should be especially familiar to viewers of late night American television: the **that's-not-all technique** (Banas & Turner, 2011; Burger, 1986; Burger, Reed, DeCesare, Rauner, & Rozolis, 1999). In this case, a consumer is offered a product at a stated price and then, before being given the opportunity to either accept or decline the purchase, the deal is sweetened by the inclusion of unexpected new incentives. Burger (1986) demonstrated the effectiveness of this during a bake sale experiment on a college campus. In the treatment condition, when students approached the table and asked about the cost of the cupcakes, they were informed that the cost was $0.75 but, after a brief pause, were told that two cookies were also included. In contrast, control group participants were initially told that the cupcake came with two cookies and the total price was $0.75. Interestingly, although both the products and the prices were identical, far more customers in the experimental group made the purchase (Burger, 1986). As in the

That's-Not-All Technique: Adding new incentives to a deal before the consumer has been given the opportunity to either accept or decline the deal and without increasing the price

FIGURE 6.2   The Give and Take of Reciprocity

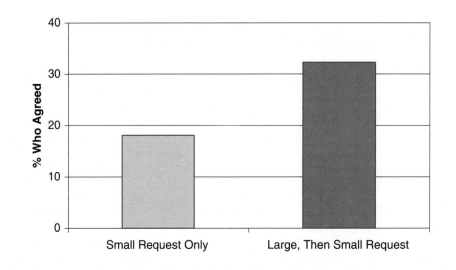

Source: Adapted from Study 2, O'Keefe, D. J., & Figgé, M. (1999). Guilt and expected guilt in the door-in-the-face technique. *Communication Monographs, 66*(4), 312–324.

DITF, the seller was perceived to have granted the potential buyer a favor, and the resulting reciprocity pressure produced increased agreement.

More recent research has enriched our understanding of the operations of the reciprocity norm. For instance, Burger and colleagues (Burger, 2007; Burger et al., 2001) have demonstrated that reciprocity may be enhanced by activation of a *liking heuristic,* a shortcut that suggests that we return favors for people we like. In contrast, reciprocity-related feelings of obligation may be lessened if the initial request is seen as benefiting the requestor more than the recipient (Keysar, Converse, Wang, & Epley, 2008; Zhang & Epley, 2009), the target is in a negative mood (Forgas, 2011), or if the request is made in a dirty- rather than clean-smelling environment (Liljenquist, Zhong, & Galinsky, 2010). Moreover, reciprocity, despite its universality and evolutionary origins (Gouldner, 1960; Sober & Wilson, 1998), varies across individuals (Matejkowski, McCarthy, & Draine, 2011) as well as cultures. For example, collectivists may be more likely to refuse a gift in order to avoid feelings of obligation, whereas individualists pay relatively more attention to the attractiveness of the gift when deciding whether or not to accept it (Shen, Wan, & Wyer, 2011) (See Research Box 6.1).

Think Again!

1. *What is the reciprocity principle?*

2. *What are the door-in-the-face and the that's-not-all techniques?*

CONFORMITY AND THE SOCIAL VALIDATION PRINCIPLE

The fifth of Cialdini's six social influence principles is called **social validation** or **social proof,** and it states that a person is more likely to enact a particular behavior to the extent that others are thought to be engaging in that same behavior (Cialdini, 2008). In short, validation or proof refers to the notion that the actual or perceived desires or behaviors of others serve as evidence for what the target should or shouldn't do. Following the group may serve either the goal of being correct or that of being approved (or both). At times the evidence that we obtain from others suggests what the objectively correct response may be, such as when we blindly but appropriately follow the route that other cars are traveling to detour around an accident. On other occasions, however, we do as others do because we believe that they will approve of us for following them, even when there is an objectively correct alternative (Aarts, Dijksterhuis, & Custers, 2003; Asch, 1952; Crutchfield, 1955; Sherif, 1966). Recall the distinction between informational and normative influence (Deutsch & Gerard, 1955). In the former case, change occurs because the target has received new evidence or arguments that lead him to rethink and consequently change a behavior, belief, or

Social Validation (or Social Proof) Principle: Increased likelihood that a person will enact a particular behavior to the extent that others are thought to be engaging in that same behavior

RESEARCH BOX 6.1
RECIPROCITY AND CULTURE

Hypothesis: Collectivists, as compared to individualists, prefer to avoid feeling indebted to people with whom they do not have a close relationship; consequently, they should be more likely to reject a gift from a stranger than from a close friend. In contrast, whether the gift-giver is a close friend or acquaintance should not matter to individualists.

Research Method: Undergraduates from relatively collectivistic Hong Kong and relatively individualistic Canada imagined accidentally encountering either a close friend or an acquaintance while at an airport and that this person offered to buy them a drink at an airport café. Participants reported how likely they would be to accept the gift and how comfortable they would be were they to accept it.

Results: As predicted, collectivists were less likely to accept a gift from an acquaintance than a close friend, but individualists did not show this difference. Furthermore, the difference between the conditions for collectivists was explained by their desire to avoid feeling indebted to the gift giver.

Conclusion: Collectivists are more strongly motivated to avoid triggering the reciprocity norm—feeling obligated to return a favor—with respect to casual acquaintances than are individualists

Source: Adapted from Shen, H., Wan, F., & Wyer, R. S., Jr. (2011). Cross-cultural differences in the refusal to accept a small gift: The differential influence of reciprocity norms on Asians and North Americans. *Journal of Personality and Social Psychology, 100*, 271–281.

attitude (Barrett, 2007). In the latter case, one's behavior, belief, or attitude are matched with those of others in order to be accepted or liked by them (Asch, 1956; Monin, 2007).

Social validation is related to one of the most studied phenomena in social psychology: **conformity**, which is a change in one's responses in order to fit in (Beran, Drefs, Kaba, Al Baz, & Al Harbi, 2015; Cialdini & Goldstein, 2004; Knapton, Bäck, & Bäck, 2015; Levine, 2007). Conformity studies focus on changes in behaviors or *expressed* attitudes or beliefs, whether or not such modifications are accompanied by *private* changes in attitudes or beliefs. Conformity is the result of normative influence. Although conformity is sometimes perceived by Americans as a dirty word because it undermines one's individuality or independence, it can often be beneficial and, at times, necessary. Can you think of some examples that illustrate the advantage of conforming?

Conformity: Change in one's responses in order to fit in

Two Types of Social Norms

As stated above, normative influence stems from the power that social norms wield over social behavior. A **social norm** is a rule and/or standard that is typically unwritten and guides the social behavior of members of a group (Cialdini & Trost, 1998; Hogg, 2010). Social rules can prescribe behavior—suggest what *should be done*—as well as proscribe behavior—indicate what *should not* be done (Cialdini & Trost, 1998; Miller & Prentice, 1996). Social standards are specific attributes of groups against which its members can compare their own behavior, attitudes, or beliefs (Miller & Prentice, 1996). In this chapter, we focus primarily on conformity-related changes in overt behavior, including the expression of attitudes and beliefs.

One of the most influential contemporary approaches to social norms is the **focus theory of normative conduct** (Cialdini, Kallgren, & Reno, 1991; Cialdini, Reno, & Kallgren, 1990; Hareli, Moran-Amir, David, & Hess, 2013). According to this theory, social norms can be divided into those that are descriptive and those that are injunctive. **Descriptive norms** indicate what most people are or are not doing in a particular context; that is, they tell us what *is* the case (Meisel & Goodie, 2014; Turner, 1991). For instance, on a highway near my home, the majority of drivers seem to drive faster than the speed limit, producing the descriptive norm that most people speed on that road. In contrast, **injunctive norms** reveal what people should or shouldn't do in a specific situation (Collins & Spelman, 2013; Jacobson, Mortensen, Jacobson, & Cialdini, 2015; Lawrence, 2015; Schultz, Nolan, Cialdini, Goldstein, & Griskevicius, 2007; Stok, de Ridder, de Vet, & de Wit, 2014). They are the norms of *ought* and as such may either prescribe or proscribe social behavior. When people speed, they are violating rather than following the injunctive norm.

These two types of social norms are more effective if they are consistent: when they jointly guide behavior in a single direction. An example of a consistent public service announcement (PSA) is one that depicts the descriptive norm that most people are driving at or below the speed limit and articulates the injunctive norm that you should follow the speed limit. In contrast, an inconsistent PSA is one that pairs the descriptive norm that most people do not obey the speed limit with the injunctive norm that you should obey it (Cialdini et al., 1991). Cialdini and his colleagues have demonstrated the power of using consistent descriptive and injunctive norms in guiding environmental behavior, including littering, recycling, and water conservation in hotels (Cialdini et al., 2006; Cialdini et al., 1991; Goldstein, Cialdini, & Griskevicius, 2008).

In one field study, Cialdini et al. (2006) examined the theft of petrified wood by tourists at the Petrified National Forest in Arizona. Theft of this valuable wood totals approximately 14 tons per year, seriously undermining the integrity and beauty of the park and nearly decimating the prior abundance of the wood. The researchers manipulated the words and images on signage such that they depicted either a descriptive or an injunctive norm regarding stealing the rare petrified wood from the forest. In addition to communicating one of these two norms, the signs varied in the strength of the normative focus; that is, one of each of the two descriptive or injunctive signs either strongly or

Social Norm: A rule and/or standard that is typically unwritten and guides social behavior

Focus Theory of Normative Conduct: Idea that social norms can be divided into those that are descriptive and those that are injunctive and that whichever norm people focus their attention on is likely to be more influential

Descriptive Norm: What most people are or are not doing in a particular context

Injunctive Norms: What people should or shouldn't do in a specific situation

weakly focused the viewer on the depicted norm. The strong focus message was negatively worded, emphasizing the fact that visitors have removed wood, whereas the weak focus message highlighted the fact that visitors have left the wood in the park. The researchers rotated placement of the norm-bearing signs across various locations in the park and discretely monitored theft of the wood along the adjoining paths.

During the five-week study period, 2,655 naïve visitors traveled on foot into the designated study areas. The researchers found that the signs with the injunctive norms significantly *reduced* stealing but only in the strong focus condition. Moreover, as expected, the descriptive/strong focus sign had the opposite result and produced *more* theft than the other conditions. Why would a sign designed to decrease an undesirable behavior actually increase it? The reason is straightforward: People tend to follow prevalent norms, even when they reflect behavior that is generally disapproved of. In this case, the descriptive/strong focus sign suggested that theft was a big problem and by implication that most people were stealing (and, by extension, getting away with it)! Unfortunately, a large number of the park signs that predated this study presented the wrong or undesirable behavior as commonplace and, as a result, likely exacerbated the problem.

Three important lessons can be drawn from this study. First, social norms can serve as powerful guides for social behavior. Second, norms will only alter behavior to the extent that they are salient or activated in the appropriate context. Finally, if improperly conceived—that is, created without regard to and perhaps contrary to social psychological principles—they can cause a boomerang effect, producing results precisely opposite their intended ones (Cialdini et al., 2006). The Cialdini et al. (2006) findings lend support to Cialdini's earlier and later conclusions from research on littering in public parking garages and water conservation by hotel visitors (Cialdini et al., 1990; Goldstein et al., 2008). Not only is it critical for a norm to be clearly discernable in the relevant context, it must be activated in the minds of the target persons. A person's attention must be focused on the correct norm in the relevant context in order for it to be influential. The work by Cialdini and his colleagues is important not only for specific demonstration of workings of social norms but also because it more generally provides evidence for their power in applied (nonlaboratory) settings. In the next section we'll turn our attention to a couple of the foundational *laboratory* studies on the influence of social norms.

Social Norms and Conformity

Imagine that you are a participant in a study of visual perception and are sitting in a dark room, facing a blank wall that is 15 feet away. A small dot of light appears on the wall and, after two seconds, you are asked to verbally indicate how far the light has traveled along the wall. At first you perform a series of trials while alone. During the next three days, you and others (who had also previously participated alone) gather in groups of three and repeat the distance estimation task, again stating aloud the distance that each thinks the light moved. In the first trial, the values that you and your two group members provide differ considerably—say, 4, 15, and 22 inches. However, on subsequent trials your estimates almost immediately converge and remain close together—say, 7, 8, and 9 inches. Following the group trials, you perform the task a third time, alone, and now offer distances that are more aligned with the norms of the group than your earlier, private estimates.

After the experiment is over, the researcher surprises you by stating that, despite what you thought you saw, the light on the wall *never* moved. Instead, the apparent movement was caused by what scientists call the *autokinetic effect:* rapid, uncontrollable movements of the eyes, called saccades, that induce the false perception of light movement in the absence of location reference points. (Try looking at a lit clock radio in a dark room, and you will likely experience this effect.) You learn that the study was not investigating visual perception but rather the development of social norms in groups, and the experimenter was interested in the extent to which the participants abandoned the estimates provided in isolation and nudged their private guesses toward those of their group members.

This is exactly what the noted Turkish American social psychologist Muzafer Sherif (1966) did in his seminal 1930s studies on the formation and maintenance of social norms in groups. Sherif (1966) demonstrated how quickly and spontaneously norms can form in a group as well as the power they continue to yield over individual behavior, even after the groups had disbanded. Furthermore, the fact that Sherif's participants changed their estimates after exposure to divergent estimates from others nicely illustrates what Deutsch and Gerrard (1955) later termed informational influence. The distances that one's fellow group members verbalized served as information, as a result of which the participants moved their guesses toward the group members' estimates in order to achieve the goal of being correct.

Sherif's research inspired another social psychologist, Solomon Asch, to further investigate the nature of group influence. Asch (1955) was somewhat skeptical of the import of the conclusions of Sherif (1966) and other researchers regarding the malleability of individual judgments in the face of contrary social pressure (Friend, Rafferty, & Bramel, 1990). He argued that the convergence in the distance estimates was primarily because of how Sherif's studies were designed and was not generalizable to other contexts (Prislin & Crano, 2008, 2012). That is, much of the variability in the individuals' judgments was a product of the ambiguity of this particular situation: The participants lacked an objective standard against which to check their personal estimates and, as a result, were influenced to an unusual extent by the perceptions of others (Asch, 1955).

In an attempt to provide empirical support for his belief in the independence of the individual, Asch conducted one of the most famous sets of experiments in the history of social psychology. Participants in his studies were informed that the researchers were studying visual judgment and that their task would be to match the length of a single vertical line—the standard line—on one card with the length of one of three lines on a second card (see Figure 6.3). Asch had previously confirmed the simplicity of the task, finding an error rate of under 1% for persons who completed it alone. The focal experiments involved seven to nine college men positioned around a table who provided their answers to the line judgment task verbally, in the order in which they were seated.

In the first two trials, all of the men correctly matched the standard line to the comparison line of the same length. However, beginning with the third trial and continuing

FIGURE 6.3   Losing Sight of Reality: Conformity in the Asch Line Judgment Task

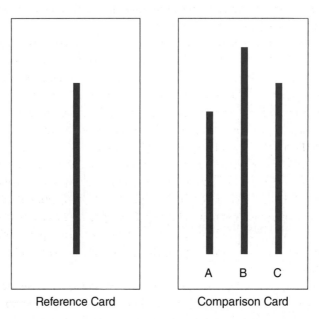

Which of the comparison lines matches the standard line? It seems obvious unless other members of your group choose a seemingly incorrect line. What would you do? Conform or follow your own intuitions?

Source: Adapted from Asch, S. E. (1955). Opinions and social pressure. *Scientific American*, *193*(5), 31–35.

intermittently throughout the 18 trials, the majority of the participants gave identical but clearly erroneous responses. The lone dissenter—who was, in fact, the only true participant—had either to reject the pressure of the majority and choose the correct line or ignore his own perception and align his responses with the majority's. The one true participant was unaware of the fact that his group members were following a predetermined script that directed them to unanimously provide incorrect answers in 12 of the trials. All told, the naïve participants deferred to the majority opinion 36.8% of the time, and about 75% of them gave at least one incorrect response in at least one of the trials (Asch, 1955).

However, again we are faced with the problem of interpretation. These numbers focus on how much people conformed, but they could just as easily be reversed to draw attention to the amount of independence of the participants: In approximately two-thirds of the trials, dissenters resisted group pressure and provided the objectively correct response, and almost one-fourth of the participants *never succumbed* to such pressure (Friend et al., 1990). In fact, Asch interpreted his findings as demonstrating how people are able to resist pressure not how they conform (Asch, 1955; Friend et al., 1990; Levine, 1999). Furthermore, although many accounts of Asch's line judgment research conceptualize such conformity as because of normative pressure, Asch argued that informational influence was primarily to blame (Asch, 1952; Levine, 1999).

When I ask my students how many of them would have given in to group influence, virtually all confidently state *not me!* This emphatic response is typically accompanied by comments such as "everyone conformed in the 1950s, but people aren't like that anymore." Social psychologists have also wondered whether conformity rates have declined over time. In order to address that question, researchers have repeatedly replicated Asch's paradigm, perhaps more times than any other study in social psychology (R. Bond & Smith, 1996b; Lalancette & Standing, 1990). The conformity rates in replications have varied considerably; the extent of conformity is dependent upon a number of contextual variables, including culture and size unanimity of the group, which we will discuss later in this chapter (R. Bond & Smith, 1996b; Cialdini & Trost, 1998). Recently, Claidière and Whiten (2012) have argued that many of the conformity-related concepts that social psychologists have developed based on human behavior may also apply to other animals. Such cross-species research provides compelling evidence for the evolutionary basis of conformity (Coultas, 2004).

As disconcerting as the conformity in these studies may be, social influence can lead to even more extreme behavior. For instance, horrific behaviors have been carried out by U.S. soldiers in the Abu Ghraib prison in Iraq as mentioned earlier (Hersh, 2004a, 2004b; Zimbardo, 2007) and during the Vietnam war in the My Lai massacre (Grossman, 1996). In the former, U.S. Army members dehumanized Iraqi war prisoners by putting leashes on them and treating them like dogs, by threatening to let loose attack dogs on them, forcing them into humiliating actions and poses, and other reprehensible behaviors (Hersh, 2004a, 2004b). In the My Lai Massacre in Vietnam in 1968, American U.S. soldiers slaughtered well over 300 Vietnamese civilians, most of whom were women, children, or elderly. Of course, as terrible as each of these was, they hardly compare to the slaughter of millions of Jews and others during the Holocaust in the 1940s or the genocide in Rwanda in the 1990s. The events in the Holocaust not only shook peoples' faith in the goodness of humanity but sent ripples through the halls of psychology and sociology departments as many sought to explain the psychology of genocide and torture. In fact, the tragedy of the Holocaust was one of the reasons Asch sought to understand the nature of independence and conformity (Asch, 1952).

Starved prisoners in a Nazi concentration camp in Ebenese, Austria, during World War II.

The Holocaust spawned some of the most famous experiments in the history of psychology: Zimbardo's Stanford Prison Experiment and Stanley Milgram's obedience studies. While it may be easy to distance ourselves from historical incidents of senseless inhumanity described above and to claim that we would never engage in such behaviors, this research should give us pause before doing so. Let's turn to Zimbardo's research next, and we will focus on Milgram's work later in the chapter.

In 1971, police in Palo Alto, California, handcuffed and arrested 12 male Stanford University students at their homes and brought them to a newly built prison in the basement of the university's psychology department (see photo). These student inmates were under the control of 12 male students assigned to be guards, who in turn were supervised by the would-be prison warden, Stanford social psychologist Philip Zimbardo. Zimbardo sought to understand the psychology of real prisons by studying the behavior of these participants (Haney, Banks, & Zimbardo, 1973; Haney & Zimbardo, 1998). The 24 students—who had been evaluated by a clinical psychologist and judged to be mentally healthy, well-adjusted individuals—were randomly assigned to be either a guard or a prisoner.

Unexpectedly, both guard and prisoner alike quickly lost sight of the fact that this was a simulation and embraced their social roles. The guards' behavior rapidly deteriorated from respectful and rule following to abusive and counternormative, whereas the inmates

Stanford Prison Experiment

Stanford University archives.

went from being rebellious to submissive. Even Zimbardo (2007), by his own admission, became so immersed in this study that he failed to maintain sufficient objectivity to see just how destructive the mock prison had become. Although he had planned for the experiment to last two weeks, he terminated it after just six days and only then because a graduate student saw what was happening and urged him to end it.

How do we explain this? Zimbardo has famously argued that the prison experiment demonstrates the power of the situation to overwhelm individual dispositions and desires and has cited his prison simulation to help explain the prisoner abuse at Abu Ghraib by U.S. soldiers and other similar atrocities. Yet Zimbardo's explanation is not without its critics. For instance, Carnahan and McFarland (2007) claim that self-selection by the participants—that people who would volunteer for a prison study are likely to be more aggressive and authoritarian and consequently more prone to abusive behavior—suggests that both dispositional and situational factors must be considered. Reicher and Haslam (Haslam & Reicher, 2007, 2012) suggest that Zimbardo himself—through the initial instructions that he gave to the guards—set the stage for the abuse and that the cruelty did not simply arise from inherent features of the prison. Given that the prison study cannot be replicated—for obvious ethical reasons—and was not a true experiment—it had no control group, no manipulate variables, and so forth—we cannot conclude with certainty why the abuse occurred. Nevertheless, it seems clear that the social behavior of the guards and inmates was a product of both situational and dispositional influences.

Think Again!

1. _Name and define the two types of social norms. How do you see these norms at work in your classroom? Home?_

2. _Describe the Asch line judgment task and explain the results. Would you have conformed had you been a participant? Why or why not?_

3. _How does the Stanford Prison Experiment shed light on the need to consider both personal and situational factors when explaining social behavior?_

Conformity Across Cultures

Whereas cross-species research demonstrates the evolutionary origins and therefore the apparent universality of conformity, there is also considerable cross-cultural variability (R. Bond & Smith, 1996; Murray, Trudeau, & Schaller, 2011; Oh, 2013). In other words, both biology and culture impact the extent to which people conform. As we have discussed, the individualism-collectivism dimension is the best-known and most studied cultural variable and not surprisingly has been extensively examined in the context of social influence and conformity (M. H. Bond & P. B. Smith, 1996; Cialdini, Wosinska,

Barrett, Butner, & Gornik-Durose, 1999; Kim & Markus, 1999). Perhaps the most widely studied paradigm across cultures is Asch's line judgment task, which has been replicated in at least 17 cultures (R. Bond & Smith, 1996).

In their meta-analysis of 133 studies conducted in nations as varied as the United States, Germany, Zimbabwe, and Kuwait, Bond and Smith (1996) found that cultures reflecting higher levels of collectivism demonstrated greater conformity than those higher in individualism. For instance, conformity rates in nations such as Portugal and France, relatively collectivistic cultures, were more than twice as high as those in Zimbabwe or Brazil, more individualistic cultures. Importantly, Bond and Smith (1996) found that culture affected compliance rates more than several noncultural factors, such as size of the majority.

The relationship between collectivism and conformity makes intuitive sense: People for whom group connections and norms are more important *should* be more responsive to group pressures to behave in a particular manner (Kim & Markus, 1999). Clearly, the power of social norms in determining behavior varies considerably across cultures (Cialdini et al., 1999; Ferreira, Fischer, Porto, Pilati, & Milfont, 2012; Fukushima, Sharp, & Kobayashi, 2009; Takano & Sogon, 2008). In one study, college students from relatively collectivistic Poland and relatively individualistic United States were asked to imagine being invited to participate in a brief survey and taste test of beverage preferences (Cialdini et al., 1999). Half of the participants in each nation were asked to consider the past agreement rates of their peers and to report the likelihood that they themselves would agree to the survey if, in the past, their classmates had agreed either all of the time, half of the time, or never. The other participants considered instead their own past behavior; previously, they had either always, half of the time, or never agreed to similar surveys. Cialdini et al. (1999) hypothesized and found that collectivists' agreement rates were more sensitive to the manipulation of the past behavior of their classmates—of social proof—whereas the respondent's own past behavior—a manipulation of personal consistency—more heavily influenced the agreement rate of individualists.

Other research has found that the influence of culture on conformity may depend on more than just the salient social norm, such as motivation to quickly arrive at decisions and conclusions (Fu et al., 2007). Fascinating recent research by Schaller and colleagues (Murray et al., 2011; Schaller & Murray, 2011) has revealed that higher rates of conformity in collectivistic cultures may be partially related to the historical prevalence of dangerous pathogens in their environment as compared to the ecologies of individualistic ones. That is, discouraging unusual and/or independent behavior may help prevent the spread of illness and disease.

Other Factors Influencing Conformity

There are many factors in addition to culture that are significantly related to conformity in the Asch line judgment paradigm, such as group size and unanimity. Asch (1956) found that conformity dramatically increased as the number of group members (not counting the participant) grew from one to three but then changed little and leveled off all the way up to 15 (his largest group). One reason that continually increasing group size does not lead to more conformity is that the lone minority member may not find the growing consensus to be believable (Insko, 1985). Variations in the unanimity of the group exerted a greater influence on conformity than did group size, such that the presence of a single dissenter significantly decreased conformity, even when the dissenter gave a different incorrect answer (Asch, 1955; Mori & Arai, 2010).

A multitude of other factors can also affect conformity. For instance, recent research has shown that people who hold power feel less pressure to conform (Galinsky, Magee, Gruenfeld, Whitson, & Liljenquist, 2008), that people who recently shared an experience with a partner conform less to that partner (Pinel, Long, & Crimin, 2010), and that older children conform less than younger children (Walker & Andrade, 1996). In an intriguing study of conformity and motivation, self-protection, and mate attraction, Griskevicius, Goldstein, Mortensen, Cialdini, & Kenrick (2006) found that, although conformity was greater for both men and women when self-protection was salient, men conformed less and women conformed more when trying to impress potential opposite sex romantic partners.

So far we have focused on conformity that, by virtue of its conscious nature, reflects the exercise of free will and the operation of the C-system. However, like so many other forms of social behavior, conformity can also occur nonconsciously or automatically via the X-system, with little or no involvement of the C-system. Research by Chartrand and Bargh (Chartrand & Bargh, 1999) on the **chameleon effect** shows how people sometimes mimic the movements of others without conscious awareness of doing so. In one study, participants paired with another person nonconsciously mirrored that person's facial expressions, postures, and mannerisms (e.g., shaking one's foot, rubbing one's face). This chameleon effect was more pronounced for people high in empathy (Chartrand & Bargh, 1999). Unfortunately, such mimicry isn't confined to these innocuous behaviors but has also been manifested in conformity to negative racial and gender stereotypes held by a person who mimicked the target (Leander, Chartrand, & Wood, 2011). Nonconscious activation of concepts relating to conformity can also increase behavioral matching (Epley & Gilovich, 1999). For instance, priming participants for either conformity or anarchy via exposure to a photo and description of either an accountant or punk rocker, respectively, produced more (or less) conformity (Pendry & Carrick, 2001).

Chameleon Effect: When people mimic the movements of others without conscious awareness of doing so

Neuroscience and Conformity

Advances in neuroscience have allowed researchers to examine some of the neurophysiological correlates of behavioral conformity (Berns et al., 2005; Harris & Fiske, 2009; Reimann & Zimbardo, 2011; Schnuerch & Gibbons, 2014). Utilizing a mental rotation task, Berns et al. (2005) found that conforming to group pressure was associated with a specific pattern of brain activation (see text box).

The Neuroscience of Conformity

Berns et al. (2005) asked participants to determine whether or not a three-dimensional object could be mentally rotated to match a comparison object. Following the Asch (1956) line judgment paradigm, the true participant went last, after the four confederates who unanimously gave some incorrect answers. Participants made errors on 41% of the trials in which the group gave incorrect answers compared with only 13.8% when performing the task on their own. Brain imaging revealed that conforming to group pressure increased activation of the occipital-parietal network, whereas independent responding was associated with the amygdala and caudate, two brain areas previously linked to fear and apprehension.

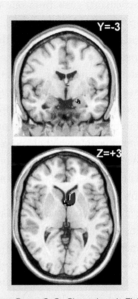

Photo from Berns, G. S., Chappelow, J., Zink, C. F., Pagnoni, G., Martin-Skurski, M. E., & Richards, J. (2005). Neurobiological Correlates of Social Conformity and Independence During Mental Rotation. *Biological Psychiatry, 58*(3), 245-253.

OBEDIENCE AND THE AUTHORITY PRINCIPLE

In a fascinating, if disturbing, article titled "The Education of a Torturer," Janice Gibson and Mika Haritos-Fatouros describe how otherwise ordinary citizens can be transformed into cold-hearted, uncaring people willing to dehumanize fellow humans (Gibson & Haritos-Fatouros, 1986; Haritos-Fatouros, 1995). During the 1960s and 1970s, Greek military police were systematically trained to torture their prisoners; these individuals—recruited from the regular military ranks for this purpose—learned to obey even the most heinous of commands from their military superiors and inflicted maximum pain on their vulnerable captives. Gibson and Haritos-Fatouros examined official military training procedures and court testimony from 21 former soldiers provided at their criminal trials for their torture-related crimes, and also interviewed 16 of them (Gibson & Haritos-Fatouros, 1986). In the process of examining their evidence they identified several elements that were keys to the training's effectiveness—and to leading otherwise good people toward the dark side of morality (Arrigo & Wagner, 2007; Suedfeld, 2007).

The education of the torturers began during the initial induction of regular soldiers into the military police; commanders recruited individuals who had both the requisite physical strength and fervent anti-communist political beliefs (their prisoners were likely to be communists). Further selection procedures ensured that only men who "kept their mouth

SELF-REFLECTION 6.1
Attitudes Toward Torture (Part 1)

How do you feel about torture? Is it ever justified? Does it work? The role of torture in a democratic society committed to promoting and protecting human rights has been hotly debated in the United States and around the world. Take a couple of minutes to reflect on your own attitudes toward and beliefs about torture and then answer the following questions. Next turn the page to see how others have responded and what experts say about torture.

TABLE 6.3   Attitudes Toward Torture

Item	Response options				
1. Clear rules against torture are crucial because any use of torture is immoral and will weaken international human rights.	Strongly disagree	Disagree	Undecided	Agree	Strongly agree
2. Torture is sometimes necessary and acceptable to gain information that may protect the public.	Strongly disagree	Disagree	Undecided	Agree	Strongly agree
3. If I were taken into custody by the authorities in my country, I am confident that I would be safe from torture.	Strongly disagree	Disagree	Undecided	Agree	Strongly agree
4. Following the September 11th, 2001 terrorist attacks, the U.S. government used interrogation methods that many consider to be torture on people suspected of terrorism. Were these methods justified or not justified?	Justified	Not Justified		Don't Know	

Questions 1–3 from International, A. (2014). *Attitudes to torture*. London: Amnesty International. https://www.amnesty.org/en/documents/act40/005/2014/en/

Question 4 from Center, P. R. (2015). Global publics back US on fighting ISIS, but are critical of post-9/11 torture. http://www.pewglobal.org/2015/06/23/methodology-5/

TURN THE PAGE TO FIND OUR ANSWERS.

SELF-REFLECTION 6.2
Attitudes Toward Torture (Part 2)

The first three questions are from Amnesty International's 2014 *Global Survey of Attitudes Toward Torture* that received responses from over 21,000 people in 21 nations (2014). The last one is drawn from the Pew Center for Research's 2015 attitude survey (2015). As you can see, people in different parts of the world have differing perspectives.

Question 1: Overall, 82% of respondents either somewhat agree or strongly agree that there should be international rules against torture. People in South Korea (89%), Greece (89%), and Canada (88%) most strongly oppose it, whereas those in Peru (71%), Argentina (72%), and India (73%) least strongly oppose it. Only 6% worldwide strongly oppose it. In the United States, 77% either somewhat or strongly agree, whereas 20% somewhat/strongly disagree.

Question 2: Worldwide, only 36% of respondents strongly/somewhat agree that torture is sometimes necessary, whereas 51% strongly/somewhat disagree. Respondents in China (74%), India (74%), and Kenya (66%) were most supportive, whereas those in Greece (12%), Argentina (15%), and Spain (17%) were most opposed. In the United States, 45% strongly/somewhat agree, and 53% strongly/somewhat disagree.

Question 3: Worldwide, 44% of people strongly/somewhat strongly disagreed, meaning they would not feel safe from torture in their own country. People feared torture the most in Brazil (80%), Mexico (64%), and Turkey, Pakistan, and Kenya (all 58%) and feared it the least in the United Kingdom (15%), Australia (16%), and Canada (21%). In the United States, 32% did not feel safe from torture.

Question 4: Worldwide, 50% of respondents indicated that it was not justified. The most supportive nations were Uganda (68%), the United States and Tanzania (58%), and Israel and Kenya (57%). Nations most strongly opposed to the U.S. methods were Venezuela (76%), Argentina (75%), Palestinian Territory (69%), and Germany (68%).

Does torture produce useful information that will save the lives of innocent people? Most experts agree that it does not (Hajjar, 2009)

shut," had demonstrated significant aggressive tendencies, were intelligent, and were loyal only to their superiors, and followed orders without question were recruited as torturers (Gibson & Haritos-Fatouros, 1986, p. 51). It was important that the soldiers feel "bound" to the superiors in such a way that they would feel comfortable with blind, unquestioning obedience. Commanders accomplished such binding through severe physical and verbal abuse of the recruits, by explaining the importance of their new mission, how lucky they were to be selected for it, and by continuously demeaning anyone not in this "elite" group. Before directly participating in abusive practices, the trainees had brief, incidental contact with brutalized prisoners and later were forced to watch others engage in torture.

Subsequently, they were individually required to use limited force on prisoners and later administer more severe punishment in groups. Slowly the soldiers became desensitized to violence, pain, and bloodshed. In addition to "binding" the recruits to their commanders, the latter also needed to overcome the "strain" of obedience experienced by the recruits—the difficulty they would have in engaging in activities that in the absence of such pressures most of them would find repulsive and, consequently, refuse to enact. That is, in order for the trainees to emotionally detach themselves from their own cruel behavior, they had to categorize their victims as less-than-human enemies of the Greeks. Unfortunately, such abusive practices are more widespread than we would like. A 2015 Amnesty International report documents instances of torture in dozens of nations around the world (2015).

Imagine you answer an ad in the local newspaper offering to pay you a small amount of money to participate in a study of the effects of punishment on learning. When you arrive at the designated building on the campus of Yale University, you and a fellow participant unknown to you are greeted by a clean-cut, white male experimenter in a lab coat. The experimenter explains that one of you will be assigned the role of teacher and the other of learner, and after drawing slips of paper from a hat you are selected as the teacher. After some introductory remarks about the study, the experimenter connects electrodes to the learner—who informs the experimenter that he has a heart condition—and then explains the procedure (see Figure 6.4). You are to test the learner's ability to remember word pairs, and each time he gives an incorrect response you are instructed to shock him. The generator has 30 switches that progress from 15 volts to 450 volts and are labeled on graded scale from *slight shock* to *danger: severe shock* and finally simply with *XXX*. Before beginning the testing procedure, the experimenter gives you a 45-volt shock to show you that the generator is authentic. In the primary, voice feedback condition, the teacher and learner are in different rooms and are unable to see one another, although they can hear each other via microphones.

During testing, the learner gives some correct and some incorrect answers and responds to the shock with progressively emphatic and pained verbalizations. While he simply says "Ugh!" after feeling 75 volts, his complaints escalate along with the voltage, eventually including such statements as "Experimenter, get me out of here! I refuse to go on!," "I can't stand the pain!," "My heart's bothering me!," "Let me out of here! Let me out of here!" as you administer escalating levels of shocks. Finally, after receiving 330 volts, the learner neither provides an answer nor makes any sound at all. Throughout the study, whenever you hesitated to deliver shocks and/or asked the experimenter if you should stop, he prodded you to continue with statements like "Please continue" or "The experiment must go on."

What is the maximum number of volts that you would have delivered before refusing to continue? Milgram (1974) asked a group of psychiatrists to predict the results, and they thought that virtually all participants would stop at or before 150 volts and that only one in a thousand would give the maximum shock. These estimates were unduly optimistic. Milgram conducted a number of variations of this experiment, and in the version

FIGURE 6.4   Milgram's Obedience Research

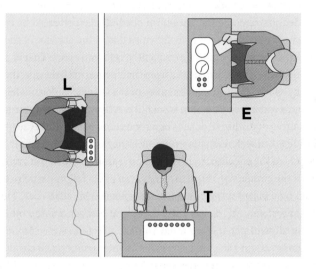

The Teacher (T), Learner (L), and Experimenter (E) in the baseline Milgram Experiment

described above, called the voice feedback condition, 62.5% of the participants were completely obedient, with the average highest voltage being 360. Think about that: in the United States, the typical wall outlet is 110 volts, and most participants went well beyond this level—they essentially continued shocking the learner long after he could have been unconscious or dead! Of course, as you may have guessed, none of the learners in Milgram's studies received any actual shock; all were confederates, and their responses were predetermined and, where possible, prerecorded.

Several alternative designs allowed Milgram to test a number of hypotheses about factors that may impact the degree of obedience and disobedience. For instance, Milgram varied the proximity or immediacy of the learner or victim to the teacher so that he was either in a different room (the voice feedback condition, described above), in the same room (the proximity condition), or in the same room with the additional requirement that the teacher physically force the learner's hand onto the shock plate (the touch-proximity condition). Not surprisingly, obedience decreased from 62.5% to 40% and to 30%, respectively (Milgram, 1974). Emotional distancing—the ability of the teacher to emotionally separate himself from the plight of the learner—was more difficult as the victim and evidence of his pain were more immediate, and therefore obedience decreased as proximity increased (Epley & Waytz, 2010; Haslam, Loughnan, Kashima, & Bain, 2008; Waytz & Epley, 2012).

Recent research has identified neural correlates of such emotional distancing: The medial prefrontal cortex—typically activated when individuals are trying to understand the mind of another person—appears to be less involved when the perceptual target is from a negatively viewed group (Harris & Fiske, 2011). Instead, the insula and amygdala regions associated with fear and disgust show increased activity when the target is a member of a dehumanized group. Related studies have pinpointed additional areas of the brain involved in empathizing with victims' suffering as a result of the actions of the self or other (Cheetham, Pedroni, Angus, Slater, & Jäncke, 2009; Decety & Ickes, 2009), a topic to which we will return in Chapter 8.

What led to such remarkable obedience? In a word, authority. As conceptualized by Cialdini (2008), the **authority principle** states that perceived authority of the source will increase the likelihood that people will do what is requested or suggested. The authority principle thus helps to explain **obedience**—a behavioral response to a direct request from an authority. At an abstract level, Milgram hypothesized that several factors contribute to obedience. One is *binding,* which refers to the strength of the bond formed between the teacher and learner or leader and follower and results in the subordinate person feeling obligated to obey and uncomfortable with disobeying. The second is the *strain* the subordinate experiences that stems from engaging in repulsive behavior (administering painful shocks) that, in the absence of significant social pressure, he would not enact. A third stems from the personal background of the individual: his religious upbringing, family experiences, schools, culture, and so forth.

In addition, there were a number of specific features of the authority as constructed by Milgram that also affected levels of obedience. First of all, the experimenter reassured the anxious teacher that he would take responsibility for harm to the learner caused by the shocks. Second, the experimenter wore a lab coat—a clear symbol of authority (Bickman, 1974; Cialdini, 2008; Milgram, 1974). Third, the initial studies took place at Yale University, a highly respected institution that further legitimized the authority of the experimenter. In fact, when the experiment was instead held in an ordinary office building in a nearby city, obedience dropped to 48% (Milgram, 1974). Fourth, Milgram varied the influence of the authority on the teacher by reducing their proximity: The experimenter, although initially in the same room as the teacher, left and gave instructions via the telephone. Not only did obedience decrease to 20.5%, but many participants lied to the experimenter, giving less shock than what they reported over the phone. In addition, when the person ordering the teacher to give the shocks was dressed in street clothes, obedience was just 20% (Milgram, 1974).

Again, I ask you, the reader, to consider how you would respond in each of these conditions. Not only do my students typically state that they would not obey the authority, they often argue that people of today think for themselves and are more likely to ignore authority. But have people become less obedient in the 21st century? In order to find out, social psychologist Jerry Burger (2009) conducted a partial replication of Milgram's experiments in 2006 at Santa Clara University in California. To avoid some of the ethical issues raised by the Milgram studies (see *Doing Research: Deception and Ethics in Psychological Research* below), Burger made some important modifications to the procedure while retaining its essential features. Before delving into the details of Burger's studies, let's review some of the ethical issues related to the original studies.

Authority Principle: Increased likelihood that people will do what is requested or suggested by a perceived authority

Obedience: Behavioral response to a request from an authority

SOCIAL PSYCHOLOGY APPLIED TO LAW
COERCED CONFESSIONS

In September 2012, Damon Theibodeaux was released after 16 years of imprisonment—15 in solitary confinement—after being cleared of the murder of a Philadelphia optometrist that he did not commit (The Innocence Project, 2015b). In March, 2014, Glenn Ford was released after three decades in prison on death row when he was declared innocent of 1983 murder of an elderly jewelry shop owner in Louisiana (Bookman, 2013). Both of these men were convicted after confessing to these crimes, despite the fact that there was no direct evidence linking them to the crimes. These false confessions and 100s more like them raise a fascinating question about human psychology while revealing a fundamental flaw in the U.S. justice system. We need to ask why do people admit to crimes that they did not—*in many cases could not have* committed (Feld, 2013; Poole, Bruck, & Pipe, 2011; Russano, Meissner, Narchet, & Kassin, 2005)?

Saul Kassin, a social psychologist and one of the foremost experts in the psychology of false confessions, has extensively examined this problem in laboratory experiments and via case studies (Kassin et al., 2010; Kassin & Gudjonsson, 2004; Kassin & Kiechel, 1996; Kukucka & Kassin, 2014). In one lab study, participants were accused of striking an incorrect key on a computer keyboard during

AP Photo/ Uncredited.

a reaction time task, which they were (falsely) told caused the researcher to lose the experimental data (Kassin & Kiechel, 1996). Participants completed either a fast-paced or slow-paced version of the task, and for half of the participants, a fellow participant—actually a confederate of the experimenter—(falsely) claimed she saw the participant make the mistake. All participants were asked to admit their guilt by signing a confession. Over two thirds of the participants agreed to do so, and even more did so when the error was "witnessed" and the task was fast paced. Perhaps more importantly, many of the participants actually thought they were guilty, again especially in the fast-paced/ witness condition. Some participants confessed to an action that they did not perform and truly believed that they had done so. Although the external validity of this study is in doubt, false confessions are common in the real world. For instance, in 330 cases of exoneration examined by The Innocence Project (2015a) approximately one fourth of the individuals falsely confessed to the murder.

Why does this happen? Kassin et al. (2010) summarize the most important situational risk factors, including physical custody and isolation from others, the presentation of false evidence by interrogators, suggestions by interrogators that the judge and/or prosecutors will be lenient if they confess. They also identified a number of dispositional risk factors, including youth and immaturity, cognitive and intellectual disabilities, and actual innocence. Given the potentially serious consequences of false confessions, the obvious public policy question is what can be done to minimize their likelihood? Suggestions from experts have ranged from electronic recording of all interrogations, shifting the presumption of guilt of suspects to the presumption of innocence, and making the interrogation less confrontational (Gudjonsson & Pearse, 2011; Kassin et al., 2010; Kassin & Gudjonsson, 2004; Narchet, Meissner, & Russano, 2011; Russano et al., 2005)

Think Again!

1. *What is obedience?*

2. *What is the authority principle?*

3. *What is emotional distancing in the context of obedience research?*

DOING RESEARCH: DECEPTION AND ETHICS IN RESEARCH

Many of the studies described in this chapter, including the conformity and obedience research, relied on misleading participants about important elements of the experimental situation. More generally, deception is an important feature of the vast majority of social psychological experiments (Epley & Huff, 1998; Hertwig & Ortmann, 2008). This widespread use of deception, along with the problem of potential harm to our research participants, has created an ongoing and important ethical discussion in social psychology (Baumrind, 1964; Kimmel, 2004; Miller, 2004b; Nicholson, 2011). In this section, we'll review the major elements of the controversy, touching on the arguments both for and against the use of deception. Afterward we will return to the Milgram paradigm and show how Burger (2009) tried to address these issues in his replication studies.

The most serious ethical objection to certain social psychological research is its potential to inflict psychological harm on its participants. Imagine, for example, how you would feel if you had just administered a 450-volt shock to an innocent person, despite his loud complaints of pain and emphatic desire to stop the experiment. Would you be upset? Feel guilty? Ashamed? Fortunately, as we'll describe in Chapter 8, a number of safeguards are now in place to prevent experiments like the obedience and prison studies from being conducted. Milgram himself was aware of the potential danger to participants and did probe for possible negative consequences, concluding that there was no irreparable harm as a result of his research (Blass, 2004; Milgram, 1974). However, a recent groundbreaking book by Australian researcher Gina Perry has uncovered compelling evidence that Milgram neither adequately explained the deception in his research nor fully explored its ill effects on the participants (Perry, 2012).

In addition to the primary threat of direct psychological harm to research participants, there is an additional risk that they may feel foolish or stupid for having been tricked and not having "seen through" the deception (Baumrind, 1964). Moreover, concern has been raised that the deception itself is disrespectful, manipulative, and inappropriate, regardless of the actual experiences of the participants (Baumrind, 1964; Cook & Yamagishi, 2008; Kelman, 1967; Stricker, 1967). These questions have bled into a related discussion about whether deception is necessary at all (Aronson, Wilson, & Brewer, 1998; Hertwig & Ortmann, 2008; Kelman, 1967).

The use of deception and the fact of possible risks of research participation together present an *ethical dilemma* for social psychologists: How can we conduct research that explores sensitive and controversial elements of peoples' thoughts, feelings, and behavior in a way that is valid and treats humans with the utmost dignity and respect? Some have argued that it may be essential to prevent participants from knowing the true purpose of an experiment while participating in the research, yet such deception may undermine the autonomy, integrity, and free will of those participants (Baumrind, 1964; Kelman, 1967; Kimmel, 2004; Rosnow & Rosenthal, 1997). One way to address this dilemma is to conduct an *a priori* analysis of the potential benefits and costs of deception (Rosnow & Rosenthal, 1999). Social psychologists Rosnow and Rosenthal (1997) created a graphical representation of how such a cost/benefit analysis may be performed (see Figure 6.5). As illustrated in the table, there are cases where the costs clearly outweigh the benefits and the research should not be conducted—such as the case of the Milgram obedience studies (Position A). In contrast, most studies include minimal or no risk of harm, and may be implemented (Position D). However, some studies fall along the diagonal of indecision (B–C line) and require more careful consideration and oversight on the part of both the researchers and regulatory bodies.

Need for Deception

Recall the research on belief perseverance in Chapter 3 in which participants were given fabricated data about the relationship between fire-fighting success and preference for

FIGURE 6.5   The Costs and Benefits of Deception

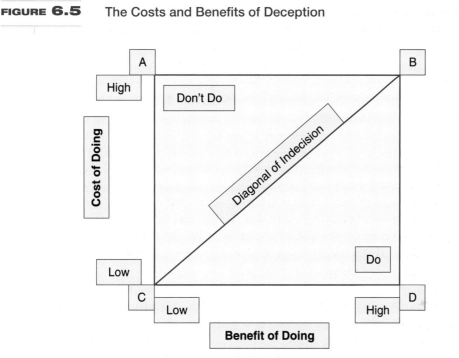

Rosnow & Rosenthal's (1999) cost-benefit analysis matrix. When the costs are high and the benefits low, the research should not be done. When the benefits are high and the costs low, it should be done. The difficult decisions fall near the diagonal of indecision.

Source: Adapted from Rosnow, R. L., & Rosenthal, R. *Beginning behavioral research: A conceptual primer* (3rd ed.). Copyright © 1999. Printed and electronically reproduced by permission of Pearson Education, Inc., New York, New York.

risk (Ross, Lepper, & Hubbard, 1975). One of the keys to producing valid conclusions about belief perseverance is that participants not be aware of the true purpose of the experiment. Do you think that participants would have reacted differently had they known that the beliefs they reported after the evidence was discredited were the real focus of interest? Had they been informed ahead of time or been able to guess the true nature of the experiment, it is likely that they would have changed their answers to appear more rational. In many cases, if the participant knows the purpose, she may either deliberately or unintentionally alter her responses and, as a result, undermine the validity of the research results.

For instance, in one study female participants were asked to report their beliefs about traditional versus nontraditional gender roles prior to meeting a highly desirable or less desirable male (Zanna & Pack, 1975). Next they were informed that the male held either traditional or nontraditional beliefs about gender roles. Zanna and Park hypothesized that women would be more likely to alter their self-reported gender role beliefs to match those of the desirable rather than those of the less desirable male. This was in fact the case. When expecting to meet the desirable male, women skewed their self-reports so that their gender role beliefs would be more similar to the male; however, the women meeting the less desirable male, the comparison condition, showed no such tendency.

Do you think that the results would have been the same had the women known what was truly being tested? If they were aware that the malleability of their beliefs was under scrutiny, would they have changed their responses? It is possible that some women would have deliberately undermined the experimenters' hypotheses and held steadfast in their beliefs, regardless of whether they were expecting to meet the desirable or less desirable man. Others may instead have tried to confirm those hypotheses. Moreover, there really was no "man" to meet (i.e., he was fictional), and had the participants been aware of this, they might have taken the experiment less seriously. As you can see, much of the research in social psychology would be difficult, if not impossible, to conduct without the use of deception.

Researchers use deception to mask a number of aspects of their experiments, and consequently the extent of deception ranges from mild to very significant. Participants may simply be given incomplete information about the experiment to prevent them from correctly guessing the hypotheses, even if other elements of the experiment are faithfully shared with participants. For instance, participants may not be told that their interactions with other participants are being recorded by a camera. A different situation occurs when the experimenter provides false information about one or more aspects of the experiment, such as when the participant is led to believe that one behavior is of primary interest when a different one is. For example, participants may be told the researcher is interested in how quickly they can complete a word puzzle, yet the researcher is actually testing how elements of the word puzzle affect a subsequent task. Some deceptive research also incorporates a **confederate** who pretends to be a naïve participant but is actually working with the experimenter, such as in Asch (1956) conformity and the Milgram (1974) obedience studies.

Confederate:
Person who pretends to be a participant but is really working with the experimenter

At other times, researchers may lead experimental participants to develop specific beliefs that they otherwise would be unlikely to hold. Sometimes these beliefs may focus on the self, such as information indicating that the participant failed a task or is lacking in an ability. All in all, most social psychologists would argue that deception is frequently necessary, even if not always preferred, in order to conduct valid experimental research.

OBEDIENCE IN THE 21ST CENTURY: MILGRAM REVISITED

As I mentioned above, many of my students are skeptical about the likelihood that they or their contemporaries would be as obedient as Milgram's participants in the 1960s. Of course we must ask the obvious question: *Why* would we expect people to respond differently now, especially given what we know about the power of the situation to influence human behavior? To assume that "we are different" today is essentially to commit the fundamental attribution error discussed in Chapter 4: ascribing the obedience of Milgram's participants to personal rather than situational forces. As mentioned earlier, social psychologist Jerry Burger wondered about this too and predicted that obedience levels would *not* change substantially in comparison to the original studies.

To test this, Burger (2009) performed what up to that time had seemed unthinkable: a replication of Milgram's obedience to authority research paradigm. In 2006, after having received IRB approval, Burger copied the key elements of Milgram's research, implementing a number of changes designed to safeguard participants without compromising experimental validity. He followed guidelines established by the American Psychological Association (APA, 2010) pertaining to informed consent, approval from his Institutional Review Board (IRB), and notifying participants of their right to withdraw from the study without penalty. Furthermore, the experiment was stopped once a participant-teacher agreed to "shock" the learner with more than 150 volts. Moreover, participants were screened by a clinical psychologist ahead of time, and the experimenter who gave the commands was a clinical psychologist who planned to terminate the procedure if a participant showed signs of excessive distress. Whether or not the safeguards that Burger implemented fully protected his participants and legitimized the experiments as "ethical" remains controversial (Nicholson, 2011).

Prior to proposing his research, Burger carefully analyzed Milgram's data, noting that 79% of the participants in the original research who chose to administer at least 150 volts also elected to give the maximum of 450 volts (Packer, 2008). Burger (2009) predicted and found the percentage of participants agreeing to the 165-volt shock to be comparable to that in Milgram's research (70% versus 82.5%, a difference that was not statistically significant). In addition to the male-participant base conditions, Burger, like Milgram, also placed females in the role of teacher. In the original study and replications as well as a number of conceptual replications conducted by other researchers, no meaningful gender differences were found (Blass, 2000). Are you surprised? In sum and contrary to what most of my students and their contemporaries claim, no clear evidence exists demonstrating that obedience has declined over the last five decades (Blass, 2004; Twenge, 2006, 2009).

Factors Influencing the Power of Authority

As you may expect, most people are disconcerted by the ability of the authorities in the research described above to produce such destructive obedience. Although simply evoking "authority" as the explanatory mechanism is accurate and, perhaps, satisfying, the story is more complicated (Miller, 2004b; Staub, 1989). Researchers need to identify specific features of these authority-related situations if we are to better understand the nature of obedience. For instance, some authorities derive their power from their assumed expertise—what French and Raven (1959) call *expert power*—in which people follow requests from an authority because they believe the authority "knows what is best." Another factor impacting obedience concerns the "symbols" of authority (Bushman, 1984; Cialdini, 2008)—features that often accompany and seemingly legitimize their right to direct the behavior of others. For instance, the garb worn by authorities, such as a white lab coat (Milgram, 1965) or police uniform (Bickman, 1974; Bushman, 1984, 1988) can increase obedience, as can "trappings" that suggest that a person is an authority, such as a business suit (Bushman, 1984). Finally, titles like "doctor" may confer automatic authority and increase obedience, even if they are erroneous (Hofling, Brotzman, Dalrymple, Graves, & Pierce, 1966).

In addition to the characteristics of the authority, features of the situation may enhance his or her power. One crucial element facilitating destructive obedience is the escalating manner in which the authority requests behavior change (Baumeister, 1996; Burger, 2009; A. G. Miller, 2004a; Zimbardo, 2007). As Milgram (1974) noted, critical to the obedience experiments was the fact that the teacher-participants initially administered a relatively insignificant shock to the learner, only gradually increasing the level and consequent (perceived) pain. Had the experimenter at first asked the participants to give, say, a 200- or 300-volt shock, it is quite likely that most or all would have refused (Gilbert, 1981). Such gradated requests are similarly effective in the training of torturers (Haritos-Fatouros, 1995) and, more innocently, in the foot-in-the-door procedure (Cialdini, 2008; Freedman & Fraser, 1966), and each of these similarly relies on the commitment/consistency principle.

The Power of the Situation Revisited: Culture, Gender, Personality

Do you think that obedience, like conformity, varies across cultures? In a recent review of the cross-cultural research on obedience in the Milgram paradigm, Blass (2012) found that obedience rates, on average, did not differ between the United States and other countries (see Table 6.4). Thus, obedience to authority within the Milgram paradigm has not been shown to be greatly influenced by cultural factors. Note, however, that Blass neither systematically identified nor examined any specific cultural variables (e.g., individualism-collectivism), and we should be cautious before concluding that culture is unrelated to obedience more generally.

One of the lessons of the research on this chapter is the power that situations have to shape peoples' thoughts, feelings, and behaviors (Asch, 1955; Benjamin & Simpson, 2009; Zimbardo, 2007). As we've seen, situational pressures can drive people to engage in what outsiders consider horrendous and immoral behavior (Fiske, Harris, & Cuddy, 2004; Milgram, 1965). Nevertheless, social psychologists argue that while situations matter, so do individuals (Ross & Nisbett, 1991). Research has examined a number of personal or dispositional variables, including gender, that may affect conformity and obedience. Consistent with the original research, virtually all replications of Milgram's focal study have found no differences in obedience based upon the sex of the participant, although women do seem to experience more personal discomfort and anxiety when shocking the learner (Blass, 1999, 2012; Milgram, 1974). The evidence is somewhat mixed when it comes to conformity. One large meta-analysis by Eagly and Carli (1981) found that women are slightly more likely to

TABLE 6.4   Obedience Across Cultures

U.S. Studies		Studies Outside the United States		
Author(s)	% Obedience Rate	Author(s)	Country	% Obedience Rate
Milgram (1974) (Average of 7 conditions)	56.43	Ancona & Pareyson (1968)	Italy	85
Holland (1967)	75	Edwards et al. (1969)	South Africa	87.5
Rosenhan (1969)	85	Mantell (1971)	Germany	85
Podd (1970)	31	Kilham & Mann (1974)	Australia	28
Ring et al. (1970)	91	Shanab & Yahya (1977)	Jordan	73
Bock (1972)	40	Shanab & Yahya (1978)	Jordan	62.5
Powers & Green (1972)	83	Miranda et al. (1981)	Spain	50
Rogers (1973)	37	Gupta (1983) (average of 4 conditions)	India	42.5
Shalala (1974)	30	Schurz (1985)	Austria	80
Costanza (1976)	81			

U.S. Mean Obedience = 60.94   Non-U.S. Mean Obedience = 65.94

Source: Adapted from Table 1 in Blass, T. (2012). A cross-cultural comparison of studies of obedience using the Milgram paradigm: A review. *Social and Personality Psychology Compass, 6*(2), 196–205.

conform than men, but this difference may be limited to situations in which men are more confident than women regarding how people should behave (Sistrunk & McDavid, 1971). Eagly (1987) has argued that the influence of gender on conformity may be related to the social roles that women and men have traditionally held rather than to genetic factors. That is, women have historically served in positions with lower status than have men and as a result have "learned" to go along in many situations.

What about personality factors? Here, too, the evidence for individual differences is underwhelming. Burger's (2009) examined two personality variables, empathic concern and desire for control, and found that neither predicted obedience rates. Some evidence suggests that the persons who are high in the need for uniqueness—to be different from others—may be less likely to conform to social pressures (Imhoff & Erb, 2009). Recent research by Bègue et al. (2015) shows that people who are higher in conscientious and/or agreeableness were willing to administer higher intensity shocks in a Milgram-like experiment. Sturman (2011) argues that there are individual differences in the tendency for "involuntary subordination," although he does not connect this to obedience to authority *per se*. Lavine (2009) has raised the interesting possibility that personality characteristics relevant to obedience in the Milgram paradigm may vary along with culture. He argues that European nations differed in their willingness to collaborate with the Nazis during the Holocaust, and that this may have been due to underlying characteristics that have not been examined in the context of obedience but that may help to explain it (Lavine, 2009). Finally, even if researchers have not always been able to identify the specific dispositional characteristics that are influential in particular situations or studies, we must continually remind ourselves of one of social psychology's guiding principles: Social behavior is a product of both personal and situational factors.

Think Again!

1. *Why did Burger's (2009) obedience study stop at 150 volts?*

2. *What is meant by the "trappings" of authority?*

3. *What does the evidence suggest about the relationship between gender and conformity?*

FINAL THOUGHTS: THE UPSIDES OF COMPLIANCE, OBEDIENCE, AND CONFORMITY

Much of the research on compliance, conformity, and obedience has focused on the negative or destructive outcomes of succumbing to these influences. However, if acquiescing to social influence produced only undesirable consequences, would it make sense, from an evolutionary perspective, that successful influence would be so ubiquitous? That is, if the core components of human psychology are the product of natural selection, then susceptibility to social influence *must* also be, on balance, adaptive. This line of reasoning is consistent with one of the fundamental principles of social psychology: that human social behavior is purposive.

Given this, what are some of the benefits of social influence? First, other people often have more information than we do, and following their requests, directives, or behavior can help us make the correct or best choices (Ent & Baumeister, 2014). Second, the need to be accepted or approved by others is of paramount importance to human emotional well-being, and often following the preferences or behaviors of others—such as by conforming—generates and strengthens meaningful social connections (Cacioppo & Patrick, 2008). Consequently, we feel better about ourselves and boost our self-esteem through our relationships to other people.

Throughout this chapter you've seen how the topic of social influence relates to four of our fundamental questions: independence, sociality, free will, and morality. *Independence* (and its lack—compliance, conformity, and obedience) is the central focus of the chapter. Conformity is often the result of our *sociality*—our need for the approval of others in order to create and/or maintain social ties. *Free will* hangs in the background of our discussion of conscious and nonconscious processes. Lastly, we have described how social forces can distort people's *moral* behavior by influencing them to act in unethical and harmful ways.

CORE CONCEPTS

- People succumb to social influence in order to be correct, accepted, and/or consistent; persuasion, compliance, conformity, and obedience are different types of influence.

- The six principles undergird most instances of social influence are scarcity, liking/friendship, commitment/consistency, reciprocity, social validation, and authority. The limited-quantity and deadline techniques work because people react to scarcity; the labeling and bait-and-switch tactics and FITD take advantage of people's need for consistency; the DITF is based on reciprocity.

- According to the focus theory of normative conduct, social norms-based interventions are most successful when descriptive and injunctive norms are in alignment. Sherif's research on the autokinetic effect, Asch's line judgment studies, and the Stanford Prison Experiment illustrate the power of social norms and conformity; nevertheless, dispositional factors also play a key role in explaining social behavior.

- The classic Milgram studies demonstrate the power of authority to command obedience and also show how factors such as proximity of the authority and immediacy of the victim impact obedience rates. Burger conducted an important replication of the Milgram research, demonstrating that obedience levels, at least in the United States, have not changed that much over time.

- The Zimbardo and Milgram research raised a number of ethical concerns, including the risk of psychological harm to participants. Psychologists are sometimes confronted with an *ethical dilemma* when balancing the tradeoffs between research goals and treating participants ethically.

- The power of authority to garner obedience is affected by factors such as expert power, symbols of authority, and the gradual escalation of the negative effects of enacting the prescribed behavior; although culture can influence obedience levels, the roles of gender and personality in obedience are uncertain.

➤ $SAGE edge™ Test your understanding of chapter content. Take the practice quiz. edge.sagepub.com/barrett

KEY TERMS

Authority Principle, 215
Bait-and-Switch, 196
Chameleon Effect, 209
Commitment/
    Consistency
    Principle, 193
Compliance, 192
Confederate , 220
Conformity, 200
Deadline Technique, 193
Descriptive Norm, 201
Door-in-the-Face
    Technique, 197
Focus Theory of Normative
    Conduct, 201

Foot-in-the-Door
    Technique (FITD), 195
Informational
    Influence, 191
Injunctive Norms, 201
Labeling Technique, 196
Liking/Friendship
    Principle, 193
Limited-Quantity
    Technique, 193
Low-Ball Tactic, 196
Normative Influence, 191

Obedience, 215
Persuasion, 191
Reactance, 193
Reciprocity Principle, 197
Scarcity Principle, 193
Social Influence, 190
Social Norm, 201
Social Validation
    (or Social Proof)
    Principle, 199
That's-Not-All
    Technique, 198

➤ $SAGE edge™   Review key terms with eFlashcards. edge.sagepub.com/barrett

THINK FURTHER!

- What are the three goals of social influence?

- Define and give examples of social influence, persuasion, informational influence, and normative influence.

- Name and define the six principles of interpersonal influence. Can you find examples of each in your own life experiences?

- What is conformity? Briefly describe the Sherif, Asch, and Zimbardo studies and explain how they illustrate the conformity.

- List six social norms (three descriptive, three injunctive) that are specific to a certain group or context (such as their family, their residence hall, workplace, etc.). Indicate whether each is positive (good), negative (bad), or neutral, from your perspective.

- How does the Stanford Prison Experiment shed light on the need to consider both personal and situational factors when explaining social behavior?

- What are obedience and the authority principle? Briefly describe the Milgram obedience studies and identify the crucial components that affected obedience.

- What is the ethical dilemma faced by social psychologists with regard to deception in research? What are the arguments for and against the use of deception? When, if ever, do you think it is justified?

SUGGESTED READINGS

Asch, S. E. (1955). Opinions and social pressure. *Scientific American, 193*(5), 31–35.

Blass, T. (2012). A cross-cultural comparison of studies of obedience using the Milgram paradigm: A review. *Social and Personality Psychology Compass, 6,* 196–205.

Cialdini, R. B. (2008). *Influence: Science and practice* (5th ed.). New York, NY: Prentice Hall.

Milgram, S. (1974). *Obedience to authority: An experimental view.* New York, NY: Harper & Row.

Murray, D. R., Trudeau, R., & Schaller, M. (2011). On the origins of cultural differences in conformity: Four tests of the pathogen prevalence hypothesis. *Personality and Social Psychology Bulletin, 37,* 318–329.

7

Attitudes and Persuasion

People often believe more strongly in the truth of a prophecy after it has failed to come true.

Jurgen Schadeberg/Premium Archive/ Getty Images.

LEARNING OBJECTIVES

7.1 Define and illustrate with examples: attitude, belief; ambivalent, indifferent, general, and specific attitudes; compare and contrast implicit and explicit attitudes; summarize the various origins of attitudes, including learning, mere exposure, and heritability.

7.2 Describe the two routes to persuasion and explain the roles of motivation, ability, and relevance in persuasion.

7.3 Identify and define key source characteristics (credibility, attractiveness, likability); explain how fear appeals work; explain the roles of self-monitoring and need for cognition in persuasion.

7.4 Describe how we measure attitudes (direct self-reports, indirect methods).

7.5 Identify the key variables in the reasoned action approach, and describe how they fit into the overall model; explain what kinds of attitudes are more likely to impact behavior.

7.6 Explain the role of consistency in persuasion, including balance theory, dissonance theory, insufficient justification, counter attitudinal advocacy, post-decisional dissonance, the Festinger and Carlsmith (1959) study, role of the self, hypocrisy induction, and self-affirmation.

⑤SAGE edge™

Get the edge on your studies.
edge.sagepub.com/barrett

Take a quiz to find out what you've learned.
Watch videos that enhance chapter content.
Explore related web and social media activities.

WHEN PROPHECIES FAIL

Late in the evening on December 20, 1954, over 20 members of a cult known as The Seekers waited in the living room of a house in greater Chicago for a mysterious visitor who they believed would whisk them off into space via a flying saucer. The Seekers were so certain of the truth of the prophecy told by their leader, Dorothy Martin, that they had given away all of their possessions, quit their jobs, and left their spouses in expectation of escaping earth for a new home in the heavens. The prophecy had been revealed to the group via Martin's "automatic writing"—writing that came from her own hand but over which she claimed she had no conscious control. December 20 was selected as the departure day because a flood would wipe out Chicago beginning in the morning of December 21, and this was The Seekers' chance to avoid that fate. To their shock and anguish, midnight on December 20 approached and then passed uneventfully. Neither visitor nor spaceship arrived and all members were present and accounted for. Shortly after midnight, however, Martin received another message stating that God had spared the earth as a result of the devout activities of The Seekers. Although entertaining in its own right, what makes this story so intriguing from a social psychological perspective are the events that followed the failed prophecy. Furthermore, unlike other prophecies that failed with no one around to study them, we know The Seekers' story because the group was covertly infiltrated and monitored by three social psychologists, Leon Festinger, Henry Riecken, and Stanley Schachter, whose findings are discussed below.

Until that December 21, The Seekers had been very secretive, carefully screening would-be members and eschewing all publicity, including requests for interviews leading up to the big event. Common sense might suggest that, following their major disappointment, the members would quietly return to their normal lives (as much as possible) and forget this misguided adventure. But that is not at all what transpired. Instead, the core group of Seekers garnered as much publicity as they could and tried to recruit new members. Why?

As you can imagine, the utter failure of the prophecy was difficult for the members to psychologically handle. According to Festinger, Riecken, and Schachter (1956), the combination of their prior confidence in their beliefs and the fact they had been clearly mistaken led to psychological discomfort or "cognitive dissonance." One way to deal with the dissonance would have been to abandon their beliefs, which some members did. Yet many members took a different path and instead bolstered their beliefs by convincing or at least trying to convince other people that they were correct. The process of trying to persuade other people of the truth of their beliefs served to strengthen their own beliefs, engaging in a form of self-persuasion in the service of dissonance reduction. The Seekers are not alone in their ability to survive failed prophecies; since then, many other apocalyptic cults have done so, although not always for the same reasons (Cooper, 2012b).

In this chapter, we examine the fundamentals of persuasion, the nature and origins of attitudes, the dominant theory of attitude change, and several variables that play major roles in persuasive communication. Recall from Chapter 6 that **persuasion** is a type of social influence and refers to attitude or belief change that may or may not be related to changes in overt behavior. Toward the end of the chapter, we investigate the important question of the relationship between attitudes and behavior. Along the way we will touch on our four social psychology perspectives and several of our fundamental themes, including free will, rationality, and the self.

Persuasion: Change in attitudes or beliefs

Think Ahead!

1. *What is an attitude?*

2. *Where do attitudes come from and how do they change? Develop?*

3. *How are attitudes and behavior related to one another?*

THE NATURE OF ATTITUDES

What do you think about allowing students to carry concealed weapons on college campuses? What about legalizing prostitution? Using capital punishment? Are you in favor of one or more of these? How you feel about these issues is your attitude toward them. An **attitude** is an evaluation of a person, thing, or idea (see photo on page 231). Attitudes can be positive, negative, neutral, or mixed. That is, you can like a person, dislike a person, or have a neutral evaluation—such as when you don't really know the person and have no opinion. The same options are available for things (e.g., buttery popcorn or Beethoven's Fifth Symphony) or ideas (e.g., freedom of speech, same-sex marriage). Attitudes are generally regarded as different from **beliefs**, which are knowledge claims about what a person thinks is true about a person, thing, or idea (Eagly & Chaiken, 1993; Wyer & Albarracín, 2005). For instance, I can believe that eating popcorn is good for my health, but my attitude towards popcorn could be either positive (because my health is important) or negative (because healthy food is tasteless). More simply, attitudes provide evaluations, and beliefs provide information. This chapter's focus is attitudes rather than beliefs, largely because of the greater attention

Attitude: Positive or negative evaluation of a person, thing, or idea

Belief: Conviction we hold about whether something is true or false

© Owen Franken/Corbis.

Protesters expressing their attitudes about abortion.

that they have received in social psychology. Do note, however, that the psychology of belief is in many ways quite similar to the psychology of attitudes. Beliefs will be discussed in more detail in the context of stereotyping (Chapter 10) and religion (Chapter 13).

Attitudes were originally viewed along a single dimension in the sense that one could favor *or* not favor an attitude object but not both (Allport, 1935; Eagly & Chaiken, 1993). However, we now understand you can have partially favorable and partially unfavorable views of a person, which is called an *ambivalent* attitude (see Table 7.1; Cacioppo, Gardner, & Berntson, 1997). In contrast, if you have neither a favorable or unfavorable attitude, you have an *indifferent* attitude. In short, attitudes don't just range from very positive to neutral to very negative but rather it is possible to have inconsistent (positive and negative) attitudes toward the same person, thing, or idea (Conner & Armitage, 2008). How is this possible? Well, take for example my own attitude toward French fries. I love the taste and therefore positively evaluate one of their features. At the same time, I loathe the fat and calorie content and therefore negatively evaluate other features. Moreover, how the attitude that I express may be affected by the situation, such as which attribute I was focusing on at that moment. In the context of a conversation about healthy eating, I am more likely to emphasize their fat content, whereas my preference for their taste may figure more prominently in a discussion about delicious foods.

Now, you may be thinking that, even though I have favorable along with unfavorable attitudes toward different characteristics of French fries, can't we just "combine" them to produce an overall, global attitude? In many cases the answer is no, for the simple

TABLE 7.1   Attitudes in Evaluative Space

Attitudes can be positive, negative, neutral, or ambivalent.		
	Low Negative	High Negative
High Positive	Positive	Ambivalent
Low Positive	Neutral (Indifferent)	Negative

[1]Source: Adapted from Cacioppo, J. T., Gardner, W. L., & Berntson, G. G. (1997). Beyond bipolar conceptualizations and measures: The case of attitudes and evaluative space. *Personality and Social Psychology Review, 1*(1), 3–25.

reason that if you were to ask me for my attitude, I would be unable to articulate a single one. Rather, I would qualify my response and offer multiple, specific attitudes toward particular attributes of the attitude object. Attitudinal ambivalence is much less likely for polarized or extreme evaluations, such as when a person is vehemently opposed to, say, immigration or bank bailouts (Conner & Armitage, 2008; Costarelli & Gerłowska, 2015a, 2015b). Take a minute and write down examples of your own positive, negative, indifferent, or ambivalent attitudes. Can you think of a couple of examples of each?

Implicit and Explicit Attitudes. In addition to reflecting differences in *valence* or how positive or negative they are, attitudes vary in other important ways. For instance, there may be times when we can articulate just one, unequivocal attitude, but we may simultaneously but not knowingly possess a competing attitude. Recall from Chapter 3 that psychological processes can occur nonconsciously, completely outside of conscious awareness (Bargh, Gollwitzer, Lee-Chai, Barndollar, & Tröschel, 2001). People are aware of and can articulate their **explicit attitudes**. In addition to their explicit attitudes, people also possess **implicit attitudes**, which are attitudes about which a person typically is not aware or conscious (Greenwald & Banaji, 1995; Wilson, Lindsey, & Schooler, 2000). Implicit attitudes may be automatically activated—or primed, as discussed previously—and guide a person's behavior, even if she is not cognizant of their effects (Bassili & Brown, 2005; Dovidio, Kawakami, & Gaertner, 2002).

For instance, say a European American grew up in a family that was overtly racist toward African Americans, but as an adult holds an egalitarian viewpoint and opposes racism. Although she may espouse positive attitudes toward African Americans and try to act in accordance with those, she may nevertheless have developed and continue to harbor negative evaluations of them at a nonconscious level. She may feel some discomfort around members of those groups, without understanding the source of this discomfort (Dovidio et al., 2002; Wilson et al., 2000). When a person holds inconsistent implicit and explicit attitudes toward a person, thing, or idea, he is said to possess **dual attitudes** (Chan & Sengupta, 2010; McConnell & Rydell, 2014; Wilson et al., 2000). Research on the antecedents and consequences of implicit attitudes is thriving in contemporary social psychology (Bassili & Brown, 2005;

Explicit Attitude:
Attitude that a person is aware of and can articulate

Implicit Attitude:
Attitude that a person is typically not aware or conscious of

Dual Attitude:
Inconsistent implicit and explicit attitudes toward a person, thing, or idea

Christensen, Drewsen, & Maaløe, 2014; Eastwick, Eagly, Finkel, & Johnson, 2011; Petty, Fazio, & Briñol, 2008); however, because most of that research is conducted in the context of stereotyping and prejudice, we will postpone further discussion until Chapter 10.

General Versus Specific Attitudes. Attitudes also vary in their generality: Some are global and represent an overall evaluation, and some are much more specific, focusing on just one feature of its object (Ajzen & Cote, 2008; Ajzen & Fishbein, 1977). For instance, a student may have a strong negative attitude about the way a professor dresses (a specific attitude) yet hold an overall very positive, global attitude about her because her liked features—teaching style, demeanor, and so forth—outweigh this small negative evaluation. Note that this inconsistency does not qualify these as dual attitudes, because the distinctions are explicit.

> ## *Think Again!*
>
> 1. *Can you define attitude and belief and think of examples of one attitude (one each of positive, negative, ambivalent, indifferent) and one belief that you hold?*
> 2. *What are implicit attitudes?*
> 3. *What are dual attitudes—can you think of any dual attitudes that you possess?*

Attitude Structure

Many theorists have proposed a **tripartite model of attitudes**, which states that they are composed of three elements: affect or feeling, cognition, and behavior (see Figure 7.1) (Breckler, 1984; Farley & Stasson, 2003; Rosenberg, Hovland, McGuire, Abelson, & Brehm, 1960). Briefly, the affective component refers to one's feelings toward or emotional response to the attitude object. In the case of French fries, my gut reaction (no pun intended) is a positive one: I like how they taste, smell, and even look. The second component is one's belief(s) about the attitude object. I believe that French fries, especially when consumed regularly and/or with other fatty foods, are bad for one's health. Thus, my affect and cognition are inconsistent with one another—I like them but know that they are bad for me. The third component is behavioral: How do I tend to act when given a chance to eat them? Do I typically consume them or avoid them?

According to the original tripartite model, each attitude includes all three elements, and together they constitute one's overall attitude. But social psychologists realize that, although attitudes can include all three components, they need not (Fazio & Olson, 2003). For instance, it is possible to have an immediate affective response to an object before cognitions have been formed, such that the feeling comes before the thinking (Zajonc, 1980). It is also clear that the three elements—affect, cognition, and behavior—are not always consistent, as illustrated by LaPiere's (1934) hospitality study discussed below and borne out by many later studies (Zanna & Rempel, 1988). Let's turn now to the reasons we have attitudes at all: What function do they serve?

Tripartite Model of Attitudes: Postulates that attitudes are composed of three elements: affect, cognition, and behavior

FIGURE **7.1**   Tripartite Structure of Attitudes

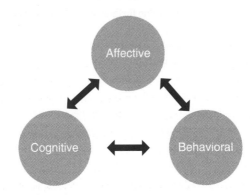

Attitudes are often considered to be composed of three elements: affective information (feelings), cognitive information (thoughts), and behavioral information (actions).

> ### *Think Again!*
>
> 1. *How is an attitude different from a belief?*
> 2. *What are implicit attitudes? Dual attitudes?*
> 3. *What is the tripartite structure of attitudes?*

THE ORIGINS OF ATTITUDES

Why do we have attitudes? To answer that, first imagine a world with no attitudes. None of us would care about our parents, the foods we eat, the music we play, or the books we read. Would you want to live in such a neutral, unattached world? Me neither. Fortunately, we have attitudes to make life more interesting. Attitudes are necessary for us to successfully navigate our worlds. One could even argue that society could not exist as we know it, because people wouldn't know what or who to approach or avoid.

How do people "get" attitudes? There are a number of avenues by which people acquire attitudes, ranging from deliberate learning to developing them with little or no conscious effort (Banaji & Heiphetz, 2010; M. A. Olson & Kendrick, 2008). We discussed one process in Chapter 5 in the context of Bem's (1967) self-perception theory; when people are uncertain about a particular attitude, they may infer their attitude from their behavior (Fazio, 1987). For instance, if a person is asked about her attitudes toward environmental conservation, she may examine her own recent behavior and, after noting that she regularly recycles and drives a compact, low-emissions vehicle, that she holds a pro-environment attitude. Self-perceptual processes are more likely at play when the attitude object is relatively unimportant and/or the person has little information about it (Wood, 1982).

Individual Experiences

In addition to inferring attitudes from one's own behavior, individuals develop attitudes via several processes that fall under the learning perspective described in Chapter 1. One process by which we can acquire attitudes should be familiar to you: simple association or classical conditioning. We can develop favorable or unfavorable attitudes toward neutral stimuli through the repeated pairing with unconditioned or previously conditioned positive or negative stimuli. In other words, people, things, and ideas that previously had little evaluative meaning for us acquire meaning. Research has shown that humans can be classically conditioned to prefer specific words, products, and other attitude objects (Grossman & Till, 1998). In one demonstration, Staats, Staats, and Crawford (1962) repeatedly paired previously neutral words with a painful noise or a shock. After the conditioning trials, participants evaluated these newly conditioned words more negatively as compared with words that were not conditioned. Classical conditioning explains why companies so often use well-liked celebrities—especially sexy ones—in their ads (Rice, Kelting, & Lutz, 2012). It also explains why many of my students report an automatic, favorable response (and also the pangs of hunger!) immediately after seeing the golden arches of McDonald's, when they were obviously not born with that tendency. Rather, repeated pairing over time created the association between the sign and a tasty meal!

Classical conditioning requires pairing of attitude objects with positive or negative stimuli. However, positive attitudes can be induced even in the absence of such pairing, simply through frequent contact with an attitude object. This **mere exposure effect** (Burger, Soroka, Gonzago, Murphy, & Somervell, 2001; Zajonc, 1968, 2001) can occur when repeated contact with or exposure to a person, thing, or idea leads one to favor or prefer it. In several demonstrations of these phenomena, Zajonc (1968) presented participants with nonsense words (but described as Turkish), Chinese symbols, or yearbook photos of strangers either 0, 1, 2, 5, 10, or 25 times. He then asked participants to rate the words, symbols, or photos on a seven-point scale, such that higher numbers reflected more positive evaluations. As you can see in Figure 7.2, greater "mere" exposure produced significantly more liking for the stimuli. Well over 200 studies have been published that support Zajonc' findings (Bornstein, 1989). The mere exposure effect is surprisingly robust, occurring via both conscious and nonconscious processes (Hicks & King, 2011; Zajonc, 2001), across a wide variety of stimuli (Zajonc, 2001) and in multiple cultures (Ishii, 2011).

If you are like my students, you will immediately question these results and report that your dislike of certain songs or people strengthens the more times you hear or see them. It turns out that this observation, too, is correct; repeated exposure can produce *less* liking if one's initial impression is a negative one (Cacioppo & Petty, 1989; Klinger & Greenwald, 1994). For instance, a study by Crisp, Hutter, and Young (2009) found that greater exposure to a threatening, negative outgroup exacerbated the unfavorable evaluation of that outgroup. Finally, overexposure to stimuli that are liked initially can lead to boredom and lowered evaluations, an experience that all of us have had to an overplayed song or over-viewed advertisement (Bornstein, 1989).

Mere Exposure Effect: Repeated contact with or exposure to a person, thing, or idea leads one to favor or prefer it

Attitudes may also be acquired via operant conditioning, in which specific positive or negative attitudes are reinforced and, consequently, more likely to be formed (Insko & Cialdini, 1969). In one well-known study, University of Hawaii college students were verbally reinforced during a phone call for voicing particular attitudes (Insko, 1965). Participants were presented with 14 statements regarding the creation of a "Springtime Aloha Week" and were randomly assigned to hear "good" after expressing either favorable or unfavorable opinions in response to each of the items. Overall attitudes toward this proposal were solicited both at the end of the interview and one week later in the context of a general paper-and-pencil attitude questionnaire. As predicted, those who had been reinforced for expressions of favorable or unfavorable opinions indicated greater or lesser support for the proposal, respectively (Insko, 1965).

Both classical and operant conditioning are based on direct experience with the attitude object; however, we often acquire attitudes from other people even in the absence of such experience. According to social learning theory, people can learn new attitudes (as well as beliefs and behaviors) by observing the actions of others and, in particular, attitudes

FIGURE 7.2   The Effects of Mere Exposure on Liking

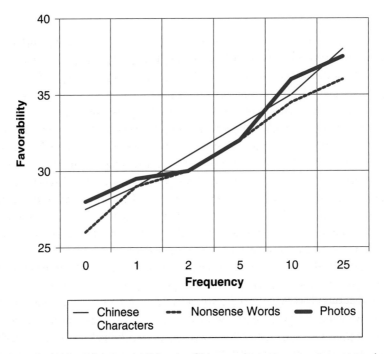

Frequency of exposure increased liking for Chinese characters, nonsense words, and photographs.

Source: Adapted from Zajonc, R. S. (1968). Attitudinal effects of mere exposure. *Journal of Personality and Social Psychology, 9,* Monograph Supplement No.2, Pt. 2.

for which those others are either reinforced or punished (Bandura, 1997). For example, children may develop favorable attitudes toward aggression after exposure to violent media or music lyrics (C. A. Anderson, Carnagey, & Eubanks, 2003) or learn racial attitudes from their parents (Räikkönen, Katainen, Keskivaara, & Kelikangas-Järvinen, 2000).

Contextual Influences

Attitudes are also absorbed from and shaped by contextual influences, including the media, schools, religions, and culture (Banaji & Heiphetz, 2010). Sometimes these are formed explicitly (or at least there is an explicit attempt to create attitudes), such as when a political campaign ad urges its audience to view an opponent unfavorably (M. A. Olson & Kendrick, 2008). Similarly, during religious instruction people are encouraged to evaluate some behaviors positively (such as sexual abstinence) and others negatively (such as sex outside of marriage). Other attitudes are formed implicitly, in the absence of a specific intent to do so, such as when exposure to cultural messages in advertising and the media leads many Americans to develop positive attitudes toward thin people and negative ones toward heavy people (Crandall, Merman, & Hebl, 2009). In Chapter 10 we'll focus more specifically on the development of prejudicial attitudes.

Biological Factors

One final route by which we acquire attitudes is based not in learning but rather in our biological and evolutionary heritage (J. M. Olson, Vernon, Harris, & Jang, 2001). Some of these attitudes may be directly, if partially, heritable (Tesser, 1993), whereas others seem to be derived indirectly from inherited personality traits and/or arousal tendencies (Albarracín & Vargas, 2010; Conway, Dodds, Towgood, McClure, & Olson, 2011; Huppertz et al., 2014). In his 1993 review of extant research, Tesser identified a large number of attitudes that may be linked to a person's genes, including job satisfaction, vocational attitudes, political conservatism, and attitudes toward drinking alcohol and conformist responding. Tesser (1993) acknowledged that it is unlikely that genes exist for, say, opinions about jazz in the way that they do for eye color. Rather, any genetic influence on attitudes probably works through other heritable features, such as intelligence, temperament, and brain structures related to hearing, taste, and other senses. A large-scale twin study by Olson et al. (2001) uncovered a genetic role in dozens of attitudes, including support for the death penalty and outlawing racial discrimination. Others have found that attitudes toward same-sex relationships (Verweij et al., 2008) and religious behavior and attendance (Button, Stallings, Rhee, Corley, & Hewitt, 2011) are partially gene based.

More recently, social psychologists have begun asking about the *types* of attitudes that should be expected to be heritable. For instance, Conway and colleagues (2011) gathered data from over 2,000 participants and found that relatively complex attitudes were more heritable than simpler ones. Brandt and Wethere (2012) predicted that, because moral attitudes are more relevant to group survival, they should have a stronger genetic basis than nonmoral ones. For example, moral attitudes such as those toward sex crimes and the death penalty were expected and found to be more heritable than nonmoral attitudes pertaining to the nature of capitalism or the treatment of refugees (Brandt & Wethere, 2012).

Keep in mind that these various sources of influence are not necessarily independent. Learning occurs within a cultural context, biology affects learning, and learning impacts our social world. Moreover, environmental influences can also impact how genes are expressed in particular individuals, which is partly why identical twins are not actually identical and may have markedly different physical features or susceptibilities to dementia (Francis, 2011).

Think Again!

1. *How can classical conditioning explain the learning of attitudes?*

2. *What is the mere exposure effect?*

3. *Specifically, what does heritability mean in the context of the genetic transmission of attitudes?*

TWO ROUTES TO PERSUASION

Although this may seem obvious today, early attitude researchers neglected the role of thought. This was the case until Anthony Greenwald (1968) argued that thinking is a crucial—perhaps the crucial—component in persuasion. More specifically, Greenwald claimed that the thoughts people had during exposure to messages—what he called their **cognitive responses**—were critical to whether or not attitude change ensued. This **cognitive response model of persuasion** posited that persuasion was more likely if targets produced a greater number of favorable than unfavorable responses to the message (Petty & Cacioppo, 1981). In a sense, the elaboration of the message arguments can produce self-persuasion if the balance of the generated thoughts is favorable.

For instance, if you are reading an article that advocates for greater government spending on the military, you may generate positive and/or negative thoughts about the message, depending on whether you agree or disagree. In general, if you produce more positive than negative thoughts, the odds are that you found the message persuasive. In contrast, the occurrence of more negative than positive responses indicates that you did not find the message convincing. How do researchers know the valence and frequency of your cognitive responses? Well, they ask participants to write them down immediately after message exposure. The resulting data are called thought listings, and the researchers will simply tally the positive and negative messages (largely ignoring the neutral or irrelevant ones), and the difference in the two sums should correlate with attitude change.

Cognitive Responses:
Thoughts a person has while processing a message

Cognitive Response Model of Persuasion:
Posits that persuasion is more likely to occur to the extent that message recipients produce a greater number of favorable than unfavorable responses to the message

Central and Peripheral Processing

Two of Greenwald's students—Richard Petty and John Cacioppo (1981)—had two key insights that transformed the cognitive response model into a more general theory of attitude change. First, Petty and Cacioppo observed that, during message exposure, people engage in two types of thinking or message processing, which they labeled central and peripheral. Second, the type of thinking that people engage in largely depends on two factors: their motivation *and* their ability to carefully process that message (Petty & Cacioppo, 1981). Petty and Cacioppo called the resulting approach to attitude change the **elaboration likelihood model of persuasion** (ELM) because it describes when people are more or less likely to engage in elaborative or deep processing of messages (Petty & Briñol, 2014; Petty, Wheeler, & Tormala, 2013).

For instance, say you are considering options for your new cell phone. You may have to choose from several providers, data plans, and models. Since a mobile can cost as much as a couple of hundred dollars and a purchase often requires a two-year service contract, you will be making a substantial commitment and will get to enjoy its fancy features or bemoan its limited capacities for what may seem like a long time. Therefore, you may go down to the local phone store and try out two or three options and compare their advantages and disadvantages. You will likely want to think carefully about the claims made by the manufacturers about the phones in order to be certain that they are valid and that the advertised features are relevant to you. Petty and Cacioppo (1981) call this deliberative or elaborative thinking **central processing**, and it is characterized by careful, relatively slower examination of the persuasion message. But people don't always engage in such scrutiny.

Let's say that you dropped your current phone into a river and are about to go on a trip during which you'll need a functional mobile. Given the lack of time to carefully consider the phone options, you are likely to make a quick decision based on relatively rapid examination of the manufacturer's claims and product features. Thinking about a message that is relatively rapid, superficial, and focused on nonargument features of the message is called **peripheral processing** (Petty & Cacioppo, 1981). Because it posits the existence of two cognitive processes or routes through which persuasion occurs, the ELM is considered a **dual process model**.

The ELM makes two specific predictions about the effects of central and peripheral processing on attitude change. One is that when we follow the central route, attitude change will depend on the *quality* of the arguments. Careful scrutiny of high quality or strong arguments—those that are logical and/or contain valid evidence—will be more persuasive than similar scrutiny of weak ones. For instance, a manufacturer's claim that their cell phones work in Kuwait is weak and would be undermined as unconvincing when carefully considered (unless one lives in Kuwait). The second prediction is that superficial, nonargument message features will determine the amount of attitude change under peripheral processing. Nonargument features include the number of arguments offered in support of a message, characteristics of the message source, and how many others agree with the message. In summary, message quality only matters when we centrally process,

Elaboration Likelihood Model of Persuasion: Postulates that persuasion occurs via central and/or peripheral processing

Central Processing: Thinking about a message that is relatively slow, careful, and focused on the quality of the arguments

Peripheral Processing: Thinking about a message that is relatively rapid, superficial, and focused on nonargument features of the message

Dual Process Model: Posits that attitudes and beliefs can change via two processes—with and without much thought

whereas nonargument features matter when we peripherally process (Petty, Cacioppo, & Goldman, 1981).

The ELM further specifies the conditions under which we are likely to engage in central or peripheral processing (Petty & Wegener, 1999). According to the ELM, in order to engage in central processing, we need both the *motivation* and the *ability* to do so (see Figure 7.3). As we discussed in Chapter 3, careful scrutiny expends precious mental resources, resources that people tend to conserve in order to devote them to important or meaningful tasks. Consequently, we will only engage in centrally processing when we are motivated to. What motivates us to do this? First, the more *personally relevant* the issue is—how much it affects us—the greater our motivation to think carefully. Topics that are highly relevant are said to be more involving, whereas low relevance topics are less so (Crano, 1995). Buying a phone for oneself engenders more involvement than buying one for someone else. Second, messages that deal with content that is important to us— that we are very concerned about—will similarly increase our desire to scrutinize them (Boninger, Krosnick, & Berent, 1995). For instance, one's attitude toward abortion could be important but not relevant for a woman who is beyond a childbearing age.

Motivation to centrally process does not, however, ensure that it will happen: We must also have the ability to do so. Sometimes we are under time pressure (Bradley & Shapiro,

FIGURE 7.3   The Two Routes to Persuasion

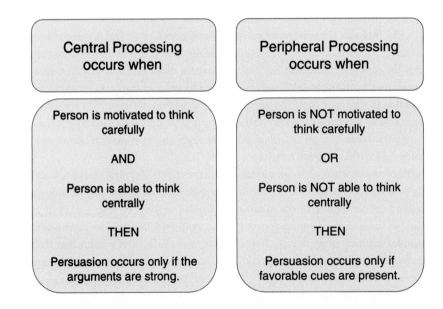

The two routes to persuasion, according to the Elaboration Likelihood Model.

Source: Adapted from Petty, R. E., & Cacioppo, J. T. (1981). *Attitudes and persuasion: Classic and contemporary approaches.* Dubuque, IA: Wm. C. Brown.

2004; Ratneshwar & Chaiken, 1991) or just don't have the mental resources available to us at that moment, such as when we are too distracted to focus (Harkins & Petty, 1981), even if we would like to. Moreover, conditions may exist that prevent us from thinking through the argument content. For example, the message content may be written in highly complex or technical language that we lack the expertise to decode (Hafer, Reynolds, & Obertynski, 1996). Central processing, then, will only occur if we have both the motivation and the ability to engage in it. If either one of these factors is absent, then we will rely on peripheral features or shortcuts to guide our decision.

Central and peripheral processing mirror the deliberative and slow and superficial and fast processing, respectively, that we discussed in Chapters 1 and 3. And you can see that there is a similar trade-off here between the two types of thinking: Greater focus on message quality reduces the effects of other factors and vice versa. Furthermore, these dual processes involve a trade-off between accuracy and speed. Typically we need to spend more time to achieve greater confidence in the accuracy of our decisions, while less time spent deliberating can lead to lower confidence in the result. Finally, attitude change that occurs via central processing is longer lasting and more resistant to counterattacks than attitude change following peripheral processing (Johnson, Maio, & Smith-McLallen, 2005; Petty & Wegener, 1999). The basic tenets of the ELM have been supported and extended in countless research articles, and it remains the most viable theory of persuasion in social psychology today (Petty & Briñol, 2012; Petty & Wegener, 1998).

Think Again!

1. *What are central and peripheral processing?*

2. *What two factors are required for a person to engage in central processing?*

3. *Pick an advertisement and identify as many nonargument messages as you can.*

Heuristic-Systematic Model

At about the same time that Petty and Cacioppo developed the ELM, another social psychologist, Shelly Chaiken (Chaiken, 1980, 1987; Chaiken, Giner-Sorolla, & Chen, 1996) proposed her own dual process approach to persuasion. Chaiken's **heuristic-systematic model of persuasion** postulates that there are two routes or modes to persuasion, called *systematic* and *heuristic,* that roughly parallel the central and peripheral processes of the ELM. Like the central route, the systematic process is marked by intensive effort or elaboration and requires both the motivation and capacity to do so. Heuristic processing, like its peripheral counterpart, is less effortful and relies on simple cues and heuristics for making decisions. We discussed heuristics in Chapter 3: They are mental shortcuts or rules of

Heuristic-Systematic Model of Persuasion: Postulates that persuasion occurs via systematic and/or heuristic processing

thumb that allow us to make rapid judgments while minimizing the expenditure of mental resources. Chaiken (Chaiken, 1987; Chaiken & Ledgerwood, 2012) describes several heuristics that message recipients may rely on to ascertain the validity of a message. "Experts' statements can be trusted" and "consensus opinions are correct" are two good examples of such heuristics, and you can see how a person might rely on these in place of engaging in systematic processing (S. Chen & Chaiken, 1999). Like the ELM, the HSM has garnered an impressive amount of empirical support across message topics and persuasion contexts (Chaiken & Ledgerwood, 2012; S. Chen & Chaiken, 1999).

ELEMENTS OF PERSUASION

We have established the central role of message processing in attitude change. Now let's examine persuasion in a different way by stripping it down to its elements. What are the elements of persuasion? These elements are identified in the classic question: *Who says what to whom with what effect?* (Hovland, Janis, & Kelley, 1953; Lasswell, 1948). As part of the Yale Communication Research Program, Hovland and his colleagues (1953) systematically examined the roles of message source (who?), message content (what?), target audience (to whom?), and target audience response (with what effect?) in persuasion. The Yale group was theoretically steeped in the psychology of behaviorism and examined persuasion primarily from a learning perspective that regarded audience members as passive recipients of information, a perspective long since disregarded (Briñol & Petty, 2012). Nevertheless, their research program proved to be quite fertile and has framed much of the thinking about persuasion since.

Source Factors

Credibility. Hovland et al. (1953) identified communicator credibility as one of the keys to successful persuasion. The **credibility** of a communicator is synonymous with believability or the extent to which message recipients accept the validity of the message. Researchers have identified three primary components of credibility: expertise, trustworthiness, and goodwill (See Table 7.2). Expertise refers to the extent to which the source is *perceived* to be knowledgeable or well informed about the message topic. As is the case with other aspects of social behavior, how people interpret or construe information is more important than what actually is true. The evidence for the role of source factors on attitude change is robust (Clark, Wegener, Habashi, & Evans, 2012; Petty & Wegener, 1998). In one classic study, participants read messages on one of four topics that were ostensibly from either a high- or low-credibility source and were generally more persuaded by the former (Hovland & Weiss, 1951). In a later study Petty, Cacioppo, and Goldman (1981) exposed individuals to education policy recommendations attributed to either a high school student or a knowledgeable expert and similarly found that, under certain conditions (described in the ELM section above), expertise enhanced persuasion.

Credibility:
Communicator characteristic based on expertise, trustworthiness, and goodwill that affects the extent to which message recipients accept the validity of the communicator's statements

TABLE 7.2 Source Characteristics

Type	Explanation
Expertise	Is the source an expert on the topic?
Trustworthiness	Can the source be trusted to offer an unbiased opinion?
Goodwill	Does the source have the best interests of the audience in mind?
Physical attractiveness, likeability, and similarity	Sources who are more attractive, better liked, and more similar to the audience are more persuasive.

The second component of credibility, trustworthiness, has also been shown to impact persuasion. For instance, Eagly, Wood, and Chaiken (1978) manipulated both source characteristics and found that participants were more convinced by sources seen as sincere and expert. Similarly, Pornpitakpan (2003) found that both the trustworthiness and expertise of celebrities enhanced persuasion among Singaporean participants. The third component of credibility, communicator good will or caring, was only identified in the 1990s and has been the subject of much less empirical research (Teven & McCroskey, 1997). This research has shown that sources who are perceived to empathize with or care about intended message recipients are more believable.

Other Factors. Several other source characteristics can also increase persuasion, such as attractiveness (Chaiken, 1979), likability (Cialdini, 2008), or similarity to the audience (Burger et al., 2001; Hung & Wyer, 2014). For instance, Chaiken (1979) found that college students were more persuaded by physically attractive (as compared to less attractive) persons who argued for changes in campus dining hall food options. In other research, students were more persuaded by a similar versus a dissimilar student (Burger et al., 2001), and African American women held more favorable attitudes towards breast self-exams after viewing recommendations from another African American woman (R. B. Anderson & McMillion, 1995).

Message Factors

The literature demonstrating the role of message content in persuasion is both deep and wide ranging (Johnson et al., 2005; Petty & Wegener, 1998). Perhaps the most important message variable is argument quality—which may or may not make a difference, depending on a variety of factors—as we discussed above with respect to the ELM. In this section, we'll focus on two other important variables: fear appeals and negativity.

Fear Appeals. We commonly see messages that rely on inducing fear to change our behaviors. They typically take the form of "if you don't stop X, then Y bad things will happen to you." If you don't stop smoking, it'll kill you! Don't vote for Candidate X, he'll wreck the economy! When I poll my students, typically about two thirds think that fear appeals work, while the remaining students are skeptical. The big question is *does inducing fear in message recipients enhance attitude and behavior change?* On the surface it seems that it should: If telling people about the potential negative consequences of their behavior doesn't stop it, then what would? But, the story is not so simple.

First of all, instilling fear in people is more difficult than you may think, and many attempts fail to engender sufficient fear to have any significant effect (Boster & Mongeau, 1984). After approximately 60 years and hundreds of studies, no overall theoretical framework that explains the mechanisms by which fear appeals affect attitudes and behavior has been developed (Mongeau, 2013). Nevertheless, investigators have identified two specific components—one emotional and one cognitive—of successful fear messages. Effective fear appeals contain both a *threat* component, which describes the feared event, disease, and so forth, and an *efficacy* component, which tells people how they can control the danger (Witte & Allen, 2000). Not surprisingly, scaring people without offering a credible and achievable way to control the threat is ineffective (Janis & Feshbach, 1953).

In one recent study of anti-smoking ads, Timmers and van der Wijst (2007) examined the effects of fear-based appeals among 268 Dutch teen and adult smokers and nonsmokers. These authors tested the impact of warnings of four types of risks: lung cancer, harming others, sexual impotence, and mouth disease. The warnings took the form of vivid images of the feared phenomena accompanied by a short textual message. All participants were exposed to all of the warnings. The researchers found that the more realistic and fear-inducing ads were viewed more positively, although they were not necessarily more persuasive. Other factors can also influence the effectiveness of fear appeals. For instance, audience members need to believe that the threat is severe and that they, individually, are susceptible to the negative outcome (Witte, 1998). In addition, fear appeals can create other emotions, such as surprise, anger, and disgust, as has been demonstrated in a number of studies (Leshner, Bolls, & Wise, 2011). Deliberately adding an element of disgust can enhance the effectiveness of fear appeals (Morales, Wu, & Fitzsimons, 2012).

Negative Messages. Fear appeals often appear in political ads and speeches (Curnalia, 2007; Westen, 2007) but represent just one type of negative message. People often complain about ads that focus on the flaws in the opposing candidate, such as integrity or honesty (Garramone, Atkin, Pinkleton, & Cole, 1990). Are they effective? The evidence is mixed (Underation, 2009); although some observers have argued that negative ads work (e.g., Westen, 2007), one recent meta-analysis of 111 studies found no evidence to support this contention (Lau, Sigelman, & Rovner, 2007). The precise reason for their ineffectiveness is unclear, but it may be due to the fact that, in general, recipients do not process them as carefully as they do positive ads (Marks, Manning, & Ajzen, 2012).

Message Sidedness. In addition to choosing whether or not to "go negative," political candidates must decide between focusing only one side—their own—or two sides—their own and their opponent's, in their ads (Czuchry & Gray, 2009; Kao, 2012). They

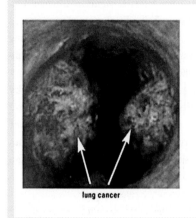

WARNING

CIGARETTES CAUSE LUNG CANCER

85% of lung cancers are caused by smoking. 80% of lung cancer victims die within 3 years.

Health Canada

Using Fear Appeals in Persuasion

Timmers, R., & van der Wijst, P. (2007). Images as anti-smoking fear appeals: The effect of emotion on the persuasion process. *Information Design Journal, 15,* 21-36.

need to ask whether it is more prudent to describe only the reasons their positions are the correct ones or to also address possible counterarguments. Early research by Hovland, Lumsdaine, and Sheffield (1949) tested radio broadcasts that either provided only statements arguing that World War II in the Pacific region would end quickly or that also included and addressed counterarguments. They found that the one-sided approach was more effective for people who already agreed with it, whereas the two-sided led to greater attitude change among those who initially disagreed with it. Again, demonstrating the self-correcting nature of science, the conclusions from Hovland et al. (1949) have been modified by subsequent research. According to meta-analyses by Allen, Hale, Mongeau, and Berkowitz-Stafford (1990) and O'Keefe (1999), two-sided messages are generally more effective as long as they refute rather than simply restate, the opposing arguments.

Audience Factors

Creating effective attitude change messages can be quite complicated and, unfortunately, is made even more so by a variety of differences in message recipient characteristics. Contrary to what many believe, there is no general persuasability personality variable. However, there are a number of more specific, person-based factors that research has demonstrated can affect persuasion. Here we will review several such variables.

Self-Monitoring. One important individual difference is self-monitoring, which we discussed in Chapter 4 (Snyder, 1974; Stukas, Snyder, & Clary, 2008). As a brief reminder, people who are high in self-monitoring are more focused on social status and on pleasing others and, consequently, adjust their behavior across contexts accordingly. In contrast, low self-monitors behave in ways that are consonant with internal standards, worry less about the preferences of others, and demonstrate more behavioral consistency across situations (Snyder, 1974). Given these differences in orientation between high and low self-monitors, one might expect that persuasive messages designed to convince people to alter their attitudes or behavior should be relatively more successful to the extent that they tap these divergent motives. Snyder and DeBono (1985) tested this prediction by asking high or low self-monitors to evaluate advertisements for whiskey, cigarettes, and coffee. The ads were manipulated to emphasize either the image they would project about the user or the quality of the product. Consistent with predictions, high self-monitors evaluated the image-focused ads more positively than the quality focused, whereas the lows showed the opposite pattern (Snyder & DeBono, 1985).

Need for Cognition. As we discussed in Chapter 3, people differ in the extent to which they enjoy and tend to engage in thinking, called their **need for cognition** (NC; Barbaro, Pickett, & Parkhill, 2015; Cacioppo & Petty, 1982; Cacioppo, Petty, Feinstein, & Jarvis, 1996; Fleischhauer, Strobel, & Strobel, 2015; Rosenbaum & Johnson, 2015). You probably have friends or acquaintances who try to avoid thinking and prefer to make decisions without really doing so. And you likely can name a person who really loves to deliberate over both large and small decisions. A person's NC can sometimes impact the success of a persuasion attempt. If a person exerts considerable effort in examining messages intended to persuade him, then whether or not his attitude is changed is affected by how strong the arguments are. Careful consideration of quality arguments is more likely to lead to persuasion than is comparable attention to weak arguments (Cacioppo & Petty, 1982). More generally, NC has a similar impact on message processing as personal relevance: Both will increase motivation and make central processing more likely, as long as they are accompanied by the ability to do so.

Other Audience Factors. In addition to these factors, researchers have examined the potential roles of many other individual differences in persuasion (Briñol & Petty, 2005). McGuire (1968) examined the roles of self-esteem and intelligence in persuasion. He argued that, contrary to what you might predict, people with moderate *self-esteem* were more easily persuaded than those who were either high or low (McGuire, 1968). His reasoning was that low self-esteem individuals are so focused on their own problems or issues that they may not attend sufficiently to persuasion messages to fully receive them and therefore they won't be affected by them. In contrast, high self-esteem persons are very confident in their attitudes and are unlikely to yield to the persuasive attempts (Rhodes & Wood, 1992). In terms of intelligence, people of relatively *lower* intelligence are more susceptible to persuasion than *highly* intelligent people (McGuire, 1968; Rhodes & Wood, 1992).

Age. Finally, a number of researchers have also examined the influence of *age* on persuasion. Although it has been argued that children, adolescents, and young adults should be

Need for Cognition: Extent to which a person enjoys and tends to engage in thinking

the most persuadable (Alwin & Krosnick, 1991; Glenn, 1980; Sears, 1986), more recent evidence indicates that both younger adults and the elderly are easier to persuade than adults in their middle years (Visser & Krosnick, 1998). The reason for this pattern is unclear, but it may be related to changes in social networks, attitude confidence, perceived knowledge, or other factors that typically change during midlife (Visser & Krosnick, 1998). Finally, Hirsh, Kang, and Bodenhausen (2012) tailored message content to individual personality profiles and found that targets rated tailored messages as more effective than others. For instance, ads that appealed to communal values and interpersonal harmony were seen as more persuasive by people relatively high on dispositional agreeability.

Think Again!

1. *What are the components of source credibility?*

2. *Under what conditions are fear appeals more likely to work?*

3. *What kind of message is most likely to change an attitude of someone who is high in need for cognition?*

THE EFFECTS OF ATTITUDES ON BEHAVIOR

The Reasoned Action Approach

Researchers have found surprisingly low correlations between attitudes and behavior (Fishbein & Ajzen, 1975, 2010; Wicker, 1969, 1971). One of the primary reasons for this is that social psychologists have often examined relationships between attitudes and behaviors that were at different levels of specification. For example, Wicker (1971) was interested in predicting religious behavior from attitudes toward religion. He found that the correlations between attitudes toward the individual's church and church attendance, donations to the church, and participation in the church's activities were low and inconsistent. After reviewing extant research that similarly found low correlations, Wicker (1969) suggested that psychologists abandon the attitude concept completely. Fortunately, other researchers disagreed with Wicker's pessimistic conclusion and endeavored to explain prior low attitude-behavior consistency and, moreover, to theorize and empirically demonstrate the conditions under which the relationship is stronger and more reliable.

In one of the most important responses to Wicker's (1969) challenge, Icek Ajzen and Martin Fishbein (1977) argued that researchers should distinguish between *global attitudes* toward a topic that do not refer to a specific behavior and *attitude toward a behavior*. For instance, a person's overall evaluation of his religion (e.g., the Catholic Church) is global, but *his* evaluation of *his* donating to *his* church is an attitude toward a specific behavior. You can easily see how a person could be religious but not donate money, and therefore the global attitude and specific behavior may not be highly correlated. Indeed, Ajzen and Fishbein's (1977) examination of 102 attitude-behavior studies that reported low attitude-behavior correlations revealed that 54 of them relied on global attitudes, and a more recent meta-analysis found much the same thing (Kraus, 1995). In order to address the inconsistent specification of variables, Ajzen and Fishbein (1980) proposed the *principle of compatibility* to improve the prediction of behavior from attitudes. Briefly, the principle states that the strength of the attitude-behavior relationship will be high only if attitudes and behavior are measured at the same level of specificity (Ajzen & Fishbein, 2008). For instance, one's attitude toward one's at-home recycling behavior should predict one's at-home recycling behavior better than one's general attitude toward the environment should.

Based partially on this principle of compatibility, Ajzen and Fishbein (1980) developed the theory of reasoned action (TRA) that they hoped would improve upon prior attempts to predict behavior from attitudes (see the dark blue components in Figure 7.4). The TRA postulated that a specific behavior can be predicted from a corresponding intention to perform that behavior, and that intention should flow from a person's corresponding attitudes and subjective or *perceived* norms. Perceived norms are the target's perceptions of what she thinks that people who are important to her want her to do with respect to the behavior in question. We can better predict a person's recycling behavior by knowing both her specific attitude toward her recycling and what she thinks her roommate, parents, and other important people think that she should do. Remember, it is what she believes they want, not what they actually want (the two may or may not be the same). The utility of the TRA in predicting behavior has been empirically demonstrated in 100s of studies (Fishbein & Ajzen, 2010). These authors later built on and improved their approach to predicting behavior (see the Social Psychology Applied to Health box).

DOING RESEARCH: MEASURING ATTITUDES

All of the theories and models of attitudes and attitude change described above would remain interesting but largely useless if psychologists were unable to measure both attitudes and attitude change. In the absence of valid measurement, it would be impossible to know whether any given intervention, ad, or argument had its intended effect on the audience. In this *Doing Research* section, we'll review the most common methods employed in social psychological research on persuasion. As you might expect, the methods used for explicit versus implicit attitudes are different. Here we'll focus primarily on direct and indirect ways to measure explicit attitudes and only touch lightly on those for implicit ones. Chapter 10 on stereotyping will delve into the latter in more detail.

SOCIAL PSYCHOLOGY APPLIED TO HEALTH
PREDICTING BEHAVIOR CHANGE

As stated in the main text, the TRA was able to improve behavioral prediction from attitudes in part because it was based on the compatibility principle. Nevertheless, Ajzen (1985) identified an important missing element and created the theory of planned behavior (TPB) by adding one component to the TRA's two determinants of intention: *perceived* behavioral control. Perceived behavioral control is the extent to which a person thinks that she has the *ability* to enact the behavior, such as riding a bike to school instead of driving (the medium blue box in Figure 7.4). Like the TRA, the TPB has received extensive support across numerous studies, especially in the realm of health behaviors (Ajzen & Cote, 2008). For example, whether or not a person intends to recycle at home will depend on his attitude toward his recycling, what he thinks important others want him to do, and whether he believes that he is able to. Perceived behavioral control may be low in this case if, for instance, the nearest recycling facility is 100 miles away.

The relationship between attitudes and behavior is more complex than either the TRA or the TPB depicted, and consequently Fishbein and Azjen developed reasoned action theory (RAT) to explain this relationship (see the entire Figure 7.4) (Fishbein & Ajzen, 2010; J. M. Olson & Stone, 2005). Reasoned action theory adds background variables (e.g., gender, education, income level, etc.) that could impact the persuasion process as well as *actual* behavioral control (see the light gray boxes in Figure 7.4). Actual control was included in the model because other factors could interfere with the relationship between intention to enact a behavior and the behavior itself: Sometimes limitations in skills and knowledge or conditions beyond our control prevent us from acting as we would like, such as when we try but lack the skills to join a basketball team or when one's car breaks down on the way to church.

For instance, say Alice is considering quitting smoking within the next four weeks. Whether or not Alice does this should depend on (a) her intention to stop within that timeframe, (b) her attitudes toward the same, (c) whether she thinks that important others (e.g., parents, close friends) want her to stop within four weeks, (d) whether she thinks she can do it, and (e) whether she actually has the ability to stop. In addition, there may be background variables that impact her behavior, such as genetics.

(Continued)

(Continued)

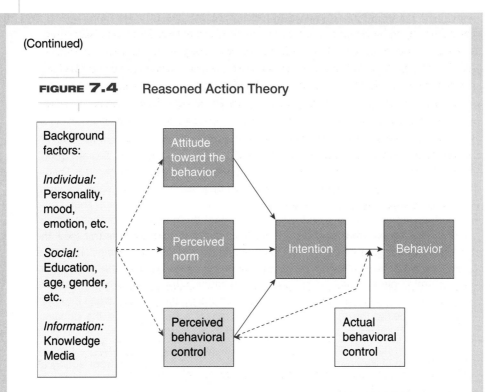

FIGURE 7.4   Reasoned Action Theory

Source: Adapted from Figure 1.1, Fishbein, M., & Ajzen, I. (2010). *Predicting and changing behavior.* New York: Psychology Press.

The RAT has been the basis for many successful smoking cessation programs (Cappella, 2007; Curtis, 2012; Guo et al., 2007; Pomery, Gibbons, Reis-Bergan, & Gerrard, 2009). Try mapping a behavior that you want to change (either start or stop) using this model. If you are having difficulty altering your behavior, the RAT may be able to help you identify why this is the case.

Direct Self-Report Methods

Closed-Ended Items. The most common way to gather data about people's attitudes is simply by directly asking them. Surveys, interviews, and other direct measures are considered **overt measures**, because respondents know that their attitudes are being examined. However, as discussed earlier, creating survey items is more complicated than is commonly believed, because there are a number of personal and contextual factors (see Chapter 4) that may prevent researchers from obtaining valid and reliable data (see Chapter 3). Attitude questions typically take the form of *Likert-type items* or rating

Overt Measures:
Obtaining information from people when they know what is being examined

scales, which ask the respondent to provide an evaluation of an attitude object and may be asked on paper, by computer, phone, text message, or online. On a true Likert scale, respondents indicate the extent to which they agree or disagree with an evaluative statement (Likert, 1932). For instance, attitudes toward the death penalty can be obtained by using the stem "the death penalty is ethical" and providing response options *strongly agree, agree, neither agree nor disagree, disagree, or strongly disagree*. An alternative approach elicits responses to a question or statement along a scale that is anchored with a highly positive evaluation at one end and a highly negative one at the other, usually with five to seven graduated response options. The anchors of these scales vary, depending on the attitude being sought or the preference of the researcher. For example, the item "government funding of research into alternative energy sources" can be evaluated on a range from *not at all important* to *very important*.

Open-Ended Items. Although closed-ended items are by far the most prevalent form of self-report, psychologists occasionally use open-ended questions that allow participants to describe in their own words how they evaluate a given attitude object. For instance, a researcher might ask participants to describe how they felt about the legalization of same-sex marriage or a new immigration policy. This format gives respondents more freedom to answer as they wish, allowing them to discuss aspects of the issues that the research may not have included on a rating scale. Researchers examine the responses for particular themes (such as Biblical references with regard to same-sex marriage) and then count how frequently the themes are mentioned. Often these results are then used in the construction of closed-ended questionnaires.

Bogus Pipeline. One of the methods that social psychologists created in hopes of avoiding social desirability considerations is the **bogus pipeline** (Jones & Sigall, 1971; Sigall & Page, 1971). In this technique, participants are hooked up to a machine that they are told records physiological indicators of a person's true feelings and are asked to "predict" what the machine will reveal about some of their own attitudes. To the extent that participants are convinced that the machine can accurately assess their attitudes, they should be more willing to provide unfiltered verbal responses to questions about those attitudes. In fact, they are. Sigall and Page (1971) found that individuals reported less favorable opinions of "Negroes" in the bogus pipeline condition than when they were not connected to it. Roese and Jamieson (1993) performed a meta-analysis of 31 studies conducted over twenty years of bogus pipeline research and found that the bogus pipeline manipulation reliably produced responses that were less socially desirable than in control conditions. More recently, Gannon, Keown, and Polashek (2007) successfully employed a modified bogus pipeline technique to induce child molesters to admit inappropriate thoughts about molestation. The bogus pipeline technique has also been applied in examining self-reported levels of anxiety (Derakshan & Eysenck, 2005), cheating (Quigley-Fernandez & Tedeschi, 1978), and adolescent smoking (Adams, Parkinson, Sanson-Fisher, & Walsh, 2008). Although the effectiveness of this technique in inducing honest responding is

Bogus Pipeline: Technique in which participants are hooked up to a machine and are told that the machine can reveal their true feelings, when in fact the machine cannot do this

clear, questions have been raised as to whether deceiving participants about the accuracy of the device is ethical (Aguinis & Henle, 2001).

Indirect Methods

In a sense all attitude measurement techniques are indirect because attitudes are really hypothetical constructs that cannot be directly observed. Nevertheless, some are more indirect or covert than others. Certain techniques are referred to as **covert** or **unobtrusive measures**, because the target is unaware that her attitude is being investigated and consequently will not have the opportunity to alter her actions in response to such awareness (Webb, Campbell, Schwartz, & Sechrest, 1966). Covert techniques should be particularly useful when assessing attitudes that the targets may, for social desirability reasons, not wish to accurately self-report (Krosnick, Judd, & Wittenbrink, 2005; Webb et al., 1966).

Sometimes behaviors are measured as indirect indicators of attitudes. The utility of doing this rests upon the strength of the attitude-behavior relationship, which has been extensively examined by social psychologists (Ajzen & Fishbein, 1977; Fishbein & Ajzen, 2010; Wicker, 1969). We will return to this relationship later in this chapter. For now, let's review two interesting examples of covert strategies for measuring behavior and subsequently inferring attitudes.

One well-known indirect measure of attitude is called the *lost-letter technique* (Milgram, 1969; Milgram, Mann, Harter, & Kass, 1965). Milgram and his colleagues sought to determine attitudes toward political groups—such as the Nazi and Communist Parties—in various locations without directly surveying the communities. In one study, the researchers randomly left 400 stamped, addressed envelopes on the ground in 10 different locations in New Haven, Connecticut. One hundred envelopes each were addressed to the Nazi Party, Communist Party, Medical Research Associates, or a fictional individual, Walter Carnap. The dependent measure was the number of envelopes received at the post office box listed in the addresses. The response rates were 25%, 25%, 72%, and 71%, respectively, and Milgram et al. (1965) inferred that attitudes toward the two parties were relatively unfavorable. Bridges and Rodriguez (2000) used a similar technique to assess attitudes toward gays and lesbians and found that lost letters addressed to clearly gay-friendly places were returned more frequently in urban than in rural communities.

Cialdini and Baumann (1981) assessed voting behavior in the 1980 presidential election using a different approach: They secretly recorded littering versus retention of political fliers placed on car windshields outside a polling station. As the cars were leaving the parking lot, the researchers asked each person whom he or she had voted for. Cialdini and Baumann (1981) found that littering of the fliers was highly correlated with voting choice, indicating that littering could be used as an indirect measure of political attitudes.

Covert or Unobtrusive Measures: Obtaining information from people when they are not aware that this is being done

Think Again!

1. *What is a Likert-type attitude question?*
2. *What is the difference between overt and covert methods?*
3. *Create your own three-item mini scale to measure attitudes toward your college.*
4. *How might you covertly measure attitudes toward your government on your college campus?*

Factors That Impact the Relationship Between Attitudes and Behavior

Social psychologists have identified a large number of factors that impact the attitude-behavior relationship, and here we'll focus on perhaps the most important, attitude *strength* (Barden & Tormala, 2014; Glasman & Albarracín, 2006; Petty & Krosnick, 1995; Visser & Holbrook, 2012). There are four prominent attitude features related to attitude strength: personal experience, accessibility, importance, and certainty.

First of all, attitudes that are based on *direct experience* are more predictive of behavior (Daugherty, Li, & Biocca, 2008; Duerden & Witt, 2010; Kraus, 1995). For instance, Fazio and Zanna (1978) surveyed college students' attitudes toward participation in psychology research and obtained data about their later participation in such research. These researchers found that attitudes were more predictive of *later* research participation for students who had *previously* participated than for those who had not. Similarly, the relationship between college student attitudes toward a housing shortage and subsequent agreement to sign a petition to the administration about the housing problem was significantly greater among those students who were directly affected by the shortage (Regan & Fazio, 1977). A recent meta-analysis of 41 studies provided substantial evidence that direct experience with the attitude object enhances the attitude-behavior relationship (Glasman & Albarracín, 2006).

Second, attitudes that are more *accessible* or easier to retrieve at the time that a person is deciding whether to not to enact the corresponding behavior are better predictors than are less accessible attitudes (Fazio, 1995; Glasman & Albarracín, 2006). When attitudes are relatively easy to retrieve from memory—such as when they are nonconsciously primed—the attitude-behavior relationship is greater (Tormala, Falces, Briñol, & Petty, 2007). Third, attitudes that are *important*—where a person is both invested and very concerned—will be more consistent with behavior (Crano, 1995; Hunt, Kim, Borgida, & Chaiken, 2010). Finally, the greater the *certainty* a person has about the correctness of an attitude, the stronger the attitude-behavior relationship (Petrocelli, Tormala, & Rucker, 2007). This makes intuitive sense—if you are very confident that an attitude is correct, you are more likely to behave in accordance with it.

COGNITIVE CONSISTENCY AND
THE EFFECTS OF BEHAVIOR ON ATTITUDES

Do you ever feel the need to behave in a particular way or express a specific attitude in order to remain consistent with what you have said or done in the past? Have you ever seen someone smoking cigarettes while at the same time acknowledging how unhealthy it is? Both of these get at the notion of cognitive consistency, which is one of the most closely scrutinized topics in the history of social psychology (Gawronski & Strack, 2012; Harmon-Jones & Mills, 1999). Many social psychologists have argued that humans have a fundamental need to be consistent in our attitudes, beliefs, and behavior (Cialdini, Trost, & Newsom, 1995; Festinger, 1957). This desire for cognitive consistency is one of the primary routes through which behavior can affect attitudes. Let's review two prominent consistency theories proposed in the mid 20th century: balance theory and the theory of cognitive dissonance.

Balance Theory

In 1946, Fritz Heider proposed that humans like to maintain consistency or balance among elements of our mental systems. For Heider, a system was in balance when there was no inconsistency-based pressure to change any of the elements (Heider, 1958; Insko, 2012; Walther & Weil, 2012). For instance, balance is present when you imitate a person you like or avoid a person you don't like, but imitating a person you don't like or avoiding a person you like produces imbalance and psychological discomfort. Heider conceptualized the existence of psychological units as triads containing three elements that could be graphically depicted as triangles (see Figure 7.5). Each unit consisted of a person (P), another person (O), and an attitude object (X). The relationships between any two elements were designated as either positive (represented by a + sign) or negative (represented by a – sign), reflecting either liking or disliking, respectively.

For instance, if Joseph (P) and Raymond (O) are close friends, but Joseph has a strong antipathy toward Raymond's girlfriend Beatrice (X), then the unit is out of balance and discomfort will ensue. The system could be balanced if, say, Joseph starts liking Beatrice, Raymond dumps her, or the two males stop being friends. Indeed, Heider (1958) proposed that the valences or signs of the relations between the three possible pairs should be multiplied; only if the product is positive is the triangle balanced. I often get a few dubious looks when I present this theory in class, although most students acknowledge its intuitive appeal. But I have no doubt that you can think of situations where it applies to you, such as when you and a close friend or partner disagree about an issue that is important to both of you (e.g., abortion, religion, etc.). Even if you are unable to come up with one at the moment, do note that empirical research on balance theory has largely supported its basic tenets (Eagly & Chaiken, 1993; Walther & Weil, 2012). If this weren't the case, then why would corporations and organizations spend billions of dollars hiring celebrities to hawk their products (Rice et al., 2012; Walther & Weil, 2012)? Think about it: If you like a celebrity and the celebrity endorses a product, then you are more likely to positively evaluate that product.

Leon Festinger recognized the central role that cognitive consistency plays in the human psyche. Festinger's (1957) theory of cognitive dissonance is one of the most influential theories in the history of social psychology (Gawronski & Strack, 2012). Briefly, Festinger's theory states that people have a basic need to be consistent in their attitudes, beliefs, and behaviors, and logical inconsistency between any pair will lead to psychological discomfort. Festinger called this discomfort **cognitive dissonance**, and argued that, given the aversive nature of dissonance, humans will seek to minimize or eliminate it. As we noted in our opening vignette, Festinger claimed that The Seekers experienced cognitive dissonance when their core beliefs were shown to be incorrect, and some members sought to reduce the dissonance by recruiting new believers. Let's elaborate on Festinger's theory using the example of smoking, one of Festinger's favorites.

Say that Richard is a regular smoker and is well aware of smoking's negative health consequences. According to Festinger (1957), this inconsistency will produce dissonance or negative arousal that can be reduced in three ways. First, Richard can eliminate it by changing the behavior (stop smoking). A second option is to change his existing cognitions in some way, perhaps by discounting the evidence that smoking really is unhealthy (the research is flawed). Third, Richard can add new cognitions to the equation that can reduce the magnitude of the inconsistency. For example, he could claim that, compared to the dangers of automobile accidents or of high cholesterol, smoking is really not *that* bad or that smoking is good because it helps keep his weight down. Any of these strategies can effectively reduce the dissonance. Can you think of times when you have acted in a way that was inconsistent with your own values, attitudes, or beliefs? For instance, have you

> **Cognitive Dissonance:**
> Unpleasant arousal stemming from inconsistencies among one's attitudes, beliefs, and/or behaviors

FIGURE 7.5 Balance Theory

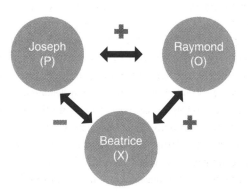

ever lied to someone without having a good reason for it and subsequently felt uneasy as a result? This very situation was the topic of a fascinating study of cognitive dissonance with surprising, counterintuitive, results.

Insufficient Justification. How would you respond to a situation in which you were paid to lie to another student about how much you enjoyed a psychology experiment that you had just finished? Would lying affect how you feel about yourself? Change your enjoyment of the task? Festinger and Carlsmith (1959) examined just this question in perhaps the most famous empirical demonstration of cognitive dissonance in all of social psychology. These researchers employed an experimental procedure called "forced" or "induced" compliance, in which participants are not actually forced to comply but rather are strongly encouraged toward a particular action desired by the experimenter. Before reading further, take a look at Figure 7.6 for the details of this study. Be sure to note how the payments that participants received differentially impacted attitude change *following* the lie. The thought process experienced by the participants is essentially "I am an honest person, yet I lied. Why?" The logical inconsistency between those two cognitions (I am honest; I lied) leads to cognitive dissonance.

Why did those who were paid *less* change their attitude *more*—that is, show greater liking for this incredibly dull experiment? Think about it. Of the two groups, which had more justification for their lies? Festinger and Carlsmith (1959) argued that the attitude change in the $1 condition resulted from the need of those participants to justify their lie. A $20 payment gave some participants a good excuse for their deception; however, receiving a meager $1 did not. Thus the $1 condition participants had an **insufficient justification** or explanation for their deceitful behavior (Chiou, 2008). The easiest method for those participants to eliminate their dissonance was to "decide" that they liked the study. In other words, if they could convince themselves that they truly liked the experiment, then the lie was not really a lie. Poof, the dissonance disappears! Dissonance reduction of this sort is deeply ingrained in us and can happen so quickly and automatically that we do not even realize that attitude change has occurred.

In general people want to justify their decisions and sometimes the need for self-justification is met by resorting to *external* justification that stems from factors outside of the self, such as receiving a sizable reward for lying (Festinger & Carlsmith, 1959). At other times, however, people will instead use *internal* justification by changing an attitude as in the $1 reward condition.

Counter Attitudinal Advocacy. When a person argues or advocates for a position with which she disagrees and that is counter or contrary to her attitudes, she is engaging in **counter attitudinal advocacy** (Festinger, 1957; Stone, 2012). Such counter attitudinal advocacy should create cognitive dissonance of the form "I believe X is true, but I just argued that X is false." The most likely route that a person will take to reconcile these discrepant cognitions is to change her true attitude so that it is closer to the one

Insufficient Justification: When a person believes that his or her explanation for their own behavior is inadequate

Counter Attitudinal Advocacy: Arguing or advocating for a position that is counter or contrary to a person's attitudes

FIGURE 7.6   Cognitive Dissonance and Attitude Change

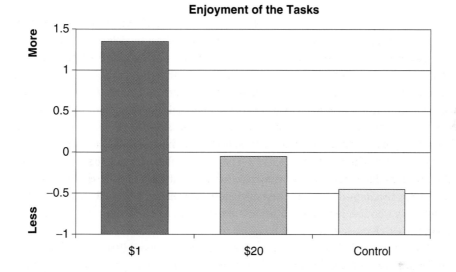

Festinger & Carlsmith (1959) hypothesized that people will sometimes change their attitudes in order to reduce cognitive dissonance. Participants completed two boring, mundane tasks and then were induced to lie to another participant (who was actually a confederate) by telling them how enjoyable the tasks had been. Participants in the two experimental conditions were given either $1 or $20 to lie; those in the control condition were not asked to lie. After the purported end of the study, all participants reported their true attitudes toward the experiment to someone not connected to the study. The experimenters predicted that the $1 participants would demonstrate greater attitude change—that is, greater liking for the experiment—than would the $20 participants, effectively reducing their dissonance. As you can see, this is exactly what they found.

Source: Adapted from Festinger, L., Carlsmith, J. M. (1959). Cognitive consequences of forced compliance. *Journal of Abnormal and Social Psychology, 58,* 203–210.

she advocated for (Festinger, 1957). In one real-world study, adolescent girls who had significant concerns about their body image were assigned to either express the disadvantages of pursuing a thin body (high dissonance) or to receive psychoeducational material that similarly indicated its disadvantages (low dissonance) (Stice, Rohde, Gau, & Shaw, 2009). The authors hypothesized and found that the dissonance-inducing intervention led to beneficial changes in body dissatisfaction, eating habits, and eating disorder symptoms as much as one year later. Other studies have demonstrated the efficacy of counter attitudinal advocacy on smoking (Simmons & Brandon, 2007) and the reduction of prejudice (Leippe & Eisenstadt, 2010).

Post-Decisional Dissonance. Making decisions requires rejecting one or more viable options in favor of another and, when one or more rejected alternative is appealing, we may immediately experience some dissonance (Chen & Risen, 2010; Festinger, 1957; Kimel, Grossmann, & Kitayama, 2012). As Heider (1958) suggested, rejecting options or people we like can be psychologically uncomfortable. For example, if you are planning to buy a cell phone, you'll probably look at several brands and models and weigh positive and negative features of each (e.g., cost, features, warranty, etc.). Ultimately, you will bring one home. Even though you presumably are happy with your decision, some doubt or discomfort may linger because you have rejected other options, and you may wonder if you made the best decision. Festinger (1957) linked this doubt to cognitive dissonance, and claimed that it stems from the fact that your decision forced you to say no to an attractive choice. He argued that people resolve this dissonance by becoming more enthusiastic about the choice they made and simultaneously downgrading the alternatives. In one supportive study, people became more certain that their chosen candidates would win an election immediately after casting their ballots (Regan & Kilduff, 1988). Similarly, individuals who had just placed a bet at a horse-racing track felt more confident about their horse's chances of winning than they had before the bet (Knox & Inkster, 1968). Festinger (1957) argued that virtually all decisions produce some dissonance, and that the magnitude of the dissonance will be greater for decisions that require more justification, such as those that are important or are between options that are relatively close in terms of attractiveness.

Advances in Dissonance Theory

Since Festinger (1957) first proposed his theory some 50 years ago, well over 2,000 empirical studies and concomitant theorizing have led to considerable advances in cognitive dissonance theory (Cooper, 1999, 2012a; Olson & Stone, 2005). Researchers have since identified a number of complexities in the model not recognized by its creator and have proposed a number of alternative interpretations of dissonance effects (Cooper, 2012a; Cooper & Fazio, 1984; Eagly & Chaiken, 1993). In this section, we'll look at a few of these developments. One of these advances has occurred in social neuroscience, where research has identified structures and processes in the brain that correlate with cognitive dissonance and dissonance reduction (see Research Box 7.1) (Harmon-Jones, Harmon-Jones, Fearn, Sigelman, & Johnson, 2008; Harmon-Jones, Harmon-Jones, Serra, & Gable, 2011).

Role of the Self. One major qualification to dissonance theory occurred when Elliott Aronson (1969) reinterpreted the basic dissonance construct by stating that, unlike what Festinger (1957) claimed, dissonance does not arise from all decisions. Rather, it occurs only as a result of threats to the self-concept. That is, if a person engages in a behavior that is discrepant with his self-concept, then it is likely to lead to dissonance (E. Aronson, 1969; Cooper, 2007; Kimel et al., 2012). For instance, the dissonance produced by the lies

RESEARCH BOX 7.1
THE NEUROSCIENCE OF COGNITIVE DISSONANCE

Hypothesis: Harmon-Jones et al. (2008) proposed an action-based model of cognitive dissonance engages our motivational system to prevent inconsistencies from interfering with implementing the corresponding decision. If we are uncertain about the correctness of a given decision, then we may be reluctant or slow to act on that decision. Such action would occur during the post-decisional phase or what Harmon-Jones et al. (2008) call the action state. The post-decisional spreading of alternatives (discussed in the text) facilitates action by increasing the attractiveness of the chosen alternative relative to the rejected one (Brehm, 1956). Research has demonstrated that the anterior cingulate cortex (ACC) is activated in the presence of cognitive inconsistency and that the left prefrontal cortex (PFC) is involved in the reduction of the corresponding dissonance. If the PFC is integral to the reduction of dissonance, then inhibiting its activity following dissonance induction should consequently prevent the expected spreading of alternatives.

Research Method: Prior to the experiment, proper participants were provided with two days of neurofeedback training in which they learned to increase or decrease left prefrontal activity. On the third day, participants completed an evaluation and ranking task similar to the Heine and Lehman (1997) CD selection procedure described in the main text, but in this case it involved expressing preferences for various psychology research experiments. After ranking the options, researchers requested that they choose one of two closely ranked experiments to participate in. Immediately afterward, all participants underwent the same neural feedback training as on the first two days. Finally, they were asked to reevaluate the two experiments they had previously selected from. The pre-decisional and post-decisional evaluations were then compared.

Results: The results were consistent with the hypotheses: Participants who had been trained to reduce activity in the PFC engaged in significantly *less* spreading of the alternatives than did those trained to increase it (see Figures 7.7).

Conclusion: Dissonance can be reduced by controlling the activation of the left PFC.

(Continued)

(Continued)

FIGURE 7.7 The Neuroscience of Cognitive Dissonance

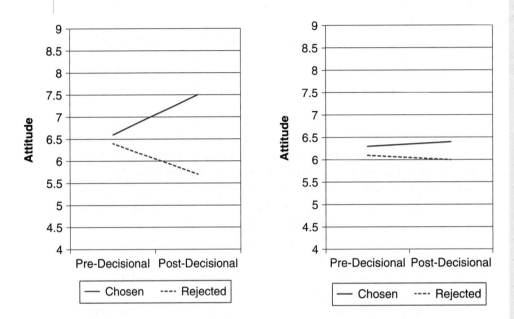

Source: Adapted from Figure 1, Harmon-Jones, E., Harmon-Jones, C., Fearn, M., Sigelman, J., & Johnson, P. (2008). Left cortical activation and spreading of alternatives: Test of the action-based model of dissonance. *Journal of Personality and Social Psychology, 94,* 1–15.

in the Festinger and Carlsmith (1959) study was because of the negative implications of lying for a central feature of the self: honesty. Aronson (1969, 1992) argued that people want to believe that they are competent, moral, consistent, and able to predict their own behavior, and dissonance will result from actions that threaten any of these. In a sense, one could say The Seekers' sense of competence was undermined because they had chosen to embrace beliefs that were patently untrue.

Hypocrisy Induction. One important implication of this assertion of the importance of the self in dissonance is that attitude change can be deliberately produced by making salient such threats to the self (Stone & Focella, 2011; Yousaf & Gobet, 2013). For instance, Aronson,

Fried, and Stone (1991) found that by leading research participants to be more mindful of their own hypocrisy regarding prior failures to use condoms, the difference between their own prior use and intention to use condoms in the future was greater, as compared to a nonmindful condition. Inducing hypocrisy produced a threat to the self, and the concomitant dissonance led participants to reduce that threat-related dissonance by strengthening their plan to use condoms in the future. This **hypocrisy induction paradigm** has been successfully employed to produce beneficial changes in attitudes and behaviors, including those related to volunteerism (Fointiat, Somat, & Grosbras, 2011), water conservation (Dickerson, Thibodeau, Aronson, & Miller, 1992), smoking (Peterson, Haynes, & Olson, 2008), and children's risky activity in a playground (Morrongiello & Mark, 2008).

Self-Affirmation. Much of the research on cognitive dissonance focused on changes in attitudes intended to directly eliminate the dissonance. However, other avenues are also available to individuals seeking to reduce dissonance, especially when the integrity of the self is threatened. Given that people want to view themselves as good, competent, and stable and that dissonance can be a response to challenges to this image of the self, then actions that help restore that self-image may also achieve dissonance reduction. Sometimes people will engage in **self-affirmation**, a process whereby the integrity of the self is restored by affirming important values or qualities (Armitage, Harris, & Arden, 2011; Aronson, Blanton, & Cooper, 1995; Sherman & Hartson, 2011; Steele, 1988). For instance, participants induced to write an essay opposing increasing state funding for handicapped persons—presumably inconsistent with their self-images as helpful and moral—demonstrated less dissonance-reducing attitude change *if* they expected to be able to volunteer later to help needy persons and thereby restore their self-concept (Steele & Liu, 1981).

The New Look. One of the biggest challenges to Festinger's original conceptualization of dissonance as stemming from inconsistencies was Cooper and Fazio's (1984) "new look" at dissonance theory. Whereas Festinger argued that mere inconsistency would produce aversive arousal, Cooper and Fazio (1984) believed this was only true if it also led to negative consequences. According to the new look, our inconsistencies are often minor or have no practical or meaningful implications and will not lead to dissonance, even though they may produce attitude change. However, if unwanted consequences ensue, then we may feel dissonance.

Culture. In addition to individual variation in the need for cognitive consistency, substantial differences also exist across cultures. This difference can explain why the traditional dissonance effects are less likely to be found among collectivists than individualists (Kokkoris & Kühnen, 2013). Recall that collectivists are more other-focused, more likely to demonstrate variety in their behavior across situations, and possess a more interdependent self. In contrast, individualists tend to be more self-focused, behave similarly across contexts, and define themselves as independent (Markus & Kitayama, 1991). Heine and Lehman (1997) investigated attitude change among Japanese and Canadian individuals under the guise of a music preference study. Participants were asked to select the ten CDs

Hypocrisy Induction Paradigm: Leading someone to recognize an inconsistency among his or her attitudes, beliefs, and behaviors

Self-Affirmation: Process whereby the integrity of the self is restored by affirming important values or qualities

that they found the most desirable from a larger list. Later they were given the option of choosing to take home one of two CDs that they had perceived to be about equally appealing, either the fifth or sixth ranked CD. Finally, they were asked to evaluate all 10 CDs. Having to make a choice between two equally attractive choices should, if Festinger (1957) was correct, lead first to dissonance and then to dissonance reduction.

Other research had shown that dissonance reduction would take the form of a post-decisional "spreading" of the alternatives such that CDs five and six (or whatever alternatives were present) would be evaluated as very different in desirability in order to rationalize their choice (Brehm, 1956; M. K. Chen & Risen, 2010; Hoshino-Browne, 2012). As a result of this spreading, participants downgraded the one not chosen as a way to justify the rejection of that option. Canadian participants responded precisely as Brehm (1956) would have predicted. However, the Japanese individuals did not exhibit the traditional dissonance effects (Heine & Lehman, 1997). Using a similar paradigm, Hoshino-Browne et al. (2005) extended this research by asking some respondents to rank and subsequently choose a restaurant dish either for themselves or a close friend. They found the expected dissonance effects in the self-condition only among Canadians and the reverse pattern among Japanese participants. Thus, the former needed to justify their choices they made for themselves but not those for others; in contrast, the latter felt the need to rationalize the decisions they made for their friends but not for themselves.

Summary. Looking back at the vast research on cognitive dissonance, several key conclusions can be drawn. Dissonance is more likely to arise when four conditions are met. First, the individual must accept *personal responsibility* for their behavior; that is, the behavior is seen as *freely chosen* and the consequences had to have been *foreseeable* prior to the behavior in question (Cooper & Fazio, 1984). Second, the behavior produced *unwanted consequences* (Cooper & Fazio, 1984). Third, the behavior had *insufficient external justification*—it could not be explained away by resorting to, say rewards for engaging in the behavior (Festinger & Carlsmith, 1959). Fourth, the behavior is *irrevocable* and cannot be changed (Festinger, 1957). Moreover, keep in mind that whether or not dissonance may be generated in any particular situation will also depend on features of the person and the culture.

Think Again!

1. *What, specifically, leads to attitude change in the forced compliance paradigm?*

2. *Think of a time when you have experienced dissonance because of conflict between two existing attitudes or behaviors. How did it feel, and how were you able to resolve the dissonance?*

3. *How does culture impact the generation of dissonance?*

SELF-REFLECTION 7.1
Preference for Consistency (Part 1)

As you know, one of social psychology's basic principles is that social behavior is a product of both the person and the situation. This is no less true for dissonance–related phenomena than for other social behavior. Dissonance effects, especially as conceptualized by Festinger (1957), largely depend on the unpleasant arousal that stems from some form of cognitive inconsistency. Festinger (1957), Heider (1958), and other psychologists have assumed that all people are similarly motivated to maintain a view of the self as consistent or stable. However, variations in the effectiveness of some purportedly consistency-based experimental manipulations led Cialdini, Trost, and Newsom (1995) to wonder whether consistency pressures are not simply situational but may be partly dispositional. In other words, do individuals vary in their desire for personal consistency? Take a few minutes to respond to the following questions and then turn the page to learn more about the scale.

TABLE 7.3   Preference for Consistency

We would like to learn more about how people perceive their own habits and behaviors. Please respond to the following items by circling the number that best describes your level of agreement with each item.

Item	Response options								
	Strongly disagree	Disagree	Some-what disagree	Slightly disagree	Neither agree nor disagree	Slightly agree	Some-what agree	Agree	Strongly agree
1. I prefer to be around people whose reactions I can anticipate.	1	2	3	4	5	6	7	8	9
2. It is important to me that my actions are consistent with my beliefs.	1	2	3	4	5	6	7	8	9
3. Even if my attitudes and actions seemed consistent with one another to me, it would bother me if they did not seem consistent in the eyes of others.	1	2	3	4	5	6	7	8	9

SELF-REFLECTION 7.1
(Continued)

Item	Response options								
	Strongly disagree	Disagree	Some-what disagree	Slightly disagree	Neither agree nor disagree	Slightly agree	Some-what agree	Agree	Strongly agree
4. It is important to me that those who know me can predict what I will do.	1	2	3	4	5	6	7	8	9
5. I want to be described by others as a stable, predictable person.	1	2	3	4	5	6	7	8	9
6. Admirable people are consistent and predictable.	1	2	3	4	5	6	7	8	9
7. The appearance of consistency is an important part of the image I present to the world.	1	2	3	4	5	6	7	8	9
8. It bothers me when someone I depend upon is unpredictable.	1	2	3	4	5	6	7	8	9
9. I don't like to appear as if I am inconsistent.	1	2	3	4	5	6	7	8	9
10. I get uncomfortable when I find my behavior contradicts my beliefs.	1	2	3	4	5	6	7	8	9

SELF-REFLECTION 7.1
(Continued)

Item	Response options								
	Strongly disagree	Disagree	Some-what disagree	Slightly disagree	Neither agree nor disagree	Slightly agree	Some-what agree	Agree	Strongly agree
11. An important requirement for any friend of mine is personal consistency.	1	2	3	4	5	6	7	8	9
12. I typically prefer to do things the same way.	1	2	3	4	5	6	7	8	9
13. I dislike people who are constantly changing their opinion.	1	2	3	4	5	6	7	8	9
14. I want my close friends to be predictable.	1	2	3	4	5	6	7	8	9
15. It is important to me that others view me as a stable person.	1	2	3	4	5	6	7	8	9
16. I make an effort to appear consistent to others.	1	2	3	4	5	6	7	8	9
17. I'm uncomfortable holding two beliefs that are inconsistent.	1	2	3	4	5	6	7	8	9
18. It doesn't bother me much if my actions are inconsistent.	1	2	3	4	5	6	7	8	9

Source: Cialdini, R. B., Trost, M. R., & Newsom, J. T. (1995). Preference for consistency: The development of a valid measure and the discovery of surprising behavioral implications. *Journal of Personality and Social Psychology, 69*, 318–328.

TURN THE PAGE TO FIND OUR ANSWERS.

SELF-REFLECTION 7.2
Preference for Consistency (Part 2)

This scale, called the Preference For Consistency (PFC) scale, was developed and validated by Cialdini et al. (1995) to capture individual differences in how important consistency in behavior is to us (Barrett, Patock-Peckham, Hutchinson, & Nagoshi, 2005; Nichols & Webster, 2014; Nolan & Nail, 2014). These researchers found that individual differences in PFC could partially explain variations in dissonance reduction in the standard counterattitudinal advocacy experiment and in responses to consistency-based compliance techniques (Heitland & Bohner, 2010). For instance, people who are relatively higher in PFC should be more vulnerable to the foot-in-the-door compliance-gaining procedure described in Chapter 6 (Cialdini et al., 1995; Guadagno & Cialdini, 2010). The PFC scale measures three types of preference: wanting to be self-consistent, to have others see oneself as consistent, and to have others be consistent. To determine your score, first reverse score the last item (1 = 9, 2 = 8, 3 = 7, 4 = 6, 5 = 5, 6 = 4, 7 = 3, 8 = 2, 9 = 1) and then add up your responses. Next divide by 18 to obtain your average response. Participants in Cialdini's original studies had a mean of 5.43; the researchers labeled anyone above that as "high" in PFC and below that as "low" PFC. How do you rate? Reflect on your own life, friends, and general preferences. Does your score make sense to you?

FINAL THOUGHTS: RESISTING PERSUASION

In this chapter, we have focused primarily on how attitudes are formed, how they change, and how they affect behavior. We saw that attitudes are acquired through a combination of biology, learning, and culture. Although attitude change was once considered mostly a matter of learning, social psychologists now know that other cognitive processes, such as message elaboration and dissonance reduction, can play important roles in attitude change. After reading the preceding discussion of persuasion, one may infer that persuasion is a process in which external forces magically change our evaluations of persons, things,

or ideas. But is this appropriate? I don't think so. It seems to me that persuasion can also be conceptualized as self-persuasion: The thoughts that we generate (our cognitive responses) or the behaviors that we engage in (such as counter attitudinal advocacy, self-affirming statements, etc.) often have the effect of changing our attitudes. No matter how we characterize it, persuasion is ubiquitous: It is everywhere around us, all of the time.

Our focus on attitude change should by no means imply that attitudes always change in the face of persuasion attempts. Knowing only one side of the story, one can legitimately ask whether people have the free will to hold firm and ward off such attempts. There are in fact numerous ways in which people can and do resist persuasion (Chen, Minson, Schöne, & Heinrichs, 2013; Dursun & Tümer Kabadayi, 2013; Knowles & Linn, 2004; Sagarin & Wood, 2007; Tormala, 2008). For instance, one way to encourage resistance is to teach people that they are vulnerable to manipulation by illegitimate authorities so that they can recognize and prevent it in the future (Sagarin, Cialdini, Rice, & Serna, 2002). Even in the absence of specific instruction, other factors, such as personality characteristics (Albarracín & Mitchell, 2004), attitude strength (Petty & Krosnick, 1995), motivation (Festinger, 1957), and warning people that a persuasion attempt is imminent (McGuire, 1964), have all been shown to reduce attitude change. So yes, people do have considerable free will with regard to persuasion. Resistance to persuasion, like persuasion itself, is ubiquitous.

The content of this chapter touches on a couple other of our fundamental questions. One question worth asking has to do with the role of rationality in the persuasion process. As depicted in dual process theory, rational, deliberative thinking can clearly impact the direction and extent of attitude change. But what about cognitive dissonance and its reduction? Does it make sense to conceptualize these processes as rational? I would say yes, it does. First of all, cognitive consistency can be said to be rooted in psycho-logic: Regardless of whether attitudes and behavior are objectively at odds, whether or not dissonance is produced depends largely on the person's perception of the cognitive fit. Secondly, the desire to justify one's thoughts and actions is itself a rational one.

The third fundamental question that I want to mention should be obvious: the centrality of the self in persuasion. Dissonance processes clearly hinge upon the need to protect the integrity of the self, explaining the roles of self-affirmation, self-justification, and self-hypocrisy in dissonance reduction. Finally, I hope that the apparently surprising responses of The Seekers to the failure of the prophecy that they had placed so much faith in now makes a little more sense.

CORE CONCEPTS

- Persuasion refers to the changes in attitudes or beliefs; an attitude is an evaluation of a person, thing, or idea; a belief is a knowledge claim about what is true about the world. Attitudes are ambivalent when they contain both positive and negative evaluations and indifferent when they contain no evaluation at all. Unlike our explicit attitudes, we tend to be unaware of our implicit attitudes.

- Attitudes may be developed and shaped by a variety of influences, including individual experiences, contextual factors, and genetic inheritance.

- Persuasion may occur via central and/or peripheral processes: The former is marked by careful thinking, whereas the latter occurs without much thought.

- A variety of source characteristics (such as expertise, trustworthiness, and goodwill), message factors (including fear and negativity), and audience factors (such as self-monitoring and need for cognition) play important roles in persuasion.

- Attitudes can be measured using direct, overt methods, or indirect, covert methods, each of which has advantages and disadvantages.

- Reasoned action theory postulates that behavior can be predicted by behavioral intention, which in turn is influenced by attitudes, perceived norms, and perceived behavioral control. Lack of actual behavioral control can disrupt the intention-behavior relationship.

- Cognitive dissonance theory can guide attempts to change behavior, such as when people recognize inconsistencies in their behavior and seek to reduce or eliminate them, when people have insufficient external justification for their behavior, and when they engage in counter attitudinal advocacy; important advances in dissonance theory include recognition of how culture may influence responses to inconsistencies, the new look reinterpretation, the realization of the centrality of the self, and how inducing hypocrisy can change behavior.

▶ $SAGE edge™ Test your understanding of chapter content. Take the practice quiz. edge.sagepub.com/barrett

KEY TERMS

Attitude, 230
Belief, 231
Bogus Pipeline, 251
Central Processing, 239
Cognitive Dissonance, 255
Cognitive Responses, 238
Cognitive Response
 Model of
 Persuasion, 238
Counter Attitudinal
 Advocacy, 256
Covert or Unobtrusive
 Measures, 252

Credibility, 242
Dual Attitude, 232
Dual Process Model, 239
Elaboration Likelihood
 Model of Persuasion, 239
Explicit Attitude, 232
Heuristic-Systematic Model
 of Persuasion, 241
Hypocrisy Induction
 Paradigm, 261

Implicit Attitude, 232
Insufficient Justification, 256
Mere Exposure Effect, 235
Need for Cognition, 246
Overt Measures, 250
Peripheral Processing, 239
Persuasion, 230
Self-Affirmation, 261
Tripartite Model
 of Attitudes, 233

▶ $SAGE edge™   Review key terms with eFlashcards. edge.sagepub.com/barrett

THINK FURTHER!

- What is an attitude? Can you define ambivalence, implicit and explicit attitudes, dual attitudes, and attitude specificity? Can you apply each of these to attitudes of your own?

- Think about how you acquired some of your attitudes. What role do you think your personal experiences and group-level influences like culture played? What attitudes do you share with your relatives that might be linked to heredity?

- What is the role of cognitive response in the two routes to attitude change? What factors impact which route a receiver is likely to take?

- Try analyzing ads that you see on TV, online, or in magazines using key features of messages, such as fear and negativity.

- How would you measure the attitudes of your partner, friends, and/or strangers? What method(s) would you use and why?

- Can you apply balance theory to your relationship with a partner or friend? What might the third element in the triangle be?

- Think of an unhealthy or destructive behavior that someone you care about engages in. How might you use hypocrisy induction to change it?

SUGGESTED READINGS

Banaji, M. R., & Heiphetz, L. (2010). Attitudes. In Fiske, S. T., Gilbert, D. T., & Lindzey, G. (Eds.), *Handbook of social psychology* (5th ed., Vol. 1, pp. 353–393). New York, NY: John Wiley & Sons.

Brandt, M. J., & Wethere, G. A. (2012). What attitudes are moral attitudes? The case of attitude heritability. *Social Psychological and Personality Science, 3,* 172–179

Festinger, L. (1957). *A theory of cognitive dissonance.* Stanford, CA: Stanford University Press.

Heine, S. J., & Lehman, D. R. (1997). Culture, dissonance, and self-affirmation. *Personality and Social Psychology Bulletin, 23,* 389–400.

Petty, R.E., & Cacioppo, J.T. (1981). *Attitudes and persuasion: Classic and contemporary approaches.* Dubuque, IA: Wm. C. Brown Company.

IV

MORAL BEHAVIOR

Helping

Volunteers donate blood on September 11, 2001 at a Park Ridge, Illinois, donation station set up to help victims of the World Trade Center attack in New York City.

Tim Boyle/Getty Images News/Getty Images.

LEARNING OBJECTIVES

8.1 Define the social responsibility norm, prosocial behavior, egoism, altruism, inclusive fitness, principle of kin selection, heritability of helping behavior, and reciprocal helping.

8.2 Describe the mood management hypothesis and compare and contrast the negative state relief and the arousal: cost reward models.

8.3 Critique bystander apathy as an explanation for failure to help; identify the characteristics of emergencies; identify the five steps in the failure-to-help model and explain the roles of diffusion of responsibility and pluralistic ignorance in failures to help.

8.4 Discuss the practices that social psychologists have established to help safeguard the well-being of participants.

8.5 Appraise the empathy-altruism hypothesis and compare and contrast the egoistic and altruistic notions of helping.

8.6 Summarize research on the impacts of personal factors, attributions, and culture on helping.

THE NATURE OF HELPING BEHAVIOR

- In December 2010, a young off-duty police officer—identified in the press only as Angel—put his life in jeopardy and jumped onto the tracks at a Madrid subway stop and pulled a fallen man out of the path of an upcoming train just moments before it passed.
- During the Holocaust, the German industrialist Oskar Schindler saved over 1,000 Jews from near certain death by protecting them from the Nazis.
- Approximately 500,000 Americans donated blood during the days following the September 11, 2001, terrorist attacks.

$SAGE edge™

Get the edge on your studies.
edge.sagepub.com/barrett

Take a quiz to find out what you've learned.
Watch videos that enhance chapter content.
Explore related web and social media activities.

Each of these cases gives us a glimpse of the countless inspiring ways that people around the world help those in need. Acts of generosity, heroism, volunteerism, helping, and other "good" deeds occur everyday, everywhere. Do you ever wonder why a soldier or police officer or bank teller puts himself in danger while trying to save another person? Or why do some people donate substantial amounts of time or money to improve the welfare of others? Unfortunately, the major news outlets focus primarily on the negative—mass killings, abuse, war, and so forth—and overlook so much of the good that we do everyday, around the globe. To be sure, specific and unusual acts of heroism and courage make their way to the headlines, but they are quickly buried in the heap of bad news.

One consequence of this unfortunate imbalance is that people often speculate about the causes of *immorality*—aggression, abuse, torture, and so forth—but spend less time wondering about the reasons people engage in *moral* behaviors. In the following pages, we will focus primarily on the enactment of moral behavior—particularly helping—often grouped under the umbrella term *prosocial behavior*. Prosocial behavior refers to the things people do—such as caring, giving, volunteering, and donating—that benefit individuals and society as a whole. In this chapter we will explain the major theories and research about why people do *good* things, particularly helping others. In contrast, the following chapter examines behavior often considered *antisocial:* aggression.

Prosocial behavior is related to several of our fundamental questions of human existence. First and foremost is the topic of morality: prosocial behavior represents the core of our moral being. Our helping, caring for, and cooperating with fellow humans is a basis for the contention that we are a moral species. Evidence for this lies in the **social responsibility norm**, which states that we should help those who need our help, and which is considered to be culturally universal (Berkowitz & Daniels, 1963). Second, prosocial behavior is also relevant to human sociality. Prosocial behavior is closely associated with group living, serving as a kind of glue that binds people together, with the reverse also being true; the failure to provide expected help can result in the offender being sanctioned and potentially

Social Responsibility Norm: Norm that states that one should help those who need one's help

outcast. Third, discussions of prosocial behavior inevitably involve questions about the nature of the self, for two reasons. One is that the type of relationship of the self to others in need—whether based in kinship, group membership, similarity, and so forth—is crucial to whether or not a person chooses to offer aid. The other is the central issue in understanding prosocial behavior—whether it can occur in the absence of any expected rewards to the self. In other words, is pure, unselfish altruism possible?

Think Ahead!

1. _Does people ever act in a truly selfless way?_
2. _Why do some people help while others turn away?_
3. _How does gender affect helping?_

WHY WE HELP

This chapter focuses on **prosocial behavior**, which we can define as behavior that is intended to benefit others. Although prosocial behavior is commonly equated with helping, it is a broader concept that also includes volunteering, cooperating, playing fairly, following norms, and being polite. Because the bulk of the social psychological research on prosocial behavior has focused on short-term, traditional helping (as opposed to cooperation or politeness more generally), we will do the same in this chapter. Cooperation is key to the effective functioning of groups and will be discussed in that context (Chapter 12).

Prosocial Behavior: Behavior that is intended to benefit others

College student volunteers help Habitat for Humanity construct a home for a low-income family during their 2012 spring break.

AP Photo/ Torin Halsey.

Understanding the origins of helping and other prosocial behavior has intrigued humans for hundreds, maybe thousands, of years (Cahn, 2009), but social psychologists only began earnestly investigating its nature in the late 20th century (Batson, 1998). Three basic motives for helping other people have been emphasized by social psychologists. The first is based in genetics: Helping behavior is primarily enacted because it is adaptive when it perpetuates the helper's gene pool. This evolution-based argument explains why we help people who are genetically related to us. The second motive is steeped in a narrower view of self-interest, called egoism. **Egoism** suggests that we help other people because it brings rewards to ourselves (Brown & Maner, 2012). These rewards may be mood based (helping feels good), material based (we help because people give us things), or status based (we receive recognition, respect, etc.). Although helping kin is egoistic in the sense that it helps one's genes survive, it is useful to separate it from nongenetic benefits because the latter are not necessarily grounded in the former. For instance, lifting one's mood by holding the door for an elderly person is not going to produce direct genetic benefits.

The third prominent motivation for helping is based in the empathic concern and compassion that we feel for other people. The principle of **altruism** states that one has a desire to benefit others purely for the sake of those others and not for one's own sake (Batson, 2011). That is, helping behavior can be motivated by something other than egoism; people can and will help in the absence of any expected meaningful benefit to the self (Macaulay & Berkowitz, 1970). We will return to the provocative question about whether or not pure, selfless behavior is possible later in the chapter.

Egoism: Helping other people because it brings internal and/or external rewards to the helper

Altruism: Acting to benefit others and not for one's own sake

ORIGINS OF HELPING BEHAVIOR

Kin Selection

One of the principle drivers of human behavior is the imperative to propagate one's genes (Darwin, 1859/1994), which easily explains why individuals help their offspring. However, an overly narrow view of evolution fails to recognize that individuals provide help to genetically related others who are not their own progeny, even while risking their own survival. The propensity to render aid to nonoffspring is seen not just in humans but also in many other species, including social insects and nonhuman primates (see photo). For instance, honey bees swarm and attack creatures that threaten their nest, despite the fact that a single sting is fatal to the honey bee. This self-sacrifice is even more puzzling when we consider that these wasps are sterile and therefore can have no offspring in the nest to protect! W.D. Hamilton (1964) offered the concept of inclusive fitness

PROSOCIAL BEHAVIOR IN THE ANIMAL KINGDOM

Chimpanzees engaged in grooming. Humans are not the only species to exhibit altruistic behavior.

Tom Brakefield]/Stockbyte/Thinkstock.

Inclusive Fitness:
Ability of one's genes
to survive both in
one's own offspring
and in one's (genetic)
relatives

Kin Selection:
Traits that tend to
facilitate the survival
of an individual's
genetic relatives are
also selected for

as a solution. According to Hamilton, **inclusive fitness** refers to the ability of one's genes to survive both in one's own offspring and in one's (genetic) relatives (Ferriere & Michod, 2011; Foster, Wenseleers, & Ratnieks, 2006; Gesselman & Webster, 2012; Jonason, Izzo, & Webster, 2007; Richardson, 2015). In other words, evolutionary fitness is not confined to just individual survival but also includes one's genetic pool. A honey bee may sacrifice itself, but by doing so, it helps to ensure the survival of its genetic relatives.

The principle of **kin selection**—a corollary of natural selection—states that traits that facilitate the survival of an individual's genetic relatives are also selected for (Cosmides & Tooby, 1992; Krebs, 2011). This principle assumes that (a) we are able to recognize our kin, and (b) we are more likely to help those who are more (versus less) genetically similar to us (Kurland & Gaulin, 2005). Consonant with the first assumption are two studies by Porter and colleagues that have demonstrated how human mothers can identify their babies simply by scent, such as the scent left by babies after contact with a shirt (Porter, Cernoch, & McLaughlin, 1983), and by photo, even if the mothers' time with the babies has been minimal (Porter, Cernoch, & Balogh, 1984). Although people can often recognize their kin, this is not always the case. Sometimes we may not realize that a stranger is genetically related, whereas other people with whom we are very familiar—such as adopted siblings—can seem genetically related and may be treated as such.

There is a great deal of evidence that supports the second assumption of kin selection, by showing that people are more likely to help genetically closer relatives than more distant relatives or strangers. For instance, in one study both adult South African Zulus

FIGURE 8.1   Helping Kin Versus NonKin

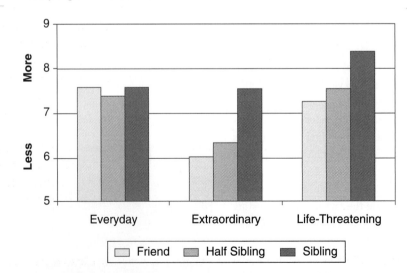

People don't distinguish much between kin and nonkin for everyday helping but do so in high-risk situations.

Source: Adapted from Fitzgerald, C. J., & Colarelli, S. M. (2009). Altruism and reproductive limitations. *Evolutionary psychology, 7* (2), 234–252.

and British undergraduates were more likely to endure pain if it financially benefited relatives as compared to nonrelatives (Madsen et al., 2007). Similarly, participants in a study by Fitzgerald and Colarelli (2009) reported a preference for helping a sibling more than a half-sibling or friend in contexts of medium or high risk to the self but not for low risk situations (see Figure 8.1). Other studies have found that genetic relatedness predicted cooperation on a difficult puzzle (Segal, 1984) and kidney donation (Borgida, Conner, & Manteufel, 1992) and a variety of other prosocial behaviors (Knafo & Israel, 2010).

Heritability

The tendency to engage in helping behavior is partially linked to one's genes. Although estimates vary, the heritability of the empathic response to the distress of other people in adults may be as high as 71% (Matthews, Batson, Horn, & Rosenman, 1981) or as low as 28% (Davis, Luce, & Kraus, 1994). A recent study of adolescent twins found that the continuity of prosocial behavior over time was largely because of genetics, whereas more specific behaviors were better predicted by nonshared environmental influences (Gregory, Light-Häusermann, Rijsdijk, & Eley, 2009). Nonshared influences refer to elements in the environment that are not experienced by both twins, such as friends, clubs or other activities, and teachers. Overall, the influence of environmental factors appears to be greater than that of genetic factors (Gregory et al., 2009).

A number of studies have examined the role that hormones—especially oxytocin—play in human social action more generally and in prosocial behavior more specifically (Campbell, 2010; Decety & Ickes, 2009). Oxytocin is a peptide hormone thought to be involved in breastfeeding, the development of maternal behaviors, mother-infant bonding, anxiety reduction, and many other aspects of mammalian social behavior (Carter, Harris, & Porges, 2009; Decety & Ickes, 2009; Kemp & Guastella, 2011; Singer et al., 2008). In her recent review of the literature, Campbell (2010) examined evidence for oxytocin's role in human behavior, concluding that under certain circumstances its presence can enhance trust in and reduce fear of other people. Oxytocin has also been shown to increase generosity in participants required to share money with another person but allowed to decide how much to share (Zak, Stanton, & Ahmadi, 2007). Thus, across a wide variety of studies, oxytocin is associated with approaching or connecting with other humans (Campbell, 2010; Poulin, Holman, & Buffone, 2012; Zak, Kurzban, & Matzner, 2005; Zak et al., 2007). The picture may be a bit more complicated, however. Other research suggests that increased oxytocin may enhance approach behavior and also inhibit avoidance behavior, leading to more conflict and possibly increasing the likelihood of aggression (Kemp & Guastella, 2011).

Group Selection

As I noted in Chapter 1, although most evolutionary theorists have argued that natural selection operates only at the level of the individual, a small but growing number have posited that evolution also occurs at the group level (Haidt & Kesebir, 2010; Sober & Wilson, 1998). The idea is that when groups compete—say, for resources—the group that contains the higher proportion of altruists will have an evolutionary advantage over the more selfish group (McAndrew, 2002). If group selection does occur, then it is possible that some prosocial behavior is rooted in the advantages that it brings to the group. That is, evolutionary processes would have led to the emergence of gene-based, group-level prosocial tendencies. For instance, an individual might sacrifice herself by covering up a hand grenade with her body in order to save unrelated members of her group. Unfortunately, as provocative as this thesis is, testing group selection in humans in an experimental setting would be quite challenging and therefore the idea remains speculative (Dovidio, Piliavin, Schroeder, & Penner, 2006).

Reciprocity

Reciprocal Helping: When people help others because the others have previously helped them or are expected to help them in the future

Norm of Reciprocity: Social rule stating that people should offer help to and avoid harming those who have helped them

There is another theory that relates prosocial behavior to evolution: the theory of **reciprocal helping** (Axelrod, 2006; Trivers, 1971). Reciprocity—as we discussed in Chapter 6—is the notion that we engage in "give and take" with others, such that when we do someone a favor, we expect that favor to eventually be repaid. Trivers (1971) argued that reciprocal helping or reciprocal benefit is an evolved mechanism that can facilitate survival of both parties. Indeed, the sociologist Alvin Gouldner (1960) postulated that a **norm of reciprocity**—entailing that we should both offer help to and avoid harming those who have helped us—is a universal feature of human societies. Note that reciprocal helping would only be beneficial if individuals were generally accurate at identifying who is likely to help and who is likely to cheat or not help. In order to accomplish that, a "cheater detector" must be an evolved component of the human cognitive system (Cosmides & Tooby, 1992). Moreover, cheaters should be shunned by others and may be punished for their transgressions (Cosmides & Tooby, 1992; Trivers, 1971).

There is ample evidence that people do in fact follow the reciprocity norm in their everyday lives (Balafoutas, Nikiforakis, & Rockenbach, 2014; Nakamura & Masuda, 2011; Trivers, 1971). For instance, participants in a study by Whatley et al. (Whatley, Webster, Smith, & Rhodes, 1999) were more likely to donate to a charity chosen by another person (actually, a confederate) if that other person had previously given them candy. In an earlier study by Kunz and Woolcott (1976), researchers sent Christmas cards to dozens of complete strangers and found that approximately one-fifth of the recipients reciprocated! Similarly, individuals given a Coca-Cola by a fellow research participant were more likely to buy raffle tickets that cost more than the soda did, as compared to those who had not been handed a Coke (Regan, 1971). People engage in both *direct* reciprocity—give and take between two individuals—and *indirect* reciprocity, when they provide benefits to individuals even when the recipient has no chance to return the favor (Bland, 2013; Delton, Krasnow, Cosmides, & Tooby, 2011; Ghang & Nowak, 2015; Roberts, 2015). In the latter case, people may, for instance, tip a waiter who they will never see again but expect that their kindness will eventually be repaid by another (Nowak & Sigmund, 2005; Stanca, 2009).

Now, you may ask why, if the reciprocity and social responsibility norms are truly universal, do some people *not* follow them? As we have said earlier, explanations for and descriptions of regularities in social behavior (a) cannot explain or predict how any particular person will behave, and (b) other social forces can prevent the enactment of that behavior. With respect to helping, not all people in the world learn these norms to the same extent. In addition, people may develop individual or personal norms that may or may not be consistent with more general social norms.

Individual Experiences

Another root of helping behavior is individual experience. Children are taught the importance of helping other people and to engage in more general prosocial behavior (e.g., respecting others, taking turns, etc.) when very young and appear to exhibit helping behavior as early as 18 months of age (Hepach, Vaish, & Tomasello, 2012). Helping behavior increases as children age, as suggested by a study by Green and Schneider (1974) in which older boys were more likely to share their candy and to help pick up dropped pencils than were younger ones. One way children may learn to help is via operant conditioning: Children who are given personal praise or other rewards for helping are more likely to do it again (Mills & Grusec, 1989), whereas those who are punished for it are less likely (Moss & Page, 1972). Furthermore, the idea that helping can bring external and internal rewards is learned as children progress from being a toddler to a teenager (Cialdini, Baumann, & Kenrick, 1981).

Social learning can also contribute to the development of prosocial behavior. For example, children who witnessed adults modeling generous behavior were more likely to donate money to a charity versus those who saw a selfish model (Rushton, 1975). Similar results were found for adults in a clever field experiment involving helping a stranded motorist on a road (Bryan & Test, 1967): Approximately 4,000 drivers passed a woman who's car had a flat tire, and about half saw a man who had stopped to help her, whereas for the others no one was helping her. Bryan and Test (1967) found that about 50% more drivers stopped to help a second stranded motorist located several hundred meters down the road in the model condition. Exposure to prosocial behavior in the media is also associated with increased prosociality in children, according to a literature review (Hearold, 1986) and a meta-analysis of 34 studies with about 5,000 participants (Mares & Woodard, 2005). Finally, playing prosocial video games has been shown to increase prosocial behavior. For instance, participants who played a prosocial versus aggressive or neutral video game subsequently spontaneously helped the experimenter pick up spilled pencils off the floor (Research Box 8.1) (Greitemeyer & Osswald, 2010).

Think Again!

1. *Can you define prosocial behavior?*
2. *What is inclusive fitness?*
3. *Have you ever helped someone because they helped you? Have you ever expected someone to reciprocate your prior helping but they didn't? How did you feel?*

RESEARCH BOX 8.1
PROSOCIAL VIDEOS GAMES AND HELPING

Hypothesis: The likelihood of helping should be higher among participants who played a prosocial video game as compared to participants who played a neutral or an aggressive video game.

Research Method: 54 male and female students at a German college participated in this study. Experimenters randomly assigned participants to one of three levels of the independent variable: a prosocial, an aggressive, or a neutral game. The prosocial game required that the player help characters navigate various worlds. Tetris (similar to the widely known Tetrix) was used as a neutral game, and the aggressive one involved killing as many beings as quickly as possible. Participants had an opportunity to help the experimenter pick up pencils that he or she "mistakenly" knocked off of a table and onto the floor while reaching for some questionnaires. The primary dependent measure was whether or not assistance was offered to the experimenter.

Results: Participants were more likely to help an experimenter pick up dropped pencils after playing a prosocial video game for eight minutes as compared to a neutral or aggressive game (67% vs. 33% vs. 28%).

Conclusion: Playing a prosocial game may increase prosocial responding.

Source: Adapted from Greitmeyer, T., & Osswald, S. (2010). Effects of prosocial video games on prosocial behavior. *Journal of Personality and Social Psychology, 98,* 211–221.

WHEN DO WE HELP?

Time Pressure

Imagine you are about to walk across campus to attend a mandatory lecture on the social psychology of helping. Imagine further that as you walk out of your residence hall, you see a man slumped down in front of the doorway with his eyes closed who you must step over in order to exit the building. Would you stop and help? Would it matter if you were late and therefore in a hurry? Darley and Batson (1973) conducted a study that largely mirrored this situation, using students from the Princeton Theological Seminary as participants. In their experiment, seminarians were instructed to walk from one building to another in order to give a talk either on the biblical parable of the Good Samaritan or a topic that was unrelated to helping. You may know this parable. Briefly, a priest walking along a road encounters a man who has been robbed and severely beaten and who lies half dead on the road. Yet the priest—presumably a person who is devoted to caring for others—ignores the plight of the injured man, passing by without offering aid.

In contrast, a Samaritan later sees the injured man and stops, tends to his wounds, brings him to an inn where he can recover, and pays for his care. In reality one would expect priests and seminarians to render aid, regardless of the circumstances but particularly when they were about to give a speech *about a priest who failed to help*. In Darley and Batson's experiment, seminarians en route to give the talk had to closely pass a man who was slumped over in an alleyway, whose eyes were closed, and who was groaning as if in pain. Yet, only 10% of those in a hurry helped, as compared to 63% of those not in a rush, regardless of the

Elderly woman being helped after falling on a street.

Mark Thomas / Science Source.

topic of their talk. Thus, time pressure negatively affected the likelihood of helping. Can you guess why? Recall that time pressure can lead to a kind of cognitive narrowing and increased reliance on rapid, superficial processing. This seems to be exactly what transpired here, leading to inattention to all but very specific elements of the available information. The reflexive X-system overwhelmed the reflective C-system (Chapter 3).

Location

I live in relative proximity to New York City and often hear complaints about how much less caring people who live in the city are in comparison to those who reside in smaller towns like my own. If there is truth to this stereotype, then we should expect to see measurable differences in helping behavior between urban and rural areas. Indeed, Amato (1983) examined several types of helping behavior—including picking up a dropped envelope, donating, and assisting a person who had collapsed—across 55 randomly selected Australian cities and towns, and found that helping was negatively correlated with population level: Locations with lower population density were generally the most helpful. A study of helping in 36 U.S. cities and towns by Levine, Martinez, Brase, and Sorenson (1994) produced similar results, as did a more recent follow-up (Levine, Reysen, & Ganz, 2008). This urban/rural difference is related to variations in the number of bystanders as well as the fact that city dwellers experience a *stimulus overload* that leads people to ignore environmental information that is not personally relevant (Milgram, 1970). Not only can *where* a person live affect likelihood of helping but so too can *how long* he has lived there (Steblay, 1987). Research by Oishi et al. (2007) found that the length of time a person has lived in a particular community is positively correlated with prosocial behavior. This tendency was present even in the context of a laboratory setting: Participants who spent more time with a small group of previously unacquainted participants helped a student struggling to answer questions more than did those in newly formed groups (Oishi et al., 2007).

Mood

Are you more likely to help when you feel good or when you feel sad? Research shows that mood can affect helping behavior in a number of ways. Positive moods sometimes will lead to more helpfulness, in part because they focus thinking on the rewards rather than the costs of helping, and helping is seen as a way to maintain a good mood (Clark & Waddell, 1983). Surprisingly, something as simple as eating a cookie can improve a person's mood and increase subsequent helping (Isen & Levin, 1972), as can smelling pleasant, as opposed to unpleasant, odors (R. A. Baron, 1997). Good moods can also increase helping behavior because they lead people to be more optimistic and to attend to the positive aspects of other people, including those in need (Forgas & Bower, 1987).

Negative State Relief Model

Negative moods may also facilitate prosocial behavior, which means that people can help themselves "feel good by doing good" (Dunn, Aknin, & Norton, 2014; Piliavin, 2005). According to the **mood management hypothesis**, people often help in order to manage their moods, especially sadness (Cialdini et al., 1981). The idea that helping can be used to manage one's moods is the basis for a broader model of helping, called the **negative state relief model** (Schaller & Cialdini, 1990). The model assumes that witnessing the distress of others causes a person to feel sadness or related negative emotions and that people are motivated to act to reduce those emotions. Sadness or distress on the part of the onlooker is exacerbated by feelings of empathy toward the victim, and therefore greater empathy should increase the likelihood of action that will reduce the negative feeling. Alleviating the suffering of another person or escaping from the situation are two ways that this can happen (Cialdini et al., 1987). Cialdini and his colleagues have garnered significant evidence to support the central tenet of this model (Cialdini et al., 1987; Maner et al., 2002). In addition to sadness, people may feel guilt upon seeing another person in distress, triggering a desire to help others in order to relieve that guilt (Cialdini, Darby, & Vincent, 1973). For instance, participants offered more help to an experimenter after being induced to feel guilty by lying to the experimenter or by breaking a rule (McMillen & Austin, 1971).

Weighing the Costs and Benefits of Helping

Like Cialdini's model, the **arousal: cost-reward model** is based on the notion that witnessing other people in distress can produce a negative arousal that can trigger attempts to relieve that arousal (Dovidio, Piliavin, Gaertner, Schroeder, & Clark, 1991; van Bommel,

---

Mood Management Hypothesis: People often help in order to manage their moods, especially when they are sad

Negative State Relief Model: Postulates that witnessing the distress of others causes a person to feel sadness or related negative emotions and that the person is motivated to act in order to reduce those emotions

Arousal: Cost-Reward Model: Postulates that seeing another person in distress causes a person to feel negative arousal, and the person will use the least costly path to reduce the arousal; decision to help is based on a cost/benefit analysis

van Prooijen, Elffers, & Van Lange, 2012). In addition to postulating that seeing distress can cause negative arousal, this model states that if the arousal is attributed to the victim's distress, then the bystander will be motivated to help, using the quickest and least costly path to reduce the arousal (Dovidio et al., 1991). Whether or not a bystander provides help depends on the expected costs and benefits. According to this model, the likelihood will increase as the (a) arousal is greater (such as for a more serious situation), (b) the bystander-victim relationship is closer, and (c) the potential rewards are larger relative to the possible costs (see Table 8.1) (Piliavin, Dovidio, Gaertner, & Clark, 1981). Factors such as shared identity, relatedness, similarity, and empathy can affect the bystander-victim relationship. The costs of helping can vary depending whether it is time consuming or effortful, the helper has some aversion to the victim (e.g., the victim is drunk), or there is the potential for the helper to be physically injured (Dovidio et al., 2006). Among the possible rewards for helping are social approval, removal of unpleasant arousal or feelings, and material benefits bestowed on the helper (Dovidio et al., 2006). As you can see, the arousal: cost-reward model, like the negative state relief model, is grounded in the notion that helping behavior is egoistically motivated. Later we will discuss an alternative hypothesis that at least some helping is truly altruistic.

Think Again!

1. *Explain the mood management hypothesis.*

2. *Have you ever helped someone when you felt sad? Did your mood change as a result?*

3. *Do you think it is possible to help someone else and not feel at least a little better afterward? Why or why not?*

Helping in Emergencies

At approximately 3 o'clock in the morning on March 13, 1964, Kitty Genovese was brutally assaulted with a knife and killed as she returned home from work to her apartment in Queens, New York. The attack lasted roughly 45 minutes, during which time the assailant Winston Mosely left the scene twice, only to finally return to make sure that she had died. According to contemporary news accounts, 38 people witnessed the attack but failed to call the police or help in any other way. Citizens of the city, state, and around the country were abhorred, and politicians and the media decried the witnesses' failure to act as apathetic, indifferent, and morally callous (Latané & Darley, 1969). Although contemporary news accounts inaccurately relayed some of the key facts of the case (e.g., as few as three people may have actually seen Genovese and Mosely together, and others only heard it;

TABLE 8.1   Arousal: Cost-Reward Model

Whether and what kind of help is offered will depend on the costs to the helper and the costs to the victim if no help is given.			
		Cost to helper of direct help	
		Low	**High**
Cost to victim if no help is given	**High**	Direct intervention	Indirect intervention OR reinterpretation of the event: not really an emergency, disparagement of the victim, diffusion of responsibility
	Low	Depends on perceived norms	Leave scene, ignore event, deny need

Source: Adapted from Figure 3.4 in Dovidio, J. F., Piliavin, J. A., Schroeder, D. A., & Penner, L. A. (2006). *The social psychology of prosocial behavior.* Mahwah, NJ: Erlbaum.

a number of people shouted and initially scared Mosely away; and reports suggest that several people contacted the police during the attack), its moral power to garner shock and disgust remains (Manning, Levine, & Collins, 2007).

Unfortunately, apparent bystander apathy is not unique to the Genovese murder. For example, similar narratives unfolded surrounding the 2008 rape of a woman in a Minnesota apartment hallway that 10 people witnessed and chose not to intervene (Gottfried, 2008) and the 1992 near-fatal beating of Reginald Denny during the Los Angeles riots in front of hundreds of people and on live television (Mathews & Meyer, 1992). More recently, on January 16, 2014, 59-year-old Radil Hebrich died after an accident in an underground subway in Montreal (Corcoran, 2015). Hebrich was drunk and staggered into a train. He fell to the ground, unconscious, not breathing, and bleeding from his head, and lay there for almost 20 minutes before helped arrived. The entire incident was captured on a security camera, and at least 40 passersby and the operators of three subway trains saw him and did nothing.

Kitty Genovese, whose murder sparked decades of social psychological research on bystander intervention.

New York Daily News Archive/New York Daily News/Getty Images.

The key question raised by these shocking events is why people fail to intervene in situations where help—especially emergency help—is clearly needed. Stimulated by the Genovese case, the social psychologists Bibb Latané and John Darley (1969) embarked on a series of empirical studies designed to uncover the true causes of so-called bystander apathy. The term **bystander apathy** refers to the explanation often given when people fail to help in emergencies: that they were uncaring or apathetic. However, research by Latané and Darley (1969) undermined this explanation. Let's walk through the groundbreaking research these authors conducted in order to identify (a) the characteristics of emergencies and (b) the social forces that can impact bystander intervention.

Bystander Apathy: Explanation that people who fail to help in emergencies do so because they are uncaring

Characteristics of Emergencies

Latané and Darley (1969) enumerate five objective characteristics of emergencies that together make them different from situations involving ordinary helping. First of all, by definition emergencies involve threat of harm or actual harm. Since intervention often poses risk to the helper and offers minimal rewards, people may be tempted to ignore or minimize their own importance and ability to help. Second, emergencies are unusual and rare, and therefore most people have little experience with which to guide their behavior. Third, the specific characteristics of emergencies differ widely, further limiting the extent to which prior experience or knowledge can be usefully applied. Fourth, emergencies tend to be unforeseen; that is, we typically are unable to predict their occurrence and consequently may not be prepared. Lastly, emergencies call for immediate action in order to prevent deterioration of the situation and the potential exacerbation of harm. The need for instant intervention puts substantial pressure on bystanders and subjects them to significant stress and can undermine the ability to engage in clear, careful thinking. Although each of these factors can affect the likelihood of effective assistance, Latané and Darley were much more interested in what they called the social determinants of **bystander intervention** or help provided by witnesses to victims or potential victims in an emergency (Darley & Latané, 1968; Fischer, Greitemeyer, Pollozek, & Frey, 2006; van Bommel et al., 2012).

Bystander Intervention: Help provided by witnesses to victims or potential victims in an emergency

Failure to Help

Imagine that you are taking a test while sitting at your desk in a classroom, and white smoke begins pouring into the room through a wall vent. Assuming you noticed the smoke, under what circumstances would you take action? This hypothetical situation mirrors one of Latané and Darley's studies in which participants completed a survey in a room either alone or with others (Darley & Latané, 1968). During the session, white smoke was pumped into the room via a wall vent. In the group conditions, the participant was joined by either two confederates who were instructed to ignore the smoke or by two other naïve participants. The experiment was run for up to six minutes, and the researchers (observing through a disguised one-way window) recorded how long it took for the smoke to be reported—if it was reported at all.

Latané and Darley (1969) proposed a five-step model that helps us understand why participants in this study and people in the real world sometimes fail to help (see Figure 8.2).

The breakdown of any one of these steps will impede helping. In order to intervene, a witness must (1) notice the event, (2) interpret it as an emergency, (3) assume responsibility for helping, (4) decide what kind of assistance is needed, and finally (5) implement that assistance. In a series of inventive experiments, Latané and Darley (Darley & Latané, 1968; Latané & Darley, 1969) provided substantial empirical support for their model. Since it was originally proposed, the Latané and Darley model of bystander intervention has enjoyed widespread empirical support across dozens of studies and a multitude of situations (Dovidio et al., 2006; Latané & Nida, 1981).

Notice the Event. Bystanders must first notice that an event is occurring before any of the ensuing steps can be undertaken. Judging by their behavior, individuals participating alone in the smoke study took an average of five seconds to notice the smoke, whereas those in the group conditions were less observant and became aware of it after about 20 seconds.

Interpret the Event as an Emergency. Once the event is noticed, the bystander must decide whether or not to interpret it as an emergency. In the smoke experiment, 75% of the solitary participants reported the smoke to the experimenter located outside of the room. Using a mathematical formulation, the experimenters estimated the likelihood that at least one of the persons in the three-person groups would report the problem at 98%. In fact, only one of the 24 participants in the eight groups brought the smoke to the attention of the experimenter within the first four minutes, and only three did so before the six-minute limit, at which time the smoke was thick enough to largely obscure the vision of the room occupants. Why the discrepancy in responding?

Darley and Latané (1968) postulated that the participants—and onlookers in emergencies in general—looked at the reactions of others who were present when deciding whether or not to construe the situation as an emergency. That is, the responses (or lack of responses) of others in the room served as *informational influence* on the participant that affected his own understanding of an uncertain reality (see Chapter 6). If those others did not appear to interpret the situation as an emergency, then the participant himself did not do so either. Latané and Darley (1969) termed this phenomenon, in which a person *incorrectly* assumes that others know more than she does, **pluralistic ignorance**. Unfortunately, pluralistic ignorance abounds and often prevents people from acting on their own, often correct, inclinations. I witness a form of this in my classroom on an all-too-regular basis when a student, confused by something I have said, looks around to see if other students appear confused. Absent a clear indication that they share her lack of comprehension, she assumes that they do understand and therefore chooses *not* to ask a question that would likely benefit her and others.

Pluralistic Ignorance: When a person *incorrectly* assumes that others know more than he or she does

Assume Personal Responsibility. Once a person has noticed an event and interpreted it as an emergency, she must then accept or reject responsibility for intervening. As you have learned, people who work on tasks or projects together share responsibility for

FIGURE 8.2   Failure to Help in Emergencies

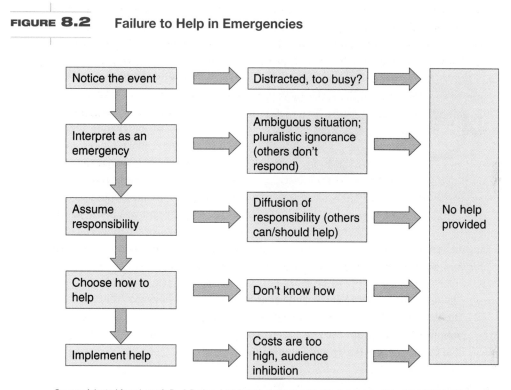

Source: Adapted from Latané, B., & Darley, J. M. (1969). Bystander "apathy." *American Scientist, 57*, 244–268.

the outcome, whereas those who work alone do not. The corollary of this is that when we witness an emergency in the presence of others, we are less likely to take *personal* responsibility than if we had been alone. Latané and Darley (1968) called this phenomenon in which, as the number of bystanders increases, individuals mentally spread responsibility for intervening to others, **diffusion of responsibility** (Pittinsky & Diamante, 2015). People in such group settings assume that other people will provide (or perhaps already have provided) the needed assistance. Together, diffusion of responsibility and pluralistic ignorance help to explain what Latané and Darley called the **bystander effect:** the fact that, as the number of onlookers in an emergency increases, the likelihood that any one person will help decreases. It is quite possible that diffusion of responsibility was key to the lack of a more timely and assertive response on the part of the witnesses to the Kitty Genovese homicide and similar cases.

Another study by Latané and Darley (1968) nicely illustrates both diffusion of responsibility and the bystander effect. In this study, college student participants were told that they'd be engaging in conversations with other students about various personal problems often experienced in college. They were situated in a separate room equipped with an

Diffusion of Responsibility: Phenomenon in which, as the number of bystanders increases, individuals mentally spread responsibility for intervening across many others

Bystander Effect: Phenomenon that, as the number of onlookers in an emergency increases, the likelihood that any one person will help decreases

AP Photo/John Badman.

A neighbor comforts a young boy Tuesday, August 4, 2015, as they wait for an ambulance to arrive on Nixon Street in Alton, Illinois, after the boy got his foot caught in the front wheel of his bicycle while riding it. Unfortunately, sometimes people don't take responsibility for helping others, especially when many bystanders are present.

intercom to enable verbal contact with what they thought were other participants but in fact were the prerecorded voices of confederates. Some conditions consisted of the participant and the "victim," others included a third person, and still others included four or six in total, all in separate rooms. Each "discussant" spoke for two minutes, with the victim going first and the true participant speaking last. In the first round the victim mentioned that he had epilepsy and was prone to seizures. The real experiment began during the second round. Again the victim was the first to speak, but shortly after he started his voice became louder and more incoherent:

> "I er um I think I I need er if if could er er . . . I'm er er h-h-having a little real problem er right now and I er if somebody could help me . . . (makes choking sounds) I'm gonna die er er I'm . . . gonna die er help er er seizure or (chokes, and then is quiet). (Darley and Latané, 1968, p. 379)

As you can guess, Darley and Latané were interested in how quickly after the onset of the seizure the participants took action by finding and telling the experimenter (who was not in the room). Thus, the primary independent variable was group size, and the dependent variable was elapsed time until the participant sought help. Can you guess the results? In the two-person conditions, 85% of the participants reported the seizure, whereas 62% did so in the four-person condition, and just 31% of those in the six-person condition did so. Like in the smoke study, we see the bystander effect at work: As the number of bystanders increased, the likelihood of help decreased. That is to say, the presence of other people served to inhibit an individual's natural tendency to respond. Clearly, the number of bystanders had a tremendous effect on emergency intervention.

Choose How to Help and Then Implement It. The last two steps are much more straightforward from a psychological perspective. The helper needs to decide whether to offer direct (such as CPR—cardiopulmonary resuscitation) or indirect (such as calling an ambulance) assistance. Nevertheless, the would-be helper of course needs to possess the knowledge and skills to effectively do so. Shotland and Heinold (1985) conducted an experiment to determine whether college students trained in first aid would intervene to help an injured person more often than untrained students. Although overall assistance rates were the same across the two groups, not surprisingly, trained students provided more effective help. Furthermore, would-be helpers, even if they know *how* to help, may refrain from doing so in order to avoid possible embarrassment, being injured, or being sued (Latané & Darley, 1969; Latané & Nida, 1981). Concerns about embarrassment or violating social norms regarding when *not* to help—such as during a family dispute—can lead to *audience inhibition* and failure to respond (Shotland & Straw, 1976).

Recent Research. More recent research has examined bystander behavior in a number of contexts, including campuses and online communities (Bennett, Banyard, & Garnhart, 2014; Fischer et al., 2011; van Bommel et al., 2012; van Bommel, van Prooijen, Elffers, & Van Lange, 2014). For instance, Rabow, Newcomb, Monto, and Hernandez (1990) found that college students reported that they were more willing to intervene to prevent another student from driving while intoxicated when there were fewer bystanders. The bystander effect has also been found online. For example, people took longer to respond to a member's request for help in an Internet chat room study as the number of chat room bystanders increased (Markey, 2000). Scholars have also become increasingly interested in reducing the bystander effect (Freis & Gurung, 2013). For example, research suggests that one of the best ways of preventing sexual violence is to educate people in particular about the bystander effect so that they become more likely to intervene (Banyard, Moynihan, Cares, & Warner, 2014; Gidycz, Orchowski, & Berkowitz, 2011).

Think Again!

1. *Does bystander apathy explain the lack of intervention in emergencies?*

2. *What would you do, if you encounter an emergency, to make sure that victims were helped?*

3. *Can you think of other, nonhelping, situations in which pluralistic ignorance could explain people's behavior?*

DOING RESEARCH: SAFEGUARDING RESEARCH PARTICIPANTS

In our discussion of social influence, we discussed the need for deception in social psychological research and the need for psychologists to weigh the benefits and costs of deceiving participants (Chapter 6). Imagine having been a participant in a study in which you failed to help someone who you thought was in need. How would you feel? Even after you were told that the apparently injured person was a confederate or was perhaps fictional, you may still feel uneasy or upset about your behavior. Psychologists have established a number of safeguards to prevent or minimize harm that may result from participation in deceptive and/or other studies that may lead a person to feel discomfort (see Table 8.2).

SOCIAL PSYCHOLOGY APPLIED TO WORK
ORGANIZATIONAL CITIZENSHIP ON THE JOB

You have likely experienced work environments in which some coworkers were enthusiastic and always trying to do their best, while others just complained a lot and did the bare minimum required to get a paycheck. I know that I have. Individuals in the first group are demonstrating greater organizational citizenship behavior than are the ones in the second group. The term *organizational citizenship behavior* (OCB) largely refers to prosocial actions that occur at the workplace. OCB includes most behaviors that go above and beyond one's normal job responsibilities (are not directly linked to job performance or formal rewards), are discretionary (an employee can choose not to do them without fear of punishment), and that provide a positive contribution to the organization (Organ, Podsakoff, & MacKenzie, 2006; Van Dyne, Graham, & Dienesch, 1994). At least in theory, such behaviors not motivated by the desire to advance one's career are rather altruistic (Finkelstein, 2012; Glomb, Bhave, Miner, & Wall, 2011; Lemmon & Wayne, 2015; Li, Kirkman, & Porter, 2014). OCB can include anything from volunteering to do extra work to help a coworker, spontaneously bringing dessert to share, driving a colleague to work, or helping organize a charity function. Social psychological research can help us better understand citizenship behaviors because they, like other social behaviors, are purposive, are a product of the person and the situation, are influenced by construal, and occur in a cultural context.

For instance, Cohen, Turan, Panter, Morse, and Yeonjeong (2014) argue that previous research tended to focus on situational explanations for OCB at the expense of dispositional ones and consequently examined the relationship between moral character and OCB. Their purpose was twofold: to predict high and low moral character from other personality traits, and to determine whether or not moral character was associated with actual workplace behavior. Based on self-report data from structured diaries and a survey of non-university workers, Cohen et al. (2014) found that high-moral character individuals valued moral behavior, had greater empathic concern for others, and were more conscientious than low-moral character persons. In addition, moral character predicted actual citizenship behaviors as reported by the participants and corroborated by their coworkers (yes, respondents freely admitted to engaging in undesirable behaviors!).

Can you think of anyone who engaged in so much OCB that he or she became burned out and stopped doing it? I have seen more than one case in which a fellow faculty member devoted many many hours of her week to service to the university (not my current institution) in her attempt to make it a better place. I have no doubt that she succeeded but at an unfortunate cost: She eventually stopped doing OCB at all. But that is just an anecdote. Bolino, Hsiung, Harvey, and LePine (2015) scientifically investigated the effects of sustaining high levels of OCB over time. Importantly, they found that people are more likely to experience *citizenship fatigue* and consequently stop engaging in OCB when (a) their organization has not provided sufficient support, (b) they have a low evaluation of the quality of teamwork at their organization, and (c) they feel social pressure from the organization to do more (Cha, Chang, & Kim, 2014).

Consider these findings as/when you become a job supervisor, team leader, and/or business owner.

One final example from the academic world: Gore, Kiefner, and Combs (2012) examined what they called *academic citizenship behavior*, which refers to student actions—such as agreeing to help other students with their homework or studying. These researchers sought to uncover personality traits of people who are more likely to engage in these behaviors. What they found probably won't surprise you: Conscientiousness and agreeableness were both significantly positively correlated with OCB. How does this apply to you? Are you conscientious? Agreeable? Willing to help other students?

The first of these requires that researchers obtain **informed consent.** According to the American Psychological Association (APA, 2010), participants must be informed of (a) the purpose of the research, expected duration, and procedures; (b) their right to decline to participate and to withdraw from the research once participation has begun; (c) the foreseeable consequences of declining or withdrawing; (d) reasonably foreseeable factors that may be expected to influence their willingness to participate such as potential risks, discomfort, or adverse effects; (e) any prospective research benefits; (f) limits of confidentiality; (g) incentives for participation; and (h) whom to contact for questions about the research and research participants' rights.

Informed Consent: Written agreement to participate in research

Second, participants must be permitted to withdraw from the research without penalty at any time. Third, information obtained from participants typically needs to be confidential and/or anonymous. That is, it should not be possible for anyone other than the researchers—and often, not even the researchers—to trace the specific data back to individual participants or even to identify who the participants in a particular study were. Fourth, research involving human subjects must be thoroughly reviewed and approved by an Institutional Review Board (IRB). IRBs were established in 1974 by the U.S. Department of Health, Education, and Welfare, and are authorized to regulate human subjects research in any institution that receives federal funding. Fifth, at the completion of research involving deception, participants must be provided additional information about its true purpose and hypotheses, a topic we'll address next.

In addition to the safeguards described above, researchers must also conduct a thorough post-experimental interview of research participants as soon after the end of the study as is reasonably possible. The post-experimental interview or **debriefing** is (a) an explanation of the true purpose of the research, (b) an exploration and reduction of possible negative effects of participation, and (c) a clarification of what actually happened during the study (if there was ambiguity or deception) (Aronson, Wilson, & Brewer, 1998). For instance, if a participant is given false negative feedback about her performance on a test or is led to believe that she harmed another person, any associated loss of self-esteem or guilt must be assuaged prior to her dismissal from the experiment. Two other components should also be included in the debriefing. First, the researcher should assess possible participant suspicion about elements of the study because such

Debriefing:
Explanation of the true purpose of the research, an exploration and reduction of possible negative effects of participation, and a clarification of what actually happened during the study (if there was ambiguity or deception)

TABLE 8.2   Safeguarding Research Participants

Informed Consent	Components
	(a) The purpose of the research, expected duration, and procedures; (b) their right to decline to participate and to withdraw from the research once participation has begun; (c) the foreseeable consequences of declining or withdrawing; (d) reasonably foreseeable factors that may be expected to influence their willingness to participate, such as potential risks, discomfort, or adverse effects; (e) any prospective research benefits; (f) limits of confidentiality; (g) incentives for participation; and (h) whom to contact for questions about the research and research participants' rights.
Right to Withdraw	Participants must be permitted to withdraw from the research without penalty at any time.
Confidentiality	Information obtained from participants typically needs to be confidential and/or anonymous.
Institutional Review	Research involving human subjects must be thoroughly reviewed and approved by an Institutional Review Board (IRB).
Debriefing	Components
	(a) An explanation of the true purpose of the research; (b) an exploration and reduction of possible negative effects of participation; (c) a clarification of what actually happened during the study; (d) an assessment of possible participant suspicion; (e) description of the expected contribution of the research to the science of psychology.

suspicion—even if inaccurate—may have affected her behavior during the experiment. Second, experimenters should inform the participants of the expected contribution of the research to the science of psychology.

The typical post-experimental interview follows a funnel approach, in which experimenters begin with a broad, somewhat vague question to assess general suspicion, such as *did you notice anything odd or unusual about the experiment?* (Aronson et al., 1998; Wilson, Aronson, & Carlsmith, 2010). Follow-up questions more specifically address the study at hand; they may, for example, ask if the participant believed that he really failed a test. After these questions are answered, the experimenter then conducts the remaining elements of the debriefing. A number of questions have been raised regarding the ability of the experimenter to accurately assess participant suspicion and, consequently, whether or not undetected suspicion may undermine the validity of the research (Epley & Huff, 1998), and these issues remain unresolved (Kimmel, 2011).

Think Again!

1. *What is the purpose of a debriefing, and what are its three essential components?*

2. *Do you think that experimenters should always obtain informed consent prior to conducting research on humans? What about studies that involve examining information from thousands of people (or more) in the public realm via social media like Facebook or Twitter? Is consent necessary? Is it even reasonable to ask researchers to obtain it?*

THE EMPATHY-ALTRUISM RELATIONSHIP

Imagine that you are a participant in an experiment and are asked to help your university's Office of Student Life assess personal accounts of problems students face at the university. Participants in your condition read an essay by Bryan Banks about how, while hurrying to class one day, he encountered an "old woman" on a sidewalk who was "wild-eyed and confused" and who asked him to help her find her house. Bryan knew where her house was and accompanied her there, making him even later for class. Shortly thereafter, while running to school, Bryan was hit by a car after emerging onto a street from between two parked cars. The accident left him with a concussion, two broken legs, a broken arm, and an inability to get to class for several weeks. After you read his account, you are asked to indicate your empathic concern for Bryan (e.g., sympathetic, compassionate, tender, and so on). Finally, since he has no computer at home, you are given the chance to help by getting copies of the notes written by fellow students in his classes.

Would you agree? Why or why not? What if you read instead that rather than helping her Bryan relayed how he was unable to help the woman but that she grabbed him and wouldn't let go? Moreover, in order to escape, Bryan jerked his arm away and, after she fell, told her she "got what she deserved." He then had the unfortunate encounter with the car, causing him to need the class notes. How much would you care about Bryan? Value him? Be likely to help him?

Batson, Eklund, Chermok, Hoyt, and Ortiz (2007) presented variations of this scenario to 80 undergraduates at the University of Kansas. The experimenters manipulated two variables. The first was how much Bryan was valued by the participants; not surprisingly, he was valued more when he helped than when he didn't. The second was perspective taking: Participants were instructed either to "imagine how the student facing this difficulty feels and how it is affecting his life" or "take an objective perspective to what is described. Try not to get caught up in how the student facing this difficulty feels." Thus, there were four conditions: objective/high valuing, imagine/high valuing, objective/low valuing, and imagine/low valuing. Batson et al. (2007) expected and found that participants would be more likely to help if they *both* valued Bryan and took his perspective, as compared to either valuing or perspective taking or doing neither.

This experiment, along with other research-based insights into the way perspective taking and perception of need, both contribute to helping behavior and are part of an underlying theoretical model that Batson (2011) calls the **theory of empathy-induced altruistic motivation**. In contrast to the egoistic approach described above, this theory postulates that altruistic—that is, non-egoistic—motivation for helping is possible, and specifies the factors that can lead to it. According to this theory, altruistic motivation stems from **empathic concern**, defined by Batson as other-oriented emotion that is elicited by and congruent with the perceived welfare of a person in need (Batson, 1991; Batson, Ahmad, & Lishner, 2009; Zaki, 2014). Such feelings as sympathy, compassion, and tenderness are encompassed by empathic concern. Building on this notion, the **empathy-altruism hypothesis** states that empathic concern produces an altruistic motivation to relieve the need(s) of a valued other (Batson, Ahmad, Powell, & Stocks, 2008). Batson's theory goes beyond postulating a relationship between empathy and altruism by specifying the two primary factors that lead to empathic concern (see Figure 8.3).

What are the antecedents of empathic concern? One is somewhat obvious: the *perception that another person is in need*. If there is no perceived need, then helping is irrelevant. As you can see in Figure 8.3, the second precursor to empathy is the *valuing of another person's welfare*. That is, a person can be aware that another is suffering yet, by virtue of the fact that the perceiver does not value the welfare of the sufferer, feel no empathy (Batson et al., 2007). For instance, when participants in the Batson et al. (2007) viewed Bryan as "nasty" because of his treatment of the old woman, empathy diminished, as did the desire to help Bryan.

At this point, the astute reader might ask about the role of perspective taking—which was manipulated by Batson et al. (2007)—in producing empathy. Why isn't it posited as

Theory of Empathy-Induced Altruistic Motivation: Idea that altruistic motivation for helping is possible and specifies the factors that can lead to it

Empathic Concern: Other-oriented emotion elicited by and congruent with the perceived welfare of a person in need

Empathy-Altruism Hypothesis: Idea that empathic concern produces an altruistic motivation to relieve the needs of a valued other

FIGURE 8.3   Empathy-Induced Altruistic Motivation

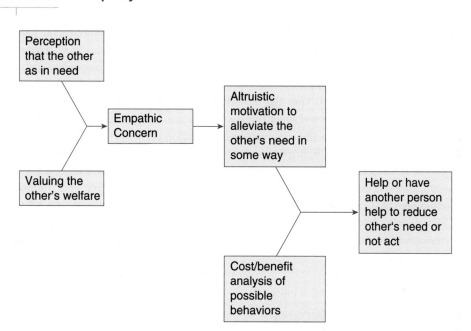

Source: Adapted from Batson, C. D., Eklund, J. H., Chermok, V. L., Hoyt, J. L., & Ortiz, B. G. (2007). An additional antecedent of empathic concern: Valuing the welfare of the person in need. *Journal of Personality and Social Psychology, 93,* 65–74.

one of the key antecedents to empathy? That is a great question! The answer is actually straightforward: Outside of the laboratory setting (and perhaps certain donation-seeking ads), people are rarely explicitly instructed to take another's perspective. Rather, perspective taking often occurs spontaneously as a result of valuing the welfare of another. Furthermore, one need not take the perspective of another to value her welfare and feel empathy for her. Thus, perspective taking can but need not play a role in empathy. An interesting side note here is that Batson's earlier versions of his theory claimed that perspective taking was the second antecedent (e.g., Batson, 1991), in addition to perception of need. However, again demonstrating the self-correcting nature of science, additional research conducted by Batson and his colleagues led to a reworking and improvement in their own model.

Neuroscience of Empathy

If Batson is correct about the role of empathy in altruistic responding, then we might be able find evidence for this in the brain. Advances in social neuroscience have in fact allowed for the identification of some brain correlates of empathy (Decety & Ickes, 2009).

One line of research has examined differences and similarities in brain activation that accompany imagining oneself in painful or embarrassing situations versus similarly imagining someone else. Participants in research by Jackson, Brunet, Meltzoff, and Decety (2006) viewed photos of people who either were or were not experiencing pain and were asked to imagine either themselves (imagine-self condition) or a stranger (imagine-other condition) as the person in the photo. One painful photo depicted a person who had just slammed a finger in a drawer, and the paired nonpainful photo merely showed the hand near the drawer. fMRI scans performed on participants revealed both differences and similarities in brain activation between the self and other conditions. For instance, the temporo-parietal junction (TPJ)—known to correspond to distinguishing the self from others—was active during the other but not the self-condition. In contrast, the anterior cingulate cortex (ACC)—understood to be associated with the experience of pain—was activated in both conditions. Jackson et al. (2006) concluded that the experience of empathy requires the *separation* of self from other (see photo). This is consonant with other research demonstrating the importance of the self-other distinction in the development of empathy in children (Kärtner, Keller, & Chaudhary, 2010).

Egoism Versus Altruism Revisited

The egoism versus altruism debate is an intriguing one, yet posing the question as an either/or dichotomy overly simplistic: Perhaps both theories have merit (Batson et al., 2009). This is partially true because there are many "egoistic" perspectives that focus on different aspects of self-interest (Batson, 1998; Dovidio et al., 2006). Moreover, although Batson's empathy-altruism hypothesis is the most prominent, others have suggested that empathy may not be the only source of altruistic motivation (e.g., Oliner & Oliner, 1988). For instance, as we will discuss below, some researchers have suggested that there is an "altruistic personality."

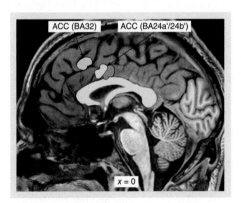

Science Source.

Advances in social neuroscience have allowed for the identification of some brain correlates of empathy. Participants in research by Jackson et al. (Jackson, Brunet, Metzloff, & Decety, 2006) viewed photos of people who either were or were not experiencing pain and asked to either imagine themselves (imagine-self condition) or a stranger (imagine-other condition) as the person in the photo. This image reflects differences in brain activation across the two conditions.

According to Batson et al. (2008), the bulk of the more than 30 studies that have directly pitted egoism against empathy-altruism have supported the existence of an altruistic motivation. But let's be clear what that means for the egoistic perspective. Researchers who advocate for the existence of altruism do not argue that *all helping is altruistic* or even *that most of it is*. Rather, they claim that *some* helping is altruistically motivated. Other helping is most certainly egoistic and merely instrumental to obtaining rewards and/or avoiding costs of not offering aid. The egoistic positions rule out the possibility of *any* truly altruistic motivation, whereas Batson's perspective allows for the existence of *both* types of motivation. Which position do you think is correct? While you consider that, let's move to some nonmotivational factors that influence the likelihood of giving and receiving help.

Think Again!

1. *What is the empathy-altruism hypothesis?*

2. *What are the two antecedents to empathy?*

PERSON FACTORS AFFECTING HELPING

Altruistic Personality

Although it is clear that people vary in their frequency of engaging in prosocial behavior and that prosocial tendencies are relatively consistent over time (Caprara, Alessandri, & Eisenberg, 2012; Oliner & Oliner, 1988), the search for dispositional variables that could explain this has been challenging (Batson, 1998; Piliavin et al., 1981). But there is some evidence that individual-level factors can affect prosocial behavior (Agnoli, Pittarello, Hysenbelli, & Rubaltelli, 2015).

Psychologists and others have wondered if there is an "altruistic personality" (Oliner & Oliner, 1988). Attempts to discover a specific, narrowly defined altruism trait over the past few decades have generally been unsuccessful (Batson, 1998; Magoo & Khanna, 1991; Piliavin & Charng, 1990). What seems to be more promising is the identification of other personality factors or groups of factors that tend to correlate with prosocial behavior, especially in the long term (Barasch, Levine, Berman, & Small, 2014; Haas et al., 2015). To this end, Samuel Oliner conducted research on Carnegie Medal of Heroism winners, rescuers of Jews during the Holocaust, and others heroes and heroines. He identified several characteristics that are related to *heroic altruism,* which he defined as helping that places the helper at risk of serious harm or death (Oliner, 2008). These characteristics include empathy, placing a high value on reciprocal helping, empathic self-efficacy (the belief that a person has that she can successfully intervene in helping situations), and strong personal morals regarding one's social responsibility for the fate of needy others

(Oliner, 2003, 2008; Oliner & Oliner, 1988) (see also Midlarsky, Jones, & Corley, 2005). We have already discussed the first two. The third, empathic self-efficacy, has been linked to sustained prosocial behavior over time in children and adults (Alessandri, Caprara, Eisenberg, & Steca, 2009; Caprara et al., 2012). Those who think they can help are more likely to do so, and people who have successfully helped in the past are more likely to believe that they can in the future. Personal norms about one's own moral responsibility to help people in need also positively correlate with actual helping behavior in specific situations (S. Schwartz, 1977; S. H. Schwartz & Howard, 1980). See this chapter's Self-Reflection: How Prosocial Are You? for more on the prosocial personality.

Gender and Helping: Who Helps More?

Who do you think helps more, men or women? Often when we think about questions like this, we imagine emergency interventions involving risk taking and awe-inspiring bravery (Ingalls, 2012; Rankin & Eagly, 2008). But helping can take a variety of forms, most of which are not heroic or courageous, which can reflect a number of goals (Stürmer & Snyder, 2010). Eagly (Eagly, 2009; Rankin & Eagly, 2008) has identified important gender-role related dimensions of helping. For instance, helping can be individually oriented or collectively oriented, with the former more associated with men and the latter with women. Females are more communal, friendly, unselfish, and relationally oriented (Hodges, Laurent, & Lewis, 2014; Hodges, Lewis, & Ickes, 2015). In contrast, males tend to be more agentic, self-assertive, dominant, and masterful, and these traits are reflected in their prosocial responding. These sex role differences are robust across cultures (Eagly & Wood, 2012; Williams & Best, 1990).

Men are more likely to help in emergency interventions involving risk of harm. In fact, over 90% of the 1904 to 2008 Carnegie Medal of Heroism winners are men (cited in Eagly, 2009). A meta-analysis by Eagly and Crowley (1986) demonstrated that men help more than women in emergencies and argued that this is partially because of differences in perceived ability to help: Men, more than women, felt that they had the strength or skill to provide effective assistance. Cases of sexual violence against women are important exceptions, as women may be more likely to help than men (Burn, 2009).

Moreover, helping behavior seems to be driven by expectations associated with traditional gender roles: Males seek to fulfill the stereotypical image of the chivalrous, heroic man, whereas females enact the role of committed long-term carer and nurturer (George, Carroll, Kersnick, & Calderon, 1998). Helping tends to mirror these gender roles; when women are the victims in emergency situations, men tend to help more than women, especially when there are bystanders present (Eagly & Crowley, 1986). However, in other risky but not imminently dangerous contexts, such as volunteering for the Peace Corps or Doctors of the World and for kidney donation, women were more likely to help (Becker & Eagly, 2004). Not all of the evidence suggests gender-based differences, however. For example, Reysen and Ganz (2006) gave 324 male and female participants in six U.S.

SELF-REFLECTION 8.1
How Prosocial Are You? (Part 1)

One very promising line of research has identified three factors that together are strong predictors of **prosociality** or the tendency to engage in prosocial behavior (Caprara et al., 2012). The first is the personality dimension *agreeableness*, which refers to how generally cooperative, trusting, and good-natured a person is, and studies show that more agreeable people tend to be more helpful (Graziano, Habashi, Sheese, & Tobin, 2007). Second, individuals who accept others as equals and are concerned about their welfare are more likely to be prosocial (Caprara et al., 2012). Finally, in line with what Oliner (2008) argued, those who express empathic self-efficacy beliefs show greater prosociality. Take a minute to answer the following questions about your prosocial tendencies and then turn the page to learn more.

> **Prosociality:**
> Tendency to engage in prosocial behavior

TABLE 8.3   How Prosocial Are You?

Instructions: The following statements describe a large number of common situations. There are no "right" or "wrong" answers; the best answer is the immediate, spontaneous one. Read each phrase carefully and mark the answer that reflects your first reaction.

Item	Response options				
	Never/ almost never true	Occasionally true	Sometimes true	Often true	Almost always/ always true
1. I am pleased to help my friends/ colleagues in their activities.	1	2	3	4	5
2. I try to help others.	1	2	3	4	5
3. I am emphatic with those who are in need.	1	2	3	4	5
4. I help immediately those who are in need.	1	2	3	4	5
5. I intensely feel what others feel.	1	2	3	4	5
6. I am willing to make my knowledge and abilities available to others.	1	2	3	4	5
7. I try to console those who are sad.	1	2	3	4	5
8. I easily lend money or other things.	1	2	3	4	5
9. I easily put myself in the shoes of those who are in discomfort.	1	2	3	4	5
10. I immediately sense my friends' discomfort, even when it is not directly communicated to me.	1	2	3	4	5

Source: Adapted from Table 1 in Caprara, G. V., Steca, P., Zelli, A., Capanna, C. (2005). A new scale for measuring adults' prosocialness. *European Journal of Psychological Assessment* 2005; Vol. 21(2):77-89. © 2005 Hogrefe & Huber Publishers (now Hogrefe Publishing). www.hogrefe.com

TURN THE PAGE TO FIND OUR ANSWERS.

SELF-REFLECTION 8.2
How Prosocial Are You? (Part 2)

Caprara et al. (Caprara et al., 2012; Caprara, Steca, Zelli, & Capanna, 2005) have recently developed and validated this prosociality scale to measure individual differences in prosocial behavior and feelings. The scale focuses more specifically on behaviors and feelings related to sharing, helping, taking care of, and empathizing with others.

To determine your score, add up your responses and divide by 16 to obtain an approximate measure of your prosociality. In one study, college age males had an average of 3.56, whereas females were higher at 3.94 (Caprara et al., 2012). In general, females score higher on this scale than do males (Alessandri et al., 2014; Caprara, Alessandri, Di Giunta, Panerai, & Eisenberg, 2010; Caprara & Steca, 2007; Caprara et al., 2005; Kanacri, Pastorelli, Eisenberg, Zuffianò, & Caprara, 2013). How do you compare to your classmates? Ask your professor to calculate a mean separately for all males and all females and see if your peers are similar to those in the study. One note of caution: This scale is particularly susceptible to social desirability effects (especially if the respondent knows what is being measured, as you do!), and therefore the scores for people in your class may be higher than they would be in another context.

opportunities to help an experimenter by picking up a dropped pen, and did not find any gender differences. In sum, it seems that neither women nor men help more; rather, they help in different ways.

Think Again!

1. *Why do men help more in emergencies?*

2. *What is the sex-role based explanation for gender differences in helping?*

3. *Ask your friends and/or classmates about their likelihood of intervening in emergencies. Do their responses differ by gender? How well do you think they can predict what they would actually do?*

WHO GETS HELPED?

Just as characteristics of the would-be helper and the situation can affect whether help is offered, so too can qualities of the person needing help. We have already discussed the role of genetic relatedness in helping behavior. What other characteristics are important?

Gender is one. According to the meta-analysis of 35 studies by Eagly and Crowley (1986) mentioned above, women tend to receive more help than men. For instance, women were more likely to be given assistance for picking up dropped pencils (Latané & Dabbs, 1975) and to be provided protection against theft (Howard & Crano, 1974). In a more recent study, however, participants alerted male and female experimenters of a dropped pen or picked it up at equal frequencies (Reysen & Ganz, 2006).

Victim attractiveness is also important, as both men and women who are attractive receive more help (Farrelly, Lazarus, & Roberts, 2007). This is particularly true in cases where men have the opportunity to assist attractive versus unattractive women (Mims, Hartnett, & Nay, 1975).

Additionally, *similarity* between the helper and the victim positively affects helping (Park & Schaller, 2005). Similarity tends to enhance liking (Byrne, 1971), and liking in turn increases helping (Eisenberg & Miller, 1987). Miller, Kozu, and Davis (2001) reviewed 16 studies in which similarity was manipulated and participants led to believe they shared a name, gender, or other characteristic and found that prosocial emotions increased along with similarity. A recent study by Kunstman and Plant (2008) found that, for instance, black victims waited longer for assistance from white helpers than did white victims, especially when experiencing a severe emergency. Black helpers did not discriminate when providing emergency assistance to white versus black victims (Kunstman & Plant, 2008) but did show such a distinction in nonurgent helping (Wegner & Crano, 1975).

One of the reasons that similarity can produce increased helping is because it indicates *shared identity* or group membership (see Chapter 12). Shared social identity can be considered a strong form of similarity because it is "all-or-nothing," whereas other types of similarity can range from slight to significant (Dovidio et al., 2006; Turner, Hogg, Oakes, Reicher, & Wetherell, 1987). That is, a victim either is or is not a member of any particular group to which the would-be helper belongs. A number of studies have shown that individuals who *perceive* that they share an identity or group membership with others are more likely to help them (Dovidio, Gaertner, Shnabel, Saguy, & Johnson, 2010; Levine, 2012). For example, research by Levine, Prosser, Evans, and Reicher (2005) manipulated shared identity between participants and staged victims. In some cases, the participants and victims were both avid fans of the Manchester United football team (what Americans call soccer), and in other cases the participants supported Manchester but the victim wore the shirt of an archrival team, Liverpool (see Figure 8.4). As predicted, participants aided victims with whom they shared an identity much more often than if they did not (92% versus 30% of the time). Moreover, the traditional bystander effect, in which likelihood of helping decreases as group size increases, depends, in part, on the extent to which the other bystanders share group membership with the would-be helper (Levine & Crowther, 2008). In one set of studies, women tended to help more when other bystanders were women, and men also were more likely to help when other bystanders were women (Levine & Crowther, 2008).

FIGURE 8.4   Shared Identity and Helping

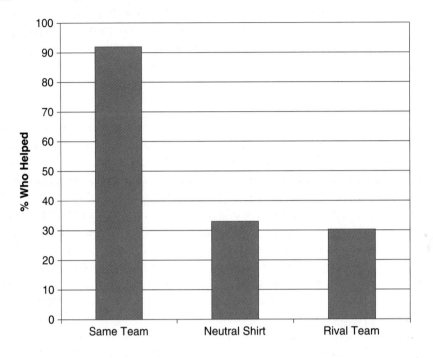

Source: Adapted from Study 1, Table 1, Levine, M., Prosser, A., Evans, D., & Reicher, S. (2005). Identity and emergency intervention: How social group membership and inclusiveness of group boundaries shape helping behavior. *Personality and Social Psychology Bulletin, 31,* 443–453.

Finally, whether or not the person needing help is perceived to be *personally responsible* for his plight can alter the responses of bystanders. In Chapter 4 we discussed how Kelley's (1967) attribution matrix provides a useful perspective on inferring the reasons why people engage in specific behaviors. In the context of prosocial behavior, people tend to be more forgiving and understanding as well as more helpful if the victim is not perceived to be at fault. Imagine you are approached by a male student while walking across campus. He tells you that you share a class and asks if he can borrow your notes from the prior week because, as evidenced by his eye patch and dark glasses, he can't currently take his own. Would you help? Schmidt and Weiner (1988) asked research participants to imagine a scenario like this and indicate their willingness to help. Those who believed that the student's problem was not his fault (he had an eye condition) were more likely to help than those who thought the student was responsible (he skipped class to go to the beach). Such "blaming the victim" is common among people who hold the **just-world hypothesis**, which states that people get what they deserve and deserve whatever they get (Barreiro, 2013; Lerner, 1980; Nudelman,

Just-World Hypothesis: Idea that people get what they deserve and deserve whatever they get

2013; Nudelman & Shiloh, 2011). If a person's problems can be attributed to her own short-comings, it can be easier to withhold assistance and empathy. The effects of attributions of responsibility are quite strong and have been found in 39 studies recently examined via meta-analysis (Rudolph, Roesch, Greitemeyer, & Weiner, 2004). Finally, men appear more likely to blame a male victim for his plight than do women, at least when conditions suggest that the victim does bear some responsibility (MacGeorge, 2003).

Helping Across Cultures

Like many dispositional factors, culture—such as levels of individualism-collectivism—can also affect helping. Research suggests that, in general, collectivists help more than individualists (Barrett et al., 2004; Bontempo, Lobel, & Triandis, 1990). In earlier chapters, we discussed the distinction between individualists and collectivists, especially how the former are more focused on the self, whereas the latter are more attentive to the group. The importance accorded to group membership across cultures has specific behavioral implications, as collectivists draw sharper category-based distinctions between ingroups and outgroups and demonstrate greater gaps between treatment of one's own group versus those in other groups, as compared to individualists (Brewer & Gardner, 1996; Triandis, 1995). Consequently, collectivists tend to help their own group members more than nongroup or outgroup members, as compared to individualists (Barrett et al., 2004; Kemmelmeier, Jambor, & Letner, 2006; Kim & Lee, 2012; J. G. Miller, Bersoff, & Harwood, 1990).

In addition to influencing who is helped, culture can also impact the kind of help that is provided. For example, research has shown that Japanese collectivists equally focus on providing emotional support and assistance with problem solving for those in need, whereas European American individualists emphasize just emotional support (Chen, Kim, Mojaverian, & Morling, 2012). Moreover, individualists deemed it important to boost the self-esteem of the helped person, as well as facilitate that person's autonomy and competence in addressing future needs.

Another recent study examined the helping of strangers in cultures that are high versus low in what is called cultural embeddedness (Knafo, Schwartz, & Levine, 2009). **Cultural embeddedness** refers to the extent to which one focuses on the family or extended ingroup, as opposed to oneself, as the primary social unit. Knafo and colleagues (2009) gathered data from three field studies conducted in 21 nations and found that less help was offered to strangers in highly embedded cultures, that is those where the focus was on the group rather than the individual.

Researchers have uncovered evidence that there is cross-cultural variation in other variables related to helping (Carlo, Koller, Eisenberg, Da Silva, & Frohlich, 1996; Kumru, Carlo, Mestre, & Samper, 2012). For instance, norms of social obligation, although universal, can range from relatively strong to relatively weak (J. G. Miller et al., 1990). Consistent with this, Baron and Miller (2000) found that Indian collectivists were more likely to endorse a social responsibility norm than were American individualists. One really interesting study demonstrated that Chinese participants felt more of an obligation

Cultural Embeddedness: Extent to which one focuses on the family or extended ingroup, as opposed to oneself, as the primary social unity

to give money to a close friend in need, whereas Americans tended to offer time (Cai, Fink, & Xie, 2012). Finally, the relationship between feelings of empathy and helping may differ across cultures. Kärtner, Keller, and Chaudhary (2010) exposed toddlers from India and the United States to the distress of another and coded their responses both in terms of how much empathy they displayed and whether they initiated prosocial behavior. The situation involved the breaking of a teddy bear's arm by the experimenter and subsequent (faked) upset and distress, and the toddler's responses were coded both for signs of distress and for prosocial behavior (e.g., hugging the experimenter, offering her an alternate toy, etc.). Kärtner et al. (2010) found that prosocial behavior among Asian Indians was more affected by situational cues that helping was called for than among Americans, for whom empathy seemed to be the driving force.

Think Again!

1. *Do you believe that the world is just? Whether you do or do not, how does your view affect who, how, and whether you help?*

2. *How does collectivism impact who gets helped?*

FINAL THOUGHTS: A BROADER VIEW OF HELPING

The egoism versus altruism question has been debated by psychologists for several decades and by other scientists and philosophers long before that. The disagreement between the two positions is not just about helping behavior in an immediate sense but also speaks to the core of our conceptualization of human nature. On the one side are those who argue that all human behavior is rooted in selfishness, competition, and aggression. On the other side is a more optimistic thread of thinking that has promulgated the view that prosociality, cooperation, and kindness are as integral to the evolution of humans as competition. Perhaps the argument is a false one marked by a meaningless dichotomy. We

are in no position to resolve this argument in these pages. However, what we can say is that human social behavior—as evidenced by the evolutionary and historical records as well as contemporary events and psychological research—demonstrates an abundance of both the "positive" and the "negative." It seems that evolution has supplied us with a variety of tools and behavioral propensities that we can selectively use to maximize our chances of survival across a variety of environments.

Humans are clearly a moral species if we take this to mean that morality is crucial to us both at the level of the individual and that of civilizations as a whole. From very early to very late in our lives we are preoccupied with good and evil, right and wrong, and many of our core beliefs—such as those concerning religion—and our social institutions—like systems of justice and prisons—have as their foundations specific conceptions of morality.

Our brief survey of research on prosocial behavior has demonstrated many of the factors that influence why, how, and when we act to benefit other people. Although we have highlighted, at various times, specific influences, be they evolutionary, developmental, cultural, and so forth, you should note that these influences are really confluences that together produce social behavior. For instance, there is a convergence of evolutionary and social/cultural explanations for social behavior with respect to the norm of reciprocity, where we have noted both its evolutionary or universalistic roots and also its cultural variability.

Lastly, we have seen how prosocial responding relates to several of our fundamental questions of human existence: morality, the self, and sociality. As we stated earlier, prosocial behavior represents the core of our moral being. In addition, the self occupies a central place in discussions of prosocial responding: The relationship of specific others to the self (similarity, closeness, etc.) affects whether we help them; moreover, we must ask if such behavior can occur in the absence of expected benefits to the self. Finally, prosocial responding is also relevant to sociality because such behavior serves as a social glue that binds groups together and has repercussions for the sanctioning of individuals who fail to provide expected help. We will continue our discussion of human moral behavior in the next chapter on aggression.

CORE CONCEPTS

- Prosocial behavior is intended to benefit others, is motivated by the drive to reproduce, by an egoistic desire for material, emotional, and status rewards, and by an altruistic desire to benefit others.

- Inclusive fitness, kin selection, and reciprocal altruism help to explain, from an evolutionary perspective, why people typically help genetic relatives more than non-relatives.

- Contextual factors that impact when we help include time pressure, environment (urban/rural), and mood. The mood management hypothesis, the negative state relief model, and the arousal:

cost reward models all assume that how we feel when we encounter a potential helping situation has a strong effect on whether or not we intervene.

- Failure to help in emergency situations can occur at any stage of the helping process; research suggest that pluralistic ignorance and diffusion of responsibility together explain much of the bystander effect, and that apathy is unlikely to be a major contributor.

- Since the 1960s a number of safeguards have been implemented to protect the well-being of research participants, including informed consent, IRB review, and debriefing.

- The theory of empathy-induced altruistic motivation postulates that purely altruistic helping is possible and that such helping is empathy based. It provides a viable alternative to a solely egoistic interpretation of helping behavior.

- Prosociality is positively correlated with helping; gender can impact the conditions under which men and women help others, but there is no overall gender difference in helping. Gender and attractiveness of the victim can impact helping, as can similarity and shared identity between the potential helper and victim and the attributions of responsibility for a person's need made by a would-be helper.

➤ ⑤SAGE edge™ Test your understanding of chapter content. Take the practice quiz. edge.sagepub.com/barrett

KEY TERMS

Altruism, 275
Arousal: Cost Reward
    Model, 282
Bystander Apathy, 285
Bystander Effect, 287
Bystander Intervention, 285
Cultural Embeddedness, 303
Debriefing, 292
Diffusion of
    Responsibility , 287
Egoism, 275
Empathic Concern, 294

Empathy-Altruism
    Hypothesis, 294
Inclusive Fitness, 275
Informed Consent, 291
Just-World Hypothesis, 302
Kin Selection , 276
Mood Management
    Hypothesis, 282
Negative State
    Relief Model, 282

Norm of Reciprocity, 278
Pluralistic Ignorance, 286
Prosocial Behavior, 274
Prosociality, 299
Reciprocal Helping, 278
Social Responsibility
    Norm, 273
Theory of Empathy-
    Induced Altruistic
    Motivation, 294

➤ ⑤SAGE edge™ Review key terms with eFlashcards. edge.sagepub.com/barrett

THINK FURTHER!

- Have you ever been faced with an emergency situation? How many of the five features of emergencies identified by Latané & Darley were applicable?

- Think about the last time you heard about an emergency in which no one offered assistance. At what stage of the five-stage model do you think emergency helping broke down? The next time you hear of emergency helping (or lack thereof), analyze the event and try to apply the model. Does it work?

- What is bystander apathy? Do you think that Latané & Darley were correct that it cannot explain why people sometimes fail to help in emergencies? Do you think that pluralistic ignorance and diffusion of responsibility provide adequate alternative explanations for the bystander effect? Why or why not?

- Think about how well-known people such as Bill Gates give large sums of money to charity. Do you think they are driven by altruistic or egoistic motives? How could you find out?

- Have you participated in psychological research? How thorough was the debriefing? Did you have suspicions about the research hypotheses? If so, how might they have affected your responses?

- If you were asked to instruct a class of seven-year-olds how to get help in emergencies, what would you tell them (beyond calling 911)? Why?

SUGGESTED READINGS

Batson, C. D. (2011). *Altruism in humans*. New York, NY: Oxford University Press.

Chen, J. M., Kim, H. S., Mojaverian, T., & Morling, B. (2012). Culture and social support provision: Who gives what and why. *Personality and Social Psychology Bulletin, 38,* 3–13.

Cialdini, R. B., Schaller, M., Houlihan, D., Arps, K., Fultz, J., & Beaman, A. L. (1987). Empathy-based helping: Is it selflessly or selfishly motivated? *Journal of Personality and Social Psychology, 52*(4), 749–758.

Latané, B., & Darley, J. M. (1969). Bystanders "apathy." *American Scientist, 57*(2), 244–268.

Levine, M., Prosser, A., Evans, D., & Reicher, S. (2005). Identity and emergency intervention: How social group membership and inclusiveness of group boundaries shape helping behavior. *Personality and Social Psychology Bulletin, 31,* 443–453.

9

Aggression

A photo from a white supremacist website showing Dylann Storm Roof holding a Confederate battle flag, March 11, 2015. Roof murdered nine members of the Emanuel African Methodist Episcopal Church in a racially motivated killing on June 17, 2015, in Charleston, South Carolina.

©Corbis.

LEARNING OBJECTIVES

9.1 Distinguish the various types of aggression; summarize the evolutionary perspective on aggression and the roles of genetics, testosterone, and brain structure/function in aggression.

9.2 Summarize the social learning approach to media violence and evaluate the evidence that supports or undermines the connection between media exposure and real-world aggression.

9.3 Compare and contrast the original frustration-aggression hypothesis and the cognitive neo-associationist theory of emotional aggression; describe the three key contextual factors that affect aggression; identify the effects of social rejection and provocation on aggression.

9.4 Explain how the culture of honor impacts aggression and discuss the Cohen and Nisbett laboratory and field research that supports it.

9.5 Outline the major components of the general aggression model and relate them to other research contained in this chapter; explain how the factors discussed throughout this chapter fall within the model.

9.6 Describe strategies that have been shown to reduce aggression.

⑤SAGE edge™

Get the edge on your studies.
edge.sagepub.com/barrett

Take a quiz to find out what you've learned.
Watch videos that enhance chapter content.
Explore related web and social media activities.

MASS SHOOTINGS

On June 17, 2015, 21-year old Dylann Roof killed nine people at the Emanuel African Methodist Episcopal Church in Charleston, South Carolina. Roof, a Caucasian American, attended a Bible study session and then, after roughly one hour, pulled out a .45 caliber handgun and shot and killed nine African Americans (Corasaniti, Pérez-Peña, & Alvarez, 2015). He fled the scene but was arrested later without incident. Roof was clearly motivated by racial bias, given his online postings, his connections to White supremacist groups, and statements he made during the shooting itself (Wines, Saul, & Bhaskar, 2015). His is awaiting trial as of this writing.

On July 20, 2012, during a Batman movie at an Aurora, Colorado, cinema, James Holmes shot 12 people and injured 70 others without provocation. Holmes was arrested just outside the theater while sitting in his car. Although his precise motives were unclear, Holmes had written down fantasies of conducting mass murder and had carefully planned his actions (Healy & Turkewitz, 2015a). Holmes plead not guilty by reason of insanity but was convicted on 165 counts of murder and attempted murder and sentenced to life in prison (Healy & Turkewitz, 2015b).

On July 22, 2011, Anders Behring Breivik, a 32-year-old Norwegian, exploded a car bomb in Norway's capital city, Oslo, killing eight people and wounding over 200 others. Later that day, Breivik shot and killed 69 youths at a summer camp, injuring over 100 more. These attacks shocked the world, especially because they occurred in a relatively peaceful nation where shootings are rare. Breivik was a right-wing extremist who was unhappy with the leftist Labor Party government and targeted both the office of the Prime Minister and a youth camp catering to children of Labor Party members. Despite the prosecutor's arguments to the contrary, Breivik was judged to be sane by a five-member judicial panel and was sentenced to 21 years in prison, the maximum sentence in Norway (Lewis & Lyall, 2012).

Although different in many respects, these events raise similar questions about the origins of aggression and violence. Acts like these are often labeled as "senseless" or "pointless," as if it were impossible to explain them in a meaningful way. As students of social psychology, however, you know that social behavior is not senseless—rather, it is purposive—and that it is possible to identify the primary reasons that it happens. We will discuss many of the most important reasons in the course of this chapter. Investigating the causes of aggression brings several of our fundamental questions into focus. First of all, people ask whether the aggressor was engaging in *rational or nonrational behavior*. In other words, did these shooters behave in a planful, calculating, and deliberate manner or were they "swept off their feet" by the heat of the moment? Second, explorations into the nature of aggressive behavior often lead to discussions of the roles of brain pathology and personal learning history. That is, were the perpetrators sane—did they have *free will* with respect to the killings? Could they have chosen not to enact them? Was there prior physical or sexual abuse that could somehow "excuse" the aggression? Determinations of sanity or insanity bear directly on the question of free will or choice. The third fundamental theme that is pertinent is, of course, *morality*. In the same way that people regard prosocial behavior as moral, we tend to view unjustified aggression as immoral.

The current chapter reviews classic and recent research on the precursors to aggressive behavior. We'll examine both dispositional and situational factors and will describe the dominant theory of aggression that attempts to integrate aggression's multiple causes into a single framework.

Think Ahead!

1. *Does aggression invariably involve physical injury?*
2. *Does exposure to media violence increase the likelihood of aggression?*
3. *What role do biological influences play in aggressive responding?*

THE NATURE OF AGGRESSION

What Is Aggression?

When you think about aggression, what images do you conjure up? Do you picture a bloody, Hollywood shoot-'em-up movie or perhaps a recent or ongoing war? Indeed, these are clear instances of aggression. But aggression includes more than such obvious examples. Think about a time when you heard ugly rumors about a political candidate, watched a professional basketball player knock another player to the ground with a sweep of her elbow, or observed a child throw a desired toy at his father (but miss) after he said "no" to the child's 14th request to buy the toy. Social psychologists classify all of these as aggression.

There are of course a number of ways to define aggression. For our purposes, **aggression** is behavior that is intended to proximately harm another person who is motivated

Aggression: Behavior that is intended to proximately harm another person, who is motivated to avoid that harm

to avoid that harm (Anderson & Bushman, 2002). Let's break this definition down. First, aggression is *behavior,* which means that it is observable. Thinking about hurting someone or feeling angry at another person does not qualify as aggression, although these thoughts or feelings may be precursors to it. Second, aggression is always *intentional* or *deliberate.* Thus, causing injury to the driver of another car as a result of an accident is not aggression. Third, as an intentional act, aggression *need not actually produce harm*: Shooting a gun at someone but missing would be categorized as aggressive behavior.

Fourth, the immediate or *proximate* goal is to cause harm, even if it is in the service of a nonaggressive goal like winning a game. As you know, social behavior often serves more than one goal, and therefore harming the target may not be the only one. Fifth, the goal of aggression is *harm* or injury to another person. Sixth, behavior intended to cause either *physical or psychological* harm counts as aggression and thus incorporates actions such as insults and spreading rumors. Moreover, merely inflicting pain by, say, strongly pinching someone, even if there is no lasting injury to the skin, is aggression. Seventh, aggression is *interpersonal,* and therefore for the purposes of this chapter, the aggressor and the target are humans. So, to the extent that incidents of animal cruelty or property damage are enacted as revenge against another person, they would fall under the umbrella of aggression only if ultimately directed at a person. Finally, aggression is nonconsensual: Pain or injury that the target desires—say in the context of sadomasochism—is not aggression.

Forms of Aggression

As you can see, the concept of aggression is not as simple as it may have at first seemed. Indeed, the picture is even more complex once we identify several different forms of aggression (Richardson, 2014). For instance, researchers commonly distinguish between aggression primarily designed to cause injury or harm and that which is done to achieve a nonaggressive end. **Hostile aggression**, sometimes called *emotional* aggression, is behavior aimed specifically at harming another person and typically stems from anger (Berkowitz, 1993). In contrast, **instrumental aggression** is similarly intended to harm another, but the behavior is a means to a nonaggressive end. Thus it serves as an instrument for achieving the true goal of the aggressor, such as winning a basketball game or a political election. These two forms are also referred to as *reactive* and *proactive* aggression, respectively, because hostile aggression is typically a reaction or response to a particular situation, whereas instrumental aggression is deliberate and future oriented (see Table 9.1).

These two forms of aggression are not completely distinct, as an instrumental act can also carry an element of hostility (Bushman & Anderson, 2001; DeWall & Anderson, 2011). For example, a basketball player may knock an opponent to the ground in order to win the game but may also be angry at that player. Another common distinction concerns the proximity of the aggressor to the target: Aggression is **direct** when the target is physically present and **indirect** when she is not (Lagerspetz, Björkqvist, & Peltonen, 1988; Lawrence & Hutchinson, 2014; Ruiz-Pamies, Lorenzo-Seva, Morales-Vives, Cosi, & Vigil-Colet, 2014).

Hostile Aggression: Behavior aimed specifically at harming another person, typically stems from anger; sometimes called emotional aggression

Instrumental Aggression: Behavior intended to harm another, but the behavior is merely a means to a nonaggressive end

Direct Aggression: Aggression that occurs when the target is present

Indirect Aggression: Aggression that occurs when the target is NOT present

TABLE 9.1   Types of Aggression

	Direct	Indirect
Hostile (reactive)	Angry Walmart customer punches another customer who took his toy	Teens angry at a police officer spray paint her car when she is away
Instrumental (proactive)	Soldier shoots an enemy soldier who was threatening him	Woman steals boyfriend's cell phone so he can't call his ex-girlfriend

Violence: Extreme
aggression that is
intended to inflict
serious harm

Although laypersons commonly use the terms aggression and violence interchangeably, social psychologists distinguish between them, defining **violence** as extreme aggression that is intended to inflict serious harm (DeWall & Anderson, 2011). Hence, all interpersonal violence is aggression, but aggression need not be violent. For instance, insulting graffiti written on a public restroom wall may be hurtful or aggressive if aimed at another person, but it is not violent. Lastly, assertive behavior is sometimes confused with aggression, yet assertiveness does not involve an attempt to hurt someone.

Think Again!

1. *What is the definition of aggression?*
2. *Can you define and give an example of instrumental aggression?*
3. *What is the relationship between aggression and violence?*

THE ORIGINS OF AGGRESSION

Social scientists have offered a number of explanations for aggressive behavior. In this section we'll review evidence from biology and learning. Later in the chapter, we will describe the social cognition-based general aggression model as well as some personal and cultural factors impacting aggression.

Evolutionary Influences

As you know, the existence of similar behavior in multiple species provides strongly suggestive evidence for the evolutionary basis of the behavior, and in the case of selective aggression, the cross-species data is vast. Contemporary evolutionary social psychologists argue that aggression is not blind though but rather is engaged in to achieve specific goals (Buss & Duntley, 2006). For instance, the fact that the frequency of aggression varies across cultures and through history suggests that nongenetic factors must play a role in the aggressive behavior, and thus aggression cannot be construed as completely instinctual (Cohen & Leung, 2011). Moreover, research has demonstrated that contextual factors impact such behavior, and therefore aggression should be considered an *optional* strategy that is selectively employed to achieve specific goals (Liddle, Shackelford, & Weekes–Shackelford, 2012). In other words, aggression, like other evolved social behaviors, is a tool to solve a variety of adaptive problems (Ainsworth & Maner, 2012; Archer, 2013; Buss & Shackelford, 1997; Cashdan & Downes, 2012; Volk, Camilleri, Dane, & Marini, 2012). Buss and Duntley (2006) suggest that aggression can serve a number of goals, including taking resources from others, injuring or killing romantic rivals, gaining status and power, and dissuading romantic partners from straying. Furthermore, to the extent that males and females face different adaptive problems, gender differences in aggressive behavior should be expected. In a later section, we'll examine how gender affects aggression.

Shutterstock.

AGGRESSION IN THE ANIMAL KINGDOM

Chimpanzee aggression. Social psychologists examine aggression in other species, especially other primates, to help understand the evolutionary origins of human aggression.

Genetics

One of the best methods for testing the influence of genes on aggression and other social behavior is through correlational studies that compare monozygotic and dizygotic twins (Rhee & Waldman, 2011). In their meta-analysis of 14 studies that examined the relationship between genes and aggression, Rhee and Waldman (2011) concluded that there is a substantial genetic component to aggression in addition to both shared and nonshared environmental influences (Brendgen et al., 2008). Not only does general aggression seem to be partially hereditary, research suggests that both reactive and proactive aggression are moderately hereditary (Brendgen, Vitaro, Boivin, Dionne, & Pérusse, 2006) (but see Vassos, Collier, and Fazel (2014) for a different perspective). Longitudinal research shows that aggressive behavior tends to remain fairly stable throughout childhood and adolescence and into adulthood and that this is largely because of genetics (Huesmann, Dubow, & Boxer, 2011). For example, one study showed that aggression levels at age eight predicted those at 48 for both males and females (Huesmann, Dubow, & Boxer, 2009).

Testosterone

Another source of biological influences on aggression is the presence of testosterone in the body (Kilduff, Hopp, Cook, Crewther, & Manning, 2013; Montoya, Terburg, Bos, &

van Honk, 2012; Platje et al., 2015; Sapolsky, 1998). Correlational studies of individu- als with high levels of testosterone find that they tend to be relatively more aggressive. For instance, prisoners convicted of violent crimes typically have elevated testosterone levels in comparison to nonviolent criminal offenders (Archer, 2006), as do members of fraternities known for being cruder and more rambunctious versus members of other fraternities (Dabbs & Dabbs, 2000). Furthermore, female-to-male transsexuals whose testosterone was increased become more aggressive, whereas male-to-female transsex- uals with decreased testosterone become less aggressive (Cohen-Ketteinis & van Goozen, 1997). However, the testosterone-aggression link is not a strong one and has been absent in some studies (Archer, Graham-Kevan, & Davies, 2005). Please note, too, that these are all correlational studies that lack the rigor of true experiments and, consequently, do not provide evidence for a cause-and-effect relationship between testosterone and aggression. Although ethical considerations prohibit the experimental manipulation of testosterone in humans without their consent, controlled studies of rats demonstrate the predicted relationship (Barr, Gibbons, & Moyer, 1976).

Serotonin

Relatively low levels of the neurotransmitter serotonin (see Chapter 2) are often associated with greater aggressive tendencies in humans and other animals (Carrillo, Ricci, Coppersmith, & Melloni, 2009; Crockett, Clark, Lieberman, Tabibnia, & Robbins, 2010; Takahashi, Quadros, de Almeida, & Miczek, 2011). However, the complexity of the human brain is such that, for instance, one study found that serotonin depletion was associated with more aggres- sion in aggressive men but not in nonaggressive men (Bjork, Dougherty, Moeller, & Swann, 2000). Similarly, administration of an antidepressant medication thought to increase seroto- nin levels reduced aggression among aggressive participants in a reaction time test (Berman, McCloskey, Fanning, Schumacher, & Coccaro, 2009). Research by Crockett et al. (2010) sug- gests that serotonin serves as an impulse inhibitor, and therefore, it may help curtail reac- tive aggression. For instance, serotonin depletion resulted in more impulsive decisions and stronger punishing behavior during a laboratory game (Crockett et al., 2010).

Brain Structures and Executive Function

The last of the biological influences on aggression that we will discuss here relates to the operation of brain structures, particularly the amygdala and prefrontal cortex (PFC). The amygdala, as we discussed in Chapter 2, is heavily involved in the response to threat and, not surprisingly, plays a key role in aggression (Matthies et al., 2012). Early research sug- gested that activation of the amygdala could enhance aggression, whereas deactivation can reduce it (Moyer, 1976). However, the amygdala is a complicated structure, and the effects of impairment will depend on where the damage occurs (Decety & Porges, 2011). In one study, left amygdala lesions increased aggressive responses, whereas right amyg- dala dysfunction appeared to induce avoidance responses (Shinoura et al., 2011).

The PFC is associated with the control of impulses, one aspect of executive function. Damage to the PFC increases the likelihood of antisocial behavior and impulsive aggression (Giancola, Godlaski, & Roth, 2012). It is interesting to note that the impact of prefrontal cortical damage on aggressive behavior resembles that of alcohol use, which we describe below (Séguin, Sylvers, & Lilienfeld, 2007).

Think Again!

1. *Can you think of any weaknesses to using twin studies to understand aggression?*

2. *What is the evidence for the effects of testosterone on aggression?*

3. *How might a brain injury to the prefrontal cortex affect a person's likelihood of aggression?*

Individual Experiences

Like most other social behaviors, aggression is partially learned. People can learn to aggress through mere association with liked conditioned stimuli (classical conditioning) or as a result of direct reinforcement (operant conditioning). However, it is unlikely that either of these can help explain most aggressive behavior (Renfrew, 1997). One reason is that people engage in many aggressive behaviors for which they have not yet been rewarded (such as bank robbery, rape, and murder) and therefore must have acquired this propensity through some other mechanism. Social learning—the third type of learning discussed in Chapter 1—may explain it. As you know, social or observational learning occurs when people notice that others have been reinforced or punished for a particular behavior and, consequently, seek the same rewards or avoid punishment by enacting similar behavior (Bandura, 1977).

In his classic "Bobo Doll" study (that was probably covered in your introductory psychology course), Albert Bandura found empirical support for his social learning theory of aggression (Bandura, Ross, & Ross, 1961). In this study, 72 children between the ages of three and six were first given the opportunity to play with a desirable set of toys. In order to increase negative arousal and thus the probability of aggressive behavior, the children were almost immediately told that they could no longer play with these toys because they were being saved for other children. They were then brought to a different room and given the chance to play with other aggressive and nonaggressive toys, including a three-foot-tall blow-up Bobo Doll. The purpose of this manipulation was to create frustration and some "readiness" to aggress in the children. The researchers tested whether prior exposure to an adult who modeled aggressive behavior by beating a Bobo doll would lead to increased aggression in exposed children, as compared to children who had not witnessed aggressive behavior. This is precisely what they found: Children in the treatment group

Dr. Albert Bandura.

who had observed the adult's aggressive behavior were more likely to aggress in a similar way (Bandura et al., 1961). It is interesting to note that modeling was associated with increased aggression even in ways that were not modeled. Bandura and his colleagues conducted numerous follow-up studies that, together, provide solid empirical support for this social learning theory of aggressive behavior (Bandura, 1986).

Since this early research, the social learning theory of aggression has been tested and supported in hundreds of studies with participants across the lifespan and in a variety of laboratory and no laboratory contexts. This theory can help us understand, for instance, why children exposed to violence at home, including spousal or partner abuse, are at increased risk of behaving violently later in life (Huesmann et al., 2009; Orue et al., 2011). One of the mechanisms that appears to facilitate the transmission of aggressive tendencies is through the construction of "scripts" for aggression (Huesmann, 1988). That is, repeated exposure to real-world violence results in the creation of mental representations of situations in which aggression is acceptable as well as scripts or guides for enacting aggressive behavior in those situations. Children can learn when to aggress and, perhaps more importantly, learn that aggression can be a tool for achieving their goals. For instance, spanking has been associated with increased aggression later in life. These scripts and exposure to violence contribute to the persistence of aggression over the long term (S. L. Brown et al., 2011; Garcia, Restubog, Kiewitz, Scott, & Tang, 2014; Huesmann et al., 2009; Underwood, Beron, Gentsch, Galperin, & Risser, 2008).

Media Influence

One of the most controversial issues in U.S. society today is whether or not exposure to violence in the media, in music, and in video or computer games increases real-world violence. Indeed, the extent of such exposure is remarkable. By the age of 12, U.S. children have observed approximately 100,000 acts of violence and an additional 8,000 murders (Eron, 2001). Moreover, as much as 61% of U.S. television shows contain acts of violence (Anderson et al., 2003). Concerns about possible adverse effects have led to the creation of parent warning labels on video and computer games and have influenced the application of the age-based ratings system used for films in the United States. Bandura provided an early test of this **media violence hypothesis** by varying the study described above and exposing children to videos of adults engaging in either violent or nonviolent behavior. He found that this too, increased aggressive behavior (Bandura, Ross, & Ross, 1963). The research on effects of media exposure and violence is vast and, for the most part, consistent with Bandura's findings (Coyne & Padilla-Walker, 2015; DeWall & Anderson, 2011). Let me summarize the basic arguments and data that support the media violence hypothesis and then briefly mention some of the criticisms of this hypothesis.

Research inside and outside of the lab has clearly demonstrated the causal link between short-term exposure to violence and short-term aggressive behavior (Grossman & DeGaetano, 1999). One meta-analysis that included over 50,000 participants in 284 laboratory studies, field experiments, longitudinal studies, and cross-sectional correlational studies demonstrates impressive consistency across this variety of methodologies (Anderson & Bushman, 2002). In light of this extensive evidence, two leading experts have argued that these effects are so well documented as to be indisputable (Bushman & Huesmann, 2010).

Causal evidence from laboratory studies of exposure to violent films is consistent with these findings (Anderson et al., 2003; Berkowitz, 1993). For example, research by Graña et al. (2004) found that children 8 to 12 years old who watched televised bullfights became more aggressive immediately afterward. Results such as these have been produced in numerous other studies (Parker & Rogers, 1981).

Numerous laboratory studies have produced causal evidence of the effects of playing violent video games on subsequent aggressive behavior (Anderson & Dill, 2000; Carnagey & Anderson, 2005). In a prototypical study, participants are randomly assigned to play either a violent or nonviolent video game. They then play a competitive video game in which they can punish their opponents. The dependent variable is a measure of the frequency and/or intensity of their punishing behavior. In one such experiment, 141 male and female undergraduates played one of three versions of a competitive car game, Carmeggedon 2 (Carnagey & Anderson, 2005, Study 3). One version rewarded drivers by giving them bonus points for killing both pedestrians and other drivers, a second version punished drivers by subtracting points for either type of

Shutterstock.

Media Violence Hypothesis: Idea that exposure to violence in the media can cause aggression in the real world

IMAGE OF MEDIA VIOLENCE

Social psychologists have extensively examined the potential effects of exposure to media violence on real-world violence.

killing, and a third version offered no opportunity for killing. After playing Carmeggedon 2 for 20 minutes, all participants received an evaluation of an essay that they had written earlier in the experiment, ostensibly from another undergraduate participant. The evaluation was harshly critical and included the statement "This is the worst essay I have ever read!" Subsequently, all participants played what is called a Taylor competitive reaction time game in which the "loser" of each trial is exposed to a blast of white noise. Although the participants did not actually administer the blast, they decided how loud and for how long it sounded. Thus participants were permitted to punish their opponent.

Carnagey and Anderson (2005) found that players of the aggressive version of the car race game were much more punishing than those who played either the version that punished violence or included no violence (See Figure 9.1). This effect remained even after experimenters controlled for differences in trait aggression that had been assessed prior to the conduct of these studies. Other studies by these authors suggest that the increase in aggressive behavior was related to cognitions and not affect and was triggered by participation in the game in which violence was rewarded (Carnagey & Anderson,

FIGURE 9.1   Violent Video Games and Aggressive Behavior

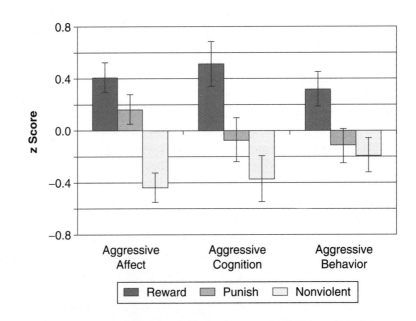

The effects of video game exposure on aggressive affect, cognition, and behavior. Some players were rewarded for their aggression, others were punished, and those in the control group played a nonviolent version of the same game.

Source: Adapted from Carnagey, N. L., & Anderson, C. A. (2005). The effects of reward and punishment in violent video games on aggressive affect, cognition, and behavior. *Psychological Science, 16*, 882–889.

2005, Studies 1 & 2). Participant gender was also important, as males were typically more aggressive than females. Finally, self-rated trait aggression was significantly, positively correlated with *prior exposure* to violent video games, and this relationship was greater for males than for females.

More impressive still is a recent meta-analysis by Anderson et al. (2010) of over 100 studies including 130,000 participants that examined the effects of playing violent video games on aggressive behavior. Their review revealed that there is a clear and consistent relationship between playing violent video games and aggressive cognition, affect, and behavior.

Criticisms of the Media Violence Hypothesis. Not all researchers concur that media violence influences real-world aggression (Elson & Ferguson, 2014). Three of the more common criticisms of the media violence hypothesis are that (1) laboratory effects tend to be of short duration, (2) what evidence there is for long-term effects is merely correlational, and (3) it is unclear whether laboratory aggression is related to real-world behavior (Ferguson & Savage, 2012; Renfrew, 1997). However, a number of researchers have offered spirited responses to these concerns. First, although laboratory studies have typically tested only short-term effects, research does show that such effects can last beyond the end of the study. For example, Carnagey, Anderson, and Bushman (2007) found that physiological arousal upon viewing real-world violence was lessened among participants who had just played a violent video game, suggesting that exposure to game violence desensitized participants to real-world violence.

In response to the second criticism, longitudinal research has clearly demonstrated that long-term exposure to violent media likely causes aggressive behavior (Friedlander, Connolly, & Craig, 2013; Gentile & Bushman, 2012). These studies rely on sophisticated designs and analysis that enable researchers to determine causal pathways. For instance, in a three-year study of young children in five countries, Huesmann and Eron (1986) found that exposure to televised violence—even when controlling for trait aggression—predicted later aggression. Huesmann, Moise-Titus, Podolski, and Eron (2003) followed the U.S. children from this sample for an additional 15 years, finding that adult aggression by both boys and girls was still positively correlated with that early exposure (see Figure 9.2). A number of others studies have revealed similar relationships between early exposure and later aggression (Johnson, Cohen, Smailes, Kasen, & Brook, 2002). Finally, the charge that laboratory aggression may be unrelated to real-world aggression has been countered by several studies documenting just such a connection (Anderson & Bushman, 1997; Anderson, Lindsay, & Bushman, 1999).

Given that the evidence for the social learning-based media violence hypothesis is overwhelming, we need to ask why this effect occurs (Bushman, Gollwitzer, & Cruz, 2015). There are many ways in which media violence can lead to real-world aggression (see Table 9.2). First, observing violence can cause physiological arousal, which, as we will describe below, can contribute to subsequent aggressive behavior. Second, aggressive or violent imagery primes aggression-related thoughts, and, as you know, priming can guide a person toward prime-consistent behavior. Third, exposure—especially if repeated—can lead to desensitization toward violence (Carnagey et al., 2007; Krahé et al., 2011). For example, two studies by Bushman and Anderson (2009) found that individuals who had just played a violent video game for 20 minutes or just viewed a full-length violent movie took longer to help an injured person. Fourth, as postulated by Bandura's social learning theory, observing behavior can lead to its imitation, particularly when the model is rewarded in some way. So-called *copycat crimes,* for instance, frequently occur after well-publicized violent events (Huesmann & Kirwil, 2007). Similarly, the incidence of suicides typically increases during the two weeks after prominent suicides (Phillips, 1979). Finally, exposure can both teach people new ways to aggress and teach them norms about when it is appropriate to aggress.

Violent Pornography and Sexual Violence. The findings reported above demonstrate linkages between exposure to media violence and general aggression. Many people are concerned about a particularly politically charged aspect of this topic: the specific effects of violent pornography on violence against women. First of all, it is quite clear that male attitudes toward sexual violence against women become more permissive as their exposure to violent pornography increases. For instance, a recent meta-analysis of nine

FIGURE 9.2   Long-Term Effects of Exposure to Violent Television

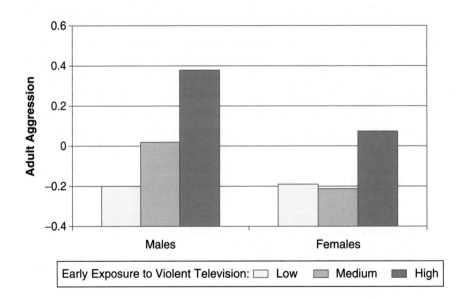

Source: Adapted from Figure 2, Huesmann, L. R., Moise-Titus, J., Podolski, C. P., & Eron, L. D. (2003). Longitudinal relations between children's exposure to TV violence and their aggressive and violent behavior in young adulthood: 1977–1992. *Developmental Psychology, 39,* 201–229.

TABLE 9.2   Effects of Media Exposure on Actual Aggression

Ways That Exposure to Media Violence Can Increase the Likelihood of Actual Aggression
Increase physiological arousal
Activate aggression-related thoughts and feelings
Desensitize people to violence
Lead to imitation
Teach new ways to be aggressive
Teach norms about when it is appropriate to be aggressive

nonexperimental studies including over 2,300 participants found a significant positive correlation between these variables and in addition found a smaller but also significant correlation between nonviolent pornography and tolerant attitudes regarding violence against women (Hald, Malamuth, & Yuen, 2010). Moreover, the results of an earlier meta-analysis of 30 experiments were consistent with a causal relationship between violent pornography and laboratory aggression by males against females (Allen, D'Alessio, & Brezgel, 1995). It is important to note that the experimental effects of violent pornography on aggressive behavior are generally short lived, and the existence of a causal link to real-world aggression has yet to be convincingly demonstrated (Kingston, Malamuth, Fedoroff, & Marshall, 2009). In response, some researchers have adopted a more nuanced and complicated model that postulates that such a relationship depends on the presence of other factors also linked to risk of sexual aggression, such as hostile masculinity or prior sexual behavior (Kingston et al., 2009; Malamuth, Hald, & Koss, 2012).

Later in this chapter, we will review the primary contextual, personal, and cultural factors that increase the likelihood of aggression. Before we do, let's take a look at several prominent theoretical frameworks for understanding the causes of aggressive behavior.

Think Again!

1. *How much exposure do you have to media violence (TV, games, etc.)? How do you think that it may have affected you?*

2. *Describe the Carmegeddon study and how it supports the media violence hypothesis.*

3. *What are the criticisms of the media violence hypothesis, and how do its proponents respond to such criticism?*

WHEN DO WE AGGRESS?

Frustration-Aggression Hypothesis

Think about a time when you were very frustrated, such as when you were desperately trying to negotiate a major traffic jam because you were late to a final exam or important job interview. How did you express this frustration? Did you yell insults at other drivers, flip them off, or pound on the steering wheel? If so, then your behavior was consistent with one of earliest theories about the causes of aggression. In 1939, John Dollard and his colleagues formulated the **frustration-aggression hypothesis** that postulated that (a) frustration always leads to aggression and (b) aggression is always produced by frustration (Dollard, Miller, Doob, Mowrer, & Sears, 1939). Frustration was defined as occurring when goal-directed activity is thwarted or blocked (Miller, 1941).

The theory is simple—too simple, in fact. By including the term "always," Dollard et al. claimed that there is a one-to-one correspondence between frustration and aggression and thus that there are no other causes of aggression. Although ample evidence exists that frustration *can* lead to aggression, even a moment's reflection will produce other possible explanations. For instance, *instrumental aggression* can be completely unrelated to frustration, such as when a sniper shoots a member of an opposing military in order to help win a war (Berkowitz, 1989). Indeed, social psychologists soon recognized that the basic frustration-aggression hypothesis ignored a large number of important influences, and these insights have led to the generation of newer, more sophisticated approaches that incorporate frustration as just one of many factors (Anderson & Bushman, 2002; Berkowitz, 1989; Breuer, Scharkow, & Quandt, 2015; Deater-Deckard et al., 2010; Renfrew, 1997).

Cognitive Neoassociationist Theory

One of the theorists who understood the shortcomings of Dollard et al.'s approach was Leonard Berkowitz, who developed the **cognitive neoassociationist theory** of hostile or emotional aggression (Berkowitz, 1993, 2012). Berkowitz's central insight was that *almost any aversive event can produce aggressive behavior, provided that that event generates negative affect* (Berkowitz, 1989). Thus he views frustration as only one example of a broader set of possible aversive events that can serve as precursors to aggression, including heat, pain, foul odors, and even depression. In the early stages of this model, automatic or X-system processes dominate: The initial event rapidly triggers negative affect or unpleasant feelings. Next, the affect automatically activates thoughts, feelings, and physiological arousal that are *associated* with the flight-or-fight response; that is, with either escape/avoidance or aggressive behavior. Which pathway a person takes will depend on such factors as prior learning, genetic endowment, and a variety of situational cues—such as nearby weapons—that can *prime* anger or fear (Berkowitz, 1989). These automatic responses may then be tempered or controlled by higher order C-system *cognitive* processes, including the generation of attributions of responsibility for the aversive

Frustration-Aggression Hypothesis: Idea that aggression is always caused by frustration, and aggression is always the result of frustration

Cognitive Neoassociationist Theory (of hostile or emotional aggression): Idea that almost any aversive event can produce aggressive behavior, provided that that event generates negative affect

event. Finally, the person enacts either aggressive or retreat/avoidance behavior. Let's turn now to some of the research that illustrates the key components of Berkowitz's cognitive neoassociationist model.

Contextual Factors

Unpleasant Events. Aversive events that produce negative affect are the contextual conditions that precipitate angry aggression. In addition to frustration, pain, heat, noise, foul odors, and other causes of physical discomfort have been shown to produce aggression in both laboratory and real-world studies (Berkowitz, 1993; Geen, 1998). In one study that examined the effects of *pain* on aggression, female participants in a study by Berkowitz, Cochran, and Embree (1981) supervised the work of another participant (actually a confederate) and administered either rewards or punishments appropriate to the quality of the work. Rewards consisted of nickels the worker could earn, and the punishments were given in the form of loud blasts of noise. During the first two of three 7-minute work periods, the participants submerged one hand in either very cold or room temperature water. Half of the women in each of these two conditions were told that punishment was likely to help improve the worker's performance, whereas the remaining learned that punishment was likely to hurt the worker's performance. By informing participants that their punishment amounted to the deliberate infliction of pain, the experimenters hoped to prime aggressive thoughts and feelings that, together with the experience of pain, would facilitate greater aggression against the worker. The results supported Berkowitz et al.'s (1981) prediction (see Figure 9.3).

Like pain, ambient *heat* can increase the likelihood of aggressive behavior, as demonstrated across a variety of laboratory and field experiments as well as naturalistic and archival studies (Anderson, 1989; Reifman, Larrick, & Fein, 1991). For instance, drivers of cars lacking air conditioning in the hot city of Phoenix blasted their horns longer when stuck behind a stalled car than those with air conditioning (Kenrick & MacFarlane, 1986). A study of major league baseball found that pitchers hit more batters on hot days, even when wild pitches, errors, passed balls, and walks are controlled for (Reifman et al., 1991). Furthermore, large-scales studies have found that violent crime (homicides, assaults, rapes, spousal abuse, and riots) increase in frequency as the relative daily and seasonal temperature increases (Anderson, 1989, 2001; Bushman, Wang, & Anderson, 2005). Importantly, data supporting this *heat hypothesis* have been obtained across both time and cultures. Why does heat have this effect? The most likely explanation is that people become physiologically—and aversively—aroused by hotter temperatures and misattribute their unpleasant arousal to causes and people in their immediate environments, thereby leading to more hostility and aggressive behavior (Anderson, 2001). We will have more to say about arousal and aggression below.

Aggressive Cues. You've seen how pain, physical discomfort, and other unpleasant events can instigate aggression. There is another feature of some situations that can trigger aggressive behavior when aversive conditions already exist: the presence of weapons. This

FIGURE 9.3   The Effects of Pain and Aggression

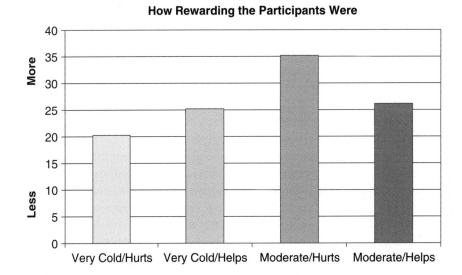

Source: Adapted from Table 2, Experiment 5, Berkowitz, L., Cochran, S. T., & Embree, M. C. (1981). Physical pain and the goal of aversively stimulated aggression. *Journal of Personality and Social Psychology, 40*, pp. 687–700.

Weapons Effect:
When the presence of a weapon—such as a rifle or a revolver—makes aggression more likely

weapons effect occurs when the presence of a weapon—such as a rifle or a revolver—makes aggression more likely (Bettencourt, Talley, Benjamin, & Valentine, 2006; Carlson, Marcus-Newhall, & Miller, 1990). Berkowitz and LePage (1967) provided the initial laboratory test of this hypothesis in a study in which they manipulated the anger of the participant and the presence of a gun. The 100 male participants were randomly assigned to either be provoked into anger by another person (a confederate) or treated nicely. In the anger, condition the participant received seven electric shocks, compared to just one in the nonanger condition. The participants were told that the shocks reflected how the confederate had evaluated their solutions to a specific problem posed by the experimenter. After receiving their shock(s), participants had an opportunity to provide feedback to the confederate in the form of shocks. In addition to the anger manipulation, the table at which the participant sat either had weapons (a revolver and a shotgun), badminton equipment (rackets and shuttlecocks), or no object. The dependent measure was the amount of shock that the participant delivered to the confederate. The results were as predicted by Berkowitz and LePage (1967): More shocks were given by the angered participants than the nonangered participants but only when a weapon was present (see Figure 9.4).

Aggressive Cues:
Words, images, and objects in the environment that trigger aggression-related thoughts can increase aggression

How does the weapons effect work? As discussed in Chapter 3, the activation of a particular concept in memory can spread to related concepts, thereby activating them and enhancing their ability to influence affect, cognition, and behavior. The weapons effect can be seen as a special case of a broader principle that the presence of **aggressive cues** in the environment that trigger aggression-related thoughts can increase aggression (Berkowitz & Lepage, 1967). Experimental evidence for the weapons effect has been supplemented by a number of field studies that have, for example, manipulated aggressive cues on a pickup truck stalled in traffic and similarly found that these cues increased aggressive horn honking (Turner, Layton, & Simons, 1975). Indeed, a meta-analysis of 56 studies testing the weapons effect provided strong support for its central prem-

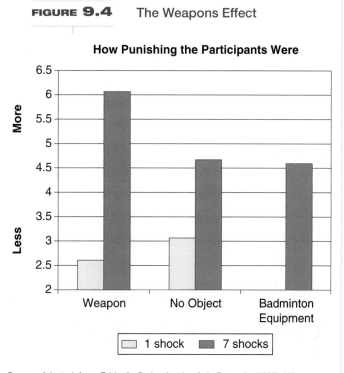

FIGURE 9.4   The Weapons Effect

Source: Adapted from Table 2, Berkowitz, L., & LePage, A. (1967). Weapons as aggression-eliciting stimuli. *Journal of Personality and Social Psychology, 7,* 202–207.

ise, and this effect is particularly strong when the target is angry (Carlson et al., 1990). Finally, consistent with the principle of spreading activation, aggressive thoughts can even be triggered by exposure to *words* related to hot temperatures (DeWall & Bushman, 2009) or aggressive images (Anderson, Anderson, & Deuser, 1996).

Think Again!

1. *What is the original frustration-aggression hypothesis?*

2. *Many people report feeling irritable when they are experiencing pain or are very hot. Do you find the same thing?*

3. *What is an "aggressive cue," and how can it influence aggressive behavior? Can you identify any aggressive cues in your environment (home, university, workplace, etc.)?*

Interpersonal Factors

Let's turn our attention now to a couple of interpersonal factors that can, like the contextual variables just described, lead to aggressive responding: social rejection and provocation. In both of the cases, individual construal plays a central role, because these events are only meaningful to the extent the target perceives them as such.

Social Rejection. Being rejected by other people, especially those who are important to us, is one of the most painful events people experience (Bowker & Etkin, 2014; Cacioppo & Patrick, 2008; Durso, Luttrell, & Way, 2015; Jacobs & Harper, 2013; Pitts, Wilson, & Hugenberg, 2013; Twenge, 2007). One might imagine, therefore, that the emotional hurt of rejection might, like physical pain, enhance aggressive responses. A number of investigations by social psychologists have shown that this is indeed the case (DeWall, Twenge, Gitter, & Baumeister, 2009; Twenge, Baumeister, Tice, & Stucke, 2001). Furthermore, social pain actually feels like physical pain, so much so that taking acetaminophen (the active ingredient in the headache medication Tylenol) seems to also reduce psychological pain, especially for women (DeWall et al., 2010; Vangelisti, Pennebaker, Brody, & Guinn, 2014). Twenge et al. (2001) manipulated social rejection in several ways—including actual rejection within the experimental session—and gave participants an opportunity to aggress against other participants. In each of their five experiments, socially rejected individuals exhibited more aggression toward another participant, whether or not they were provoked into anger by that participant (Twenge et al., 2001). Other research by Twenge and her colleagues showed that social exclusion can also decrease prosocial behavior, which is incompatible with aggression; such rejection may indirectly increase aggression (Twenge, Baumeister, DeWall, Ciarocco, & Bartels, 2007).

Social rejection can be painful.

Ray Pietro/Taxi/Getty Image.

Provocation. It has been argued that provocation may be the most potent trigger of human aggression (Anderson & Huesmann, 2003; Berkowitz, 1993). **Provocation** occurs when one person intentionally elicits an aggressive response from another through the use of insults, physical aggression, blocking goal attainment, teasing, or

Provocation: When a person intentionally elicits an aggressive response from another through the use of insults, physical aggression, blocking goal attainment, teasing, or similar behaviors

similar behaviors (Anderson & Huesmann, 2003). In one study, Baron (1988) tested the effects of provocation on aggression by giving participants either constructive or destructive criticism of their work on an experimental task. Those in the destructive condition were more likely to adopt an inflexible, less cooperative position in possible future negotiations with the criticizer.

Cultural Influences

The situational influences described so far can be considered proximal in that they are immediately present and directly affect social behavior. Although in some ways culture may also seem to be a situational or contextual variable, it is much broader and deeper than factors such as ambient temperature or aggressive cues that may amplify aggressive tendencies. As you've seen in previous chapters, culture pervades all aspects of social behavior. Culture not only influences people's thoughts, feelings, and behaviors, but it also gives them meaning (Cohen & Leung, 2011). Not surprisingly, aggressive behavior also varies across cultures and nations (Bergmüller, 2013; Bernards & Graham, 2013; Negy, Ferguson, Galvanovskis, & Smither, 2013). In this section, we'll discuss research on one important culture-related variable that has been closely tied to aggression both in the laboratory and in field studies: personal honor.

Culture of Honor. Imagine that you have arrived at the psychology building at your college to take part in a study of human judgment under time pressure. Upon reporting to the lab room, you are given a survey to complete and then deliver to a room down a long, narrow hallway. As you begin walking down the corridor, a man enters ahead of you and opens a file cabinet drawer that blocks your path. When you approach, the man closes the drawer to allow you to pass. After dropping off your survey at a table, you turn and head back up the hallway to the room you started in. The man has again opened the file drawer and again your path is blocked. As you approach, the man slams the drawer closed, bumps you with his shoulder, and calls you an "asshole." What would you do? Laugh it off or respond aggressively? Well, according to the authors of just such a study, your response would depend on your cultural background. More specifically, the primary factor determining how aggressively the participants responded was whether or not they were raised in a southern or northern region of the United States. That is, the researchers predicted that Southern males would be significantly more aggressive than would Northern males.

This culture-based difference in aggressive responding is exactly what Cohen, Nisbett, Bowdle, and Schwartz (1996) found in a number of studies based on the procedure just described. The experimenters measured the strength of aggressive responses in a number of ways: how cognitively primed for aggression participants were (as measured by the amount of aggression embedded in a story they completed); how likely the participants were to feel that their masculinity was threatened; how upset they were (as measured by the level of the stress hormone cortisol in their saliva); how physiologically primed for aggression they were (as indicated by the testosterone level in their saliva); and finally how likely they were to demonstrate aggressive and dominant behavior. In three laboratory studies and across many dependent measures, Southern participants consistently exhibited significantly stronger aggression response patterns than did the Northerners (see Figure 9.5). In an illustrative field experiment, Cohen and Nisbett (1997) found that Southern businesses were more receptive to job queries from admitted murderers than were Northern businesses, provided that the murder was honor related. The key question is, of course, why are there differences?

According to research by Cohen and others, the Southern states are characterized by **a culture of honor** in which people—especially males—are highly protective of their reputation and very sensitive and reactive to personal insults, humiliation, and other threats to their honor (Cohen & Nisbett, 1997; Fiske & Rai, 2015; Henry, 2009; Nisbett & Cohen, 1996). These perceived insults produce anger that tends to give rise to hostility

Culture of Honor:
Society in which people, especially males, are highly protective of their reputation and very sensitive and reactive to personal insults, humiliation, and other threats to their honor

FIGURE 9.5   Aggression and the Culture of Honor

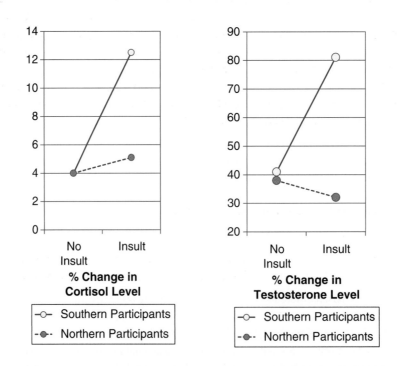

Source: Adapted from Study 2, Cohen, D., & Nisbett, R. E., Bowdle, B. F., & Schwarz, N. (1996). Insult, aggression, and Southern culture of honor: An "experimental ethnography". *Journal of Personality and Social Psychology, 70,* 945–960.

and increase the likelihood of aggression (Ijzerman, van Dijk, & Gallucci, 2007; E. J. Pedersen, Forster, & McCullough, 2014). The U.S. South, like several other geographic regions around the world, has developed norms for social behavior that permit—or encourage—harsh, aggressive behaviors for specific purposes, including self-protection and responding to an insult or humiliation (Nisbett & Cohen, 1996; Vandello, Cohen, Grandon, & Franiuk, 2009). A study by Brown, Osterman, and Barnes (2009) demonstrates how high school students from states described as culture of honor states (Cohen, 1998) are more likely to bring weapons to school and that approximately 75% of high school shootings occurred in those states.

Nisbett and Cohen (1996) argue that cultures of honor tend to exist in regions in which herding and shepardry—as opposed to agriculture—are or were dominant. They reason that herds are much more susceptible to theft than are products of agriculture, and therefore the psychological mechanism of honor and its concomitant norms for aggressive retaliation would ward off potential thieves. Nisbett, Cohen and other researchers have amassed impressive evidence from the United States and around the world for this hypothesis (Vandello et al., 2009). In the United States, the South was settled primarily by herders from Scotland and Ireland, whereas the North was populated by English and Dutch farmers (Nisbett & Cohen, 1996). This norm of aggressive retaliation extend to other insults or humiliations that questioned a person's honor or character and indeed persist to this day. A recent related study revealed that Southern men are more likely than Northern men to perceive that other men are relatively more aggressive (compared to themselves); Southerners also perceive bystanders of interpersonal conflicts to be more encouraging of aggression than do Northerners (Vandello, Cohen, & Ransom, 2008). Moreover, these and other researchers found similar herding conditions and violence-related norms in other places, including Brazil and Chile (Campbell, 1965; Figueredo, Tal, McNeil, & Guillén, 2004; Vandello et al., 2009).

Think Again!

1. _How can social rejection affect aggression?_

2. _What is the culture of honor?_

3. _In some places, the legal system is more forgiving of honor-related killings in comparison to other killings. Do you agree with this distinction? Why or why not?_

THE GENERAL AGGRESSION MODEL

The most comprehensive psychological theory of aggression is the general aggression model (GAM), which attempts to gather several more specific theories under a single framework

(Anderson & Bushman, 2002; DeWall & Anderson, 2011; Hosie, Gilbert, Simpson, & Daffern, 2014). The GAM focuses on a single episode or cycle of aggression that occurs during a particular social situation and accounts for both proximate influences (e.g., arousal) as well as more distal ones (such as genetic endowment). Furthermore, the effects of that interaction on subsequent episodes are built into the model, and therefore it can also serve as a window into repeated aggressive behavior that unfolds over time (Anderson & Bushman, 2002). Perhaps the most impressive aspect of this general model is that it incorporates all of the specific influences on aggressive behavior described in this chapter.

The GAM views social cognitive processes as the core through which the other influences operate. That is, background factors like genes and personality only alter the likelihood of aggressive behavior to the extent that they impact mental processing at the moment at which aggression is enacted (or avoided). As can be seen in the simplified model in Figure 9.6, the GAM identifies three components of an aggressive episode: personal and situational inputs, internal states, and outcomes. Examples of situational inputs described earlier in this chapter include frustration, pain, heat, provocation, violent media, and the presence of weapons. Later in this chapter we will discuss several person-based inputs such as cognitive biases, gender, and a few personality traits. The second component is the internal state of the individual, and this serves as a *route* through which the two types of inputs have their effects on the third component, the outputs. According to

FIGURE 9.6   The General Aggression Model

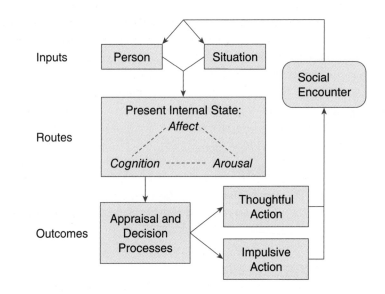

Source: Anderson, C. A., & Bushman, B. J. (2002). The general aggression model: An integrated social-cognitive model of human aggression. *Annual Review of Psychology, 53,* 27–51.

this model, a person's internal state is a combination of her existing affect, cognitions, and level of arousal. The individual's appraisal and potential reappraisal of the situation—such as making an attribution about the source of her frustration or pain—are one set of outputs that lead to the second set, her resultant actions. Finally, the outputs from that episode can cycle back to influence subsequent social interactions and aggressive episodes.

DOING RESEARCH: ARCHIVAL STUDIES OF HISTORICAL AGGRESSION

The majority of the social psychological research discussed in this book—and in our professional journals—is laboratory based and experimental. However, some questions that are important to psychologists can only be answered through alternative methods. For instance, if a psychologist were to hypothesize that a recent downward trend in murder rates was a continuation of long-term changes, then she would have to look at historical records of the relevant time periods and cultures or nations. In doing so, the psychologist would be engaging in what is called **archival research**, which examines data from preexisting sources or archives, such as newspapers, historical records, speeches, and so forth. This is exactly what Daly and Wilson (Daly & Wilson, 1988) did in their highly regarded book on the history of murder, *Homicide*. These authors sought to assess historical trends in homicide rates across many cultures and time periods. To do so, they gathered data from a variety of archival sources and demonstrated the decline in homicide over time. Much more recently, in his ambitious *The Better Angels of Our Nature: Why Violence Has Declined,* Steven Pinker (2011) conducted his own archival research and analyzed many archival studies performed by others—creating what could be called a *meta*-archival study—and concluded (as the title implies) that the Western world has experienced a decrease in violent behavior over several millennia. Some of the research by Nisbett and Cohen (1996) on the culture of honor similarly relied on historical records of violence and immigration in the southern and northern United States.

> **Archival Research:** Examines data from preexisting sources or archives, such as newspapers, historical records, and speeches

What do you suppose are the advantages and disadvantages of archival research? The primary advantage is that data can be obtained about social behavior that is impossible to collect in any other way. One of the major drawbacks is that causal relationships cannot be established, because the researcher is unable to manipulate variables and control other factors. Determining the validity of the historical records may be difficult, as can finding data that answer the question being asked. For instance, if only last names are listed in an accounting of murderers and victims in a particular city in a specific time period, researchers would be unable to conclude anything about gender and homicide in that era.

PERSON FACTORS AFFECTING AGGRESSION

As you now know, the general aggression model incorporates personal factors as inputs that, along with situational features, provide the material that creates the internal states of the focal individual. In this section we will examine the role that several person-based influences play in the generation of aggressive behavior. We will look at certain influences that are largely fixed—gender and personality—and one that is variable—alcohol.

Gender. Who is more aggressive, males or females? When asked this question, most of my students emphatically state that males are. However, a few of them, typically females, provide a more nuanced view, suggesting that it depends on what kind of aggression is being considered. It turns out that women's beliefs are closer to the truth, which is somewhat complicated.

Males are more aggressive in most animal species, including mice, rats, dogs, and many primates (Hood & Cairns, 1988; Lagerspetz, 1979; Wrangham & Peterson, 1996). In humans, gender-based differences in aggression emerge as early as the preschool years, when males begin to show more physical aggression (Loeber & Hay, 1997). The difference in physical aggression increases during elementary school, strengthened by the fact that females exhibit more indirect and nonphysical aggression (Card, Stucky, Sawalani, & Little, 2008; Lagerspetz et al., 1988). Females consistently engage in more **relational aggression**—which is intended to disrupt relationships—including gossip, rumor spreading, and social exclusion (Coie et al., 1999; Martin, Miller, Kubricht, Yorgason, & Carroll, 2015; Rivera-Maestre, 2015). Females are actually more physically aggressive with romantic partners (Archer, 2000). Nevertheless, males continue to be much more physically aggressive overall as adults, and comprise 87% of people arrested for assault and 88% of those arrested for murder (Kimmel, 2004; Walker, Richardson, & Green, 2000). Moreover, Bettencourt and Miller's (1996) meta-analysis of 64 laboratory experiments concluded that men were consistently more aggressive than women, although under conditions of provocation, this disparity is significantly diminished. Finally, recent evidence suggests that the once wide gender difference in indirect aggression may have narrowed or disappeared (Richardson & Hammock, 2007).

A crucial question is, of course, why these gender differences exist. An obvious answer may be that greater levels of testosterone can lead to more aggression; however, there is more to the story. In fact there are two complementary perspectives on the origins of gender differences in aggression, one based in evolutionary theory and other in social role theory. The evolutionary argument starts with the assumption (discussed in Chapter 1) that psychological traits are present because they helped solve adaptive problems in our ancestral past (Buss & Shackelford, 1997). Differences between men and women should emerge whenever the two sexes faced divergent, adaptive problems. For instance, males must engage in greater intrasexual competition (competition against other males) to gain access to females than do females seeking male partners (Daly & Wilson, 1988; Wilson & Daly, 1985). We will discuss this idea in greater detail in Chapter 11. Among the many lines of evidence for the evolutionary-based perspective is the prevalence of this gender difference across cultures and across species (Buss & Shackelford, 1997; Daly & Wilson, 1988).

Although there is a great deal of data that supports the evolutionary approach, it is clear that socialization also has a key role in these differences. From an early age, children are

Relational Aggression:
Aggression that is intended to disrupt relationships, such as gossip, rumor spreading, and social exclusion

taught that males are expected to be more physically aggressive, and females ought to show more concern for the victims and for their own safety (Eagly & Steffen, 1986). In addition, the fact that gender differences in both indirect and direct aggression appear to be decreasing suggests that such differences are not biologically determined but are products of the interaction between social influences and evolutionary predispositions (Richardson & Hammock, 2007). Nevertheless, the existence of some cross-cultural and historical variation in aggression does not necessarily undermine evolutionary explanations, as the latter allow for multiple influences on human behavior (Kenrick, Nieuweboer, & Buunk, 2010; Liddle et al., 2012). It is most likely the case that both evolutionary pressures and social roles are at play here.

Personality. Psychologists have examined the relationship between aggression and a number of personality traits (Bettencourt et al., 2006; Webster et al., 2014, 2015; White, Gordon, & Guerra, 2015). Although many believe that people with low self-esteem are more aggressive than those with moderate or high levels, the evidence is inconsistent with this (Baumeister & Boden, 1998; Locke, 2009). Bushman et al. (2009) argue that, if anything, high self-esteem is related to aggression, especially when a person is also high in *narcissism* and is facing a threat to his ego (Baumeister & Boden, 1998). Narcissists are people who possess an inflated view of the self, are highly self-admiring, have a sense of entitlement or believe that the world owes them something even if they haven't earned it, and are overly confident (Twenge & Campbell, 2009). Narcissists are particularly sensitive to insults, slights, and other threats to their ego and hence often exhibit verbally or physically aggressive responses (Thomaes & Bushman, 2011).

Problems with *self-control* and *impulsivity* have also been linked to aggressive tendencies and are seen as a major personal factor predisposing a person to violent crime (Gottfredson, 2011; Hecht & Latzman, 2015). In addition, people exhibiting a *Type "A" personality*—who are constantly in a hurry, very competitive, and often difficult—are also more likely to exhibit hostile aggression when provoked (Bettencourt et al., 2006). Bettencourt et al. (2006) also found that *trait irritability,* which is the tendency to anger quickly and take offense easily, is positively correlated with aggression. Finally, individuals diagnosed with *antisocial personality disorder,* also called *psychopathy,* are more likely to be aggressive (Nouvion, Cherek, Lane, Tcheremissine, & Lieving, 2007). Psychopaths seem to lack feelings of empathy or a moral conscience and engage in frequent deception and manipulation, yet may come across as charming and friendly.

Alcohol. As you probably know—and as many studies show—alcohol reduces a person's self-control and facilitates impulsive and aggressive behavior (Taylor & Chermack, 1993). The link is rather strong, and in fact alcohol is involved in over half of all murders and other violent crimes in the United States (Murdoch, Pihl, & Ross, 1990). This *correlational* evidence, although interesting, does not itself establish causality. However, the results of both individual laboratory studies and meta-analyses are quite clear: Alcohol consumption, even in small quantities, increases the likelihood of aggression (Ito, Miller, & Pollock, 1996).

For example, in one study male and female participants either drank alcohol or a placebo that they believed was alcohol before engaging in a competitive reaction time test against a same sex (fictitious) opponent (Giancola et al., 2009). Each time they won one of the 34 trials they had the opportunity to shock their opponents and were subject to being shocked when they lost. The experimenters were interested in whether alcohol would impact aggressive responding as the opponent progressively increased the shock delivered to the participants. Their hypothesis was confirmed: Both male and female participants more frequently delivered shocks and, notably, administered the highest available shock more often, when under the influence of alcohol. Males were more aggressive overall, and alcohol affected their responses more than it did for females (Giancola et al., 2009) (See Figure 9.7). Can merely priming alcohol increase aggression? Look at this chapter's research box to find out.

A number of explanations have been offered regarding why alcohol has these effects, and all may be partially correct. First, people's expectations about the effects of alcohol on aggression can themselves increase such behavior (Bègue et al., 2009). Second, alcohol may reduce a person's natural inhibitions or misgivings about aggression (Gailliot &

FIGURE 9.7   Can Alcohol Increase Aggression?

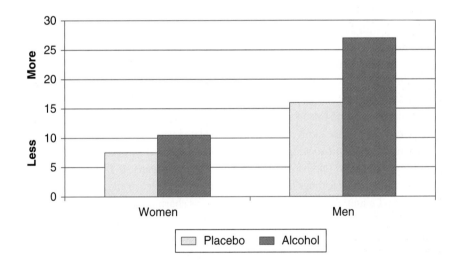

Participants who drank alcohol provided maximum punishment in the form of electric shocks against competitors in a reaction time task. Males were also more aggressive than females.

Source: Adapted from Giancola et al. (2009). Men and women, alcohol and aggression. *Experimental and Clinical Psychopharmacology, 17,* 154–164.

SELF-REFLECTION 9.1
How Aggressive Are You? (Part 1)

Chapter 8 has a scale that allows you to assess how prosocial you are. Below is a complimentary scale with which you can measure how aggressive you are. As you know, both dispositional and situational factors influence social behavior. While researchers have utilized a plethora of experimental strategies and a variety of dependent variables to gauge *state*—situational—aggressiveness, there have been few attempts to assess *trait*—dispositional—aggressiveness. Perhaps the mostly widely used approach to trait aggressiveness is the agreeableness scale that is tied to the five-factor model of personality (Costa & McCrae, 2009). The questions below are part of a different, standalone scale of aggressiveness. Take a minute to answer the following questions and then turn the page to learn more.

TABLE 9.3   How Aggressive Are You?

Item	Response options				
	Extremely uncharacteristic	Uncharacteristic	Neither uncharacteristic nor characteristic	Characteristic	Extremely characteristic
1. Given enough provocation, I may hit another person. (P)	1	2	3	4	5
2. If I have to resort to violence to protect my rights, I will. (P)	1	2	3	4	5
3. There are people who pushed me so far that we came to blows. (P)	1	2	3	4	5
4. I tell my friends openly when I disagree with them. (V)	1	2	3	4	5
5. When people annoy me, I may tell them what I think of them. (V)	1	2	3	4	5
6. My friends say that I'm somewhat argumentative. (V)	1	2	3	4	5
7. I am an even-tempered person. (A)	1	2	3	4	5
8. Sometimes I fly off the handle for no good reason. (A)	1	2	3	4	5
9. I have trouble controlling my temper. (A)	1	2	3	4	5
10. Other people always seem to get the breaks. (H)	1	2	3	4	5
11. I sometimes feel that people are laughing at me behind my back. (H)	1	2	3	4	5
12. When people are especially nice, I wonder what they want. (H)	1	2	3	4	5

Source: Scale from Webster, G. D., DeWall, C. N., Pond, R. S., Jr., Deckman, T., Jonason, P. K., Le, B. M., . . . Bator, R. J. (2014). The brief aggression questionnaire: Psychometric and behavioral evidence for an efficient measure of trait aggression. *Aggressive Behavior, 40*, 120–139.

TURN THE PAGE TO FIND OUR ANSWERS.

SELF-REFLECTION 9.2
How Aggressive Are You? (Part 2)

These items compose the 12-Item Brief Aggression Questionnaire (Webster et al., 2014, 2015). To determine your score, reverse score item 7 (1 = 7, 2 = 6, 3 = 5, 4 = 4, 5 = 3, 6 = 2, 7 = 1) and then add up your responses. Next divide by 12 to obtain your average aggressiveness score. Webster et al. designed the scale to measure four types of aggression: physical aggression (P), verbal aggression (V), anger (A), and hostility (H). Thus, in addition to providing an overall measure, you can calculate your level of each type by averaging its three corresponding items. As a basis for comparison, here are the means from a 307 undergraduate participants from the University of Kentucky: physical = 2.75, verbal = 3.56, anger = 2.31, hostile = 2.36, and total = 2.74. Where do you rate in comparison to these students or others in your class? Does your level of aggressiveness on this scale make sense in the light of your level of prosociality from Chapter 8? Should they be consistent? Why or why not?

Baumeister, 2007). Third, alcohol consumption can interfere with a person's ability to reason, organize, and plan behavior, as well as consider its consequences, all of which are related to the executive function (Bushman, Giancola, Parrott, & Roth, 2012; Giancola et al., 2012). Fourth, consumption can produce an alcohol myopia, that is a narrowing of one's attention, leading to misperceptions of the acts and intentions of others (Giancola, Duke, & Ritz, 2011). Finally, alcohol and alcohol-related images, such as an advertisement for or a bottle of alcohol, can act as cues that prime aggressive thoughts (Bartholow & Heinz, 2006; S. L. Brown et al., 2011). One very recent study found that alcohol-related primes can increase retaliatory behavior as well (see Research Box 9.1) (W. C. Pedersen, Vasquez, Bartholow, Grosvenor, & Truong, 2014).

Think Again!

1. _What is archival research, and what are its advantages and disadvantages?_

2. _What are the differences in the general patterns of aggression between males and females? Why do you think these exist?_

3. _Have you witnessed or heard about situations in which alcohol seemed to make people more aggressive? How would you know if alcohol really was a contributing factor?_

RESEARCH BOX 9.1
CAN ALCOHOL PRIMES INCREASE AGGRESSION?

Hypothesis: Participants exposed to alcohol-related word primes would demonstrate more retaliatory aggression toward another person than participants exposed to non-alcohol-related primes but only following an ambiguous provocation from that other person.

Research Method: 182 male and female undergraduate participants were randomly assigned to one of the six conditions in this 2 (alcohol/neutral prime) x 3 (unambiguous/ambiguous/no provocation) design. Participants wrote either a pro-choice or pro-life essay that they submitted to the experimenter for evaluation by another (fictional) participant. Next they performed a task requiring them to decide whether or not strings of letters presented rapidly on a computer screen were English words. Half of the participants were exposed to alcohol-related words (such as beer/wine) and half to non-alcohol-related words (such as milk/water). Next they received what they were told was the evaluation of their essay by the other participant. The feedback in the unambiguous condition was "this is one of the worst essays I have ever read," in the ambiguous one was "I don't even know where to begin," and in the control condition no feedback was given. Finally, participants had an opportunity to retaliate against the participant who they thought authored the evaluation by recommending how long he or she should be forced to hold his or her hand in a bucket of very cold water. Recommending a longer (versus shorter) duration was used as a measure of greater (versus lesser) aggression.

Results: As predicted, aggression was greater in the alcohol-prime condition, but only among participants in the ambiguous condition. That is to say, the unambiguous, clearly hostile, provocation was equally likely to produce an aggressive response regardless of the type of priming. However, participants in the alcohol-related prime condition were more aggressive than those in the non-alcohol-related prime conditions when the feedback was relatively ambiguous.

Conclusion: Activating alcohol-related thoughts through priming leads people to become aggressive when confronted with an ambiguous but potentially negative or hurtful situation. Such activation causes people to become aggressive in the same way as giving them alcohol does. A follow-up study reported in the same article found that the difference between the alcohol-primed and the non-alcohol-primed participants was that the latter perceived his or her evaluator to have more hostile intent. Both thinking about alcohol and drinking alcohol increase the likelihood that a person will demonstrate the hostile attribution bias.

Source: Adapted from Study 1, Pedersen, W. C., Vasquez, E. A., Bartholow, B. D., Grosvenor, M., & Truong, A. (2014). Are you insulting me? Exposure to alcohol primes increases aggression following ambiguous provocation. *Personality & Social Psychology Bulletin, 40,* 1–13.

THE ROUTE TO AGGRESSION: FROM INPUTS TO OUTPUTS

Anderson and Bushman's (2002) general aggression model asserts that a person's internal state, comprised of physiological arousal, cognitions, and affect, serves as the pathway from the personal and situational inputs to the cognitive and behavioral outputs. Temporary physiological arousal—as indicated by increased heart rate, heavier breathing, sweating, and so forth—has been linked to increased likelihood of aggression (Patrick & Verona, 2007). In fact, heat, violent media, loud noises, and other factors may influence aggression through their effects on arousal. There are several ways that arousal may enhance aggressive responding. One is through a process call **excitation transfer**, in which arousal produced by one stimulus can "spill over" and strengthen a person's emotional response to a different one (Zillmann, 2003). For example, participants in a study by Zillmann, Katcher, and Milavsky (1972) who completed a strenuous bike ride were more aggressive after being provoked by a confederate versus those who engaged in light exercise on a stationary bicycle.

The second pathway involves the activation of aggressive, hostile thoughts and/or scripts through the priming process described earlier, such as during exposure to violent films or when playing a violent video game (Anderson & Bushman, 2002; Anderson & Dill, 2000). Such priming can trigger a **hostile attribution bias** in which a person tends to interpret the intentions and behavior of others as hostile or threatening (Pettit & Mize, 2007; Wu, Zhang, Chiu, Kwan, & He, 2014). This bias is common among chronically aggressive children (MacBrayer, Milich, & Hundley, 2003) and adults (Dill, Anderson, & Deuser, 1997). Dodge et al. (2015) have uncovered evidence for the hostile attribution bias in children in 12 distinct cultural groups around the world and also that the frequency of the bias was positively correlated with actual child aggression. Recent research by DeWall et al. (2009) and a meta-analysis of 41 studies strongly support the causal link between interpreting the intent of others as hostile and subsequent aggression (Orobio de Castro, Veerman, Koops, Bosch, & Monshouwer, 2002). Finally, the third pathway comes into play when, as described earlier, negative emotions are triggered by frustration and other conditions, which can then lead to aggressive responses.

Outputs: Appraisals, Decisions, and Actions

The final component of the general aggression model consists of the cognitive and action outputs stemming from the internal states just described. According to Anderson and Bushman (2002), people engage in appraisal and reappraisal of the overall situation, which drives their decisions to enact either aggressive or nonaggressive behavior. Appraisals are automatic and effortless and can lead to impulsive actions, unless a more deliberate, thoughtful reappraisal occurs and corrects the initial appraisal. Anderson and Bushman (2002) provide an example of a person who is bumped by another while thinking aggressive thoughts and may interpret the bump as aggressive and proceed to

Excitation Transfer: Arousal produced by one stimulus spilling over and strengthening a person's emotional response to a different one

Hostile Attribution Bias: Tendency to interpret the intentions and behavior of others as hostile or threatening

retaliate. In contrast, if that person has been focusing on how many people are jammed into a small room, then the bump may be seen as accidental and will not lead to aggression. If the person has time, motivation, and the cognitive resources to engage in more effortful processing, then the person may reappraise or reinterpret the situation, which could either strengthen the initial appraisal or generate an alternative attribution or construal of it. As we have seen at many points in the text, deliberative, C-system processes can be congruent with or can override automatic, X-system processes.

REDUCING AGGRESSION

If you casually skim through the news channels or major online news outlets leads, you can easily be overwhelmed by the plethora of mass shootings, genocide, murder, and civil strife that seem to dominate the headlines. Moreover, it would not be unreasonable to infer from these reports that the world is a very violent place, at least as violent if not more so than at any time in the past. But such a conclusion would be incorrect. Psychologists, anthropologists, historians, and others have examined short- and long-term trends in violence over the past millennia. As mentioned earlier, the psychologist Steven Pinker (2011) has gathered data from hundreds of sources and has concluded that, as a whole, violence has been steadily decreasing. Pinker is not arguing that the *absolute* number of violent incidents has gone down but rather that the *relative* number has decreased. For example, according to the criminologist Manuel Eisner, the murder rate among the English has decreased from 24 per 100,000 persons some 600 years ago to .6 per 100,000 in the mid-twentieth century (cited in Pinker, 2011). Pinker also points out that much of the brutality that used to be accepted as a ordinary—such as animal cruelty, torture, and systematic war-related rape—has largely disappeared in the West, reflecting changing norms and values.

These are clearly welcome global trends, yet they don't absolve us of the responsibility to try to reduce aggression even further. Let me mention a few strategies that can positively impact the incidence of aggression, although space limitations will preclude me from describing them in detail. One strategy is to appropriately *punish aggression.* Punishment in the form of imprisonment for violent crimes is a necessary component of civil society. However, the conditions under which punishment is effective—including occurring immediately after the aggressive incident, being implemented consistently, being perceived as justified—are not generally present in the real world (Berkowitz, 1993). Unfortunately, because it is not immediate, consistently applied, or perceive as justified, punishment is often ineffective and may, under certain situations, increase aggression. Punishment models undesirable behavior and may, especially in the case of children, inflict long-lasting psychological harm.

Another approach is to *teach, model, and reward behaviors that are incompatible with aggression* (Berkowitz, 1993). For example, school intervention programs intended to reduce bullying and other aggression often focus on conflict resolution skills, teaching respect for others, and reinforcing children who avoid or prevent peer aggression (Krahé & Busching, 2014; Mayseless & Scharf, 2011). Attempts to *build empathy* have also successfully curbed aggression. For instance, Konrath, Bushman, and Campbell (2006) found that participants given the chance to retaliate against another participant who had just given them harsh, negative feedback on an essay were *less* like to do so if they believed that they had something in common with that person, in this case, a shared a birthday.

One strategy that many people believe can prevent hostile aggressive behavior is to redirect the underlying anger by acting aggressively in some other way. For instance, a college student angered by his roommate may choose to hit the punching bag at the gym as a means to "blowing off the steam" in a harmless manner, in hopes that this will decrease the likelihood of subsequent aggression. Unfortunately, this *catharsis hypothesis*—the idea that acting aggressively in a directed, nonharmful manner can reduce aggression—is contradicted by the evidence, which suggests that the opposite may be true (Bushman, Baumeister, & Phillips, 2001). Hitting a punching bag or a wall may actually increase subsequent aggressive responding (See Figure 9.8). However, programs that teach people how to appropriately manage their anger have been shown to reduce aggression (Novaco, 2011).

FIGURE 9.8   The Catharsis Hypothesis: Fact or Fiction?

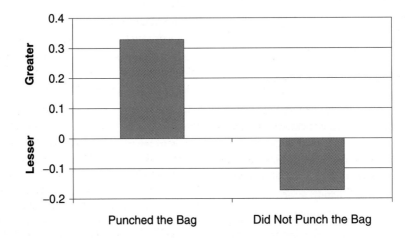

Participants led to believe in *catharsis*—the idea that acting aggressively can reduce aggression—in fact were *more* aggressive after hitting a punching bag than were participants who did not punch the bag. The bottom line: acting aggressively is likely to increase, not decrease, aggression. The catharsis hypothesis is fiction.

Source: Adapted from Bushman, B. J., Baumeister, R. F., & Phillips, C. M. (2001). Do people aggress to improve their mood? Catharsis beliefs, affect regulation opportunity, and aggressive responding. *Journal of Personality and Social Psychology, 81,* 17–32.

SOCIAL PSYCHOLOGY APPLIED TO WORK

BULLYING ON THE JOB

Have you ever been insulted, humiliated, or threatened while at work? If you have, then you may have been subjected to workplace bullying. Bullying at the workplace occurs when an individual or group is repeatedly on the receiving end of hostile actions over a period of time and can include actions ranging from social isolation to verbal hostility to being the target of unpleasant jokes (Nielsen & Einarsen, 2012; Sansone & Sansone, 2015; Tuckey & Neall, 2014). Although estimates of the frequency of the problem range around the world, from 3% in Sweden to 30% in Italy, somewhere in the vicinity of one or two out of every 10 U.S. employees is/are experiencing bullying at any given time (Jacobson, Hood, & Van Buren, 2014; Nielsen, Matthiesen, & Einarsen, 2010; Sansone & Sansone, 2015). One survey found that 27% of Americans have firsthand experience with workplace bullying (Namie, 2014). Two of the challenges to making accurate estimates are that people define bullying in different ways and that question order and question structure can lead to widely divergent estimates (Huang & Cornell, 2015; Nielsen et al., 2010).

What do you think are some of the antecedents to bullying (I hope both situational and disposition factors are coming to mind!)? Environmental factors such as high stress, conflict with management, little autonomy, and monotonous work are all associated with bullying (Astrauskaite, Kern, & Notelaers, 2014; Pilch & Turska, 2015). Perpetrators of bullying often have relatively low self-esteem, feelings of inferiority, and poor social skills, whereas victims are often anxious, sensitive, introverted, emotionally unstable, and may struggle with adjusting to others at work (Astrauskaite et al., 2014; Glasø, Nielsen, & Einarsen, 2009).

As you may imagine, exposure to bullying can lead to a number of negative outcomes for victims. For some, being bullied can create or exacerbate mental health problems (e.g., depression, post-traumatic stress), lower job satisfaction, poorer job performance, emotional exhaustion, and greater intention to change jobs, as well as physical health problems related to stress (Nielsen & Einarsen, 2012; Pilch & Turska, 2015).

How do we prevent workplace bullying? According to Namie and Namie and other experts, the institution needs to have and implement a clear anti-bullying policy that provides both support for the victim, training for all employees (in part to prevent the bystander effect described in Chapter 8), counseling for the victim and perpetrator, and effective sanctions for punishing the perpetrator (Branch, Ramsay, & Barker, 2013; S. L. Johnson, 2011; Namie, 2014; Namie & Namie, 2009; Saam, 2010; Yamada, 2009).

Think Again!

1. *Why is the general aggression model considered a social cognitive model?*

2. *Have you been in a situation in which someone who had been drinking became aggressive? If so, do you think alcohol played a role or would the aggression have occurred anyway?*

3. *Does Pinker's argument that violence is in the decline surprise you? How do you think violence is changing in your community?*

FINAL THOUGHTS: THE MULTIPLE CAUSES OF AGGRESSION

We began this chapter with a description of three violent incidents that represent two types of aggression. Although these events represent different types of aggression, keep in mind that the instrumental/hostile distinction is not dichotomous: Any given aggressive act may have both instrumental and hostile components. Similarly, although we have described both the automatic or reactive and controlled or deliberate outputs of aggression, it is difficult, if not impossible, to draw a sharp line between these two categories. Furthermore, it is clear that aggression, like other social behavior, can be examined through the lenses of different levels of analysis and that each level can contribute to the explanation of aggression. The broader lesson here— and a theme that permeates this text—is that social behavior is determined by both the person and the situation and, moreover, that the words *person* and the *situation* merely serve as labels for a myriad of factors underlying each. Whenever you see or hear

another person offering a simple, one-factor explanation for an act of aggression, remind them, and remind yourself, that social behavior cannot be so easily distilled to a single cause.

As I mentioned at the beginning of the chapter, the topic of aggressive behavior relates to several of our fundamental themes. One question that people often ask when confronted with an act of aggression is whether it was *rational* or *irrational*. What they usually mean here is whether the behavior was justified in some way by a prior action. So, for instance, an honor-related killing may be seen as legitimate in the U.S. South—and thus rational—but illegitimate in the North and therefore irrational. A second fundamental theme is the extent to which the perpetrator acted out of his free will. This issue is often couched along the lines of whether, for instance, prior physical and/or sexual abuse or brain pathology were so influential that they overwhelmed the person's control of his behavior. Did her brain "make" her do it? Psychiatrists, psychologists, juries, and even judges sometimes struggle with this issue, because it can have a direct effect both on guilt and on sentencing. Finally, discussions of aggression almost invariably contain assumptions about the morality of a specific behavior and about the human species more generally. Are humans fundamentally moral and, if so, how can we reconcile our morality with the countless acts of horrendous brutality that mark our history? The obvious rejoinder to this question is that, although we are capable of unspeakable acts of cruelty, we are equally capable of incredible acts of kindness and compassion.

CORE CONCEPTS

- Aggression has three primary goals: to gain social and material rewards, to express negative feelings and thoughts, and to attract and retain romantic partners.

- Aggression is defined as behavior that is intended to proximately harm another person, who is motivated to avoid that harm; hostile aggression stems from anger, whereas instrumental aggression serves a nonaggressive end.

- Recent evolutionary theory proposes instead that aggression is an optional strategy that can be used to solve particular adaptive problems.

- The media violence hypothesis—that exposure to violent video games and television can lead to real-world aggression—has been supported by both laboratory and real-world research.

- The original frustration aggression hypothesis has been broadened to include other conditions that lead to aggression, such as pain, heat, noise, foul odors, and other unpleasant events that trigger negative thoughts and feelings.

- Interpersonal factors, such as social rejection and provocation, can contribute to aggressive responding; specific types of threats and insults are much more likely to lead to aggression in cultures of honor than in other cultures.

- The GAM provides an overarching framework for understanding the personal and situational factors that impact the enactment of aggressive behaviors.

- Archival research examines data from preexisting sources or archives, such as newspapers, historical records, and speeches.

- A number of personal factors can impact the likelihood of aggression, including gender, personality, use of alcohol, and the hostile attribution bias.

- Aggression can be reduced by a combination of teaching, modeling, and rewarding behaviors that are incompatible with aggressive behavior.

▶ $SAGE edge™ Test your understanding of chapter content. Take the practice quiz. edge.sagepub.com/barrett

KEY TERMS

Aggression, 310
Aggressive Cues, 325
Archival Research, 331
Cognitive Neoassociationist
    Theory (of hostile
    or emotional
    aggression), 322
Culture of Honor, 328
Direct Aggression, 311
Excitation
    Transfer, 338

Frustration-Aggression
    Hypothesis, 322
Hostile Aggression, 311
Hostile Attribution
    Bias, 338
Indirect Aggression, 311
Instrumental
    Aggression, 311

Media Violence
    Hypothesis, 317
Provocation, 327
Relational
    Aggression, 332
Violence, 312
Weapons Effect, 324

> **⑤SAGE edge**™   Review key terms with eFlashcards.
>   edge.sagepub.com/barrett

THINK FURTHER!

- People use the term "aggression" in everyday conversation on a regular basis. When you hear people do this, think about what they mean by the term and how closely it matches the one in this text. Ask them to explain what they may mean. Does their definition make sense to you? Why or why not?

- Before you watch a particular film or TV show, estimate how many instances of each type of aggression you will see. Perhaps do this with a friend so that you each make guesses. Then try keeping track of how many of each type there were. How were your estimates?

- Think about the Carmegeddon study and how it supports the media violence hypothesis. Do you or your friends play violent video games? If so, how do you feel and/or how do they feel afterward? More aroused? More relaxed?

- What are the criticisms of the media violence hypothesis and how do its proponents respond to these criticisms?

- Given the evidence on the effects of aggressive cues, such as weapons and alcohol-related words and images, what do you suppose the public policy implications are? Do think there should be any curbs on advertisements?

- Can you map out the general aggression model? Try doing this and list examples of each component and compare your result with the text. How did you do?

SUGGESTED READINGS

Anderson, C. A., & Bushman, B. J. (2002). Human aggression. *Annual Review of Psychology, 53*(1), 27–51.

Bandura, A., Ross, D., & Ross, S. A. (1963). Imitation of film-mediated aggressive models. *The Journal of Abnormal and Social Psychology, 66*(1), 3–11.

Berkowitz, L. (1993). *Aggression: Its causes, consequences, and control.* New York, NY: McGraw-Hill.

DeWall, C. N., Twenge, J. M., Gitter, S. A., & Baumeister, R. F. (2009). It's the thought that counts: The role of hostile cognition in shaping aggressive responses to social exclusion. *Journal of Personality and Social Psychology, 96,* 45–59.

Pedersen, W. C., Vasquez, E. A., Bartholow, B. D., Grosvenor, M., & Truong, A. (2014). Are you insulting me? Exposure to alcohol primes increases aggression following ambiguous provocation. *Personality & Social Psychology Bulletin, 40,* 1–13.

10

Prejudice, Stereotyping, and Discrimination

A protester stands in front of the Immigration and Customs Enforcement (ICE) offices in Phoenix, Arizona, in 2012. About 100 immigration supporters held a protest against ICE and continued deportations by the Obama administration, and also celebrated the US Supreme Court decision to overturn most of SB1070, Arizona's tough anti-immigration law.

ZUMA Press/Alamy.

LEARNING OBJECTIVES

10.1 Define intergroup bias, stereotype, prejudice, discrimination, and modern and aversive racism; outline the three waves of research on racism.

10.2 Explain social identity and self-categorization theories and how they help us understand prejudice; define ingroups, outgroups, ingroup favoritism, minimal group paradigm, and outgroup homogeneity effect.

10.3 Describe how stereotypes can be automatically activated.

10.4 Summarize the Robbers Cave study and its flaws and relate it to realistic group conflict theory; discuss scapegoating and the research on culture and prejudice. Explain the IAT, how it works, and what it is intended to measure.

10.5 Discuss how illusory correlation, the ultimate attribution error, social dominance orientation, and right-wing authoritarianism relate to prejudice.

10.6 Identify types of sexism; contrast interpersonal and institutional discrimination, glass ceiling, and stereotype threat; identify ways to reduce intergroup conflict.

ANTI-IMMIGRANT ATTITUDES AROUND THE GLOBE

In recent decades, as global immigration has continued to rise, so too have anti-immigrant attitudes, particularly in the United States and Europe (Wagner, Christ, & Heitmeyer, 2010). A recent survey found that the majority of citizens in seven European nations perceived immigrants to have generally adverse effects on their country (Duffy, 2012). In the United States, anti-illegal immigrant laws in Alabama and Arizona attest to the growth of negative attitudes toward immigrants. It is now unlawful in Alabama for many organizations and companies to provide even basic services, such as water and electricity, to individuals who have illegally immigrated. Furthermore, police officers in Arizona are now allowed to stop, interrogate, and detain people if there is "reasonable suspicion" they are undocumented or illegal immigrants—essentially, if they look like stereotypical illegal Latino immigrants. Even worse are the horrific examples of prejudice-based attempted genocides in Europe and Africa during the 20th century.

How do we explain such hateful feelings and behavior? It won't surprise you to find out that social psychologists have extensively investigated these and related phenomena over the last century. This chapter reviews some of the most fruitful theory and research on the nature, causes, and consequences of prejudice, stereotypes, and discrimination. We will examine the multiple origins of prejudice, and we will explore the major situational and personal factors that contribute to its emergence and maintenance in individuals and groups. Towards the end of the chapter, we will describe some of the negative effects of prejudice, stereotyping, and discrimination on individuals and society and, finally, several ways to reduce or eliminate them. Despite the fact that social psychologists have learned a lot about these topics, there is much more work to be done and many questions to be addressed.

Three of our fundamental questions are particularly relevant to this chapter: rationality, self, and morality. People often view prejudices as irrational, abnormal, and maladaptive. Yet social psychology reveals to us that prejudice and stereotyping are surprisingly *rational* in that they can help achieve particular goals. Moreover, some stereotypes may contain a kernel of truth, which provides a grounded basis for their existence, even if they are exaggerations or distortions of that kernel. Another feature of prejudice is its tie to the *self:* Derogating others can provide a self-esteem boost. Finally, when we judge others negatively and treat them in hurtful ways, especially when we dehumanize them, we are perpetuating injustice and engaging in *immoral* behavior.

Think Ahead!

1. *Why do people have prejudices?*

2. *How do prejudice and stereotyping affect their targets?*

3. *Are prejudice and stereotyping inevitable? How can we overcome them?*

THE NATURE OF PREJUDICE, STEREOTYPING, AND DISCRIMINATION

Intergroup Bias:
Tendency of one group to hold prejudice toward, stereotype, and discriminate against another group

As you know, one of our guiding principles of social psychology is that social behavior is purposive. This is true even for behaviors and related thoughts and feelings that we may not "like," such as prejudices, stereotyping, and discrimination. What do you suppose are the reasons we have these? How can they be seen as adaptive or useful? Well, social psychologists have identified three primary goals for what we call **intergroup bias**—which refers to prejudice, stereotyping, and discrimination collectively (Dovidio & Gaertner, 2010; Kang, Gray, & Dovidio, 2014; Perry, Dovidio, Murphy, & van Ryn, 2015). First, intergroup bias can serve the motivational goal of enhancing the self and group, in part through its role in shaping and bolstering our social identity. For instance, when we degrade or devalue members of other groups, we simultaneously upgrade or enhance the value of our own.

Second, intergroup bias can serve the cognitive goal of simplifying the world, and thereby conserving our mental resources so that they are available when they are really needed. For example, stereotypes serve as heuristics or rules of thumb that allow us to "know" what a man is like before we have met him, as long as we know what group he belongs to and we possess stereotypic beliefs about the characteristics of that group. Third, these three phenomena allow groups to justify and preserve social positions, resources, and power. By preventing members of another group from, say, moving up the hierarchy in a corporation or government, the existing elite can preserve control of valuable resources. As you know, any given social behavior can simultaneously serve more than one goal.

According to social psychologist Gordon Allport, "The human mind must think with the aid of categories. . . . Once formed, categories are the basis for normal prejudgment. We cannot possibly avoid this process" (Allport, 1954, p. 20). In a similar vein, psychologist Jerome Bruner articulated the "rather bold assumption that . . . all perceptual experience is necessarily the end product of a categorization process" (Bruner, 1957, p. 124). The point that these two psychologists are making is that the human mind cannot *not* categorize. That is, in order for our minds to function, distinctions must be made between objects, ideas, and people: Thought, feeling, and action depend on them. Can you imagine a world without perceptual categories? That would be an impossible world.

If we did not group things together and simplify the world, we'd have to examine each perceptual object individually to ascertain its qualities or properties; we simply do not have the time or mental capacity to do so. As we'll see in this chapter, categorizing the self and others, what we call *social categorization,* forms the basis for prejudices, stereotypes, and, therefore, discrimination.

Stereotypes partially stem from the inevitable process of categorizing people. A **stereotype** is a belief about the characteristics, attributes, and behaviors of a group and its members. Stereotypes help us simplify and navigate the social world by allowing us to automatically apply these general beliefs to specific individuals; they do not necessarily assign value to the beliefs, good or bad. Fortunately, once having used stereotyping to make quick judgments, we often go beyond them when forming impressions of individuals. Although we begin with a general, automatic categorization, when given the motivation and opportunity, we engage in individuation (Fiske & Neuberg, 1990). Individuation is the process of discerning the specific features of a particular target person, including how those features may diverge from category-based features. People commonly and rapidly categorize—and then stereotype—others based upon skin color, age, and sex—what Fiske, Cuddy, and Glick (2007) called the "Big 3" (see Chapter 5). We see a woman and we infer that she has particular characteristics—such as being warm and nurturing—based on her sex.

In contrast to a stereotypic belief, prejudice is an attitude. An attitude, as you know from Chapter 8, is an evaluation of a person, idea, or object. **Prejudice,** then, is an evaluation of a particular group and its members. It is an affective prejudgment that is typically but not always negative (Czopp, Kay, & Cheryan, 2015). If a person harbors negative feelings toward a person because of her group membership—such as if she is Iranian—then that person has a prejudice. Finally, the stereotypes and prejudices that people hold often affect their behavior toward the targets. **Discrimination** is the unequal treatment of individuals based on their group membership. For instance, if the coach of a basketball team gives a White center more playing time than a Black one based solely on race, the coach is discriminating. Although these are conceptually separate, prejudice, stereotypes, and discrimination often occur simultaneously and therefore I refer to them together as intergroup bias.

Stereotype:
Belief about the characteristics, attributes, and behaviors of a group and its members

Prejudice:
Evaluation or prejudgment of a group and its members

Discrimination:
Unequal treatment of individuals based on their group membership

THE THREE WAVES OF RESEARCH ON RACISM

Before we delve into the antecedents and consequences of prejudice, stereotyping, and discrimination, we need to address one important question that students and others often ask: Aren't racial prejudice, stereotyping, and discrimination a thing of the past

Hopes were high that racism in the US would decline after the election of President Barack Obama.

©iStockphoto.com/EdStock.

or at least no longer much of a problem in the United States? People will point to the election and reelection of Barack Obama as U.S. president as proof of racial progress. But is that accurate? Research has shown that perceptions of racial progress following the 2008 election were much rosier than before (Valentino & Brader, 2011). For instance, approximately one in four perceived there to be *less* discrimination immediately after the election than they had perceived prior to it (Valentino & Brader, 2011). However, another longitudinal survey found that perceptions of discrimination in 2012 were about the same as in 1987, although tolerance for interracial dating has increased significantly (see Table 10.1) (Pew Research Center, 2012). To be sure, the ascension of a Black man to president is historic and is changing more than just the face of this country. However, as we will see in this chapter, the reality is much more complicated.

First of all, realize that prejudice does not refer just to anti-Black sentiment, although in the United States that is typically what initially comes to mind. In the United States and around the world, there are a wide variety of targets of prejudice, such as females, people who are overweight or gay, immigrants, and Muslims, just to name a few. However, since most of the core theories and research on intergroup bias—especially those in the United States—focus on White-Black relations, our discussion will spend more time on these. Obviously, other forms of bias, such as sexism and anti-immigrant prejudice, are prevalent in the United States and around the world; unfortunately, detailed treatment of these is not possible within the space constraints of this text.

Second, even as some of the more outward expressions of anti-Black prejudice have become less prevalent in the United States over the past several decades, other, less visible, manifestations continue to be quite influential (Brown, 2010; Katz & Hoyt, 2014; King et al., 2011). That is, whereas prejudice used to be blatant or overt, it is now, at least in the United States, largely hidden or disguised. The realization of this newer form of prejudice was largely due to the recognition that people hold both implicit and explicit attitudes, as we discussed in Chapter 7. Social psychologists have identified three waves of research on racial prejudice that help to illustrate the changes in thinking about the nature of prejudice

TABLE 10.1   Changes in Overt Racial Attitudes

	1987	1999	2012
Discrimination against Blacks is rare today	34%	22%	34%
Not much improvement in position of Blacks	36%	38%	38%
Alright for Blacks and Whites to date each other	48%	73%	86%

Americans have become more tolerant of interracial dating, but views on discrimination and the position of Blacks in the U.S. are similar to what they were in 1987.

[1]Source: Pew Research Center Press (2012). Trends in American Values, 1978–2012.

TABLE 10.2   Three Waves of Psychologists' Thinking About Prejudice

Wave	Years	Description
First Wave	1920s–1950s	As individual pathology (abnormal)
Second Wave	1960s–1980s	As stemming from normal individual and social processes, such as categorization and intergroup competition
Third Wave	1990s–present	As multidimensional, with research focused on implicit processes and measurement, automatic activation of negative associations

Source: Dovidio, J. F. (2001). On the nature of contemporary prejudice: The third wave. *Journal of Social Issues, 57,* 829–849.

(see Table 10.2) (Dovidio, 2001). According to Dovidio, the first wave of research spanned the four decades between 1920 and 1960 and understood prejudice to be abnormal, deviant, and pathological. Prejudice was like a cancer that needed to be treated and, hopefully, could be eradicated. Measurements of prejudice relied on self-reports that were, at that time, considered to be valid reflections of people's attitudes.

In contrast to this focus on the explicit nature of attitudes, the second wave recognized that (a) norms against the expression of prejudice reduce the validity of explicit measures; (b) people may harbor implicit prejudicial attitudes that they may not be aware of; (c) prejudice was seen as the outgrowth of *normal* social cognitive processes; and (d) because prejudicial feelings violated emerging social norms, overt manifestation of prejudice largely disappeared and, in its place, more *subtle* racism emerged. The third wave of social psychological research on racial attitudes built on the conceptual advances of the second wave, clarifying the distinctions between implicit and explicit attitudes by developing new techniques to measure implicit ones. As you know from Chapter 7, people are typically not aware of their **implicit attitudes** and therefore cannot report on them. The relationship between implicit and explicit attitudes appears to be quite complicated, and researchers are still trying to understand the nature of that relationship.

Types of Racism

Social psychologists have examined two related types of subtle racism. One is **modern racism**, which exists when a person overtly professes egalitarian views but has negative feelings that result in opposition to giving disadvantaged groups special consideration or opportunities (McConahay, 1986). Modern racists distance themselves from "old-fashioned" explicit prejudice and agree that Blacks and Whites are equal and should be treated the same way, but are against affirmative action or other formal attempts to help Blacks overcome historical social and economic disadvantages. A second type of subtle racism is **aversive racism**, which refers to the coexistence of explicit claims of

Implicit Attitude:
Attitude that a person is typically not aware or conscious of

Modern Racism:
Overtly professing egalitarian views of racial groups but holding negative feelings that result in opposition to giving disadvantaged groups special consideration or opportunities

Aversive Racism:
Coexistence of explicit claims of being nonprejudiced with implicit reactions and behaviors that reveal prejudiced feelings

being nonprejudiced with implicit reactions and behaviors that reveal prejudiced feelings (Pearson, Dovidio, & Gaertner, 2009; Rodenborg & Boisen, 2013). Aversive racists will make extra efforts to appear nonprejudiced, such as when a White female is overly friendly to a Black female. Aversive racism is typically examined using implicit techniques to reveal underlying nonconscious attitudes (Dovidio, Kawakami, Smoak, & Gaertner, 2008). This chapter's *Doing Research* segment will detail the most common methods contemporary social psychologists use for assessing implicit attitudes.

Think Again!

1. *What prejudices and/or stereotypes do you hold? How do you think they affect your behavior?*

2. *Can you think of possible benefits of prejudice, stereotyping, and discrimination?*

3. *How much old-fashioned racism do you still see or hear about? Why do you think that it persists, even if it has diminished over the years?*

THE ORIGINS OF PREJUDICE, STEREOTYPING, AND DISCRIMINATION

Evolutionary Influences

Evolutionary history has handed down to us countless numbers of psychological characteristics that helped our ancestors survive and reproduce. Accordingly, when we ponder the origin of specific psychological mechanisms, we should ask whether and in what way they may be or have been beneficial to our genetic predecessors. Although students initially cringe when faced with the proposition that prejudice might have advantages (as well as its obvious disadvantages), careful consideration illuminates its potential benefits (McDonald, Navarrete, & Van Vugt, 2012; Schaller, Conway, & Peavy, 2010). Social psychologists Steven Neuberg and Catherine Cottrell (2006) have laid out a persuasive case regarding the adaptive, evolutionary benefits of prejudice. They argue that prejudices are intimately connected with the human threat detection and response system. In a sense, they serve as defense mechanisms against potential dangers from unfamiliar groups and warnings to members of the ingroup to be cautious of those outgroups, just in case they may pose a threat. As the old American adage goes, *it is better to be safe than sorry.*

Brain Structure and Process

Recent research has begun exploring the physiological bases of prejudice (See Research Box 10.1 for one surprising link). For instance, examination of event-related potentials

(ERPs) reveals that the brain recognizes each of the Big 3 person variables—race, gender and age—very quickly, noticing race within about 120 milliseconds, faster than gender (145 milliseconds) or age (180 milliseconds) (Fiske et al., 2007; Kubota & Ito, 2009). Participants in another brain study indicated how much they liked or disliked images of White or Black faces set against a background of positive or negative stimuli, such as cute puppies or rotting animals (Ito, Thompson, & Cacioppo, 2004). The researchers found that participants had stronger ERP responses to pairing of White faces and negative images or Black faces and positive images in comparison to the opposite pairings, indicating that participants viewed the White-negative and Black-positive pairs as more discrepant or surprising. In other words, their brains were less accustomed to seeing White faces associated with negative things than with positive things. The opposite was true for Black faces. Moreover, participants in the Ito et al. (2004) study had previously completed a scale measuring racism, and their controlled self-reports of racist feelings matched their automatic brain activity as measured by these discrepancy scores. Thus, what people are accustomed to seeing can influence the kinds of associations that are stored in memory, and these can affect the judgments we make about people.

Individual Experiences

Humans seem to have a "built-in" evolutionary and biological readiness for particular types of prejudices. Nevertheless, individuals learn prejudices and stereotypes that are specific to their culture and to culture-relevant groups. Such learning begins early in life and is likely a product of classical and operant conditioning as well as social learning (Aboud, 2003; Allport, 1954; Carr, Dweck, & Pauker, 2012; Dunham, Stepanova, Dotsch, & Todorov, 2015; Le Pelley et al., 2010). For example, American children as young as two or three are already easily categorizing people according to race and gender (Williams & Morland, 1976). Preference for faces of ingroup versus outgroup members has been found in three-month old infants (Kelly et al., 2005). We obviously cannot ask infants what they prefer, so instead psychologists present infants with faces from the infants' own and other races/ethnicities. In general, they attend more to same-race faces than other faces, and researchers assume that infants prefer the former.

Researchers are still trying to uncover how children learn prejudicial attitudes. Parental attitudes undoubtedly play a role, but exactly how they influence their children is unclear. For instance, adult children of parents who espouse egalitarian views are more likely to share their parents' attitudes, whereas adult children whose parents are highly prejudiced are less likely to feel the same (Rohan & Zanna, 1996). Although we may expect that peer attitudes or media exposure would significantly affect the development of prejudice, there is little empirical evidence for either (Aboud & Amato, 2001). Given the lack of strong evidence linking children's prejudice to any of the likely sources of social learning, much more research is needed before we can conclude with any certainty how children become prejudiced (Aboud & Amato, 2001). Nevertheless, it is clear that children learn the predominant cultural messages pertaining to preferred

RESEARCH BOX 10.1
FACIAL STRUCTURE AND PREJUDICE

Hypotheses: (a) White adult males with greater facial width-to-height ratios (fWHR) would admit to stronger anti-Black prejudice than would those with lower ratios, but fWHR would not be related to implicit bias (Study 1). fWHR is the ratio of the distance between the cheekbones to the distance between the upper lip and midbrow. This hypothesis is based on the idea that greater ratios reflect the presence of more testosterone during puberty and also the motive for social dominance and weakened desire to follow conventional norms. Consequently, males with greater fWHR should be more willing to break the norm against explicitly expressing prejudice. (b) Participants would base their assessment of the racial prejudice of targets based on fWHR (Study 2). (c) Participants assessment of the racial prejudice of targets would be positively correlated with the targets' self-reported prejudice (Study 2).

Research Method: In Study 1, 70 White males completed a scale measuring their overt prejudice toward Blacks. Two weeks later, they completed the Black/White IAT, a measure of their implicit bias (the IAT), were photographed, and their fWHR was calculated. In Study 2, 102 White male and female participants evaluated the racial prejudice of 20 of the Study 1 participants who represented the full range of fWHR and admissions of prejudice.

Results: In Study 1, as expected, fWHR was positively correlated with explicit statements of prejudice but was unrelated to implicit bias. In Study 2, not only did participants rate targets with greater fWHR as being more prejudiced than those with lower fWHR, but their assessments of prejudice were in fact positively correlated with the self-reports obtained in Study 1.

Conclusion: White males with relatively wider and short faces are more likely to admit their anti-Black prejudice than are those with relatively longer and narrower faces. The authors speculate that high fWHR correlates with self-reported prejudice because it is a reflection of greater testosterone exposure during puberty and with the desire to be socially dominant. Consequently, these males are less rule-bound and more prone to not conforming to conventional norms. In addition, untrained individuals accurately, if intuitively, connect a male's fWHR to his prejudice.

Source: Hehman, E., Leitner, J. B., Deegan, M. P., & Gaertner, S. L. (2013). Facial structure is indicative of explicit support for prejudicial beliefs. *Psychological Science, 24,* 289–296.

and nonpreferred groups during the socialization process, even if it is difficult to trace the specific pathways through which such influence works (Devine, 1989).

SOCIAL IDENTITY THEORY

As discussed above, people develop and maintain prejudices partially for motivational purposes: They can boost our self-esteem by enhancing our social identity. Our identity is comprised of **personal identity**—characteristics and qualities that distinguish us from others—and **social identity**—characteristics and qualities that are linked to group membership. **Social identity theory** (SIT), one of the most influential approaches to understanding prejudice, reflects the fundamental role of social identity in social perception. SIT begins with the notion that people have a need to feel good about themselves, and one major factor in self-esteem is the groups to which people belong (Tajfel & Turner, 1979). When people maintain an emotional investment in or tie to their group, they are likely to engage in social comparison with other groups they can look down upon, which in turn produces a more positive view of their own group in relation to those groups (Abrams & Hogg, 2010; Sim, Goyle, McKedy, Eidelman, & Correll, 2014).

According to the related **self-categorization theory** (SCT), the fact that we recognize social categories is not sufficient for the generation of prejudice (Cadinu, Galdi, & Maass, 2013; Tate, Youssef, & Bettergarcia, 2014; Turner & Reynolds, 2012). In addition, we must place ourselves within a category, and we then satisfy self-esteem needs by more positively evaluating our group as compared to other groups. Given that all of us are members of variety of groups, we can self-categorize in many ways. The category that is most influential and likely to influence thought, feelings, and behavior in a given context is the one that is most salient within that context, such as if it had recently been activated by priming. For example, your membership on a basketball team will likely affect your thoughts and feelings during a game to a greater extent than it will while you are at your job.

SIT postulates that we automatically prefer our **ingroups** (the groups to which we belong), relative to **outgroups** (the groups we are not members of). The positive evaluations we provide to the salient ingroup constitute an **ingroup bias**. People can develop these biases toward groups that they have been long-term members of as well as those they have just joined. Ingroup bias can lead to more positive treatment of ingroups as compared to outgroups, a phenomenon called **ingroup favoritism** (Scheepers, Spears, Doosje, & Manstead, 2006). Although people tend to prefer their own group members, they do not necessarily downgrade or derogate outgroup members. We can like our ingroups without *dis*liking corresponding outgroups (Quattrone & Jones, 1980).

Ingroup bias has been demonstrated in research utilizing the **minimal group paradigm,** in which participants are divided into groups, usually for trivial reasons such as by the color of their eye or the roll of the dice (Dunham, 2013; Tajfel, Billig, Bundy,

Personal Identity: Characteristics and qualities that distinguish us from others

Social Identity: Component of the self-concept that is derived from membership in various groups.

Social Identity Theory (SIT): Idea that people have a need to feel good about themselves and that one major component of their self-esteem derives from the groups to which they belong.

Self-Categorization Theory (SCT): Idea that people place themselves within a category and can satisfy self-esteem needs by more positively evaluating their group as compared to other groups

Ingroup: Group to which a person belongs

Outgroup: Group to which is a person does not belong

Ingroup Bias: Tendency to positively evaluate one's ingroup

Ingroup Favoritism: More favorable treatment of ingroups as compared to outgroups

Minimal Group Paradigm: Research method in which participants are divided into groups, usually for trivial reasons, such as by the color of their eye or the roll of the dice.

Shutterstock.

Shutterstock.

& Flament, 1971). Consequently, the groups have *minimal* differences between them. For instance, Locksley, Ortiz, and Hepburn (1980) randomly assigned participants to a minimal group on the basis of a rigged lottery and subsequently asked them to allocate chips or desirable traits to their own or another group. Participants overwhelming gave more to their own group (see Figure 10.1). Similar results occurred when Tajfel and Bilig (1974) asked students to judge a number of modern paintings and falsely grouped those students as either preferring paintings by Vassily Kandinsky or Paul Klee. When given the opportunity to divide money between the groups, participants favored their fellow group members. It seems that, no matter how arbitrary or trivial, minimal groups lead to ingroup favoritism (Brown, 2000). Given that such brief and fairly weak group affiliations can produce meaningful ingroup loyalties, it is easy to see how longer-lasting and stronger ingroup bonds can lead to greater discrepancies in treating ingroups and outgroups and can contribute to more serious intergroup conflict.

The ease with which people begin discriminating on the basis of trivial differences was dramatically illustrated by Jane Elliott, the U.S. elementary school teacher who created the famous Blue Eye/Brown Eye exercise in 1968. In response to the assassination of Martin Luther King Jr., Elliott divided her third-grade class into blue-eyed and brown-eyed groups and subsequently induced the latter to treat the former in unfriendly and discriminatory ways. The exercise was remarkably effective, and Elliott subsequently made a career out of conducting similar exercises with adults around the world. The takeaway message from the minimal group research and Elliott's exercises is that it is surprisingly easy to create an *us versus them* mentality.

Once we have drawn the ingroup/outgroup line, we quickly create stereotypes about the characteristics, attributes, and behaviors of outgroup members and, consequently, tend to apply these stereotypes to *all* of its members. The belief that all members of a given group are more similar to each other than members of our group are to each other is called the **outgroup homogeneity effect** (Boldry, Gaertner, & Quinn, 2007;

FIGURE 10.1   Preference for the Ingroup

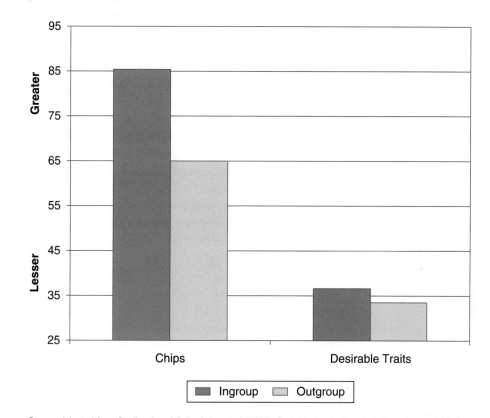

Source: Adapted from Studies 1 and 2, Locksley et al. (1980). Social categorization and discriminatory behavior: Extinguishing the minimal intergroup discrimination effect. *Journal of Personality and Social Psychology, 39,* 773–783.

Ishii & Kitayama, 2011). For example, men may assume that all women are nurturing, and Whites may believe that all Asians are good at math. In contrast, people rarely see their ingroup in this way, instead recognizing the diversity in personality traits, abilities, and behaviors within their own group (Tajfel & Turner, 1979). This propensity to view outgroups as "all the same" even applies to physical appearance, as when eyewitnesses struggle to differentiate among possible suspects in crimes if those suspects are of another race (Pauker et al., 2009). This effect can be minimized when people are motivated to distinguish outgroup members from each other, such as when scrutinizing angry faces of a threatening outgroup (Ackerman et al., 2006).

SIT focuses on how people may use their group membership or social identity to improve their self-esteem by positively evaluating the relevant group. Cialdini proposed a similar, albeit more circumscribed idea: People often bask in the reflected glory of successful individuals or groups by highlighting their association with them (Cialdini et al., 1976). People make themselves look better by virtue of their ties to highly regarded others. In both cases, individuals are motivated to identify with or belong to groups that will enhance their self-esteem. Remember, however, that self-concept is composed of both social identity and personal identity and that we derive our self-esteem from both of these elements. There is a danger that very strong identification with even positively regarded groups can overwhelm our personal identity, thus eliminating important distinctions between ourselves and the group (Brewer, 1991). To prevent this from occurring, people seek to join groups that allow them to satisfy their need to belong *and* their desire to be distinct from others.

Recognition of the need to balance these motivations led Marilyn Brewer to develop **optimal distinctiveness theory**, which holds that people will join groups that facilitate the satisfaction of both the need to belong and the desire to be unique (Abrams, 2009; Brewer, 1991; Jang Ho & Yong Jun, 2015; Slotter, Duffy, & Gardner, 2014). For instance, membership in very large groups prevents people from feeling distinct, whereas membership in very small ones can interfere with the need for inclusion (Brewer & Caporael, 2006). Therefore, people prefer groups that balance these two needs.

Optimal Distinctiveness Theory: Postulates that people will join groups that facilitate the satisfaction of both their need to belong and their desire to be unique

Think Again!

1. *Again think about the prejudices and stereotypes that you may hold. Can you identify factors in your experiences that may have contributed to their development?*

2. *Can you think of a minimal group that you are or have been a member of? How has it affected the way you view and treat members versus nonmembers?*

3. *Given that eyewitnesses sometimes have a trouble distinguishing members of other races/ethnicities from each other, what can police do to address this?*

CONTEXTUAL FACTORS

Automatic Activation of Stereotypes

Prejudice, stereotyping, and discrimination can be manifested in both automatic and controlled ways. As you know from Chapter 3, concepts in memory—including biased evaluations and stereotypes—can be automatically activated and subsequently guide a person's social behavior without his knowledge, even when he does not overtly endorse them (Devine, 1989). This is particularly likely when stereotypes are activated outside of conscious awareness (Dijksterhuis, Spears, & Lepinasse, 2001). Recall the study described in Chapter 1 in which exposure to words related to being elderly led undergraduates to walk more slowly down a hallway versus others who were not so exposed—thus exhibiting a behavior that they implicitly associate with older individuals (Bargh, Chen, & Burrows, 1996). Using a different approach, Spencer et al. (1998) activated racial stereotypes by subliminally presenting either a White or a Black face to participants. Next, participants finished a series of incomplete word stems such as ste__, stu__, and hos__. Participants in the "White" condition were more likely to create words not associated with racial stereotypes (e.g., step, student, or hospital), whereas those in the "Black" condition provided more stereotype-related words (e.g., steal, stupid, and hostile). All told, there is a rather large body of research demonstrating the many ways in which stereotype activation can influence subsequent judgments and behaviors (Bennett & Gaines, 2010; Clark, Thiem, Barden, Stuart, & Evans, 2015; Gawronski & Bodenhausen, 2007).

But is the activation and influence of stereotypes under such situations inevitable? The answer is no (Kawakami, Dion, & Dovidio, 1998). For instance, once people move beyond mere categorization to *personalization* or individuation, in which they learn about specific individuals with stereotype-inconsistent attributes, the influence of stereotypes wanes (Fiske & Neuberg, 1990). For example, upon meeting David, a young, physically imposing Black male, Maria, a petite White female, may initially apply commonly held stereotypes that suggest that he is dangerous. However, if given a chance to get to know David as a kind and sensitive man who enjoys classical music, the influence of the anti-Black stereotype on Maria's perceptions of and behavior toward David may be reduced or eliminated (Steele, 2010).

Realistic Group Conflict Theory

Another source of prejudice, stereotyping, and discrimination is direct competition between groups over limited resources. One of the classic field experiments in social psychology explored the nature of resource-based intergroup conflict and resolution in a mid 20th century series of studies at a boys' camp near Oklahoma City, Oklahoma (Sherif, Harvey, White, Hood, & Sherif, 1988/1961). In their 1954 study, Muzafer Sherif and his colleagues brought together twenty-two 11 and 12 year-old, middle class White boys, who had been carefully screened to ensure that they had similar family, school, and religious backgrounds, were well adjusted and psychologically "normal," and did not know one another. The boys were divided into two 11-person groups that arrived and were housed separately at Robbers Cave State Park. Initially the groups—who nicknamed themselves the Eagles and the Rattlers—were unaware of the other's existence, and in the first phase of the study each had time to develop its own hierarchy, culture, and norms.

Sherif and his colleagues held two assumptions: (1) When groups had goals that could only be achieved at the expense of the other group, intergroup hostility would ensue; and (2) when groups work together to achieve a common, overarching goal, intergroup relations would become more harmonious (Sherif, 1956). These two assumptions formed the core of what was later termed **realistic group conflict theory** (Campbell, 1965). To test the first hypothesis, the experimenters allowed the groups to "accidentally" discover each other's

Realistic Group Conflict Theory: Postulates that (a) when a group has goals that could only be achieved at the expense of another group, intergroup hostility would ensue; and (b) when groups work together to achieve a common, overarching goal, intergroup relations should become more harmonious

existence and subsequently arranged for a series of sports and games competitions between them. Each of these competitive interactions produced one winner and one loser, and mutual hostility developed that was manifested in intergroup insults, physical scuffles, and raids on each other's cabins. Thus, competition for shared material resources—points and money awarded to the winners—led to intergroup conflict, supporting Sherif's hypothesis. Moreover, this conflict increased the solidarity, cohesiveness, and cooperativeness within each of the groups (see Chapter 12).

In order to test the second hypothesis, the experimenters created three "problems" that required cooperation between the groups in order to solve. The challenges that the campers faced were to find and fix a break in the pipe carrying the camp water supply, to pull a large truck with a rope to get it started, and to pool money from both groups for the purposes of renting a movie. These **superordinate goals** transcended the interests of these specific groups, required mutual cooperation to solve, and did in fact facilitate intergroup harmony.

Although Sherif et al.'s studies (1988/1961) provided a number of important insights into the role of material resources in intergroup hostility and have been supported in numerous later studies (Brewer & Brown, 1998), as field experiments, they have a number of shortcomings. First was the limited ability of the experimenters to control extraneous variables (Platow & Hunter, 2012). For instance, two of the boys from one of the groups left camp during the experiment, and it is unclear what effects their departure may have had. Second, the *experimenters* were also *participants* in the study and were obviously not blind to the hypotheses (Billig, 1976). Moreover, the studies were designed to confirm rather than test the experimental hypotheses (Brannigan, 2006). Third, despite their focus on *realistic* conflict, Sherif et al. (1988/1961) failed to distinguish between hostility stemming from competition for *material* versus *symbolic* resources, such as the prestige and status associated with winning (Brewer & Brown, 1998). Consequently, the study does not provide clear support for Sherif's theory. However, it has spurred dozens of controlled studies designed to overcome the limitations of Sherif's research.

Intergroup Threat Theory

As you can see, intergroup conflict can arise from either competition for limited material resources—for example, money, land, and so forth—or symbolic ones—for example, prestige, status, esteem, and so forth (Stephan, Ybarra, & Morrison, 2009). Realistic group conflict theory focuses on the former, whereas social identity theory emphasizes the latter. Both of these theories explain competition and conflict over actual resources, yet intergroup hostilities may also be caused by threats to resources. Walter Stephan's intergroup threat theory postulates that perceptions of threats to symbolic or material resources can produce prejudice, stereotyping, and discrimination (Legault & Green-Demers, 2012; Stephan & Renfro, 2003; Stephan & Stephan, 2000). This theory provides a framework for understanding the antecedents and behavioral and psychological consequences of intergroup threat.

Superordinate Goals: Goals that transcend the interests of specific groups and require mutual cooperation to solve and which facilitate intergroup harmony

According to intergroup threat theory, these threats can occur at either the group or individual level. Group-level threats may involve the material resources described above and/or symbolic resources, such as belief systems, religion, and values. Individual-level threats may not be synonymous with group ones. For example, a claim by one political party that another party's ideology and worldview are wrong headed can threaten the legitimacy of the group-level belief system, but it can also threaten the self-esteem of individuals in the group, because they are thereby associated with a flawed group (Corneille, Yzerbyt, Rogier, & Buidin, 2001). Moreover, research has demonstrated that stereotypes may also precede threat, such as when a negative stereotype about the intellectual capacities of Blacks threatens the honor or self-esteem of Blacks (Stephan et al., 2002). Although threats to material and symbolic resources were previously viewed as independent, more recent conceptualizations have emphasized their interrelatedness, such as when a dominant political party is concerned about losing the "battle" of ideas and values among its electorate, yet also recognizes that such a loss will reduce its access to economic resources (Esses, Jackson, Dovidio, & Hodson, 2005).

Scapegoating

Perceptions of threat as well as actual losses can lead people to search for explanations, and they frequently blame others for their problems. As you know from Chapter 4, this is one component of the self-serving bias, in which we take credit for our successes but attribute our failures to situational factors. When groups similarly attribute their problems to other groups, they are engaging in what is called scapegoating. **Scapegoating** occurs when one group unfairly claims that another group has intentionally caused its misfortunes (Allport, 1954). The attempted extermination of Jews by the Nazi Party in Germany, the Rwandan genocide committed by the Hutu against the Tutsi, and the mass killing of Armenians by the Turks, are often cited as consequences of scapegoating, as the perpetrators blamed the victims for social and economic problems in their nation (Staub, 2003). More recently, one study of perceptions of threat in Northern Ireland found that Protestants felt more challenged by immigrants than did Catholics and not surprisingly held stronger anti-immigrant attitudes (Pehrson, Gheorghiu, & Ireland, 2012).

Recognition of its shortcomings led to a recasting of scapegoating as resulting not from absolute loss but rather from relative loss or deprivation. **Relative deprivation** (RD) is the discontent that individuals feel when they believe that they are in a worse situation than they should be, either as compared to their previous situation or the situation of other groups (Smith, Pettigrew, Pippin, & Bialosiewicz, 2012; Stouffer, Suchman, Devinney, Star, & Williams, 1949). **Relative deprivation theory** (RDT) argues that such discontent can breed resentment toward minorities and lead people to blame those others for their own situation, sometimes resulting in violence (Davis, 1959; Gurr, 1970; Hovland & Sears, 1940; Osborne, Smith, & Huo, 2012). More recently, RDT has been applied to conflict over jobs between individuals in former East Germany

Scapegoating:
When one group unfairly claims that another group has intentionally caused its misfortunes

Relative deprivation (RD):
Discontent that individuals feel when they believe that they are in a worse situation than they should be, either as compared to their previous situation or the situation of other groups

Relative Deprivation Theory (RDT): Idea that discontent can breed resentment toward others and lead people to blame minorities for their own situation, sometimes resulting in violence

and those in former West Germany (Mummendey, Kessler, Klink, & Mielke, 1999), over workplace conditions in California universities (Osborne et al., 2012), and to interracial prejudices in South Africa (Duckitt & Mphuthing, 2002). Research has generally provided mixed support for RD; however, after conducting a recent meta-analysis, Smith and colleagues (2012) argue that, as long as the researchers use carefully constructed measures and clearly specify the comparison groups, RD can help explain intergroup biases and conflict (Brown, 2010).

Cultural Influences

Prejudice and stereotyping are probably present in all cultures, although their specific content varies considerably across cultures and groups. While research on the effects of culture on prejudice and stereotyping has been relatively scarce (Williams & Spencer-Rodgers, 2010), the research that has been conducted has produced a number of interesting findings. Triandis (1995) argued that collectivists are generally more likely to demonstrate prejudice and discrimination than are individualists, primarily because they tend to identify more strongly with their ingroup and to make clearer distinctions between ingroups and outgroups. For instance, a recent study by Spencer-Rodgers, Williams, Hamilton, Peng, and Wang (2007) found Chinese participants to more readily stereotype hypothetical others, in comparison to American ones. In contrast, other researchers have suggested that ingroup favoritism and outgroup derogation are greater among individualists (Gouveia, Milfont, Martinez, & Paterna, 2011). While there is inconsistency in the research to date, a recent integrated review of the stereotyping and culture literatures concludes that stereotyping is probably more prevalent among collectivists (Williams & Spencer-Rodgers, 2010). Furthermore, relative to individualists, collectivists tend to communicate—such as when describing one person to another person—more stereotype-consistent information to others, thereby facilitating the persistence of stereotypes across time (See Figure 10.2) (Yeung & Kashima, 2012).

Think Again!

1. *Think about a couple of groups on your campus or in your community that are working at cross-purposes (competing rather than cooperating). Is there a way to bring the groups together using superordinate goals?*

2. *Take a look at Figure 10.2. Why do you suppose there are differences between individualists and collectivists? What do you suppose might be the motives for sharing more or less stereotype-consistent information?*

3. *How well does the Robbers Cave study illustrate realistic group conflict theory? How might it have been done differently in order to better test this theory?*

FIGURE 10.2   Perpetuating Stereotypes

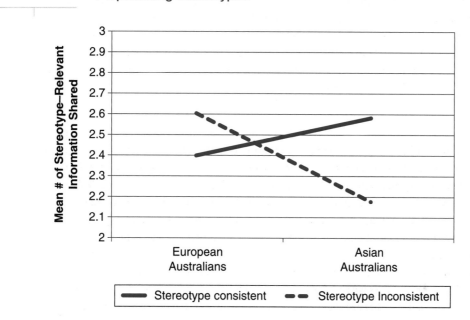

Collectivists (Asian Australians) shared more information about a person that was consistent with the stereotype than did individualists (European Australians), thereby perpetuating a common stereotype. The reverse pattern was found for stereotype-inconsistent information.

Source: Adapted from Study 1, Yeung, V. W. L., & Kashima, Y. (2012). Culture and stereotype communication: Are people from Eastern cultures more stereotypical in communication? *Journal of Cross-Cultural Psychology, 43*, 446–463.

DOING RESEARCH: MEASURING IMPLICIT ATTITUDES

In earlier chapters we discussed how social psychologists use self-reports to learn about people's explicit attitudes and beliefs. We also reviewed the strengths and weaknesses of overt or direct methods such as self-reporting for assessing attitudes and beliefs (see Chapter 7). Although they are often relatively easy and inexpensive to administer, self-reports may be affected by social desirability concerns in part because people are often reluctant to report attitudes that may be counter normative, controversial, or offensive. In response to these issues, social psychologists have developed a number of covert or indirect approaches that mask the true purpose of the research (e.g., lost-letter technique). However, it is important to recognize that some indirect measures may in fact be reactive if participants perceive their intent and change their responses accordingly.

As we've said, in addition to *explicit* attitudes or prejudices, people have *implicit* prejudices that they are typically unaware of and therefore unable to report and therefore require specialized methods for their measurement. Let's now turn to the primary ways in social psychologists have examined implicit attitudes.

Implicit Association Test (IAT). Perhaps the most popular method for assessing implicit attitudes is the computer-based implicit association test (IAT), which has been reported in over 500 publications (Greenwald, McGhee, & Schwartz, 1998; Greenwald, Poehlman, Uhlmann, & Banaji, 2009). The IAT does not ask respondents to provide their attitudes, *per se,* but rather examines the strength of associations between, for example, positive and negative words and members of categories, such as Black/White or old/young. The underlying idea is that the strength of the associations between the person categories and the evaluative words reflects implicit attitudes.

How does it work? In the case of the Black/White race IAT, respondents view a series of words and categorize them as either positive or negative by hitting a particular key (see Figure 10.3). Next, they sequentially view a number of faces and indicate whether they are African American (AA) and European American (EA), again by striking a corresponding key. During the third stage both words and faces are presented, one at a time, and respondents hit one key if they see a negative word or an AA face and a different key for positive words or EA faces. Finally, the pairing of the words and faces is reversed, so that positive words or AA faces are assigned to one key, and negative words or EA faces are assigned to the other. Participants are told to respond as quickly as possible without sacrificing accuracy. The critical measure is the **response latency** or how long it takes participants to categorize a stimulus after it is presented. If response latencies for categorizing negative words and AA faces using the same key are faster than those for positive words and AA faces, then this indicates a preference for EA faces. If instead the negative words and EA faces are categorized more quickly than positive words and EA faces, a preference for AA faces is likely. At the end of the test, respondents are informed that they strongly, moderately, or slightly prefer one group over the other or that they show no preference. I urge you to try the Black/White or other IAT yourself to become familiar with the test and to determine whether or not you harbor any implicit attitudes (https://implicit.harvard.edu/implicit/).

Affective or Evaluative Priming

There is another set of well-known techniques that, like the IAT, rely on response latencies to measure implicit attitudes. These are collectively called **affective or evaluative priming** techniques, because they subliminally present an attitude object to respondents and then ask them to categorize words or other stimuli as positive or negative (Alexopoulos, Fiedler, & Freytag, 2012; Fazio, 2001; Fazio, Jackson, Dunton, & Williams, 1995; Huntsinger, 2014; Villepoux, Vermeulen, Niedenthal, & Mermillod, 2015). In each trial an initial stimulus—usually a word, such as *spinach* or an EA or AA face—is presented below the threshold of consciousness in order to prime positivity or negativity. The prime stimulus is followed by string of target stimuli that the respondent classifies

Response Latency: How long it takes participants to categorize a stimulus after it is presented

Affective or Evaluative Priming: Subliminal presentation of attitude objects in order to measure their effects on subsequent categorization of stimuli

FIGURE 10.3   Measuring Your Implicit Associations

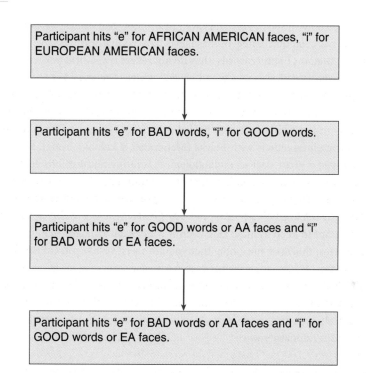

Participant hits "e" for AFRICAN AMERICAN faces, "i" for EUROPEAN AMERICAN faces.

Participant hits "e" for BAD words, "i" for GOOD words.

Participant hits "e" for GOOD words or AA faces and "i" for BAD words or EA faces.

Participant hits "e" for BAD words or AA faces and "i" for GOOD words or EA faces.

Most people are faster at pairing BAD words with AFRICAN AMERICAN faces and GOOD words with EUROPEAN AMERICAN faces as opposed to pairing GOOD words with AFRICAN AMERICAN faces and BAD words with EUROPEAN AMERICAN faces. This suggests an automatic preference for White or European American faces.

Sources: The IAT has been used to explore a wide variety of attitudes in addition to race, including gender (Nosek, Banaji, & Greenwald, 2002), heavy/normal weight individuals (Bessenoff & Sherman, 2000), sexual orientation (Dasgupta & Rivera, 2006), and voting behavior in Germany (Friese, Bluemke, & Wänke, 2007).

as positive or negative. The response latency again serves as the dependent measure. According to Fazio (2001), latencies should be lower on trials in which the prime and the target stimuli share an evaluative connotation—that is, when they are *both* evaluated as either positive or negative by the participant—as compared to trials where the prime and target are evaluatively inconsistent—one positive, one negative. Thus, a person harboring anti-Black prejudice should have lower latencies for negative words than positive words after being primed with a Black face.

The primary advantage of the IAT and other response latency techniques is that they are designed to measure automatic responding and to reduce or eliminate the ability of a person to consciously hide what are often socially undesirable attitudes. In addition, since they tend to be computer-based measures, once the hardware and software are properly configured, it is easy and inexpensive to run large numbers of participants.

The IAT and other implicit measures are not without their critics. Perhaps the greatest complaint has been that results of these tests have no implications beyond the immediate testing situation: In other words, they do not reflect real-world behavior. However, a recent meta-analysis by Greenwald and his colleagues (Greenwald et al., 2009) of 184 studies that included 14,900 participants concluded that the IAT predicts behavior in a wide variety of domains. For example, response patterns on the Black-White IAT are significantly correlated with the nonverbal behavior (e.g., eye contact, body posture, etc.) of Whites during interactions with Blacks (McConnell & Leibold, 2001). Moreover, the IAT has survived a great deal of methodological scrutiny and exhibits test-retest and internal reliability as well as internal validity (Greenwald, Banaji, & Nosek, 2015; Nosek, Greenwald, & Banaji, 2007; Yang, Shi, Luo, Shi, & Cai, 2014). Nevertheless, questions about its validity remain.

It is important to keep in mind that even if your results suggest that you have preferences or biases, this does not imply that you are racist or a bigot. Rather, it suggests that you have stronger associations between particular pairs of concepts as compared to other pairs. Typically these associations are learned at an early age and are reinforced by culture and the media (Devine, 1989). Awareness of these biases and their possible effects on thinking, feeling, and behavior can help us compensate for or overcome them and treat people in nondiscriminatory ways.

PERSON FACTORS

Cognitive Biases

Research has uncovered a number of ways in which normal social cognitive processes can lead us astray as we try to understand ourselves and other people. For instance, we often rely on mental shortcuts or *heuristics* when making inferences and judgments, although they can produce cognitive errors (see Chapter 3). Stereotypes serve as such shortcuts, allowing us to conserve mental resources and allocate them for other purposes (Bodenhausen, 1990). Earlier in this chapter, we mentioned the fundamental nature of categorization and the largely automatic way that we develop ingroup preferences. There are a number of other ways in which relatively normal cognitive processes can contribute to prejudice.

First of all, people tend to notice individuals who stand out or are different and to exaggerate the behaviors of those individuals (Taylor, Crocker, Fiske, Sprinzen, & Winkler, 1979) and to remember them differently (Lord & Saenz, 1985). Second, people often fall victim to an **illusory correlation**, which occurs when people overestimate the extent to which two variables are correlated (Kutzner & Fiedler, 2015; Meiser & Hewstone, 2006).

Illusory Correlation: Overestimation of the extent to which two variables are correlated

This illusion is particularly likely when the variables are distinctive, such as when a member of a minority group engages in an unusual or infrequent behavior (Risen, Gilovich, & Dunning, 2007; Vogel, Kutzner, Fiedler, & Freytag, 2013). For example, if one of the few Latinos in a school is discovered painting graffiti on the university president's car, then people may associate Latinos in general with painting graffiti, even though no actual correlation exists. Illusory correlations may be related to our tendency to allow atypical past behavior to exert undue influence on our expectations for future behavior. In other words, when we predict how a target will behave, we give more weight to her infrequent past behavior than to her more frequent past behavior (Morewedge & Todorov, 2012).

A third cognitive bias, introduced in Chapter 3, is called the *confirmation bias,* and it occurs when people's expectations lead them to search primarily for evidence that supports their expectations, often ignoring or downplaying evidence to the contrary (Rassin, Eerland, & Kuijpers, 2010). For instance, Australian students were more likely to remember and pass on information that confirmed existing stereotypes about Australian football players (e.g., that they drink beer), as compared to stereotype inconsistent behavior (e.g., they like classical music) (Lyons & Kashima, 2001). Thus, stereotypes can serve as *expectations* as well as shortcuts.

Not only can expectations affect the mental formation and maintenance of stereotypes, they can also lead to the *behavioral* confirmation of those stereotypes. In Chapter 5, we described the self-fulfilling prophecy, which occurs when an initially inaccurate expectation leads to behaviors that cause that expectation to come true (Madon, Willard, Guyll, & Scherr, 2011). Treating someone *as if* a stereotype about that person were true can result in that person engaging in behavior consistent with that stereotype (Word, Zanna, & Cooper, 1974).

There is one final cognitive bias that is particularly relevant. In Chapter 5, we discussed the *fundamental attribution error* (FAE) that occurs when people overestimate the influence of dispositional factors on an individual's social behavior, simultaneously underestimating the influence of situational factors. There is a corollary bias that is often exhibited when people explain the behavior of groups. This **ultimate attribution error** is evident when the negative behavior of outgroups is attributed to dispositional factors, and positive outgroup behavior is attributed to situational influences (Coleman, 2013; Hewstone, 1990). In contrast, positive ingroup behavior is seen as stemming from dispositional factors and negative behavior from situational ones. The ultimate attribution error helps people maintain a positive image of their own group and a negative image of outgroups. For instance, during the conflict between Catholics and Protestants in Northern Ireland, each group tended to demonstrate this error when explaining the positive and negative behaviors of the other (Hunter, Stringer, & Watson, 1991). The ultimate attribution error is often found when people explain the successes and failures of their favored as opposed to disliked sports teams (Winkler & Taylor, 1979), such as when New York Yankees fans describe the behavior of the arch nemesis Boston Red Sox players.

Ultimate Attribution Error: Attributing the negative behavior of outgroups to dispositional factors and positive outgroup behavior to situational influences

SELF-REFLECTION 10.1
How Egalitarian Are You? (Part 1)

Do you think that all groups of people are essentially the same and should be treated in the same way by society, or are some groups better suited to "be on top," and therefore, we should allow them to determine what is good for the rest of us? In your opinion, how much should the government intervene to ensure that all groups have equal access to opportunities and the riches of society? The answers you provide to questions like these are closely related to your intergroup biases that you may (or may not) hold. The items below come from the social dominance orientation (SDO) scale, which was intended to measure preference for hierarchical and unequal relationships among groups, including the belief that one's own group should dominate other groups (Ho et al., 2012; Pratto et al., 2013; Pratto, Sidanius, Stallworth, & Malle, 1994; Sidanius & Pratto, 1999). Take a few minutes to answer the following, and then turn the page to learn more about SDO.

TABLE 10.3　　Social Dominance Orientation

There are many kinds of groups in the world: men and women, ethnic and religious groups, nationalities, political factions. How much do you support or oppose the ideas about groups in general?

Item	Response option						
	Extremely oppose	Oppose	Somewhat oppose	Undecided	Somewhat favor	Favor	Extremely favor
1. Some groups of people are simply inferior to other groups. (D)	1	2	3	4	5	6	7
2. In getting what you want, it is sometimes necessary to use force against other groups. (D)	1	2	3	4	5	6	7
3. Superior groups should dominate inferior groups. (D)	1	2	3	4	5	6	7
4. To get ahead in life, it is sometimes necessary to step on other groups. (D)	1	2	3	4	5	6	7

SELF-REFLECTION 10.1

Item	Response option						
	Extremely oppose	Oppose	Somewhat oppose	Undecided	Somewhat favor	Favor	Extremely favor
5. If certain groups stayed in their place, we would have fewer problems. (D)	1	2	3	4	5	6	7
6. It's probably a good thing that certain groups are at the top and other groups are at the bottom. (D)	1	2	3	4	5	6	7
7. Inferior groups should stay in their place. (D)	1	2	3	4	5	6	7
8. Sometimes other groups must be kept in their place. (D)	1	2	3	4	5	6	7
9. It would be good if groups could be equal. (E)	1	2	3	4	5	6	7
10. Group equality should be our ideal. (E)	1	2	3	4		6	7
11. All groups should be given an equal chance in life. (E)	1	2	3	4	5	6	7
12. We should do what we can to equalize conditions for different groups. (E)	1	2	3	4	5	6	7
13. Increased social equality. (E)	1	2	3	4	5	6	7
14. We would have fewer problems if we treated people more equally. (E)	1	2	3	4	5	6	7
15. We should strive to make incomes more equal. (E)	1	2	3	4	5	6	7
16. No one group should dominate in society. (E)	1	2	3	4	5	6	7

Source: Jost, J. T., & Thompson, E. P. (2000). Group-based dominance and opposition to equality as independent predictors of self-esteem, ethnocentrism, and social policy attitudes among African Americans and European Americans. *Journal of Experimental Social Psychology, 36*, 209–232.

TURN THE PAGE TO FIND OUR ANSWERS.

SELF-REFLECTION 10.2
How Egalitarian Are You? (Part 2)

To determine your score, reverse score items 9 through 16 (1 = 7, 2 = 6, 3 = 5, 4 = 4, 5 = 3, 6 = 2, 7 = 1) and then add up your responses. Next divide by 16 to obtain your overall dominance score. The scale actually measures two correlated aspects of SDO: dominance (D) and egalitarianism (E). Thus, in addition to providing an overall measure, you can calculate your level of each type by averaging its eight corresponding items. The SDO scale has been used with different response options as well as different numbers of response options. Where do you rate in comparison to others in your class? Does your relative level of dominance/egalitarianism on this scale make sense in the light of your level of prosociality from Chapter 8 and aggressiveness from Chapter 9? Should they be consistent? Why or why not?

Slightly different versions of the SDO scale have been used in many nations throughout the world, and the two-dimensional structure is robust (Pratto et al., 2013; Sidanius et al., 2013). Research supporting the relationship between SDO and prejudice is rather impressive: high SDO has been correlated with prejudice against women, gays, Blacks, Muslims, and immigrants, and many other groups (Ho et al., 2012; Sidanius & Pratto, 1999). People scoring high on SDO are more likely to believe that men should dominate women sexually, tend to be more politically conservative, to be more supportive of strict immigration policies, and less supportive of discrimination claims by Blacks against Whites (Craig & Richeson, 2014; Crawford, Jussim, Cain, & Cohen, 2013; Rosenthal, Levy, & Earnshaw, 2012; Unzueta, Everly, & Gutiérrez, 2014).

Individual Differences

Situational factors obviously contribute to intergroup bias but of course leave out important person factors. Let's turn our attention to two individual difference variables that have been closely tied to prejudice: authoritarianism and social dominance orientation. Authoritarianism was first linked to prejudice by the German researcher Theodor Adorno and his colleagues (Adorno, Frenkel-Brunswik, Levinson, & Sanford, 1950). Adorno et al. (1950) defined authoritarianism as a personality dimension that reflects the likelihood that a person will engage in rigid, simplistic thinking, accept blind obedience to authority, and demonstrate prejudice. Although some research demonstrated that authoritarianism was correlated with certain types of prejudice, its reliance on Freudian theory, along with psychometric problems with the scale created to measure it, the *F-scale*, led researchers to develop newer constructs and scales (Brown, 2010). One of most researched and best supported replacement theories is **right-wing authoritarianism** (RWA), which focuses on the three core elements of authoritarianism: submission to legitimate authority, aggression against outgroups or deviants, and endorsement of conventional social norms and morality (Altemeyer, 1996). People

Right-Wing Authoritarianism (RWA): Individual difference variable comprised of three core elements: submission to legitimate authority, aggression against outgroups or deviants, and endorsement of conventional social norms and morality

high in RWA exhibit inflexible, black/white thinking, a tendency toward conformity and obe-dience, and greater prejudice against groups that legitimate authorities oppose (Altemeyer, 1996; Duckitt, 2001). The RWA scale has demonstrated good reliability and validity and is correlated with hostility toward homosexuals and ethnic minorities as well as other groups seen as deviant or as threats to conventional attitudes (Altemeyer, 1996).

A second individual difference variable, **social dominance orientation** (SDO), also reliably predicts prejudice against a variety of groups (Sidanius & Pratto, 1999, 2012). SDO is the degree to which a person generally endorses hierarchy and inequality among social groups and specifically prefers that his ingroup dominate others. (To assess your own SDO, see the Self-Reflection box in this chapter). People who are high in SDO agree with such statements as "some groups are simply inferior to other groups" and "it is unjust to try to push for group equality" (Ho et al., 2012).

> **Social Dominance Orientation (SDO):** Degree to which a person generally endorses hierarchy and inequality among social groups, and specifically prefers that his ingroup dominate others

Think Again!

1. *Take one or more versions of the IAT. What do you think about the results of these tests? Are they valid, in your opinion? Why or why not?*

2. *Do you think that the likelihood that people will adopt unflattering illusory cor-relations about other groups is affected by their overall attitudes toward those groups? For instance, if a person holds a negative attitude toward a certain immigrant group, is she more likely to generalize from a single negative act by one member and assume that it is indicative of the entire group?*

3. *Can you think of any other person variables, in addition to RWA and SDO, that may be related to prejudice?*

RWA and SDO are individual difference variables, but are they measures of personal-ity? Many researchers do not think so, suggesting that they reflect attitudes or ideologies (belief systems) that can change over time and across contexts for particular groups or individuals (Duckitt, 2001; Ho et al., 2012). One prominent researcher has gone even further, arguing that the personality approach to prejudice fails as an adequate expla-nation for its existence (Brown, 2010). Obviously, there is much more to prejudice than individual differences, demonstrating once again how the person and the situation jointly produce social behavior.

The Content of Prejudice and Stereotypes

Stereotype Content Model

The targets of prejudice vary across cultures and times. Nevertheless, as we suggested earlier in this chapter, the content of prejudice is not arbitrary. For instance, from an evo-lutionary perspective, prejudice is an adaptive response to actual and potential threats to ingroup goals posed by outgroups (Neuberg & Cottrell, 2006). Consequently, prejudices and stereotypes about particular groups are more likely to be related to the threats potentially posed by those groups. Take as a hypothetical example a situation in which Group A is concerned that Group B is a threat to Group A's physical well-being because members of Group B tend to be larger and stronger than those in Group A. Group A is more likely to exhibit negative stereotypes about the characteristics relevant to safety and security, such as by making claims that Group B males are actively seeking to physically assault or rape females in Group A.

A complementary approach seeks to identify the major ways in which stereotypes differ across cultures and groups. The **stereotype content model** (SCM) postulates that, cross-culturally, stereotypes vary along two major dimensions: competence and warmth (Fiske, Cuddy, & Glick, 2003; Fiske et al., 2007; Kervyn, Fiske, & Yzerbyt, 2013, 2015). According to Fiske and her colleagues, the competence dimension reflects the relative status of the perceiving group and the target group, such that the target group will be judged competent when they have high status and are powerful but as incompetent when they have low status and are powerless. Outgroups are seen as warm when they do not compete with the ingroup and cold when they do. As shown in Table 10.4, the SCM depicts these two dimensions as sides of a 2 x 2 table that produces four boxes representing four possible combinations. The box in which an outgroup is placed by a specific ingroup determines the content of its corresponding stereotype. For instance, groups seen as not competing with the ingroup and of low status, such as the elderly or the disabled, will be placed in the warm, incompetent category and will receive pity and sympathy from the ingroup. Using this approach, Fiske and her colleagues have been able to predict the content of stereotypes both in the United States and across ten different nations, including Belgium, the United Kingdom, Japan, and South Korea (Cuddy et al., 2009).

Stereotype Content Model (SCM): Postulates that stereotypes universally vary along two major dimensions: competence and warmth

SPECIFIC TYPES OF INTERGROUP BIAS

Sexism

Although much of this chapter focuses on Whites' anti-Black prejudice in the United States, there are countless other groups in the United States and around the world that are subject to negative prejudice, stereotypes, and discrimination. For instance, gender biases—sexism—can be found around the world. When we think of sexism we usually conjure up images of men behaving badly toward women; however, women are also capable of sexist behavior. Consequently, we will define **sexism** so that it encompasses the negative prejudices, stereotypes, and discrimination directed at individuals based on their gender and/or institutional practices that support the unequal status of men and women (Swim & Hyers, 2009). Sex, as you recall, is one of the Big 3 characteristics that people most quickly recognize about others (Fiske, 1998). Because most research has investigated anti-female sexism, we will focus on that here. Paralleling the distinction between old-fashioned racism

Sexism: Negative prejudices, stereotypes, and discrimination directed at individuals based on their gender, and/or institutional practices that support the unequal status of men and women

TABLE 10.4   The Content of Stereotypes

Warmth	Competence	
	Low	High
High	Paternalistic prejudice Pity, sympathy (e.g., elderly, disabled, housewives)	Admiration Pride, admiration (e.g., ingroup, close allies)
Low	Contemptuous prejudice Contempt, disgust, anger, resentment (e.g., welfare recipients, poor people)	Envious prejudice Envy, jealousy (e.g., Asians, Jews, rich people, feminists)

Source: Adapted from Fiske, Cuddy, Glick, & Xu. (2002). A model of (often mixed) stereotype content: Competence and warmth respectively follow from perceived status and competition. *Journal of Personality and Social Psychology, 82,* 878–902.

and modern racism is the separation of old-fashioned sexism from modern sexism (Glick & Fiske, 1996). Traditional or **hostile sexism** is what the layperson typically envisions when thinking about sexism: derogatory views of women as seeking to control men via marital commitment and sex, along with perceptions of women as sex objects (Becker & Wright, 2011; Glick & Fiske, 2011). In contrast, **benevolent sexism** combines stereotypical views of women as different from (e.g., more emotionally sensitive and warmer) and inferior (e.g., weak and in need of protection) to men (Akrami, Ekehammar, & Yang-Wallentin, 2011; Glick & Fiske, 1996). Although dubbed the "women are wonderful effect" because the characterization of women is superficially positive, benevolent sexism actually produces a number of negative consequences for women (Eagly & Mladinic, 1989). For instance, the portrayal of men and women as possessing complementary qualities leads to the view that men are competent and independent, whereas women are incompetent and dependent. This in turn is related to efforts to maintain male dominance and traditional gender roles via discriminatory behavior (Eagly & Sczesny, 2009).

Because people often hold both hostile and benevolent sexist views, Glick and Fiske coined the term **ambivalent sexism,** to refer to the simultaneous perception of women in negative and positive terms, and developed the ambivalent sexism inventory (ASI) to measure individual differences in this dimension (Clow, Ricciardelli, & Bartfay, 2014; Glick & Fiske, 1996, 2011). In studies involving thousands of participants in over 19 countries, Glick and his colleagues have found that these two components of sexism are moderately correlated (Glick et al., 2004). Moreover, levels of ambivalent sexism predict a number of other attitudes and behaviors, including negative perceptions of women who engage in premarital sex in Turkey and tolerant attitudes toward wife abuse in Turkey

Hostile Sexism:
Derogatory views of women as seeking to control men via marital commitment and sex, along with perceptions of women as sex objects

Benevolent Sexism:
Stereotypical views of women as very different from (e.g., more emotionally sensitive and warmer) and inferior (e.g., weak and in need of protection) to men

Ambivalent Sexism:
Simultaneous perception of women in negative and positive terms

Students at Scotland's Glasgow University protest sexism on campus, on International Women's Day.

AP Photo/Danny Lawson.

and Brazil (Sakalli-Uğurlu & Glick, 2003). Finally, ambivalent sexism toward men, where men are seen as powerful and immoral or as benevolent protectors and providers who need women to nurture them, is also present in cultures around the globe (Glick et al., 2004).

Other Forms

There are of course many other forms of prejudice beyond racism and sexism, including those focusing on immigrants, age, sexual orientation, religion, and weight (Dovidio, Hewstone, Glick, & Esses, 2010; Phelan et al., 2014; Vanhove & Gordon, 2014). One form, *anti-immigrant prejudice,* has been linked to competition for economic resources, especially when immigrants are believed capable of successfully competing with the native population (Esses, Dovidio, Jackson, & Armstrong, 2001; Wagner, Christ, & Heitmeyer, 2010). For instance, one study conducted in the United States and Canada manipulated participant perceptions of the economic benefits of immigration and found that participants' anti-immigrant prejudices were greater when they believed that immigration would threaten their economic livelihood (Esses et al., 2001). Anti-immigrant attitudes are also related to beliefs in the virtues of diversity: Where diversity is highly valued, immigrants are evaluated in a more favorable light (Kauff & Wagner, 2012). Indeed, specific stereotypes of immigrants can be predicted by their relative status and the likelihood that they will compete for resources, as predicted by the stereotype content model described above (Lee & Fiske, 2006).

Intergroup bias against people based on their age, **ageism,** is prevalent in many—but certainly not all—parts of the world, a fact that is not surprising given that age is the third of the Big 3 attributes that people notice first (Cuddy et al., 2009; Fiske, 1998; Nelson, 2009). Ageism tends to focus mainly on the elderly (over 65) and includes perceptions that they are, among other characteristics, frail, unhealthy, and unattractive (Bennett & Gaines, 2010; Giles et al., 2003; Lieberman & Peskin, 1992). Across many cultures, including Belgium, Costa Rica, and Japan, the "old" stereotype typically falls in the warm but incompetent category in the stereotype content model (Cuddy, Norton, & Fiske, 2005). The mixed positive and negative evaluation of the elderly suggests the

Ageism: Prejudice against people based on their age

presence of an ambivalent ageism. A very recent study that gathered data on age-related personality traits from over 3,000 participants in 26 nations found a number of striking similarities (Chan et al., 2012). For instance, adolescents were typically seen as impulsive and rebellious, adults as more assertive and competent, and older adults as more agreeable and leading more routine-based lives.

I want to briefly mention two more targets of frequent prejudice: gay men and lesbians. Like sexism, **hetero-sexism** encompasses negative prejudices, stereotypes, and discrimination directed at individuals based on their nonheterosexual orientation and/or institutional practices that support the unequal status of heterosexuals and nonheterosexuals (Hebl, Law, & King, 2010). One core element of heterosexism is **homophobia**, which is a particularly strong fear of homosexuals or homosexual behavior (Herek, 2004). Although heterosexism has declined in recent decades (Herek, 2009), its persistence—at least in the United States—is evident in the political debates over the policies regarding gays in the military as well as the right to same-sex civil union and/or marriage.

AP Photo/ Susan Walsh.

Man supporting legislative efforts in Washington to repeal the U.S. military's "Don't Ask, Don't Tell" policy regarding gay and lesbian soldiers. The policy was repealed in September 2011.

Heterosexism: Negative prejudices, stereotypes, and discrimination directed at individuals based on their nonheterosexual orientation and/or institutional practices that support the unequal status of heterosexuals and nonheterosexuals

Homophobia: Particularly strong fear of homosexuals or homosexual behavior

Accuracy of Stereotypes

One of the principal concerns people have about stereotypes is that they are inaccurate and, consequently, unfair. Most social psychologists have traditionally assumed that stereotypes are, by definition, inaccurate beliefs about the characteristics of members of a group (Jussim, Cain, Crawford, Harber, & Cohen, 2009). Others have argued, however, that at least some stereotypes may contain a "kernel of truth." In order to test this hypothesis, we need to define accuracy. If people believe that men are more physically aggressive than women, and if the data demonstrate that they are, does this mean that the stereotype is accurate? Even if people have the direction of the difference right (i.e., men are more aggressive), wouldn't we also want them to correctly perceive the magnitude of the difference (i.e., *how much* more aggressive are men)? Janet Swim (1994) conducted a meta-analytic examination of a number of gender stereotypes in the United States and found that both male and female respondents were relatively accurate about the direction of and magnitude of many stereotypes (that women are happier), underestimated several (e.g., mathematical abilities and helping in emergencies), and overestimated only two (male aggression and female's verbal abilities). More recently, Jussim et al. (2009) found that, across a range of domains, many racial/ethnic and gender stereotypes are surprisingly accurate. However, in at least one domain, stereotypes are quite inaccurate: in the United States, Democrats tend to see Republicans as more conservative than they are, and Republicans overestimate the liberalness of Democrats (Judd & Park, 1993). Nevertheless, as you can see, there is a kernel of truth to some—but certainly not all—stereotypes (Hřebíčková & Graf, 2014; Jussim et al., 2009; Lönnqvist, Konstabel, Lönnqvist, & Verkasalo, 2014).

Think Again!

1. *Not all of my students accept the idea that benevolent sexism is harmful in any way. What do you think?*

2. *Anti-immigrant bias often increases during difficult economic times. Why might this be so?*

3. *Can you think of any stereotypes not listed above that may be at least partially accurate? How would you find out if they are/are not?*

THE EFFECTS OF PREJUDICE, STEREOTYPING, AND DISCRIMINATION

Discriminatory Practices

Interpersonal Discrimination: Unequal treatment of specific individuals based on their group membership (contrast with institutional discrimination)

Institutional Discrimination: Unequal treatment of individuals that is embedded in the norms, policies, and practices of an institution, producing unequal outcomes for members of different groups (contrast with interpersonal discrimination)

Glass Ceiling: When qualified women are prevented from attaining high-level positions

So far we have focused on attitude (prejudice) and belief (stereotypes) components of intergroup bias. Let's turn now to its behavioral component, discrimination. When we think about discrimination, we commonly envision an individual who provides opportunities to some while denying those same opportunities to others, based on irrelevant variables. For instance, a store manager may chose to promote a White worker over an equally (or more) qualified Indian worker or a man over an equally (or more) qualified woman. These are examples of **interpersonal discrimination,** because specific individuals are the targets of discrimination (Benokraitis & Feagin, 1997).

There is a second type of discrimination that is more systematic and perpetrated by institutions, such as governments, corporations, or educational systems. **Institutional discrimination** is embedded in the norms, policies, and practices of an institution, producing unequal outcomes for members of different groups (Feagin & Feagin, 1986). Even though institutional discrimination is usually not overtly discriminatory—that is, no policy explicitly prescribes differential treatment for one race, ethnicity, and so forth over another—*subtle discrimination* is *de facto* evident because the affected group never achieves equal status. For instance, if women are underrepresented in the upper tiers of a corporation despite being well represented at lower tiers, then one may infer institutional discrimination. Such a situation is indicative of the so-called **glass ceiling**, which is present when qualified women

SOCIAL PSYCHOLOGY APPLIED TO WORK
MICROAGGRESSIONS

Workplace discrimination—unequal treatment with regarding to hiring, performance appraisals, compensation, promotion, and so forth—is a widespread problem in the United States and around the world. Such discrimination can range from being relatively overt to quite subtle. In recent years, scholars have identified and begun examining a new category of discriminatory behaviors called microaggressions (Sue, 2010; Wang, Leu, & Shoda, 2011). **Microaggressions** are "brief and commonplace daily verbal, behavioral, and environmental indignities, whether intentional or unintentional, that communicate hostile, derogatory, or negative racial, gender, sexual-orientation, and religious slights and insults to the target person or group" (Sue, 2010, p. 5). They are little things people say or do that may, on the surface, seem harmless, but can carry with them subtle messages that undermine the target's self-esteem or question his competence, legitimacy, and so on. For instance, an ethnic microaggression would be asking someone who appears to be of Asian descent where she was born, which carries with it the subtle message that she is not a real American. An example of a racial microaggression is a Caucasian American man putting his hands over his wallet as an African American man walks

nearby or crossing the street so as to avoid an African American male walking toward him. Finally, a gender microaggression (one that I witnessed not that long ago) was a man saying to a subordinate female employee "you look all dolled up," essentially equating her to a plastic children's toy rather than acknowledging her as a grown woman.

Sue and his colleagues developed a taxonomy of microaggressions that included three types (Sue, 2010; Sue et al., 2007). *Microinsults* are rude, insensitive statements that may demean a person's heritage, such as asking a person of color how she got into Harvard Law School. *Microassaults* are more overt behaviors or statements that are meant to harm someone, such as using a racial slur or conspicuously hanging a noose from a tree. *Microinvalidations* are statements that exclude or question the validity of a target's feelings, thoughts, or experiences, such as claiming not to "see" race in others or stating that there is no gender discrimination in today's workforce. Researchers have begun developing scales intended to measure the experiences of individuals who are targets of microaggressions (as opposed to trying to determine how likely people are to engage in microaggressions) (Forrest-Bank,

(Continued)

Microaggressions: Ordinary, daily interactions that send negative messages to an individual based upon the person's group membership(s)

(Continued)

Jenson, & Trecartin, 2015; Nadal, 2011; Torres-Harding, Andrade, & Romero Diaz, 2012). To give you a feel for the kinds of items that are included, here are a couple of examples: *I am singled out by police or security because of my race,* or *others ask me to serve as a "spokesperson" for people in my racial group* (Torres-Harding et al., 2012). Although the microaggressive nature of the first item is probably obvious, what about the second one? What assumptions does that make about a person and/or group?

Microaggressions are quite common in the workplace, and they can, like other forms of discrimination, have negative consequences for targets, as described in the main text (Basford, Offermann, & Behrend, 2014; Torres & Taknint, 2015; Wang et al., 2011). Many companies, organizations, and educational institutions have developed policies designed to deal with microaggressions and provide training to staff so that they might be avoided entirely. Asking people to more closely monitor what they say or do—especially when typically acknowledging that those same persons are not old-fashioned racists—has been controversial. Some critics have raised concerns that such programs may undermine freedom of speech or that they represent political correctness run amok (Campbell & Manning, 2015; Schmidt, 2015). What do you think?

are prevented from attaining high-level positions (Danaher & Branscombe, 2010). Despite the fact that discrimination is often unfair and/or offensive, it is not necessarily illegal. Think about the ban on women serving in combat brigades in the U.S. military or rules preventing children from working in dangerous occupations.

Threats to Self-Esteem and Performance

Stigma. Individuals who are categorized in groups about which there is a negative stereotype are called *stigmatized,* because they "possess (or are believed to possess) some attribute, or characteristic, that conveys a social identity that is devalued in a particular social context" (Crocker, Major, & Steele, 1998, p. 505). The specific characteristic that distinguishes a stigmatized group from other groups is a **stigma**, a term that can include a wide variety of personal attributes, such as race, ethnicity, gender, age, mental illness, and physical disability (Goffman, 1963). One point to keep in mind is that stigmas are context dependent, meaning an attribute need not always be seen as a stigma. For instance, being overweight is currently stigmatized in the United States, but that was not always the case, nor is it stigmatized in many parts of the world (Crandall, 1995; Crandall, Merman, & Hebl, 2009; Major, Eliezer, & Rieck, 2012; Phelan et al., 2014). Stigmatized individuals

Stigma: Specific characteristic (such as a personal attribute, facial mark, mental illness, and so forth) that distinguishes a stigmatized group from other groups

face threats to their self-image as socially valued, good, and competent (Crocker & Garcia, 2009). Moreover, self-image threats can also undermine the self-esteem of targets, although this need not be the case (Crocker & Garcia, 2010; Crocker & Major, 1989). A meta-analysis by Twenge and Crocker (2002) found that, contrary to what many believe, the self-esteem of stigmatized persons is not consistently lower that that of other groups and, in the case of African Americans, may be higher.

Stereotype Threat. Not all differences in outcomes across groups are the result of discrimination. For example, social psychologist Claude Steele and his colleagues sought to explain gaps in school achievement and in standardized test scores between Black and White students in the United States (Steele, 2010; Steele & Aronson, 1995). They identified and provided convincing evidence for a previously unrecognized but surprisingly potent threat posed by stereotypes. According to Steele and his colleagues, **stereotype, or social identity, threat** is the discomfort or anxiety that targets feel when concerned that they may confirm a negative stereotype held about their group (Abdou & Fingerhut, 2014; J. Aronson & McGlone, 2009; Ihme & Möller, 2015; Steele & Aronson, 1995). In a seminal set of studies, Steele and Aronson (1995) demonstrated how merely being aware of a negative stereotype relevant to task performance can lead to a decrease in performance on that task by the stereotyped group.

In one study, Black and White male college students responded to a series of questions pulled from the verbal graduate record examination (GRE), one of the tests used to determine a person's qualifications for graduate school in the United States. Half of the participants were informed that the test was diagnostic or indicative of their verbal ability (diagnostic condition), whereas the remainder were told that it was a laboratory problem-solving task (nondiagnostic condition). The experimenters expected that the mere mention of the diagnosticity of the exam would activate a negative stereotype about the intellectual abilities of African Americans relative to European Americans, even if the participants did not endorse that stereotype. The consequence of making the stereotype salient would be different for the White and Black students. Since the stereotype did not threaten the social identity of the former, activating the stereotype should not affect their performance. However, the Black students would likely experience an increased mental burden as they worried about confirming the negative stereotype while simultaneously trying to do well. Therefore, the performance of the Black students in the diagnostic condition should be reduced as compared to the nondiagnostic condition. This is, in fact, precisely what Steele and Aronson (1995) found (see Figure 10.4). This performance decrement is the result of anxiety and resulting physiological arousal as well as a reduction in attentional resources devoted to task performance stemming from additional demands on working memory (Schmader & Johns, 2003).

Although often discussed in the context of race, stereotype threat can affect any group for which there is a negative performance-related stereotype that is activated in a relevant context (J. Aronson & McGlone, 2009; Steele & Aronson, 1995). Effects similar to those

Stereotype (or Social Identity) Threat: Discomfort or anxiety that targets feel when concerned that they may confirm a negative stereotype held about their group

FIGURE 10.4   The Effects of Stereotype Threat

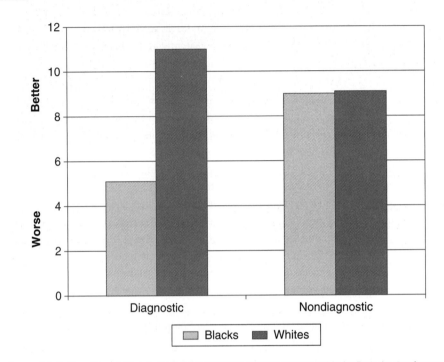

Source: Adapted from Figure 2, Study 2, Steele & Aronson (1995). Stereotype threat and the intellectual test performance of African Americans. *Journal of Personality and Social Psychology, 69,* 797–811.

described above have been demonstrated for women (vs. men) (Danaher & Crandall, 2008) and girls (vs. boys) (Huguet & Régner, 2007) on math exams, psychology (vs. other science students) on a science ability test (Croizet et al., 2004), and White men (vs. Asian men) on a math tests (J. Aronson et al., 1999). Importantly, in each of these studies, the experimenters controlled for possible alternative explanations for their findings, such as intelligence, differences in school achievement, and the like. Stereotype threat is a robust phenomenon that has been empirically demonstrated in over 200 studies across a number of performance domains and stigmatized groups (Aronson & McGlone, 2009).

Threats to Physical Well-Being

The negative effects of prejudice, stereotyping, and discrimination extend to the physical well-being of targets, as demonstrated by a large number of studies across many nations, races, and ethnicities, and for a wide range of physical health indicators (Penner, Albrecht, Orom, Coleman, & Underwood III, 2010). Blacks, Latinos, and other minorities experience worse health outcomes and lesser quality care in the United States and other majority-White

Correll, J. Park, P., Judd, C., & Wittenbrink, B. (2002). The police officer's dilemma: Using ethnicity to disambiguate potentially threatening individuals. *Journal of Personality and Social Psychology, 83,* 1314–1329 (Figure 1).

RACE OF TARGET AND DECISIONS TO SHOOT

Under time pressure, who would you shoot? Participants in one study "shot" a Black target more quickly than a White target if he held a gun. They also decided against shooting an unarmed White target more rapidly than an unarmed Black target.

nations, including the United Kingdom and Canada (Banks, Marmot, Oldfield, & Smith, 2006; Millett, Gray, Bottle, & Majeed, 2008). These indicators include greater alcohol, drug, and nicotine use associated with depression and anxiety (Gibbons, Gerrard, Cleveland, Wills, & Brody, 2004) and reduced life expectancy and increased infant mortality (National Center for Health Statistics, 2006).

Another key social domain in which race- or ethnicity-based discrepancies are prevalent, at least in the United States, is in the criminal justice system. For example, Americans with more stereotypically Black African facial features receive more severe punishments (Blair, Judd, & Chapleau, 2004) and are more likely to be given the death penalty for capital crimes (Eberhardt, Davies, Purdie-Vaughns, & Johnson, 2006). Finally, both Black and White participants are more likely to "shoot" first and ask questions later when faced with Black targets, who may or may not be armed, versus White targets, who may nor may not be armed (see photo) (Correll, Park, Judd, & Wittenbrink, 2002). This racial bias in decisions to shoot is also evident among trained police officers (Correll et al., 2007).

Think Again!

1. *How are interpersonal and institutional discrimination different?*

2. *How can stereotypes undermine task performance?*

3. *What are the negative effects of stigma?*

OVERCOMING PREJUDICE, STEREOTYPING, AND DISCRIMINATION

Fortunately, as severe as the consequences of prejudice, stereotyping, and discrimination are, there are a number of effective ways in which they can be counteracted and/or

**Contact
Hypothesis:** Idea
that contact between
members of different
groups can reduce
intergroup hostility
and facilitate positive
intergroup relations

**Intergroup Contact
Theory:** Postulates
that intergroup
contact can reduce
intergroup bias
as long as several
conditions are
present: Individuals
must perceive that
the groups have equal
status; the groups
must pursue common,
superordinate
goals; the groups
must cooperate to
achieve those goals;
and the contact
must be sanctioned
or supported by
authorities, laws, and/
or customs

Subtype: Part of the
group that is seen
as a deviation from
the larger group,
allowing a global
stereotype about
that overall group to
persist

overcome. The research literature on this topic is quite extensive, and here I will present some of the highlights. Much of the contemporary research on reducing intergroup conflict originates in what is called the **contact hypothesis**: the idea that *mere* contact between members of groups can reduce intergroup hostility and enhance positive intergroup relations. The most basic version of this hypothesis suggests that contact in and of itself is sufficient. However, early research—including the Sherif et al. (1988/1961) Robbers Cave experiment described earlier as well as real-world implementation of desegregation in U.S. schools—demonstrated unequivocally that mere contact or familiarity is an inadequate solution (E. Aronson & Bridgeman, 1979). For example, recall how initially facilitating interactions between the two groups of boys at Robbers Cave increased rather than decreased tensions between them (Sherif et al., 1988/1961).

The initial contact hypothesis was refashioned by Allport (1954), whose **intergroup contact theory** specified that contact could be effective as long as several conditions were present: Individuals must perceive that the groups have equal status; the groups must pursue common, superordinate goals; the groups must cooperate to achieve those goals; and the contact must be sanctioned or supported by authorities, laws, and/or customs (See Table 10.5). A recent meta-analysis by Pettigrew and Tropp (2006) of 515 studies testing intergroup contact theory provided support for the positive effects of these factors, especially when all are present. However, a more fine-grained analysis revealed that, although each of these conditions *facilitated* the reduction of hostilities, none of them were *essential,* as Allport suggested. Pettigrew and Tropp (2006) argue that, up to a point, mere contact will help reduce intergroup tensions because, in general, familiarity breeds liking (Chapter 7). Pettigrew and Tropp (2008) empirically demonstrated that intergroup contact can reduce hostility by (a) increasing knowledge of the outgroup, (b) lessening anxiety about that contact, and (c) facilitating empathy and perspective taking. Moreover, greater cross-group friendship as measured by more time spent with members of the outgroup and more self-disclosure to outgroup members also reduce negative intergroup attitudes (Davies, Tropp, Aron, Pettigrew, & Wright, 2011).

One potential obstacle preventing positive individual-level contact from reducing prejudice more generally is that people often create subcategories of negatively valued outgroups. That is, even when people do get to know individuals who violate a stereotype, they can often maintain that stereotype by creating a **subtype** of the group that is a deviation from the larger group, allowing that global stereotype to persist (Richards & Hewstone, 2001). For instance, Michael Jordan may be perceived as a "special case" of a more negative stereotype of the African American male as angry, loud, and threatening, which acknowledges his deviation from the stereotype while preserving the validity of that stereotype. Nevertheless, Pettigrew and Tropp (2008) found that intergroup contact that reduces bias toward specific individuals—such as members of subtypes—can also lead people to rethink stereotypes and generalize these new, more positive perceptions to the outgroup as a whole.

One type of intergroup contact—termed the jigsaw classroom—was designed by Elliot Aronson and his colleagues in the 1970s to overcome intergroup bias in Texas elementary

TABLE 10.5   When and Why Intergroup Contact Helps

Intergroup Contact Is Particularly Likely to Reduce Intergroup Bias When	
1.	Individuals perceive that the groups have equal status
2.	The groups pursue common, superordinate goals
3.	The groups cooperate to achieve those goals
4.	The contact is sanctioned or supported by authorities, laws, and/or customs
5.	Contact is at the individual level
Intergroup Contact, Including Mere Contact, Can Reduce Intergroup Bias Because It	
1.	Increases knowledge/familiarity with the outgroup
2.	Lessens anxiety about contact with the outgroup
3.	Facilitates empathy and perspective taking

Sources: Allport, G. (1954). *The nature of prejudice*. Reading, MA: Addison-Wesley Publishing. Company. Pettigrew, T. F. & Tropp, L. R. (2011). *When groups meet. The dynamics of intergroup contact*. New York: Psychology Press. Kenworthy, J. B. Turner, R. N., Hewstone, M., Voci, A. (2005). Intergroup contact: When does it work and why? In *On the nature of prejudice: Fifty years after Allport* (J. F. Dovidio, P. Glick, & L. A. Rudman (Ed.) (pp. 278–292). Malden: Blackwell Publishing, 2005.

schools (E. Aronson, Blaney, Sikes, Stephan, & Snapp, 1975; Aronson & Bridgeman, 1979; Kilic, 2013). The **jigsaw classroom** requires children from different ethnic and/or racial backgrounds to cooperatively solve problems (Perkins & Tagler, 2011; Williams, 2004). The students are presented with a metaphorical jigsaw puzzle and need to assemble the pieces. Students from different backgrounds are each responsible for tracking down a piece of the puzzle, and they must depend on each other to put the pieces together to complete the project. The jigsaw approach is consistent with the basic tenets of intergroup contact theory and has been successfully implemented in both lab experiments and real-world settings (Aronson, 2004; Slavin & Cooper, 1999).

At the outset of this chapter, we discussed Allport's (1954) contention that categorization is fundamental to human cognition and subsequently reviewed some ways in which categorization can lead to intergroup bias and conflict. Let's bring the discussion full circle by describing how categorization can be used to reduce intergroup bias.

When encouraged to do so, people are able to change the way they categorize individuals. **Recategorization** occurs when people see ingroup and outgroup members primarily as members of a larger, mutually inclusive group, thereby diminishing the importance of the initial intergroup differences (Gaertner & Dovidio, 2000). The concept of recategorization represents the core of the **common ingroup identity model**, which posits

Jigsaw Classroom:
Teaching strategy that requires persons from different ethnic and/or racial backgrounds to cooperatively solve problems

Recategorization:
Viewing ingroup and outgroup members primarily as members of a larger, mutually inclusive group, thereby diminishing the importance of intergroup differences

Common Ingroup Identity Model:
Posits that at the core of intergroup bias is the categorization of individuals into ingroups and outgroups

that the basis for intergroup bias is the categorization of individuals into ingroups and outgroups (Gaertner & Dovidio, 2000; Gaertner, Dovidio, & Houlette, 2010). Therefore, to the extent that individuals are able to downplay those group boundaries and instead emphasize commonalities with outgroup members, bias and hostility can be reduced.

Although recategorization can occur by symbolically merging the groups into a super-ordinate entity, it can also happen when people focus on dimensions, attributes, and characteristics that they share with outgroup members (Gaertner et al., 2010). For instance, male engineering students may define male art students as outgroup members based on their college major. However, they could engage in recategorization by recognizing that both groups are members of a larger group (the "university) or by focusing instead on the fact that they are all males. The effectiveness of interventions based on common ingroup identity model has been demonstrated in a number of studies (Gaertner & Dovidio, 2000, 2009). One particularly interesting study asked Jewish Americans to focus either on differences between them and Germans or as common members of a superordinate group—humans (Wohl & Branscombe, 2005). Consistent with the common ingroup identity model, participants in the first group were much less forgiving of the atrocities committed by Germans against the Jews during World War II.

FINAL THOUGHTS:
THE CHANGING LANDSCAPE OF PREJUDICE

According to some measures, the prevalence of prejudice, stereotyping, and discrimination has decreased over the last 60 years, at least in the United States. In fact, in much of the Western world, strong social norms against the open expression of prejudice, along with genuine changes in intergroup bias, have together helped to greatly reduce its overt manifestations and have led to the removal of many legal barriers to equal opportunity. However, as you have seen throughout this chapter, the landscape has changed: Prejudice, stereotyping, and discrimination can be said to have gone "underground" as it were, remaining less visible but nevertheless both prevalent and influential. Not only do many people harbor hidden or implicit prejudices, but these prejudices have implications for the behavior of the perceiver as well as the feelings and behavior of the target. Moreover, targets must contend with invisible discriminatory practices that are often more difficult to prove and resistant to change.

Advances in theory and research have helped social psychologists to see the "bigger picture," by identifying similarities and regularities in the content and function of prejudice and stereotypes across time and across cultures. As a result of gaining a better understanding of the nature of prejudice, we can craft effective interventions that are based on empirically tested broader principles yet take into account specific groups, persons, and local conditions.

In this chapter we have taken a whirlwind tour of the rapidly growing body of theory and research on prejudice, stereotypes, and discrimination. We have seen how they are rooted in evolutionary pressures and are shaped by contextual factors and individual experiences. It is also evident that these social behaviors, like others we have investigated, are produced by the interaction between the person and the situation.

The relevance of several of our fundamental questions—especially rationality, the self, and morality—to the content of this chapter is quite clear. First of all, early 20th century treatments suggested that prejudice and stereotyping were pathological—abnormal and irrational. These views were supplanted by newer conceptualizations of prejudice and stereotyping as normal consequences of the necessity of social categorization, along with

conflicts over power, status, and/or limited material resources. Intergroup bias can be rational, functional, and adaptive.

Moreover, the centrality of the self to intergroup bias is reflected in the fact that social categorization is simultaneously a categorization of the self as a member of a particular ingroup. The "us" in "us versus them" obviously includes the self, and the self is clearly at the core of prejudice. Furthermore, one of the functions of prejudice and stereotyping is the maintaining or enhancing self-esteem. Finally, prejudices and stereotypes often guide—for better or worse—our moral behavior. These biases have driven people to treat others in hurtful, occasionally dehumanizing, and often atrocious ways. Fortunately, recognition of the presence and operation of these biases allows us to override them and preserve and/or restore human dignity.

CORE CONCEPTS

- A stereotype is a belief about the characteristics, attributes, and behaviors of a group and its members; prejudice is an evaluation of a group and its members; discrimination is unequal treatment of individuals based on their group membership; intergroup bias encapsulates all three of these.

- Although old-fashioned racism has diminished in recent years, at least in the United States, aversive racism is prevalent. Modern racists profess egalitarian views of racial groups but have negative feelings that result in opposition to giving

disadvantaged groups special consideration or opportunities.

- Social identity theory ties intergroup bias to peoples' need to feel good about themselves and is based on the fact that one major component of self-esteem derives from the groups to which people belong.

- Priming stereotypes can affect subsequent cognitive processing of relevant groups and can lead to discrimination.

- Realistic group conflict theory suggests that intergroup bias is often because of competition for resources, as was illustrated by the Robbers Cave Study. Intergroup threat theory postulates that even perceptions of threat to symbolic or material resources can produce prejudice, stereotyping, and discrimination.

- Researchers have used response latency techniques, including the IAT and evaluative priming, to assess implicit associations; a number of cognitive biases are relevant to stereotypes, including exaggerating the behaviors of minorities, illusory correlation, confirmation bias, self-fulfilling prophecy, ultimate attribution error; right-wing authoritarianism and social dominance orientation are individual difference variables that are correlated with intergroup bias.

- Intergroup bias carries many material and physical costs as well as posing threats to self-esteem.

- The reformulated intergroup contact theory shows that mere contact can help reduce intergroup bias but is more effective when the groups share equal status; pursue common, superordinate goals; cooperate to achieve those goals; and, are supported by norms, laws, customs, and authorities; the jigsaw classroom and the common identity intergroup model are empirically supported strategies that can reduce intergroup bias.

▶ ⓈSAGE edge™ Test your understanding of chapter content. Take the practice quiz. edge.sagepub.com/barrett

KEY TERMS

Ageism, 376

Ambivalent Sexism, 375

Aversive Racism, 353

Benevolent Sexism, 375

Common Ingroup Identity Model, 385

Contact Hypothesis, 384

Discrimination, 351

Glass Ceiling, 378

Heterosexism, 377

Homophobia, 377

Hostile Sexism, 375

Illusory Correlation, 368

Implicit Attitude, 353

Ingroup, 357

Ingroup Bias, 357

Ingroup Favoritism, 357

Institutional Discrimination, 378

Intergroup Bias, 350

Intergroup Contact Theory, 384

Interpersonal Discrimination, 378

Jigsaw Classroom, 385

Microaggressions, 379

Minimal Group Paradigm, 357

Modern Racism, 353

Optimal Distinctiveness Theory, 360

Outgroup, 357

Outgroup Homogeneity Effect, 358

Personal Identity, 357

Prejudice, 351

Realistic Group Conflict Theory, 361

Recategorization, 385

Relative deprivation (RD), 363

Relative Deprivation Theory (RDT), 363

Response Latency, 366

Right-Wing Authoritarianism (RWA), 370

Scapegoating, 363

Self-Categorization Theory (SCT), 357

Sexism, 374

▶ **⑤SAGE edge™**   Review key terms with eFlashcards.
                    edge.sagepub.com/barrett

THINK FURTHER!

- Do you hold any negative prejudices and/or stereotypes that you wish you didn't hold? If so, do you think you can change those? How? If you were to try recategorization, what larger categories would you use?

- Do you think it is possible to eliminate negative prejudices and stereotypes from a society? Why or why not?

- Ask some of your female friends about benevolent sexism. Does it bother them? Ask your mother or other women who are of a different generation than you. What do they think?

- If there were two groups in your community or society that you wish could eliminate the negative prejudices and stereotypes each has about the other, which would they be? How could the common ingroup identity model be used to do that?

- The jigsaw classroom is used for small groups and therefore is limited in the extent to which can change society as a whole. Can you think of ways that this approach could be modified to use it on a larger scale (like towns or communities)?

- Have you experienced interpersonal and/or institutional discrimination? What was the situation? Was the discrimination justifiable?

- Have you ever been the target of a negative stereotype that has undermined your performance in some way?

SUGGESTED READINGS

Allport, G. W. (1954). *The nature of prejudice.* Oxford, UK: Addison-Wesley.

Dovidio, J. F., & Gaertner, S. L. (1998). On the nature of contemporary prejudice: The causes, consequences, and challenges of aversive racism. In J. L. Eberhardt & S. T. Fiske (Eds.), *Confronting racism: The problem and the response* (pp. 3–32). Thousand Oaks, CA: Sage.

Ho, A. K., Sidanius, J., Pratto, F., Levin, S., Thomsen, L., Kteily, N., & Sheehy-Skeffington, J. (2012). Social dominance orientation: Revisiting the structure and function of a variable predicting social and political attitudes. *Personality & Social Psychology Bulletin, 38,* 583–606.

Risen, J. L., Gilovich, T., & Dunning, D. (2007). One-shot illusory correlations and stereotype formation. *Personality and Social Psychology Bulletin, 33,* 1492–1502.

Steele, C. M. (2010). *Whistling Vivaldi: And how other clues to stereotypes affect us.* New York, NY: W.W. Norton.

11

Affiliation and Love

In the last decade, new forms of interpersonal relationships have sprung up, including "friends with benefits."

PYMCA/Universal Images Group/Getty Images.

LEARNING OBJECTIVES

11.1 Define relationship, close relationship, need for affiliation, need to belong, reinforcement-affect model, social exchange theory, equity theory, and communal and exchange relationships.

11.2 Summarize the study on I-sharing and liking, the influence of proximity, familiarity, and similarity on liking, and the matching hypothesis.

11.3 List the physical features that heterosexual men and women tend to find attractive in the other gender as well as the perceived and actual benefits of physical attractiveness; explain the evolutionary and the social role theory perspectives on mate selection.

11.4 Define passionate and companionate love, outline the triangular theory, two-factor theory (and the bridge study); summarize the evolutionary perspective on the function of love, the three motivation systems associated with love, and the research on the origins of homosexuality.

11.5 Discuss the obstacles to relationship research and how event sampling can help overcome some of them.

11.6 Identify the four attachment styles and how they affect adult romantic relationships; describe the influences of positive illusions and self-disclosure on relationship satisfaction.

FRIENDS WITH BENEFITS

What is a friend? What is a lover? Not that many years ago the distinction between friends and romantic partners was generally pretty clear. When we think of friendships, we typically imagine relationships ranging from little more than mere acquaintances to close, enduring emotional bonds. The term *friendship* has traditionally referred to nonsexual relationships, although romantic relationships often incorporate many aspects of friendships. However, in recent years, new types of interpersonal arrangements have emerged in many Western cultures that are neither traditional nonsexual friendships nor romantic and sexual relationships—*friends with benefits* and *hooking up*. Friends with benefits are stable friendships that involve occasional sex but neither romantic love nor commitment (Garcia, Reiber, Massey, & Merriwether, 2012; Williams & Jovanovic, 2015). People who hook up meet primarily for sex, are often just acquaintances, and are not emotionally involved or committed to each other, although there frequently are not any rules about what is or is not to be done (Garcia et al., 2012; Owen, Quirk, & Fincham, 2014; Paul & Hayes, 2002; Quirk, Owen, & Fincham, 2014). This loosening of the connection between love and sex is reflected in the fact that 60% to 80% of U.S. undergraduates report having engaged in casual sex at least once, some at as early as 12 years of age (Garcia et al., 2012). These sexual encounters do not necessarily involve sexual intercourse and are often limited to "petting" or oral sex (Reiber & Garcia, 2010). Although casual sex has been increasing in frequency in the West in the past few decades, it is not clear if this trend will continue or whether it will spread to other nations or societies.

Despite the emergence of these new arrangements, the vast majority of people will have many more friendships that are strictly platonic or nonsexual, in addition to one or more relatively long-term sexual relationships, over the course of their lives. Not surprisingly, most relationship research has investigated these two more common and culturally universal arrangements, and consequently the current chapter will focus primarily on them (Berscheid & Reis, 1998). A **relationship** between two people exists when they influence each other, and that relationship is considered **close** when the influence is strong, frequent, and enduring, and the two individuals are interdependent (Berscheid & Reis, 1998;

Relationship: When two people influence each other

Close Relationship: When the influence between two people is strong, frequent, enduring, and characterized by interdependence

Clark & Lemay, 2010). We'll review a variety of aspects of interpersonal relationships, ranging from factors that influence who we like and who we choose as romantic partners to the nature and purpose of attachment and romantic love.

Two of our six fundamental questions of human existence, self and sociality, are most relevant to the topics of platonic and romantic relationships. First, as we'll discuss in more detail below, meaningful connections between the self and others are essential to the psychological and physical well-being of the *self;* without these connections to nourish us, we would, in essence, wither away. Second, affiliation, friendship, and romance are universal features of human life that reflect a core human trait—*sociality*. We do not simply *want* to form relationships with other people. Rather, we *need* to.

Think Ahead!

1. *Why do we form relationships with others?*
2. *Who do we find attractive and why?*
3. *What is love?*

THE NATURE OF AFFILIATION AND LOVE

Why do we expend so much effort to connect with and maintain relationships with other people? Meaningful contact with other people satisfies two related, fundamental human motives: affiliation and belongingness. The **need for affiliation** is our desire to be around and interact with other people (Baumeister & Leary, 1995; Hofer, Busch, & Schneider, 2015; Leary, 2010). We may fulfill this need by chatting with a casual acquaintance before class, going alone to a coffee shop to study, or interacting with others on Facebook. The second motive is the **need to belong**: our desire to form and maintain close and durable relationships with others (Baumeister, 2012). This belongingness need can be met by establishing close bonds with others that provide emotional intimacy, with or without a romantic dimension. While in practice it is difficult to completely separate affiliation and belongingness, we can conceptually distinguish them: Mere affiliation will not meet our need for close relationships, and close relationships can be formed and maintained without frequent contact (Baumeister & Leary, 1995).

The need for affiliation is associated with four types of social rewards (C. A. Hill, 1987, 2009). First, merely being in the presence of others—sometimes even strangers—can help us feel good. A second reason for affiliation is to allow us to obtain the positive attention or praise that others can give us. Third, other people can provide emotional support that reduces negative emotions, such as anxiety or fear. For instance, talking with fellow students just before an exam may help relieve exam-related stress. The fourth reason

Need for Affiliation: Desire to be around and interact with other people

Need to Belong: Desire to form and maintain close and durable relationships with others

for affiliation is that it provides opportunities for us to engage in social comparison (see Chapter 4). Social comparison allows us to gather information from others regarding how we are doing and is primarily helpful in the absence of objective feedback or standards (Festinger, 1954). In addition to these social rewards, developing connections with others can help us obtain material resources and knowledge that we are unable to secure on our own. For example, people often rely on their social networks to find jobs or to utilize connections with others by exchanging the money they earn for products and services that they cannot independently obtain. Lastly, humans have historically needed to form enduring bonds with romantic partners in order to nourish and protect our offspring (notwithstanding recent social and scientific developments that have lessened this need).

One reason for affiliation is that spending time with and connecting with others can make us feel good. This notion is consistent with the **reinforcement-affect model of interpersonal attraction**, which states that we prefer to interact with and befriend people who we find to be emotionally rewarding (Clore & Byrne, 1974). In addition, we also gravitate toward people with whom we associate positive or reinforcing experiences, such as a memorable summer trip or terrific concert (Hofmann, De Houwer, Perugini, Baeyens, & Crombez, 2010). In other words, we tend to affiliate with and befriend people who make us feel better.

A different perspective on interpersonal relationships assumes that they operate as social exchanges in which people seek a balance between relationship benefits and costs. This **social exchange theory** postulates that people view their interactions with others in terms of the trade-off between what they put into and what they get out of the relationships, and they seek to maximize the gains and minimize the losses (Chang & Hsiao, 2013; Thibaut & Kelley, 1959). Although it loosely resembles an economic model, social exchange theory extends to nonmaterial aspects of relationships, including mutual affection, esteem, and approval (Foa & Foa, 1975). If conceptualizing our relationships in terms of benefits and costs may seem overly cold and calculating, take a minute to apply it to one of your friendships. What happens if the costs outweigh the benefits and you "give" more emotional support or invest far greater effort or material resources than the other person, who seems to "take" more? How would you feel about that? For many, this type of imbalance can doom a friendship.

While we care about the actual benefit-to-cost ratio, people often want to ensure that each partner feels that she or he is getting the same fair "deal" out of the relationship. We are more satisfied when each partner has the same *ratio* of benefits to costs. In other words, if one could assign numeric values to the benefits and costs of relationships, people want their own ratio to be equivalent to the other person's. Thus, if Sandy receives twice as many benefits as she gives in costs, then she would likely prefer that her friend Diane's benefit/cost ratio is also approximately two-to-one. This perspective is elaborated in Elaine Hatfield's **equity theory**, which postulates that people prefer relationships—including close relationships—in which each partner enjoys the same ratio (Hatfield & Rapson, 2012; McKown, 2013; Sechrist, Suitor, Howard, & Pillemer, 2014). Think about

---

Reinforcement-Affect Model of Interpersonal Attraction: Postulates that people prefer to interact with and befriend others who they find to be emotionally rewarding

Social Exchange Theory: Idea that people view their interactions with others in terms of the trade-off between benefits and costs and that they seek to maximize the benefits and minimize the costs

Equity Theory: Idea that people prefer relationships— including close relationships—in which each partner enjoys the same ratio of benefits to costs

SOCIAL PSYCHOLOGY APPLIED TO HEALTH
THE IMPORTANCE OF BEING SOCIAL

The importance of healthy, stable social relationships to our well-being is hard to overemphasize (Cacioppo, Cacioppo, & Boomsma, 2014; Cacioppo & Cacioppo, 2012). Hundreds of studies have demonstrated the harmful effects of social rejection and isolation on peoples' physical and mental health (Bastian et al., 2012; Cacioppo & Patrick, 2008; Ford & Collins, 2013). For instance, people who are chronically lonely are more susceptible to a variety of physical problems, including cancer, high blood pressure, and other ailments (Cacioppo & Patrick, 2008; Chou, Cacioppo, Kumari, & Song, 2014; Hawkley, Thisted, Masi, & Cacioppo, 2010; Kurina et al., 2011; Stickley et al., 2015). They tend to have lower subjective well-being (discussed in Chapter 13), are even more vulnerable to the common cold, and may have shorter lifespans (Y. Luo, Hawkley, Waite, & Cacioppo, 2012; Pressman et al., 2005; VanderWeele, Hawkley, & Cacioppo, 2012). Loneliness can interfere with academic success and hasten burnout (Quan, Zhen, Yao, & Zhou, 2014; Stoliker & Lafreniere, 2015). Moreover, as discussed in Chapter 9, rejection can lead people to experience physical pain and increase aggression and decrease prosocial behavior. In short, even temporarily removing the "social" from our "social lives" leaves us emotionally and physically depleted and can have serious, deleterious consequences for our well-being.

There are some important aspects to loneliness that need to be mentioned. First, loneliness is in the eye of the beholder—if a person reports feeling lonely or perceives himself as being lonely, then he probably is. That is, it is the perception of loneliness or of being isolated that is associated with negative effects. As I am sure you are aware, just because a person seems to have many friends and a number of apparent sources of social support, it does not mean that she is not lonely.

Second, loneliness is partially heritable and consequently is more prevalent in pairs of identical as opposed to fraternal twins or other siblings: Some people are simply more sensitive at birth to social rejection than are others (Distel et al., 2010). Interestingly, lonely people tend to marry and have children with other lonely people and the nonlonely partner with the nonlonely (Distel et al., 2010).

Third, as odd as this may seem, lonely people tend to be found in clusters in social networks, which means they are often connected to other lonely people. Cacioppo, Fowler, and Christakis (2009) examined a large network of people who were enrolled in the Framingham Heart Study, and not only discovered the clustering but also learned that loneliness can also be contagious and spread across a social network.

some of your friendships—how important is it to you that they be equitable? Take a look at the questions in Table 11.1 to gauge how equitable your relationship is. Hatfield and her colleagues argue that fairness—the extent to which the relationship is rewarding—and the degree of equity are correlated with sexual satisfaction, marital happiness, and marital stability (Hatfield & Rapson, 2012).

Clearly, many relationships are based on the equitable exchange of benefits and costs. But are they all? The psychologists Margaret Clark and Judson Mills proposed that many follow a different model, one in which the parties do not keep track of the relative costs and benefits. Clark and Mills call this a **communal relationship**, which they define as one in which the individuals are primarily concerned about the welfare of the other and they give without expecting anything in return (Clark & Lemay, 2010; Clark & Mills, 1979). Clark and Mills distinguish a communal from an **exchange relationship**, which is one based on the reciprocal exchange of benefits. In exchange relationships, people keep an accounting of what benefits and costs each has received or accrued and expect that, overall, exchanges will be balanced. Marriages, families, and close friendships, are typically communally based, whereas business partnerships, relationships between acquaintances, buyers and sellers, and strangers are more apt to be exchange based.

Communal Relationship:
Relationship in which individuals are primarily concerned about the welfare of the other and that they give to each other without expecting to receive anything in return

Exchange Relationship:
Relationship that is based on the reciprocal exchange of benefits

TABLE 11.1   Measuring Equity in Relationships

How would you rate the equity of your relationship? Do you think that your partner agrees with you?

+3	I am getting a much better deal than my partner.
+2	I am getting a somewhat better deal.
+1	I am getting a slightly better deal.
0	We are both getting an equally good or bad deal.
-1	My partner is getting a slightly better deal.
-2	My partner is getting a somewhat better deal.
-3	My partner is getting a much better deal than I am.

Source: Hatfield, E., & Rapson, R. L. (2012). Equity theory in close relationships. In P. A. M. Van Lange, A. W. Kruglanski, & E. T. Higgins (Eds.), *Handbook of theories of social psychology* (Vol. 2, pp. 200–217). Thousand Oaks, CA: Sage Publications Ltd.

Think Again!

1. _How strong is your need for affiliation? Do you think you are average, below average, or above? Why do you think that?_

2. *Can both reinforcement-affect theory and social exchange theory apply to the same relationship? If so, how?*

3. *Think of a particular friend or partner and complete the Equity Scale in Table 11.1. Ask the other person to do the same. Are there differences in your perceptions? How do you explain them? How would being overbenefited (getting more from the relationship than you give) make you feel?*

CONTEXTUAL FACTORS

Liking

As we discussed in Chapter 6 on social influence, *liking* plays an important role in inter-personal relationships. In addition to liking those who make us feel good and/or with whom we associate positive experiences, we also like people who like us: liking leads to liking. As we've mentioned, people often actively attempt to *ingratiate* themselves to others—to make others like them. Flattery can be an effective way to ingratiate others: When others think we like them, they generally like us more (Jones, 1990; Medler-Liraz & Yagil, 2013). The converse is also true: when we think others like us, our liking for them increases (Montoya & Horton, 2012). For example, participants in one study had greater liking for paired partners who they believed liked them, and they were also warmer and more agreeable in their interactions with their partners (Curtis & Miller, 1986). In another study, merely sharing a recent experience led participants to like an outgroup member more than an ingroup member with whom they did not have that shared experience (see Research Box 11.1) (Pinel & Long, 2012). In addition to the reciprocal effects of liking on liking, there are several other factors that influence who we like, including their proximity, familiarity, and similarity to us.

Proximity

People tend to like and develop friendships with others who are in relatively close physical proximity to them or who are geographically near them (Newcomb, 1961). One famous early demonstration of the effects of proximity on liking was conducted by Festinger, Schachter, and Back (1950) at a married student-housing complex at the Massachusetts Institute of Technology near Boston. Incoming students—who were World War II veterans—and their families were randomly assigned to units in 17 different buildings. Festinger et al. surveyed the students and found that two-thirds of the friendships that developed within the complex were between individuals in the same building, and 40% of the same-building friendships were between students who lived in adjacent units. More recently, Nahemow and Lawton (1975) analyzed friendship patterns in a multi-building housing project in Manhattan, New York. The residents were a diverse mix of Black, White, and Puerto Rican

RESEARCH BOX 11.1
SHARING, LIKING, AND GROUP MEMBERSHIP

Hypotheses: This research focused on *I-sharing,* which involves the in-the-moment sharing of experiences (in contrast with sharing of past experiences). The researchers hypothesized that I-sharing with an outgroup member would lead to greater liking for that member than for an ingroup member who did not I-share. In addition, liking would be greater for an ingroup member who I-shared than for an outgroup member who did not I-share.

Research Method: 115 male and female heterosexual participants played a computer game with a partner who was identified as either heterosexual or lesbian/gay. The game involved responses to hypothetical, nonsensical questions about the resemblances of celebrities to various objects, such as what tool Jennifer Aniston would be, if she were a tool. The experimenters manipulated I-sharing by varying whether the participant and partner had identical responses either 75% of the time or not at all. At the end of the game, participants indicated how much they liked their partners.

Results: Participants generally liked ingroup members (heterosexuals) with whom they shared 75% of their responses than outgroup members (lesbians/gays) who gave completely different responses. However, participants liked outgroup members with whom they I-shared better than ingroup members who gave completely different responses.

Conclusion: In-the-moment shared experiences were able to trump cross-group differences and lead participants to like outgroup members more than ingroup members. Thus, merely sharing experiences can increase liking. This research suggests a method of reducing prejudice between groups different than the ones described in Chapter 10.

Source: Based on Pinel, E. C., & Long, A. E. (2012). When I's meet: Sharing subjective experience with someone from the outgroup. *Personality and Social Psychology Bulletin, 38,* 296–307.

individuals of various ages. These authors found that, although similarity in race/ethnicity was one important predictor, proximity was also correlated with friendship: Almost 50% of the residents listed someone on the same floor as their best friend, and 88% listed someone in the same building.

Familiarity

Why does proximity matter? One reason is that people are simply more likely to interact with people who live or work nearby, and therefore there is a higher probability that they will become acquainted with them. In addition, people who we see more often become *familiar* to us. Familiarity or *mere exposure* often leads to liking, as you learned in Chapter 7 (de Zilva, Newell, & Mitchell, 2015; Hansen & Wänke, 2009). Recently, Back, Schmukle, and Egloff (2008) randomly assigned students to desks in an introductory psychology class in Germany. The researchers assessed students' liking for other students at the beginning of the course and after one year and found that proximity predicted both initial attraction ratings and assessments of friendship intensity one year later (see Figure 11.1). This familiarity principle even applies to the *self*: We prefer images of ourselves that are mirror reflections of our faces (what we see) as compared to photographs of our faces (how others see us), whereas we prefer images of others that are not their mirror reflections (Mita, Dermer, & Knight, 1977). Try this by standing in front of a mirror and comparing your mirror image to a photograph of you—which do you like better?

Similarity

Do *birds of a feather flock together* or do *opposites attract?* These two lay theories make opposite predictions regarding how romantic partners are drawn to each other. My students

FIGURE 11.1   Familiarity and Attraction

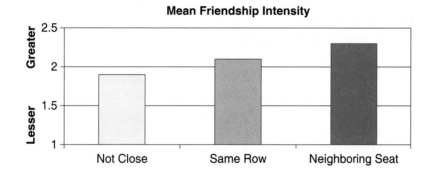

Students developed a greater liking (greater friendship intensity) for other students who sat in neighboring seats, in comparison to those who sat less close but in the same row or who did not sit close to them, as measured one year later.

Source: Adapted from Back, M. D., Schmuckle, S. D., & Egloff, B. (2008). Becoming friends by chance. *Psychological Science, 19,* 439–440.

People tend to associate with others who are similar to them.

© Richard Olivier/CORBIS.

will agree with either one, as long as they are thinking about only one of them! However, they find themselves in a bind when I ask about the other theory, because they want to endorse that one too! Let's try to resolve this conundrum by reviewing the evidence for each.

Similarity is unquestionably predictive of who people associate with in both platonic and romantic relationships. A vast amount of research supports the general principle of **homophily:** the preference we have for spending time and/or connecting with people who are like us (Mackinnon, Jordan, & Wilson, 2011). Possessing common attitudes, demographic characteristics, experiences, and level of attractiveness can lead to greater interpersonal attraction (S. Luo & Klohnen, 2005). For example, participants in one study were asked to complete a detailed attitude questionnaire and later received responses from the same questionnaire ostensibly provided by another student (Byrne, 1971). The similarity of the responses was (you guessed it) manipulated so as to vary from high to moderate to low. Not surprisingly, students expected to like that other person more to the extent that they believed they shared attitudes. People with similar *demographic* characteristics, including race/ethnicity, religion, age, and socioeconomic status, also tend to associate with one another (McPherson, Smith-Lovin, & Cook, 2001; Nahemow & Lawton, 1975). For instance, Liu, Campbell, and Condie (1995) surveyed Latino, Asian, African, and European Americans and found that they generally preferred to date people of their own ethnicity. Moreover, a recent longitudinal study of over 400 adolescents revealed that similarities in sex (male/female), acceptance by peer, physical aggressiveness, and academic ability in seventh grade predicted which friendships remained intact and how long they lasted through Grades 8 through 12 (Hartl, Laursen, & Cillessen, 2015).

Finally, although many would prefer a romantic partner who is very handsome or beautiful, the reality is that such individuals are unattainable for most people. Consequently, people end up settling for someone else. According to the **matching hypothesis**, people typically select romantic partners who are at approximately the same

Homophily: Preference people have for spending time with and/or connecting with people who are like them

Matching Hypothesis: Idea that people typically select romantic partners who are at approximately the same "level" of attractiveness as they are

"level" of attractiveness as they are, even if they would prefer a more attractive person (Montoya, 2008). A meta-analysis by Feingold (1988) found evidence of the matching phenomenon in romantic couples and male same-sex friendships but, interestingly, not among female same-sex friendships. Other research has found that matched couples may also stay together longer and be happier (Luo & Klohnen, 2005). A set of studies by Mackinnon et al. (2011) found that similarity in physical appearance (e.g., wearing glasses, hair color) even predicted who tended to sit together in college classrooms.

Think Again!

1. *Of the four situational influences on who we like, which do you think is the strongest and why?*

2. *Why do you suppose that the matching hypothesis is supported for male same-sex but not female same-sex relationships?*

3. *Sometimes we see couples who do not have the same level of attractiveness. Why do you think this is so? Why are some people able to find a partner who is much more attractive than they are?*

WHO IS ATTRACTIVE?

The Components of Attractiveness

Although most people would agree that beauty is not *only* skin deep, what is skin deep can exert enormous influence on interpersonal perceptions and interactions. The effects of physical attractiveness operate in both platonic and romantic relationships (Berscheid & Reis, 1998). Around the world, people who are physically attractive are, all else being equal, liked more (Kniffin & Wilson, 2004). One of the key determinants of judgments of physical beauty is of course the face, and its effects can be quite powerful.

What makes a face attractive? I ask my students this question each semester and they accurately identify the eyes, nose, and mouth as important features. However, they frequently overlook one feature that is not so obvious: symmetry. A face is symmetrical if one side of the face is a mirror image of the other side, and a number of studies have demonstrated the association between facial symmetry and attractiveness (Rhodes et al., 2007). Why might symmetry matter? It is mostly likely because of the fact that symmetry acts as a proxy for or signal of biological health and fertility. People's preference for symmetry extends from the face to the body: Research clearly shows that both sexes find symmetrical bodies more attractive than asymmetrical ones, even if they are not consciously aware of it (Gangestad & Thornhill, 1997).

Of course facial beauty is composed of more than symmetry (Danel & Pawlowski, 2007; Scott et al., 2014; Swami et al., 2010). For instance, research by Cunningham and his colleagues found that U.S. college females rated male faces with large eyes, a big, expressive smile, a large chin, and prominent cheekbones as more attractive (Cunningham, Barbee, & Pike, 1990). In contrast, males preferred women's faces with large eyes, large pupils, high and expressive eyebrows, a big smile, a small nose, a small chin, and narrow cheeks but prominent cheekbones—which combine baby face features with signs of maturity (Cunningham, 1986). These features were seen as attractive whether the women were other college students or Caucasian, African, or Asian international beauty pageant contestants—suggesting that there may be some cross-cultural agreement about the elements of female beauty. In fact, a number of other studies have found evidence of cross-cultural universality in facial attractiveness (Langlois et al., 2000). For instance, Cunningham, Roberts, Barbee, Druen, and Wu (1995) asked recent Asian and Hispanic immigrants to the United States, Chinese-speaking Taiwanese students living in Taiwan, and Caucasian Americans to rate the attractiveness of Asian, Hispanic, Black, and Caucasian women and found a surprisingly high correlation of over .91 among the raters.

Much of the research on physical attractiveness asks raters to judge the beauty of existing, unretouched photos. There is another group of studies that takes a very different approach: actual photos are digitally combined to produce an array of stimuli that allow researchers to systematically vary particular facial components. For example, a number of researchers merge increasingly large numbers of photos in order to create images that are more or less average across important features, such as eye size (Langlois & Roggman, 1990; Rhodes & Tremewan, 1996). Langlois and Roggman (1990) created composites of 4, 8, 16, or 32 undergraduate male or female Hispanic, Asian, and Caucasian faces and asked undergraduates to rate the composites as well as the 550 individual faces they were created from (see photo). These researchers found very high agreement among the male and female raters regarding how attractive the photos were. Importantly, the composite or "averaged" photos were seen as more attractive when they were created from 16 or 32 separate faces versus 4 or 8. In other words, the more "average" the faces, the more attractive they were deemed to be! Although in many respects average is better, cross-cultural research demonstrates that not all averages are the same (DeBruine, Jones, Unger, Little, & Feinberg, 2007; Said & Todorov, 2011). Perrett, May, and Yoshikawa (1994) asked individuals from

AVERAGE FACES ARE MORE ATTRACTIVE

Ratings of attractiveness go up as the number of faces averaged increases.

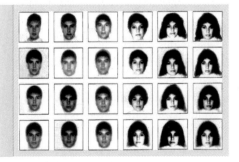

Langlois, J. H., & Roggman, L. A. (1990). Attractive faces are only average. *Psychological Science, 1,* 115–121.

Japan and Great Britain to rate composites created from women previously rated as average or highly attractive and found that people largely agreed that the latter were more attractive. Thus, averaging highly attractive faces produces more desirable faces than does averaging average faces.

After presenting this evidence to my students, many ask—appropriately—about individual variation in perceptions of attractiveness, given that they know that people often disagree. Indeed, despite the universality in some judgments of beauty, both individual and cross-cultural differences do exist, and beauty remains, in many respects, in the eye of the beholder (Hönekopp, 2006).

Perceived Benefits of Physical Attractiveness

One advantage of physical attractiveness, then, is that it can increase liking. There are a number of other benefits to being beautiful. One is that physically attractive people are commonly thought to have other positive characteristics. That is, many people subscribe to the *what is beautiful is good* stereotype (Eagly, Ashmore, Makhijani, & Longo, 1991; Lemay, Clark, & Greenberg, 2010). Dion, Berscheid, and Walster (1972) provided evidence for the existence of this stereotype when they asked male and female college students to make inferences about people, based only on their photos. Each participant viewed a photo of one attractive, one average looking, and one unattractive target and predicted the target's personality traits as well as the likelihood that she or he would experience certain positive life events. Dion et al. found that participants believed that attractive individuals had more socially desirable traits (e.g., altruistic, sociable, warm, sophisticated), would be more competent spouses, and have happier marriages, better jobs, and greater overall happiness. In short, physical attractiveness was significantly correlated with being "good." Support for this *what is beautiful is good* effect has been found in a number of other studies as a well as two meta-analyses (Eagly et al., 1991; Jackson, Hunter, & Hodge, 1995).

There are some limits to this stereotype, as attractive people are not generally seen as better parents and are often viewed as immodest (Dion et al., 1972; Wheeler & Kim, 1997). Moreover, although physical attractiveness enhances perceptions of other qualities in both individualistic and collectivistic societies, the specific attributes associated with beauty differ (Anderson, Adams, & Plaut, 2008). According to research by Wheeler and Kim (1997), individualists tend to see attractive persons as dominant and assertive, whereas collectivists perceive them to have integrity and be empathetic and generous.

Actual Benefits of Physical Attractiveness

As we discussed in Chapter 10, stereotypes sometimes have a kernel of truth. Psychologists have investigated whether attractive people really do have other socially desirable traits and more positive social experiences and have found some evidence that they do.

Attractive people tend to be more popular, to date more, and to have better social skills (Rhodes, Halberstadt, Jeffery, & Palermo, 2005). Why, do you suppose, attractive people are more socially adept? This is a challenging question to answer, but researchers think that these skills develop as a result of more positive interactions with and treatment from others that likely began early in their lives (Langlois et al., 2000). Moreover, research suggests that attractive persons may in fact be happier and more satisfied with their lives (Meier, Robinson, Carter, & Hinsz, 2010).

In addition to these social benefits, attractiveness bestows other "gifts" (Ma & Hu, 2015; Rosar, Klein, & Beckers, 2012; Tsai, Huang, & Yu, 2012). For instance, attractive persons receive shorter prison sentences than do less attractive ones (Gunnell & Ceci, 2010). They are also more likely to be hired for a job and to earn more (Frieze, Olson, & Russell, 1991; Judge, Hurst, & Simon, 2009). One study revealed that there is a positive correlation between attractiveness and earnings, such that, as attractiveness ratings increase, so too does annual income (Frieze et al., 1991). University professors get "bonus points" for being attractive, as students tend to rate them more favorably than nonattractive ones (Hamermesh & Parker, 2005). Finally, even infants benefit from being attractive, as they may receive better care from nurses (Badr & Abdallah, 2001) and are seen as more sociable, competent, and easier to care for (Karraker & Stern, 1990).

Of course, physical attractiveness is not limited to the face—body size and shape are also important. For example, women tend to prefer males who are strong and athletic, at least when specifically seeking *sexual* partners (Frederick & Haselton, 2007; Li & Kenrick, 2006). Perhaps the most crucial body feature that is tied to attractiveness is weight. Study after study has demonstrated that individuals who are heavyweight or obese—at least according to U.S. standards—are stigmatized, often shunned, and denied opportunities provided to so-called normal weight persons (Brownell, Puhl, Schwartz, & Rudd, 2005; Crandall, Merman, & Hebl, 2009). For instance, heavyweight individuals are more likely to be teased in school (Neumark-Sztainer & Eisenberg, 2005), evaluated more harshly in the workplace (Zemanek, McIntyre, & Zemanek, 1998), and seen as less desirable romantic partners (Regan, 1996). Even parents discriminate against their heavyweight children, providing less financial support for their college education (Crandall, 1995). In the next section we'll discuss other physical and nonphysical features that are desired by males and females in their romantic partners.

Think Again!

1. *What facial features do men and women find attractive in each other?*

2. *Explain what is meant by "what is beautiful is good."*

3. *What are two benefits of being attractive?*

EVOLUTIONARY PERSPECTIVE ON MATE SELECTION

Evolutionary pressures have been a powerful influence on who people choose as romantic partners (Buss, 2003). The most important adaptive problems faced by mammals are survival, reproduction, and ensuring the survival of offspring. As you recall, *natural selection* is the engine that drives the evolution of features necessary for the survival of individual members of a species. There is a second, related evolutionary process identified by Darwin (1871) called **sexual selection**, which is the evolution of characteristics that provide a *reproductive* advantage. According to Darwin (1871), there are two aspects of sexual selection: competition between members of the same sex (intrasexual competition) for access to members of the opposite sex and the selection of opposite sex mating partners based on specific features (intersexual selection).

Building on Darwin's work, Trivers's (1972) **theory of differential parental investment and sexual selection** makes two hypotheses about these two aspects of sexual selection: (1) the sex that is more invested in the offspring will be more selective in choosing sexual partners, and (2) the less invested sex will engage in more intrasexual competition in order to gain access to the more invested sex. Parental investment refers to the time and effort that parents expend in the creation and nurturance of the offspring.

In humans, females are more invested because they carry the unborn fetus, feed the newborn child, and typically have a significantly greater role in child rearing. There is also a tremendous disparity in the biological investments of the parents at conception: Whereas the male contributes just one sperm among the millions and millions of sperm he produces, the female contributes a much larger ovum (egg) that includes not just half of the genes but also the immediate nutrition and protection provided in what will become the placenta. Furthermore, females are generally capable of conceiving and bearing just one child at a time—notwithstanding relatively rare multiple births. In contrast, males can impregnate many women over the course of one partner's nine-month pregnancy. All told, the human female is by far the more invested sex. Consequently, because each pregnancy is much costlier for the female than for the male, she must be more selective in choosing mates in order to ensure that her child has both the "best" genes and the greatest likelihood of survival to its own reproductive age (Trivers, 1972).

Although both sexes want to maximize the likelihood of reproductive success, differences in biology and parental investment suggest that the sexes will demonstrate distinct, evolved partner selection strategies (Buss, 2003; Conroy-Beam, Buss, Pham, & Shackelford, 2015). Females would be expected to favor males who demonstrate the capacity to provide the resources and protection needed to successfully raise children. Therefore, females seek males who have these resources (e.g., wealth) or demonstrate the ability to obtain them (e.g., industriousness, intelligence, strength). Females should prefer males who have status, power, and material resources they are willing to commit to her and her offspring, as compared to those who do not. In contrast, evolutionary theory suggests that males should seek women who are disease-free and fertile and, therefore, likely to produce healthy offspring.

Sexual Selection: Genes that provide a reproductive advantage are more likely to be passed on to a new generation

Theory of Differential Parental Investment and Sexual Selection: Idea that (a) the sex that is more invested in the offspring will be more selective in choosing sexual partners, and (b) the less invested sex will engage in more intrasexual competition in order to gain access to the more invested sex

How do men "know" when a woman is healthy and fertile? For one thing, features associated with physical attractiveness—lustrous hair, full lips, smooth skin—suggest health (Ford & Beach, 1951; Hinsz, Matz, & Patience, 2001; Singh, 1995). In addition, characteristics suggestive of youth and fertility—such as large eyes and a smaller waist than hips—should also be preferred (Cunningham et al., 1990; Cunningham et al., 1995). In fact, males do typically prefer a figure with a rather specific waist-to-hip ratio of 7/10, which means that the waist is approximately 30% narrower than the hips (Singh, 1995). This ratio is particularly likely to be found in females who are at the height of their fertility, old enough to bear children but not yet menopausal, and not very thin or very heavy (Buss, 2003). Recently, Lewis, Russell, Al-Shawaf, and Buss found that men prefer a particular curvature from the lower back to the buttocks—a 45.5 degree, on average, irrespective of the size of the buttocks—perhaps because this would have allowed a pregnant woman to have maximal stability and to avoid falling while pregnant or carrying small children (Lewis, Russell, Al-Shawaf, & Buss, 2015)

A substantial amount of research supports the predictions of the evolutionary approach to mate selection (Eastwick, Luchies, Finkel, & Hunt, 2014; Gallup & Frederick, 2010; Hinsz, Stoesser, & Matz, 2013; Wood & Brumbaugh, 2009). For instance, Buss and his colleagues asked approximately 10,000 people from 37 cultures in 33 nations on six continents to rate the importance of 18 characteristics in potential mates (Buss, 1989). In general, the results were consistent with the predictions. Although males and females both ranked intelligence and kindness as most important, several key differences did emerge (Buss, 1989, 2003). Females valued mates with financial resources, social status, ambition, industriousness, and who are older than they are. In contrast, males preferred females who are younger and physically attractive. However, males in their teens actually prize *older* females because many of their peers and younger females have yet to reach sexual maturity (Kenrick, Gabrielidis, Keefe, & Cornelius, 1996). Similar results were found in a number of studies of personal ads, online dating services, and actual marriages, and in a variety of nations, including the United States, Canada, and India (Alterovitz & Mendelsohn, 2011; Gustavsson, Johnsson, & Uller, 2008).

Further Considerations on Mate Selection

Social Role Theory
Postulates that biological and social factors together can sufficiently explain sex differences in mate preferences

Although there is strong support for the evolutionary perspective, some investigators have suggested that there is more to the story. For instance, social psychologists Eagly and Wood (2012) propose a **social role theory** that postulates that biological and social factors together can sufficiently explain sex differences in mate preferences, thus dispensing with genetically based psychological propensities. First, they claim that, as a result of their smaller size, lesser strength, and childbearing status, females have long assumed less dominant roles in society. Second, these social roles in turn produce differences in social behaviors, such aggression, passivity, and emotional supportiveness. Social role disparities lead women to seek men who are dominant, of high status, and able to provide the material resources and protection needed to raise children. Since men have histori-cally controlled wealth and monopolized positions of power, women have had no choice but to obtain these through their male partners. In contrast, males seek females who are more likely to successfully fulfill their biological roles as mothers (young, healthy, attrac-tive) and social roles as caregivers in the family (peacemakers, nurturers, etc.).

Eagly and Wood's (1999) re-analysis of Buss's (1989) data showed, consistent with their hypotheses, that sex-based differences in mate preferences correlated with cross-cultural variations in socioeconomic conditions (Zentner & Mitura, 2012). That is, women's pref-erences for older, high-status, wealthy men, and men's preferences for younger, domesti-cally oriented women, were more pronounced in cultures where greater gender inequality existed and women had little access to resources, such as Kenya and Haiti, in contrast with those with more gender equality, such as the United States. The evolutionary argument is also rendered less compelling by the fact that females place a much greater emphasis on male physical attractiveness when seeking short-term rather than long-term partners (Li, Bailey, Kenrick, & Linsenmeier, 2002; Li & Kenrick, 2006), when they experience greater gender equality (Gangestad, 1993) and when they are rating real-world—as opposed to hypothetical—potential partners (Eastwick & Finkel, 2008). However, Gan-gestad, Haselton, and Buss (2006) found that, by controlling for variables not taken into account by Eagly and Wood (1999), variations in gender inequality *could not* account for gender differences in mate preferences.

It is important to note that the evolutionary argument does not postulate that gender-based preferences will never vary across time or context. For instance, women do not unwaveringly prefer fully masculine features in male partners. Although women who are ovulating favor masculine-looking men, women tend to prefer androgynous—that is more feminized—men at other times in their menstrual cycle (Perrett et al., 1998). Fur-thermore, evolutionary theory predicts that male and female mating strategies should vary in response to specific environmental conditions (Neuberg, Kenrick, & Schaller, 2010). Moreover, as people age and become more agreeable and communally oriented, they tend to prefer more similar traits in their opposite sex partners (Wood & Brumbaugh, 2009). For example, older females and males place less emphasis on sexually suggestive features and more on being sensitive, conventional, and formal, than do their younger counterparts (See Table 11.3).

Sexual Selectivity and Sexual Behavior

Whenever I introduce the topic of gender and sexual behavior, students inevitably comment about how males seem to seek more sexual partners, have lower standards for potential sexual partners, and think women are more interested in sex with them than they really are. As it turns out, each of these stereotypes has a kernel of truth. A number of studies—including one that had over 16,000 participants from around the world—have found that men are more interested in casual sex and in a greater variety of

TABLE 11.3   Mate Preferences Change With Age

Preference Increased With Age		Preference Decreased With Age	
Males	Females	Males	Females
Sensitive	Sensitive	Sexually suggestive	Sexually suggestive
Conventional	Conventional	–	Trendy
Formal	Formal	–	Smaller frame
Intelligent	Intelligent		
Well groomed	Well groomed		
Smiling	Smiling		

About 30,000 heterosexual men and women from around the world (including Europe, Asia, South Africa, Australia, the Middle East, and the United States) rated the attractiveness of males and females depicted in 98 photos. Across most regions older respondents preferred males and females who appeared to be more communally oriented (e.g., sensitive, friendly), and placed less emphasize on sexuality.

Source: Adapted from Brumbaugh, C. C., & Wood, D. (2012). Mate preferences across life and across the world. *Social and Personality Psychology Compass, 4*, 101–107.

sexual partners than are women (Greitemeyer, 2005; Schmitt, 2003; Shackelford, Goetz, LaMunyon, Quintus, & Weekes-Shackelford, 2004). In one study in which respondents were asked to indicate how many sexual partners they wanted during the next month, 25% of men but only 5% of women hoped for more than one (Schmitt, 2003). Another study showed that, over the course of their lifetimes, men would like more than twice as many sexual partners (7.69) as women (2.78) (Pedersen, Miller, Putcha-Bhagavatula, & Yang, 2002). Nevertheless, many members of both sexes hope to eventually settle down with a single, lifelong mate (Pedersen et al., 2002).

In addition, males do seem to have lower standards, at least for one-night stands involving just sex (Kenrick, Sadalla, Groth, & Trost, 1990). In one study done in 1989, male and female college students were approached by attractive opposite-sex strangers (confederates) and asked either whether they would "go out tonight," "come over to my apartment," or "go to bed with me" (Clark & Hatfield, 1989). Before asking the question, the confederate informed the participant she or he had previously noticed the participant on campus and thought that she or he was attractive. Can you guess the results? Not surprisingly, most men—in fact well more than half—readily agreed to the apartment and bed requests, whereas very few women agreed to the apartment and none to the bed requests. Men and women similarly responded to the date question, with about half saying yes.

Twenty years later, in a partial replication with students from the United States, Germany, and Italy, Schützwohl and his colleagues found that men were again much more likely to agree to going to the apartment or straight to bed than were women (although a few women did assent to the bed request) (Schützwohl, Fuchs, McKibbin, & Shackelford, 2009). These researchers also varied the attractiveness of the requestor and found that the requestor's attractiveness affected women's likelihood of saying yes to a greater extent than men's. Interestingly, perhaps the biggest reversal from the Clark and Hatfield study was that more men agreed to just the date than to either of the other requests. Finally, a recent study of over 21,000 heterosexual males and females indeed found that females tended to have more restrictive standards for mates than did males, except with regard to physical attractiveness, where males were more selective (Schwarz & Hassebrauck, 2012).

Not only are there gender–based variations in attitudes toward causal sex, but males and females also have different perceptions of the sexual interest of others in them. According to error management theory, humans possess cognitive biases in their perception of potential opposite sex partners that have evolved as responses to sex-based adaptive problems (Delton, Nemirow, Robertson, Cimino, & Cosmides, 2013; Haselton & Buss, 2000, 2009; Henningsen & Henningsen, 2010; Kohl & Robertson, 2014; McKay & Efferson, 2010). That is, males face the adaptive problem of finding females willing to procreate with them, whereas females must be able to find male partners who are willing to commit their resources to her and her offspring. Haselton and Buss (2000) argue that men tend to *overperceive* the sexual interest that women have in men, whether it be themselves or another man; that is, they "see" sexual interest, even when it is not present, by picking up on even the slightest cues.

Indeed, a plethora of studies have demonstrated that men do in fact exhibit this bias (Bendixen, 2014; Haselton & Buss, 2000; Henningsen, Henningsen, & Valde, 2006; Kunstman & Maner, 2011; La France, Henningsen, Oates, & Shaw, 2009). Given that females are more selective in choosing sexual partners than are males, the latter face the adaptive problem of finding females willing to reproduce with them. Therefore, they must be vigilant so as to detect any possible opportunity for sex and often commit this overperception bias. Haselton and Buss (2009) point out that the costs involved in overperception are minimal, typically amounting to no more than simple rejection, whereas the costs of missing actual opportunities could be the end of the man's genetic lineage.

As mentioned earlier, the more heavily invested female needs to secure the resources and protection of the less-invested male. An unconditional commitment by the male to the relationship is of paramount importance, and consequently females will require that a potential male meet a high threshold to convince her that he *truly* is committed. This need to be very confident in the commitment claims of the male will lead a female to *underperceive* or remain skeptical about the seriousness of that commitment. This underperception bias serves as a complement to the male overperception bias.

Romantic Jealousy

Admit it—most of us like it when our romantic partner expresses a little jealousy from time to time, such as when we give extra attention to or receive it from a possible alternative mate. Of course I am referring to jealousy of the mild, measured sort and not hostile, extreme, or violent jealousy. Like other evolved psychological tendencies, jealousy serves an adaptive function. What do you think it is?

Each semester I ask my students whether they would be more bothered if their romantic partner (a) had sex with *or* (b) become emotionally attached to another person. Although a difficult choice—either would be upsetting for the majority of people—most males select sexual infidelity and most females say emotional infidelity. Controlled research is consistent with my anecdotal findings. For example, one study found that approximately 60% of college males expected to be more bothered by potential sexual infidelity, whereas 83% of college females chose emotional infidelity (Buss, Larsen, Westen, & Semmelroth, 1992). A number of other researchers have replicated these results (Burchell & Ward, 2011; Guadagno & Sagarin, 2010; Schützwohl, 2004; Shackelford, Voracek et al., 2004). Why, do you suppose, men and women differ on this?

First, a definition of **romantic or sexual jealousy**: It is an uncomfortable psychological arousal that occurs in response to an infidelity threat to a romantic or sexual relationship (Buss, 2003; S. E. Hill, DelPriore, & Vaughan, 2011; Muscanell, Guadagno, Rice, & Murphy, 2013; Seiffge-Krenke & Burk, 2015). Second, jealousy is understood to be a form of *mate guarding* that can help prevent the loss of a partner via *mate poaching* (Adams & Williams, 2014; Buss, 2000; Zengel, Edlund, & Sagarin, 2013). Expressions or suggestions of jealousy-based responses can ward off others from trying to steal or poach one's partner as well as deter one's partner from engaging in infidelity.

Buss and others further argue that, since the consequences of infidelity are not the same for the two sexes, the experience of jealousy is also different. Males are faced with the problem of **paternity uncertainty**, which refers to the fact that they have, historically, never truly known whether the children of their female partners are genetically the male's own (Buss, 2003; Buss et al., 1992; Goetz & Shackelford, 2009). Romantic jealousy—especially when particularly focused on sexual infidelity—helps to reduce that uncertainty. In contrast, the loss of the male's investment in the offspring, which becomes more likely if the male develops an emotional attachment to another female—threatens the survival of the offspring, and thus presents an adaptive problem for the female. In fact, female jealousy is heightened when the male partner flirts with increasingly attractive women, and male jealousy was stronger if his partner flirted with a dominant male (Dijkstra & Buunk, 1998). Although some investigators have questioned the validity of the sex differences in jealousy (Harris, 2003, 2005), most of the research supports this finding (Ward & Voracek, 2004). Research has obtained similar results in countries as varied as Mexico, Hungary, and Ireland (Buunk & Hupka, 1987), for noncollege-aged adults (Tagler, 2010), for situations involving actual infidelity (Zengel et al., 2013), and for online threats to infidelity (Guadagno & Sagarin, 2010).

Romantic or Sexual Jealousy: An uncomfortable psychological arousal that often occurs in response to an infidelity threat to a sexual relationship

Paternity Uncertainty: Fact that throughout evolutionary history males have never really known whether the children of their female partners are truly genetically their own

Think Again!

1. *Try listing traits that you think are more likely to have survived as a result of sexual selection than natural selection and vice versa.*

2. *Try stating, in your own words, the two primary hypotheses of the theory of differential parental investment.*

3. *Can you think of any species in which the male is more invested in the offspring than the female? Which sex would you expect to be the choosier sex and why?*

WHAT IS LOVE?

The phrase *"love is a many splendored thing,"* the title and theme song of a popular 1955 American movie, suggests that love is not as simple as it may at first appear. Pause for a minute and write down 10 or so words that you associate with love. Ask a friend or partner to do the same and compare lists to see how much you agree. When I ask my students, their

© Marc Dozier/Corbi.

Love is a many splendored thing.

answers frequently mention honesty, caring, trust, supportive, sexual passion, physical attraction, among others. These features cover a wide range of emotions, thoughts, and behaviors that would be very difficult to distill into a simple definition. Because of love's inherent complexity, psychologists have generally resisted the one-definition-fits-all approach, preferring instead to focus on the varieties of love. In this section we will examine several prominent attempts to understand the nature and components of love.

Passionate and Companionate Love

One of the most influential perspectives on love emerged from early research that identified two types of love: passionate and companionate (Hatfield & Walster, 1978). **Passionate love** is an intense longing for union with another person, characterized by physiological arousal, strong attraction, and frequent thoughts about that person (Lieberman & Hatfield, 2006). Passionate love that is reciprocated brings fulfillment and ecstasy but, when unreciprocated, despair and emptiness ensue (Baumeister, Wotman, & Stillwell, 1993). Passionate love tends to be associated with the early stages of relationships (at least in Western cultures) and is often referred to as erotic love, obsessive love, or infatuation.

Passionate Love: Intense longing for union with another person, characterized by physiological arousal, strong attraction, and frequent thoughts about that person

Companionate Love: Feelings of affection and intimacy that occur in the context of a relatively stable, trusting relationship that may or may not involve passionate love

In order to more closely study it, Hatfield and Sprecher (1986) developed The Passionate Love Scale, which reliably measures individual experiences of passionate love within the context of a romantic relationship. Take a look at the sample items in Table 11.4 to get a feel for how this may be measured (also see this chapter's Self-Reflection for an alternative perspective). In contrast, **companionate love** refers to feelings of affection and intimacy that occur in the context of a relatively stable, trusting relationship that may or may not involve passionate love (Hatfield & Rapson, 1993). Companionate love also describes our close nonsexual or platonic friendships.

Triangular Theory of Love

A second influential psychological approach to love posits *seven* different types of love that result from combinations of three basic components: passion, intimacy, and commitment (Madey & Rodgers, 2009; Sternberg, 1986). These three elements can be represented as the points on a triangle in which the lines represent their presence or absence, and various combinations produce the seven forms of love (see Figure 11.2). Sternberg's passion and intimacy aspects correspond to passionate and companionate, respectively. Passion is closely

TABLE 11.4   The Passionate Love Scale

Hatfield and Sprecher's (1986) Passionate Love Scale asks respondents to indicate, using the scale below, how they felt the last time they were passionately in love with someone. Here only 10 of the 30 items are listed.

Not at all true				Moderately true				Definitely true
1	2	3	4	5	6	7	8	9

1.	Since I have been involved with _____, my emotions have been on a roller coaster.
2.	I would feel deep despair if _____ left me.
3.	Sometimes I can't control my thoughts; they are obsessively on _____.
4.	I'd get jealous if I thought _____ were falling in love with someone else.
5.	I yearn to know all about _____.
6.	I melt when looking deeply into _____'s eyes.
7.	I sometimes find it difficult to concentrate on work because thoughts of _____ occupy my mind.
8.	I want _____ to know me—my thoughts, my fears, and my hopes.
9.	In the presence of _____, I yearn to touch and be touched.
10.	I possess a powerful attraction for _____.

Source: Hatfield, E., & Sprecher, S. (1986). Measuring passionate love in intimate relationships. *Journal of Adolescence, 9*, 383–410.

tied to sexual desire and is a *motivation* for romantic love. (See this chapter's Self-Reflection to see how passion might be measured.) Intimacy refers to the closeness or bond between two individuals and can be thought of as love's *emotion* aspect. Finally, the commitment component represents the decision to love another and to make a long-term commitment to that person and as such is largely *cognitive*. Although the decision to love someone and the commitment to that person do not necessarily go together, they often coincide.

According to Sternberg (1986), the type of love that people ultimately seek in romantic relationships is *consummate love,* which incorporates all three components. Love that includes only passion is called *infatuation,* only intimacy is termed *liking,* and only commitment is called *empty love.* Hooking up is often at least partially based on infatuation. In addition to the other types of love shown in the figure, Sternberg described *nonlove* as the absence of all three components, a condition that applies to casual interactions with strangers or acquaintances.

Two-Factor Theory

One characteristic of sexual attraction is physiological arousal. Yet, given that physiological arousal can stem from a wide variety of activities, including exercise, caffeine, and a

FIGURE 11.2   Triangular Theory of Love

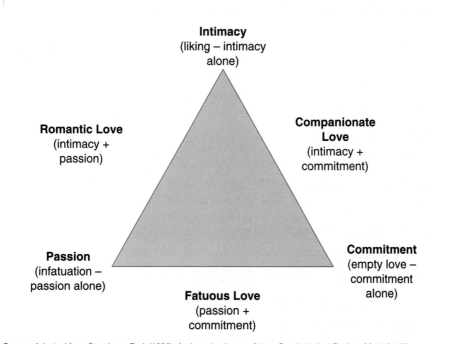

Source: Adapted from Sternberg, R. J. (1986). A triangular theory of love. *Psychological Review, 93,* 119–135.

rollercoaster ride, why do people sometimes interpret the arousal as interpersonal attraction? More broadly, how do we know what we are feeling? According to the **two-factor theory of emotion**, two distinct processes together lead to the experience of specific emotions: general physiological arousal (increased pulse, faster breathing, sweaty palms, etc.) and an emotion label (Mezzacappa, Katkin, & Palmer, 1999; Moors, 2013; Schachter, 1964; Schachter & Singer, 1962). Stanley Schachter argued that arousal generated by many different sources feels the same, regardless of its source. Consequently, a second step must occur before we can experience specific emotions, such as love, fear, or anger. That is, we must *attribute* that arousal to an identifiable cause, which we do by searching the environment for a likely trigger. That trigger could, for example, be another person or some other proximal stimulus. According to Schachter and Singer (1962), we may sometimes *misattribute* the arousal to an environmental stimulus that had little to no effect and thus inaccurately label our emotional state. This theory nicely illustrates how emotions are a product of both the person and the situation—what we are feeling depends on the situation we are in.

An inventive field experiment by Donald Dutton and Arthur Aron (Dutton & Aron, 1974) provided additional support for the two-factor theory. Imagine that you were a male visiting the Capilano Suspension Bridge Park in British Columbia, Canada. You arrive at the park and decide to cross a 230-foot long suspension footbridge that spans a 450-foot deep gorge. The bridge is made of five-foot long wooden planks that are held together by thick wires, and it bounces and sways in the wind as you walk. Midway across the bridge you are stopped by an attractive woman who explains that she is conducting an experiment. She asks you to complete a survey, shows you a picture, and requests that you write a brief story about that picture. The picture is intentionally ambiguous—the woman is bent over, hand across her face, outside of a room in which a man lies on a bed. After you complete the tasks, the experimenter offers you her phone number and invites you to call her later if you have any questions about the study. Unbeknownst to you, other participants encounter the same experimenter and complete identical tasks, but do so while crossing a much sturdier solid bridge just 10 feet above the ground.

Dutton and Aron were primarily interested in differences between the conditions on two measures. First, they expected that participants on the high bridge would be more likely to call the experimenter and, second, that their stories would contain more sexual language, versus those on the low bridge. Can you guess why? Dutton and Aron (1974) hypothesized that the physiological arousal created by the high, unsteady bridge would be attributed to and labeled as sexual attraction for the experimenter, and this in turn would lead the men to both inject sex into their stories and to call her. In other words, the men would look to their environment for the cause of their arousal and, because an attractive woman was present, would interpret the arousal as sexual attraction to her. Dutton and Aron's hypotheses were supported; the experienced emotion was a product of general arousal *plus* a label.

Although Schachter and Singer's two-factor theory has received a fair amount of empirical support, a number of studies have produced inconsistent or contradictory results (Ruys, Aarts, Papies, Oikawa, & Oikawa, 2012). For instance, one study found that even

Two-Factor Theory of Emotion. Idea that the experience of emotion is comprised of two distinct processes: general physiological arousal and an emotion label

SELF-REFLECTION 11.1
How Passionate Is Your Relationship? (Part 1)

The main text describes the triangular theory of love that conceptualizes consummate love as composed of passion, intimacy, and commitment. Although Sternberg (1986) considered passion to be part of love and roughly equivalent to sexual desire, this is not the only way to understand it. For instance, Vallerand and his colleagues view romantic passion as broader than love in that it contains both desire and decision or commitment (Ratelle, Carbonneau, Vallerand, & Mageau, 2013; Vallerand et al., 2003). Take a few minutes to answer the following and then turn the page to learn more about romantic passion.

TABLE 11.5   Romantic Passion Scale

Think about your current or a past romantic relationship when responding.

Item	Response options						
	Strongly disagree	Disagree	Some-what disagree	Undecided	Some-what agree	Agree	Strongly agree
1. My partner allows me to live memorable experiences. (HP)	1	2	3	4	5	6	7
2. I'm completely carried away by my relationship with my partner. (HP)	1	2	3	4	5	6	7
3. My relationship with my partner is in harmony with my other life domains. (HP)	1	2	3	4	5	6	7
4. The new things that I discover within our relationship allows me to appreciate my partner even more. (HP)	1	2	3	4	5	6	7
5. For me, my relationship with my partner is a passionate one but one that I'm still able to control. (HP)	1	2	3	4	5	6	7
6. My relationship with my partner reflects the qualities I like about myself. (HP)	1	2	3	4	5	6	7
7. My relationship with my partner allows me to live varied experiences. (HP)	1	2	3	4	5	6	7
8. I can't manage without my partner. (OP)	1	2	3	4	5	6	7
9. I'm emotionally dependent on my partner. (OP)	1	2	3	4	5	6	7
10. My mood depends on whether I can see my partner. (OP)	1	2	3	4	5	6	7
11. I have difficulty controlling my need to see my partner. (OP)	1	2	3	4	5	6	7
12. I have almost obsessive feelings for my partner. (OP)	1	2	3	4	5	6	7
13. I have difficulty imagining my life without my partner. (OP)	1	2	3	4	5	6	7
14. The urge is so strong, I cannot separate from my partner. (OP)	1	2	3	4	5	6	7

Source: Ratelle, C. F., Carbonneau, N., Vallerand, R. J., & Mageau, G. (2013). Passion in the romantic sphere: A look at relational outcomes. *Motivation and Emotion, 37*, 106–120.

TURN THE PAGE TO FIND OUR ANSWERS.

SELF-REFLECTION 11.2
How Passionate Is Your Relationship? (Part 2)

To determine your score, add up your responses and divide by 14 to obtain your average overall rating of the passion in your relationship. These 14 items compose the Romantic Passion Scale, and it is designed to measure two more specific kinds of passion: *harmonious* and *obsessive* (Ratelle et al., 2013; Vallerand et al., 2003). People feel harmonious passion when they willingly enter and remain in a romantic relationship, and this relationship, while important, does not consume people's lives. People feel obsessive passion when they are more strongly driven or compelled to be with their partner and feel as if the passion controls them. Unlike harmonious passion, which can easily coexist with other aspects of a person's life, obsessive passion can undermine or hinder those because a person is focused primarily on their relationship. In addition to providing an overall measure, you can calculate your level of each type by averaging its seven corresponding items (HP = harmonious passion, OP = obsessive passion). Feel free to compare your scores to other students, but what might be more interesting is if you were to compare your evaluation of your relationship with your partner. Try that—how closely do your ratings match up? If they are significantly different, why might that be the case?

when men were told their physiological arousal was caused by exercise they just completed, they still reported greater sexual attraction for a target female (Allen, Kenrick, Linder, & McCall, 1989). Despite the controversial nature of these findings, one conclusion that can be drawn with confidence is that people are most likely to generate mistaken attributions when they are uncertain about the actual cause of their arousal (Reisenzein, 1983).

An Evolutionary Perspective

The final perspective on love that we will discuss is the evolutionary one, which focuses on the *function* of love rather than its components. As you know, evolutionary psychologists view emotions and other aspects of human psychology as mechanisms that evolved as solutions to particular adaptive problems. Humans are unique in the primate world because our offspring are vulnerable for a relatively long portion of their lives. Consequently, they require the effort, energy, and protection of both the mother and the father over the course of many years. In order to ensure that both parents remain involved in the child rearing, a bond of some sort must emerge. This bond, according to evolutionary psychologists, is love, and love is, in short, a commitment device (Buss, 2003). The evolutionary argument posits that love also serves a number of other functions critical to successful long-term relationships, including increasing the likelihood of sexual fidelity, providing easy sexual access to the partner, and signaling parental investment (Buss, 1988). Not very romantic, is it?

If love is rooted in our evolutionary heritage, then we should expect to find evidence for it across all cultures and across time (See photo). Indeed, researchers engaging in archival research have examined historical and anthropological records that indicate the existence of passionate love everywhere from ancient Sumer to isolated groups in Micronesia and Kenya (Schmitt, 2006; Sprecher et al., 1994). Cross-cultural research has found that large percentages of people all over the world report being "in love" at any given time (Sprecher et al., 1994). Data collected from interviews with 1667 women and men found that 63% of women and 41% of men in Japan, 73% and 61%, respectively, in Russia, 63% and 53%, respectively, in the United States were "in love" (Sprecher et al., 1994). Additional evidence for the universality of love comes from research in which

Jupiterimages/Creatas/Thinkstock.

BananaStock/BananaStock/Thinkstock.

Love is a cultural universal.

Jupiterimages/Creatas/Thinkstock.

people are asked whether or not they would marry someone in the absence of loving that person. In Levine et al.'s 11-nation survey, college students from eight nations—including the United States, England, Japan, and Mexico—overwhelming reported that they would not marry someone they did not love, even if their would-be partner possessed all of the other qualities that the respondent thought were important (Levine, Sato, Hashimoto, & Verma, 1995). In the study mentioned earlier, Sprecher et al. (1994) found that no more than 20% of American and Japanese respondents said they would marry without love, with Russians being a little higher (37%). Although some cultural variation in conceptions of love does exist, many of these differences are quickly disappearing as a result of Westernization and globalization (Lieberman & Hatfield, 2006).

Think Again!

1. *Consider the different types of love in Sternberg's model. Which have you experienced, and when?*

2. *How might you take advantage of your knowledge of the two-factor theory of emotion while trying to woo a potential mate?*

3. *If love is, at its base, merely a commitment device, why don't people see it that way?*

4. *Compare and contrast the two "passion" scales in this chapter. What differences do you notice and how do you explain them?*

Love on the Brain

The experience of love has also garnered significant attention from social neuroscientists (Acevedo, Aron, Fisher, & Brown, 2011; Fisher, 2006). According to biological anthropologist Helen Fisher (2006), there are three brain systems associated with love: the attraction/romantic love, lust/sex drive, and attachment systems. These three emotion/motivation systems overlap and interact, jointly directing courtship, mating, reproduction, and parenting. Fisher and her colleagues have conducted numerous studies that have shed light on the patterns of brain activation associated with various aspects of these systems (Acevedo et al., 2011; Aron et al., 2005). For instance, one such study used fMRI to examine participants' neural responses to the viewing of faces of individuals in various types of relations with them (Acevedo et al., 2011). Each of the 10 women and seven men were in long-term monogamous romantic relationships characterized by self-reported intense love. While undergoing fMRI, participants looked at photos of their own long-term partner, a close (platonic) long-term friend, a highly familiar person with whom they were not emotionally bonded, and a person with whom they were not that familiar. As expected, the researchers found much greater activation in two brain regions—specifically, in the right ventral tegmental area (VTA) and the caudate nucleus—in response to the romantic partner compared to the other individuals. Furthermore, these differences in brain activity are closely connected to the brain's dopamine system, which is associated with rewards and motivation. Interestingly, these patterns of brain activation were in many ways similar to patterns found in persons who were experiencing new love relationships (Aron et al., 2005).

Same-Sex Attraction

During our discussion of evolution, mate preferences, and romantic love, my students usually ask how same-sex attraction and same-sex relationships fit into the picture. Worded differently, if reproduction is the ultimate underlying motive for romantic relationships, then why would people be attracted to those of their own sex? A great question, especially if you consider the fact that people who engage exclusively in same-sex relationships would have no direct progeny and therefore their unique gene pool would cease to exist. The same argument does not apply to bisexuality, as their same-sex attraction, even if very strong, would not preclude having children—such as in the case of the Irish poet and writer, Oscar Wilde (Miller, 2000).

How common is homosexuality? First of all, there are plenty of examples of sexual activity between members of the same sex in other species, including bonobos, macaques, and over 400 other species (de Waal, 2005). Second, estimates of homosexual behavior in humans vary, but seem to hover around approximately 2% to 4% of men and 0.5% to 2% of women (Burri, Cherkas, Spector, & Rahman, 2011). Homosexual behavior is likely present in all societies and cultures and has been documented on all six settled continents. Third, the homosexuality-heterosexuality distinction is not always a clear one. Not only do some people self-identify as bisexual, others may change their sexual preference over the course of their lives (Chivers, Seto, & Blanchard, 2007). For example, in the Sambian culture in New Guinea, boys aged seven to 15 routinely provide oral sex for older boys, then become the recipient for a few years, and finally, after settling down with a female partner, they become exclusively heterosexual (Herdt, 2006). In general though, women seem to display more *erotic plasticity* or changes in sexual desires for women and men over the course of their lives (Diamond, 2003, 2007; Herdt, 2006; Vrangalova & Savin-Williams, 2012).

AP Photo/Natacha Pisarenko.

Researchers are trying to understand why some people are more strongly attracted to members of the same sex than are other people.

Although there is no scientific consensus regarding the origins of same-sex attraction, researchers have offered a number of plausible explanations (LeVay, 2011). Some evolutionary psychologists have argued that, at least for males, homosexuals confer benefits to heterosexual relatives—including nieces and nephews—by providing them with the resources that would otherwise be expended on their own children (Vasey & VanderLaan, 2012, 2014). The fact that sisters of gay men may be more fertile and consequently have need of greater support from their brothers lends support to this notion (Vasey & VanderLaan, 2010). The social psychologist Daryl Bem (2000) proposed instead that the genetic influence on sexual orientation is indirect. Genes strongly influence childhood temperament, and this leads some boys to play more with girls and some girls to play mostly with boys. Consequently, when these kids grow into adolescence and reach puberty, they see members of their own sex as *exotic,* which, says Bem, makes them more *erotic.* Although Bem's *exotic becomes erotic* theory is intriguing, it has yet to receive substantial empirical support (Peplau, Garnets, Spalding, Conley, & Veniegas, 1998).

Finally, there is some evidence for a biological basis for homosexuality, at least for men. Researchers point to brain differences between gay and straight men (LeVay, 1991) as well as to the fact that the concordance of homosexual orientation between identical male twins is much higher than would be expected by chance (Bailey, Dunne, & Martin, 2000). However, a very recent study of 4,426 British identical or fraternal twin females found that genetic factors explained about 25% of the variation in sexual orientation and 31% of gender nonconformity (defined in terms of engaging in behavior atypical for one's sex during childhood) (Burri et al., 2011). In sum, much more research is clearly needed to uncover the evolutionary, biological, and nonbiological influences on same-sex attraction.

Attachment Style

Attachment Style: Patterns of expectations, needs, and behaviors a person typically exhibits in close relationships

We have spent quite a bit of time discussing what constitutes love and friendship, and why such relationships exist. In this section, we talk about some of the factors that affect the types of relationships people prefer: attachment style. **Attachment style** refers to the patterns of expectations, needs, and behaviors a person typically exhibits in close relationships. John Bowlby and his colleagues formulated attachment theory in the context of their studies of young children's relationships to their parents and primary caregivers (Bowlby, 1982). According to Bowlby (1982), infants have an innate propensity for forming strong bonds with their primary caregiver that facilitate protection and survival. Other psychologists extended attachment theory, hypothesizing that these early attachments form the basis of later connections with significant others, especially romantic partners (Hazan & Shaver, 1987; Mikulincer & Shaver, 2007).

Although early research provided evidence for three styles of attachment (Hazan & Shaver, 1987), more recently psychologists have identified two major dimensions along which attachments vary and have consequently added a fourth style (Collins & Feeney, 2004). These two dimensions, anxiety and avoidance, refer to mental models of the self and other, respectively (see Figure 11.3). Briefly, the anxiety dimension reflects the positivity (or negativity) of a person's self-worth and refers to a person's desire for a close, dependent relationship with a partner, along with concern that the partner will be available and responsive. The avoidance dimension reflects discomfort with a close, dependent relationship coupled with a fear of intimacy and desire for emotional distance.

Crossing these two dimensions produces four attachment styles: secure, anxious/ambivalent or preoccupied, dismissing avoidant, and fearful avoidant (Chopik & Edelstein, 2014; Collins & Feeney, 2004; Shaver & Mikulincer, 2012b). *Secure* individuals have both low anxiety (high self-worth) and avoidance, are comfortable with close relationships, and are not afraid of dependence or of abandonment. *Preoccupied* individuals have high anxiety (low self-worth) and low avoidance; they desire close relationships with others who can validate the self, but they also worry about abandonment. *Dismissing* avoidant persons have low anxiety (high self-worth) and avoid close relationships, essentially dismissing them as unnecessary. Finally, people who exhibit the *fearful* avoidant style have high anxiety (low self-worth) and high avoidance and tend not enter into close relationships.

These four attachment styles have ramifications for close relationships (Shaver & Mikulincer, 2012a). Secure individuals are comfortable entering into committed, stable,

FIGURE 11.3   The Four Attachment Styles

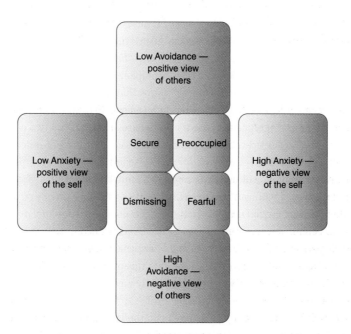

Source: Adapted from Griffin, D. W., & Bartholomew, K. (1994). Models of the self and other: Fundamental dimensions underlying measures of adult attachment. *Journal of Personality and Social Psychology, 67*, 430–445.

close relationships. Preoccupied persons want excessively close relationships but need constant reassurance that their partner will not abandon them. Dismissing individuals develop relationships that are marked by low commitment and emotional distance. Fearful persons do not trust their partners and will keep them at a safe emotional distance.

The dominant attachment pattern that people develop also affects their sex lives. For instance, securely attached individuals tend to have healthy sex lives that are relatively problem free. In contrast, those who are dismissive or fearful avoidant seem to prefer sex without emotional intimacy, are more likely to have one-night stands and many sex partners, and engage in sex to garner prestige and popularity (Schachner & Shaver, 2004). People with a preoccupied or anxious attachment style also have many sexual experiences but tend to do so in order to please potential or actual partners and to increase emotional intimacy, even when they may not want to have sex (Bogaert & Sadava, 2002; Schachner & Shaver, 2004).

DOING RESEARCH: EXAMINING INTERPERSONAL RELATIONSHIPS

As you know, studying people scientifically poses a number of challenges, many of which social psychologists have been able to overcome through carefully designed and controlled studies, sophisticated statistical techniques, and innovative technological applications. We have addressed a number of those challenges in other chapters. Here we'll focus on several concerns that arise primarily when studying platonic and romantic interpersonal relationships (Berscheid, 1999; Campbell & Rubin, 2012; Finkel, Eastwick, & Reis, 2015; Reis, Aron, Clark, & Finkel, 2013). First of all, since by definition relationship science investigates phenomena that exist *between* people, its object is essentially invisible (Berscheid, 1999). Second, relationships emerge from the interactions between two people—what we call a *dyad*—and are more than the sum of their parts (Gonzalez & Griffin, 2004). Thus, even if we gather data separately from each member of a dyad, we are likely to miss significant elements of their relationship that we could only glean by collecting data from them during their interaction. Examples of potential data of interest include measuring eye contact, physical proximity, or the authenticity of smiles during conversations. Recall our discussion in Chapter 5 about how Gottman (Gottman & Levenson, 1999, 2000) was able to predict relationship longevity by *observing* brief interactions between married couples—something he obviously could not do via other research methods. A third obstacle that relationship scientists encounter is the difficulty of getting ongoing participation from both partners, especially if it requires coming into a laboratory setting. The experimenters can alleviate this problem in a variety of ways, such as by offering special incentives for continued study participation and completion or allowing for maximum flexibility in scheduling.

Although observing couples' behavior in the laboratory can be quite useful, the vast majority of their interactions occur out in the real world. While it is possible to ask research participants to report in the lab on experiences that transpired at home, these self-reports are subject to the limitations that we described in Chapter 4, such as misremembering and various biases. In addition, we are unable to recreate the "relationship situation" in the laboratory, and data collected there may not reflect real-world interactions. One technique for minimizing this is called **event sampling** or **experience sampling,** and it requires that participants report on their life experiences while they are happening or just after they have happened. For instance, in one study, college students were asked to record social interactions that lasted at least 10 minutes during specific weeks in the academic year (Nezlek, 1993). The purpose of this research was to examine student adjustment during the first year, and students reported their interactions during several two-week periods across that year. One of the many findings was that students experienced increased consistency in their interactions with close friends over the course of the year, suggesting that they were in fact adjusting to college life. Event sampling is useful but not perfect and is just one of dozens of other data collection methods that have helped scientists to better understand the dynamics of interpersonal relationships.

> **Event Sampling or Experience Sampling:** Obtaining participants' report on their life experiences while they are happening or just after they have happened

Think Again!

1. _What do you think of the "exotic becomes erotic theory" of same sex attraction?_

2. _Say you were going to participate in a relationship study that involved event sampling. Do you think that knowing that you were supposed to be reporting on particular feelings or behaviors might change what you feel or do? Would you be more or less likely to be honest if you were reporting electronically versus in person, in a lab?_

3. _What kinds of relationship behaviors would be more or less difficult to study in the laboratory?_

RELATIONSHIP SATISFACTION

The early stages of romantic relationships—when people report falling or being "in love"—are flowing with excitement, novelty, and passion (Hatfield & Rapson, 1987). As mentioned above, the experience of falling in love seems to be culturally universal, even if not all people experience it in precisely the same way (Hendrick & Hendrick, 2006). Unfortunately, the emotional highs and overly positive perceptions of one's partner that so often typify the beginning of a relationship—the intense passion—tend to diminish over time (Traupmann & Hatfield, 1981). Fortunately, though, that gradual reduction in passion is often counterbalanced by a strengthening of intimacy and commitment.

Positive Illusions

People who are satisfied in relationships often hold **positive illusions** about the traits and attributes of partners (Barelds & Dijkstra, 2011; Dijkstra, Barelds, Groothof, & van Bruggen, 2014; Gordon, Johnson, Heimberg, Montesi, & Fauber, 2013). That is, they typically perceive their partner to be higher on many characteristics (attractive, intelligent, etc.) than the partners see themselves (Murray, Holmes, & Griffin, 1996). Moreover, they often demonstrate biases that reflect an overly optimistic view of the relationship itself and view it as better than the relationships of other people (Murray & Holmes, 1994). For example, in one five-year longitudinal study of dating couples, the partners rated their relationship as higher in satisfaction, love and affection, and commitment at each of five recording times than at the prior recording times (Sprecher, 1999). However, the actual ratings showed *no change* in these ratings over that time, indicating that the couples' beliefs that the relationship continually improved were inaccurate; in some of these cases, the relationship in fact went downhill (Levenson & Gottman, 1983).

What is the impact of positive illusions on actual relationship satisfaction? The answer may depend on what stage the relationship is in. Some research shows that when people are dating, they tend to prefer it when partners judge them in an overly optimistic way (De La Ronde & Swann, 1998). In contrast, some research indicates that in longer lasting, more committed relationships, accuracy is closely tied to satisfaction, perhaps because what we really want is a long-term partner who sees us accurately and accepts both our good and bad characteristics. However, other researchers argue that idealization may contribute to long-term happiness, which suggests that people might consider withholding their most negative attributes from their partners (Murray et al., 2011; Murray et al., 1996).

Self-Disclosure

The fact that positive illusions can help to maintain a relationship does not imply that people should refrain from sharing their true selves, including their less flattering thoughts, feelings, and experiences with their partners, in an effort to maintain those illusions. On the contrary, genuine self-disclosure is one of the hallmarks of a successful, satisfying relationship, and it plays a critical role in whether or not the relationship develops into a long-term bond (Altman & Taylor, 1973; Derlega, Winstead, & Greene, 2008). Typically, self-disclosure between partners includes a wider range of topics—increasing breadth—as well as a more intimate, personal, and sensitive issues—greater depth—over time (Altman & Taylor, 1973). For instance, prerelationship or early relationship conversations may go no deeper than weekend plans or superficial family history, whereas later they may extend to emotional insecurities or family problems. Why does self-disclosure follow this pattern? In general, we like those who self-disclose because it suggests that they like or trust us, and the act of self-disclosing to others leads us to like them more (Collins & Miller, 1994). Obviously, self-disclosure must be a two-way street: We are unlikely to continue to share intimate details with someone unless that person engages in reciprocal disclosure.

Attributions

In addition to self-disclosure, the kinds of attributions people make about their partners are also linked to satisfaction. Those who are more satisfied engage in *relationship-enhancing attributions* that help to maintain these rosy perceptions (Bradbury, Fincham, & Beach, 2000; Fincham, Beach, & Davila, 2007). For instance, individuals perceive the positive behaviors of their partners as because of internal, dispositional factors and the negative ones as resulting from external, situational ones, consistent with the fundamental attribution error (Ross, 1977). In contrast, couples who are dissatisfied exhibit *distress-maintaining attributions,* which reflect the opposite pattern: internal attributions for undesirable behaviors and external attributions for desirable ones (Graham & Conoley, 2006; Miller & Rempel, 2004). It interesting to note that, upon breaking up, people may reexamine their earlier, positive perceptions of the relationship—essentially throwing a splash of cold reality on them, resulting in more balanced or, perhaps overly negative, assessments (Vaughn, 1986).

Satisfaction Over Time

How does relationship satisfaction change over time? Well, it depends. First, in love marriages, relationships that are most commonly associated with the Western world, satisfaction tends to decline. A 10-year longitudinal study of 522 newlyweds by Kurdek (1999) revealed two stages at which the drop-off was most evident: during the first year, and again during the eighth year (see Figure 11.4). The first dramatic reduction may not surprise you, as it corresponds to adjustment following the traditional honeymoon period. The reasons for the second decline are less clear, but it is interesting to note that it roughly matches up to the so-called "seven-year itch." Karney and Bradbury (1997) conducted a smaller study of 60 newlywed couples over four years and found a similar decrease in satisfaction during the first year. The decrease was steeper in couples who were less satisfied at the outset as compared to those who were initially more satisfied. Interestingly, in both of these studies male and female satisfaction declined at about the same rates, although females were generally more satisfied throughout the relationships.

Second, in contrast to the studies just mentioned of heterosexual relationships, same-sex couples tend not to show the same rapid decrease in satisfaction, although the reason for this is not clear (Kurdek, 2008). Finally, people in arranged marriages may experience an *increase* in love over time. In one study of 50 Indian couples, mutual love was initially lower among those in arranged marriages but was significantly higher in comparison to levels in love marriages after ten years (Gupta & Singh, 1982).

FIGURE 11.4   Marital Satisfaction Over Time

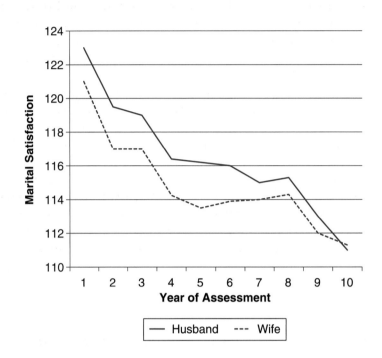

Source: Adapted from Kurdek, L. A. (1999). The nature and predictors of the trajectory of change in marital quality for husbands and wives over the first 10 years of marriage. *Developmental Psychology, 35*, 1283–1296.

DATING IN THE VIRTUAL WORLD

This chapter would not be complete without a discussion of online dating, because, like the hook-up culture described earlier, it is a rapidly growing and influential factor in romantic relationships (Finkel, Eastwick, Karney, Reis, & Sprecher, 2012; Lin & Lundquist, 2013). According to a Pew study, 37% of single individuals seek a romantic partner through online dating sites (Madden & Lenhart, 2006). There are two major questions my students ask when we discuss online dating: Does it work, and do people really tell the truth about themselves?

First, as you probably know, the major dating sites use sophisticated algorithms in their efforts to create compatible pairings. Sizable numbers

DATING IN THE VIRTUAL WORLD
Tinder and other apps have given rise to "mobile dating" by helping people hook up with others in their physical vicinity.

© Iain Masterton/incamerastock/Corbis.

of heterosexual (22%) and same-sex couples (61%) report meeting online (Finkel et al., 2012), and some evidence indicates that these relationships are more likely to persist for two years than are those that begin with face-to-face encounters (Bargh & McKenna, 2004). Nevertheless, after an extensive review of the literature, Finkel et al. conclude that, overall, dating that is initiated online is no more successful than dating that begins with in-person interactions (Finkel et al., 2012).

Second, the potential for deception in advertising the self is obviously much greater in the virtual world, and users are indeed wise to be skeptical of the photos, profiles, and claims of others (Hancock & Toma, 2009; Toma & Hancock, 2010). For instance, one study found that people engage in subtle, perhaps even nonconscious, deception by virtue of the photos that they post online (Hancock & Toma, 2009). Independent judges compared people's profile photos with those taken during the study, and they concluded that almost one-third of the profile photos were misleading (e.g., they made the person look better than he or she really was). Furthermore, another study by the same research team revealed that people who were less attractive were more likely to post deceptive photographs, sometimes by digitally manipulating them (Toma & Hancock, 2010).

Think Again!

1. *Name and describe the two dimensions along which attachment varies.*

2. *What are the advantages and disadvantages of online dating as opposed to in-person dating?*

3. *What kind of attachment style do you think you have? What about your current (or past) romantic partner? How do you think these styles have impacted your relationship?*

FINAL THOUGHTS: DOES FACEBOOK MAKE YOU LONELY?

One of the most intriguing research questions about friendship and love is understanding the ways in which technology has changed them in recent decades, yet not losing track of the elements that have remained the same over the last 10,000 years. Whereas the fundamental human needs that motivate friendship and love—the need to affiliate, to belong, to find mates and reproduce, and so forth—are based in our evolutionary past, new forms of interpersonal relationships have emerged and profoundly altered the social landscape in contemporary society. Although computer technology and the Internet have provided the basis for these changes, perhaps the most visible and recent shaper of this new landscape is Facebook. As of this writing, there are well over 1.2 billion active users of Facebook strewn across the world. Not surprisingly, psychological research on Facebook and other social networking sites has begun in earnest, appearing in our most prestigious journals and conferences (Wilson, Gosling, & Graham, 2012). Before I conclude this chapter, I'd like to briefly touch on the possible relationship between Facebook and loneliness.

On the one hand, one would expect that people would feel *less* lonely because they have easy access to most of their friends, acquaintances, and often family. They can keep in touch with people in their social networks, even across geographic distances, and monitor their activities, see photos, engage in discussions, and send private messages. On the other hand, much of online communication is relatively superficial and not particularly focused on meaningful topics and events. Moreover, the specific motivations individuals have for spending time on Facebook and how they interact with it may impact how satisfying they find the experience (Burke, Marlow, & Lento, 2010; Wilson et al., 2012).

For instance, a correlational study found that people who are relatively passive while looking at their newsfeed may be more likely to feel lonely after spending time on Facebook as compared to more active users who click and comment on postings (Burke et al., 2010). In another study, college students randomly assigned to the experimental group were asked to artificially increase the frequency of their status updates, whereas those in the control condition were given no Facebook-related instructions (Deters & Mehl, 2013). Participant scores on a loneliness scale were compared before and after the study, and the experimental participants became significantly *less* lonely, whereas the control participants' loneliness did not change. Deters and Mehl (2013) argued that the decrease was because of a greater feeling of social connectedness produced by the additional updates. More recently, Steers, Wickham, and Acitelli (2014) studied several hundred college students who were frequent Facebook users and found that, in general, individuals who spent more time engaging in social comparison (discussed in Chapter 4) experienced more depressive symptoms. As interesting as these early findings are, at this point much more research is needed before we can draw firm conclusions about the cost and benefits of omnipresent electronic social networking on our social well-being.

Given the depth and breadth of the topic, a chapter on relationships is particularly hard to summarize. What I hope you got out of the discussion above is that social psychologists understand friendship and love to be complex and multifaceted phenomena resulting from evolutionary pressures and shaped by social, cultural, and individual forces. Both affiliation and love strongly affect and, in turn, are themselves influenced by the self and our sociality. The *self* cannot thrive in isolation but needs relationships with others—in short, our *sociality*—to remain healthy and sound.

CORE CONCEPTS

- People have fundamental needs to affiliate and to belong and participate in communal and exchange relationships to help fulfill them; the lack of healthy connections with others and rejection by others can lead to problems with both mental and physical health.

- The reinforcement-affect model and social exchange theory are two complementary theories that help explain who we develop and maintain relationships with; liking, proximity and familiarity are important predictors of friendship and liking.

- Physical attractiveness has a number of benefits: People who are physically attractive tend to be popular, more socially skilled, and receive shorter prison sentences.

- Darwin postulated a second evolutionary process (in addition to natural selection), called sexual selection. The theory of differential parental investment proposes that male/female differences in mate preferences stem from sexual selection, which has two elements: intrasexual competition and intersexual selection. Social role theory postulates that male/female differences in mate preferences are because of biological and social factors.

- Passionate love is an intense longing for union with another person, whereas companionate love refers to feelings of affection and intimacy. The triangular theory of love proposes seven types of love that reflect varying amounts of passion, intimacy, and commitment.

- According to two-factor theory, love—like other emotions—consists of physiological arousal and an attributional label that identifies an environmental cause of the arousal.

- Researchers have developed specific procedures, such as event sampling, to overcome obstacles to studying relationships.

- Attachment style can predict relationship qualities and duration; relationship satisfaction tends to diminish over time; positive illusions and self-disclosure can improve relationship satisfaction.

▶ $SAGE edge™ Test your understanding of chapter content. Take the practice quiz. edge.sagepub.com/barrett

KEY TERMS

➤ ⑤SAGE edge™   Review key terms with eFlashcards.
edge.sagepub.com/barrett

THINK FURTHER!

- What are the two primary emotional needs that interpersonal relationships fulfill? What kinds of relationships are more likely to fulfill one or both?

- For what types of relationships might the reinforcement-affect model and social exchange theory predict different outcomes? In other words, when are the models complementary, and when are they exclusive?

- Take a look at the situational influences on who we like. Think about how they might have contributed to the development of relationships with one of your acquaintances, close friends, and current or former romantic partner.

- People often state that *beauty is only skin deep*. Given the research described in this chapter, do you think that this is always true?

- How is sexual selection different from natural selection? Can you come up with some examples of each?

- How does the finding that love and satisfaction decline fit with the evolutionary explanation of the function of love?

- How could you "diagnose" someone's attachment style from their behavior?

- The text mentions how changes over time differ for love and arranged marriages. Why might that be so?

SUGGESTED READINGS

Back, M. D., Schmukle, S. C., & Egloff, B. (2008). Becoming friends by chance. *Psychological Science, 19,* 439–440.

Buss, D. M. (2003). *The evolution of desire: Strategies of human mating* (Rev. ed.). New York, NY: Basic Books.

Dion, K., Berscheid, E., & Walster, E. (1972). What is beautiful is good. *Journal of Personality and Social Psychology, 24,* 285–290.

Finkel, E. J., Eastwick, P. W., Karney, B. R., Reis, H. T., & Sprecher, S. (2012). Online dating: A critical analysis from the perspective of psy-chological science. *Psychological Science in the Public Interest, 13,* 3–66.

Reiber, C., & Garcia, J. R. (2010). Hooking up: Gender differences, evolution, and pluralis-tic ignorance. *Evolutionary Psychology, 8,* 390–404.

WANT A BETTER GRADE?

Get the tools you need to sharpen your study skills. Access practice quizzes, eFlashcards, web exercises, and multimedia at edge.sagepub.com/barrett

⑤SAGE edge™

12

Group Processes

Soccer fans rioting
at a soccer match between
Al-Ahly and Al-Masry
in Egypt in 2012.

© STRINGER/epa/Corbis.

LEARNING OBJECTIVES

12.1 Define group, groupiness, social selection, common-identity and common-bond groups, cohesiveness, and entitativity.

12.2 Summarize the early research on social facilitation and examine how the three theories discussed in the chapter explain it.

12.3 Discuss social loafing and free riding, explain why they occur, how to prevent or reduce them; describe deindividuation, Zimbardo's explanation for it, and the social identity alternative explanation.

12.4 Outline the ODDI; analyze the groupthink model, including its major antecedents, symptoms, and risks, and the strategies to prevent it; describe group polarization and compare and contrast the three explanations for it.

12.5 Compare and contrast majority and minority influence and explain conversion theory, social comparison and validation routes, and what minorities can do to maximize their influence.

12.6 Identify the major advantages and disadvantages of the case study approach.

12.7 Describe the great person, contingency, and social identity perspectives on effective leadership, transactional and transformational leaders, and the research on gender and leadership.

⑤SAGE edge™

Get the edge on your studies.
edge.sagepub.com/barrett

Take a quiz to find out what you've learned.
Watch videos that enhance chapter content.
Explore related web and social media activities.

SPORTS-RELATED RIOTS

On February 1, 2012, 74 people were killed during a riot that began after a soccer (football, to people outside the Americas) game in Egypt between rivals El Masry and Al Ahly. Although there had been some relatively minor scuffles in the stands during the event, what became the deadliest soccer riot in recent history began almost immediately after the game-ending whistle was blown, with the final score three to one. As angry fans flooded the field, police and military personnel mostly stood aside and watched the violence unfold, choosing not to intervene. The locker rooms were transformed into veritable emergency rooms where fans who had been trampled, stabbed, or otherwise bloodied were brought for shelter and care. Eventually the fighting subsided, but the incident spurred additional violent clashes between citizens and security forces in the ensuing days. Unfortunately, this was not an isolated incident. In the past few years, similar, albeit less deadly, sports-related riots have occurred in cities around the world, including Buenos Aries, Sydney, Montreal, and Los Angeles.

Although pinpointing the precise causes of the Egypt riot is difficult, social psychological research has identified a number of factors that affect how people behave in group situations. A few of these have been covered earlier in this book, such as overt requests from others and unspoken social norms prescribing or proscribing specific behaviors. The current chapter focuses our analysis of social psychology on the nature of groups, group behavior, and group influence. For instance, people's ability to perform a specific task can be either improved or worsened simply by the presence of others, and we'll examine the conditions under which one or the other occurs. Our extended discussion of this phenomenon, *social facilitation,* will illustrate the complexity of social behavior and is also a nice example of the self-corrective nature of science.

One important theoretical approach to behavior in groups that we will revisit is social identity theory, which we discussed earlier in the context of stereotyping. Social identity theory helps to explain bonds between group members, the relationship between the self and the group, and also why some leaders are more effective than others. This chapter also examines some of the pitfalls of group decision-making and the nature of effective leadership. The Doing Research section evaluates the pros and cons of case studies.

Several of our fundamental questions of human existence, including sociality, the self, and rationality, are clearly relevant to group-based behavior. *Sociality* is of course located at the core of group living, and the human propensity for cooperating with others and developing and maintaining alliances evolved along with communal existence itself. The *self* is implicated in group processes with regard to the social identity component of the self and the ways in which involvement in groups can result in either the expression or the inhibition of the self. Groups can also interfere with good decision-making by suppressing or distorting *rationality*.

Think Ahead!

1. *What is a group, and why do we join them?*

2. *Do people work harder or perform better in a group or when alone?*

3. *What makes group leaders effective?*

THE NATURE OF GROUPS

What Is a Group?

When you conjure up the image of a group, what do you picture? The audience at a concert? The band on the stage? Perhaps you and a couple of friends participating in an online chat about the concert the next day? Or a special interest group on Facebook devoted to the band? As different as each of these entities is, all are often characterized as groups. Here, we'll define a **group** as two or more individuals who perceive themselves as part of a unit and who influence each other and are interdependent. There are four key elements to this definition.

First, a group (obviously) includes at least two people. You may wonder why two is considered a group, since we typically refer to two people as a couple or pair. That is a good question. The reason is that once a second person is added to the mix, we start seeing the mutual influence and interdependence that are commonly associated with a group. In other words, the *psychological* difference between one and two is far greater than that between two and three. While we will focus primarily on groups of three or more, keep in mind that many of the principles and findings from research on larger groups will also apply to dyads or pairs.

The second component of the definition is that the individuals must perceive themselves to be members of a group—if they do not believe they are in a group, then it makes

Group: Two or more individuals who perceive themselves as part of a unit and who both influence each other and are interdependent

little sense for us to say they are. Third, the individuals must influence each other to some degree, and this requires some form of interaction. Fourth, they must be interdependent, which means that they share a common goal. Go back and look at the examples above as well as the ones that you thought of. Do they qualify as groups?

One of the problems with being too strict with our definition is that it sometimes forces us to draw an artificial line between groups and nongroups, even though it can be difficult to draw that distinction. Therefore, it is easier to think about groups in terms of **groupiness** or the degree to which a collection of individuals is grouplike (Cartwright & Zander, 1960; Moreland, 1987; van Veelen, Otten, & Hansen, 2013). For instance, some sets of individuals clearly constitute a group, such as a close-knit family or a professional basketball team. Yet other collections of individuals would not be accurately described that way, such as strangers in a shuttle van to the airport who do not interact. Nongroups, such as the van occupants, can become groups, however. For example, if the shuttle gets stuck in the mud and the passengers work together to pull it out, then the set of occupants becomes more grouplike.

Groupiness: Degree to which a collection of individuals is grouplike

Why We Join Groups

Humans are among the most social of all species, and groups are so pervasive that it is almost impossible to imagine life without them (Wilson, Van Vugt, & O'Gorman, 2008). With the possible exception of a self-sufficient hermit living alone in the mountains, all humans would identify themselves as members of at least one group. Take a moment and reflect on why groups are so prevalent. What are the benefits of group membership?

The reasons people have for joining and forming groups should be somewhat familiar, as they overlap with the purposes of developing and maintaining affiliative and romantic relationships. First, joining groups can help satisfy our needs for affiliation and belongingness (Chapter 11) (Baumeister & Leary, 1995). Second, groups can accomplish tasks that individuals simply cannot. For instance, one person cannot pull a van out of a ditch or wage war. Third, there are many activities that groups can perform more easily or efficiently, such as building a house. A person could build a house on her own, but that would obviously take much longer. Fourth, groups can help to protect us and our families. Finally, individuals can obtain material resources and information through our group affiliations that would otherwise be unattainable. For example, becoming part of a network of traders allows a person in London to eat pineapples or other tropical fruit without traveling to the tropics. Accurate information received from others can also be essential to survival, such as when we learn about dangers posed by the environment or by other groups (Levine, 2013).

Evolutionary theorists argue that group life is not simply an optional way of meeting specific needs but rather is an essential part of our evolved human nature—what I refer in this text to our *sociality,* and what others term *ultrasociality* (Crosier, Webster, & Dillon, 2012; DeWall & Richman, 2011; Neuberg & Cottrell, 2006; Portin, 2015; Turchin, Whitehouse, François, Slingerland, & Collard, 2012). In other words, humans as we

Social Selection:
Genes that facilitate successful social living are more likely to be passed to a new generation

know ourselves would not exist were it not for our immersion in groups. The importance of group living is such that specific traits needed for successful social living may have been selected for, a process known as **social selection** (Van Vugt & Kameda, 2013). As we discussed in Chapter 1, some individual traits may have evolved because they help benefit the group via a process called group selection (Wilson et al., 2008). For instance, the human capacity for empathy may be the result of pressures to cooperate with ingroup members when resources are threatened by outgroups.

Think Again!

1. *Take a few minutes and try to count how many groups (including subgroups) you participate in on a given day—I bet the number will be higher than you expect.*

2. *Why do social psychologists prefer the use of "groupiness" over "group"?*

3. *Can you think of any reasons people join groups not mentioned above?*

KEY FEATURES OF GROUPS

Types of Groups

It is obvious that not all groups are alike. One important distinction is between two kinds of groups based on the primary bonds that hold them together. The first, called **common-identity groups**, are built upon the attachments members have to the group itself, even in the absence of direct interaction among group members (Prentice, Miller, & Lightdale, 1994; Ufkes, Otten, Van der Zee, Giebels, & Dovidio, 2012). People are members of these groups by virtue of their identification with the group as a whole, derive part of their *social identity* from them, and normally will not know many or most of the other members (Tajfel & Turner, 2010; Turner, Hogg, Oakes, Reicher, & Wetherell, 1987). Ethnicities, nationalities, and university communities are examples of common-identity groups.

The second type are **common-bond groups**, which are primarily based on the attachments that members have to each other (Prentice et al., 1994). Members of common-bond groups typically know each other and regularly interact. Sports teams—such as El Masry and Al Ahly mentioned at the beginning of this chapter—are common-bond groups, as are work teams and students collaborating in small groups on a class assignment. The strength of an individual's attachment to the common-bond group can vary from weak to strong but is weaker than the bonds members have to each other (Prentice et al., 1994). Before reading further, take a moment and write down two to three of the common-identity and common-bond groups that you belong to.

Common-Identity Group: Group primarily based on the attachments members have to the group itself (rather than to other members), even in the absence of direct interaction among group members

Common-Bond Group: Group primarily based on the attachments that members have to each other (rather than to the group itself)

Cohesiveness

As you may know from experience, some groups are relatively close knit—what psychologists call cohesive—whereas other groups have looser connections among members. **Group cohesiveness** refers to the strength of the bonds that hold the members together and keep them in the group (Cartwright & Zander, 1960; Karau & Williams, 1997). Highly cohesive groups have a strong sense of "we-ness" and, because they cooperate to achieve common goals, are more likely to be successful in comparison to less cohesive groups (Ellemers, De Gilder, & Haslam, 2004). For instance, basketball and other sports teams that are cohesive work more closely together to finish plays and, consequently, win more games (Carron, Colman, Wheeler, & Stevens, 2002). Which—the high performance or high cohesion—is the cause, and which is the effect? Although the mere correlation cannot tell us, carefully controlled studies can. The research shows that it can work both ways: Cohesiveness often leads to better group performance, but also group success enhances cohesiveness. However, the bulk of the evidence suggests that the impact of cohesiveness on success is more potent than that of success on cohesiveness (Castaño, Watts, & Tekleab, 2013; Tekleab, Quigley, & Tesluk, 2009; van Woerkom & Sanders, 2010).

> **Group Cohesiveness:** Strength of the bonds that hold group members together and keep them in the group

Entitativity

One of the hallmarks of cohesive groups is that they are easily identifiable as groups. That is, outside observers can easily conceptualize that particular collection of individuals as a true group, which is a characteristic called **entitativity** (Brewer, 2015; Campbell, 1958; Effron & Knowles, 2015). Loosely formed groups, such as citizens of the United States—who vary considerably in appearance, ethnicity, and so forth—are low in entitativity, whereas tightly formed groups—including uniformed sports teams or families—are high (Lickel et al., 2000). When group members are very similar, interact frequently, share goals, and rank the group as important, then they are considered high on this dimension (Ip, Chiu, & Wan, 2006; Lickel et al., 2000). How collections of individuals fall on the cohesion and entitativity dimensions largely determines their level of groupiness, as illustrated in Figure 12.1. Sets of individuals are more like groups as cohesion and entitativity increase. Sets with very low cohesion and low entitativity are not very grouplike.

> **Entitativity:** Extent to which outside observers can easily conceptualize a collection of individuals as a true group

Thinkstock Images/Stockbyte/Thinkstock.

A GROUP WITH HIGH ENTITATIVITY

High entitativity groups are easy to recognize as groups.

FIGURE 12.1   Groupiness

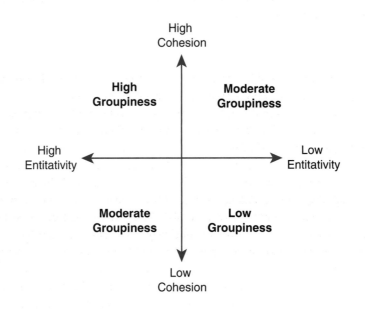

Social Norms

Social norms—a concept that we explored in the context of social influence in Chapter 6—constitute another important feature of groups. Norms are rules, typically unwritten, about how people should or should not behave. As you may recall, Sherif's (1966) research on the *autokinetic effect* demonstrated how social norms can develop over time and be transmitted among members. For instance, norms may influence people to engage in or refrain from certain behaviors, use particular words, or adopt specific attitudes, such as prejudice toward outgroups. Indeed, they can develop quite rapidly to bring member behavior into alignment with a particular standard. Bryant and Marmo (2012) examined norms governing appropriate and inappropriate behavior on Facebook. On the one hand, there are explicit rules that a person must consent to when joining the network (e.g., do not bully or intimidate, refrain from illegal activity, etc.). On the other hand, the regular Facebook users they studied identified a number of implicit norms pertaining to interaction with others.

REUTERS/Eric Thayer.

For example, users should not engage in behavior that hurts their Facebook friends or that is deceptive but should occasionally post on their friends' walls and comment on their postings (Bryant & Marmo, 2012).

Roles

Social norms are not the only factor influencing behavior in groups. People take on roles—which may be voluntary or dictated by the group—that prescribe (direct) or proscribe (restrict) what people do (Bales, 1958). For example, members of a military squad may occupy a variety of roles, including captain, communications officer, medic, and so forth. One advantage of such role differentiation is that groups will often be more productive as a result, especially when roles are clearly defined (Lu, While, & Barriball, 2008). However, when roles are ambiguous, people are assigned roles that do not match their skills and abilities, or they simultaneously hold two or more roles that conflict with one another, performance is likely to decrease (Talley, Kocum, Schlegel, Molix, & Bettencourt, 2012; van Veelen et al., 2013). A basketball player who is also the coach has to balance two very different roles and consequently may not fulfill either well and may detract from team performance. In a meta-analysis that included over 11,000 participants in 74 studies, Tubre and Collins (2000) found that productivity reliably decreased the less clearly defined the roles and responsibilities of group members were. Think about it: If you are working with other students on a complex class project, would you be more likely to produce a higher quality paper if each member knew precisely what her or his responsibilities were or if the roles were ambiguous?

Think Again!

1. _Consider various religious groups and cults that you have some knowledge of. Would you place them in the common-bond or common-identity category, and why?_

2. _What do you think are the most important social norms on Facebook or another social media site that you belong to?_

3. _What are common consequences of violating social norms in groups that you belong to?_

GROUPS AND BEHAVIOR

Groups Can Improve Performance: Social Facilitation

How do you feel about giving a class presentation? Many of my students tell me that the very thought of it stirs feelings of anxiety and fear of looking foolish and makes their heart pound and their palms sweat. Other students, though, look forward to such an opportunity with excitement. As you'll see, the degree of comfort you have about performing in front of groups partially depends on how confident you are in your presentation skills, which in turn is related to how finely honed those skills are.

The relationship between performance and the presence of others was initially explored by Triplett in the late 19th century (Stroebe, 2012; Triplett, 1897). You may recall from Chapter 1 that Triplett observed that children turned a fishing reel more quickly when competing against other children and concluded that competition *enhanced* individual performance. Some subsequent research was consistent with Triplett's work, and more broadly found that the *mere presence* of others—even when they were only observing and not competing—led to better performance (Cottrell, Wack, Sekerak, & Rittle, 1968).

However, the inference that social situations produce better outcomes was challenged by research by Ringelmann (also mentioned in Chapter 1) and others who found that the presence of others *decreased* performance (Aiello & Douthitt, 2001). Poorer performance in group-based situations has been found across a wide variety of situations, including driving (for new drivers) and billiards (for unskilled players) (Michaels, Blommel, Brocato, Linkous, & Rowe, 1982; Rosenbloom, Shahar, Perlman, Estreich, & Kirzner, 2007). This reduction can appear in the strangest places—even public restrooms, where

FIGURE 12.2   Social Facilitation

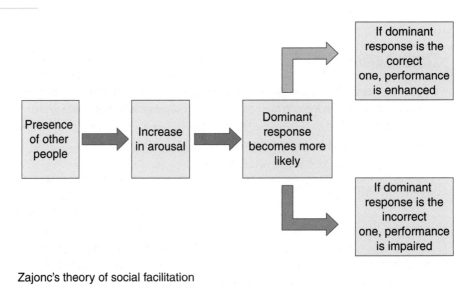

Zajonc's theory of social facilitation

Source: Adapted from Zajonc, R. B. (1965). Social facilitation. *Science, 149*, 269–274.

the proximity of other men can increase the amount of time it takes a man to begin urinating (Middlemist, Knowles, & Matter, 1976).

Okay, so which is it—does the presence of others enhance or inhibit performance? Well, like many other aspects of social behavior, it depends. In 1965, social psychologist Robert Zajonc published a paper that resolved these contradictory findings (Zajonc, 1965). He argued that the presence of others improves performance on well-learned or easy tasks but decreases it on novel or difficult ones, a phenomenon known as **social facilitation** (Feinberg & Aiello, 2006). Stated differently, an organism's *dominant* response becomes more likely in the presence of others, whereas the *nondominant* response becomes less likely. If the dominant response is the correct one, then performance is said to have improved; however, if it is the incorrect one, then performance is worsened (see Figure 12.2).

For example, a person who is a skilled free throw shooter will sink more shots in front of an audience than when alone. In contrast, an unskilled player will likely make fewer shots in the presence of others versus alone. In one study, college students played better billiards when they had an audience but only if they were already relatively skilled (Michaels et al., 1982). Otherwise, they did worse. The existence of social facilitation has been demonstrated in a large number of studies conducted on humans across a variety of tasks and in other species, including rats and cockroaches (Rosenbloom et al., 2007; Zajonc, 1965). Zajonc and his colleagues found that cockroaches ran a straight path—an easy task—more quickly, but solved a maze—a difficult task—more slowly in the presence of other cockroaches than when alone (Zajonc, Heingartner, & Herman, 1969).

Explaining Social Facilitation

Psychologists have offered a number of different explanations for social facilitation. Zajonc (1980a) proposed that the **mere presence** of others while one is performing a task leads to physiological arousal, which in turn affects how well the person does it. But this explanation is incomplete: Mere presence does not always affect performance and does not always cause arousal (Guerin, 1986). Therefore, one or more other processes must be involved (Blascovich, Mendes, Hunter, & Salomon, 1999).

One of the reasons that people may be less successful in the presence of others lies in their self-presentational concerns. That is, people often worry about how others are going to judge their performance, something social psychologists refer to as **evaluation apprehension** (Cottrell, 1972; Feinberg & Aiello, 2006). Evaluation apprehension improves completion of easy or well-learned tasks but can have the opposite effect for difficult or novel ones (Seta, Crisson, Seta, & Wang, 1989). For example, if you enjoy public speaking, you may do better when you expect to be evaluated than if you do not. Similar results have been found for solving math problems or completing other nonphysical tasks (Kors, Linden, & Gerin, 1997; Park & Catrambone, 2007). This explanation, however, is

Social Facilitation:
Presence of others improves performance on well-learned or easy tasks but decreases it on novel or difficult ones

Mere Presence:
Presence of others while one is performing a task leads to physiological arousal, which in turn affects how well the person performs

Evaluation Apprehension:
Concern about how others are going to judge one's performance

also not the whole story, as social facilitation has been found in the absence of evaluation and in species in which evaluation is not likely to be a concern, such as cockroaches (Platania & Moran, 2001).

Given the shortcomings of the mere presence and evaluation apprehension explanations for social facilitation, psychologists have proposed a third one: that the presence of other people can siphon off our attention, leading to a performance decrement (Huguet, Galvaing, Monteil, & Dumas, 1999). This **distraction-conflict theory** hypothesizes that the actor is distracted from focusing on the task at hand, thereby creating a conflict between the need to concentrate on that task while minimizing the distraction caused by others, and distraction tends to interfere only with performance for difficult or novel tasks (Baron, Moore, & Sanders, 1978). Once again, however, distraction does not always lead to task impairment and therefore by itself cannot fully explain social facilitation (Huguet et al., 1999).

As you can see, the evidence for social facilitation is both wide and deep. Not only are its effects seen in face-to-face situations, but they are even found when the observer is a virtual human (see Research Box 12.1). At the same time, social psychologists have expended considerable effort in attempting to explain social facilitation. Which explanation is correct? Well, it appears that each of them is valid in some circumstances or conditions and that, as a whole, they illustrate how complex social behavior can require multiple explanations (Nijstad, 2013). The history of social facilitation research nicely illustrates how science is a process of discovery rather than a set of findings carved in stone.

Groups Can Degrade Performance: Social Loafing and Free Riding

As we mentioned at the beginning of the last section, research by Ringelmann and others demonstrates how the presence of others can decrease our performance. Ringelmann was particularly interested in situations where efforts are pooled—group members are working together—and a single group output is produced. An example of this is trying to push a car out of a ditch: If there are multiple people working together, each person pushes less vigorously than if she had been alone. Following Ringelmann, the psychologist Ivan Steiner (1972) postulated two reasons for the reduction in individual performance that lowers group output (as compared to the hypothetical output, were individual productivity simply added up). First, completing tasks in groups can sometimes reduce peoples' *motivation* to work hard. That is, they don't try as hard. Second, poor *coordination* of activities among individuals in groups can lead to inefficient task performance and reduced productivity.

I am sure that you have had experience working in groups, whether for class projects or paid jobs, in which one or more members seemed to slack off a bit. Why do you suppose your fellow group members or people working in groups more generally choose not to work as hard when in groups? Social psychological research suggests two primary explanations: social loafing and free riding (Nijstad, 2013).

Distraction-Conflict Theory: Idea that the actor is distracted from focusing on the task at hand, thereby creating a conflict between the need to concentrate on that task and minimizing the distraction caused by others

RESEARCH BOX 12.1
SOCIAL FACILITATION IN THE VIRTUAL WORLD

Hypothesis: Performance of a simple task will be enhanced in the presence of a virtual human, but performance of a difficult task will be impaired.

Research Method: Participants completed anagrams, mazes, and mathematical computations that were either simple or difficult. Tasks were completed either alone, in the presence of a human, or in the presence of a virtual human face on a computer that exhibited simple facial expressions and occasionally blinked. The independent variables were presence (alone, a human present, or a virtual human present) and task complexity (simple, difficult). The dependent variable was task completion time.

Results: The results confirmed the hypothesis. For difficult tasks, completion times were significantly longer when either a virtual human or actual human was present as compared to when the participant was alone. For simple tasks, presence reduced completion time.

Conclusion: The presence of a virtual human produced the expected social facilitation effects.

Source: Park, S., & Catrambone, R. (2007). Social facilitation effects of virtual humans. *Human Factors, 49,* 1054–1060.

When individuals exert less effort when working in a group as opposed to when working alone, they are exhibiting **social loafing** (Latané, Williams, & Harkins, 1979; Ying, Li, Jiang, Peng, & Lin, 2014). Social loafing is particularly likely in situations where individual contributions to the group output are not identifiable, such as in Ringelmann's rope-pulling task or in pushing a car (Ingham, Levinger, Graves, & Peckham, 1974; Williams, Harkins, & Latané, 1981). People often socially loaf when other group members or evaluators are unable to determine or assess that they are not doing their fair share.

Why does working in groups reduce individual effort? Social psychologist Bibb Latané and his colleagues designed several clever experiments intended to better understand social loafing (Latané et al., 1979; Williams et al., 1981). The advantages of these studies were that individual contributions to the group output were identifiable, and thus the experimenters

Social Loafing:
When individuals exert less effort when working in a group as opposed to working alone

could assess how hard each person worked. Participants in one study—who were blind-folded and placed in soundproof rooms but wore headsets through which the experimenters could manipulate the sounds they heard—were asked to shout as loudly as possible, either alone or in groups of two or six persons (Latané et al., 1979). Unbeknownst to the partici-pants, some of the two- or six-person groups were actually fake or pseudo groups, and in those trials the participants falsely believed they were shouting with other participants.

Latané et al. (1979) found that participants' individual efforts depended on whether or not they believed that others were shouting at the same time. Although overall pooled sound output increased as group size increased, it did not do so to the extent that would be expected by simply adding the individual contributions. People slacked off during group performance. Importantly, these researchers were able to differentiate between loss of motivation and loss of coordination. Participant effort was lower in pseudo groups as compared to shouting alone where there was no need for coordination and only moti-vation mattered. It was even lower still in the actual groups where coordination of effort did matter, reflecting productivity loss because of both reduced motivation *and* lack of coordination. The basic findings of the Latané et al. experiments have been supported by many other studies conducted in situations ranging from working collaboratively on a farm, playing soccer (European football), and swimming in a relay (Hoeksema-van Orden, Gaillard, & Buunk, 1998; Høigaard & Ommundsen, 2007; Miles & Greenberg, 1993).

Free riding (Brooks & Ammons, 2003; Swaray, 2012) occurs when individuals reduce their effort because they believe that their contribution to the group task is dispensable or not important to the overall group output (Kerr, 1983). Consequently, they get something for nothing, such as a meal without paying for it or a good grade on a class project by piggybacking on the efforts of others. For instance, a person with limited skills or ability with regard to a par-ticular group task—such as renovating a house—may not work as hard because she feels that her contribution won't make much of a difference to the overall project (Kerr & Bruun, 1983).

Free Riding: When group members exert little or no effort because they believe that their contribution to the group task is dispensable or not important to the overall group output

Solutions to Social Loafing and Free Riding

Psychologists have offered several research-based solutions to social loafing and free rid-ing. First, make sure that individual contributions are identifiable. Second, see that they feel valued by ensuring that members believe that each effort is critical to successful task completion (Shepperd & Taylor, 1999). Third, keep groups relatively small, because that can increase individual accountability (Aggarwal & O'Brien, 2008). Fourth, set goals that are meaningful or important to members, so that they are motivated to work hard to accomplish them (Karau & Williams, 1993).

Social Loafing Across Cultures

Social loafing becomes more likely when people are less committed to group outcomes. This negative correlation between loafing and commitment implies that individualists,

SELF-REFLECTION 12.1
How Much Do You Like Group Work? (Part 1)

Many work environments (and some college classes) require that employees (and students) work cooperatively to plan, achieve tasks, and complete projects. For a variety of reasons, some people (and some students) prefer to do things on their own and not in a group. The below scale is one way to measure people's preferences for group work. Take a minute to answer the following and then turn the page to learn more.

TABLE 12.1   Preference for Group Work

Item	Response options				
	Strongly disagree	Disagree	Undecided	Agree	Strongly agree
1. When I have a choice, I try to work in a group instead of by myself.	1	2	3	4	5
2. I prefer to work on a team rather than individual tasks.	1	2	3	4	5
3. Working in a group is better than working alone.	1	2	3	4	5
4. Given the choice, I would rather do a job where I can work alone rather than do a job where I have to work with others in a group.	1	2	3	4	5
5. I prefer to do my own work and let others do theirs.	1	2	3	4	5
6. I like to interact with others when working on projects.	1	2	3	4	5
7. I personally enjoy working with others.	1	2	3	4	5

Source: Wagner, J. A. (1995). Studies of individualism-collectivism: Effects on cooperation in groups. *Academy of Management Journal, 38*, 152–172.

TURN THE PAGE TO FIND OUR ANSWERS.

SELF-REFLECTION 12.2
How Much Do You Like Group Work? (Part 2)

To determine your score, first reverse score Items 4 and 5 (1 = 7, 2 = 6, 3 = 5, 4 = 4, 5 = 3, 6 = 2, 7 = 1) and then add up your responses. Next divide by seven to obtain your average response. These items are actually part of a larger scale of individualism-collectivism, but these specific questions are designed to measure a person's preference for group work (PGW) (Shaw, Duffy, & Stark, 2000; Stark, Shaw, & Duffy, 2007; Wagner, 1995). Shaw and colleagues (2000) administered the scale to 566 students in 17 upper-level business administration courses—all of which include substantial group work—and obtained a mean of 4.49. They found that females preferred group work more than males and that, in general, GPA was negatively correlated with liking group work. How does your score compare to this and to students in your class? What do you think of the items in the scale? Do they adequately capture what they are trying to measure?

who are less group-focused than collectivists, should be more likely to loaf. In other words, the stronger bonds that collectivists have toward their group should discourage them from reducing effort when working in their groups. This is in fact what empirical research reveals (Haslam, 2004). Moreover, although social loafing certainly is not absent among collectivists, it is less common among East Asian collectivists (Karau & Williams, 1993; Klehe & Anderson, 2007). For instance, in one study of ninth graders, Chinese children actually worker harder in pairs than they did when alone, whereas American children showed the opposite pattern (Gabrenya, Wang, & Latané, 1985). However, if the group norm is that members do not need to work hard, then norm-following collectivists may instead be more likely to loaf (Hong, Wyer, & Fong, 2008). Finally, social loafing is negatively related to preference for group work (PGW): People who don't like group work tend not to put in as much effort as those who do (Stark et al., 2007).

Think Again!

1. *Can you think of times when your performance on a task has been affected by the presence of others? Which explanation seems most relevant in those examples?*

2. *Can you come up with any other possible explanations for social facilitation?*

3. *Imagine you were a manager at a small store or restaurant. What concrete steps could you take to prevent social loafing among your employees?*

LOSING ONESELF IN THE GROUP: DEINDIVIDUATION

At the outset of this chapter, we described instances in which soccer fans displayed surprising, atypical, and violent behavior at the conclusion of high-stakes matches. These incidents both shock and puzzle many observers, especially because the individuals involved are normally law-abiding citizens. Aspects of the situation interact with features of the person, and the result is that some individuals appear to feel free to disregard social norms regarding sportsmanship and the humane treatment of others. In these cases, the boundary between individuals and groups is temporarily dissolved, such that the individual no longer feels as if she exists separate from the group. Social psychologists refer to this state of immersion in a group as **deindividuation**, which is defined as a psychological state characterized by loss of self-awareness and the sense of personal responsibility (Zimbardo, 1969). Deindividuation is likely to occur when people are anonymous, experience a reduced sense of individuality, and do not feel personally accountable for their behavior; it has been primarily associated with negative, often violent, behavior (Hughes & Louw, 2013; M. Levine & Cassidy, 2010; Staub, 2003; Zimbardo, 1969).

In one fun study of 1,352 Halloween trick-or-treaters mentioned in Chapter 1, Diener and his colleagues measured how much candy children took from houses under a variety of conditions (Diener, Fraser, Beaman, & Kelem, 1976). The experimenter posed as the homeowner and told the children to take one piece of candy from a bowl on the porch while he left them alone by going back into the house. Before disappearing into the house, the experimenter randomly asked some children their names and where they lived but asked nothing of the remaining children. The researchers unobtrusively counted how many *extra* pieces of candy children took either when they were alone or in a group, and found that those who were both anonymous and in a group grabbed the most (See Table 12.2).

In a more serious study, Zimbardo (1969) had women participants dress in Ku Klux Klan (KKK) robes and hoods or remain in their street clothes and asked them to shock learners (actually, confederates) for mistakes made in a paired-association task. As

Deindividuation:
Psychological state characterized by loss of self-awareness and the sense of personal responsibility

TABLE 12.2   Deindividuation on Halloween

	Percentage Stealing Candy	
	Alone	In a group
Personally identifiable	7.5	20.8
Anonymous	21.4	57.2

Halloween trick-or-treaters who were in a group and were anonymous stole the most candy.

Source: Adapted from Diener, E., Fraser, S. C., Beaman, A. L., & Kelem, R. T. (1976). Effects of deindividuation variables on stealing among Halloween trick-or-treaters. *Journal of Personality and Social Psychology, 33,* 178–183.

expected, participants in the KKK robes and hoods administered more shock. A related study by Johnson and Downing (1979) found that women dressed in KKK outfits administered more shocks than those wearing nurse uniforms; since all participants wore uniforms, it is clear that anonymity caused by the uniform alone does not necessarily facilitate antisocial behavior.

Other research has shown that preventing people from becoming self-aware can increase aggressive responding (Batson, Thompson, Seuferling, Whitney, & Strongman, 1999). For example, Prentice-Dunn and Rogers (1982) put participants in a dark room with blasting rock music—conditions which likely reduced self-awareness—and found that they gave more shocks to a mistake-prone confederate than other participants who sat in a bright, quiet room.

Finally, people who feel less accountable for their actions often engage in behavior that is against their personal norms. For example, the savagery of lynchings in the United States between 1899 and 1946 was positively correlated with group size, according to an archival study by Mullen (1986). Similarly, the baiting of individuals contemplating jumping off a high perch increases along with size of the group (Mann, 1981). As we discussed in the context of prosocial behavior in Chapter 8, individual responsibility for behavior can become diffused as groups become larger (Darley & Latané, 1968).

Although deindividuation is often associated with the reduction of the ability of social norms to guide desirable behavior, resulting in negative, undesirable behaviors, it is not always the case. For example, female participants in nurse uniforms in the Johnson and Downing (1979) study mentioned above were *less* likely to administer a shock to a "learner" when they were not individually identified by a name tag as compared to when their name was prominently displayed. The authors argued that participants—who were not actually nurses—essentially disappeared into their role as nurses implied by their uniforms and acted in accordance with the norm that states that nurses take care of and do not harm other people.

A more recent examination of deindividuation, consistent with these findings, argues that rather than releasing a person from social norms it actually leads to norm-following behavior. Thus, whether the dominant norm is to engage in prosocial or antisocial behavior, deindividuation will make *either* more likely. Building on social identity theory, Stephen Reicher and his colleagues proposed the **social identity model of deindividuation effects** (SIDE), which states that immersion in groups can *heighten* one's sense of self (Le Hénaff, Michinov, Le Bohec, & Delaval, 2015; Levine, Cassidy, & Jentzsch, 2010; Reicher, Spears, & Postmes, 1995). As you recall from the chapter on prejudice, Tajfel and Turner (1986) suggested that individuals possess both a personal identity that distinguishes us from others and a social identity that is connected to the groups we belong to. SIDE focuses on how social identity can become more salient and influential, resulting in greater adherence to group norms (Cronin & Reicher, 2009). For instance, a basketball coach may emphasize how important it is for each member to focus on being a teammate (their social identity) instead of trying to win the game as individuals (personal identity). Therefore, one aspect of identity is affirmed rather than suppressed in a group setting.

Social Identity Model of Deindividuation Effects (SIDE): Postulates that immersion in groups can heighten one's sense of self

Think Again!

1. *Have you experienced deindividuation? How did it feel, and what did you do?*

2. *Which theory of deindividuation is correct, in your opinion? Why do you think that?*

3. *In situations where deindividuation is not desirable, how might a leader prevent it from happening? What about the opposite situation, when it is desirable?*

GROUP DECISION-MAKING

Pause for a moment: In your experience, are decisions made by groups more or less sound than individual decisions? Are two (or more) heads really better than one? Although complaints about the inefficiencies or ineffectiveness of committees are rampant among my academic and corporate friends, groups generally make better decisions than individuals, although groups are by no means free from error (Tindale, Talbot, & Martinez, 2013). Below we describe two of the most prominent kinds of decisional shortcomings of groups, but before doing so, let's review the steps that lead to effective group decision-making.

According to the **orientation-discussion-decision-implementation** (ODDI) model, effective decision-making is enhanced when groups move through four stages of deliberation and subsequent action (Bonner & Baumann, 2012; Hollingshead et al., 2005; Wittenbaum, Hollingshead, & Botero, 2004). During the *orientation* stage, group members define the problem, establish goals, gather information, and develop a plan for the overall decision-making process. One of the products of this stage is a *shared mental model* of the nature of the problem to be addressed and a general idea of how to solve it (Cannon-Bowers, Salas, & Converse, 1993; Lim & Klein, 2006).

For instance, let's say that students in a class on the psychology of persuasion are assigned the task of creating and implementing a program to increase recycling on their campus. Before they can make any meaningful progress, they need to have a common understanding of their task. If some members mistakenly believe they are expected to simply write a 10-page paper on the history of recycling, whereas others think they need to create a YouTube video, there clearly is not shared mental model. Difficulty in agreeing on the nature of the problem or task or misunderstanding what its goals are hampers the effectiveness of the group. Researchers refer to the reduction in the ability of the group to engage in good problem solving that stems from shortcomings in group interaction as **process loss** (Hurley & Allen, 2007; Steiner, 1972). Process loss can result from a variety of sources, including the selection of an ineffective leader, poor communications among members, or failure to cooperate.

Orientation-Discussion-Decision-Implementation (ODDI) Model: Postulates that effective decision-making consists of four stages of deliberation and subsequent action: orientation, discussion, decision, and implementation

Process Loss: Reduction in the ability of a group to engage in good problem solving that stems from shortcomings in group interaction

The second stage consists primarily of *discussion* of the information gathered during the orientation stage. Group members must remember, share, and process (think carefully about) that information, in this case the reasons that people recycle less than they should. If some withhold vital information needed to solve the problem or forget to pass it on to the rest of the group, then process loss has occurred and the final project may be weakened.

Unfortunately, failure to share important information—called the **shared information bias**—is common in groups, which in fact tend to spend too much time on information that all members possess and consequently that warrant little attention (Larson, 2010; Mojzisch, Grouneva, & Schulz-Hardt, 2010; Stasser, 1999; Stasser & Titus, 1985). When individual members of a group withhold relevant information, this undermines the advantage of what is called **transactive memory**, which is the idea that group memory is the combination of the memories of individuals and thus provides a problem-solving advantage (Moreland, 1999; Peltokorpi, 2008; Siegel Christian, Pearsall, Christian, & Ellis, 2014; Wegner, 1987). You have very likely benefited from the transactive memory of your family or friends when recalling shared experiences in which different people remembered different parts of the events. In our class project example, individual students may have been tasked to research and report on specific and nonoverlapping aspects of the topic, and their transactive memory of this information—assuming it is shared—will enhance the final product (Jackson & Moreland, 2009).

The advantages of transactive memory for group performance have been demonstrated in both laboratory and field settings (DeChurch & Mesmer-Magnus, 2010; Mesmer-Magnus & DeChurch, 2009; van Ginkel & van Knippenberg, 2009). Fortunately, researchers have uncovered a number of strategies that groups can use to encourage information exchange, such as making sure members know that they alone hold important information (Stewart & Stasser, 1995).

In the third stage of the ODDI, a group comes to a *decision*. Let's say that in the class project example, the students are allowed to select just one intervention to increase recycling. How do they decide which strategy to choose? The group can follow any one of a number of decision rules, ranging from allowing the leader or a majority to choose or requiring a consensus wherein all members must agree (Kameda, Tsukasaki, Hastie, & Berg, 2011). There are times when delegating decisional authority to a specific individual makes sense, such as when that person truly possesses the most expertise or experience, when there is little time or opportunity for extended group discussion, or for relatively unimportant issues. For instance, students may allow their group leader to make decisions about paper color or typeface but are more likely to strive for a majority or consensus regarding important issues, such as which strategy for increasing recycling to advocate. In general, allowing the majority or super-majority (two-thirds) to decide results in the best decisions (Hastie & Kameda, 2005).

The final stage consists of the *implementation* of the decision, along with an evaluation of the merits or success of the plan. In our class example, the students would first roll out their recycling program and, at a later date, evaluate how much recycling has changed on their campus.

Shared Information Bias: Tendency for groups to spend too much time discussing information that all members possess rather than unshared information

Transactive Memory: Group memory that is the combination of the memories of individuals

Shortcomings in Group Decisions: Groupthink

Although the ODDI presents an ideal vision of group processes, in reality groups take many different approaches to deliberation and action. It is important to recognize that groups are subject to some of the same cognitive biases as are individuals. For instance, as we described in Chapter 3 on social cognition, people may seek only information that confirms their initial opinion or may engage in biased processing of that information in ways that favor their preferred outcome. Groups can also fail to adequately gather and evaluate the evidence and rush to decisions without sufficient knowledge of the problem or forethought of the possible undesirable outcomes of those decisions.

One of the most researched and consequential failures of groups to live up to their potential to make reasoned decisions occurs when members of a group behave as if they are of one mind rather than many separate ones. Psychologist Irving Janis called this phenomenon **groupthink**, which is a type of faulty thinking in groups that strive to maintain cohesion and achieve unanimity at the expense of adequately evaluating the information and options available to them (Janis, 1972, 1982). In other words, it is important to members of the group that everyone agrees and, consequently, they will ignore or downplay inconsistent opinions and information. Janis developed the idea of groupthink based on several case studies in U.S. history in which poor decisions led to catastrophic consequences.

Groupthink: Type of faulty thinking in groups that strives to maintain cohesion and achieve unanimity at the expense of adequately evaluating the information and options available to the group

Examples of Groupthink

Perhaps Janis's most prominent example of groupthink unfolded during John F. Kennedy's presidency in the early 1960s. Kennedy, acting on the unanimous recommendation of his top advisors, ordered an invasion of Cuba in an effort to overthrow its leader, Fidel Castro. In April 1961, approximately 1,400 Cuban exiles trained by the U.S. Central Intelligence Agency landed at the Bay of Pigs. By the third day, virtually all of the exiles were captured or killed. Needless to say, the invasion did not live up to the rosy expectations of the Kennedy administration, humiliating the United States in the eyes of the world. Janis (1972, 1982) also analyzed the U.S. decision in 1941 *not* to take seriously the threat of a Japanese attack on Pearl Harbor and found good evidence that groupthink was at work. The result of not making adequate preparations proved to be disastrous, as thousands of Americans were killed and a substantial portion of the U.S. Navy was destroyed.

Researchers have argued that the explosion of the Space Shuttle Challenger soon after liftoff resulted from faulty decision making.

Two more contemporary fiascoes further illustrate problems with groupthink. One began in 2003 when U.S. President George Bush ordered a full-scale attack on Iraq and the overthrow of Saddam

Hussein. Bush, Vice President Dick Cheney, Secretary of State Colin Powell, and other close advisors justified the invasion on the grounds that Hussein possessed weapons of mass destruction (WMDs) and posed a serious and imminent threat to the United States and its interests in the Middle East. History has shown that the evidence of WMDs was weak at best and fabricated at worst and that there were stupendous blunders by both the Americans and the British in the planning and implementation of the invasion and subsequent occupation (Houghton, 2008; Rodrigues, Assmar, & Jablonski, 2005).

A second example was the 1986 decision by administrators of the U.S. National Aeronautic and Space Administration (NASA) to launch the space shuttle *Challenger* despite warnings that critical O-ring seals in the rocket boosters would fail in the cold temperatures on launch day (Esser, 1998). This fateful decision resulted in the disintegration of the shuttle just moments after lift-off and the death of the entire crew.

Antecedents and Symptoms of Groupthink

What causes groupthink? Janis (1982) identified three antecedents of groupthink: high cohesion, certain features of the structure and organization of the group, and stressful situations (See Figure 12.3). First, members of cohesive groups are unlikely to dissent and they feel pressure to conform to group norms. Second, the presence of a strong, directive leader, homogeneity among members, the lack of procedures to ensure open discussion and consideration of alternatives, and isolation of the group from outside influences that may contradict the leader's preferences increase the likelihood of groupthink. Third, like individuals, groups under time pressure often forego accuracy in order to make rapid decisions. Evidence that groupthink has occurred includes an illusion of invulnerability to failure, belief in the superiority of the group (more moral, intelligent, etc.), closemindedness, and pressures toward uniformity. Moreover, even when individuals have reservations about a group decision, they often engage in self-censorship and, consequently, foster an illusion of group unanimity.

Evaluation of the Groupthink Model

Although Janis made a compelling argument for the existence of groupthink, there are a number of flaws with his analysis and problems with the groupthink model itself (Ahlfinger & Esser, 2001; Baron, 2005; Burnette, Pollack, & Forsyth, 2011; Choi & Kim, 1999; Kramer, 1998; Post, 2011; Turner, Pratkanis, & Struckman, 2007). First, there are difficulties associated with drawing causal conclusions from case studies, as we discuss below in our Doing Research section. Second, subsequent examinations of the Bay of Pigs and the escalation of the Vietnam War (another of the examples Janis used to bolster his theory) suggest that political considerations were at least as influential as groupthink in producing ill-fated decisions (Kramer, 1998). That is to say, these decisions were made by the leaders to score political points or garner popularity rather than because the leader was truly blinded by the process. Other researchers have questioned whether all of the antecedents identified by Janis are necessary for groupthink to occur (Henningsen, Henningsen, Eden, & Cruz, 2006). For instance, high cohesion is not always present in groups that display groupthink (Burnette et al., 2011).

Preventing Groupthink

Despite some weaknesses in the original conceptualization of groupthink, groups interested in making a good decision about an important topic would be wise to avoid the antecedents identified by Janis. There are a number of empirically supported actions that groups and their leaders can take to minimize the likelihood of poor decisions (Smith & Collins, 2009). Janis (1982) suggested that leaders should encourage dissent, avoid making their own preferences known prior to discussion, and invite individuals with diverse opinions to participate in group proceedings. In addition, the leader could establish subgroups that can tackle specific aspects of the problem and meet apart from the full group, subsequently reporting their findings to the full group. Finally, the full group should convene a second time after a cooling off period to reconsider its decision prior to implementation.

Think Again!

1. *What antecedents to groupthink are the most or least crucial?*

2. *Before reading the Doing Research section below, can you identify some of the strengths and weaknesses of the case study approach?*

Group Polarization

One of the lessons from research on groupthink is that groups do not always make better decisions than individuals do. As the Bay of Pigs and Challenger fiascoes illustrate, groups sometimes take risks that some members would likely have objected to, had they been asked independently. Indeed, early research on the social psychology of groups found that their decisions tended to be riskier than what most or perhaps all of the members originally preferred (Wallach, Kogan, & Bem, 1962).

For instance, say one of your friends—we'll call her Elsa—currently works as an assistant manager in a local Italian restaurant. She makes a decent salary and enjoys the benefits of relatively secure job, health insurance, and paid sick days. However, Elsa has just been offered a higher paying manager position at a new trendy restaurant, but it is located in a spot that has seen a lot of turnover in restaurants, and thus the job is much less secure. Let's say Elsa is leaning toward taking the job but wants to first poll her closest friends. When she asks them individually, via email, one of the five says take the job. However, she later learns that her friends discussed this over coffee and now four of the five

FIGURE 12.3   Janis's Model of Groupthink

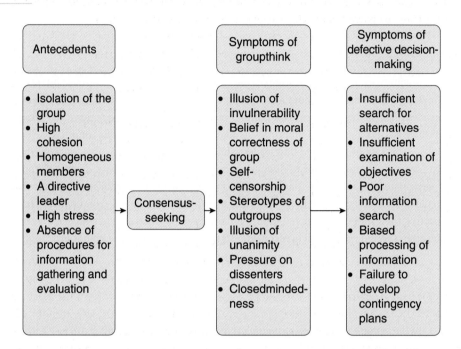

Source: Adapted from Janis, I. L. (1972). *Victims of groupthink: A psychological study of foreign-policy decisions and fiascoes*. Oxford England: Houghton Mifflin. Janis, I. L. (1982). *Groupthink: Psychological studies of policy decisions and fiascoes* (2nd ed.). Boston: Houghton Mifflin.

suggest taking it. What changed? In this case, the group was willing to accept (on behalf of Elsa) a greater risk than the individuals would have alone. Elsa's friends exhibited a *risky shift* that some early research showed can follow group deliberation (Wallach et al., 1962).

Despite early indications that group decisions are typically riskier than individual ones, other research found the opposite: Discussion shifted group opinion toward *more* conservative, *less* risky, positions (Moscovici & Zavalloni, 1969). Which is correct? Does discussion lead to more conservative or riskier decisions? It turns out that *both* occur. Research has found that group discussion typically leads groups to more extreme positions in the direction that they were already leaning. This phenomenon is called **group polarization**, and it refers to the tendency for group discussion to enhance the initial *prior* tendencies of its individual members (Aikin, 2013; Krizan & Baron, 2007; Moscovici & Zavalloni, 1969; Myers & Bishop, 1971).

Group polarization is not limited to decisions involving risk but rather can occur for almost any issue on which groups may discuss and arrive at a conclusion or judgment, including such topics as racial attitudes and investment decisions (Chandrashekaran, Walker, Ward, & Reingen, 1996; Myers & Bishop, 1971). For example, research in France

Group Polarization:
Tendency for group discussion to enhance the initial leanings of the individuals prior to discussion

found that French opinions of their president were more favorable after deliberation, but those toward U.S. citizens were less so, reflecting an overall more favorable impression of the French president than of U.S. citizens (Moscovici & Zavalloni, 1969).

One of the ways that psychologists have studied group polarization is to ask participants to indicate what is the lowest probability of success (from among a number of options) for which they would recommend taking a particular risk (see Table 12.3). Participants are given a brief scenario in which a fictional person—such as Elsa above—must choose between a conservative option (keeping a secure job) and a riskier one (moving to a less secure but more rewarding position). Participants make this recommendation twice, once before group discussion and again following it. Experimenters compare the average response before discussion and then again following it. Typically, they find that, after discussion, the group average has moved toward whichever pole the individuals were leaning before discussion. That is, initial leanings toward a conservative choice will lead to an even more conservative final recommendation; the same would hold for an initial risky preference (see Figure 12.4).

Why do you suppose groups experience such polarization? Social psychologists offer three explanations, two of which are closely related to concepts we discussed in Chapter 6 on social influence. First, consider that, prior to discussion, group members held some knowledge in common, but each individual also possessed unique information. During discussion, the uniquely held information is shared with others and, consequently, will impact the deliberations. If more individuals preferred caution (or risk) prior to discussion, then more arguments in favor of caution (or risk) will be aired and accepted, shifting the average opinion in the cautious (or risky) direction. This is referred to as the *persuasive arguments* explanation, which accounts for attitude change resulting from exposure to arguments that are (a) novel, (b) compelling, and (c) supportive of members' initial

TABLE 12.3   Group Discussion and Risk Taking

Liam, a college senior with considerable musical talent, must choose between the secure course of going on to medical school and becoming a physician or the risky course of embarking on the career of a concert pianist.

Please indicate the lowest probability of success that they would consider acceptable to advise Liam to skip medical school and try to make a career as a pianist.

_____ 1 in 10 chance of succeeding	_____ 7 in 10 chance of succeeding
_____ 3 in 10 chance of succeeding	_____ 9 in 10 chance of succeeding
_____ 5 in 10 chance of succeeding	_____ I would not recommend taking the chance.

Source: Adapted from Wallach, M. A., Kogan, N., & Bem, D. J. (1962). Group influence on individual risk taking. *The Journal of Abnormal and Social Psychology, 65*, 75–86.

FIGURE 12.4   Group Polarization

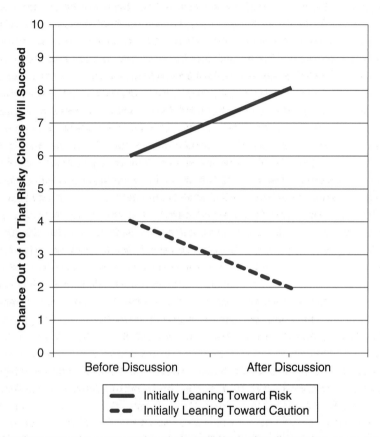

Initial leanings toward a conservative choice will lead, after discussion, to an even more conservative final recommendation; the same would hold for an initial risky recommendation.

opinion (Brauer, Judd, & Gliner, 1995; Burnstein & Vinokur, 1977). A number of studies have shown that individual attitudes become more extreme after reading or hearing the arguments others have made that are consistent with their own (Pavitt, 2003). The persuasive arguments explanation is synonymous with *informational influence* that we discussed in Chapter 6.

Can you think of any other reasons why groups may polarize? As you know, people will sometimes change their attitudes in order to follow a group norm, which in this case would be the opinion verbalized by the majority in a group. We often want to believe what others do, wear clothes that are similar to what our friends wear, and generally fit in with others. Consequently, we may change our opinions following group discussion as a result of *social comparison* processes (Festinger, 1954). Remember that individuals are particularly likely to engage in social comparison when objective standards for evaluating how they are doing are not available, and as a result, they rely on the opinions of others to determine what they should do. This explanation for group polarization is closely related to the concept of *normative influence* we described in Chapter 6. Indeed, research has shown that people become more extreme in their attitudes after learning that most members of their group are more extreme in their attitudes (Sanders & Baron, 1977).

The third major explanation for group polarization, in addition to the persuasive arguments and social comparison accounts, is based on social identity theory. The *social identity* explanation combines elements of both other explanations (Krizan & Baron, 2007; Turner et al., 1987). According to the social identity approach, people shift their opinions on an issue in order to align it with that of the person or position they see as prototypical of their group—the person or position that seems to best represent what the group stands for or believes. This component is closely related to social comparison theory. In addition, the persuasive arguments approach is incorporated by virtue of the fact that arguments from group members become particularly important to the extent that an individual identifies with that group (Van Knippenberg & Wilke, 1988). A person who closely identifies with the group will be more convinced by the arguments of the other members than will someone who is loosely connected to it. Furthermore, when outgroups with opinions that are different from the ingroup become salient, people seem motivated to draw clear distinctions between their ingroup and outgroups, and then the likelihood of polarization increases (Mackie, 1986).

Which account of group polarization is correct? It turns out that all three can help us understand group polarization. A meta-analysis of 21 studies testing the persuasive arguments and social comparison explanations found empirical support for both (Isenberg, 1986). These two processes are most likely to be operative when a group is newly formed and members do not already know the views of their fellow members (Brown, 2000a). Thus, learning about the opinions of others provides new informational arguments and/or knowledge about the positions held by others. However, social identity does a better job of explaining why polarization occurs in existing groups and when group identity is made particularly salient, such as when it may be threatened by the outgroup (Brown, 2000a). For instance, attitudes can polarize by becoming more patriotic in a nation after that nation has been threatened by another.

If group polarization were limited to just the laboratory, it wouldn't be of much interest. However, many real-world groups demonstrate this opinion shift to more extreme positions. For instance, terrorist organizations evolve in part as a result of the way like-minded individuals congregate and share opinions and complaints about other groups that are seen as threats (McCauley, 2007). They often insulate themselves from divergent or more moderate opinions and become progressively radicalized as their interpersonal bonds strengthen (Moghaddam, 2005). Similar polarization has been observed in extremist hate groups online (Gerstenfeld, Grant, & Chiang, 2003) and in fraternities and sororities on college campuses (Pascarella & Terenzini, 1991).

Please note that the social psychological concept of group polarization is sometimes confused with what people outside of psychology mean when they say that a nation is *politically* polarized. Political polarization refers to a sharply divided electorate in which citizens tend to be either very conservative or very liberal, with relatively few individuals occupying a more moderate political position. In group polarization, all members of a group lean *in the same direction*.

Think Again!

1. *If you were a member of a group that was becoming polarized in a way that you did not support, what might you do to lessen or prevent it?*

2. *How is group polarization different from groupthink?*

3. *Under what conditions might group polarization be desirable?*

Brainstorming

Before reading further, take a minute and write down all of the uses you have for a plastic ballpoint that has run out of ink. How many did you think of? Now, imagine that you were sitting around a table with four other students and brainstormed this task together. How do you think the group would perform? How about you—would you come up with more ideas if in a group setting? Most of my students (as well as nonstudents I ask), are usually

PEOPLE
BRAINSTORMING

Are two or more heads always better than one?

©iStockphoto.com/Rawpixel Ltd.

quick to answer that brainstorming in a group is much more effective than alone. Indeed, the advertising executives who developed and popularized this idea were convinced of its advantages (Osborn, 1953, 1957). Today, brainstorming groups are commonly used in governments, corporations, and generally thought to be effective.

Osborn (1953, 1957) claimed that **brainstorming**—a procedure in which members of a group are encouraged to generate as many ideas as they can within a specific amount of time—would result in a higher quantity of and better quality ideas than if members did this on their own. Osborn argued that the ideal size of a group is 12, that members should be of relatively equal status or rank, and that they should

- refrain from criticism, no matter how good or bad an idea may seem;
- offer any idea, even if it sounds wild or strange;
- generate as many ideas as possible, because as more ideas are offered, the quality will improve; and
- try to build off and improve the ideas of others.

Unfortunately, as intuitively appealing as it is, brainstorming does not produce either a larger number or better quality suggestions (Deuja, Kohn, Paulus, & Korde, 2014; Diehl & Stroebe, 1987; Larson, 2010; Mullen, Johnson, & Salas, 1991). Even the evidence supplied by Osborn to justify his claims was questionable, as it was based only on case studies (see this chapter's Doing Research section). In fact, the bulk of the research as well as a meta-analysis by Mullen, Johnson, and Salas (1991) of eighteen studies found that brainstorming in interactive groups produced *fewer* ideas, as compared to individuals working in what are called *nominal groups* (Henningsen & Henningsen, 2013; Jones & Lambertus, 2014; Michinov, Jamet, Métayer, & Le Hénaff, 2015; Nijstad & Stroebe, 2006; Paulus & Brown, 2007; Paulus & Coskun, 2013). Nominal groups include the same number of people as interactive ones and are given identical instructions, but they work separately, without communication. In other words, your group of five students would have been better off generating ideas individually rather than in a face-to-face group.

Despite the fact that interactive brainstorming is not effective, both people who participate in them and those who are aware of them tend to believe that they are, reflecting an illusion of group effectiveness (Nijstad & Stroebe, 2006; Paulus, Dzindolet, Poletes, & Camacho, 1993; Stroebe, Diehl, & Abakoumkin, 1992). Moreover, participants rate their experience as more enjoyable than do those working alone and take credit for the ideas of others and, consequently, overestimate their own productivity (Paulus et al., 1993).

There is one notable exception to the findings of brainstorming ineffectiveness: when interaction among group members occurs electronically. Research has shown that electronic groups are more productive than face-to-face ones, as long as the group has at least four members (Dennis & Williams, 2005; DeRosa, Smith, & Hantula, 2007). Why is brainstorming in electronic groups more effective? It seems that they avoid some of the pitfalls of face-to-face ones. For instance, group conversations require turn taking, and

Brainstorming: Procedure in which members of a group are encouraged to generate as many ideas as they can within a specific amount of time

people forget ideas while waiting for their chance to speak. Moreover, when contributions are anonymous, participants are not concerned about how they are being evaluated by other group members. Finally, the free riding that can occur during in-person brainstorming can be reduced if each person's contributions are electronically tracked (Dennis & Williams, 2005). Thus, if you are assigned the task of group brainstorming, you may want to do it online!

DOING RESEARCH: CASE STUDIES

Throughout this text, we have discussed how important it is for social psychologists to eliminate confounds in experiments. As you may recall, a confound is present when a variable other than the independent variable is allowed to change along with the independent variable. As we have noted, psychologists try to avoid confounds by maximizing control of extraneous factors in the experimental situation and by randomly assigning participants to experimental conditions. These features increase our confidence in making causal inferences about the relationships between independent and dependent variables. Other types of research, including archival and correlational research described earlier, do not incorporate these features. Let's turn our attention to another alternative to controlled experimentation, the **case study**, which we define as a close examination of an event, person, or group.

Case Study: Close examination of an event, person, or group

Note that some of the most influential studies in the history of social psychology are case studies, including the investigation of The Seekers by Festinger et al. (1956) and Sherif's Robbers Cave Study (Sherif, Harvey, White, Hood, & Sherif, 1988/1961). Case studies have also figured prominently in research on groups, such as in Janis's studies of groupthink mentioned earlier in this chapter.

Pause for a moment and consider some of the drawbacks of the case study approach. I alluded to one moments ago: Case studies do not allow researchers to establish causality. Why do you suppose that might be? There are several reasons for this. First, the lack of control of all of the possible influences on the situation means that researchers cannot isolate and examine specific variables. Second and relatedly, control or comparison groups are rare, and this further limits the ability to detect the effects of particular variables on the outcomes of interest. Third, the cases under investigation occur only once and are not replicable, and therefore the reliability of the data cannot be established. Finally, because each situation is truly unique, inferences drawn from a case study are not easily generalizable to other events, persons, or groups.

Given their shortcomings, why do case studies at all? Well, investigating real-world events can be fascinating. Because case studies tend to be in-depth, they also provide an abundance of detail that cannot be obtained from experimental research. More importantly from a research perspective, they can be rich ground for the generation of hypotheses about the causes of social behavior. These hypotheses, in turn, can be tested under properly controlled conditions where variables can be teased apart and individually examined. Janis's case studies of groupthink have provided social psychologists with ample hypotheses regarding the roles of cohesion, leadership style, and diversity in group membership on group decision-making (Janis, 1982).

MINORITY INFLUENCE

Our treatment of attitude and behavior change in earlier chapters focused primarily on how a *majority* in a group influences a *minority*. For instance, social influence research in the United States has typically investigated when and why individuals change their public attitudes and behavior to match those of the majority (Cialdini & Trost, 1998). As mentioned earlier, even though Asch (1956) emphasized how minorities resisted conforming in his seminal research involving the line judgment task, later researchers highlighted how the group successfully altered the responses of minorities (Moscovici & Faucheux, 1972). More broadly, social psychologists have demonstrated what has been termed a *conformity bias,* which is the tendency to understand group influence only in terms of how the majority affects the minority (Moscovici, 1976). In this section, we are going to turn the tables, so to speak, and look at the leading theories and research describing when majorities succumb to minority influence. **Minority influence** occurs when a numerical minority in a group changes the attitudes, beliefs, or behaviors of a majority (Baron & Bellman, 2007; Crano & Seyranian, 2007; Gardikiotis, 2011; J. M. Levine & Prislin, 2013; Mucchi-Faina, Pacilli, & Pagliaro, 2010).

We know simply by looking at the real world that minorities have the ability to create social change on a mass scale—think about Gandhi's ability to transform politics in India and U.S. civil rights activists in the 1960s. In both cases, opinions initially held by a small segment of the population became rather widespread and influenced the law and public policy. Leaders, too, are minorities and of course can be very influential. We will discuss leaders in the next section.

The French social psychologist Serge Moscovici, seeking to understand how social change or innovation happens, pioneered research on minority influence. Moscovici started from the premise that societal or group change is initiated by the minority, not the majority, because the majority is content with the status quo. Then he sought to understand how minorities, despite being numerically outnumbered, are able to influence majorities. For example, participants in one of his early studies were asked to publicly declare whether slides were either blue or green (Moscovici, Lage, & Naffrechoux, 1969). Participants completed this task in groups of six, but unbeknownst to them, two were actually confederates. Moreover, the slides were in fact all different shades of blue. Depending on the condition, the confederates either stated that the slides were green every time, two-thirds of the time, or one-third of the time. When faced with a consistent minority, participants conformed (declaring the slide to be green) 8% of the time. In contrast, participants conformed only 1% of the time when the minority was inconsistent—about as often as they did in the control in which there were no confederates. Importantly, the effects of the minority on the majority spilled over into a second stage

Minority Influence:
When a numerical minority in a group changes the attitudes, beliefs, or behaviors of the majority

SOCIAL PSYCHOLOGY APPLIED TO LAW
JURY DECISION-MAKING

In earlier chapters, we touched on some pretrial aspects of the U.S. criminal justice system. Chapters 2 and 5 describe the challenges involved in trying to detect lies in suspects, whether by using fMRI or simple observation. And in Chapter 6, you were introduced to a couple of famous instances of individuals who confessed to and were imprisoned for crimes that they did not do. In this section, we describe some of the potential flaws in one of the key components of the trial itself: the jury. Social psychology is relevant to every step in the jury process, from how juries are selected, to how they process information during a trial, to the ways in which they make decisions about guilt or innocence. Here we'll briefly focus on some of the potential flaws in the jury system.

There are inherent tensions within the process of jury selection to the extent that the prosecution, defense, and judge disagree about who should serve on any given case. The prosecution wants to seat a jury that is most likely to convict, the defense one that is most likely going to acquit or at least be lenient, and the judge is (or should be) primarily interested in fairness (Baldus, Woodworth, Zuckerman, Weiner, & Broffitt, 2001). Attorneys on both sides of a case have the ability to

©iStockphoto.com/PatrickPoendl.

disqualify potential jurors from serving without giving a justification for doing so, using what are called peremptory challenges. Although they often hire psychologists or other consultants to help them select their ideal jury, it is by no means clear whether this increases the chances that they will obtain a favorable jury (Lieberman, 2011). Despite the fact that these disqualifications are not permitted to be based on social categories—such as gender, race, income, and so forth—attorneys will often offer a "legal" reason that in fact merely masks a category-based decision (Norton, Sommers, & Brauner, 2007). However, racial and other biases may influence judgments below the level of awareness (Chapter 10), and consequently, these bias surely affect the selection process (Mitchell, Haw, Pfeifer, & Meissner, 2005; Sommers & Norton, 2008). This is an unfortunate outcome, because diverse juries tend to be the most impartial (Sommers, 2008, 2010; Sommers & Ellsworth, 2009).

Race—or other person features of jury members—is of course not the only source of potential bias (Bornstein & Greene, 2011b; Gastil, Burkhalter, & Black, 2007; McAuliff, Kovera, & Nunez, 2009). You have read about many other phenomena that can introduce less than optimal

decision-making, including overreliance on anecdotes at the expense of base rate information, the confirmation bias, and various heuristics. For instance, Bornstein and Greene (Bornstein & Greene, 2011a; showed how juries may use the number provided by attorneys as an anchor when determining the dollar amounts of financial awards. Juries are similar to many other groups in that they are subject to the same kinds of group influences discussed in this book, such as group polarization and groupthink (Devine, Clayton, Dunford, Seying, & Pryce, 2001; Howard, Brewer, & Williams, 2006; Thompson, Kaasa, & Peterson, 2013).

of the experiment, in which participants exposed to the consistent minority "saw" more green slides than did those in the inconsistent conditions, even though participants in this second stage performed the task alone.

Why do you think such influence persists? In answer to this question, Moscovici proposed **conversion theory**, which postulates that dissent within a group leads to an uncomfortable conflict that members are motivated to reduce and, consequently, either change their own opinions or try to change those of others (Curşeu, Schruijer, & Boroş, 2012; Moscovici, 1994). According to Moscovici, minorities respond to majority influence by engaging in *social comparison,* considering the negative consequences of dissent, and may publicly comply in order to avoid those consequences. Thus, majority influence is primarily normative, direct or overt, and immediate in the sense that additional deliberation by the minority is not necessary. The minority may publicly agree with the majority but retain their private attitudes and beliefs.

In contrast, majorities respond to minority dissent via a *validation process,* in which they evaluate the merit of the minority view. If they determine that the minority position is valid, then their private attitudes and beliefs are thereby converted to the minority position. Minority influence, then, is informational, indirect or private, and delayed because the majority must think about the minority position before adopting it. Moscovici further claimed that validation creates longer-lasting change than does comparison

Conversion Theory: Idea that dissent within a group leads to an uncomfortable conflict that members are motivated to reduce and, consequently, either change their own opinions or try to change those of others because the new attitudes are internalized or accepted, whereas comparison produces only external compliance.

A meta-analysis by Wood et al. of 97 studies provided empirical support for the basic tenets of conversion theory, as has additional research conducted later (Levine & Prislin, 2013; Wood, Lundgren, Ouellette, Busceme, & Blackstone, 1994). When are minorities likely to be successful in changing majority opinion? Moscovici's blue-green studies described above demonstrated that *consistency* on the part of the minority is key (Moscovici & Nemeth, 1974). In addition to remaining consistent in their position, minorities are more influential to the extent that they exhibit *confidence* in their opinions (Maass & Clark, 1984), as long as they also are competent and willing to work with rather than against the majority (Levine & Russo, 1987). Finally, minority members are more likely to create *strong arguments* in support of their position than are majority members, and these arguments enhance the chances of effective influence (Guinote, Brown, & Fiske, 2006).

Think Again!

1. *Have you experienced the discomfort that can stem from disagreements between the majority and minority in a group? How was it resolved?*

2. *Why do you think that majority and minority influence tend to occur through different processes?*

3. *If you could conduct a case study on a historical event, what would you choose? Try listing some of the aspects of the event that would be relatively easier or more difficult to capture via a case study.*

LEADERSHIP

It is impossible to truly understand the psychology of groups without examining one of the most potent influences on group behavior: leadership. Virtually every group we can think of—including nations, companies, and sports teams—contains some form of leadership, most commonly a single individual. **Leadership** is the process by which a person influences group members to work toward common goals. Leadership can be contrasted with other forms of social influence, such as compliance, in that it produces internal acceptance in the target of the ideas and beliefs of the person making the request. Compliance, like conformity and obedience, does not necessarily mean that a target agrees *with* the requestor but only that he agrees *to* the request. Here we'll concentrate on leaders who can achieve results without simple reliance on mere punishment or reward to motivate group members.

Leadership:
Process by which a person influences group members to work toward common goals

Types of Leaders

Have you ever worked with or known a leader who was very focused on getting the job done and not particularly concerned with how she related to her group members? What about the opposite, a leader who was more concerned about the feelings of his group than about achieving group goals? Researchers have termed leaders who are primarily interested in group efficiency and productivity as *task oriented* and those who prioritize maintaining good interpersonal relationships as *relations oriented* (Derue, Nahrgang, Wellman, & Humphrey, 2011; Yuki, 2013). Although Bales (1950) and other early researchers argued that people could be high on one but not the other, more recent investigators have found that it is possible to be high on both of them and that those who are may be particularly effective leaders (Sorrentino & Field, 1986).

Theories of Leadership

Great Person Theories. What makes an outstanding leader—someone who has been able to rally a nation or people to achieve great things—so effective? Is it a product of particular dispositional characteristics, such as charisma, charm, and assertiveness? Much of the early research on the nature of effective leaders focused on their personality traits (Stogdill, 1948). This *trait* or *great person* approach attempted to identify the innate or dispositional factors that were possessed by all exceptional leaders but ultimately could not uncover any such general leaderships traits (Arvey & Chaturvedi, 2011). Nevertheless, there are several specific traits that are correlated—though not causally related—with effective leadership. Individuals who are high on extraversion, conscientiousness, and openness to experience and low on neuroticism are generally better leaders, but none of these traits are *essential* to good leadership (Judge, Colbert, & Ilies, 2004). Researchers have also found that good leaders tend to be intelligent, competent, assertive, self-confident, and honest (Hogan & Kaiser, 2005). But as you know, any complete theory of social behavior must account for both the person and the situation. The great person approach obviously leaves out a critical component: the situation. The great person perspective on leadership reflects the fundamental attribution error (Maruna & Mann, 2006). Let's turn to other theories that better capture the complexity of the social psychology of leadership (see Table 12.4).

Contingency Model. In contrast to the person-centered models of leadership, Fiedler (1978) proposed a **contingency model of leadership**, which postulated that leadership effectiveness is *contingent* or dependent upon both the behavior of the leader and the context (Vroom & Jago, 2007). According to the contingency model, a satisfactory explanation of leadership must take into account both dispositional and situational features. For example, Prime Minister Winston Churchill was a highly successful leader of the

Contingency Model of Leadership: Postulates that leadership effectiveness is contingent upon both the behavior of the leader and aspects of the situation

TABLE 12.4   Theories of Leadership

Theory	Description
Great person theory	• Great leaders are naturally born. • They inherent personality traits that facilitate leadership. • These traits are common to all great leaders.
Contingency model	• The effectiveness of leaders depends on both traits and situational factors. • Task-oriented leaders will be especially effective when situational control is either high or low. • Relations-oriented leaders will be particularly effective when they have moderate situational control.
Social identity theory	• Leaders and group members share a social identity, at least to some degree • Leaders will be more effective when group members perceive them to be prototypical, as representing the true values, attitudes, or positions of the group. • Shared social identity is particularly important when group identity is made salient.

United Kingdom during World War II but may very well have been a failure had he been in power during the 1980s. Fiedler adopted Bales's distinction between task-oriented and relations-oriented leadership styles and found that the effectiveness of each depended on the ability of the leader to control the situation or group. Fiedler (1978) specified three factors that together predict *situational control:* leader-member relations, task structure, and how much power the leader wielded.

According to the contingency model, leaders have high situational control when the relations between the leader and the members are positive, the leader is powerful, and the task is very structured. In other words, when the members like their leader, the leader has the power to make things happen, and when it is clear what needs to be accomplished, then the leader can control the situation. In contrast, poor leader-member relations, low power, and an unstructured task with vague goals together produce low situational control.

Fiedler argued that task-oriented leaders would be effective for difficult groups (low control), because they could keep the group on task, whereas relations-oriented leaders would not provide the direction the group needs to stay focused on the goals. Task-oriented leaders will also thrive when dealing with easy groups (high control) that are already working hard and interpersonal relationships do not need to be fostered. In contrast, relations-oriented leaders may derail the group by focusing too much on interpersonal relationships. However, they will be effective when situational control is moderate, because good interpersonal relationships are crucial to motivating members and critical to goal accomplishment. Although some studies in the military, hospitals, and sports teams have supported the model, some researchers have questioned its reliability and/or validity (Ayman, Chemers, & Fiedler, 2007; Schriesheim, Tepper, & Tetrault, 1994; Snyder & Cantor, 1998; Strube & Garcia, 1981).

Transactional and Transformational Leaders. The contingency model represented an advance over the great person approach because it accounted for the role of the situation in determining leader effectiveness. However, it also has a weakness: It focuses primarily on how the leader influences the group and treats group members largely as passive recipients of that influence. In reality, leader-follower relationships, like those between other individuals, involve the mutual, ongoing reciprocal exchange of benefits in which leaders and followers influence each other (Hollander, 1985; Messick, 2005). **Transactional leaders** use transactions—which means offering benefits (e.g., money, promotion, etc.) to members in exchange for their energy and effort—to motivate the group to work toward shared goals (Bass, 1997; Burns, 1978; Eagly, Johannesen-Schmidt, & van Engen, 2003; Hollander, 1985; Kastenmüller et al., 2014). Most leaders are probably best described as primarily transactional, and most of the interactions between leaders and followers hinge on ordinary exchanges of benefits.

As quickly as you can, name 10 exceptional leaders. Who came to mind? Winston Churchill, Mahatma Gandhi, Mao Tse-Tung, Martin Luther King, Franklin Delano Roosevelt, Steve Jobs. These individuals go beyond merely transactional. Each electrified and motivated their followers and served as change agents for nations, organizations, or companies. It is safe to say that the most memorable and well-known leaders in history are those who were able to transform their

> **Transactional Leaders:** Individuals who use transactions—offering benefits (e.g., money, promotion, etc.) to members in exchange for their energy and effort—to motivate the group to work toward shared goals

©iStockphoto.com/Ken Brown.

©iStockphoto.com/PeopleImages.

> TRANSFORMA-TIONAL VERSUS TRANSACTIONAL LEADERS
>
> An example of a transformational leader (top; Martin Luther King, Jr.) and an ordinary transactional leader (bottom).

group. Burns (1978) called such individuals such as these **transformational leaders,** because they offer a compelling vision that inspires followers to set aside personal needs and interests and work hard toward loftier, overarching goals (Ayman, Korabik, & Morris, 2009; Bass & Riggio, 2006; Judge & Piccolo, 2004).

Transformational leaders are differentiated from other leaders because they (a) provide inspirational motivation (as opposed to simply monetary reward); (b) demonstrate concern for individual needs, abilities, and preferences; and (c) encourage followers to rethink assumptions, beliefs and old solutions and develop new perspectives and novel solutions (Bass, 1997). Research by Bernard Bass and others has shown that transformational leaders tend to be more successful than transactional ones (Bass & Riggio, 2006).

Social Identity Theory. Another approach to understanding leadership is based on social identity theory (Ellemers & Haslam, 2012). Given that leaders and followers are part of the same group, to some extent they share a social identity. According to the social identity theory of leadership, members will accept, support, and follow their leader to the degree that the leader is seen as reflecting the social identity of the group (Hogg, 2010). Leadership effectiveness, then, depends on member identification with the leader—including whether the leader is seen as belonging to the ingroup, as opposed to an outgroup (Ellemers et al., 2004).

Gender and Leadership

Given that males dominate leadership positions in governments, organizations, and companies around the globe, people may assume that men are more effective leaders than are women (Eagly & Carli, 2007; Hoyt & Chemers, 2008). Since social behavior is a product of both the person and the situation, we need to ask not *which* gender is more effective at leading but rather *when* there might be differences (Ayman & Korabik, 2010). First of all, it probably will not surprise you that women are generally more communal, relations oriented, and democratic than men (Leaper & Ayres, 2007). Second, some researchers have argued that, since leaders tend to be perceived more favorably and be more effective when their behavior matches what their followers expect, women may perform better when the situation calls for relations-oriented leadership, whereas men may when task-orientation is required (Karau & Williams, 1993). Third, women assert or claim authority less often than men, but when they do are perceived to be equally authoritative (Bowles & McGinn, 2005). Unfortunately, women continue to face negative stereotypes and biases about their leadership style and ability, and this can undermine their effectiveness (Forsyth & Nye, 2008; Paustian-Underdahl, Walker, & Woehr, 2014). For instance, women who are directive, who express their anger, or otherwise appear "masculine" are criticized for not being more traditionally feminine (Brescoll & Uhlmann, 2008).

Recently, Paustian-Underdalh and colleagues (2014) conducted a meta-analysis of 99 samples from 95 studies that examined gender and leadership. Their findings are perhaps the most definitive statements to date on gender and leadership. First, although earlier studies found that, when averaged across all leadership contexts, men were *perceived* as more effective leaders, more recent studies show a reversal of that trend. Second, context matters: In organizations that are stereotypically seen as more "masculine" and are male dominated (e.g., the military, government), men are perceived to be more effective, but this was not the case in "feminine" or female-dominated organizations (e.g., social service, education). Third, women were seen to be better leaders in middle-management positions, but there were no gender differences at the upper- and lower-management. Fourth, men tended to rate themselves as more effective than women rated themselves, but women were rated as more effective than men when other people did the ratings (e.g., peers, bosses, etc.). Are you surprised? What does this suggest about changes in gender roles over time?

Think Again!

1. *What kind of a leader are you, and why do you say that? Would your followers agree?*

2. *Think about the leader of your company, city, or state—is she or he more transactional or transformational? How do you think this person's gender affects how effective she or he is perceived to be?*

3. *Are the transactional and transformational categories mutually exclusive, or is there room for people to be a little bit of both?*

FINAL THOUGHTS: CROWD WISDOM AND SMART MOBS

Groups sometimes engage in unpredictable, violent, or dysfunctional behavior—such as the riots mentioned at the outset of this chapter—in ways that the individuals in isolation would not. However, groups can also be rational, peaceful, and productive and can solve problems that individuals are ill equipped to do on their own. For example, James Surowiecki (2004) relays how the British scientist Francis Galton learned about the cumulative wisdom of crowds. While attending an agricultural fair in 1906, Galton came across a competition in which visitors would win a prize if they correctly guessed the weight of an oxen. Although he expected a wide range of guesses—some of which would be wildly inaccurate—what he was really interested in was how close the *average* guess was. Therefore, he secured all of the written entries and was surprised to find that the "crowd" as a whole was remarkably accurate: The actual weight was just one pound more than the average guess, which was 1,198 pounds! In his book *the Wisdom of Crowds,* Surowiecki provides example after example—ranging from predicting the outcomes of sporting events to influencing Google's system of website ranking—of how crowds can be wiser than individuals, even outperforming the most intelligent or knowledgeable member. A number of apps for smartphones, such as the mapping/GPS program *Waze,* gather reports from individual users and then aggregate and send information to other users.

The growing electronic connectedness of billions of people around the globe will only hasten the impact of crowd wisdom on society. Howard Rheingold (2003) describes in his book *Smart Mobs: The Next Social Revolution* how people who are physically distant but electronically connected can cooperate to solve problems, search for intelligent life on other planets, and depose the president of the Philippines. More recently, we have seen how social connections played a pivotal role in the Arab Spring of 2011, during which crowds massed and protested, creating mass social upheaval that resulted in the overthrowing of several governments, including those in Tunisia, Libya, and Egypt.

Despite the fact that some of the ways that groups and crowds form and communicate have changed over the past two millennia, the role that they play in human social life is as critical now as at any other time in our history. The group processes described in this chapter are closely connected to several of our fundamental questions of human existence. As we discussed at the beginning of this chapter, group life has been a central part of our evolutionary past, and social selection has favored the propagation of *sociality*— person traits that foster cooperative group living. In addition, the *self* is inextricably tied up in the social identity provided by our group affiliation. Groups can help to express the self, but they can also inhibit or suppress individual identity. Finally, human *rationality* can be undermined by social forces associated with group decision-making although, as we have seen, groups can also demonstrate intelligence and wisdom that is superior to that of the individual.

CORE CONCEPTS

- A *group* is two or more individuals who perceive themselves as part of a unit and who influence each other and are interdependent. Important features of groups include their cohesiveness, entitativity, social norms, and role differentiation.

- Groups help us satisfy our needs for affiliation and belongingness, accomplish tasks that we cannot complete individually, meet goals more efficiently than we are able to without assistance, and obtain material resources and information that otherwise would be difficult or impossible to acquire.

- Common-identity groups are built upon attachment to the group, whereas common-bond groups are based on the bonds members have to each other.

- Via social facilitation, groups can undermine or enhance individual performance, depending on a number of individual and contextual factors, and through deindividuation can induce people to engage in behavior that they might otherwise refrain from.

- Group decisions ideally follow the ODDI model but can sometimes be compromised by groupthink and the polarization of opinions toward a more extreme position.

- Majorities and minorities typically affect each through other through distinct influence processes.

- A case study is a close examination of an event, person, or group. Although case studies can be useful for hypothesis generation, the lack of experimental control prevents researchers from drawing causal inferences from them.

- Leadership success depends on a number of personal and group variables, including matching the leader's task versus relations orientation to that of the group and also on whether leaders are transactional or transformational.

▶ **⑤SAGE** edge™ Test your understanding of chapter content. Take the practice quiz. edge.sagepub.com/barrett

KEY TERMS

▶ **⑤SAGE** edge™ Review key terms with eFlashcards. edge.sagepub.com/barrett

THINK FURTHER!

- Why do researchers prefer the *groupiness* concept to a strict definition of groups?

- Identify two or three or your groups that are the most important to you. Would you characterize them as common-identity or common-bond groups? Why?

- What is social facilitation? What are the three explanations for it? Can you give an example of each?

- Imagine you were a manager at a small store or restaurant. What concrete steps could you take to prevent social loafing among your employees?

- Say your department, unit, or team at work was discussing whether and how to restructure itself. Before discussion there was lukewarm support, but after deliberation, the group decided to radically restructure itself. Describe how the decision-making process may have unfolded, using each of the three explanations for group polarization.

- Apply the classic distinction between task-orientation and social relations-orientation to your own parenting style, if you are a parent, or to each of your parents' styles. Where type are you/they most similar to?

Suggested Readings

Janis, I. L. (1982). *Groupthink: Psychological studies of policy decisions and fiascoes* (2nd ed.). Boston, MA: Houghton Mifflin.

Moscovici, S. (1976). *Social influence and social change*. London, UK: Academic Press.

Mullen, B. (1986). Atrocity as a function of lynch mob composition: A self-attention perspective. *Personality and Social Psychology Bulletin, 12*, 187–197.

Wilson, D. S., Van Vugt, M., & O'Gorman, R. (2008). Multilevel selection theory and major evolutionary transitions: Implications for psychological science. *Current Directions in Psychological Science, 17*, 6–9.

Zajonc, R. B., & Sales, S. M. (1966). Social facilitation of dominant and subordinate responses. *Journal of Experimental Social Psychology, 2*, 160–168.

VI

EMERGING TOPICS IN SOCIAL PSYCHOLOGY

13

Three Emerging Trends

THE SOCIAL PSYCHOLOGY OF HAPPINESS, RELIGION, AND SUSTAINABILITY

Psychologist Mary Pipher

JOSE MORE/KRT/Newscom.

LEARNING OBJECTIVES

13.1 Contrast hedonic and eudaimonic happiness and subjective well-being; relate the concept of affective forecasting to the durability bias, focalism, and immune neglect.

13.2 Summarize the research regarding how social relationships, children, personal wealth, and culture can affect happiness; relate happiness to adaptation-level theory.

13.3 Describe the benefits of happiness and explain the sustainable happiness model and what people can do to become happier.

13.4 Discuss religiousness and its four dimensions; distinguish them from the three forms of religious orientation; identify the functions and sources of religion; explain how religion impacts physical and mental health as well as happiness.

13.5 Identify the primary and secondary effects of overconsumption and resulting pollution; explain how the environment affects well-being.

13.6 Compare and contrast tragedy of the commons, social dilemmas, and one-person, missing-hero, and collective traps; summarize how to overcome the problem of sustainability, the seven categories of obstacles, and the major ways that society can help improve sustainability.

⑤SAGE edge™

Get the edge on your studies.
edge.sagepub.com/barrett

Take a quiz to find out what you've learned.
Watch videos that enhance chapter content.
Explore related web and social media activities.

THE INTERSECTION OF HAPPINESS, RELIGION, AND SUSTAINABILITY

In *The Green Boat,* psychologist Mary Pipher (2013) relays the story of how she became involved in community-based environmental activism. Although joining a social movement was not what she originally intended, it was the outcome of conversations she engaged in with friends about their concerns surrounding the proposed construction of the Keystone XL Pipeline. The pipeline was intended to bring oil products from Canada to the U.S. Gulf Coast, and the initial plans called for it to pass through the nation's largest sensitive wetlands, located in the Midwestern state of Nebraska. While Pipher's life prior to her involvement in the environmental movement was not without purpose—she is a clinical psychologist and author of many books, including the bestseller *Reviving Ophelia* (1994), which focused on the troubled lives of adolescent girls—one of the unexpected side effects of her activism was a sense of renewed meaning and connection to other people and to nature itself. It seems there was something deeply satisfying about her experiences, which she describes as spiritual, working toward a greener world. Thus her advocacy proved satisfying, spiritually meaningful, and environmentally important. Pipher's story nicely illustrates the intersection of the three topics of this chapter—happiness (closely connected to life satisfaction), religion (a major source of meaning), and sustainability (environmental activism).

Research around these three topics is evidence of exciting, emerging trends in social psychology. Whereas our earlier chapters covered classic subject areas found in most social psychology textbooks, this chapter is different as it looks at new research areas, with an extended discussion of happiness and sustainability research and a much more in-depth coverage of the psychology of religion.

Three of our fundamental questions of human existence are particularly relevant to this chapter. First, the *self* is quite clearly at the core of both happiness and religion. After all, happiness and the meaning that can be provided by religion hinge upon the self, as they only exist if the person believes that they do. Observers cannot determine whether a person is happy, nor can they decide what is meaningful to that person. Second, happiness is partially contingent upon a person's *sociality* or the connections he develops to other people. Similarly, one of the central components of religious involvement is the social support and sense of community or belonging it provides to its adherents. Moreover, creating a truly sustainable world will require considerable cooperation among individuals, communities, and nations. Third, religion serves as a basis or justification for *morality* for most of the world. Many people even view humanity's treatment of the environment and other species in moral terms, arguing that humans have a moral obligation to be good stewards of both.

Think Ahead!

1. *Do people really know what makes them happy?*
2. *Why do people become religious, and how does religiousness affect happiness?*
3. *How do we promote environmentally sustainable living?*

THE SOCIAL PSYCHOLOGY OF HAPPINESS

Hedonic Happiness: Short-term pleasure people derive from things like chocolate, sex, or a new pair of pants

Eudaimonic Happiness: Deep, longer-lasting contentment or general satisfaction with life associated with living a meaningful life

Positive Psychology: Focuses on optimal human functioning, including what is good and/or adaptive about humans

What makes us happy? This is a deceptively simple question posed by people all over the world. For example, take a look at the psychology/self-help section of your nearest bookstore or online book retailer, and you will find a plethora of books either partly or wholly devoted to how to live the happy life. If you add to this all of the books on combating depression and other happiness-inhibiting mental disorders, it seems that being happy is one of humanity's central preoccupations. The fact that it has been examined by the ancient philosophers—including Socrates and Aristotle in the West and Lao Tzu and Confucius in the East—right down to the present day, further attests to its importance.

Philosophers have distinguished between *hedonic* and *eudaimonic* happiness. **Hedonic happiness** refers to the short-term pleasures people derive from things like chocolate, sex, or a new pair of pants. **Eudaimonic happiness** is considered to be a deeper, longer-lasting contentment or general satisfaction with life and is associated with living a meaningful life (Peterson, Park, & Seligman, 2005). Recently there has been a virtual explosion of social psychological interest in the United States in the roots and nature of these two types of happiness, and a number of prominent researchers have published books on the topic for the layperson (Gilbert, 2006; Lyubomirsky, 2013). Research on happiness is an emerging focus of a wider, positive psychology movement that has blossomed over the last couple of decades. **Positive psychology** focuses on optimal human functioning, including what is good and/or adaptive about humans (Snyder, Lopez, & Pedrotti, 2011). It is the study of the positive elements of human life, emotions, thoughts,

John Lund Blend Images/Newscom.

The many faces of happiness.

and behaviors, such as happiness, hope, optimism, wisdom, and courage (Seligman & Csikszentmihalyi, 2000). The positive psychology movement arose partly in response to the emphasis of traditional psychology on human weaknesses and shortcomings, such as mental illness, violence, and cognitive biases and errors.

THE NATURE OF HAPPINESS

What is happiness? **Happiness** or **subjective well-being** (SWB) has two components: temporary or short-term positive and negative feelings that may fluctuate from day-to-day or moment-to-moment and longer-lasting life satisfaction (Kahneman, 1999). The first component can be referred to as one's *online* or in-the-moment happiness and can be influenced by anything from a good (or bad) joke to a good meal to a bad headache (Aknin, Dunn, & Norton, 2012; Diener, Ng, Harter, & Arora, 2010; Larsen & Green, 2013). Although we often think of positive and negative experiences as being the opposite of one another—such that having more of one results in fewer of the other—researchers have found that they are relatively independent. This means that people may alternate between highs and lows. When people politely ask "How are you today?" they are typically asking about in-the-moment happiness. Needless to say, people who say they are happy enjoy many more positive than negative in-the-moment experiences (Fredrickson & Losada, 2005).

Happiness or Subjective Well-Being (SWB): Combination of temporary positive and negative feelings and overall life satisfaction

The second component of SWB is a global or broader evaluation of how one is doing and is often called *life satisfaction* (Diener et al., 2010). Life satisfaction is based in part on the discrepancy between how much one likes one's life as a whole versus how one would like that life to be (Caunt, Franklin, Brodaty, & Brodaty, 2013; Diener, Tamir, & Scollon, 2006). Note here that both day-to-day happiness and life satisfaction are *subjective* in that they are defined or decided by the person. Thus it will not surprise you to learn that SWB is primarily measured by self-report, because only the person can decide how happy she is. No one else, even one's therapist, can determine this. (See this chapter's Self-Reflection: Measuring Life Satisfaction, to measure your life satisfaction).

Do you know what makes you happy? A good exam grade, a job promotion, the purchase of a new car, or a meal with a close friend? This may seem like a silly question, because of course you do! Perhaps surprisingly, social psychological research has shown that people often *do not know* what makes them happy. Sure, we realize that we feel better after eating a piece of chocolate cake or watching a good movie or worse when suffering from a stomach virus or being stuck in a big traffic jam. Nonetheless, our insight often fails us when we engage in what is called **affective forecasting** or trying to predict the intensity and duration of our emotional responses to future events (Marroquín & Nolen-Hoeksema, 2015; Marroquín, Nolen-Hoeksema, & Miranda, 2013; T. D. Wilson & Gilbert, 2005; Zelenski et al., 2013). For instance, one study found that university professors who were denied tenure—which, when awarded, provides us with a permanent position—were about as happy several years later as those who received it (Gilbert, Pinel, Wilson, Blumberg, & Wheatley, 1998). This finding is contrary to the expectation most professors would have had: that the denial of tenure would lead to long-term unhappiness. Similarly, people expect that ending a romantic relationship will be much more devastating than it actually is (Gilbert et al., 1998).

This tendency to overestimate how long one's emotional reactions to future events will last is called the **durability bias** (Gilbert, Lieberman, Morewedge, & Wilson, 2004; Wood & Bettman, 2007). Think about a recent, emotion-laden event in your life. Were you as happy or sad for as long as you expected? One of the reasons we have trouble forecasting our future feelings is that we tend to focus narrowly on just the event that we are thinking about and fail to take into account the effects of other events or circumstances on our future emotional state. Wilson and his colleagues call this tendency **focalism**, because we place too much emphasis on the *focal* event that we are thinking about and too little on nonfocal events (Lench, Safer, & Levine, 2011; Wilson, Wheatley, Meyers, Gilbert, & Axsom, 2000). For instance, when couples predict how happy their upcoming marriage will make them, they are likely to ignore other events, routines, and stresses that will continue to be present in their lives and may interfere with their happiness, such as an undesirable job or the car that keeps breaking down. Moreover, they may fail to take into account all of the other, less wonderful aspects of a marriage, such as arguments and disagreements, overbearing in-laws, and so forth.

Affective Forecasting: Predicting the intensity and duration of our emotional responses to future events

Durability Bias: Tendency to overestimate how long one's emotional reactions to future events will last

Focalism: Placing too much emphasis on the focal event and too little on the nonfocal events

SELF-REFLECTION 13.1
Measuring Life Satisfaction (Part 1)

How satisfied with your life are you? Stated another way, how much of your life would you change, if you could? The below scale is one way to measure people's life satisfaction. Take a minute to answer the following and then turn the page to learn more.

TABLE 13.1   Measuring Life Satisfaction

Using the 1 through 7 scale, indicate your agreement with each item by placing the appropriate number on the line.

Item	Response options						
1. In most ways my life is close to my ideal.	1	2	3	4	5	6	7
2. The conditions of my life are excellent.	1	2	3	4	5	6	7
3. I am satisfied with my life.	1	2	3	4	5	6	7
4. So far I have gotten the important things I want in life.	1	2	3	4	5	6	7
5. If I could live my life over, I would change almost nothing.	1	2	3	4	5	6	7

Source: Pavot, W., & Diener, E. (1993). Review of the Satisfaction with Life Scale. *Psychological Assessment, 5,* 164–172.

TURN THE PAGE TO FIND OUR ANSWERS.

SELF-REFLECTION 13.2
Measuring Life Satisfaction (Part 2)

As you see in the main text, social psychologist Ed Diener has taken strong interest in life satisfaction and subjective well-being and, along with colleagues, created this Satisfaction with Life Scale (Diener, Emmons, Larsen, & Griffin, 1985; Pavot & Diener, 1993). To determine your score, simply add up your responses. According to Diener (2006) respondents who have a *highly satisfied* (30+) are happy with all major aspects of their lives (e.g., family, recreation, work/school, personal development); those with a *high* score (25–29) think that most aspects of their lives are going well but could be a little better; people with an *average* score (20–24) may be satisfied with their lives over-all, but they would like to experience a significant improvement in some domains or a little improvement in most of them; those with a slightly below average score (15–19) may either being doing very poorly in one major domain or somewhat poorly in many domains; respondents with a *dissatisfied* score (10–14) are experiencing significant problems in several domains or very significant problems in one or two domains; those with an *extremely dissatisfied* score (5–9) are very unhappy and wish for very substantial changes in their lives.

A second reason for the durability bias is that people may not keep in mind their own ability to recover or bounce back from negative events. People possess a *psychological immune system* that operates much like their biological one in that it helps to ward off or eliminate the effects of undesirable occurrences. For example, after being rejected by a romantic partner, people may alter their initial construal of the event as totally negative to one that recognizes its positive consequences, such as affording the opportunity to find someone who suits them better. How often has a friend said that a job loss or relationship breakup was "probably for the best"?

We often reinterpret negative events after they occur as "not so bad," which allows us to emotionally recover more quickly. In addition, such reassessment can facilitate a reduction in the dissonance we may experience from, say, being rejected by a desired other or fired from a job we liked. Our tendency to ignore or forget about our ability to psychologically rebound from emotional setbacks and negative events is called **immune neglect** (Gilbert et al., 1998; Hoerger, 2012). In other words, we neglect to take into consideration our psychological immune system when we predicting our reactions to future events.

Immune Neglect: Tendency for people to ignore their ability to psychologically rebound from emotional setbacks and negative events

Think Again!

1. *Take a look at your overall life satisfaction (Table 13.1). Can you identify pos-sible reasons why you are or are not satisfied?*

2. *Do you think it would preferable were we better able to predict how we will feel after future events? Why?*

3. *What are some ways that we could improve our affective forecasting?*

THE ANTECEDENTS AND BENEFITS OF HAPPINESS

Contextual Factors

Although people may struggle to pinpoint what makes them happy, psychologists have been able to identify some of the contextual and dispositional factors that impact subjective well-being.

©iStockphoto.com/Pekic.

One predictor of personal happiness is the quality of a person's romantic and platonic relationships.

Social Relationships. One predictor of personal happiness lies in the quality of a person's romantic and platonic relationships. This makes intuitive sense, considering how such relationships can satisfy our fundamental need to belong. A number of studies have shown that, on average, people who have quality relationships with others report being happier than those lacking them (Lakey, 2013). For instance, Diener and Seligman (2002) have shown that spending more time with others and being more satisfied with our interpersonal relationships are positively correlated with happiness.

People often wonder how important romantic relationships are, as compared to platonic ones, in determining subjective well-being. The research is mixed, although it generally supports the notion that married people are happier than the nonmarried (Saphire-Bernstein & Taylor, 2013). For instance, it appears as they transition from being single to being married, people experience an increase in subjective well-being (Kamp Dush & Amato, 2005). Unfortunately, this happiness boost tends to deflate after a couple of years, dropping the newlyweds back to their individual premarital levels (Lucas, Clark, Georgellis, & Diener, 2003). Consistent with the notion that marriage can increase happiness is the fact that SWB significantly decreases upon divorce or death of a spouse (Lucas, 2005). Although marital status does impact happiness, research has shown that the *quality* of the marriage has a stronger effect than simply whether or not a person is married (Proulx, Helms, & Buehler, 2007).

Children. Lately there has been a lot of discussion in the news about the effect of children on people's overall well-being. Most people want to have children and believe that having them will make them happy. However, the bulk of the research shows that childless couples are generally happier than those with children, and a recent meta-analysis of over 100 studies found that relationship satisfaction tends to drop significantly once couples have one or more children (Luhmann, Hofmann, Eid, & Lucas, 2012). Furthermore, satisfaction tends to rebound once the children have moved out of the house (Gorchoff, John, & Helson, 2008). Does all of this mean that you shouldn't have children? Absolutely not. Although the emotional and financial stresses and strains of parenthood can be challenging, parents generally report that their children have brought meaning into their lives and, in retrospect, tend not to regret having them (Nelson, Kushlev, English, Dunn, & Lyubomirsky, 2013).

Personal Wealth. We have probably all heard the old adage that money can't buy happiness. Yet at the same time, many people feel that if they just had a little more money, then they would be a little happier. So just what is the actual relationship between wealth and happiness? Well, it depends. People do tend to be less happy at the lower end of the socioeconomic ladder, where they are struggling to satisfy basic needs for food and shelter, and as their income begins to rise, so too does their happiness (Diener et al., 2010). However, once these basic needs are met, more money does not necessarily increase a person's happiness, although it can (Kahneman & Deaton, 2010; Mohanty, 2014). Interestingly, a study of homeless individuals staying at a shelter in Madrid revealed that about half of them consider themselves happy (Panadero, Guillén, & Vázquez, 2015). In fact, at the other end of the spectrum, a study of the 400 wealthiest Americans found that they were on average no more satisfied with their lives than East African Masai, a group of herders who live without running water or electricity (Diener & Seligman, 2004; Tay, Morrison, & Diener, 2014). Perhaps even more surprisingly, people who win huge amounts of money in the lottery experience only a short-term gain in happiness, returning to their prior level after the novelty of it all has worn off (Brickman, Coates, & Janoff-Bulman, 1978).

Several hypotheses have been proposed to explain why money is not strongly associated with happiness at the individual level. First, once people are able to meet their needs for food, shelter, employment, and so forth, earning a little extra money does not change their lives in meaningful ways. Second, people's satisfaction with their current wealth or income is based not on how much they actually have—their *absolute wealth*—but rather how they fare in comparison to other people—their *relative wealth* (Boyce, Brown, & Moore, 2010). As we have discussed in Chapter 6 on social influence, people often engage in social comparisons and are more concerned with how they are doing in relation to how referent others are doing. A third hypothesis for why personal wealth is not strongly associated with happiness is that, after experiencing an increase, people quickly get used to their new income level and begin comparing themselves to those who have even more.

The idea that people adapt to new situations in life and then return to their previous level of well-being forms the basis of **adaptation-level theory** (Brickman et al., 1978). The idea originally emerged from studies of paraplegics and lottery winners, who seemed to psychologically adapt to their losses or gains and return to their earlier level

Adaptation-Level Theory: Idea that people adapt to new situations in life and then return to their previous level of well-being of well-being. Brickman et al. (1978) provided evidence that people who lost the ability to use their legs experienced only a short-term dip in their life satisfaction.

Adaptation-level theory may make intuitive sense, but newer research has questioned its validity (Headey, 2013). Even one of its early champions has begun having second thoughts about the explanatory power of adaptation-level theory (Easterlin, 2010). For instance, chronic health problems, significant physical disabilities, death of a spouse, and long-term and/or frequent unemployment can all lead to enduring or even permanent declines in SWB (Clark, Diener, Georgellis, & Lucas, 2008).

Fourth, of the two components of subjective well-being, wealth is correlated more strongly with life satisfaction than with our daily positive and negative affect (Diener et al., 2010). This suggests that how good or bad we feel from day-to-day has little to do with how much money we have. Age also matters: Income is more closely related to life satisfaction for people ages 30 to 50 than for people who are above or below that age range (Cheung & Lucas, 2015). Finally, as people grow wealthier, they also tend to become more materialistic, and materialism—the continuous striving to accumulate wealth and possessions—is related to a reduction in happiness (Kasser, 2004).

Culture and Subjective Well-being

Like individuals, nations as a whole differ in their level of happiness (Curhan et al., 2014). You may have seen news reports indicating how nations rank in their Gross National Happiness. For instance, according to the World Data of Happiness (WDH), Ireland, Norway, and Finland ranked highest in general life satisfaction, whereas Burundi, Zimbabwe, and Tanzania were lowest (see Table 13.2) (Tov & Au, 2013). Remember, though, that there is a hedonic component of well-being, and the rankings change if we focus on just day-to-day emotions. Iceland, Djibouti, and Kenya possess the greatest ratio of positive to negative emotions, whereas Armenia, Georgia, and Iraq are lowest.

Unlike personal wealth, societal wealth has a strong positive relationship to happiness, and may well be more influential. Correlations of SWB with personal wealth are in the .1 to three range, as compared with roughly .5 for national wealth (Diener & Biswas-Diener, 2002). This is true when we compare the relative wealth and well-being of different countries as well as the income gap between the very poor and the rich within a country (Diener, Tay, & Oishi, 2013). Importantly, income and well-being are most closely connected in nations where people are also becoming more optimistic, more satisfied with their financial situation, and *feel* that they personally are better off (Diener et al., 2013).

Differences in wealth are not the only explanations for the variation in well-being across nations. Some research suggests that people in individualistic nations are generally happier than those in collectivistic ones (Veenhoven, 1999). One reason for this is that individualistic nations tend to be wealthier. Why might this be so? Well, people in collectivistic cultures are more likely to sacrifice the fulfillment of their personal, instinctual needs and desires in favor of gaining the approval of others and maintaining social

TABLE 13.2   Well-Being Across Nations

The top and bottom five nations on the general life satisfaction measure of well-being.

	Nation	General Life Satisfaction Score
Top 5	Ireland	8.14
	Norway	8.09
	Finland	8.02
	Sweden	7.90
	Australia	7.88
Bottom 5	Liberia	3.43
	Benin	3.02
	Burundi	2.94
	Zimbabwe	2.83
	Tanzania	2.45

Source: Tov, W., & Au, E. W. M. (2013). Comparing well-being across nations: Conceptual and empirical issues. In S. A. David, I. Boniwell, & A. Conley Ayers (Eds.) *The Oxford handbook of happiness* (pp. 449–464). New York: Oxford University Press.

harmony (Suh & Koo, 2008). Consistent with this idea is the finding that more individualistically oriented people in collectivistic cultures report higher levels of happiness than their more collectivistic fellow citizens (Heine, Lehman, Markus, & Kitayama, 1999). In addition, individualistic countries grant their citizens more personal freedom and guarantee more individual rights, which may also lead to greater happiness (Diener, 2000).

As you are reading this section on culture and happiness, you may be wonder whether the meaning of happiness varies around the globe (at least I hope you are!). The answer is both yes and no (Diener, 2012; Joshanloo & Weijers, 2014). To be sure, individualists associate well-being with autonomy and independence more than collectivists do, whereas collectivists more heavily emphasize connections with others as a source of happiness (Joshanloo, 2014; Kitayama & Markus, 2000). In addition, people are happier to some extent when they possess characteristics that are preferred in their cultures (Fulmer et al., 2010). For instance, in individualistic nations—which value high self-esteem—self-esteem predicts satisfaction, whereas in collectivistic nations—which do not place importance on self-esteem—individual self-esteem is not correlated with life satisfaction (Diener & Diener, 1995; Steele & Lynch, 2013). Nevertheless, as we just mentioned, fulfilling individual needs is associated with greater happiness across both types of cultures.

Person Factors

Situational factors clearly influence personal happiness. What about dispositional ones? First, the fact that happiness is fairly stable over time for most people suggests that it may have a genetic basis (Lucas, 2008; Pavot & Diener, 2013). Second, two personality variables, extraversion and neuroticism, have been reliably linked to SWB, such that extraversion is *positively* correlated with positive affect and neuroticism is *positively* correlated with negative affect (Lucas, 2008). That is, extraverted people tend to be happier than introverted ones, and neurotic individuals less happy than emotionally stable persons (McCrae & Costa, 1991).

Think Again!

1. *Before reading this section, did you think that you would be happier if you had a little more money? Are you convinced by the research? Why or why not?*

2. *Ask your parents or other people about their level of happiness before and after having children. What do they say? Remember, though, that self-reports are not always reliable.*

3. *Can you think of other personality variables that may also correlate with happiness?*

Benefits of Happiness

Why should we strive for happiness? Well, one obvious answer is that it feels good. But there is much more to the story, and research has revealed many other important benefits to being happy. In a meta-analysis examining 225 studies, Lyubomirsky, King, & Diener (2005) pinpointed a number of them. First, happiness leads to greater work success, including higher income, more prestigious jobs, greater productivity, and better evaluations (Jacobs Bao & Lyubomirsky, 2013; Oishi, 2012). Second, greater well-being is not only positively *correlated* with getting married and marital satisfaction but, as several longitudinal studies have demonstrated, is *causally* related (Lucas et al., 2003).

Third, individuals high on SWB are seen as warmer and friendlier (Schimmack, Oishi, Furr, & Funder, 2004), more intelligent, competent, physically attractive, and moral (Diener & Fujita, 1995; King & Napa, 1998). Finally, people who are happy tend to be healthier, both physically and mentally. In brief, it pays to be happy, both literally and figuratively.

Improving Your Happiness

Given the tremendous benefits of living a happy life, what can you do about it? How much of your total happiness can you control, and how much is rooted in factors that you cannot change? Sonia Lyubomirsky, one of the leading happiness researchers, developed the sustainable happiness model (SHM) that suggests that people *can* affect their day-to-day happiness by making small changes in their behavior and outlook (Lyubomirsky, Sheldon, & Schkade, 2005; Sheldon & Lyubomirsky, 2006a). She estimates that genes (including a portion of personality) account for about only 50% of people's happiness (see Figure 13.1).

This portion reflects a person's **set point** or adaptation level for SWB, which is the level to which a person typically returns after experiencing significant life events (e.g., a job change, the end of a relationship, etc.). People seem to walk on a virtual **hedonic treadmill**, which means that they move forward through life but their level of day-to-day happiness remains about the same (Brickman et al., 1978; Frederick & Loewenstein, 1999; Mancini, Bonanno, & Clark, 2011).

Circumstances such as ethnicity, gender, income, health, and geographic location together contribute about 10%. Together that means that we lack the ability to affect about 60% of our happiness. If our level of happiness were only based on genes and external circumstances, it would indeed be difficult to substantially improve it.

Fortunately for you and me, the remaining 40% of people's happiness is related to one's day-to-day activities and can be altered relatively easily. For instance, regularly taking time to reflect on and write about the good aspects of one's life, identifying things for which one is grateful, or focusing on and recording optimistic thoughts about the future can all boost one's mood and overall well-being (Catalino, Algoe, & Fredrickson, 2014; Layous, Nelson, & Lyubomirsky, 2013; Sheldon & Lyubomirsky, 2006b). Another effective way to increase one's happiness is to engage in behaviors that are designed to achieve goals that are personally satisfying or meaningful (Diener, Fujita, Tay, & Biswas-Diener, 2012). Such activities could be as simple as reading or learning a new instrument or as complex as working toward an advanced educational degree. Please note that the percentages above refer to the influences on people's happiness in

Set Point: The level of well-being to which a person typically returns after experiencing significant life events

Hedonic Treadmill: Idea that people move forward through life but their level of happiness remains about the same

FIGURE 13.1   Sustainable Happiness Model

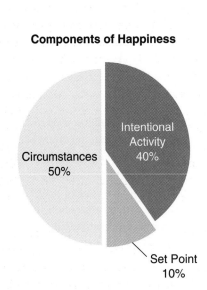

Components of Happiness

Source: Adapted from Sheldon, K. M., Boehm, J., & Lyubomirsky, S. (2013). Variety is the spice of happiness: The hedonic adaptation prevention model. In S. A. David, I. Boniwell & A. Conley Ayers (Eds.), *The Oxford handbook of happiness* (pp. 901–914). New York, NY US: Oxford University Press.

general, not for any particular individual. In other words, it would be incorrect to assume that exactly 40% of your happiness is easy to change as the intensity and types of influences are different for different people.

In summary, you can see that happiness is not the simple, straightforward notion that so many of us believe it to be. We may know when we are happy, but we struggle with identifying the factors that influences our happiness. I hope reading this section will help you better understand the roots of happiness and allow you to make positive changes in your life.

DOING RESEARCH: GENERALIZING TO THE REAL WORLD

In Chapter 5, we discussed the need for researchers to monitor and maintain both internal and external validity. As you have learned, internal validity refers to the confidence that the manipulations of the independent variable and only those manipulations produced changes in the dependent variable. In the case of the bystander research, the researchers would need to be certain that their manipulation of group size and only that manipulation was the cause of differences in responding across the conditions. Researchers frequently also want their research to have **external validity** or **generalizability**, which refers to how well the results of the study can be applied to other settings and populations (Shadish, Cook, & Campbell, 2002). Do the results apply to different laboratory and non-laboratory settings, to additional populations, and across a variety of manipulations and forms of the variables? For instance, do the effects of thinking about god that are found in the laboratory hold true in the outside world? Contrary to what some may assume, studies conducted in applied settings are not necessarily more (or less) generalizable than laboratory studies. The reason is there will be limits to the extent to which the findings of *any* given study hold true beyond the original conditions (Aronson, Ellsworth, Carlsmith, & Gonzales, 1990). It is also important to note that researchers are not always hoping to generalize to all populations. For instance, one might only be interested in the effects of oxytocin on affiliation among Japanese women who have given birth in the last three months and whether or not the findings apply to women who do not meet these criteria is irrelevant.

When designing a study, researchers need to decide, ahead of time, to what population they wish to generalize the findings from the sample of individuals who participate in the study (e.g., college students, single women, etc.). If one wants experimental research on the bystander to apply to both males and females, then participants should obviously be both men and women. Researchers can increase the confidence they have in the external validity of the study in several ways. First, ensure that the sample is **representative** of the relevant population on the variables that matter, such as frequencies of gender, age, language, ethnicity, education level, and so forth. Recall that findings based on WEIRD samples should only be generalized to WEIRD populations (see Chapter 5). Scientists will often conduct **random selection** or **sampling**—which means that every individual in

External Validity: Extent to which the results of a study can be generalized or applied to other settings and populations (also called generalizability)

Generalizability: The extent to which the results of a study can be generalized or applied to other settings and populations (also called external validity)

Representative Sampling: When a study sample mirrors the relevant population on the variables that matter, such as frequencies of gender, age, language, or ethnicity

Random Selection or Sampling: That every individual in a population has an equal probability of being chosen for inclusion in the study

a population has an equal probability of being chosen for inclusion in the study—as a way to produce a representative sample (Shadish et al., 2002).

Second, the study should be replicated across settings and populations to which one seeks to generalize—the more the better. Third, the experimental setting should match, as much as possible, the conditions to which one wants to generalize. For instance, a laboratory experiment should have what is called **mundane realism**, which means that it is reasonably similar to the relevant real-world setting in all important respects (Aronson et al., 1990). In the bystander studies, the researchers hoped the experiment's participants would feel the same way that bystanders would feel when witnessing a real-world event.

THE SOCIAL PSYCHOLOGY OF RELIGION

According to recent estimates, approximately 80% of the world's adults identify with a religious group, and about 68% regard religion as an important part of their daily lives (Diener, Tay, & Myers, 2011; Pew Religion and Public Life Project, 2012). At the present time, Christians comprise the single largest religious group (31.5% of the world), followed by Muslims (23.2%), those not affiliated with any organized religion (16.3%), and Hindus (15%) (see Figure 13.2). The pervasiveness of religion attests to the need for social psychological analysis. Yet, with the exception of a classic book by Gordon Allport (1950) and the work of a relatively small number of other researchers, the study of religion has historically been only a minor concern to social psychologists. As a result, not surprisingly, coverage of the psychology of religion is either absent or scant in most social psychology textbooks. I have included this section on religion for two reasons. First, the psychological study of religion is becoming more prevalent in social psychology, and second, recent research has begun connecting religious belief and practice to a number of other topics that are central to social psychology, including prosocial and moral behavior, prejudice, and happiness (Saroglou, 2014b).

THE NATURE OF RELIGIOUS BELIEF

Religiousness

Before going further, we need to clarify exactly what aspects of religion we are and are not examining. The most important distinction is the one between studying the validity of religious institutions, beliefs, and practices, and investigating how religious beliefs "work." We are not addressing whether or what people ought to believe in but rather how religious beliefs and practices interact with people's psychological functioning. Asking how beliefs work means looking at the psychological mechanisms, personality traits, and contextual characteristics that lead people to affiliate with religious groups and/or believe in a supernatural being. In addition, religious beliefs and practices have the capacity to affect other aspects of our social being, including our emotions, thoughts, well-being, and behavior.

Mundane Realism: When a study is similar to the relevant real-world setting in all important respects

Jupiterimgaes/Photos.com/Thinkstock.

Yawar Nazir /Getty Images News/Getty Images.

Religious
leaders around
the world.

Pacific Press /LightRocket/Getty Images.

In this chapter, we will focus on *individual* or *personal* religion and not religion as a social institution. The extent to which a person is involved in religion is called **religiousness**, which incorporates behaviors, attitudes, cognitions, and emotion with respect to some sort of transcendent entity (Saroglou, 2014a). Transcendent entities are beings that are postulated to be greater than humans and transcend or go beyond the physical world. Although religions vary considerably in their precise conception of the transcendent being, all of them incorporate one or more into their theology. For instance, ancient Greeks believed in the existence of Zeus and many other gods, whereas Christians believe in one God.

Religiousness:
Extent to which a
person is involved
religion

FIGURE 13.2   Religions Around the World

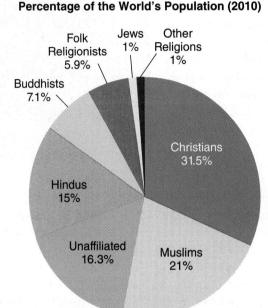

Percentage of the World's Population (2010)

Source: Pew Research Center's for Religion and Public Life Project, *The Global Religious Landscape* (2012).

According to Saroglou (Saroglou, 2011, 2014a), there are four universal dimensions of religiousness: believing, bonding, behaving, and belonging (the four "Bs"). First, people hold religious *beliefs* about spiritual and physical worlds, such as that an otherworldly heaven exists. Second, people develop emotional connections or *bonds* with other religious people and with the transcendent being. They may "love" their god or become emotionally attached to members of their religious community, church, synagogue, mosque, and so forth. Third, people *behave* in accordance with the dictates, tenets, or principles of their religion. Fourth, religious people *belong* to and identify with a group of fellow believers. Taken together, these four criteria are the hallmarks of religion and can help us distinguish religion from other cultural institutions or groups.

Religious Orientation

What motivates people to become or stay involved in religion? One of the classic approaches to the social psychology of religion proposes that people are either internally or externally motivated to participate in religion (Allport & Ross, 1967; D. W. Barrett, Patock-Peckham, Hutchinson, & Nagoshi, 2005; Batson, Schoenrade, & Ventis, 1993; Hunter & Merrill, 2013) (see Table 13.3). Those who have an internal or **intrinsic orientation** view religion as an end in itself and arrange their lives around their religious beliefs and practices. Intrinsic

Intrinsic Orientation: View of religion as an end in itself

orientation is correlated with devout, often fundamentalist, adherence to religious tenets, norms, and prohibitions (Altemeyer & Hunsberger, 1992). In contrast, people with an **extrinsic orientation** use religion as a means to nonreligious ends, such as socialization, status, and emotional security against anxiety-provoking thoughts of death (Doane, Elliott, & Dyrenforth, 2014; Maltby & Day, 2003). Their beliefs tend to be more superficial and less strict than more intrinsically oriented individuals.

A woman receives communion at a Catholic church in Kinshasa, the capital city of the Democratic Republic of the Congo.

REUTERS/Peter Andrews.

Batson et al. (1993) recognized that these two dimensions failed to account for those individuals who experience religion as a spiritual journey for truth and meaning. Batson and his colleagues proposed that people who hold a **quest orientation** perceive religion as an open-ended process of trying to answer existential questions, such as the meaning of life and the role or place of humans in the greater universe (Batson, Denton, & Vollmecke, 2008). People exhibiting a quest orientation raise doubts about established religious beliefs and practices and may change their beliefs if they don't seem to fit with their own experiences of the world. Gandhi and Martin Luther King are often cited as prominent examples of quest-oriented individuals. Although people generally approach religion from just one of these orientations, it is important to note that a person may have mixed motives. For instance, one can be a devout Catholic, adhering to its doctrines and rituals for their own sake, but yet also enjoy related, nonreligious benefits of attending a church, such as making and maintaining social connections.

Extrinsic Orientation: View of religion as a means to nonreligious ends

Quest Orientation: View of religion as an open-ended process of trying to answer existential questions

Think Again!

1. *How religious are you (if you are)? Examine your religiousness using the four Bs of religion.*

2. *If you are religious, would you say you are more intrinsically, extrinsically, or quest oriented? Why? If you are not part of organized religion, can you still have a religious orientation? If so, how?*

3. *In your opinion, are the three orientations independent of each other? For instance, can you be high on more than one?*

TABLE 13.3   Sample Items From Religious Orientation Scales

Selected items from the Intrinsic, Extrinsic, and Quest Orientation Scales.

Strongly disagree (1) to strongly agree (9)	Item
	Intrinsic Orientation
	It is important to me to spend periods of time in private religious thought and meditation.
	I try hard to carry my religion over into all of my other dealings in life.
	My religious beliefs are really what lie behind my whole approach to life.
	Extrinsic Orientation
	Although I believe in my religion, I feel there are many more important things in my life.
	A primary reason for my interest in religion is that my church is a congenial social activity.
	Occasionally I find it necessary to compromise my religious beliefs in order to protect my social and economic standing.
	Quest Orientation
	I was not very interested in religion until I began to ask questions about the meaning and purpose of my life.
	It might be said that I value my religious doubts and uncertainties.
	There are many religious issues on which my views are still changing.

Sources: Allport, G. W., & Ross, J. M. (1967). Personal religious orientation and prejudice. *Journal of Personality and Social Psychology, 5*, 432–443. Batson, C. D., & Schoenrade, P. A. (1991). Measuring religion as Quest II: Validity concerns. *Journal for the Scientific Study of Religion, 30*, 430–447.

The Functions of Religion

As you can see, people vary in their motivation for joining religions. In addition to uncovering these motivational differences, research on religion demonstrates that it can serve several different functions for its adherents. The two most important functions fulfilled by religion are the provision of meaning and the facilitation of coping with stress (Batson et al., 1993; Kirkpatrick, 2005). Humans are meaning-seeking creatures driven to know why events happen as they do and why the world is as it is (Park, 2012). Religions tell us why we exist at all and what our purpose is, thereby endowing our lives with meaning. The provision of *meaning* is one of the primary functions of religion (Hood, Hill, & Spilka, 2009).

A second major function of religion is *coping*. People often turn to religion, including prayer and participation in religious rituals, to cope with and adapt to negative events in their lives. When faced with the death of a loved one, a life-threatening disease, or other major trauma, religious persons tend to exhibit more religion-based behavior, such as prayer and attendance at church services (Cummings & Pargament, 2012). For example, religion became much more important to Americans immediately after the September 11, 2001, terrorist attacks (Seirmarco et al., 2012).

ORIGINS AND BENEFITS OF RELIGIOUS BELIEF

Evolutionary Origins

One of the most interesting questions about religion is how it emerged over the course of human history. Why did people begin to develop superstitions and supernatural explanations for the natural and social worlds? Evolutionary theorists have offered two answers: religion as either a psychological adaptation or a by-product of other psychological adaptations (Atran, 2008; Bellah, 2011; Dow, 2006; Sosis, 2009).

According to the former perspective, religious beliefs and practices evolved and spread among humans because they solved one or more adaptive problems. For instance, some researchers have claimed that religiosity is associated with better physical and mental health. In addition to these proposed *direct* benefits, engaging in religious activity may also provide individuals with the *indirect* advantages, such as those resulting from cohesion and cooperation within their religious groups (Matthews, 2012).

The second perspective on the evolutionary basis for religion posits that it is not an adaptation in and of itself but rather it is a consequence of other cognitive adaptations (Shariff, Norenzayan, & Henrich, 2010). For instance, people seem to be predisposed to be sensitive to and detect the role of humans in causing events in our environments (Guthrie, 2007). This tendency can lead to the belief that invisible and hence supernatural others affect the environment (Atran, 2008). Both theories are plausible, and at this point there is no consensus among evolutionary psychologists as to whether religion is an adaptation or the product of other adaptations.

One of the questions that you should be asking with regard to the evolutionary explanation for religion is whether religion, given its ancient roots, has a genetic basis. Unfortunately, high quality research is scarce in this area (Hood et al., 2009). However, one solid study involving over 800 pairs of twins found that about half of the variation in religious orientation between twins was because of genetic factors, which is comparable to the variation of many personality traits (Waller, Kojetin, Bouchard, Lykken, & Tellegen, 1990). More recently, Bradshaw and Ellison (2008) examined data on four measures of religiosity from over 350 fraternal and identical twins. They concluded that the genes accounted for between 19% (for childhood religiosity) and 65% (for claiming to be "born again") of the variation in religiosity, depending on the measure. Moreover, the heritability of religiosity appears to increase as people transition from adolescence to adulthood (L. B. Koenig, McGue, & Iacono, 2008). The remaining variance is attributable to various environmental factors and to gene-environment interactions.

Individual Experiences

A person's developmental and socialization history are major influences on her or his religiosity and religious affiliation (Desrosiers, 2012). Uncovering the relationship between parental and child religiosity is complicated by the fact that the parents' religious beliefs themselves affect parenting, which in turn impacts the children's own beliefs (Bartkowski, Xu, & Levin, 2008). For instance, children of authoritative parents—who strike a balance between being authoritarian and being permissive—tend to develop an intrinsic religious orientation, whereas those of permissive parents are more likely to be extrinsically oriented (Giesbrecht, 1995). At the same time, parents who have more fundamental or extreme religious views tend toward the authoritarian parenting style, which emphasizes obedience and conformity, which can then affect their children's religious views.

Probably the most influential theory linking development and religion is Kirkpatrick's compensation hypothesis: Children with insecure attachments to their parents are likely to seek a secure, personal relationship with a god as adults (Granqvist, 2006; Granqvist, Mikulincer, & Shaver, 2010; Kirkpatrick, 2012). The theory has garnered substantial empirical support. For instance, one longitudinal study found that women reporting an insecure relationship with their parents were significantly more likely to have developed a relationship with God, thereby compensating or making up for their earlier insecurities (Kirkpatrick, 1997).

Other research has demonstrated how religious beliefs change over the course of child and adolescent development. For example, concepts of God held by three- to six-year-old U.S. children commonly resemble those of fairy tale characters, whereas 12- to 18-year olds show a much greater variety in their beliefs (Fowler, 1981; Harms, 1944). Finally, religious attitudes and behaviors, like other attitudes and behaviors, are enhanced or suppressed by social learning and punishment and reinforcement (Granqvist, 2014; Kirkpatrick, 2005).

Earlier in this book we postulated that there is something special about social cognition that sets it apart from nonsocial cognition and argued that there are specific brain processes devoted to social cognition (Chapter 3). When considering the evolution of religious cognition, we can ask if there is anything unique about *religious* cognition in contrast to other forms of cognition. According to Gervais (2014), religious cognition utilizes the same cognitive mechanisms as routine social cognition, which is consistent with the religion as by-product position described above. That is, religious and nonreligious social cognition rely on the same brain regions, show the same developmental trajectory in children, exhibit the same types of biases, and demonstrate other similarities (J. L. Barrett, 2000; Gervais, 2014).

One example of the parallel between religious and social cognition is the fact that people's public self-awareness increases when thinking about either people or god, in comparison to a nonsocial control condition (Gervais & Norenzayan, 2012). Moreover, people respond in more socially desirable ways when thinking about god than about a control topic (Gervais & Norenzayan, 2012). Thus, research seems to suggest that there is nothing about religious cognitive processes that distinguishes them from other social cognitive processes.

Based on your knowledge and experiences, do you think that people who are religious differ in one or more important personality traits from nonreligious people? The question is an interesting one. It has been suggested that religiosity itself is a personality dimension because it varies systematically between people and seems to be relatively stable, at least in adulthood (Allport, 1950; Hood et al., 2009; Schaefer & Gorsuch, 1991). However, Saroglou's (2012) four "Bs" concept of religiousness is much broader than a particular personality trait and includes the beliefs people hold and the groups they belong to, neither of which are considered components of personality (Ashton, 2013; Ashton & Lee, 2014). Moreover, widely accepted measures of personality traits like extraversion or neuroticism do not assess either specific beliefs or membership in specific groups, and it is unlikely that they ever could (Costa & McCrae, 2009).

Although religiousness is not itself a personality trait, it may be correlated with true personality variables (Argyle, 2000; Ashton & Lee, 2014; Batson et al., 1993). For instance, a meta-analysis of 71 mostly Christian samples examining these links found that people who were more religious were generally also more conscientious and agreeable than less religious persons (Saroglou, 2010). Other research shows that religiosity is positively correlated with measures of honesty and humility (Lee, Ogunfowora, & Ashton, 2005).

There has been great interest in the relationship between religiosity and a variable called right-wing authoritarianism (RWA), which we discussed in Chapter 10 in the context of prejudice. As you may recall, RWA—the tendency to submit to authority, support aggression toward outgroups, and endorse conventional norms and morality—is positively associated with prejudicial attitudes (Altemeyer, 1996, 1998; Duckitt, 2001). Research has shown that people who are more religious—thus holding more traditional beliefs and attitudes—are also higher on RWA (Bouchard, 2009; de Regt, 2012; M. K. Johnson et al., 2011). Importantly, this relationship between religiosity and RWA is present across different religions, including Hindus, Muslims, Jews, and Christians, and in both Eastern Europe and the United States (Altemeyer & Hunsberger, 1992; Flere & Klanjšek, 2009).

Finally, although not a personality dimension, a number of studies have shown that intelligence is negatively associated with both religious fundamentalism and how strongly a person identifies with and how devoutly he practices his religion (Ganzach, Ellis, & Gotlibovski, 2013; Lewis, Ritchie, & Bates, 2011; Nyborg, 2009). Interestingly, a recent meta-analysis of 63 studies found this negative correlation to be stronger for college students and other adults than for younger participants (Zuckerman, Silberman, & Hall, 2013).

Cultural Influences

Like other beliefs and practices, those pertaining to religion are embedded in culture. Religion and culture influence each other; moreover, religion has been characterized as a kind of culture (Johnson & Cohen, 2014). Like cultures, religions provide meaning, strongly affect how their members perceive the world, what attitudes and beliefs they hold, their identity, and the practices in which they should or should not engage.

Unpacking the relationship between religion and culture is further complicated by the vast differences between religions and the ways in which beliefs in practices within a given religion vary both across and within national and local cultures. Moreover, differences between religions may mirror those between cultures and therefore can be difficult to distinguish from them. For example, Cohen and Hill (2007) found that, at least among their U.S. samples, Jews and Catholics were less individualistic than Protestants.

Prosociality and Prejudice

Prosociality

People tend to hold the stereotype that individuals who are religious are more moral than the nonreligious and, consequently, that they are more prosocial (Galen, 2012). Although this may be accurate to some extent (and religious individuals certainly *report* being more helpful), the relationship between religion and prosocial behavior is more complicated and depends on many factors (Galen, 2012; Mattis et al., 2000; Preston, Ritter, & Hernandez, 2010; Saroglou, 2012). First of all, prosociality seems to be greater among intrinsically rather than extrinsically oriented persons (Batson & Flory, 1990; Benson et al., 1980; Hunsberger & Platonow, 1986). Whereas the intrinsically oriented are more likely to help similar others and to do so in a planned fashion, those higher in quest orientation exhibit a more universal helping ethic, will help a wider range of people, and will do so in a more spontaneous fashion (Batson et al., 2008; Batson, Eidelman, Higley, & Russel, 2001; Hansen, Vandenberg, & Patterson, 1995).

Prejudice

What do you think: Are religious persons more or less likely to be accepting of others than the nonreligious? You may be surprised to learn that, if anything, greater religiosity predicts more prejudice and less tolerance, despite the fact that tolerance is explicitly advocated by many religions (Hall, Park, Song, & Cody, 2010; Hood et al., 2009; Whitley, 2009). As is the case with prosociality, the religiosity-prejudice relationship depends on what aspect of religiosity is measured, what religion a person belongs to, who the targets of prejudice are, and a variety of situational features (Doehring, 2013; Hunsberger & Jackson, 2005; Leak & Finken, 2011; Ramsay, Pang, Shen, & Rowatt, 2014; Rowatt, Carpenter, & Haggard, 2014).

For instance, intrinsic religiosity seems related to *less* racial/ethnic prejudice but *more* anti-gay/lesbian prejudice (Hunsberger & Jackson, 2005). Context also matters. LaBouff,

Rowatt, Johnson, and Finkle (2012) conducted an inventive field study in England and The Netherlands. The experimenters asked 99 adults who were passing by either a religious or a nonreligious building to complete a brief attitude survey. The researchers found that people who were surveyed outside the religious structures (but did not enter them) held more negative attitudes—more prejudice—toward 11 of 12 target groups, including Africans, Arabs, the rich, the poor, and gays and lesbians. The only exception was for Christians. The authors hypothesized that priming of religious concepts occurred naturally as a result of exposure to the religious building and consequently also primed prejudicial attitudes. Indeed, priming of religious concepts conducted in controlled laboratory settings has shown that it increases thoughts and behavior related to the tenets of a person's religion (Johnson, Rowatt, & LaBouff, 2010; Johnson, Rowatt, & LaBouff, 2012).

In sum, it is clear that the relationships between religion and prosocial behavior and prejudice are complex. Note that, like other social behavior, these relationships illustrate one of our core principles of social psychology: how personal and situational factors *together* determine social behavior.

Religion, Mental Health, and Happiness

If religion can lead to improvements in physical health (see Social Psychology Applied to Health section in this chapter), what then are its effects on mental health and happiness? Before we examine the research, let's first acknowledge that the division between physical and mental health can be muddy at times, in part because changing one can change the other, and in part because they simply overlap. For example, people who feel depressed may also feel more tired, and treating one may alleviate the other.

The weight of the evidence indicates that greater religious involvement is positively correlated with a number of indicators of mental functioning, including higher self-esteem, lower levels of depression, better stress management, and less death-related anxiety (Hogg, Adelman, & Blagg, 2010; Laurencelle, Abell, & Schwartz, 2002; Smith, McCullough, & Poll, 2003). Moreover, religious individuals tend to be more optimistic and hopeful about the future and report being higher on well-being (Hackney & Sanders, 2003; Lomas, Cartwright, Edginton, & Ridge, 2014; Myers, 2013). It seems then, that there is something about religion that facilitates or at least is largely compatible with individual SWB.

Determining exactly how religious involvement enhances SWB is complicated by the fact that their relationship is not straightforward (Gebauer, Nehrlich, Sedikides, & Neberich, 2013). In a massive study involving over 420,000 individuals from 153 nations, Diener et al. (2011) found that the strength of the religiosity-SWB correlation depends on other societal factors. First of all, in nations and U.S. states where religiosity is high, religiosity has a stronger positive correlation with well-being, as compared to those with low religiosity. Second, nations and states that are more economically prosperous and in which people experience relatively greater safety and security, religiosity is less important for SWB. In other words, religious involvement is more critical

SOCIAL PSYCHOLOGY APPLIED TO HEALTH
DOES RELIGION MAKE YOU HEALTHY?

Recently there has been a great deal of coverage in the popular press describing the benefits of religious practice on physical health (Luhrmann, 2013). Reviews of the empirical research confirm this (Koenig, McCullough, & Larson, 2001). Church or worship attendance—perhaps the most frequently studied component of religiousness—has been linked with a variety of healthy behaviors and better outcomes (Park, 2007). For instance, one study of over 71,000 women found that church attendance positively correlated with many health behaviors, including preventive care (such as mammograms), although not with regular exercise or saturated fat intake (Salmoirago-Blotcher et al., 2011). Other research has shown that attendance is negatively related to mortality due to all causes (Schnall et al., 2010). For example, people who attend service several times a week live an average of seven years longer than those who never attend (Hummer, Rogers, Nam, & Ellison, 1999).

There are three qualifications to the religiosity-health link that should be kept in mind. First, the health benefits of religiosity depend in part on what religion a person subscribes to. For example, Christian Scientists are prohibited from seeing physicians or receiving immunizations and are therefore especially vulnerable to certain illnesses and diseases. Second, many of the studies rely on self-reported health and worship attendance, and, as you know, self-reports are often unreliable. Third, the direction of the influence between religion and health is impossible to determine from the correlational studies from which most of the relevant data are gathered (Hayward & Krause, 2014). Nevertheless, we can now at least confidently say that religiosity is more likely to be positively associated with better rather than worse health.

The more interesting question is why might religiosity have these effects. Oman and Thoresen (2005) have offered several explanations, three of which are related to *mental* health. One is that a religion may overtly encourage health behaviors and in some cases may prohibit followers from engaging in unhealthy activities, such as smoking or drinking. Alternately, belonging to a church community can enhance mental health by bolstering social support and reducing loneliness, as we discussed earlier.

Another way that religion can improve physical health is by offering ways of coping over and above those available to nonreligious people. For example, religion-based *positive* coping, such as perceiving God to be a partner in achieving health and framing adverse events as God's will and as potentially beneficial are positively linked to health (Ano & Vasconcelles, 2005). However, people who engage in *negative* religious coping, such as being angry at and/or blaming God or believing that health problems are caused by a devil can undermine their physical and mental health (Ano & Vasconcelles, 2005). In short, religion can either hamper or boost physical health.

to providing social support for people living in difficult societal circumstances than it is for those in more comfortable ones. Third, individuals who are highly religious had higher SWB only if they live in a highly religious nation or state, suggesting that the person-culture fit is important for individual well-being. Finally, Diener et al. (2011) found that the religiosity-SWB relationship was similar across all four of the world's major religions (Buddhism, Christianity, Hinduism, and Islam).

In addition, recent research has shown that the relationship between religion and well-being depends on biology as well as culture. For example, Sasaki, Kim, and Xu (2011) found that a genetically based predisposition toward being more sensitive to the needs of others was related to greater well-being among Koreans but not among European Americans. In other words, both genes and culture affect whether or not greater religiosity is correlated with well-being.

Let's return to the question as to why religiosity can enhance physical and mental health. We already mentioned that some religions prohibit and thus reduce unhealthy behaviors and that religious involvement can provide needed social support and better methods of coping with adversity. There is one additional, well-supported hypothesis regarding why religion can enhance mental and physical health. Some researchers postulate that it is not religion, *per se,* that leads to better health outcomes, but rather the belief that one's life has meaning, regardless of the source of that meaning (Oman & Thoresen, 2005; Park, 2007, 2013; Park, Edmondson, & Hale-Smith, 2013).

Religion is a major source of meaning for people around the world, but the secularization of the Western world has resulted in people turning to other systems of meaning, such as work or prosocial causes (Park, 2011). Psychological research has shown that having a meaning in life can motivate us to take better care of ourselves, which can produce both physical and mental health benefits (Park, 2012). A recent study even found that meaning may be more important for physical health than happiness is (Fredrickson et al., 2013).

Recently, psychologists and others have become interested in the relationships among meditation, mindfulness, and SWB (Malinowski, 2013). Although meditation is historically rooted in the Eastern tradition of Buddhism, it can be practiced without adhering or subscribing to Buddhism's theological principles or even being aware of them (Fredrickson, Cohn, Coffey, Pek, & Finkel, 2008). Various forms of meditation have been experimentally linked to a number of desirable outcomes, including improved mood, achieving a balance between negative and positive emotions, and finding meaning and satisfaction in life (Fredrickson et al., 2008; Garland et al., 2010). Please take a look at Research Box 13.1 for an in-depth look at a recent study examining the benefits of meditation on emotions and life satisfaction.

Think Again!

1. *Can you identify some of the elements in your background that affected your religious beliefs or lack of belief?*

2. *Do you think that religion is an adaptation or a by-product of evolution? Why?*

3. *Do you think that religion is a form of culture or separate from and related to culture? Why?*

THE SOCIAL PSYCHOLOGY OF SUSTAINABILITY

Our Environmental Crisis and How Social Psychology Can Help

In *Collapse,* geographer Jared Diamond (2005) identifies five sets of factors that can lead to the failure of human societies. Three of these are becoming increasingly important for the future of our species—ecological damage, climate change, and how a society responds to environmental problems—and are relevant to this chapter. Human civilization around the globe may not be sustainable if current patterns of resource consumption and pollution continue (The Worldwatch Institute, 2013). There is a consensus among leading scientists around the world that our environment is in crisis as a result of human activity, and the only way to avert disaster is to change human attitudes, beliefs, and behavior (NASA, 2013). Overconsumption and resulting pollution create two categories of problems. The *primary* problem is the direct long-term or permanent damage to the environment and loss of nonrenewable resources. A serious *secondary* negative consequence of our behavior is the harm it does to human well-being. Fortunately, social psychology—as you know from reading earlier chapters—can be applied to a range of social problems and has repeatedly produced desirable results (McKenzie-Mohr, Lee, Schultz, & Kotler, 2012).

We encounter the terms *sustainable* and *sustainability* in the news, television and movies, and even in advertisements for products that claim to be environmentally friendly. But what does the term sustainable mean? According to The Worldwatch

RESEARCH BOX 13.1

MEDITATION, MINDFULNESS, AND LIFE SATISFACTION

Hypothesis: Participants who learned and practiced loving-kindness meditation (LKM) would experience more positive emotions that would strengthen personal resources (e.g., mindfulness, purpose in life, resilience, positive relations with others, etc.) in comparison to those who had not learned or practiced it.

Research Method: 202 adults were randomly assigned to either a seven-week LKM training course or to a control group whose members were told that they were on a waiting list for the course. Participants in both groups recorded their emotions daily. Participants completed surveys of life satisfaction, depressive symptoms, and other related measures before and after the seven-week course. LKM involves quietly sitting with one's eyes closed and concentrating on feelings of warmth and kindness for the self and for others.

Results: Participants who practiced LKM showed improvements in positive emotions, which led to increased mindfulness, greater purpose in life, and fewer symptoms of illness. These changes also led to increased life satisfaction.

Conclusion: Engaging in regular loving-kindness meditation can increase positive emotions and life satisfaction.

Source: Fredrickson, B. L., Cohn, M. A., Coffey, K. A., Pek, J., & Finkel, S. M. (2008). Open hearts build lives: Positive emotions, induced through loving-kindness meditation, build consequential personal resources. *Journal of Personality and Social Psychology, 95,* 1045–1062.

Institute, a sustainable activity is one that "can be maintained in existence without interruption or diminution" indefinitely (2013, p. 3). The term can be applied to a specific activity (e.g., coal mining), an industry (e.g., automobile manufacturing), or even a nation (referring to the sum total of its activities and industries).

For example, the automobile industry—because it both directly depletes natural resources as a result of its manufacturing practices and indirectly severely damages the environment by creating vehicles that use nonrenewable, emissions producing gasoline engines—is unsustainable in its current configuration. At a broader level, many people are asking whether our global ecosystem can survive, given the tremendous growth in nonsustainable activities, including the manufacture and use of automobiles, around the world.

©iStockphoto.com/Christopher Futcher.

Research has demonstrated the mental health benefits of spending time in nature.

Human overconsumption has led to the depletion of many of our limited natural resources and caused serious—and in some cases irreversible—adverse changes to and pollution of our environment (Oskamp, 2000). For instance, approximately 1 billion people lack easy access to fresh water, a figure that could rise to 3 billion by 2025 (Corral-Verdugo, Frías-Armenta, Tapia-Fonllem, & Fraijo-Sing, 2012; The Worldwatch Institute, 2013). Global climate change, driven by increases in the average worldwide temperature, is leading to droughts, flooding, glacial melting, rising sea levels, and other problems. Moreover, approximately 70% of the world's fisheries are being depleted faster than they are naturally replenished, threatening a significant source of protein for approximately 3 billion people (The Worldwatch Institute, 2013). These are just three examples of the many disastrous environmental problems caused by human behavior; the list can go on and on and is quite depressing indeed. In addition to these primary adverse consequences of human behavior, environmental damage also has unwanted, secondary, psychological effects, to which we will now turn.

How the Environment Affects Well-Being

How do you feel when you stroll through an urban park, hike a forest path, or sit on the shore of a lake or sea and just listen to the waves? Many people—including me—find connecting to nature in these and other ways to be both relaxing and mentally therapeutic. In other words, I feel better during and following time spent in natural environments. The psychological benefits of exposure to natural settings have been demonstrated in a number of studies. Unfortunately these benefits may be undermined by human-caused damage to these environments. Moreover, the depletion of and/or lack of availability of natural resources such as water can exact a toll on human well-being by creating severe psychological hardships associated with hunger, poverty, and even violence.

There are two main ways in which time spent in natural environments can enhance mental health: by reducing stress and by restoring cognitive functioning (Scopelliti, Carrus, & Bonnes, 2012). A wide body of research has shown that spending time in natural environments, such as a taking a walk through the woods, can significantly reduce a person's stress.

Scientists have garnered evidence from both self-reports of people's emotional states prior to and following exposure to natural environments and direct physiological measures, such as blood pressure and level of muscle relaxation (Hartig, Mang, & Evans, 1991; Laumann, Gärling, & Stormark, 2003; Ulrich et al., 1991). For instance, in one study, participants viewed a stressful video and then either videos of natural outdoor settings or urban settings (Ulrich et al., 1991). Participants exposed to the natural setting demonstrated lower levels of stress on both self-report and physiological measures.

In addition to the stress-reducing effects of natural landscapes, people can also restore their attentional capacities by exposing themselves to nature (Russell, 2012). For example, Hartig et al. (1991) found that participants who were randomly assigned to walk through a natural setting experienced greater recovery of their mental resources after being cognitively fatigued than did participants who walked through an urban setting or sat and relaxed in an enclosed room. A meta-analysis of 28 studies that included over 3,000 children and adolescents demonstrated that programs that provided substantial wilderness experiences had positive effects on delinquency (Wilson & Lipsey, 2000). Similar beneficial effects of nature on both stress and cognition have emerged from other research conducted both in the lab and in the field (Hartig et al., 1991).

Researchers have found that the quality of the green space also matters. For example, in a recent study experimenters gathered data on several indicators of psychological well-being from visitors to urban parks that varied in their biodiversity of plants, birds, and number of specific habitats (Fuller, Irvine, Devine-Wright, Warren, & Gaston, 2007). Visitors received greater psychological benefit from green spaces that contained greater diversity in all three features (see Figure 13.3).

Think Again!

1. _What are the primary and secondary problems associated with human overuse of the environment?_

2. _In what ways do you or could you contribute to sustainability?_

3. _When you spend time in natural environments, how does it make you feel?_

Social Dilemmas as Social Traps

Resource depletion and environmental pollution are growing concerns around the world. Governments, experts, and ordinary people readily acknowledge this, yet not enough is being done to reverse these trends. The question that is begging to be asked is _why?_ More specifically, why do most people (and governments, corporations, etc.) seem to focus on their short-term gains and ignore the long-term costs of their overconsumption and pollution?

FIGURE 13.3   Biodiversity and Well-Being

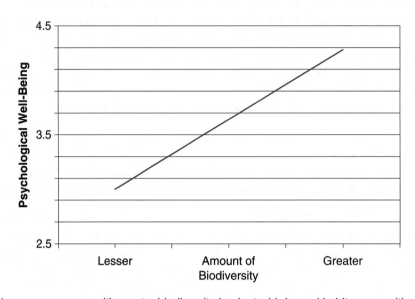

Urban green spaces with greater biodiversity in plants, birds, and habits are positively correlated with psychological well-being.

Source: Fuller, R. A., Irvine, K. N., Devine-Wright, P., Warren, P. H., & Gaston, K. J. (2007). Psychological benefits of greenspace increase with biodiversity. *Biology Letters, 3*, 390–394.

Stated differently, why do they sacrifice the greater good in favor of their individual pleasure or goals? Let's explore this tradeoff with a fable that reflects a basic truth about human behavior: the tragedy of the commons. Hardin (1968, p. 1244) describes it thus:

> "Picture a pasture open to all. It is to be expected that each herdsman will try to keep as many cattle as possible on the commons. Such an arrangement may work reasonably satisfactorily for centuries because the tribal wars, poaching, and disease keep the numbers of both man and beast well below the carrying capacity of the land. Finally, however, comes the day of reckoning, that is, the day when the long-desired goal of social stability becomes a reality. At this point, the inherent logic of the commons remorselessly generates tragedy . . . As a rational being, each herdsman seeks to maximize his gain . . . he asks, "What is the utility to me of adding one more animal to my herd?"

This widespread pursuit of individual self-interest and the sacrifice of the greater good is what Hardin (1968) calls the *tragedy of the commons*. The commons tragedy is an example of a **social dilemma**, which is a situation in which individuals choose between maximizing their own beneficial outcomes and maximizing those of the group (Van Lange, Joireman, Parks, & Van Dijk, 2013; Wang & Ng, 2015). Researchers call these **social traps** and argue that they exist when, as more and more individuals pursue their self-interest, the group as a whole suffers negative consequences (Platt, 1973; Van Lange et al., 2013). Throughout our evolutionary history, humans have encountered a wide variety of social dilemmas when faced with limited resources or opportunities (Ridley, 1996). Platt (1973) outlined three types of social traps, each of which represents a tradeoff between immediate gratification and harm to either the self or to the self and others.

One-Person Trap. First, there is the **one-person trap**, which is present when a person satisfies her short-term needs at the expense of her long-term ones. For instance, a person who gains immediate gratification by subsisting mostly on high-fat and high-sugar junk food and gets no substantial exercise is at risk of developing a number of medical problems.

Missing-Hero Trap. Second is the **missing-hero trap**, wherein action or information is required to solve a problem, but no one steps forward to take the action or supply the information, despite being able to do so (Platt, 1973). An example of this is when a mattress falls off a truck onto a highway, and person after person drives around it without stopping to move it. Traffic slows down and people may be swerving and braking to avoid it, and consequently, the risk of an accident increases. The bystander effect discussed in Chapter 8, in which people refrain from helping others when help is clearly needed is an example of the missing-hero dilemma.

Collective Trap. Platt's third category is the purely **collective trap** or the individual goods-collective bads dilemma, which has been the focus of the bulk of the research on social dilemmas. The collective dilemma is evident when individuals seek to maximize their own gains in a rational manner, and problems arise when too many others also try to maximize their personal gains. In other words, the situation is good for the individual but bad for the collective or group (Kramer, 2011). The difference between this category and other types of social traps is that resolution or avoidance of the problem can only be achieved if the members of the group cooperate with one another. The one-person trap needs the action of just one person to resolve, and the missing-hero trap can be overcome by one person or a small group. The tragedy of the commons is an example of a collective trap, as the common green can only be saved if many farmers refrain from adding extra cattle and remove excessive cattle that are already grazing.

Tackling the Problem

Solving the problem of environmental sustainability has three components: changing attitudes, beliefs, and behaviors; developing new technology; and making structural changes to our cities and landscapes (Heberlein, 2012). The first—changing people, not things—is the primary focus of this section and is discussed is more detail below. Although altering

Social Dilemmas or Social Traps: Situations in which individuals choose between maximizing their own beneficial outcomes and maximizing those of the group

One-Person Trap: Present when a person satisfies his short-term needs at the expense of his/her long-term ones

Missing-Hero Trap: Situation in which action or information is required to solve a problem, but no one steps forward to take the action or supply the information, despite being able to do so

Collective Trap: Situation in which many individuals seek to maximize their own gains in a rational manner, resulting in cumulative damage or harm

human behavior will go far toward solving our environmental problems, overcoming and averting potential crises will also need technological and structural solutions. For instance, substantially reducing CO_2 emissions from vehicles can only partly be accomplished through behavior change, as the creation of affordable, cleaner, and more fuel-efficient vehicles is necessary.

Developing new technology is largely a problem of business innovation and market economics, which for the most part, cannot be dictated or legislated. However, in some cases, governments can establish rules that facilitate technological innovation. For instance, the U.S. government establishes standards for fuel efficiency and emissions for automobiles and trucks. Moreover, without changes in the structure and infrastructures of our cities (e.g., efficient and affordable mass transportation), people have no choice but to rely on automobiles. Infrastructure is largely a public policy issue, as governments must choose to create and support trains, subways, and other types of mass transportation in order to reduce dependence on the automobile.

These categories of solutions are not independent; new technology will only be effective if people adopt it, and infrastructure will not be built unless key people favor it. Therefore, changes in attitudes, beliefs, and behaviors are still required. Given that this is a social psychology text, our discussion will focus primarily on affecting individuals and not governments and corporations. At the individual level, the relevant environmental social behaviors are *consumption* and *pollution*. In short, achieving sustainability will require substantial changes in how people consume goods and how we handle the by-products of those goods.

Think Again!

1. *Can you think of any commons dilemmas in your community? Before reading ahead, try to write down some suggestions for solving them.*

2. *What are the similarities and differences between the missing-hero trap and the bystander intervention problem?*

Psychological Barriers to Implementing Solutions

Given the severity of the environmental problems facing humans, something needs to be done. How can social psychology help? Let's start by identifying some of the psychological barriers to changing environmental behaviors. Gifford (2011, 2013) identified 29 barriers to addressing the problem of climate change, most of which also apply to other environmental problems. He called these the "dragons of inaction" and grouped them into seven categories: limited cognition of the problem, ideological worldviews, social comparison, sunk costs and behavioral momentum, rejection of experts and authorities, perceived risks of change, and positive but inadequate behavior change (see Table 13.4).

TABLE 13.4   The Dragons of Inaction

The seven "Dragons of Inaction" that are obstacles to increasing environmentally friendly behaviors.

General Psychological Barrier	Some Specific Manifestations
Limited cognition	Ignorance, uncertainty, optimism bias, low perceived control
Ideologies	Worldviews, magical solutions from nature, supreme being, or technology
Comparisons with others	Social comparisons with others who are not environmentally conscious
Sunk costs	Invested time, money, effort in current behaviors
Disbelief	Disbelief and/or rejecting experts and authorities, reactance
Perceived risks	Risks of engaging in sustainable behavior seen as too great
Limited behavior	Token behavior, rebound effect

Source: Gifford, R. (2011). The dragons of inaction: Psychological barriers that limit climate change mitigation and adaptation. *American Psychologist, 66,* 290–302.

The first category, *limited cognition,* refers to people's lack of knowledge of the extent of existing environmental damage and its consequences and uncertainty about whether and how humans can reverse this damage (Wals & Dillon, 2012). In addition, people may downplay or simply not recognize the extent to which climate change and other problems will affect them. Gifford likens this *optimistic bias* about the environment to people's tendency to underestimate their likelihood of experiencing other setbacks or problems, such as a heart attack (Shepperd, Klein, Waters, & Weinstein, 2013; Shepperd, Waters, Weinstein, & Klein, 2015). Even among those who do acknowledge the threats to the environment, many may mistakenly believe that they individually have little control over the overall problem and are thus unable to do anything about it (Olson, 1965).

The second category of psychological barriers is grounded in the *ideologies and worldviews* that people hold (Scopelliti et al., 2012). For instance, a person may have strong beliefs in the virtues of free-market capitalism and not recognize that it can also have undesirable consequences. Others believe that climate change or other environmental problems will be magically cured—by technology, a religious being, or nature itself—and therefore they do not need to change their behavior. Gifford's third category is one that should be quite familiar to you: *social comparison* or how we evaluate ourselves by comparing our progress, behavior, or status to relevant others. Peoples' reliance on others as a guide to behavior can increase either desirable or undesirable behavior, depending on which the others are engaging in, as we discussed in Chapter 6.

Sunk-Cost Effect:
Tendency for people to be reluctant to give up on a course of action that they have invested time, money, and/or effort into, even if it is in their best interest to do so

The fourth set of barriers stems from the fact that people have *invested time, money, and effort into their present lifestyles,* and this may lead them to devalue and ignore alternative behaviors. Psychologists refer to this as the **sunk-cost effect,** and it is present when people are reluctant to give up on a course of action into which they have invested time, money, and/or effort, even if it is in their best interest to do so (Tykocinski & Ortmann, 2011). For instance, imagine you have paid $200 for a weekend trip to Boston and $100 for a different weekend trip to New York City and that you prefer New York to Boston. Imagine further that you have just realized that the trips are scheduled for the same weekend, and therefore you can only select one of them. Which would it be? Arkes and Blumer (1985) posed a similar scenario for participants in one of their experiments and found that participants tended to choose the more expensive trip over the one they would find more enjoyable, despite the fact that they will have spent the exact same total amount of money ($300). Why choose the *less* desirable trip? According to researchers, people feel like they will have wasted more money were they to skip the option in which they invested the most (Arkes & Blumer, 1985; Navarro & Fantino, 2009).

The psychology of sunk cost also applies to entrenched habits that, like a boulder rolling down a hill, have momentum and are hard to redirect or change (Gifford, 2011; Neal, Wood, Wu, & Kurlander, 2011). The notion of *behavioral momentum* is clearly applicable to environmentally related behavior, such as when people feel obligated to drive an expensive, gas guzzling car instead of a more efficient one, simply because they made a bigger investment into it (Eriksson, Garvill, & Nordlund, 2008). In addition, people may hold values and/or goals that are inconsistent with sustainable living and which they do not want to change, consequently undermining the desire to engage in more sustainable living. For instance, a fast-rising, status-seeking business executive may decide to buy a sports car, despite the fact that she knows that doing so will conflict with her pro-environment attitudes.

Gifford's fifth category, *disbelief and/or rejecting the expertise of authorities,* has to do with how a person responds to scientists and other authorities who argue that humans have played a substantial role in altering the natural environment. People may mistrust experts and authorities in general or simply those expressing concern about climate change and the need for us to take appropriate actions. Others engage in denial, claiming that the climate is not changing or that humans have no role in the change that is occurring. In addition, people may demonstrate reactance—which we discussed in Chapter 6— to being told what to do/not do and therefore engage in behavior expressly contrary to the recommendations.

The last two categories—*perceived risk* and *limited behavior*—refer to the possible or actual consequences of adopting more environmentally friendly behavior. According to research by Schiffman, Kanuk, and Das (2006), some individuals may be concerned that change may not be worth risk of adverse outcomes. For instance, people may not want to spend money on solar panels or an expensive hybrid vehicle because they may never gain back their investments, despite realizing long-term energy savings. Finally, even when people do enact limited environmentally friendly behavior, they may do so in ways that

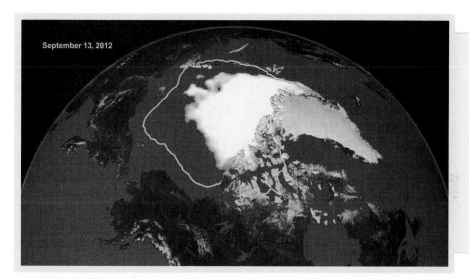

September 13, 2012

An image of the Arctic sea ice on September 16, 2012, the day that the National Snow and Ice Data Center identified to be the minimum reached in 2012. The outline shows the average sea ice minimum from 1979 through 2010, revealing the melting of the icecaps.

NASA/Goddard Space Flight Center Scientific Visualization Studio. The Blue Marble data are courtesy of Reto Stockli (NASA/GSFC).

have little to no positive impact on the environment, such as turning off lights when not in use (Whitmarsh, 2009).

Alternatively, engaging in some green behavior, even a token or ineffectual one, may lead people to permit themselves to be less green in other ways, often resulting in a net negative impact on the environment (Mazar & Zhong, 2010). For instance, a recent study found a rebound effect of an intervention that, on its surface, seemed likely to succeed. There, research participants wasted *more* paper when they were able to recycle it, as compared to when recycling was not an obvious option (Catlin & Wang, 2013).

Regulation. Since most corporations are more interested in profits than in sustainability, they typically do not voluntarily protect the environment. Consequently, governments around the world make laws that regulate their activities, including resource use and pollution. The United States created the federal Environmental Protection Agency (EPA), and the European Union established the European Environment Agency to protect the environment against human activity (e.g., pollution from factories), which in turn protects human health from the consequence of living in a polluted or degraded environment.

Education. Another approach to creating a sustainable society is to educate people by teaching them about the damaging effects of their behavior as well as how to change it. Education provides people with important information, but in the absence of other interventions, it generally falls short of spurring significant behavior change, in part because it may not address the structural obstacles or psychological barriers (McKenzie-Mohr et al., 2012). Nevertheless, education is not without value, as it may activate thoughts about the

Recycling Icon

©iStockphoto.com/heibaihu.

environment and leave people more susceptible to subsequent behavior change messages (Steg & Vlek, 2009). Education can also be useful in changing the ways governments respond to environmental problems, such as instituting incentives and penalties, as described below.

Changing Reinforcements and Punishments. Platt (1973) suggests that, if existing reinforcements and punishments are insufficient to effect sufficient behavior change, then they should be changed. For instance, governments can strengthen reinforcements by offering (or increasing) tax breaks for purchasing hybrid vehicles or highly efficient home air conditioners. One fascinating variant of this approach was successfully implemented in Niger when it tried to prevent desertification caused by the over harvesting of trees. Citizens had little incentive to protect trees because they could not own them and therefore were unable to make money by selling their fruit and bark (Polgreen, 2007). Instead, they would simply use the wood for heating or other one-time activities that would destroy it. Niger passed a law that allowed tree ownership, and subsequently people had a good reason to conserve them and plant more. Consequently, over 7 million acres have been planted with trees over the past three decades. Thus, reinforcements and punishments can be effective, although by themselves will not solve the global problem.

Inducing Dissonance and Hypocrisy Induction. As we saw in Chapter 6, inducing people to make commitments, particularly ones that are public, written, and voluntary, can effectively increase pro-environment behavior (McKenzie-Mohr, 2011). Hypocrisy induction techniques also induce dissonance by making salient the inconsistencies between people's beliefs, values, and/or attitudes and their behavior (Stone, Aronson, Crain, Winslow, & Fried, 2003). People do not want to see themselves and do not want others to see them as hypocritical and will often change their behavior to avoid it. Imagine, for instance, that you claim that you are serious about conserving trees but choose not to buy recycled paper products, such as toilet paper and paper for your printer, even though these are readily available, of high quality, and cost the same as non-recycled products. Say one day you have a basketful of these products at the store and run into a good friend, boss, or (!) professor, who is aware of your attitudes and points out this discrepancy. You have been unmasked as a hypocrite and may very well change your behavior. Another demonstration of hypocrisy induction is a study in which college students asked to sign a publicly displayed poster urging people to conserve water significantly reduced the length of their showers on campus (Dickerson, Thibodeau, Aronson, & Miller, 1992).

Norm-Based Interventions. As you know, social norms can be effective in changing behavior, and they have repeatedly and successfully been used to increase pro-environment behavior (Göckeritz et al., 2010). Informing targets that most people engage in and/or approve of conservation behaviors will increase the likelihood that they will too. In addition, many people believe that they have a moral obligation to preserve the natural environment; consequently, framing sustainable behavior in moral terms can increase their intention to engage in sustainable behavior (Feinberg & Willer, 2013).

Think Again!

1. _Can you think of examples from your community of changing reinforcements and punishments in order to encourage sustainable behavior?_

2. _Pick a couple of sustainable behaviors on your campus and think of whether and how hypocrisy induction could be used to increase them._

3. _How might you create a norm-based campaign to change the same behaviors?_

FINAL THOUGHTS: SUBJECTIVE WELL-BEING AND SUSTAINABILITY

At the beginning of this chapter we described how the psychologist Mary Pipher became involved in a local environmental group fighting against the construction of the Keystone XL Pipeline through a fragile and important Nebraska ecosystem. In her memoir, Pipher (2013) relays the satisfaction she gained and the spiritual and deeply meaningful relationship she developed with the natural world. This work contributed both to her own psychological well-being and to the sustainability of the local habitat. Pipher's story nicely connects the three themes of this chapter: happiness and life satisfaction,

religion and meaning, and sustainability. Pipher's experiences are of course anecdotal, but they illustrate the findings of a vast quantity of research linking these topics.

For example, a recent meta-analysis of dozens of studies found that social conflict increased around the globe as a result of two components of climate change—hotter temperatures and extreme rainfall (Hsiang, Burke, & Miguel, 2013). To the extent that climate change and other results of overconsumption and insufficient attention to environmental damage continue to occur, nature's ability to restore our mental health is imperiled. Research has also shown that higher SWB is related to more sustainable lifestyles (Thompson, Marks, & Jackson, 2013), and others have argued that religion should and sometimes does foster environmentally conscious behaviors (Adriance et al., 2010).

These topics have implications for three of our fundamental questions. Happiness and SWB obviously revolve around the *self,* as they are inherently subjective. Similarly, the extent to which religion can provide people with meaning—if it can at all—of course depends on the person. *Sociality* is strongly related to a person's happiness because our connections to others impact our psychological and physical well-being. Religious involvement—and for many, such as Pipher, environmental engagement—can provide important social contacts and emotionally support, especially when a person is facing adverse circumstances. Finally, one of the pillars of human *morality* is religion. Understanding the interplay among well-being, religion, and sustainability provides insight into human nature and may help to ensure the future survival of the human race.

CORE CONCEPTS

- Happiness or subjective well-being (SWB) has two components: hedonic or in-the-moment happiness and eudaimonic happiness or life satisfaction. Positive psychology focuses on optimal human functioning, including what is good and/o r adaptive about humans. Accurate affective forecasting can be challenging, partially because people succumb to the durability bias and neglect their psychological immune system.

- The quality of social relationships, having children, personal wealth, and culture can all contribute to people's happiness. There are a number of documented benefits of happiness, including greater work success, higher income, greater marital satisfaction, being perceived in a more positive light, and physical and mental health.

- Religiousness has four dimensions: believing, bonding, behaving, and belonging; the three religious orientations (intrinsic, extrinsic, quest) reflect people's motivation for engaging in religious activity.

- Religion's two most important functions are to provide meaning and cope with stress, adversity, and fear of death; two perspectives on the evolutionary origins of religious belief are that it is a psychological adaptation or a by-product of other psychological adaptations.

- People who are religious tend to enjoy greater physical health, typically obtain more preventive care, live longer, and have healthier mental functioning.

- The tragedy of the commons is a situation in which the widespread pursuit of individual self-interest in consuming common resources results in a sacrifice of the greater good. Variants on social traps include the one-person, missing-hero, and collective traps.

- Solving the sustainability problem will require three kinds of solutions: changing attitudes, beliefs, and behaviors; developing new technology; and making structural changes to our cities and landscapes. Gifford has outlined seven categories of what he has called the "dragons of inaction," each of which contributes to the unsustainability of contemporary levels of consumption.

- There are many strategies that governments and others can use to help create a more sustainable world, including regulation, education, changing reinforcements and punishments to increase their effectiveness, and others.

➤ ⑤SAGE edge™ Test your understanding of chapter content. Take the practice quiz. edge.sagepub.com/barrett

KEY TERMS

Adaptation-Level Theory, 484
Affective Forecasting, 480
Collective Trap, 507
Durability Bias, 480
External Validity, 489
Eudaimonic Happiness, 478
Extrinsic Orientation, 493
Focalism, 480
Generalizability, 489
Happiness (Subjective Well-Being), 479

Hedonic Happiness, 478
Hedonic Treadmill, 488
Immune Neglect, 482
Intrinsic Orientation, 492
Missing-Hero Trap, 507
Mundane Realism, 490
One-Person Trap, 507
Positive Psychology, 478
Quest Orientation, 493

Random Selection or Sampling, 489
Religiousness, 491
Representative Sampling, 489
Set Point, 488
Social Dilemmas or Social Traps, 507
Sunk-Cost Effect, 509

➤ ⑤SAGE edge™ Review key terms with eFlashcards. edge.sagepub.com/barrett

THINK FURTHER!

- Try examining your own ability to correctly forecast your future emotions by writing down how you expect to feel if a given future event occurs (such as a course grade or salary boost). After it happens compare how you actually felt with how you expected to feel.

- Why, do you suppose, do people seem to think that money will buy them happiness, even though the evidence does not support this (except at the low end of the economic scale)? Ask your friends and family if they believe money will make them happier? Do you think people will answer this question honestly?

- What function, if any, does religion serve for you? If you are not religious, from where do you derive meaning in your life, and what/whom do you turn to for support in difficult times?

- What manifestations of the primary and secondary problems associated with human overuse of the environment do you see on your campus or in your community?

- Given that mental health is positively related to exposure to natural environments, what could be done on your campus or in your community to increase such exposure?

- If you could tackle just one of the psychological barriers to sustainable behavior, which would it be and why? If you could use just one of the strategies described in the chapter, which would it be and why?

SUGGESTED READINGS

Boyce, C. J., Brown, G. D. A., & Moore, S. C. (2010). Money and happiness: Rank of income, not income, affects life satisfaction. *Psychological Science, 21,* 471–475.

Diener, E. (2000). Subjective well-being: The science of happiness and a proposal for a national index. *American Psychologist, 55,* 34–43.

Feinberg, M., & Willer, R. (2013). The moral roots of environmental attitudes. *Psychological Science, 24,* 56–62.

Galen, L. W. (2012). Does religious belief promote prosociality? A critical examination. *Psychological Bulletin, 138,* 876–906.

Pipher, M. (2013). *The green boat: Reviving ourselves in our capsized culture.* New York, NY: Riverhead Books.

Glossary

Acquiescence Bias: Tendency to agree with or say "yes" to questions (Chapter 4)

Actor/Observer Effect: When the attributions for a person's behavior vary according to whether one is the actor (doing the behavior) or an observer (of the behavior) (Chapter 5)

Actual Self: Who one is (Chapter 4)

Adaptation-Level Theory: Idea that people adapt to new situations in life and then return to their previous level of well-being (Chapter 13)

Affective Forecasting: Predicting the intensity and duration of our emotional responses to future events (Chapter 13)

Affective or Evaluative Priming: Subliminal presentation of attitude objects in order to measure their effects on subsequent categorization of stimuli (Chapter 10)

Ageism: Prejudice against people based on their age (Chapter 10)

Aggression: Behavior that is intended to proximately harm another person who is motivated to avoid that harm (Chapter 9)

Aggressive Cues: Words, images, and objects in the environment that trigger aggression-related thoughts can increase aggression (Chapter 9)

Alleles: Gene variants that carry the information essential for the expression of traits (Chapter 2)

Altruism: Acting to benefit others and not for one's own sake (Chapter 8)

Ambivalent Sexism: Simultaneous perception of women in negative and positive terms (Chapter 10)

Anchoring and Adjustment Heuristic: Mental shortcut in which people use readily available information on which to base estimation and then adjust that estimate up or down to arrive at a final judgment (Chapter 3)

Anthropology: Seeks culture-level explanations for human behavior by exploring a specific culture in depth, utilizing primarily observational research (Chapter 1)

Appraisal Model of Stress: States that people engage in two appraisal processes—primary and secondary—of a potential stressor that impact how they emotionally respond to it

Archival Research: Examines data from preexisting sources or archives, such as newspapers, historical records, and speeches (Chapter 9)

Arousal: Cost Reward Model: Postulates that seeing another person in distress causes a person to feel negative arousal, and the person will use the least costly path to reduce the arousal; decision to help is based on a cost/benefit analysis Chapter 8)

Attachment Style: Patterns of expectations, needs, and behaviors a person typically exhibits in close relationships (Chapter 11)

Attitude: Positive or negative evaluation of a person, thing, or idea (Chapter 7)

Attribution: Judgment about the cause of behavior (Chapter 5)

Authority Principle: Increased likelihood that people will do what is requested or suggested by a perceived authority (Chapter 6)

Automaticity: Extent to which a given event is unintentional, occurs without conscious awareness, is accomplished efficiently, and, once begun, cannot be controlled (Chapter 3)

Availability Heuristic: Mental shortcut in which people judge the frequency or likelihood of an event based on how easily relevant examples come to mind (Chapter 3)

Aversive Racism: Coexistence of explicit claims of being nonprejudiced with implicit reactions and behaviors that reveal prejudiced feelings (Chapter 10)

Bait-and-Switch: Social influence tactic in which a person psychologically commits to a product and then, suddenly, the product is replaced with a related product that is more expensive (Chapter 6)

Base Rate: Frequency at which a given phenomenon occurs (Chapter 3)

Base Rate Fallacy: Judging how likely an event is to occur, based on unusual or atypical instances while ignoring its actual base rate or probability of occurrence (Chapter 3)

Belief: Conviction we hold about whether something is true or false (Chapter 7)

Belief Perseverance: Phenomenon of holding onto a belief when its validity has been undermined by the facts (Chapter 3)

Benevolent Sexism: Stereotypical views of women as very different from (e.g., more emotionally sensitive and warmer) and inferior (e.g., weak and in need of protection) to men (Chapter 10)

Better-Than-Average Effect: Judging that one is above average on most desirable characteristics (Chapter 4)

Bias Blind Spot: Believing that one is immune to cognitive biases that affect others (Chapter 4)

Biased Assimilation: Construing information so that it seems similar to or consistent with one's preferred perspective (Chapter 3)

Biological/Physiological Psychology: Examines the influence of genes, hormones, brain functioning and structure, and other elements of the nervous system, on all kinds of human behavior (Chapter 1)

Blended Emotions: Wherein an expression reflects more than one emotion (Chapter 5)

Bogus Pipeline: Technique in which participants are hooked up to a machine and are told that the machine can reveal their true feelings, when in fact the machine cannot do this (Chapter 7)

Brainstorming: Procedure in which members of a group are encouraged to generate as many ideas as they can within a specific amount of time (Chapter 12)

Bystander Apathy: Explanation that people who fail to help in emergencies do so because they are uncaring (Chapter 8)

Bystander Effect: Phenomenon that, as the number of onlookers in an emergency increases, the likelihood that any one person will help decreases (Chapter 8)

Bystander Intervention: Help provided by witnesses to victims or potential victims in an emergency (Chapter 8)

C-system: Largely reflective, sequential, conscious, or deliberative mental processing system (Chapter 3)

Case Study: Close examination of an event, person, or group (Chapter 12)

Causal Relationship: Relationship that exists when a change in one variable can be shown to produce a change in another one (Chapter 3)

Central Processing: Thinking about a message that is relatively slow, careful, and focused on the quality of the arguments (Chapter 7)

Chameleon Effect: When people mimic the movements of others without conscious awareness of doing so (Chapter 6)

Classical Conditioning: Form of learning in which a previously neutral stimulus becomes a conditioned stimulus after being paired with an unconditioned stimulus (Chapter 1)

Clinical Psychology: Examines the nature, causes, and consequences of mental disorders and dysfunction of individuals who deviate from the norm and seeks ways to treat them (Chapter 1)

Close Relationship: When the influence between two people is strong, frequent, and enduring, and characterized by interdependence (Chapter 11)

Cognitive Dissonance: Unpleasant arousal stemming from inconsistencies among one's attitudes, beliefs, and/or behaviors (Chapter 7)

Cognitive Neoassociationist Theory (of hostile or emotional aggression): Idea that almost any aversive event can produce aggressive behavior, provided that that event generates negative affect (Chapter 9)

Cognitive Psychology: Seeks to explain mental processes such as memory, problem solving, decision-making, language, and the nature of consciousness (Chapter 1)

Cognitive Responses: Thoughts a person has while processing a message (Chapter 7)

Cognitive Response Model of Persuasion: Posits that persuasion is more likely to occur to the extent that message recipients produce a greater number of favorable than unfavorable responses to the message (Chapter 7)

Collective Trap: Situation in which many individuals seek to maximize their own gains in a rational manner, resulting in cumulative damage or harm (Chapter 13)

Collectivistic Culture: Type of society in which people's self-concepts tend to be intimately tied to and defined by their group memberships, people subordinate personal preferences and goals to the group's, and where individual choice is not highly valued (Chapter 1)

Commitment/Consistency Principle: Increased likelihood that people will enact a behavior that is consistent with their own past behavior and allows them to follow through on prior commitments (Chapter 6)

Common-Bond Group: Group primarily based on the attachments that members have to each other (rather than to the group itself) (Chapter 12)

Common-Identity Group: Group primarily based on the attachments members have to the group itself (rather than to other members), even in the absence of direct interaction among group members (Chapter 12)

Common Ingroup Identity Model: Posits that the core of intergroup bias is the categorization of individuals into ingroups and outgroups (Chapter 10)

Communal Relationship: Relationship in which individuals are primarily concerned about the welfare of the other, and they give to each other without expecting to receive anything in return (Chapter 11)

Companionate Love: Feelings of affection and intimacy that occur in the context of a relatively stable, trusting relationship that may or may not involve passionate love (Chapter 11)

Compliance: Behavioral response to a request (Chapter 6)

Confederate: Person who pretends to be a participant but is really working with the experimenter (Chapter 6)

Confirmation Bias: Tendency to search only for evidence that supports one's beliefs and to ignore information that disagrees with them (Chapter 3)

Conformity: Change in one's responses in order to fit in (Chapter 6)

Confound: In an experiment, a factor that changes along with the independent variable and can prevent a clear assessment of the effects of the IV on the DV

Considering the Opposite: Imagining how one's beliefs could be false (Chapter 3)

Contact Hypothesis: Idea that contact between members of different groups can reduce intergroup hostility and facilitate positive intergroup relations (Chapter 10)

Context Effects: Variations in responding because of survey features encountered prior to answering a question (Chapter 4)

Contingency Model of Leadership: Postulates that leadership effectiveness is contingent upon both the behavior of the leader and aspects of the situation (Chapter 12)

Conversion Theory: Idea that dissent within a group leads to an uncomfortable conflict that members are motivated to reduce and, consequently, either change their own opinions or try to change those of others (Chapter 12)

Control Group: Group of participants that did not receive the treatment and serves as a comparison to assess the effects of the treatment (Chapter 3)

Correlation: Two variables are correlated when a change in one variable is associated with a change in the other variable

Correspondence Bias: Tendency to assume that outward *behavior* corresponds to inward *attitudes* and to ignore situational influences (Chapter 5)

Counter Attitudinal Advocacy: Arguing or advocating for a position that is counter or contrary to a person's attitudes (Chapter 7)

Counterfactual Thinking: Imagining what *could* have happened (but did not) (Chapter 4)

Covert or Unobtrusive Measures: Obtaining information from people when they are not aware that this is being done (Chapter 7)

Credibility: Communicator characteristic based on expertise, trustworthiness, and goodwill that affects the extent to which message recipients accept the validity of the communicator's statements (Chapter 7)

Culture: System of enduring meanings, perceptions, attitudes, beliefs, and practices shared by a large group of people (Chapter 1)

Cultural Embeddedness: Extent to which one focuses on the family or extended ingroup, as opposed to oneself, as the primary social unity (Chapter 8)

Culture of Honor: Society in which people, especially males, are highly protective of their reputation and very sensitive and reactive to personal insults, humiliation, and other threats to their honor (Chapter 9)

Deadline Technique: Setting a specific end date for an opportunity, such as a sale or service, in order to increase its desirability (Chapter 6)

Debriefing: Explanation of the true purpose of the research, an exploration and reduction of possible negative effects of participation, and a clarification of what actually happened during the study (if there was ambiguity or deception) (Chapter 8)

Decoding: Interpretation of facial expressions and other nonverbal behavior (Chapter 5)

Deindividuation: Psychological state characterized by loss of self-awareness and the sense of personal responsibility (Chapter 12)

Dependent Variable: Measured variable that is expected to be affected by manipulation of the independent variable

Descriptive Norm: What most people are or are not doing in a particular context (Chapter 6)

Diffusion of Responsibility: Phenomenon in which, as the number of bystanders increases, individuals mentally spread responsibility for intervening across many others (Chapter 8)

Direct Aggression: Aggression that occurs when the target is present (Chapter 9)

Discrimination: Unequal treatment of individuals based on their group membership (Chapter 10)

Display Rules: Rules indicating which facial expressions are appropriate in a given context (Chapter 5)

Distraction-Conflict Theory: Idea that the actor is distracted from focusing on the task at hand, thereby creating a conflict between the need to concentrate on that task and minimizing the distraction caused by others (Chapter 12)

Door-in-the-Face Technique: Sequential procedure of (a) making a relatively large request, (b) waiting until the request has been refused, and (c) subsequently scaling back to a smaller request (Chapter 6)

Downward Social Comparison: Contrasting one's own performance, ability, or situation with individuals who did less well, have weaker abilities, or are in worse situations (Chapter 4)

Dual Attitude: Inconsistent implicit and explicit attitudes toward a person, thing, or idea (Chapter 7)

Dual Process Model: Posits that attitudes and beliefs can change via two processes—with and without much thought (Chapter 7)

Dualism: The philosophical position that the mind and body are separate (Chapter 2)

Durability Bias: Tendency to overestimate how long one's emotional reactions to future events will last (Chapter 13)

Egoism: Helping other people because it brings internal and/or external rewards to the helper (Chapter 8)

Elaboration Likelihood Model of Persuasion: Postulates that persuasion occurs via central and/or peripheral processing (Chapter 7)

Empathic Concern: Other-oriented emotion elicited by and congruent with the perceived welfare of a person in need (Chapter 8)

Empathy-Altruism Hypothesis: Idea that empathic concern produces an altruistic motivation to relieve the needs of a valued other (Chapter 8)

Entitativity: Extent to which outside observers can easily conceptualize a collection of individuals as a true group (Chapter 12)

Equity Theory: Idea that people prefer relationships—including close relationships—in which each partner enjoys the same ratio of benefits to costs (Chapter 11)

Eudaimonic Happiness: Deep, longer-lasting contentment or general satisfaction with life associated with living a meaningful life (Chapter 13)

Evaluation Apprehension: Concern about how others are going to judge one's performance (Chapter 12)

Event Sampling or Experience Sampling: Obtaining participants' report on their life experiences while they are happening or just after they have happened (Chapter 11)

Event-Related Potentials (ERPs): Changes in electrical activity in the brain that reflect how it responds to particular stimuli (Chapter 2)

Exchange Relationship: Relationship that is based on the reciprocal exchange of benefits (Chapter 11)

Excitation Transfer: Arousal produced by one stimulus spilling over and strengthening a person's emotional response to a different one (Chapter 9)

Experiment: Study in which one or more variables are systematically varied in order to examine the effects on one or more other variables

Explicit Attitude: Attitude that a person is aware of and can articulate (Chapter 7)

External Validity: Extent to which the results of a study can be generalized or applied to other settings and populations (also called **generalizability**) (Chapters 3 & 13)

Extremity Bias: Tendency to provide answers that are at the extremes of the response options (Chapter 4)

Extrinsic Motivation: Desire to perform a behavior as a result of external rewards or pressures (Chapter 4)

Extrinsic Orientation: View of religion as a means to nonreligious ends (Chapter 13)

Facial Feedback Hypothesis: Idea that people infer their feelings from their facial expressions (Chapter 4)

False Consensus Effect: Believing that one's opinions or behaviors are more common than they actually are (Chapter 4)

False Uniqueness Effect: Holding incorrect beliefs about how different one is from others (Chapter 4)

Focalism: Placing too much emphasis on the *focal* event and too little on the nonfocal events (Chapter 13)

Focus Theory of Normative Conduct: Idea that social norms can be divided into those that are

descriptive and those that are injunctive and that whichever norm people focus their attention on is likely to be more influential (Chapter 6)

Foot-in-the-Door Technique (FITD): Sequential procedure in which (a) a small request is made and, following compliance, (b) a larger request is made (Chapter 6)

Free Riding: When group members exert little or no effort because they believe that their contribution to the group task is dispensable or not important to the overall group output (Chapter 12)

Frustration-Aggression Hypothesis: Idea that aggression is always caused by frustration, and aggression is always the result of frustration (Chapter 9)

Fundamental Attribution Error: Attributing behavior to dispositional factors while ignoring situational ones (Chapter 5)

Gambler's Fallacy: Believing that the odds of a coin coming up heads are greater after having just come up tails rather than heads in the last flip (Chapter 5)

Generalizability: Extent to which the results of a study can be generalized or applied to other settings and populations (also called **external validity**) (Chapter 13)

Glass Ceiling: When qualified women are prevented from attaining high-level positions (Chapter 10)

Group: Two or more individuals who perceive themselves as part of a unit and who both influence each other and are interdependent (Chapter 12)

Group Cohesiveness: Strength of the bonds that hold group members together and keep them in the group (Chapter 12)

Groupiness: Degree to which a collection of individuals is grouplike (Chapter 12)

Group Polarization: Tendency for group discussion to enhance the initial leanings of the individuals prior to discussion (Chapter 12)

Groupthink: Type of faulty thinking in groups that strives to maintain cohesion and achieve unanimity at the expense of adequately evaluating the information and options available to the group (Chapter 12)

Happiness (Subjective Well-Being): Combination of temporary positive and negative feelings and overall life satisfaction (Chapter 13)

Hedonic Happiness: Short-term pleasure people derive from things like chocolate, sex, or a new pair of pants (Chapter 13)

Hedonic Treadmill: Idea that people move forward through life but their level of happiness remains about the same (Chapter 13)

Heterosexism: Negative prejudices, stereotypes, and discrimination directed at individuals based on their nonheterosexual orientation and/or institutional practices that support the unequal status of heterosexuals and nonheterosexuals (Chapter 10)

Heuristic: Mental shortcut that facilitates rapid inferences without much thought (Chapter 3)

Heuristic-Systematic Model of Persuasion: Postulates that persuasion occurs via systematic and/or heuristic processing (Chapter 7)

Hindsight Bias: Incorrect belief that, after a person has already learned the outcome of a particular event, he or she would have accurately predicted the outcome before it occurred (Chapter 1)

Homophily: Preference people have for spending time with and/or connecting with people who are like them (Chapter 11)

Homophobia: Particularly strong fear of homosexuals or homosexual behavior (Chapter 10)

Hostile Aggression: Behavior aimed specifically at harming another person, typically stems from anger; sometimes called *emotional* aggression (Chapter 9)

Hostile Attribution Bias: Tendency to interpret the intentions and behavior of others as hostile or threatening (Chapter 9)

Hostile Sexism: Derogatory views of women as seeking to control men via marital commitment and sex, along with perceptions of women as sex objects (Chapter 10)

Hot Hand Illusion: Incorrectly thinking that identical random outcomes are "streaks" (Chapter 5)

Hypocrisy Induction Paradigm: Leading someone to recognize an inconsistency among his or her attitudes, beliefs, and behaviors (Chapter 7)

Hypothesis: Prediction about the nature of social phenomena, oftentimes in the form of a proposition about how two factors are related to one another (Chapter 1 & 3)

Ideal Self: Image of a hypothetical self that possesses the qualities and features that a person wishes she or he had (Chapter 4)

Illusion of Transparency: Incorrect belief that others can "read" our emotions or detect our lies merely by looking at our facial expressions (Chapter 4)

Illusion of Control: False belief that one can control or influence random or chance events (Chapter 5)

Illusory Correlation: Overestimation of the extent to which two variables are correlated (Chapter 5 & 10)

Immune Neglect: Tendency for people to ignore their ability to psychologically rebound from emotional setbacks and negative events (Chapter 13)

Implicit Attitude: Attitude that a person is typically not aware or conscious of (Chapter 7 & 10)

Impression Management: Efforts to project the image of the self that a person wants others to have (Chapter 4)

Implicit Personality Theory: Lay or unscientific theory about the kinds of person characteristics that are typically found together (Chapter 5)

Inclusive Fitness: Ability of one's genes to survive both in one's own offspring and in one's (genetic) relatives (Chapter 8)

Independent Variable: Manipulated variable that is expected to change the dependent variable

Indirect Aggression: Aggression that occurs when the target is NOT present (Chapter 9)

Individualistic Culture: Type of society in which people's self-concepts tend to be stable, not tied to particular groups, and people place their personal preferences and goals above those of the group and value individual choice (Chapter 1)

Informed Consent: Written agreement to participate in research (Chapter 8)

Informational Influence: Adoption of other's behaviors, attitudes, and/or beliefs because those individuals are perceived as sources of valid information about objective reality (Chapter 6)

Ingratiation: Attempts to get particular persons to like us (Chapter 4)

Ingroup: Group to which a person belongs (Chapter 10)

Ingroup Bias: Tendency to positively evaluate one's ingroup (Chapter 10)

Ingroup Favoritism: More favorable treatment of ingroups as compared to outgroups (Chapter 10)

Injunctive Norms: What people should or shouldn't do in a specific situation (Chapter 6)

Instrumental Aggression: Behavior intended to harm another, but the behavior is merely a means to a nonaggressive end (Chapter 9)

Institutional Discrimination: Unequal treatment of individuals that is embedded in the norms, policies, and practices of an institution, producing unequal outcomes for members of different groups (contrast with interpersonal discrimination) (Chapter 10)

Instrumental Conditioning: Form of learning in which reinforcement is given or punishment is administered in order to increase or decrease a specific behavior (Chapter 1)

Insufficient Justification: When a person believes that his or her explanation for their own behavior is inadequate (Chapter 7)

Intergroup Bias: Tendency of one group to hold prejudice toward, stereotype, and discriminate against another group (Chapter 10)

Intergroup Contact Theory: Postulates that intergroup contact can reduce intergroup bias as long as several conditions are present: Individuals must perceive that the groups have equal status; the groups must pursue common, superordinate goals; the groups must cooperate to achieve those goals; and the contact must be sanctioned or supported by authorities, laws, and/or customs (Chapter 10)

Internal Validity: Extent to which an experimenter can be sure that the purported cause—the IV—is the only factor influencing the purported effect—the DV (Chapter 3)

Interpersonal Discrimination: Unequal treatment of specific individuals based on their group membership (contrast with institutional discrimination) (Chapter 10)

Interpersonal Self: Way we present ourselves to other people (Chapter 4)

Intrinsic Motivation: Desire to engage in a behavior simply because it is interesting or enjoyable (Chapter 4)

Intrinsic Orientation: View of religion as an end in itself (Chapter 13)

Introspection: Looking internally at the self to examine who one is, how one feels, and so forth (Chapter 4)

Ironic Process of Mental Control: Trying to control one's thoughts or behavior in a way that produces the very thoughts or behavior that one is trying to avoid (Chapter 4)

Jigsaw Classroom: Teaching strategy that requires persons from different ethnic and/or racial backgrounds to cooperatively solve problems (Chapter 10)

Just-World Hypothesis: Idea that people get what they deserve and deserve whatever they get (Chapter 8)

Kin Selection: Traits that tend to facilitate the survival of an individual's genetic relatives are selected for (Chapter 8)

Labeling Technique: Bestowing a positive label on a person in order to gain compliance to a request (Chapter 6)

Lay Theory: Explanation for social behavior that is possessed by an ordinary (lay) person without advanced training in psychology and without using scientific methods (Chapter 1)

Leadership: Process by which a person influences group members to work toward common goals (Chapter 12)

Liking/Friendship Principle: People are more likely to adhere to a request from a positively evaluated other, such as a friend or an admired person (Chapter 6)

Limited-Quantity Technique: Restricting the quantity of a product, service, or opportunity in order to increase its desirability (Chapter 6)

Looking-Glass Self: Imagining how other people perceive and judge one's self, which in turn can affect that sense of self (Chapter 3)

Low-Ball Tactic: Enticing consumers to agree to purchase something and then subsequently inform them that the price is higher than initially promised (Chapter 6)

Matching Hypothesis: Idea that people typically select romantic partners who are at approximately the same "level" of attractiveness as they are (Chapter 11)

Media Violence Hypothesis: Idea that exposure to violence in the media can cause aggression in the real world (Chapter 9)

Mere Exposure Effect: Repeated contact with or exposure to a person, thing, or idea leads one to favor or prefer it (Chapter 7)

Mere Presence: Presence of others while one is performing a task leads to physiological arousal, which in turn affects how well the person performs (Chapter 12)

Meta-analysis: Combines multiple studies, usually by different researchers, into one analysis that allows the researcher to draw conclusions about the set of studies as a whole (Chapter 5)

Microaggression: Ordinary, daily interactions that send negative messages to an individual based upon the person's group membership(s) (Chapter 10)

Mind/Body Problem: Challenge of determining how the mind and the body are related (Chapter 2)

Minimal Group Paradigm: Research method in which participants are divided into groups, usually for trivial reasons, such as by the color of their eye or the roll of the dice (Chapter 10)

Minority Influence: When numerical minority in a group changes the attitudes, beliefs, or behaviors of the majority (Chapter 12)

Missing-Hero Trap: Situation in which action or information is required to solve a problem, but no one steps forward to take the action or supply the information, despite being able to do so (Chapter 13)

Modern Racism: Overtly professing egalitarian views of racial groups but holding negative feelings that result in opposition to giving disadvantaged groups special consideration or opportunities (Chapter 10)

Mood Management Hypothesis: People often help in order to manage their moods, especially when they are sad (Chapter 8)

Motivated Reasoning: Person's mental processing is influenced by her or his desires, feelings, or goals (Chapter 3)

Mundane Realism: Making a study similar to the relevant real-world setting in all important respects (Chapter 13)

Natural Selection: Genes that tend to increase the chances of survival of their carrier are more likely to be passed on to a new generation (Chapter 1)

Need for Affiliation: Desire to be around and interact with other people (Chapter 11)

Need to Belong: Desire to form and maintain close and durable relationships with others (Chapter 11)

Need for Cognition: Extent to which a person enjoys and tends to engage in thinking (Chapter 7)

Negative State Relief Model: Postulates that witnessing the distress of others causes a person to feel sadness or related negative emotions and that the person is motivated to act in order to reduce those emotions (Chapter 8)

Neocortex Ratio: Quotient of the neocortex volume divided by the volume of the rest of the brain (Chapter 2)

Nonverbal Behavior: Perceptible social behavior that is extra linguistic and not primarily intended to manipulate the physical world (Chapter 5)

Norm of Reciprocity: Social rule stating that people should offer help to and avoid harming those who have helped them (Chapter 8)

Normative Influence: Alteration of one's behaviors, attitudes, or beliefs in order to be accepted by another person or group (Chapter 6)

Obedience: Behavioral response to a request from an authority (Chapter 6)

One-Person Trap: Present when a person satisfies his or her short-term needs at the expense of long-term ones (Chapter 13)

Optimal Distinctiveness Theory: Postulates that people will join groups that facilitate the satisfaction of both their need to belong and their desire to be unique (Chapter 10)

Orientation-Discussion-Decision-Implementation (ODDI) Model: Postulates that effective decision-making consists of four stages of deliberation and subsequent action: orientation, discussion, decision, and implementation (Chapter 12)

Ought Self: Image of a hypothetical self who a person believes important others think he or she should be (Chapter 4)

Outgroup: Group to which is a person does not belong (Chapter 10)

Outgroup Homogeneity Effect: Perception that all members of a given group are more similar to each other than members of one's own group are to each other (Chapter 10)

Overjustification Effect: When one's intrinsic motivation—such as enjoyment experienced by simply enacting the behavior—is weakened by the presence of extrinsic motivation (Chapter 4)

Overt Measures: Obtaining information from people when they know what is being examined (Chapter 7)

Passionate Love: Intense longing for union with another person, characterized by physiological arousal, strong attraction, and frequent thoughts about that person (Chapter 11)

Paternity Uncertainty: Fact that throughout evolutionary history, males have never really known whether the children of their female partners are truly genetically their own (Chapter 11)

Peripheral Processing: Thinking about a message that is relatively rapid, superficial, and focused on non-argument features of the message (Chapter 7)

Personal Identity: Characteristics and qualities that distinguish us from others (Chapter 10)

Personality Psychology: Investigates the development and nature of personality traits over the lifespan (Chapter 1)

Persuasion: Change in attitudes or beliefs (Chapters 6 & 7)

Pluralistic Ignorance: When a person *incorrectly* assumes that others know more than he or she does (Chapter 8)

Positive Illusion: An overly rosy view of the self, others, or situations (Chapter 11)

Positive Psychology: Focuses on optimal human functioning, including what is good and/or adaptive about humans (Chapter 13)

Prejudice: Evaluation or prejudgment of a group and its members (Chapter 10)

Priming: When a concept or other knowledge structure is automatically triggered or activated by an environmental stimulus, thereby becoming more likely to affect subsequent related thoughts, feelings, and behaviors (Chapter 3)

Process Loss: Reduction in the ability of a group to engage in good problem solving that stems from shortcomings in group interaction (Chapter 12)

Prosocial Behavior: Behavior that is intended to benefit others (Chapter 8)

Prosociality: Tendency to engage in prosocial behavior (Chapter 8)

Provocation: When a person intentionally elicits an aggressive response from another through the use of insults, physical aggression, blocking goal attainment, teasing, or similar behaviors (Chapter 9)

Quest Orientation: View of religion as an open-ended process of trying to answer existential questions (Chapter 13)

Random Assignment: Each participant in a study has an equal chance of being assigned to any condition

Random Selection or Sampling: When every individual in a population has an equal probability of being chosen for inclusion in the study (Chapter 13)

Reactance: Unpleasant arousal that triggers behavior intended to protect or reinstate freedoms that are restricted or threatened (Chapter 6)

Realistic Group Conflict Theory: Postulates that (a) when a group has goals that could only be achieved at the expense of another group, intergroup hostility would ensue; and (b) when groups work together to achieve a common, overarching goal, intergroup relations should become more harmonious (Chapter 10)

Recategorization: Viewing ingroup and outgroup members primarily as members of a larger, mutually inclusive group, thereby diminishing the importance of intergroup differences (Chapter 10)

Reciprocal Helping: When people help others because the others have previously helped them or are expected to help them in the future (Chapter 8)

Reciprocity Principle: Increased likelihood that an individual will comply with a request from a person or an entity who has previously done a favor to that individual (Chapter 6)

Reductivism: Idea that we need only study the brain to fully understand the causes of social behavior (Chapter 2)

Reinforcement-Affect Model of Interpersonal Attraction: Postulates that people prefer to interact with and befriend others who they find to be emotionally rewarding (Chapter 11)

Relational Aggression: Aggression that is intended to disrupt relationships, such as gossip rumor spreading, and social exclusion (Chapter 9)

Relationship: When two people influence each other (Chapter 11)

Relative Deprivation (RD): Discontent that individuals feel when they believe that they are in a worse situation than they should be, either as compared to their previous situation or the situation of other groups (Chapter 10)

Relative Deprivation Theory (RDT): Idea that discontent can breed resentment toward others and lead people to blame minorities for their own situation, sometimes resulting in violence (Chapter 10)

Reliability: How consistently each measurement of the same phenomenon using the same measurement tool produces approximately the same result under the same conditions (Chapter 3)

Religiousness: Extent to which a person is involved religion (Chapter 13)

Representative Sampling: When a study sample that mirrors the relevant population on the variables that

matter, such as frequencies of gender, age, language, or ethnicity (Chapter 13)

Representativeness Heuristic: Mental shortcut in which people categorize a particular instance based on how similar the instance is to a typical member of that category (Chapter 3)

Response Effects: Unintended variations in question responses that stem from procedural aspects or features of the survey instrument, such as the wording of a question or the order of the questions (Chapter 4)

Response Latency: How long it takes participants to categorize a stimulus after it is presented (Chapter 10)

Right-Wing Authoritarianism (RWA): Individual difference variable comprised of three core elements: submission to legitimate authority, aggression against outgroups or deviants, and endorsement of conventional social norms and morality (Chapter 10)

Romantic or Sexual Jealousy: Uncomfortable psychological arousal that often occurs in response to an infidelity threat to a sexual relationship (Chapter 11)

Scapegoating: When one group unfairly claims that another group has intentionally caused its misfortunes (Chapter 10)

Scarcity Principle: People are more likely to value options and items when they are difficult to obtain or otherwise limited in their availability (Chapter 6)

Schemas: Cognitive structures that organize knowledge about particular objects of thought, such as concepts, experiences, or roles (Chapter 4)

Self: Psychological apparatus that gives a person the capacity to consciously think about him or herself (Chapter 4)

Self-Affirmation: Process whereby the integrity of the self is restored by affirming important values or qualities (Chapter 7)

Self-Categorization Theory (SCT): Idea that people place themselves within a category and can satisfy self-esteem needs by more positively evaluating their group as compared to other groups (Chapter 10)

Self-Concept: Set of beliefs a person has about the characteristics she or he possesses (Chapter 4)

Self-Discrepancy Theory: Idea that each person has an actual, ideal, and ought self (Chapter 4)

Self-Esteem: Overall positive or negative evaluation of oneself (Chapter 4)

Self-Evaluation Maintenance Model (SEM): Postulates that a person typically only makes social comparisons when this will improve her or his self-evaluation (Chapter 4)

Self-Fulfilling Prophecy: When an initially inaccurate expectation leads to behaviors that cause that expectation to come true (Chapter 5)

Self-Handicapping: Arranging events that may reduce one's likelihood of success but also protect one's self-esteem by serving as excuses for possible failure (Chapter 4)

Self-Monitoring: Extent to which people chronically think about how they appear to others and, as a consequence, change their appearance and behavior to fit the circumstances (Chapter 4)

Self-Perception Theory: Idea that people sometimes infer their own attitudes in the same way that a third party might infer their attitudes: by watching their behavior (Chapter 4)

Self-Promotion: Efforts designed to enhance one's self-image (Chapter 4)

Self-Protection: Efforts intended to maintain or defend one's positive self-image (Chapter 4)

Self-Regulation: The capacity to control one's thoughts, feelings, and behavior (Chapter 4)

Self-Report: Individual's conscious response to a question or situation (Chapter 4)

Self-Schema: Schema that organizes information about oneself with respect to specific domains of one's life (Chapter 4)

Self-Serving Attributional Bias: Taking credit for one's successes but blaming outside factors for one's failures (Chapter 4)

Self-Verification: Seeking information that will confirm one's self-concept (Chapter 4)

Set Point: The level of well-being to which a person typically returns after experiencing significant life events (Chapter 12)

Sexism: Negative prejudices, stereotypes, and discrimination directed at individuals based on their gender and/or institutional practices that support the unequal status of men and women (Chapter 10)

Sexual Selection: Genes that provide a reproductive advantage are more likely to be passed on to a new generation (Chapter 11)

Shared Information Bias: Tendency for groups to spend too much time discussing information that all members possess rather than unshared information (Chapter 12)

Social Cognition: Mental processes involved in perceiving, attending to, remembering, thinking about, and making sense of oneself and others (Chapter 1)

Social Comparison: Monitoring how one is doing and adjusting one's behavior accordingly in an effort to be liked by important others (Chapter 4)

Social Dilemmas or Traps: Situations in which individuals choose between maximizing their own beneficial outcomes and maximizing those of the group (Chapter 13)

Social Dominance Orientation (SDO): Degree to which a person generally endorses hierarchy and inequality among social groups and specifically prefers that her or his ingroup dominate others (Chapter 10)

Social Exchange Theory: Idea that people view their interactions with others in terms of the trade-off between benefits and costs and that they seek to maximize the benefits and minimize the costs (Chapter 11)

Social Facilitation: Presence of others improves performance on well-learned or easy tasks but decreases it on novel or difficult ones (Chapter 12)

Social Identity: Component of the self-concept that is derived from membership in various groups (Chapter 10)

Social Identity Model of Deindividuation Effects (SIDE): Postulates that immersion in groups can *heighten* one's sense of self (Chapter 12)

Social Identity Theory (SIT): Idea that people have a need to feel good about themselves and that one major component of their self-esteem derives from the groups to which they belong (Chapter 10)

Social Influence: Internal or external change in a person caused by real or imagined pressure from others (Chapter 6)

Social Learning: Learning by observing or hearing that someone else was reinforced or punished for engaging in a particular behavior (Chapter 1)

Social Loafing: When individuals exert less effort when working in a group as opposed to working alone (Chapter 12)

Social Neuroscience: Interdisciplinary field devoted to the study of neural, hormonal, cellular, and genetic mechanisms, and to the study of the associations and influences between social and biological levels of organization (Chapter 2)

Social Norm: A rule and/or standard that is typically unwritten and guides social behavior (Chapter 6)

Social Psychology: Scientific study of the social experiences and behaviors of individuals. (Chapter 1)

Social Responsibility Norm: Norm that states that one should help those who need one's help (Chapter 8)

Social Role Theory: Postulates that biological and social factors together can sufficiently explain sex differences in mate preferences (Chapter 11)

Social Selection: Genes that facilitate successful social living are more likely to be passed to a new generation (Chapter 12)

Social Validation (or Social Proof) Principle: Increased likelihood that a person will enact a particular behavior to the extent that others are thought to be engaging in that same behavior (Chapter 6)

Sociology: Examines group-level phenomena—such as societal trends, cultural norms, the effects of race or social class, and so forth (Chapter 1)

Sociometer Hypothesis: Idea that people have a psychological mechanism—the sociometer—that assesses the strength and importance of social relationships and that these relationships strongly influence self-esteem (Chapter 4)

Spotlight Effect: Overestimation of the extent to which other people are observing and noticing one (Chapter 4)

Spreading Activation: Activation of one node in the mental system leads to the activation of other concepts that are closely associated with it in memory (Chapter 3)

Stereotype: Belief about the characteristics, attributes, and behaviors of a group and its members (Chapter 10)

Stereotype Content Model (SCM): Postulates that stereotypes universally vary along two major dimensions: competence and warmth (Chapter 10)

Stereotype (or Social Identity) Threat: Discomfort or anxiety that targets feel when concerned that they may confirm a negative stereotype held about their group (Chapter 10)

Stigma: Specific characteristic (such as a personal attribute, facial mark, mental illness, and so forth) that distinguishes a stigmatized group from other groups (Chapter 10)

Subtype: Part of the group that is seen as a deviation from the larger group, allowing a global stereotype about that overall group to persist (Chapter 10)

Sunk-Cost Effect: Tendency for people to be reluctant to give up on a course of action that they have invested time, money, and/or effort into, even if it is in their best interest to do so (Chapter 13)

Superordinate Goals: Goals that transcend the interests of specific groups and require mutual cooperation to solve and which facilitate intergroup harmony (Chapter 10)

Surveys: Questionnaires that consist entirely of self-report items that can be administered on paper, computer, online, or in interviews (Chapter 4)

That's-Not-All Technique: Adding new incentives to a deal before the consumer has been given the opportunity to either accept or decline the deal and without increasing the price (Chapter 6)

Theory: Set of interrelated statements that explain and predict patterns of observable events (Chapter 1)

Theory of Empathy-Induced Altruistic Motivation: Idea that altruistic motivation for helping is possible and specifies the factors that can lead to it (Chapter 8)

Theory of Differential Parental Investment and Sexual Selection: Idea that (a) the sex that is more invested in the offspring will be more selective in choosing sexual partners, and (b) the less invested sex will engage in more intrasexual competition in order to gain access to the more invested sex (Chapter 11)

Theory of Social Comparison Processes: Idea that people will evaluate how they are doing using subjective standards when objective standards are not available (Chapter 4)

Transactional Leaders: Individuals who use transactions—offering benefits (e.g., money, promotion, etc.) to members in exchange for their energy and effort—to motivate the group to work toward shared goals (Chapter 12)

Transactive Memory: Group memory that is the combination of the memories of individuals (Chapter 12)

Transformational Leaders: Individuals who offer a compelling vision that inspires followers to set aside personal needs and work hard toward loftier, overarching goals (Chapter 12)

Treatment Group: Group of participants assigned to receive the treatment

Tripartite Model of Attitudes: Postulates that attitudes are composed of three elements: affect, cognition, and behaviour (Chapter 7)

Two-Factor Theory of Emotion: Idea that the experience of emotion is comprised of two distinct processes: general physiological arousal and an emotion label (Chapter 11)

Ultimate Attribution Error: Attributing the negative behavior of outgroups to dispositional factors and positive outgroup behavior to situational influences (Chapter 10)

Unobtrusive Measures or Covert: Obtaining information from people when they are not aware that this is being done (Chapter 7)

Upward Social Comparison: Contrasting one's performance, ability, or situation with individuals who performed better, have stronger abilities, or are in better situations (Chapter 4)

Validity: Extent to which a particular measurement tool provides accurate results (Chapter 3)

Violence: Extreme aggression that is intended to inflict serious harm (Chapter 9)

Weapons Effect: When the presence of a weapon—such as a rifle or a revolver—makes aggression more likely (Chapter 9)

Willpower: Mental energy needed to change the activities of the self to meet the desired standards (Chapter 4)

X-system: Primarily reflexive, nonconscious, or automatic parallel processing system (Chapter 3)

References

Aamodt, M. G., & Custer, H. (2006). Who can best catch a liar?: A meta-analysis of individual differences in detecting deception. *The Forensic Examiner, 15,* 6–11.

Aarts, H., Dijksterhuis, A., & Custers, R. (2003). Automatic normative behavior in environments: The moderating role of conformity in activating situational norms. *Social Cognition, 21,* 447–464.

Abdou, C. M., & Fingerhut, A. W. (2014). Stereotype threat among Black and White women in health care settings. *Cultural Diversity and Ethnic Minority Psychology, 20,* 316–323.

Abell, L., & Brewer, G. (2014). Machiavellianism, self-monitoring, self-promotion and relational aggression on Facebook. *Computers in Human Behavior, 36,* 258–262.

Aboud, F. E. (2003). The formation of in-group favoritism and out-group prejudice in young children: Are they distinct attitudes? *Developmental Psychology, 39,* 48–60.

Aboud, F. E., & Amato, M. (2001). Developmental and socialization influences on intergroup bias. In R. J. Brown & S. L. Gaertner (Eds.), *Blackwell handbook of social psychology* (pp. 65–85). Oxford, UK: Blackwell.

Abrams, D. (2009). Social identity on a national scale: Optimal distinctiveness and young people's self-expression through musical preference. *Group Processes & Intergroup Relations, 12,* 303–317.

Abrams, D., & Hogg, M. A. (2010). Social identity and self-categorization. In J. F. Dovidio, M. Hewstone, P. Glick & V. M. Esses (Eds.), *Sage handbook of prejudice, stereotyping, and discrimination* (pp. 179–193). Los Angeles, CA: Sage.

Acevedo, B. P., Aron, A., Fisher, H. E., & Brown, L. L. (2011). Neural correlates of long-term intense romantic love. *Social Cognitive and Affective Neuroscience, 7,* 145–159.

Ackerman, J. M., Shapiro, J. R., Neuberg, S. L., Kenrick, D. T., Becker, D. V., Griskevicius, V., . . . Schaller, M. (2006). They all look the same to me (unless they're angry): From out-group homogeneity to out-group heterogeneity. *Psychological Science, 17,* 836–840.

Adam, H., Obodaru, O., & Galinsky, A. D. (2015). Who you are is where you are: Antecedents and consequences of locating the self in the brain or the heart. *Organizational Behavior and Human Decision Processes, 128,* 74–83.

Adams, H. L., & Williams, L. R. (2014). "It's not just you two": A grounded theory of peer-influenced jealousy as a pathway to dating violence among acculturating Mexican American adolescents. *Psychology of Violence, 4,* 294–308.

Adams, J., Parkinson, L., Sanson-Fisher, R. W., & Walsh, R. A. (2008). Enhancing self-report of adolescent smoking: The effects of bogus pipeline and anonymity. *Addictive Behaviors, 33,* 1291–1296.

Adorno, T. W., Frenkel-Brunswik, E., Levinson, D. J., & Sanford, R. N. (1950). *The authoritarian personality.* Oxford, UK: Harpers.

Adriance, P., Aiken, W., Brown, P., Carmichael, C., Coddington, N., Dobb, R. F., . . . Wood, J. (2010). Religion in a sustainable world: What is the role of religious institutions in fostering ecological sustainability? *Ecopsychology, 2,* 5–11.

Aggarwal, P., & O'Brien, C. L. (2008). Social loafing on group projects. *Journal of Marketing Education, 30,* 255–264.

Agnoli, S., Pittarello, A., Hysenbelli, D., & Rubaltelli, E. (2015). "Give, but give until it hurts": The modulatory role of trait emotional intelligence on the motivation to help. *PLoS ONE, 10,* 1–22.

Aguinis, H., & Henle, C. A. (2001). Empirical assessment of the ethics of the bogus pipeline. *Journal of Applied Social Psychology, 31,* 352–375.

Ahlfinger, N. R., & Esser, J. K. (2001). Testing the groupthink model: Effects of promotional leadership and conformity predisposition. Social Behavior and Personality, 29, 31–41.

Aiello, J. R., & Douthitt, E. A. (2001). Social facilitation from Triplett to electronic performance monitoring. *Group Dynamics: Theory, Research, and Practice, 5,* 163–180.

Ainsworth, S. E., & Maner, J. K. (2012). Sex begets violence: Mating motives, social dominance, and physical aggression in men. *Journal of Personality and Social Psychology, 103,* 819–829.

Ajzen, I. (1985). From intentions to actions: A theory of planned behavior. In J. Kuhl & J. Beckman (Eds.), *Action-control: From cognition to behavior* (pp. 11–39). Heidelberg: Springer.

Ajzen, I., & Cote, N. G. (2008). Attitudes and the prediction of behavior. In W. D. Crano & R. Prislin (Eds.), *Attitudes and attitude change* (pp. 289–311). New York, NY: Psychology Press.

Ajzen, I., & Fishbein, M. (1977). Attitude-behavior relations: A theoretical analysis and review of empirical research. *Psychological Bulletin, 84,* 888–918.

Ajzen, I., & Fishbein, M. (1980). *Understanding attitudes and predicting social behavior.* Englewood Cliffs, NJ: Prentice Hall.

Ajzen, I., & Fishbein, M. (2008). Attitudinal and normative variables as predictors of specific behaviors. In R. H. Fazio & R. E. Petty (Eds.), *Attitudes: Their structure, function, and consequences* (pp. 425–443). New York, NY: Psychology Press.

Akimoto, S. A., Sanbonmatsu, D. M., & Ho, E. A. (2000). Manipulating personal salience: The effects of performance expectations on physical positioning. *Personality and Social Psychology Bulletin, 26,* 755–761.

Aknin, L. B., Dunn, E. W., & Norton, M. I. (2012). Happiness runs in a circular motion: Evidence for a positive feedback loop between prosocial spending and happiness. *Journal of Happiness Studies, 13,* 347–355.

Akrami, N., Ekehammar, B., & Yang-Wallentin, F. (2011). Personality and social psychology factors explaining sexism. *Journal of Individual Differences, 32,* 153–160.

Albarracín, D., & Mitchell, A. L. (2004). The role of defensive confidence in preference for proattitudinal information: How believing that one is strong can sometimes be a defensive weakness. *Personality and Social Psychology Bulletin, 30,* 1565–1584.

Albarracín, D., & Vargas, P. (2010). Attitudes and persuasion: From biology to social responses to persuasive intent. In S. T. Fiske, D. T. Gilbert & G. Lindzey (Eds.), *Handbook of social psychology* (Vol. 1, 5th ed., pp. 394–427). Hoboken, NJ: John Wiley & Sons.

Alessandri, G., Caprara, G. V., Eisenberg, N., & Steca, P. (2009). Reciprocal relations among self-efficacy beliefs and prosociality across time. *Journal of Personality, 77,* 1229–1259.

Alessandri, G., Kanacri, B. P. L., Eisenberg, N., Zuffianò, A., Milioni, M., Vecchione, M., & Caprara, G. V. (2014). Prosociality during the transition from late adolescence to young adulthood: The role of effortful control and ego-resiliency. *Personality and Social Psychology Bulletin, 40,* 1451–1465.

Alexopoulos, T., Fiedler, K., & Freytag, P. (2012). The impact of open and closed mindsets on evaluative priming. *Cognition and Emotion, 26,* 978–994.

Alicke, M. D., & Sedikides, C. (2009). Self-enhancement and self-protection: What they are and what they do. *European Review of Social Psychology, 20,* 1–48.

Allen, J. B., Kenrick, D. T., Linder, D. E., & McCall, M. A. (1989). Arousal and attraction: A response-facilitation alternative to misattribution and negative-reinforcement models. *Journal of Personality and Social Psychology, 57,* 261–270.

Allen, M., D'Alessio, D., & Brezgel, K. (1995). A meta-analysis summarizing the effects of pornography: II. Aggression after exposure. *Human Communication Research, 22,* 258–283.

Allen, M., Hale, J., Mongeau, P., & Berkowtiz-Stafford, S. (1990). Testing a model of message sidedness: Three replications. *Communication Monographs, 57,* 275–291.

Allport, F. H. (1924). *Social psychology.* London: Routledge/Thoemmes Press.

Allport, G. W. (1935). Attitudes. In C. Murchison (Ed.), *Handbook of social psychology* (pp. 798–844). Worcester, MA: Clark University Press.

Allport, G. W. (1950). *The individual and his religion: A psychological interpretation.* Oxford, UK: Macmillan.

Allport, G. W. (1954). *The nature of prejudice.* Oxford, UK: Addison-Wesley.

Allport, G. W. (1985). The historical background of social psychology. In G. Lindzey & E. Aronson (Ed.), *Handbook of social psychology* (3rd ed., Vol. 1, pp. 1–46). New York, NY: Random House.

Allport, G. W., & Ross, J. M. (1967). Personal religious orientation and prejudice. *Journal of Personality and Social Psychology, 5,* 432–443.

Altemeyer, B. (1996). *The authoritarian specter.* Cambridge, MA: Harvard University Press.

Altemeyer, B. (1998). The "other" authoritarian personality. In M. P. Zanna (Ed.), *Advances in Experimental Social Psychology* (Vol. 30, pp. 47–92). New York, NY: Academic Press.

Altemeyer, B., & Hunsberger, B. E. (1992). Authoritarianism, religious fundamentalism, quest, and prejudice. *International Journal for the Psychology of Religion, 2,* 113–133.

Alter, A. L., & Oppenheimer, D. M. (2006). From a fixation on sports to an exploration of mechanism: The past, present, and future of hot hand research. *Thinking & Reasoning, 12,* 431–444.

Alterovitz, S. S. -R., & Mendelsohn, G. A. (2011). Partner preferences across the life span: Online dating by older adults. *Psychology of Popular Media Culture, 1,* 89–95.

Altman, I., & Taylor, D. A. (1973). *Social penetration: The development of interpersonal relationships.* Oxford, UK: Holt, Rinehart & Winston.

Alwin, D. F., & Krosnick, J. A. (1991). Aging, cohorts, and the stability of sociopolitical orientations over the life span. *American Journal of Sociology, 97,* 169–195.

Amato, P. R. (1983). Helping behavior in urban and rural environments: Field studies based on a taxonomic organization of helping episodes. *Journal of Personality and Social Psychology, 45,* 571–586.

Ambady, N. (2010). The perils of pondering: Intuition and thin slice judgments. *Psychological Inquiry, 21,* 271–278.

Ambady, N., & Rosenthal, R. (1992). Thin slices of expressive behavior as predictors of interpersonal consequences: A meta-analysis. *Psychological Bulletin, 111,* 256–274.

Ambady, N., & Rosenthal, R. (1993). Half a minute: Predicting teacher evaluations from thin slices of nonverbal behavior and physical attractiveness. *Journal of Personality and Social Psychology, 64,* 431–441.

Ambady, N., & Weisbuch, M. (2010). Nonverbal behavior. In S. T. Fiske, D. T. Gilbert, & G. Lindzey (Eds.), *Handbook of social psychology* (Vol. 1, 5th ed., pp. 464–497). Hoboken, NJ: John Wiley & Sons.

American Psychological Association. (2010). Ethical principles of psychologists and code of conduct. Retrieved from http://www.apa.org/ethics/code/principles.pdf

Amiot, C. E., de la Sablonniere, R., Smith, L. G. E., & Smith, J. R. (2015). Capturing changes in social identities over time and how they become part of the self-concept. *Social and Personality Psychology Compass, 9,* 171–187.

Amnesty International. (2014). *Attitudes to torture.* London, UK: Amnesty International.

Amnesty International. (2015). *The state of the world's human rights.* London, UK: Amnesty International.

Andersen, S. M., Moskowitz, G. B., Blair, I. V., & Nosek, B. A. (2007). Automatic thought. In A. W. Kruglanski & E. T. Higgins (Eds.), *Social psychology: Handbook of basic principles* (2nd ed., pp. 138–175). New York, NY: Guilford Press.

Andersen, S. M., Moskowitz, G. B., Blair, I. V., & Nosek, B. A. (2007). Automatic thought. In A. W. Kruglanski & E. T. Higgins (Eds.), *Social psychology: Handbook of basic principles* (2nd ed., pp. 138–175). New York, NY: Guilford Press.

Anderson, C. A. (1982). Inoculation and counterexplanation: Debiasing techniques in the perseverance of social theories. *Social Cognition, 1,* 126–139.

Anderson, C. A. (1983). Abstract and concrete data in the perseverance of social theories: When weak data lead to unshakeable beliefs. *Journal of Experimental Social Psychology, 19,* 93–108.

Anderson, C. A. (1989). Temperature and aggression: Ubiquitous effects of heat on occurrence of human violence. *Psychological Bulletin, 106,* 74–96.

Anderson, C. A. (2001). Heat and violence. *Current Directions in Psychological Science, 10,* 33–38.

Anderson, C. A., & Bushman, B. J. (1997). External validity of "trivial" experiments: The case of laboratory aggression. *Review of General Psychology, 1,* 19–41.

Anderson, C. A., & Bushman, B. J. (2002). Human aggression. *Annual Review of Psychology, 53,* 27–51.

Anderson, C. A., & Dill, K. E. (2000). Video games and aggressive thoughts, feelings, and behavior in the laboratory and in life. *Journal of Personality and Social Psychology, 78,* 772–790.

Anderson, C. A., & Huesmann, L. R. (2003). Human aggression: A social-cognitive view. In M. A. Hogg & J. Cooper (Eds.), *The Sage handbook of social psychology* (pp. 296–323). London, UK: Sage.

Anderson, C. A., Anderson, K. B., & Deuser, W. E. (1996). Examining an affective aggression framework: Weapon and temperature effects on aggressive thoughts, affect, and attitudes. *Personality and Social Psychology Bulletin, 22,* 366–376.

Anderson, C. A., Berkowitz, L., Donnerstein, E., Huesmann, L. R., Johnson, J. D., Linz, D., . . . Wartella, E. (2003). The influence of media violence on youth. *Psychological Science in the Public Interest, 4,* 81–110.

Anderson, C. A., Carnagey, N. L., & Eubanks, J. (2003). Exposure to violent media: The effects of songs with violent lyrics on aggressive thoughts and feelings. *Journal of Personality and Social Psychology, 84,* 960–971.

Anderson, C. A., Carnagey, N. L., Flanagan, M., Benjamin, A. J., Eubanks, J., & Valentine, J. C. (2004). Violent video games: Specific effects of violent content on aggressive thoughts and behavior. In M. P. Zanna (Ed.), *Advances in experimental social psychology* (Vol. 36, pp. 199–249). San Diego, CA: Elsevier Academic Press.

Anderson, C. A., Lepper, M. R., & Ross, L. (1980). Perseverance of social theories: The role of explanation in the persistence of discredited information. *Journal of Personality and Social Psychology, 39,* 1037–1049.

Anderson, C. A., Lindsay, J. J., & Bushman, B. J. (1999). Research in the psychological laboratory: Truth or triviality? *Current Directions in Psychological Science, 8,* 3–9.

Anderson, C. A., Shibuya, A., Ihori, N., Swing, E. L., Bushman, B. J., Sakamoto, A., . . . Saleem, M. (2010). Violent video game effects on aggression, empathy, and prosocial behavior in Eastern and Western countries: A meta-analytic review. *Psychological Bulletin, 136,* 151–173.

Anderson, R. B., & McMillion, P. Y. (1995). Effects of similar and diversified modeling on African American women's efficacy expectations and intentions to perform breast self-examination. *Health Communication, 7,* 327–343.

Anderson, S. L., Adams, G., & Plaut, V. C. (2008). The cultural grounding of personal relationship: The importance of attractiveness in everyday life. *Journal of Personality and Social Psychology, 95,* 352–368.

Ano, G. G., & Vasconcelles, E. B. (2005). Religious coping and psychological adjustment to stress: A meta-analysis. *Journal of Clinical Psychology, 61,* 461–480.

Anseel, F., & Lievens, F. (2006). Certainty as a moderator of feedback reactions? A test of the strength of the self-verification motive. *Journal of Occupational and Organizational Psychology, 79,* 533–551.

Archer, J. (2000). Sex differences in aggression between heterosexual partners: A meta-analytic review. *Psychological Bulletin, 126,* 651–680.

Archer, J. (2006). Testosterone and human aggression: An evaluation of the challenge hypothesis. *Neuroscience and Biobehavioral Reviews, 30,* 319–345.

Archer, J. (2013). Can evolutionary principles explain patterns of family violence? *Psychological Bulletin, 139,* 403–440.

Archer, J., Graham-Kevan, N., & Davies, M. (2005). Testosterone and aggression: A reanalysis of Book, Starzyk, and Quinsey's (2001) study. *Aggression & Violent Behavior, 10,* 241–261.

Argyle, M. (2000). *Psychology of religion: An introduction.* London, UK: Routledge.

Arkes, H. R. (2013). The consequences of the hindsight bias in medical decision making. *Current Directions in Psychological Science, 22,* 356–360.

Arkes, H. R., & Blumer, C. (1985). The psychology of sunk cost. *Organizational Behavior and Human Decision Processes, 35,* 124–140.

Armitage, C. J., Harris, P. R., & Arden, M. A. (2011). Evidence that self-affirmation reduces alcohol consumption: Randomized exploratory trial with a new, brief means of self-affirming. *Health Psychology, 30,* 633–641.

Aron, A., & Aron, E. N. (1989). *The heart of social psychology: A backstage view of a passionate science* (2nd ed.). Lexington, MA: Lexington Books.

Aron, A., Fisher, H., Mashek, D. J., Strong, G., Li, H., & Brown, L. L. (2005). Reward, motivation, and emotion systems associated with early-stage intense romantic love. *Journal of Neurophysiology, 94,* 327–337.

Aronson, E. (1969). The theory of cognitive dissonance: A current perspective. In L. Berkowitz (Ed.), *Advances in Experimental Social Psychology* (Vol. 4, pp. 1–34). New York, NY: Academic Press.

Aronson, E. (1992). The return of the repressed: Dissonance theory makes a comeback. *Psychological Inquiry, 3,* 303–303.

Aronson, E. (2001). *Nobody left to hate: Teaching compassion after Columbine.* New York, NY: Holt.

Aronson, E. (2004). Reducing hostility and building compassion: Lessons from the jigsaw classroom. In A. G. Miller (Ed.), *The social psychology of good and evil* (pp. 469–488). New York, NY: Guilford Press.

Aronson, E., & Bridgeman, D. (1979). Jigsaw groups and the desegregated classroom: In pursuit of common goals. *Personality and Social Psychology Bulletin, 5,* 438–446.

Aronson, E., Blaney, N., Sikes, J., Stephan, C., & Snapp, M. (1975). Busing and racial tension: The jigsaw route to learning and liking. *Psychology Today, 8,* 43–59.

Aronson, E., Ellsworth, P. C., Carlsmith, J. M., & Gonzales, M. H. (1990). *Research methods in social psychology* (2nd, ed.). New York, NY: McGraw-Hill.

Aronson, E., Fried, C., & Stone, J. (1991). Overcoming denial and increasing the intention to use condoms through the induction of hypocrisy. *American Journal of Public Health, 81,* 1636–1636.

Aronson, E., Wilson, T. D., & Brewer, M. B. (1998). Experimentation in social psychology. In D. T. Gilbert, S. T. Fiske, & G. Lindzey (Eds.), *The handbook of social psychology,* (Vols. 1 & 2, 4th ed., pp. 99–142). New York, NY: McGraw-Hill.

Aronson, J., & McGlone, M.S. (2009). Stereotype and social identity threat. In T. D. Nelson (Ed.), *Handbook of prejudice, stereotyping, and discrimination* (pp. 153–178). New York, NY: Psychology Press.

Aronson, J., Blanton, H., & Cooper, J. (1995). From dissonance to disidentification: Selectivity in the self-affirmation process. *Journal of Personality and Social Psychology, 68,* 986–996.

Aronson, J., Lustina, M. J., Good, C., Keough, K., Steele, C. M., & Brown, J. (1999). When White men can't do math: Necessary and sufficient factors in stereotype threat. *Journal of Experimental Social Psychology, 35,* 29–46.

Arrigo, J. M., & Wagner, R. V. (2007). Psychologists and military interrogators rethink the psychology of torture. *Peace and Conflict: Journal of Peace Psychology, 13,* 393–398.

Arvey, R. D., & Chaturvedi, S. (2011). Examining the genetic basis of leadership. In S. E. Murphy & R. J. Reichard (Eds.), Series in applied psychology. Early development and leadership: Building the next generation of leaders (pp. 59–69). New York, NY: Routledge.

Asch, S. E. (1946). Forming impressions of personality. *The Journal of Abnormal and Social Psychology, 41,* 258–290.

Asch, S. E. (1952). *Social psychology.* Englewood Cliffs, NJ: Prentice Hall.

Asch, S. E. (1955). Opinions and social pressure. *Scientific American, 193,* 31–35.

Asch, S. E. (1956). Studies of independence and conformity: I. A minority of one against a unanimous majority. *Psychological Monographs: General and Applied, 70,* 1–70.

Asencio, E. K. (2013). Self-esteem, reflected appraisals, and self-views: Examining criminal and worker identities. *Social Psychology Quarterly, 76,* 291–313.

Ashton, M. C. (2013). *Individual differences and personality* (2nd ed.). San Diego, CA: Academic Press.

Ashton, M. C., & Lee, K. (2014). Personality and religiousness. In V. Saroglou (Ed.), *Religion, personality, and social behavior* (pp. 31–45). New York, NY: Psychology Press.

Astrauskaite, M., Kern, R. M., & Notelaers, G. (2014). An individual psychology approach to underlying factors of workplace bullying. *The Journal of Individual Psychology, 70,* 25–25.

Atran, S. (2008). The evolutionary psychology of religion. In C. Crawford & D. Krebs (Eds.), *Foundations of evolutionary psychology* (pp. 477–498). New York, NY: Taylor & Francis Group/Lawrence Erlbaum.

Axelrod, R. (2006). *The evolution of cooperation* (Rev. ed.). New York, NY: Basic Books.

Ayman, R., & Korabik, K. (2010). Leadership: Why gender and culture matter. American Psychologist, 65, 157–170.

Ayman, R., Chemers, M. M., & Fiedler, F. (2007). The contingency model of leadership effectiveness: Its levels of analysis. In R. P. Vecchio (Ed.), *Leadership: Understanding the dynamics of power and influence in organizations* (2nd ed., pp. 335–360). Notre Dame, IN: University of Notre Dame Press.

Ayman, R., Korabik, K., & Morris, S. (2009). Is transformational leadership always perceived as effective? Male subordinates' devaluation of female transformational leaders. *Journal of Applied Social Psychology, 39,* 852–879.

Bachman, J. G., & O'Malley, P. M. (1984). Yea-saying, nay-saying, and going to extremes: Black-White differences in response style. *Public Opinion Quarterly, 48,* 491–509.

Back, M. D., Schmukle, S. C., & Egloff, B. (2008). Becoming friends by chance. *Psychological Science, 19,* 439–440.

Back, M. D., Stopfer, J. M., Vazire, S., Gaddis, S., Schmukle, S. C., Egloff, B., & Gosling, S. D. (2010). Facebook profiles reflect actual personality, not self-idealization. *Psychological Science, 21,* 372–374.

Badr, L. K., & Abdallah, B. (2001). Physical attractiveness of premature infants affects outcome at discharge from the NICU. *Infant Behavior & Development, 24,* 129–133.

Baer, J., Kaufman, J. C., & Baumeister, R. F. (2008). *Are we free? Psychology and free will.* New York, NY: Oxford University Press.

Baghurst, T., & Kelley, B. C. (2014). An examination of stress in college students over the course of a semester. *Health Promotion Practice, 15,* 438–447.

Bailey, J. M., Dunne, M. P., & Martin, N. G. (2000). Genetic and environmental influences on sexual orientation and its correlates in an Australian twin sample. *Journal of Personality and Social Psychology, 78,* 524–536.

Balafoutas, L., Nikiforakis, N., & Rockenbach, B. (2014). Direct and indirect punishment among strangers in the field. *PNAS Proceedings of the National Academy of Sciences of the United States of America, 111,* 15924–15927.

Baldus, D. C., Woodworth, G. G., Zuckerman, D., Weiner, N. A., & Broffitt, B. (2001). The use of peremptory challenges in capital murder trials: A legal and empirical analysis. *University of Pennsylvania Journal of Constitutional Law, 3,* 3–169.

Bales, R. F. (1950). *Interaction process analysis; a method for the study of small groups.* Oxford UK: Addison-Wesley.

Bales, R. F. (1958). Task roles and social roles in problem-solving groups. In E. E. Maccoby, T. M. Newcomb, & E. L. Hartley (Eds.), *Readings in social psychology* (pp. 437–447). New York, NY: Holt, Rinehart, & Winston.

Banaji, M. R., & Heiphetz, L. (2010). Attitudes. In S. T. Fiske, D. T. Gilbert & G. Lindzey (Eds.), *Handbook of social psychology* (Vol. 1, 5th ed., pp. 353–393). Hoboken, NJ: John Wiley & Sons.

Banas, J., & Turner, M. M. (2011). Exploring the "that's -not-all" effect: A test of theoretical explanations. *Southern Communication Journal, 76,* 305–322.

Bandura, A. (1977). *Social learning theory.* Oxford, UK: Prentice-Hall.

Bandura, A. (1986). *Social foundations of thought and action: A social cognitive theory.* Englewood Cliffs, NJ: Prentice-Hall.

Bandura, A. (1997). *Self-efficacy: The exercise of control.* New York, NY: W. H. Freeman/Times Books/Henry Holt & Co.

Bandura, A. (2012). Social cognitive theory. In P. A. M. Van Lange, A. W. Kruglanski, E. T. Higgins, P. A. M. Van Lange, A. W. Kruglanski, & E. T. Higgins (Eds.), *Handbook of theories of social psychology* (Vol. 1, pp. 349–373). Thousand Oaks, CA: Sage Publications Ltd.

Bandura, A., & Walters, R. H. (1963). *Social learning and personality development.* New York, NY: Holt, Rinehart, & Winston.

Bandura, A., Ross, D., & Ross, S.A. (1963). Imitation of film-mediated aggressive models. *The Journal of Abnormal and Social Psychology, 66,* 3–11.

Bandura, A., Ross, R., & Ross, S. (1961). Transmission of aggression through imitation of aggressive models. *Journal of Abnormal and Social Psychology, 63,* 575–582.

Banks, J., Marmot, M., Oldfield, Z., & Smith, J. P. (2006). Disease and disadvantage in the United States and in England. *JAMA: Journal of the American Medical Association, 295,* 2037–2045.

Banyard, V. L., Moynihan, M. M., Cares, A. C., & Warner, R. (2014). How do we know if it works? Measuring outcomes in bystander-focused abuse prevention on campuses. *Psychology of Violence, 4,* 101–115.

Bar-Anan, Y., Wilson, T. D., & Hassin, R. R. (2010). Inaccurate self-knowledge formation as a result of automatic behavior. *Journal of Experimental Social Psychology, 46,* 884–894.

Barasch, A., Levine, E. E., Berman, J. Z., & Small, D. A. (2014). Selfish or selfless? On the signal value of emotion in altruistic behavior. *Journal of Personality and Social Psychology, 107,* 393–413.

Barbaro, N., Pickett, S. M., & Parkhill, M. R. (2015). Environmental attitudes mediate the link between need for cognition and pro-environmental goal choice. *Personality and Individual Differences, 75,* 220–223.

Barden, J., & Tormala, Z. L. (2014). Elaboration and attitude strength: The new meta-cognitive perspective. *Social and Personality Psychology Compass, 8,* 17–29.

Barelds, D. P. H., & Dijkstra, P. (2011). Positive illusions about a partner's personality and relationship quality. *Journal of Research in Personality, 45,* 37–43.

Bargh, J. A. (1994). The four horsemen of automaticity: Awareness, intention, efficiency, and control in social cognition. In R. S. Wyer & T. K. Srull (Eds.), *Handbook of social cognition, Vol. 1: Basic processes; Vol. 2: Applications* (2nd ed., pp. 1–40). Hillsdale, NJ: Lawrence Erlbaum.

Bargh, J. A. (2008). Free will is un-natural. In J. Baer, J. C. Kaufman, & R. F. Baumeister (Eds.), *Are we free? Psychology and free will* (pp. 128–154). New York, NY: Oxford University Press.

Bargh, J. A., & McKenna, K. Y. A. (2004). The Internet and social life. *Annual Review of Psychology, 55,* 573–590.

Bargh, J. A., Chen, M., & Burrows, L. (1996). Automaticity of social behavior: Direct effects of trait construct and stereotype activation on action. *Journal of Personality and Social Psychology, 71,* 230–244.

Bargh, J. A., Gollwitzer, P. M., Lee-Chai, A., Barndollar, K., & Tröschel, R. (2001). The automated will: Nonconscious activation and pursuit of behavioral goals. *Journal of Personality and Social Psychology, 81,* 1014–1027.

Bar-Hillel, M. (1980). The base-rate fallacy in probability judgments. *Acta Psychologica, 44,* 211–233.

Bar-Hillel, M. (1990). Back to base rates. In R. M. Hogarth (Ed.), *Insights in decision making: A tribute to Hillel J. Einhorn* (pp. 200–216). Chicago, IL: University of Chicago Press.

Baron, J., & Miller, J. G. (2000). Limiting the scope of moral obligations to help: A cross-cultural investigation. *Journal of Cross-Cultural Psychology, 31,* 703–725.

Baron, R. A. (1988). Negative effects of destructive criticism: Impact on conflict, self-efficacy, and task performance. *Journal of Applied Psychology, 73,* 199–207.

Baron, R. A. (1997). The sweet smell of . . . helping: Effects of pleasant ambient fragrance on prosocial behavior in shopping malls. *Personality and Social Psychology Bulletin, 23,* 498–503.

Baron, R. S. (2005). So right it's wrong: Groupthink and the ubiquitous nature of polarized group decision making. In M. P. Zanna (Ed.), *Advances in experimental social psychology,* (Vol. 37, pp. 219–253). San Diego, CA: Elsevier Academic Press.

Baron, R. S., & Bellman, S. B. (2007). No guts, no glory: Courage, harassment and minority influence. *European Journal of Social Psychology, 37,* 101–124.

Baron, R. S., Moore, D., & Sanders, G. S. (1978). Distraction as a source of drive in social facilitation research. Journal of Personality and Social Psychology, 36, 816–824.

Barr, G. A., Gibbons, J. L., & Moyer, K. E. (1976). Male-female differences and the influence of neonatal and adult testosterone on intraspecies aggression in rats. *Journal of Comparative and Physiological Psychology, 90,* 1169–1183.

Barreiro, A. (2013). The appropriation process of the belief in a just world. *Integrative Psychological & Behavioral Science, 47,* 431–449.

Barrett, D. W. (2007). Informational influence. In R. F. Baumeister & K. D. Vohs (Eds.), *Encyclopedia of social psychology* (Vol. 1, pp. 480–481). Thousand Oaks, CA: Sage.

Barrett, D. W., Patock-Peckham, J. A., Hutchinson, G. T., & Nagoshi, C. T. (2005). Cognitive motivation and religious orientation. *Personality and Individual Differences, 38,* 461–474.

Barrett, D. W., Wosinska, W., Butner, J., Gornik-Durose, M., Cialdini, R. B., & Petrova, P. (2004). Individual differences in the motivation to comply across cultures: The impact of social obligation. *Personality and Individual Differences, 37,* 19–31.

Barrett, J. L. (2000). Exploring the natural foundations of religion. *Trends in Cognitive Sciences, 4,* 29–34.

Barrett, L. F., Mesquita, B., & Gendron, M. (2011). Context in emotion perception. *Curent Directions Psychological Science, 20,* 286–290.

Barrick, M. R., Shaffer, J. A., & DeGrassi, S. W. (2009). What you see may not be what you get: Relationships among self-presentation tactics and ratings of interview and job performance. *Journal of Applied Psychology, 94,* 1394–1411.

Bartels, J. M., & Magun-Jackson, S. (2009). Approach-avoidance motivation and metacognitive self-regulation: The role of need for achievement and fear of failure. *Learning and Individual Differences, 19,* 459–463.

Bartholow, B. D., & Dickter, C. L. (2007). Social cognitive neuroscience of person perception: A selective review focused on the event-related brain potential. In E. Harmon-Jones & P. Winkielman (Eds.), *Social neuroscience: Integrating biological and psychological explanations of social behavior* (pp. 376–400). New York, NY: Guilford Press.

Bartholow, B. D., & Heinz, A. (2006). Alcohol and aggression without consumption: Alcohol cues, aggressive thoughts, and hostile perception bias. *Psychological Science, 17,* 30–37.

Bartkowski, J. P., Xu, X., & Levin, M. L. (2008). Religion and child development: Evidence from the Early Childhood Longitudinal Study. *Social Science Research, 37,* 18–36.

Basford, T. E., Offermann, L. R., & Behrend, T. S. (2014). Do you see what I see? Perceptions of gender microaggressions in the workplace. *Psychology of Women Quarterly, 38,* 340–349.

Bass, B. M. (1997). Does the transactional–transformational leadership paradigm transcend organizational and national boundaries? *American Psychologist, 52,* 130–139.

Bass, B. M., & Riggio, R. E. (2006). Transformational leadership (2nd ed.). Mahwah, NJ: Lawrence Erlbaum.

Bassili, J. N., & Brown, R. D. (2005). Implicit and explicit attitudes: Research, challenges, and theory. In D. Albarracín, B. T. Johnson, & M. P. Zanna (Eds.), *The handbook of attitudes* (pp. 543–574). Mahwah, NJ: Lawrence Erlbaum.

Bastian, B., Jetten, J., Chen, H., Radke, H. R. M., Harding, J. F., & Fasoli, F. (2012). Losing our humanity: The self-dehumanizing consequences of social ostracism. *Personality & Social Psychology Bulletin, 39,* 156–169.

Batson, C. D. (1991). *The altruism question: Toward a social-psychological answer.* Hillsdale, NJ: Lawrence Erlbaum.

Batson, C. D. (1998). Altruism and prosocial behavior. In D. T. Gilbert, S. T. Fiske, & G. Lindzey (Eds.), *The handbook of social psychology* (Vols. 1 & 2, 4th ed., pp. 282–316). New York, NY: McGraw-Hill.

Batson, C. D. (2011). *Altruism in humans.* New York, NY: Oxford University Press.

Batson, C. D., & Flory, J. D. (1990). Goal-relevant cognitions associated with helping by individuals high on intrinsic, end religion. *Journal for the Scientific Study of Religion, 29,* 346–360.

Batson, C. D., Ahmad, N., & Lishner, D.A. (2009). Empathy and altruism. In S. J. Lopez & C. R. Snyder (Eds.), *Oxford handbook of positive psychology* (2nd ed., pp. 417–426). New York, NY: Oxford University Press.

Batson, C. D., Ahmad, N., & Stocks, E. L. (2011). Four forms of prosocial motivation: Egoism, altruism, collectivism, and principlism. In D. Dunning (Ed.), *Social motivation* (pp. 103–126). New York, NY: Psychology Press.

Batson, C. D., Ahmad, N., Powell, A. A., & Stocks, E. L. (2008). Prosocial motivation. In J. Y. Shah & W. L. Gardner (Eds.), *Handbook of motivation science* (pp. 135–149). New York, NY: Guilford Press.

Batson, C. D., Denton, D. M., & Vollmecke, J. T. (2008). Quest religion, anti-fundamentalism, and limited versus universal compassion. *Journal for the Scientific Study of Religion, 47,* 135–145.

Batson, C. D., Eidelman, S. H., Higley, S. L., & Russel, S. A. (2001). "And who is my neighbor?" II: Quest religion as a source of universal compassion. *Journal for the Scientific Study of Religion, 40,* 39–50.

Batson, C. D., Eklund, J. H., Chermok, V. L., Hoyt, J. L., & Ortiz, B. G. (2007). An additional antecedent of empathic concern: Valuing the welfare of the person in need. *Journal of Personality and Social Psychology, 93,* 65–74.

Batson, C. D., Schoenrade, P., & Ventis, W. L. (1993). *Religion and the individual: A social-psychological perspective.* New York, NY: Oxford University Press.

Batson, C. D., Thompson, E. R., Seuferling, G., Whitney, H., & Strongman, J. A. (1999). Moral hypocrisy: Appearing moral to oneself without being so. *Journal of Personality and Social Psychology, 77,* 525–537.

Bauman, C. W., & Skitka, L. J. (2010). Making attributions for behaviors: The prevalence of correspondence bias in the general population. *Basic and Applied Social Psychology, 32,* 269–277.

Baumeister, R. F. (1987). How the self became a problem: A psychological review of historical research. *Journal of Personality and Social Psychology, 52,* 163–176.

Baumeister, R. F. (1996). *Evil: Inside human cruelty and violence.* New York, NY: W H Freeman/Times Books/Henry Holt.

Baumeister, R. F. (2005). *The cultural animal: Human nature, meaning, and social life.* New York, NY: Oxford University Press.

Baumeister, R. F. (2008). Free will, consciousness, and cultural animals. In J. Baer, J. C. Kaufman, & R. F. Baumeister (Eds.), *Are we free? Psychology and free will* (pp. 65–85). New York, NY: Oxford University Press.

Baumeister, R. F. (2010). The self. In R. F. Baumeister & E. J. Finkel (Eds.), *Advanced social psychology: The state of the science* (pp. 139–175). New York, NY: Oxford University Press.

Baumeister, R. F. (2011). The unity of self at the interface of the animal body and the cultural system. *Psychological Studies, 56,* 5–11.

Baumeister, R. F. (2012). Need-to-belong theory. In P. A. M. Van Lange, A. W. Kruglanski, & E. T. Higgins (Eds.), *Handbook of theories of social psychology* (Vol. 2, pp. 121–140). Thousand Oaks, CA: Sage.

Baumeister, R. F., & Bargh, J. A. (2014). Conscious and unconscious: Toward an integrative understanding of human mental life and action. In J. W. Sherman, B. Gawronski, Y. Trope, J. W. Sherman, B. Gawronski, & Y. Trope (Eds.), *Dual-process theories of the social mind* (pp. 35–49). New York, NY: Guilford Press.

Baumeister, R. F., & Boden, J. M. (1998). Aggression and the self: High self-esteem, low self-control, and ego threat. In R. G. Geen & E. Donnerstein (Eds.), *Human aggression: Theories, research, and implications for social policy* (pp. 111–137). San Diego, CA: Academic Press.

Baumeister, R. F., & Leary, M. R. (1995). The need to belong: Desire for interpersonal attachments as a fundamental human motivation. *Psychological Bulletin, 117,* 497–529.

Baumeister, R. F., Bratslavsky, E., Muraven, M., & Tice, D. M. (1998). Ego depletion: Is the active self a limited resource? *Journal of Personality and Social Psychology, 74,* 1252–1265.

Baumeister, R. F., Campbell, J. D., Krueger, J. I., & Vohs, K. D. (2003). Does high self-esteem cause better performance, interpersonal success, happiness, or healthier lifestyles? *Psychological Science in the Public Interest, 4,* 1–44.

Baumeister, R. F., Schmeichel, B. J., & Vohs, K. D. (2007). Self-regulation and the executive function: The self as controlling agent. In A. W. Kruglanski & E. T. Higgins (Eds.), *Social psychology: Handbook of basic principles* (2nd ed., pp. 516–539). New York, NY: Guilford Press.

Baumeister, R. F., Wotman, S. R., & Stillwell, A. M. (1993). Unrequited love: On heartbreak, anger, guilt, scriptlessness, and humiliation. *Journal of Personality and Social Psychology, 64,* 377–394.

Baumrind, D. (1964). Some thoughts on ethics of research: After reading Milgram's "Behavioral Study of Obedience." *American Psychologist, 19,* 421–423.

Beadle, J., & Tranel, D. (2011). Social neuroscience: A neuropsychological perspective. In J. Decety & J. T. Cacioppo (Eds.), *Oxford handbook of social neuroscience* (pp. 49–68). Oxford, UK: Oxford University.

Becker, J. C., & Wright, S. C. (2011). Yet another dark side of chivalry: Benevolent sexism undermines and hostile sexism motivates collective action for social change. *Journal of Personality and Social Psychology, 101,* 62–77.

Becker, S. W., & Eagly, A. H. (2004). The heroism of women and men. *American Psychologist, 59,* 163–178.

Bègue, L., Beauvois, J. L., Courbet, D., Oberlé, D., Lepage, J., & Duke, A. A. (2015). Personality predicts obedience in a Milgram paradigm. *Journal of Personality, 83,* 299–306.

Bègue, L., Subra, B., Arvers, P., Muller, D., Bricout, V., & Zorman, M. (2009). A message in a bottle: Extrapharmacological effects of alcohol on aggression. *Journal of Experimental Social Psychology, 45,* 137–142.

Beilock, S. (2015). *How the body knows its mind: The surprising power of the physical environment to influence how you think and feel.* New York, NY: Atria Books.

Bellah, R. N. (2011). *Religion in human evolution: From the Paleolithic to the axial age.* Cambridge, MA: Belknap Press.

Bem, D. J. (1967). Self-perception: An alternative interpretation of cognitive dissonance phenomena. *Psychological Review, 74,* 183–200.

Bem, D. J. (2000). Exotic becomes erotic: Interpreting the biological correlates of sexual orientation. *Archives of Sexual Behavior, 29,* 531–548.

Bem, D. J., & McConnell, H. K. (1970). Testing the self-perception explanation of dissonance phenomena: On the salience of premanipulation attitudes. *Journal of Personality and Social Psychology, 14,* 23–31.

Bendixen, M. (2014). Evidence of systematic bias in sexual over- and underperception of naturally occurring events: A direct replication of Haselton (2003) in a more gender-equal culture. *Evolutionary Psychology: An International Journal of Evolutionary Approaches to Psychology and Behavior, 12,* 1004–1021.

Benjamin, L. T., Jr., & Simpson, J. A. (2009). The power of the situation: The impact of Milgram's obedience studies on personality and social psychology. *American Psychologist, 64,* 12–19.

Bennett, S., Banyard, V. L., & Garnhart, L. (2014). To act or not to act, that is the question? Barriers and facilitators of bystander intervention. *Journal of Interpersonal Violence, 29,* 476–496.

Bennett, T., & Gaines, J. (2010). Believing what you hear: The impact of aging stereotypes upon the old. *Educational Gerontology, 36,* 435–445.

Benokraitis, N. V., & Feagin, J. R. (1997). *Modern sexism.* Englewood Cliffs, NJ: Prentice-Hall.

Benson, P. L., Dehority, J., Garman, L., Hanson, E., Hochschwender, M., Lebold, C., . . . Sullivan, J. (1980). Intrapersonal correlates of nonspontaneous helping behavior. *The Journal of Social Psychology, 110,* 87–95.

Beran, T., Drefs, M., Kaba, A., Al Baz, N., & Al Harbi, N. (2015). Conformity of responses among graduate students in an online environment. *Internet & Higher Education, 25,* 63–69.

Bergmüller, S. (2013). The relationship between cultural individualism-collectivism and student aggression across 62 countries. *Aggressive Behavior, 39,* 182–200.

Berkowitz, L. (1989). Frustration-aggression hypothesis: Examination and reformulation. *Psychological Bulletin, 106,* 59–73.

Berkowitz, L. (1993). *Aggression: Its causes, consequences, and control.* New York, NY: Mcgraw-Hill.

Berkowitz, L. (2012). A cognitive-neoassociation theory of aggression. In P. A. M. Van Lange, A. W. Kruglanski, & E. T. Higgins (Eds.), *Handbook of theories of social psychology* (Vol. 2, pp. 99–117). Thousand Oaks, CA: Sage.

Berkowitz, L., & Daniels, L. R. (1963). Responsibility and dependency. *The Journal of Abnormal and Social Psychology, 66,* 429–436.

Berkowitz, L., & Lepage, A. (1967). Weapons as aggression-eliciting stimuli. *Journal of Personality and Social Psychology, 7,* 202–207.

Berkowitz, L., Cochran, S. T., & Embree, M. C. (1981). Physical pain and the goal of aversively stimulated aggression. *Journal of Personality and Social Psychology, 40,* 687–700.

Berman, M. E., McCloskey, M. S., Fanning, J. R., Schumacher, J. A., & Coccaro, E. F. (2009). Serotonin augmentation reduces response to attack in aggressive individuals. *Psychological Science, 20,* 714–720.

Bernards, S., & Graham, K. (2013). The cross-cultural association between marital status and physical aggression between intimate partners. *Journal of Family Violence, 28,* 403–418.

Berns, G. S., Chappelow, J., Zink, C. F., Pagnoni, G., Martin-Skurski, M. E., & Richards, J. (2005). Neurobiological correlates of social conformity and independence during mental rotation. *Biological Psychiatry, 58,* 245–253.

Berry, J. W. (2015). Culture and cognition: A forty-year overview. In T. C. Papadopoulos, R. K. Parrila, J. R. Kirby, T. C. Papadopoulos, R. K. Parrila, & J. R. Kirby (Eds.), *Cognition, intelligence, and achievement: A tribute to J. P. Das* (pp. 101–115). San Diego, CA: Elsevier.

Berry, J. W., Poortinga, Y. H., Segall, M. H., & Dasen, P. R. (2002). *Cross-cultural psychology: Research and applications* (2nd ed.). New York, NY: Cambridge University Press.

Berscheid, E. (1999). The greening of relationship science. *American Psychologist, 54,* 260–266.

Berscheid, E., & Reis, H. T. (1998). Attraction and close relationships. In D. T. Gilbert, S. T. Fiske, & G. Lindzey (Eds.), *The handbook of social psychology* (Vols. 1 & 2, 4th ed., pp. 193–281). New York, NY: McGraw-Hill.

Beruchashvili, M., Moisio, R., & Heisley, D. D. (2014). What are you dieting for? The role of lay theories in dieters' goal setting. *Journal of Consumer Behaviour, 13,* 50–59.

Bessenoff, G. R., & Sherman, J. W. (2000). Automatic and controlled components of prejudice toward fat people: Evaluation versus stereotype activation. *Social Cognition, 18,* 329–353.

Bettencourt, B. A., & Miller, N. (1996). Gender differences in aggression as a function of provocation: A meta-analysis. *Psychological Bulletin, 119,* 422–447.

Bettencourt, B. A., Talley, A., Benjamin, A. J., & Valentine, J. (2006). Personality and aggressive behavior under provoking and neutral conditions: A meta-analytic review. *Psychological Bulletin, 132,* 751–777.

Bickman, L. (1974). The social power of a uniform. *Journal of Applied Social Psychology, 4,* 47–61.

Billig, M. G. (1976). *Social psychology and integroup relations.* London, UK: Academic Press.

Bizzi, E., Hyman, S. E., Raichle, M. E., Kanwisher, N., Phelps, E. A., Morse, S. J., . . . Greely, H. T. (Eds.). (2009). *Using imaging to identify deceit: Scientific and ethical questions.* Cambridge, MA: American Academy of Arts and Sciences.

Bjork, J. M., Dougherty, D. M., Moeller, G., & Swann, A. C. (2000). Differential behavioral effects of plasma trytophan depletion and loading in aggressive and nonagressive men. *Neuropsychopharmacology, 22,* 357–369.

Blair, C., Ursache, A., Vernon-Feagans, L., & Greenberg, M. (2015). Multiple aspects of self-regulation uniquely predict mathematics but not letter-word knowledge in the early elementary grades. *Developmental Psychology, 51,* 459–472.

Blair, I. V., Judd, C. M., & Chapleau, K. M. (2004). The influence of Afrocentric facial features in criminal sentencing. *Psychological Science, 15,* 674–679.

Bland, C. G. (2013). Evidence of direct reciprocity norms in US preschoolers. *College of St. Elizabeth Journal of the Behavioral Sciences,* 1–35.

Blanton, H., Buunk, B. P., Gibbons, F. X., & Kuyper, H. (1999). When better-than-others compare upward: Choice of comparison and comparative evaluation as independent predictors of academic performance. *Journal of Personality and Social Psychology, 76,* 420–430.

Blascovich, J. (2000). Using physiological indexes of psychological processes in social psychological research. In H. T. Reis & C. M. Judd (Eds.), *Handbook of research methods in social and personality psychology* (pp. 117–137). New York, NY: Cambridge University Press.

Blascovich, J., & Seery, M. D. (2007). Visceral and somatic indexes of social psychological constructs: History, principles, propositions, and case studies. In A. W. Kruglanski & E. T. Higgins (Eds.), *Social psychology: Handbook of basic principles* (2nd ed., pp. 19–38). New York, NY: Guilford Press.

Blascovich, J., Mendes, W. B., Hunter, S. B., & Salomon, K. (1999). Social "facilitation" as challenge and threat. *Journal of Personality and Social Psychology, 77,* 68–77.

Blass, T. (1999). The Milgram Paradigm after 35 years: Some things we now know about obedience to authority. *Journal of Applied Social Psychology, 29,* 955–978.

Blass, T. (2000). *Obedience to authority: Current perspectives on the Milgram paradigm.* Mahwah, NJ: Lawrence Erlbaum.

Blass, T. (2004). *The man who shocked the world: The life and legacy of Stanley Milgram.* New York, NY: Basic Books.

Blass, T. (2012). A cross-cultural comparison of studies of obedience using the Milgram paradigm: A review. *Social and Personality Psychology Compass, 6,* 196–205.

Bocchiaro, P., & Zimbardo, P. G. (2010). Defying unjust authority: An exploratory study. *Current Psychology: A Journal for Diverse Perspectives on Diverse Psychological Issues, 29,* 155–170.

Bodenhausen, G. V. (1990). Stereotypes as judgmental heuristics: Evidence of circadian variations in discrimination. *Psychological Science, 1,* 319–322.

Bogaert, A. F., & Sadava, S. (2002). Adult attachment and sexual behavior. *Personal Relationships, 9,* 191–204.

Boldry, J. G., Gaertner, L., & Quinn, J. (2007). Measuring the measures: A meta-analytic investigation of the measures of outgroup homogeneity. *Group Processes & Intergroup Relations, 10,* 157–178.

Bolino, M. C., Hsiung, H. -H., Harvey, J., & LePine, J. A. (2015). "Well, I'm tired of tryin'!" Organizational citizenship behavior and citizenship fatigue. *Journal of Applied Psychology, 100,* 56–74.

Bond, C. F., & DePaulo, B. M. (2006). Accuracy of Deception Judgments. *Personality and Social Psychology Review, 10,* 214–234.

Bond, C. F., Jr., & DePaulo, B. M. (2008). Individual differences in judging deception: Accuracy and bias. *Psychological Bulletin, 134,* 477–492.

Bond, M. H., & Smith, P. B. (1996a). Cross-cultural social and organizational psychology. *Annual Review of Psychology, 47,* 205–235.

Bond, R., & Smith, P. B. (1996b). Culture and conformity: A meta-analysis of studies using Asch's (1952b, 1956) line judgment task. *Psychological Bulletin, 119,* 111–137.

Boninger, D. S., Krosnick, J. A., & Berent, M. K. (1995). Origins of attitude importance: Self-interest, social identification, and value relevance. *Journal of Personality and Social Psychology, 68,* 61–80.

Bonner, B. L., & Baumann, M. R. (2012). Leveraging member expertise to improve knowledge transfer and demonstrability in groups. *Journal of Personality and Social Psychology, 102,* 337–350.

Bontempo, R., Lobel, S., & Triandis, H. (1990). Compliance and value internalization in Brazil and the U.S.: Effects of allocentrism and anonymity. *Journal of Cross-Cultural Psychology, 21,* 200–213.

Bookman, M. (2013). The confessions of innocent men. *The Atlantic.* http://www.theatlantic.com/national/archive/2013/08/the-confessions-of-innocent-men/278363/

Borgida, E., Conner, C., & Manteufel, L. (1992). Understanding living kidney donation: A behavioral decision-making perspective. In S. Spacapan & S. Oskamp (Eds.), *Helping and being helped: Naturalistic studies* (pp. 183–211). Thousand Oaks, CA: Sage.

Bornstein, B. H., & Greene, E. (2011a). Consulting damage awards. In R. L. Weiner & B. H. Bornstein (Eds.), *Handbook of trial consulting* (pp. 281–295). New York, NY: Springer.

Bornstein, B. H., & Greene, E. (2011b). Jury decision making: Implications for and from psychology. *Current Directions in Psychological Science, 20,* 63–67.

Bornstein, R. F. (1989). Exposure and affect: Overview and meta-analysis of research, 1968–1987. *Psychological Bulletin, 106,* 265–289.

Bos, M. W., & Dijksterhuis, A. (2011). Unconscious thought works bottom-up and conscious thought works top-down when forming an impression. *Social Cognition, 29,* 727–737.

Boster, F. J., & Mongeau, P. (1984). Fear-arousing persuasive messages. *Communication Yearbook, 8,* 330–375.

Bouchard, T. J., Jr. (2009). Authoritarianism, religiousness, and conservatism: Is "obedience to authority" the explanation for their clustering, universality and evolution? In E. Voland & W. Schiefenhövel (Eds.), *The biological evolution of religious mind and behavior* (pp. 165–180). New York, NY: Springer Science + Business Media.

Bourdage, J. S., Wiltshire, J., & Lee, K. (2015). Personality and workplace impression management: Correlates and implications. *Journal of Applied Psychology, 100,* 537–546.

Bowker, J. C., & Etkin, R. G. (2014). Mixed-grade rejection and its association with overt aggression, relational aggression, anxious-withdrawal, and psychological maladjustment. *The Journal of Genetic Psychology, 175.*

Bowlby, J. (1982). *Attachment and loss: Vol 1, attachment* (2nd ed.). New York, NY: Basic Books.

Bowles, H. R., & McGinn, K. L. (2005). Claiming authority: Negotiating challenges for women leaders. In D. M. Messick & R. M. Kramer (Eds.), *The psychology of leadership: New perspectives and research* (pp. 191–208). Mahwah, NJ: Lawrence Erlbaum.

Bowles, S., & Gintis, H. (2011). *A cooperative species: Human reciprocity and its evolution.* Princeton, NJ: Princeton University Press.

Boyce, C. J., Brown, G. D. A., & Moore, S. C. (2010). Money and happiness: Rank of income, not income, affects life satisfaction. *Psychological Science, 21,* 471–475.

Boyd, R., & Richerson, P. J. (2007). Group selection: A tale of two controversies. In S. W. Gangestad & J. A. Simpson (Eds.), *The evolution of mind: Fundamental questions and controversies* (pp. 221–225). New York, NY: Guilford Press.

Bradbury, T. N., Fincham, F. D., & Beach, S. R. H. (2000). Research on the nature and determinants of marital satisfaction: A decade in review. *Journal of Marriage and the Family, 62,* 964–980.

Bradley, S. D., & Shapiro, M. A. (2004). Parsing reality: The interactive effects of complex syntax and time pressure on cognitive processing of television scenarios. *Media Psychology, 6,* 307–333.

Bradshaw, M., & Ellison, C. G. (2008). Do genetic factors influence religious life? Findings from a behavior genetic analysis of twin siblings. *Journal for the Scientific Study of Religion, 47,* 529–544.

Braga, J. N., Ferreira, M. B., & Sherman, S. J. (2014). The effects of construal level on heuristic reasoning: The case of representativeness and availability. *Decision.* (Supplemental)

Branch, S., Ramsay, S., & Barker, M. (2013). Workplace bullying, mobbing, and general harassment: A review. *International Journal of Management Reviews, 15,* 280–299.

Brandt, M. J., & Wethere, G. A. (2012). What attitudes are moral attitudes? The case of attitude heritability. *Social Psychological and Personality Science, 3,* 172–179.

Brannigan, A. (2006). Introduction to the AldineTransaction edition of M. Sherif: Social interactions: Processes and products. Piscataway, NJ: Aldine Transaction Publishers.

Brannon, T. N., Markus, H. R., & Taylor, V. J. (2015). "Two souls, two thoughts," two self-schemas: Double consciousness can have positive academic consequences for African Americans. *Journal of Personality and Social Psychology, 108,* 586–609. [Supplemental]

Brauer, M., Judd, C. M., & Gliner, M. D. (1995). The effects of repeated expressions on attitude polarization during group discussions. *Journal of Personality and Social Psychology, 68,* 1014–1029.

Breckler, S. J. (1984). Empirical validation of affect, behavior, and cognition as distinct components of attitude. *Journal of Personality and Social Psychology, 47,* 1191–1205.

Breen, J. O. (2014). Personal statement to personal physician: bait and switch? *The Hastings Center Report, 44,* 25–27.

Brehm, J. W. (1956). Postdecision changes in the desirability of alternatives. *The Journal of Abnormal and Social Psychology, 52,* 384–389.

Brehm, J. W. (1966). *A theory of psychological reactance.* New York, NY: Academic Press.

Brendgen, M., Boivin, M., Vitaro, F., Bukowski, W. M., Dionne, G., Tremblay, R. E., & Pérusse, D. (2008). Linkages between children's and their friends' social and physical aggression: Evidence for a gene-environment interaction? *Child Development, 79,* 13–29.

Brendgen, M., Vitaro, F., Boivin, M., Dionne, G., & Pérusse, D. (2006). Examining genetic and environmental effects on reactive versus proactive aggression. *Developmental Psychology, 42,* 1299–1312.

Brescoll, V. L., & Uhlmann, E. L. (2008). Can an angry woman get ahead? Status conferral, gender, and expression of emotion in the workplace. *Psychological Science, 19,* 268–275.

Breuer, J., Scharkow, M., & Quandt, T. (2015). Sore losers? A reexamination of the frustration–aggression hypothesis for colocated video game play. *Psychology of Popular Media Culture, 4,* 126–137.

Brewer, M. B. (1988). A dual process model of impression formation. In T. K. Srull & R. S. Wyer (Eds.), *A dual process model of impression formation* (pp. 1–36). Hillsdale, NJ: Lawrence Erlbaum Associates.

Brewer, M. B. (1991). The social self: On being the same and different at the same time. *Personality and Social Psychology Bulletin, 17,* 475–482.

Brewer, M. B. (2015). Motivated entitativity: When we'd rather see the forest than the trees. In S. J. Stroessner, J. W. Sherman, S. J. Stroessner, & J. W. Sherman (Eds.), *Social perception from individuals to groups* (pp. 161–176). New York, NY: Psychology Press.

Brewer, M. B., & Brown, R. J. (1998). Intergroup relations. In D. T. Gilbert, S. T. Fiske, & G. Lindzey (Eds.), *The handbook of social psychology* (Vols. 1 & 2, 4th ed., pp. 554–594). New York, NY: McGraw-Hill.

Brewer, M. B., & Caporael, L. R. (2006). An evolutionary perspective on social identity: Revisiting groups. In M. Schaller, J. A. Simpson, & D. T. Kenrick (Eds.), *Evolution and social psychology* (pp. 143–161). Madison, CT: Psychosocial Press.

Brewer, M. B., & Gardner, W. (1996). Who is this "We"? Levels of collective identity and self representations. *Journal of Personality and Social Psychology, 71,* 83–93.

Brickman, P., Coates, D., & Janoff-Bulman, R. (1978). Lottery winners and accident victims: Is happiness relative? *Journal of Personality and Social Psychology, 36,* 917–927.

Bridges, F. S., & Rodriguez, W. I. (2000). Gay-friendly affiliation, community size, and color of address in return of lost letters. *North American Journal of Psychology, 2,* 39–45.

Briñol, P., & Petty, R. E. (2005). Individual Differences in Attitude Change. In D. Albarracín, B. T. Johnson & M. P. Zanna (Eds.), *The handbook of attitudes* (pp. 575–615). Mahwah, NJ: Lawrence Erlbaum.

Briñol, P., & Petty, R. E. (2012). A history of attitudes and persuasion research. In A. W. Kruglanski & W. Stroebe (Eds.), *Handbook of the history of social psychology* (pp. 283–320). New York, NY: Psychology Press.

Brislin, R. W. (1970). Back-translation for cross-cultural research. *Journal of Cross-Cultural Psychology, 1,* 185–216.

Brodsky, S. L., & Cannon, D. E. (2006). Ingratiation in the courtroom and in the Voir dire process: When more is not better. *Law & Psychology Review, 30,* 103–117.

Brooks, C. M., & Ammons, J. L. (2003). Free riding in group projects and the effects of timing, frequency, and specificity of criteria in peer assessments. *Journal of Education for Business, 78,* 268–272.

Brown, M. A., & Stopa, L. (2007). The spotlight effect and the illusion of transparency in social anxiety. *Journal of Anxiety Disorders, 21,* 804–819.

Brown, R. (2000a). *Group processes* (2nd ed.). Malden, MA: Blackwell.

Brown, R. (2000b). Social identity theory: Past achievements, current problems and future challenges. *European Journal of Social Psychology, 30,* 745–778.

Brown, R. (2010). *Prejudice: Its social psychology* (2nd ed.). West Sussex, UK: Wiley-Blackwell.

Brown, R. P., Osterman, L. L., & Barnes, C. D. (2009). School violence and the culture of honor. *Psychological Science, 20,* 1400–1405.

Brown, S. L., & Maner, J. K. (2012). Egoism or altruism? Hard-nosed experiments and deep philosophical questions. In D. T. Kenrick, N. J. Goldstein, S. L. Braver, D. T. Kenrick, N. J. Goldstein, & S. L. Braver (Eds.), *Six degrees of social influence: Science, application, and the psychology of Robert Cialdini* (pp. 109–118). New York, NY: Oxford University Press.

Brown, S. L., Lipka, S., Coyne, S. M., Qualter, P., Barlow, A., & Taylor, P. (2011). Implicit alcohol-aggression scripts and alcohol-related aggression on a laboratory task in 11- to 14-year-old adolescents. *Aggressive Behavior, 37,* 430–439.

Brownell, K. D., Puhl, R. M., Schwartz, M. B., & Rudd, L. (2005). *Weight bias: Nature, consequences, and remedies.* New York, NY: Guilford Publications.

Bruner, J. S. (1957). On perceptual readiness. *Psychological Review, 64,* 123–152.

Bruner, J. S. (1990). *Acts of meaning.* Cambridge, MA: Harvard University Press.

Bruner, J. S., & Taiguri, R. (1954). Person perception. In G. Lindzey (Ed.), *Handbook of social psychology* (Vol. 2, pp. 634–654). Reading, MA: Addison-Wesley.

Bryan, J. H., & Test, M. A. (1967). Models and helping: Naturalistic studies in aiding behavior. *Journal of Personality and Social Psychology, 6,* 400–407.

Bryant, E. M., & Marmo, J. (2012). The rules of Facebook friendship: A two-stage examination of interaction rules in close, casual, and acquaintance friendships. Journal of Social and Personal Relationships, 29, 1013–1035.

Bui, N. H. (2014). I don't believe it! Belief perseverance in attitudes toward celebrities. *Psychology of Popular Media Culture, 3,* 38–48.

Burchell, J. L., & Ward, J. (2011). Sex drive, attachment style, relationship status and previous infidelity as predictors of sex differences in romantic jealousy. *Personality and Individual Differences, 51,* 657–661.

Burger, J. M. (1986). Increasing compliance by improving the deal: The that's-not-all technique. *Journal of Personality and Social Psychology, 51,* 277–283.

Burger, J. M. (2007). Fleeting attraction and compliance with requests. In A. R. Pratkanis (Ed.), *The science of social influence: Advances and future progress* (pp. 155–166). New York, NY: Psychology Press.

Burger, J. M. (2009). Replicating Milgram: Would people still obey today? *American Psychologist, 64,* 1–11.

Burger, J. M., & Caldwell, D. F. (2003). The effects of monetary incentives and labeling on the foot-in-the-door efect: Evidence for a self-perception process. *Basic and Applied Social Psychology, 25,* 235–241.

Burger, J. M., & Cornelius, T. (2003). Raising the price of agreement: Public commitment and the lowball compliance procedure. *Journal of Applied Social Psychology, 33,* 923–934.

Burger, J. M., & Guadagno, R. E. (2003). Self-concept clarity and the foot-in-the-door procedure. *Basic and Applied Social Psychology, 25,* 79–86.

Burger, J. M., & Petty, R.E. (1981). The low-ball compliance technique: Task or person commitment? *Journal of Personality and Social Psychology, 40,* 492–500.

Burger, J. M., Horita, M., Kinoshita, L., & Roberts, K. (1997). Effects of time on the norm of reciprocity. *Basic and Applied Social Psychology, 19,* 91–100.

Burger, J. M., Reed, M., DeCesare, K., Rauner, S., & Rozolis, J. (1999). The effects of initial request size on compliance: More about the that's-not-all technique. *Basic and Applied Social Psychology, 21,* 243–249.

Burger, J. M., Sanchez, J., Imberi, J. E., & Grande, L. R. (2009). The norm of reciprocity as an internalized social norm: Returning favors even when no one finds out. *Social Influence, 4,* 11–17.

Burger, J. M., Soroka, S., Gonzago, K., Murphy, E., & Somervell, E. (2001). The effect of fleeting attraction on compliance to requests. *Personality and Social Psychology Bulletin, 27,* 1578–1586.

Burke, M., Marlow, C., & Lento, T. (2010). *Social network activity and social well-being.* Paper presented at the Conference on Human Factors in Computing Systems, Atlanta, GA.

Burkley, E., Curtis, J., Burkley, M., & Hatvany, T. (2015). Goal fusion: The integration of goals within the self-concept. *Self and Identity, 14,* 348–368.

Burn, S. M. (2009). A situational model of sexual assault prevention through bystander intervention. *Sex Roles, 60,* 779–792.

Burnette, J. L., Pollack, J. M., & Forsyth, D. R. (2011). Leadership in extreme contexts: A groupthink analysis of the May 1996 Mount Everest disaster. *Journal of Leadership Studies, 4,* 29–40.

Burns, J. M. (1978). *Leadership.* Oxford, UK: Harper & Row.

Burnstein, E., & Vinokur, A. (1977). Persuasive argumentation and social comparison as determinants of attitude polarization. *Journal of Experimental Social Psychology, 13,* 315–332.

Burri, A., Cherkas, L., Spector, T., & Rahman, Q. (2011). Genetic and environmental influences on female sexual orientation, childhood gender typicality and adult gender identity. *PLoS ONE, 6,* 1–8.

Burusic, J., & Ribar, M. (2014). The moderating role of self-presentation tactics: Judgments of personality traits and self-presentation of others based on a limited amount of information. *Swiss Journal of Psychology, 73,* 235–242.

Bushman, B. J. (1984). Perceived symbols of authority and their influence on compliance. *Journal of Applied Social Psychology, 14,* 501–508.

Bushman, B. J. (1988). The effects of apparel on compliance: A field experiment with a female authority figure. *Personality and Social Psychology Bulletin, 14,* 459–467.

Bushman, B. J., & Anderson, C. A. (2001). Is it time to pull the plug on hostile versus instrumental aggression dichotomy? *Psychological Review, 108,* 273–279.

Bushman, B. J., & Anderson, C. A. (2009). Comfortably numb: Desensitizing effects of violent media on helping others. *Psychological Science, 20,* 273–277.

Bushman, B. J., & Baumeister, R. F. (1998). Threatened egotism, narcissism, self-esteem, and direct and displaced aggression: Does self-love or self-hate lead to violence? *Journal of Personality and Social Psychology, 75,* 219–229.

Bushman, B. J., & Huesmann, L. R. (2010). Aggression. In S. T. Fiske, D. T. Gilbert, & G. Lindzey (Eds.), *Handbook of social psychology* (Vol. 2, 5th ed., pp. 833–863). Hoboken, NJ: John Wiley & Sons.

Bushman, B. J., Baumeister, R. F., & Phillips, C. M. (2001). Do people aggress to improve their mood? Catharsis beliefs, affect regulation opportunity, and aggressive responding. *Journal of Personality and Social Psychology, 81,* 17–32.

Bushman, B. J., Baumeister, R. F., Thomaes, S., Ryu, E., Begeer, S., & West, S.G. (2009). Looking again, and harder, for a link between low self-esteem and aggression. *Journal of Personality, 77,* 427–446.

Bushman, B. J., Giancola, P. R., Parrott, D. J., & Roth, R. M. (2012). Failure to consider future consequences increases the effects of alcohol on aggression. *Journal of Experimental Social Psychology, 48,* 591–595.

Bushman, B. J., Gollwitzer, M., & Cruz, C. (2015). There is broad consensus: Media researchers agree that violent media increase aggression in children, and pediatricians and parents concur. *Psychology of Popular Media Culture, 4,* 200–214.

Bushman, B. J., Wang, M. C., & Anderson, C. A. (2005). Is the curve relating temperature to aggression linear or curvilinear? Assaults and temperature in Minneapolis reexamined. *Journal of Personality and Social Psychology, 89,* 62–66.

Buss, D. M. (1988). The evolution of human intrasexual competition: Tactics of mate attraction. *Journal of Personality and Social Psychology, 54,* 616–628.

Buss, D. M. (1989). Sex differences in human mate preferences: Evolutionary hypotheses tested in 37 cultures. *Behavioral and Brain Sciences, 12,* 1–49.

Buss, D. M. (2000). *The dangerous passion: Why jealousy is as necessary as love and sex.* New York, NY: Free Press.

Buss, D. M. (2003). *The evolution of desire: Strategies of human mating* (Rev. ed.). New York, NY: Basic Books.

Buss, D. M., & Duntley, J. D. (2006). The evolution of aggression. In M. Schaller, J. A. Simpson & D. T. Kenrick (Eds.), *Evolution and social psychology* (pp. 263–285). Madison, CT: Psychosocial Press.

Buss, D. M., & Shackelford, T. K. (1997). Human aggression in evolutionary psychological perspective. *Clinical Psychology Review, 17,* 605–619.

Buss, D. M., Larsen, R. J., Westen, D., & Semmelroth, J. (1992). Sex differences in jealousy: Evolution, physiology, and psychology. *Psychological Science, 3,* 251–255.

Button, T. M. M., Stallings, M. C., Rhee, S. H., Corley, R. P., & Hewitt, J. K. (2011). The etiology of stability and change in religious values and religious attendance. *Behavior Genetics, 41,* 201–210.

Buunk, B. P., & Oldersma, F. L. (2001). Enhancing satisfaction through downward comparison: The role of relational discontent and individual differences in social comparison orientation. *Journal of Experimental Social Psychology, 37,* 452–452.

Buunk, B., & Hupka, R. B. (1987). Cross-cultural differences in the elicitation of sexual jealousy. *Journal of Sex Research, 23,* 12–22.

Byrne, D. (1971). *The attraction paradigm.* New York, NY: Academic Press.

Cacioppo, J. T., & Bernston, G. G. (1992). Social psychological contributions to the decade of the brain: Doctrine of multilevel analysis. *American Psychologist, 47,* 1019–1028.

Cacioppo, J. T., & Berntson, G. G. (2005). *Social neuroscience: Key readings.* New York, NY: Psychology Press.

Cacioppo, J. T., & Patrick, W. (2008). *Loneliness: Human nature and the need for social connection.* New York, NY: W. W. Norton & Co.

Cacioppo, J. T., & Petty, R. E. (1981). Electromyograms as measures of extent and affectivity of information processing. *American Psychologist, 36,* 441–456.

Cacioppo, J. T., & Petty, R. E. (1982). The need for cognition. *Journal of Personality and Social Psychology, 42,* 116–131.

Cacioppo, J. T., & Petty, R. E. (1989). Effects of message repetition on argument processing, recall, and persuasion. *Basic and Applied Social Psychology, 10,* 3–12.

Cacioppo, J. T., Berntson, G. G., & Crites, S. L. (1996). Social neuroscience: Principles of psychophysiological arousal and response. In E. T. Higgins & A. W. Kruglanski (Eds.), *Social psychology: Handbook of basic principles* (pp. 72–101). New York, NY: Guilford Press.

Cacioppo, J. T., Cacioppo, S., & Boomsma, D. I. (2014). Evolutionary mechanisms for loneliness. *Cognition & Emotion, 28,* 3–21.

Cacioppo, J. T., Fowler, J. H., & Christakis, N. A. (2009). Alone in the crowd: The structure and spread of loneliness in a large social network. *Journal of Personality and Social Psychology, 97,* 977–991.

Cacioppo, J. T., Gardner, W. L., & Berntson, G. G. (1997). Beyond bipolar conceptualizations and measures: The case of attitudes and evaluative space. *Personality and Social Psychology Review, 1,* 3–25.

Cacioppo, J. T., Lorig, T. S., Nusbaum, H. C., & Berntson, G. G. (2004). Social neuroscience: Bridging social and biological systems. In C. Sansone, C. C. Morf, & A. T. Panter (Eds.), *The Sage handbook of methods in social psychology* (pp. 383–404). Thousand Oaks, CA: Sage.

Cacioppo, J. T., Petty, R. E., & Kao, C. F. (1984). The efficient assessment of need for cognition. *Journal of Personality Assessment, 48,* 306–307.

Cacioppo, J. T., Petty, R. E., Feinstein, J. A., & Jarvis, W. B. G. (1996). Dispositional differences in cognitive motivation: The life and times of individuals varying in need for cognition. *Psychological Bulletin, 119,* 197–253.

Cacioppo, J. T., Petty, R. E., Losch, M. E., & Kim, H. S. (1986). Electromyographic activity over facial muscle regions can differentiate the valence and intensity of affective reactions. *Journal of Personality and Social Psychology, 50,* 260–268.

Cacioppo, S., & Cacioppo, J. T. (2012). Decoding the invisible forces of social connections. *Frontiers In Integrative Neuroscience, 6,* 51–51.

Cadinu, M., Galdi, S., & Maass, A. (2013). Chameleonic social identities: Context induces shifts in homosexuals' self-stereotyping and self-categorization. *European Journal of Social Psychology, 43,* 471–481.

Cahn, S. M. (2009). *Exploring ethics.* New York, NY: Oxford University Press.

Cai, D. A., Fink, E. L., & Xie, X. (2012). "Brother, can you spare some time, or a dime?": Time and money obligations in the United States and China. *Journal of Cross-Cultural Psychology, 43,* 592–613.

Campbell, A. (2010). Oxytocin and human social behavior. *Personality and Social Psychology Review, 14,* 281–295.

Campbell, B., & Manning, J. (2015). Microaggression and changing moral cultures. Available from EBSCOhost nmr Retrieved from http://search.ebscohost.com/login.aspx?direct=true&db=nmr&AN=WBN04D81C C831C2EEAE1A17F385B8D45E4019DBFC95&login .asp&site=ehost-live&scope=site

Campbell, D. T. (1958). Common fate, similarity, and other indices of the status of aggregates of persons as social entities. *Behavioral Science, 3,* 14–25.

Campbell, D. T. (1965). *Ethnocentrism and other altruistic motives.* Lincoln, NE: University of Nebraska.

Campbell, D. T., & Stanley, J. C. (1963). *Experimental and quasi-experimental designs for research.* Boston, MA: Houghton, Mifflin.

Campbell, J. D. (1990). Self-esteem and clarity of the self-concept. *Journal of Personality and Social Psychology, 59,* 538–549.

Campbell, J. K. (1965). Honour and the devil. In J. G. Peristiany (Ed.), *Honour and shame: The values of Mediterranean society* (pp. 112–175). London, UK: Weidenfeld & Nicholson.

Campbell, L., & Rubin, H. (2012). Modeling dyadic processes. In L. Campbell, J. G. La Guardia, J. M. Olson, & P. Zanna Mark (Eds.), *The science of the couple: The Ontario Symposium* (Vol. 12, pp. 1–15). New York, NY: Psychology Press.

Cannon-Bowers, J. A., Salas, E., & Converse, S. (1993). Shared mental models in expert team decision making. In N. J. Castellan (Ed.), *Individual and group decision making: Current issues* (pp. 221–246). Hillsdale, NJ: Lawrence Erlbaum.

Cappella, J. N. (2007). The role of discrete emotions in the theory of reasoned action and its successors: Quitting smoking in young adults. In I. Ajzen, D. Albarracín, R. Hornik, I. Ajzen, D. Albarracín, & R. Hornik (Eds.), *Prediction and change of health behavior: Applying the reasoned action approach* (pp. 43–51). Mahwah, NJ: Lawrence Erlbaum.

Caprara, G. V., & Steca, P. (2007). Prosocial agency: The contribution of values and self-efficacy beliefs to prosocial behavior across ages. *Journal of Social and Clinical Psychology, 26,* 218–239.

Caprara, G. V., Alessandri, G., & Eisenberg, N. (2012). Prosociality: The contribution of traits, values, and self-efficacy beliefs. *Journal of Personality and Social Psychology, 102,* 1289–1303.

Caprara, G. V., Alessandri, G., Di Giunta, L., Panerai, L., & Eisenberg, N. (2010). The contribution of agreeableness and self-efficacy beliefs to prosociality. *European Journal of Personality, 24,* 36–55.

Caprara, G. V., Steca, P., Zelli, A., & Capanna, C. (2005). A new scale for measuring adults' prosocialness. *European Journal of Psychological Assessment, 21,* 77–89.

Card, N. A., Stucky, B. D., Sawalani, G. M., & Little, T. D. (2008). Direct and indirect aggression during childhood and adolescence: A meta-analytic review of gender differences, intercorrelations, and relations to maladjustment. *Child Development, 79,* 1185–1229.

Carey, J. M., & Paulhus, D. L. (2013). Worldview implications of believing in free will and/or determinism: Politics, morality, and punitiveness. *Journal of Personality, 81,* 130–141.

Carlo, G., Koller, S. H., Eisenberg, N., Da Silva, M. S., & Frohlich, C. B. (1996). A cross-national study on the relations among prosocial moral reasoning, gender role orientations, and prosocial behaviors. *Developmental Psychology, 32,* 231–240.

Carlson, E. N., Vazire, S., & Furr, R. M. (2011). Meta-insight: Do people really know how others see them? *Journal of Personality and Social Psychology, 101,* 831–846.

Carlson, M., Marcus-Newhall, A., & Miller, N. (1990). Effects of situational aggression cues: A quantitative review. *Journal of Personality and Social Psychology, 58,* 622–633.

Carlston, D. E. (2013). *The Oxford handbook of social cognition* (D. E. Carlston Ed.). New York, NY: Oxford University Press.

Carmichael, C. L., Tsai, F.- F., Smith, S. M., Caprariello, P. A., & Reis, H. T. (2007). The self and intimate relationships. In C. Sedikides & S. J. Spencer (Eds.), *The self* (pp. 285–309). New York, NY: Psychology Press.

Carnagey, N. L., & Anderson, C. A. (2005). The effects of reward and punishment in violent video games on aggressive affect, cognition, and behavior. *Psychological Science, 16,* 882–889.

Carnagey, N. L., Anderson, C. A., & Bushman, B. J. (2007). The effect of video game violence on physiological desensitization to real-life violence. *Journal of Experimental Social Psychology, 43,* 489–496.

Carnahan, T., & McFarland, S. (2007). Revisiting the Stanford prison experiment: Could participant self-selection have led to the cruelty? *Personality and Social Psychology Bulletin, 33,* 603–614.

Carr, P. B., Dweck, C. S., & Pauker, K. (2012). "Prejudiced" behavior without prejudice? Beliefs about the malleability of prejudice affect interracial interactions. *Journal of Personality and Social Psychology, 103,* 452–471.

Carraro, L., Negri, P., Castelli, L., & Pastore, M. (2014). Implicit and explicit illusory correlation as a function of political ideology. *PLoS ONE, 9,* e96312-e96312.

Carrillo, M., Ricci, L. A., Coppersmith, G. A., & Melloni, R. H., Jr. (2009). The effect of increased serotonergic neurotransmission on aggression: A critical meta-analytical review of preclinical studies. *Psychopharmacology, 205,* 349–368.

Carron, A. V., Colman, M. M., Wheeler, J., & Stevens, D. (2002). Cohesion and performance in sport: A meta analysis. *Journal of Sport & Exercise Psychology, 24,* 168–188.

Carter, C. S., Harris, J., & Porges, S. W. (2009). Neural and evolutionary perspectives on empathy. In J. Decety & W. Ickes (Eds.), *The social neuroscience of empathy* (pp. 169–182). Cambridge, MA: MIT Press.

Cartwright, D., & Zander, A. (1960). *Group dynamics: Research and theory* (2nd ed.). Oxford England: Row, Peterson & Co.

Cashdan, E., & Downes, S. M. (2012). Evolutionary perspectives on human aggression: Introduction to the special issue. *Human Nature, 23,* 1–4.

Castaño, N., Watts, T., & Tekleab, A. G. (2013). A reexamination of the cohesion–performance relationship meta-analyses: A comprehensive approach. *Group Dynamics: Theory, Research, and Practice, 17,* 207–231.

Castelli, L., & Carraro, L. (2011). Ideology is related to basic cognitive processes involved in attitude formation. *Journal of Experimental Social Psychology, 47,* 1013–1016.

Catalino, L. I., Algoe, S. B., & Fredrickson, B. L. (2014). Prioritizing positivity: An effective approach to pursuing happiness? *Emotion, 14,* 1155–1161.

Catlin, J. R., & Wang, Y. (2013). Recycling gone bad: When the option to recycle increases resource consumption. *Journal of Consumer Psychology, 23,* 122–127.

Caunt, B. S., Franklin, J., Brodaty, N. E., & Brodaty, H. (2013). Exploring the causes of subjective well-being: A content analysis of peoples' recipes for long-term happiness. *Journal of Happiness Studies, 14,* 475–499.

Cavallo, J. V., Holmes, J. G., Fitzsimons, G. M., Murray, S. L., & Wood, J. V. (2012). Managing motivational conflict: How self-esteem and executive resources influence self-regulatory responses to risk. *Journal of Personality and Social Psychology, 103,* 430–451.

Centers for Disease Control (n.d.). *Deaths: Final data for 2013.* Retrieved from http://www .cdc.gov/nchs/fastats/homicide.htm

Cerasoli, C. P., Nicklin, J. M., & Ford, M. T. (2014). Intrinsic motivation and extrinsic incentives jointly predict performance: A 40-year meta-analysis. *Psychological Bulletin, 140,* 980–1008.

Cesario, J. (2014). Priming, replication, and the hardest science. *Perspectives on Psychological Science, 9,* 40–48.

Cha, J., Chang, Y., & Kim, T. -Y. (2014). Person-organization fit on prosocial identity: Implications on employee outcomes. *Journal of Business Ethics, 123,* 57.

Chaiken, S. (1979). Communicator physical attractiveness and persuasion. *Journal of Personality and Social Psychology, 37,* 1387–1397.

Chaiken, S. (1980). Heuristic versus systematic information processing and the use of source versus message cues in persuasion. *Journal of Personality and Social Psychology, 39,* 752–766.

Chaiken, S. (1987). The heuristic model of persuasion. In M. P. Zanna, J. M. Olson, & C. P. Herman (Eds.), *Social influence: The Ontario symposium* (Vol. 5., pp. 3–39). Hillsdale, NJ: Lawrence Erlbaum.

Chaiken, S., & Baldwin, M. W. (1981). Affective-cognitive consistency and the effect of salient behavioral information on the self-perception of attitudes. *Journal of Personality and Social Psychology, 41,* 1–12.

Chaiken, S., & Ledgerwood, A. (2012). A theory of heuristic and systematic information processing. In P. A. M. Van Lange, A. W. Kruglanski, & E. T. Higgins (Eds.), *Handbook of theories of social psychology* (Vol. 1, pp. 246–266). Thousand Oaks, CA: Sage.

Chaiken, S., Giner-Sorolla, R., & Chen, S. (1996). Beyond accuracy: Defense and impression motives in heuristic and systematic information processing. In P. M. Gollwitzer & J. A. Bargh (Eds.), *The psychology of action: Linking cognition and motivation to behavior* (pp. 553–578). New York, NY: Guilford Press.

Chaiken, S., Liberman, A., & Eagly, A. H. (1989). Heuristic and systematic information processing within and beyond the persuasion context. In J. S. Uleman & J. A. Bargh (Eds.), *Unintended thought* (pp. 212–252). New York, NY: Guilford Press.

Chan, E., & Sengupta, J. (2010). Insincere flattery actually works: A dual attitudes perspective. *Journal of Marketing Research (JMR), 47,* 122–133.

Chan, W., McCrae, R. R., De Fruyt, F., Jussim, L., Löckenhoff, C. E., De Bolle, M., . . . Terracciano, A. (2012). Stereotypes of age differences in personality traits: Universal and accurate? *Journal of Personality and Social Psychology, 103,* 1050–1066.

Chandrashekaran, M., Walker, B. A., Ward, J. C., & Reingen, P. H. (1996). Modeling individual preference evolution and choice in a dynamic group setting. *Journal of Marketing Research, 33,* 211–223.

Chang, T. -S., & Hsiao, W. -H. (2013). Factors influencing intentions to use social recommender systems: A social exchange perspective. *Cyberpsychology, Behavior, and Social Networking, 16,* 357–363.

Chapman, G. B., & Bornstein, B. H. (1996). The more you ask for, the more you get: Anchoring in personal injury verdicts. *Applied Cognitive Psychology, 10,* 519–540.

Chapman, G. B., & Johnson, E. J. (2002). Incorporating the irrelevant: Anchors in judgments of belief and value. In T. Gilovich, D. Griffin, & D. Kahneman (Eds.), *Heuristics and biases: The psychology of intuitive judgment* (pp. 120–138). New York, NY: Cambridge University Press.

Chapman, L. J. (1967). Illusory correlation in observational report. *Journal of Verbal Learning & Verbal Behavior, 6,* 151–155.

Chartrand, T. L., & Bargh, J. A. (1996). Automatic activation of impression formation and memorization goals: Nonconscious goal priming reproduces effects of explicit task instructions. *Journal of Personality and Social Psychology, 71,* 464–478.

Chartrand, T., & Bargh, J. A. (1999). The chameleon effect: The perception-behavior link and social interaction. *Journal of Personality and Social Psychology, 76,* 893–910.

Chartrand, T., Pinckert, S., & Burger, J. M. (1999). When manipulation backfires: The effects of time delay and requester on the foot-in-the-door technique. *Journal of Applied Social Psychology, 29,* 211–221.

Cheetham, M., Pedroni, A. F., Angus, A., Slater, M., & Jäncke, L. (2009). Virtual Milgram: Empathic concern or personal distress? Evidence from functional MRI and dispositional measures. *Frontiers in Human Neuroscience, 3.*

Chen, C., Lee, S.-y., & Stevenson, H. W. (1995). Response style and cross-cultural comparisons of rating scales among East Asian and North American students. *Psychological Science, 6,* 170–175.

Chen, F. S., Minson, J. A., Schöne, M., & Heinrichs, M. (2013). In the eye of the beholder: Eye contact increases resistance to persuasion. *Psychological Science, 24,* 2254–2261.

Chen, J. M., Kim, H. S., Mojaverian, T., & Morling, B. (2012). Culture and social support provision: Who gives what and why. *Personality and Social Psychology Bulletin, 38,* 3–13.

Chen, M. K., & Risen, J. L. (2010). How choice affects and reflects preferences: Revisiting the free-choice paradigm. *Journal of Personality and Social Psychology, 99,* 573–594.

Chen, S., & Chaiken, S. (1999). The heuristic-systematic model in its broader context. In S. Chaiken & Y. Trope (Eds.), *Dual-process theories in social psychology* (pp. 73–96). New York, NY: Guilford Press.

Chen, Y. -F. (2011). Auction fever: Exploring informational social influences on bidder choices. *Cyberpsychology, Behavior, and Social Networking, 14,* 411–416.

Cheung, F., & Lucas, R. E. (2015). When does money matter most? Examining the association between income and life satisfaction over the life course. *Psychology and Aging, 30,* 120–135.

Chiao, J. Y. (2011). Cultural neuroscience: Visualizing culture-gene influences on brain function. In J. Decety & J. T. Cacioppo (Eds.), *Oxford handbook of social neuroscience* (pp. 742–761). Oxford, UK: Oxford University.

Chiou, W. -B. (2008). Induced attitude change on online gaming among adolescents: An application of the less-leads-to-more effect. *CyberPsychology & Behavior, 11,* 212–216.

Chiu, C. -y., Hong, Y. -y., & Dweck, C. S. (1997). Lay dispositionism and implicit theories of personality. *Journal of Personality and Social Psychology, 73,* 19–30.

Chiu, C. -y., Leung, A. K. y., & Kwan, L. (2007). Language, cognition, and culture: Beyond the Whorfian hypothesis. In S. Kitayama & D. Cohen (Eds.), *Handbook of cultural psychology* (pp. 668–688). New York, NY: Guilford Press.

Chiu, C. -y., Morris, M. W., Hong, Y. -y., & Menon, T. (2000). Motivated cultural cognition: The impact of implicit cultural theories on dispositional attribution varies as a function of need for closure. *Journal of Personality and Social Psychology, 78,* 247–259.

Chiu, C.-y., & Hong, Y.-y. (2007). Cultural processes: Basic principles. In A. W. Kruglanski & E. T. Higgins (Eds.), *Social psychology: Handbook of basic principles* (2nd ed., pp. 785–804). New York, NY: Guilford Press.

Chivers, M. L., Seto, M. C., & Blanchard, R. (2007). Gender and sexual orientation differences in sexual response to sexual activities versus gender of actors in sexual films. *Journal of Personality and Social Psychology, 93,* 1108–1121.

Choi, B. K., Moon, H. K., & Chun, J. U. (2015). Impression management motive and voice: Moderating effects of self-monitoring, self-efficacy, and voice instrumentality. *Asian Journal of Social Psychology.*

Choi, I., Dalal, R., Kim-Prieto, C., & Park, H. (2003). Culture and judgement of causal relevance. *Journal of Personality and Social Psychology, 84,* 46–59.

Choi, I., Nisbett, R. E., & Norenzayan, A. (1999). Causal attribution across cultures: Variation and universality. *Psychological Bulletin, 125,* 47–63.

Choi, J. N., & Kim, M. U. (1999). The organizational application of groupthink and its limitations in organizations. *Journal of Applied Psychology, 84,* 297–306.

Chopik, W. J., & Edelstein, R. S. (2014). Age differences in romantic attraction around the world. *Social Psychological and Personality Science, 5,* 892–900.

Chou, K. -L., Cacioppo, J. T., Kumari, M., & Song, Y. Q. (2014). Influence of social environment on loneliness in older adults: Moderation by polymorphism in the CRHR1. *The American Journal of Geriatric Psychiatry: Official Journal of the American Association for Geriatric Psychiatry, 22,* 510–518.

Christensen, B. T., Drewsen, L. K., & Maaløe, J. (2014). Implicit theories of the personality of the ideal creative employee. *Psychology of Aesthetics, Creativity, and the Arts, 8,* 189–197.

Chua, S. N., Carbonneau, N., Milyavskaya, M., & Koestner, R. (2015). Beyond the self in self-control: The role of relational interdependent self-construal in goal pursuit. *Journal of Social and Personal Relationships, 32,* 330–343.

Church, A. T., Katigbak, M. S., Arias, R. M., Rincon, B. C., Vargas-Flores, J. d. J., Ibáñez-Reyes, J., . . . Ortiz, F. A. (2014). A four-culture study of self-enhancement and adjustment using the social relations model: Do alternative conceptualizations and indices make a difference? *Journal of Personality and Social Psychology, 106,* 997–1014.

Churchland, P. M. (1988). *Matter and consciousness: A contemporary introduction to the philosophy of mind* (Rev. ed.). Cambridge, MA: The MIT Press.

Cialdini, R. B. (2008). *Influence: Science and practice* (5th ed.). New York, NY: Prentice Hall.

Cialdini, R. B., & Ascani, K. (1976). Test of a concession procedure for inducing verbal, behavioral, and further compliance with a request to give blood. *Journal of Applied Psychology, 61,* 295–300.

Cialdini, R. B., & Baumann, D. J. (1981). Littering: A new unobtrusive measure of attitude. *Social Psychology Quarterly, 44,* 254–259.

Cialdini, R. B., & Goldstein, N. J. (2004). Social influence: Compliance and conformity. *Annual Review of Psychology, 55,* 591–621.

Cialdini, R. B., & Trost, M. R. (1998). Social influence: Social norms, conformity and compliance. In D. T. Gilbert, S. T. Fiske, & G. Lindzey (Eds.), *The handbook of social psychology* (Vols. 1 & 2, 4th ed., pp. 151–192). New York, NY: McGraw-Hill.

Cialdini, R. B., Baumann, D. J., & Kenrick, D. T. (1981). Insights from sadness: A three-step model of the development of altruism as hedonism. *Developmental Review, 1,* 207–223.

Cialdini, R. B., Borden, R. J., Thorne, A., Walker, M. R., Freeman, S., & Sloan, L. R. (1976). Basking in reflected glory: Three (football) field studies. *Journal of Personality and Social Psychology, 34,* 366–375.

Cialdini, R. B., Borden, R. J., Thorne, A., Walker, M. R., Freeman, S., & Sloan, L. R. (1976). Basking in reflected glory: Three (football) field studies. *Journal of Personality and Social Psychology, 34,* 366–375.

Cialdini, R. B., Cacioppo, J. T., Bassett, R., & Miller, J. A. (1978). Low-ball procedure for producing compliance: Commitment then cost. *Journal of Personality and Social Psychology, 36,* 463–476.

Cialdini, R. B., Darby, B. L., & Vincent, J.E. (1973). Transgression and altruism: A case for hedonism. *Journal of Experimental Social Psychology, 9,* 502–516.

Cialdini, R. B., Demaine, L. J., Sagarin, B. J., Barrett, D. W., Rhoads, K., & Winter, P. L. (2006). Managing social norms for persuasive impact. *Social Influence, 1,* 3–15.

Cialdini, R. B., Eisenberg, N., Green, B. L., Rhoads, K., & Bator, R. (1998). Undermining the undermining effect of reward on sustained interest. *Journal of Applied Social Psychology, 28,* 249–263.

Cialdini, R. B., Kallgren, C. A., & Reno, R. R. (1991). A focus theory of normative conduct: A theoretical refinement and reevaluation of the role of norms in human behavior. *Advances in Experimental Social Psychology, 21,* 201–234.

Cialdini, R. B., Petrova, P., & Goldstein, N. J. (2004). The hidden costs of organizational dishonesty. *Sloan Management Review, 45,* 67–73.

Cialdini, R. B., Reno, R. R., & Kallgren, C. A. (1990). A focus theory of normative conduct: Recycling the concept of norms to reduce littering in public places. *Journal of Personality and Social Psychology, 58,* 1015–1026.

Cialdini, R. B., Schaller, M., Houlihan, D., Arps, K., Fultz, J., & Beaman, A.L. (1987). Empathy-based helping: Is it selflessly or selfishly motivated? *Journal of Personality and Social Psychology, 52,* 749–758.

Cialdini, R. B., Trost, M. R., & Newsom, J. T. (1995). Preference for consistency: The development of a valid measure and the discovery of surprising behavioral implications. *Journal of Personality and Social Psychology, 69,* 318–328.

Cialdini, R. B., Vincent, J. E., Lewis, S. K., Catalan, J., Wheeler, D., & Darby, B. L. (1975). Reciprocal concessions procedure for inducing compliance: The door-in-the-face technique. *Journal of Personality and Social Psychology, 31,* 206–215.

Cialdini, R. B., Wosinska, W., Barrett, D. W., Butner, J., & Gornik-Durose, M. (1999). Compliance with a request in two cultures: The differential influence of social proof and commitment/consistency on collectivists and individualists. *Personality and Social Psychology Bulletin, 25,* 1242–1253.

Cialdini, R. B., Wosinska, W., Barrett, D. W., Butner, J., & Gornik-Durose, M. (1999). Compliance with a request in two cultures: The differential influence of social proof and commitment/consistency on collectivists and individualists. *Personality and Social Psychology Bulletin, 25,* 1242–1253.

Ciarocco, N. J., Echevarria, J., & Lewandowski, G. W. (2012). Hungry for love: The influence of self-regulation on infidelity. *The Journal of Social Psychology, 152,* 61–74.

Claidière, N., & Whiten, A. (2012). Integrating the study of conformity and culture in humans and nonhuman animals. *Psychological Bulletin, 138,* 126–145.

Clark, A. E., Diener, E., Georgellis, Y., & Lucas, R. E. (2008). Lags and leads in life satisfaction: A test of the baseline hypothesis. *Economic Journal, 118,* F222–F243.

Clark, J. K., Thiem, K. C., Barden, J., Stuart, J. O. R., & Evans, A. T. (2015). Stereotype validation: The effects of activating negative stereotypes after intellectual performance. *Journal of Personality and Social Psychology, 108,* 531–552.

Clark, J. K., Wegener, D. T., Habashi, M. M., & Evans, A. T. (2012). Source expertise and persuasion: The effects of perceived opposition or support on message scrutiny. *Personality and Social Psychology Bulletin, 38,* 90–100.

Clark, M. S., & Lemay, E. P., Jr. (2010). Close relationships. In S. T. Fiske, D. T. Gilbert, & G. Lindzey (Eds.), *Handbook of social psychology* (Vol. 2, 5th ed., pp. 898–940). Hoboken, NJ: John Wiley & Sons.

Clark, M. S., & Mills, J. (1979). Interpersonal attraction in exchange and communal relationships. *Journal of Personality and Social Psychology, 37,* 12–24.

Clark, M. S., & Waddell, B. A. (1983). Effects of moods on thoughts about helping, attraction and information acquisition. *Social Psychology Quarterly, 46,* 31–35.

Clark, R. D., & Hatfield, E. (1989). Gender differences in receptivity to sexual offers. *Journal of Psychology & Human Sexuality, 2,* 39–55.

Clore, G. L., & Byrne, D. E. (1974). A reinforcement-effect model of attraction. In T. L. Huston (Ed.), *Foundations of interpersonal attraction* (pp. 143–170). New York, NY: Academic Press.

Clow, K. A., Ricciardelli, R., & Bartfay, W. J. (2014). Attitudes and stereotypes of male and female nurses: The influence of social roles and ambivalent sexism. *Canadian Journal of Behavioural Science / Revue canadienne des sciences du comportement, 46,* 446–455.

Cohen, A. B., & Hill, P. C. (2007). Religion as culture: Religious individualism and collectivism among American Catholics, Jews, and Protestants. *Journal of Personality, 75,* 709–742.

Cohen, D. (1998). Culture, social organization, and patterns of violence. *Journal of Personality and Social Psychology, 75,* 408–419.

Cohen, D. (2007). Methods in cultural psychology. In S. Kitayama & D. Cohen (Eds.), *Handbook of cultural psychology* (pp. 196–236). New York, NY: Guilford Press.

Cohen, D., & Leung, A. K.y. (2011). Violence and character: A CuPS (culture x person x situation) perspective. In P. R. Shaver & M. Mikulincer (Eds.), *Human aggression and violence: Causes, manifestations, and consequences* (pp. 187–200). Washington, DC: American Psychological Association.

Cohen, D., & Nisbett, R. E. (1997). Field experiments examining the culture of honor: The role of institutions in perpetuating norms about violence. *Personality and Social Psychology Bulletin, 23,* 1188–1199.

Cohen, D., Nisbett, R. E., Bowdle, B. F., & Schwarz, N. (1996). Insult, aggression, and the Southern culture of honor: An "experimental ethnography." *Journal of Personality and Social Psychology, 70,* 945–960.

Cohen, T. R., Turan, N., Panter, A. T., Morse, L., & Yeonjeong, K. (2014). Moral Character in the Workplace. *Journal of Personality & Social Psychology, 107,* 943–963.

Cohen-Ketteinis, P. T., & van Goozen, S. H. M. (1997). Sex reassignment of adolescent transsexuals: A follow-up study. *Journal of the American Academy of Child & Adolescent Psychiatry, 36,* 263–271.

Coie, J. D., Cillessen, A. H. N., Dodge, K. A., Hubbard, J. A., Schwartz, D., Lemerise, E. A., & Bateman, H. (1999). It takes two to fight: A test of relational factors and a method for assessing aggressive dyads. *Developmental Psychology, 35,* 1179–1188.

Coleman, M. D. (2013). Emotion and the ultimate attribution error. *Current Psychology: A Journal for Diverse Perspectives on Diverse Psychological Issues, 32,* 71–81.

Collier, G., Minton, H. L., & Reynolds, G. (1991). *Currents of thought in American social psychology.* New York, NY: Oxford University Press.

Collins, A. M., & Loftus, E. F. (1975). A spreading-activation theory of semantic processing. *Psychological Review, 82,* 407–428.

Collins, N. L., & Feeney, B. C. (2004). Working models of attachment shape perceptions of social support: Evidence from experimental and observational studies. *Journal of Personality and Social Psychology, 87,* 363–383.

Collins, N. L., & Miller, L. C. (1994). Self-disclosure and liking: A meta-analytic review. *Psychological Bulletin, 116,* 457–475.

Collins, S. E., & Spelman, P. J. (2013). Associations of descriptive and reflective injunctive norms with risky college drinking. *Psychology of Addictive Behaviors, 27,* 1175–1181.

Conner, M., & Armitage, C. J. (2008). Attitudinal ambivalence. In W. D. Crano & R. Prislin (Eds.), *Attitudes and attitude change* (pp. 261–286). New York, NY: Psychology Press.

Conroy-Beam, D., Buss, D. M., Pham, M. N., & Shackelford, T. K. (2015). How sexually dimorphic are human mate preferences? *Personality and Social Psychology Bulletin, 41,* 1082–1093.

Conway, L. G., III, Dodds, D. P., Towgood, K. H., McClure, S., & Olson, J. M. (2011). The biological roots of complex thinking: Are heritable attitudes more complex? *Journal of Personality, 79,* 101–134.

Cook, K. S., & Yamagishi, T. (2008). A defense of deception on scientific grounds. *Social Psychology Quarterly, 71,* 215–221.

Cooley, C. C. (1902). *Human nature and social order.* New York, NY: Charles Scribner.

Cooper, J. (1999). Unwanted consequences and the self: In search of the motivation for dissonance reduction. In E. Harmon-Jones & J. Mills (Eds.), *Cognitive dissonance: Progress on a pivotal theory in social psychology* (pp. 149–173). Washington, DC: American Psychological Association.

Cooper, J. (2007). *Cognitive dissonance: Fifty years of a classic theory.* Thousand Oaks, CA: Sage.

Cooper, J. (2012a). Cognitive dissonance theory. In P. A. M. Van Lange, A. W. Kruglanski, & E. T. Higgins (Eds.), *Handbook of theories of social psychology* (Vol. 1, pp. 377–397). Thousand Oaks, CA: Sage.

Cooper, J. (2012b). Cognitive dissonance: Revisiting Festinger's end of the world study. In S. A. Haslam & J. R. Smith (Eds.), *Social psychology: Revisiting the classics* (pp. 42–56). Los Angeles, CA: Sage.

Cooper, J., & Fazio, R. H. (1984). A new look at dissonance theory. In L. Berkowitz (Ed.), *Advances in experimental social psychology* (Vol. 17, pp. 229–264). Orlando, FL: Academic Press.

Corallo, G., Sackur, J., Dehaene, S., & Sigman, M. (2008). Limits on introspection: Distorted subjective time during the dual-task bottleneck. *Psychological Science, 19,* 1110–1117.

Corasaniti, N., Pérez-Peña, R., & Alvarez, L. (2015, June 18). CHARLESTON MASSACRE SUSPECT HELD AS CITY GRIEVES: Races unite for nine killed by gunman at Black church. (Cover story). *New York Times, 164,* A1-A16.

Corcoran, K. (2015). Radil Hebrich died bleeding on Montreal platform for over 15 MINUTES before anybody helped. *The Daily Mail.* Retrieved from http://search.ebscohost.com/login.aspx?direct=true&db=nmr&AN=WBN14638717AEAFE855C84E6A7BC576925586F0BE5E&login.asp&site=ehost-live&scope=site

Corneille, O., Yzerbyt, V. Y., Rogier, A., & Buidin, G. (2001). Threat and the group attribution error: When threat elicits judgments of extremity and homogeneity. *Personality and Social Psychology Bulletin, 27,* 437–446.

Corr, P. J. (2010). Automatic and controlled processes in behavioural control: Implications for personality psychology. *European Journal of Personality, 24,* 376–403.

Corral-Verdugo, V., Frías-Armenta, M., Tapia-Fonllem, C. O., & Fraijo-Sing, B. S. (2012). Protecting natural resources: Psychological and contextual determinants of freshwater conservation. In S. Clayton (Ed.), *The Oxford handbook of environmental and conservation psychology* (pp. 581–597). Oxford, UK: Oxford University Press.

Correll, J., Park, B., Judd, C. M., & Wittenbrink, B. (2002). The police officer's dilemma: Using ethnicity to disambiguate potentially threatening individuals. *Journal of Personality and Social Psychology, 83,* 1314–1329.

Correll, J., Park, B., Judd, C. M., Wittenbrink, B., Sadler, M. S., & Keesee, T. (2007). Across the thin blue line: Police officers and racial bias in the decision to shoot. *Journal of Personality and Social Psychology, 92,* 1006–1023.

Cosmides, L., & Tooby, J. (1992). Cognitive adaptations for social exchange. In J. H. Barkow, L. Cosmides, & J. Tooby (Eds.), *The adapted mind: Evolutionary psychology and the generation of culture* (pp. 163–228). New York, NY: Oxford University Press.

Costa, P. T., Jr., & McCrae, R. R. (2009). The five-factor model and the NEO inventories. In J. N. Butcher (Ed.), *Oxford handbook of personality assessment* (pp. 299–322). New York, NY: Oxford University Press.

Costarelli, S., & Gerłowska, J. (2015a). Ambivalence, prejudice and negative behavioural tendencies towards out-groups: The moderating role of attitude basis. *Cognition and Emotion, 29,* 852–866.

Costarelli, S., & Gerłowska, J. (2015b). I am not prejudiced towards "them" . . . I am ambivalent! The moderating roles of attitudinal basis and motivation to respond without prejudice. *Group Dynamics: Theory, Research, and Practice, 19,* 1–14.

Cottrell, N. B. (1972). Social facilitation. In C. G. McClintock (Ed.), Experimental social psychology (pp. 185–236). New York, NY: Holt, Rinehart & Wilson.

Cottrell, N. B., Wack, D. L., Sekerak, G. J., & Rittle, R. H. (1968). Social facilitation of dominant responses by the presence of an audience and the mere presence of others. *Journal of Personality and Social Psychology, 9,* 245–250.

Coultas, J. C. (2004). When in Rome . . . An Evolutionary Perspective on Conformity. *Group Processes & Intergroup Relations, 7,* 317–331.

Coyne, S. M., & Padilla-Walker, L. M. (2015). Sex, violence, & rock n' roll: Longitudinal effects of music on aggression, sex, and prosocial behavior during adolescence. *Journal of Adolescence, 41,* 96–104.

Craig, M. A., & Richeson, J. A. (2014). Not in my backyard! Authoritarianism, social dominance orientation, and support for strict immigration policies at home and abroad. *Political Psychology, 35,* 417–429.

Crandall, C. S. (1995). Do parents discriminate against their heavyweight daughters? *Personality and Social Psychology Bulletin, 21,* 724–735.

Crandall, C. S., Merman, A., & Hebl, M. (2009). Anti-fat prejudice. In T. D. Nelson (Ed.), *Handbook of prejudice, stereotyping, and discrimination* (pp. 469–487). New York, NY: Psychology Press.

Crandall, C. S., Silvia, P. J., N'Gbala, A. N., Tsang, J. -A., & Dawson, K. (2007). Balance theory, unit relations, and attribution: The underlying integrity of Heiderian theory. *Review of General Psychology, 11,* 12–30.

Crano, W. D. (1995). Attitude strength and vested interest. In R. E. Petty & J. A. Krosnick (Eds.), *Attitude strength: Antecedents and consequences* (pp. 131–157). Hillsdale, NJ: Lawrence Erlbaum.

Crano, W. D., & Brewer, M. B. (1973). *Principles of research in social psychology.* New York, NY: McGraw-Hill.

Crano, W. D., & Seyranian, V. (2007). Majority and minority influence. *Social and Personality Psychology Compass, 1,* 572–589.

Crawford, J. T., Jussim, L., Cain, T. R., & Cohen, F. (2013). Right-wing authoritarianism and social dominance orientation differentially predict biased evaluations of media reports. *Journal of Applied Social Psychology, 43,* 163–174.

Crisp, R. J., Hutter, R. R. C., & Young, B. (2009). When mere exposure leads to less liking: The incremental threat effect in intergroup contexts. *British Journal of Psychology, 100,* 133–149.

Critcher, C. R., & Dunning, D. (2009). Egocentric pattern projection: How implicit personality theories recapitulate the geography of the self. *Journal of Personality and Social Psychology, 97,* 1–16.

Crocker, J., & Garcia, J. A. (2009). Downward and upward spirals in intergroup interactions: The role of egosystem and ecosystem goals. In T. D. Nelson (Ed.), *Handbook of prejudice, stereotyping, and discrimination.* (pp. 229–245). New York, NY: Psychology Press.

Crocker, J., & Garcia, J. A. (2010). Internalized devaluation and situational threat. In J. F. Dovidio, M. Hewstone, P. Glick, & V. M. Esses (Eds.), *SAGE handbook of prejudice, stereotyping, and discrimination* (pp. 395–409). London, UK: Sage.

Crocker, J., & Major, B. (1989). Social stigma and self-esteem: The self-protective properties of stigma. *Psychological Review, 96,* 608–630.

Crocker, J., & Park, L. E. (2004). The costly pursuit of self-esteem. *Psychological Bulletin, 130,* 392–414.

Crocker, J., & Wolfe, C. T. (2001). Contingencies of self-worth. *Psychological Review, 108,* 593–623.

Crocker, J., Luhtanen, R. K., Cooper, M. L., & Bouvrette, A. (2003). Contingencies of self-worth in college students: Theory and Measurement. *Journal of Personality and Social Psychology, 85,* 894–908.

Crocker, J., Luhtanen, R., Blaine, B., & Broadnax, S. (1994). Collective self-esteem and psychological well-being among White, Black, and Asian college students. *Personality and Social Psychology Bulletin, 20,* 503–513.

Crocker, J., Major, B., & Steele, C. (1998). Social stigma. In D. T. Gilbert, S. T. Fiske, & G. Lindzey (Eds.), *The handbook of social psychology* (Vols. 1 & 2, 4th ed., pp. 504–553). New York, NY: McGraw-Hill.

Crockett, M. J., Clark, L., Lieberman, M. D., Tabibnia, G., & Robbins, T. W. (2010). Impulsive choice and altruistic punishment are correlated and increase in tandem with serotonin depletion. *Emotion, 10,* 855–862.

Croizet, J. -C., Després, G., Gauzins, M. -E., Huguet, P., Leyens, J. -P., & Méot, A. (2004). Stereotype threat undermines intellectual performance by triggering a disruptive mental load. *Personality and Social Psychology Bulletin, 30,* 721–731.

Cronin, P., & Reicher, S. (2009). Accountability processes and group dynamics: A SIDE perspective on the policing of an anti-capitalist riot. *European Journal of Social Psychology, 39,* 237–254.

Crosier, B. S., Webster, G. D., & Dillon, H. M. (2012). Wired to connect: Evolutionary psychology and social networks. *Review of General Psychology, 16,* 230–239.

Crusius, J., & Mussweiler, T. (2012). When people want what others have: The impulsive side of envious desire. *Emotion, 12,* 142–153.

Crutchfield, R. S. (1955). Conformity and character. *American Psychologist, 10,* 191–198.

Cuddy, A. J. C., Fiske, S. T., Kwan, V. S. Y., Glick, P., Demoulin, S. p., Leyens, J. -P., . . . Ziegler, R. (2009). Stereotype content model across cultures: Towards universal similarities and some differences. *British Journal of Social Psychology, 48,* 1–33.

Cuddy, A. J. C., Norton, M. I., & Fiske, S. T. (2005). This old stereotype: The pervasiveness and persistence of the elderly stereotype. *Journal of Social Issues, 61,* 267–285.

Cummings, J. P., & Pargament, K. I. (2012). Religious coping with workplace stress. In P. C. Hill & B. J. Dik (Eds.), *Psychology of religion and workplace spirituality* (pp. 157–177). Charlotte, NC: IAP Information Age Publishing.

Cunningham, M. R. (1986). Measuring the physical in physical attractiveness: Quasi-experiments on the sociobiology of female facial beauty. *Journal of Personality and Social Psychology, 50,* 925–935.

Cunningham, M. R., Barbee, A. P., & Pike, C. L. (1990). What do women want? Facialmetric assessment of multiple motives in the perception of male facial physical attractiveness. *Journal of Personality and Social Psychology, 59,* 61–72.

Cunningham, M. R., Roberts, A. R., Barbee, A. P., Druen, P. B., & Wu, C. -H. (1995). "Their ideas of beauty are, on the whole, the same as ours": Consistency and variability in the cross-cultural perception of female physical attractiveness. *Journal of Personality and Social Psychology, 68,* 261–279.

Curhan, K. B., Levine, C. S., Markus, H., Kitayama, S., Park, J., Karasawa, M., . . . Ryff, C. D. (2014). Subjective and objective hierarchies and their relations to psychological well-being: A U.S./Japan comparison. *Social Psychological and Personality Science.*

Curnalia, R. M. L. (2007). Fear appeals in political ads: Threats to health, safety, and financial security in the 2004 presidential election. *Ohio Communication Journal, 47,* 55–76.

Curşeu, P. L., Schruijer, S. G. L., & Boroş, S. (2012). Socially rejected while cognitively successful? The impact of minority dissent on groups' cognitive complexity. British Journal of Social Psychology, 51, 570–582.

Curtis, B. (2012). Understanding tailored Internet smoking cessation messages: A reasoned action approach. *Annals of the American Academy of Political and Social Science, 640,* 136–149.

Curtis, R. C., & Miller, K. (1986). Believing another likes or dislikes you: Behaviors making the beliefs come true. *Journal of Personality and Social Psychology, 51,* 284–290.

Czopp, A. M., Kay, A. R., & Cheryan, S. (2015). Positive stereotypes are pervasive and powerful. *Perspectives on Psychological Science, 10,* 451–463.

Czuchry, M., & Gray, B. (2009). Influence of message sidedness, pictures, and need for cognition on beliefs and behavior: The Terri Schiavo case. *Journal of Applied Social Psychology, 39,* 762–789.

D'Lima, G. M., Pearson, M. R., & Kelley, M. L. (2012). Protective behavioral strategies as a mediator and moderator of the relationship between self-regulation and alcohol-related consequences in first-year college students. *Psychology of Addictive Behaviors.*

Dabbs, J. M., & Dabbs, M. G. (2000). *Heroes, rogues, and lovers: Testosterone and behavior.* New York, NY: McGraw-Hill.

Daly, M., & Wilson, M. (1988). *Homicide.* Hawthorne, NY: Aldine de Gruyter.

Damasio, A. R. (1994). *Descartes' error: Emotion, reason, and the human brain.* New York, NY: Quill.

Damasio, A. R. (2010). *Self comes to mind: Constructing the conscious brain.* New York, NY: Pantheon/Random House.

Damasio, H., Grabowski, T., Frank, R., Galaburda, A. M., & Damasio, A. R. (2005). The Return of Phineas Gage: Clues about the Brain from the Skull of a Famous Patient. In J. T. Cacioppo & G. G. Berntson (Eds.), *Social neuroscience: Key readings* (pp. 21–28). New York, NY: Psychology Press.

Danaher, K., & Branscombe, N. R. (2010). Maintaining the system with tokenism: Bolstering individual mobility beliefs and identification with a discriminatory organization. *British Journal of Social Psychology, 49,* 343–362.

Danaher, K., & Crandall, C. S. (2008). Stereotype threat in applied settings re-examined. *Journal of Applied Social Psychology, 38,* 1639–1655.

Danel, D., & Pawlowski, B. (2007). Eye-mouth-eye angle as a good indicator of face masculinization, asymmetry, and attractiveness (Homo sapiens). *Journal of Comparative Psychology, 121,* 221–225.

Darley, J. M., & Batson, C. D. (1973). "From Jerusalem to Jericho": A study of situational and dispositional variables in helping behavior. *Journal of Personality and Social Psychology, 27,* 100–108.

Darley, J. M., & Latané, B. (1968). Bystander intervention in emergencies: Diffusion of responsibility. *Journal of Personality and Social Psychology, 8,* 377–383.

Darwin, C. (1871). *The descent of man and selection in relation to sex.* London: Murray.

Darwin, C. (1872). *The expression of the emotions in man and animals.* London, UK: John Murray.

Darwin, C. (1994). *On the origin of species by means of natural selection or the preservation of favored races in the struggle for life.* London, UK: Senate. (Originally published in 1859)

Dasgupta, N., & Rivera, L. M. (2006). From automatic antigay prejudice to behavior: The moderating role of conscious beliefs about gender and behavioral control. *Journal of Personality and Social Psychology, 91,* 268–280.

Daugherty, T., Li, H., & Biocca, F. (2008). Consumer learning and the effects of virtual experience relative to indirect and direct product experience. *Psychology & Marketing, 25,* 568–586.

Davies, K., Tropp, L. R., Aron, A., Pettigrew, T. F., & Wright, S. C. (2011). Cross-group friendships and intergroup attitudes: A meta-analytic review. *Personality and Social Psychology Review, 15,* 332–351.

Davies, M. F. (1997). Belief persistence after evidential discrediting: The impact of generated versus provided explanations on the likelihood of discredited outcomes. *Journal of Experimental Social Psychology, 33,* 561–578.

Davis, J. A. (1959). A formal interpretation of the theory of relative deprivation. *Sociometry, 22,* 280–296.

Davis, M. H., Luce, C., & Kraus, S. J. (1994). The heritability of characteristics associated with dispositional empathy. *Journal of Personality, 62,* 369–391.

De Houwer, J., & Moors, A. (2015). Levels of analysis in social psychology. In B. Gawronski, G. V. Bodenhausen, B. Gawronski, & G. V. Bodenhausen (Eds.), *Theory and explanation in social psychology* (pp. 24–40). New York, NY: Guilford Press.

De La Ronde, C., & Swann, W. B., Jr. (1998). Partner verification: Restoring shattered images of our intimates. *Journal of Personality and Social Psychology, 75,* 374–382.

de Regt, S. (2012). Religiosity as a moderator of the relationship between authoritarianism and social dominance orientation: A cross-cultural comparison. *International Journal for the Psychology of Religion, 22,* 31–41.

de Ridder, D., Kuijer, R., & Ouwehand, C. (2007). Does confrontation with potential goal failure promote self-regulation? Examining the role of distress in the pursuit of weight goals. *Psychology & Health, 22,* 677–698.

de Waal, F. B. M. (2005). *Our inner ape: A leading primatologist explains why we are who we are.* New York, NY: Riverhead Books.

de Zilva, D., Newell, B. R., & Mitchell, C. J. (2015). Multiple context mere exposure: Examining the limits of liking. *Quarterly Journal Of Experimental Psychology (2006),* 1–35.

Deater-Deckard, K., Beekman, C., Wang, Z., Kim, J., Petrill, S., Thompson, L., & DeThorne, L. (2010). Approach/positive anticipation, frustration/anger, and overt aggression in childhood. *Journal of Personality, 78,* 991–1010.

DeBruine, L. M., Jones, B. C., Unger, L., Little, A. C., & Feinberg, D. R. (2007). Dissociating averageness and attractiveness: Attractive faces are not always average. *Journal of Experimental Psychology: Human Perception and Performance, 33,* 1420–1430. [Supplemental]

Decety, J., & Cacioppo, J. T. (Eds.). (2011). *The Oxford handbook of social neuroscience.* Oxford: Oxford University.

Decety, J., & Ickes, W. (2009). *The social neuroscience of empathy.* Cambridge, MA: MIT Press.

Decety, J., & Porges, E. C. (2011). Imagining being the agent of actions that carry different moral consequences: An fMRI study. *Neuropsychologia, 49,* 2994–3001.

DeChurch, L. A., & Mesmer-Magnus, J. R. (2010). Measuring shared team mental models: A meta-analysis. Group Dynamics: Theory, Research, and Practice, 14, 1–14.

Delton, A. W., Krasnow, M. M., Cosmides, L., & Tooby, J. (2011). Evolution of direct reciprocity under uncertainty can explain human generosity in one-shot encounters. *Proceedings of the National Academy of Sciences of the United States of America, 108,* 13335–13340.

Delton, A. W., Nemirow, J., Robertson, T. E., Cimino, A., & Cosmides, L. (2013). Merely opting out of a public good is moralized: An error management approach to cooperation. *Journal of Personality and Social Psychology, 105,* 621–638.

Demarque, C., Apostolidis, T., & Joule, R. -V. (2013). Consideration of future consequences and pro-environmental decision making in the context of persuasion and binding commitment. *Journal of Environmental Psychology, 36,* 214–220.

Dennett, D. C., & Weiner, P. (1991). *Consciousness explained.* New York, NY: Little, Brown.

Dennis, A.R., & Williams, M. L. (2005). A meta-analysis of group size effects in electronic brainstorming: More heads are better than one. *International Journal of e-Collaboration, 1,* 24–42.

Depaulo, B. M., & Friedman, H. S. (1998). Nonverbal communication. In D. T. Gilbert, S. T. Fiske, & G. Lindzey (Eds.), *The handbook of social psychology* (Vols. 1 & 2, 4th ed., pp. 3–40). New York, NY: McGraw-Hill.

DePaulo, B. M., & Kashy, D. A. (1998). Everyday lies in close and casual relationships. *Journal of Personality and Social Psychology, 74,* 63–79.

DePaulo, B. M., Kashy, D. A., Kirkendol, S. E., Wyer, M. M., & Epstein, J. A. (1996). Lying in everyday life. *Journal of Personality and Social Psychology, 70,* 979–995.

DePaulo, B. M., Lindsay, J. J., Malone, B. E., Muhlenbruck, L., Charlton, K., & Cooper, H. (2003). Cues to deception. *Psychological Bulletin, 129,* 74–118.

Derakshan, N., & Eysenck, M. W. (2005). When the bogus pipeline interferes with self-deceptive strategies: Effects on state anxiety in repressors. *Cognition and Emotion, 19,* 83–100.

Derlega, V. J., Winstead, B. A., & Greene, K. (2008). Self-disclosure and starting a close relationship. In S. Sprecher, A. Wenzel, & J. Harvey (Eds.), *Handbook of relationship initiation* (pp. 153–174). New York, NY: Psychology Press.

DeRosa, D. M., Smith, C. L., & Hantula, D. A. (2007). The medium matters: Mining the long-promised merit of group interaction in creative idea generation tasks in a meta-analysis of the electronic group brainstorming literature. *Computers in Human Behavior, 23,* 1549–1581.

Derue, D. S., Nahrgang, J. D., Wellman, N., & Humphrey, S. E. (2011). Trait and behavioral theories of leadership: An integration and meta-analytic test of their relative validity. *Personnel Psychology, 64,* 7–52.

Descartes, R. (1960). *Meditations* (L. J. Lafleur, Trans.). Indianapolis, IN: Bobbs-Merrill. (Original work published in 1641)

Desrosiers, A. (2012). Development of religion and spirituality across the life span. In J. D. Aten, K. A. O'Grady, & E. L. Worthington (Eds.), *The psychology of religion and spirituality for clinicians: Using research in your practice* (pp. 13–37). New York, NY: Routledge/Taylor & Francis Group.

Deters, F. g., & Mehl, M. R. (2013). Does posting Facebook status updates increase or decrease loneliness? An online social networking experiment. *Social Psychological and Personality Science, 4,* 579–586.

Deuja, A., Kohn, N. W., Paulus, P. B., & Korde, R. M. (2014). Taking a broad perspective before brainstorming. *Group Dynamics: Theory, Research, and Practice, 18,* 222–236.

Deutsch, M., & Gerard, H. B. (1955). A study of normative and informational social influences upon individual judgment. *The Journal of Abnormal and Social Psychology, 51,* 629–636.

Devine, D. J., Clayton, L. D., Dunford, B. B., Seying, R., & Pryce, J. (2001). Jury decision making: 45 years of empirical research on deliberating groups. *Psychology, Public Policy, and Law, 7,* 622–727.

Devine, P. G. (1989). Stereotypes and prejudice: Their automatic and controlled components. *Journal of Personality and Social Psychology, 56,* 5–18.

DeVoe, S. E., & Pfeffer, J. (2011). Time is tight: How higher economic value of time increases feelings of time pressure. *Journal of Applied Psychology, 96,* 665–676.

DeWall, C. N., & Anderson, C. A. (2011). The general aggression model. In P. R. Shaver & M. Mikulincer (Eds.), *Human aggression and violence: Causes, manifestations, and consequences* (pp. 15–33). Washington, DC: American Psychological Association.

DeWall, C. N., & Bushman, B. J. (2009). Hot under the collar in a lukewarm environment: Words associated with hot temperature increase aggressive thoughts and hostile perceptions. *Journal of Experimental Social Psychology, 45,* 1045–1047.

DeWall, C. N., & Richman, S. B. (2011). Social exclusion and the desire to reconnect. *Social and Personality Psychology Compass, 5,* 919–932.

DeWall, C. N., MacDonald, G., Webster, G. D., Masten, C. L., Baumeister, R. F., Powell, C., . . . Eisenberger, N. I. (2010). Acetaminophen reduces social pain: Behavioral and neural evidence. *Psychological Science, 21,* 931–937.

DeWall, C. N., Masten, C. L., Powell, C., Combs, D., Schurtz, D. R., & Eisenberger, N. I. (2012). Do neural responses to rejection depend on attachment style? An *f*MRI study. *Social Cognitive and Affective Neuroscience, 7,* 184–192.

DeWall, C. N., Twenge, J. M., Gitter, S. A., & Baumeister, R. F. (2009). It's the thought that counts: The role of hostile cognition in shaping aggressive responses to social exclusion. *Journal of Personality and Social Psychology, 96,* 45–59.

Diamond, J. (2005). *Collapse: How societies choose to fail or succeed.* New York, NY: Penguin.

Diamond, L. M. (2003). Was it a phase? Young women's relinquishment of lesbian/bisexual identities over a 5-year period. *Journal of Personality and Social Psychology, 84,* 352–364.

Diamond, L. M. (2007). A dynamical systems approach to the development and expression of female same-sex sexuality. *Perspectives on Psychological Science, 2,* 142–161.

Dickerson, C. A., Thibodeau, R., Aronson, E., & Miller, D. (1992). Using cognitive dissonance to encourage water conservation. *Journal of Applied Social Psychology, 22,* 841–854.

Diehl, M., & Stroebe, W. (1987). Productivity loss in brainstorming groups: Toward the solution of a riddle. *Journal of Personality and Social Psychology, 53,* 497–509.

Diener, E. (2000). Subjective well-being: The science of happiness and a proposal for a national index. *American Psychologist, 55,* 34–43.

Diener, E. (2006). *Understanding scores on the Satisfaction with Life Scale.* Retrieved from http://internal.psychology.illinois.edu/~ediener/Documents/Understanding SWLS Scores.pdf

Diener, E. (2012). New findings and future directions for subjective well-being research. *American Psychologist, 67,* 590–597.

Diener, E., & Biswas-Diener, R. (2002). Will money increase subjective well-being? *Social Indicators Research, 57.*

Diener, E., & Diener, M. (1995). Cross-cultural correlates of life satisfaction and self-esteem. *Journal of Personality and Social Psychology, 68,* 653–663.

Diener, E., & Fujita, F. (1995). Resources, personal strivings, and subjective well-being: A nomothetic and idiographic approach. *Journal of Personality and Social Psychology, 68,* 926–935.

Diener, E., & Seligman, M. E. P. (2002). Very happy people. *Psychological Science, 13,* 81–84.

Diener, E., & Seligman, M. E. P. (2004). Beyond money: Toward an economy of well-being. *Psychological Science in the Public Interest, 5,* 1–31.

Diener, E., Emmons, R. A., Larsen, R. J., & Griffin, S. (1985). The Satisfaction With Life Scale. *Journal of Personality Assessment, 49,* 71–75.

Diener, E., Fraser, S. C., Beaman, A. L., & Kelem, R. T. (1976). Effects of deindividuation variables on stealing among Halloween trick-or-treaters. *Journal of Personality and Social Psychology, 33,* 178–183.

Diener, E., Fujita, F., Tay, L., & Biswas-Diener, R. (2012). Purpose, mood, and pleasure in predicting satisfaction judgments. *Social Indicators Research, 105,* 333–341.

Diener, E., Ng, W., Harter, J., & Arora, R. (2010). Wealth and happiness across the world: Material prosperity predicts life evaluation, whereas psychosocial prosperity predicts positive feeling. *Journal of Personality and Social Psychology, 99,* 52–61.

Diener, E., Tamir, M., & Scollon, C. N. (2006). Happiness, life satisfaction, and fulfillment: The social psychology of subjective well-being. In P. A. M. Van Lange (Ed.), *Bridging social psychology: Benefits of transdisciplinary approaches* (pp. 319–324). Mahwah, NJ: Lawrence Erlbaum.

Diener, E., Tay, L., & Myers, D. G. (2011). The religion paradox: If religion makes people happy, why are so many dropping out? *Journal of Personality and Social Psychology, 101,* 1278–1290.

Diener, E., Tay, L., & Oishi, S. (2013). Rising income and the subjective well-being of nations. *Journal of Personality and Social Psychology, 104,* 267–276.

Dijksterhuis, A. (2010). Automaticity and the unconscious. In S. T. Fiske, D. T. Gilbert, & G. Lindzey (Eds.), *Handbook of social psychology* (Vol. 1, 5th ed., pp. 228–267). Hoboken, NJ: John Wiley & Sons.

Dijksterhuis, A., Spears, R., & Lepinasse, V. (2001). Reflecting and deflecting stereotypes: Assimilation and contrast in impression formation and. *Journal of Experimental Social Psychology, 37.*

Dijksterhuis, A., Strick, M., Bos, M. W., & Nordgren, L. F. (2014). Prolonged thought: Proposing Type 3 processing. In J. W. Sherman, B. Gawronski, Y. Trope, J. W. Sherman, B. Gawronski, & Y. Trope (Eds.), *Dual-process theories of the social mind* (pp. 355–368). New York, NY: Guilford Press.

Dijkstra, P., & Buunk, B. P. (1998). Jealousy as a function of rival characteristics: An evolutionary perspective. *Personality and Social Psychology Bulletin, 24,* 1158–1166.

Dijkstra, P., Barelds, D. P. H., Groothof, H. A. K., & van Bruggen, M. (2014). Empathy in intimate relationships: The role of positive illusions. *Scandinavian Journal of Psychology, 55,* 477–482.

Dill, K. E., Anderson, C. A., & Deuser, W. E. (1997). Effects of aggressive personality on social expectations and social perceptions. *Journal of Research in Personality, 31,* 272–292.

Dillard, J. P. (1990). Self-inference and the foot-in-the-door technique: Quantity of behavior and attitudinal mediation. *Human Communication Research, 16,* 422–447.

Dillard, J. P., Hunter, J. E., & Burgoon, M. (1984). Sequential-request persuasive strategies: Meta-analysis of foot-in-the-door and door-in-the-face. *Human Communication Research, 10,* 461–488.

Dion, K., Berscheid, E., & Walster, E. (1972). What is beautiful is good. *Journal of Personality and Social Psychology, 24,* 285–290.

Distel, M. A., Rebollo-Mesa, I., Abdellaoui, A., Derom, C. A., Willemsen, G., Cacioppo, J. T., & Boomsma, D. I. (2010). Familial resemblance for loneliness. *Behavior Genetics, 40,* 480–494.

Doane, M., Elliott, M., & Dyrenforth, P. (2014). Extrinsic religious orientation and well-being: Is their negative association real or spurious? *Review of Religious Research, 56,* 45–60.

Dodge, K. A., Malone, P. S., Lansford, J. E., Sorbring, E., Skinner, A. T., Tapanya, S., . . . Pastorelli, C. (2015). Hostile attributional bias and aggressive behavior in global context. *Proceedings of the National Academy of Sciences of the United States of America.*

Doehring, C. (2013). An applied integrative approach to exploring how religion and spirituality contribute to or counteract prejudice and discrimination. In K. I. Pargament, A. Mahoney, & E. P. Shafranske (Eds.), *APA handbook of psychology, religion, and spirituality: An applied psychology of religion and spirituality* (Vol. 2, pp. 389–403). Washington, DC: American Psychological Association.

Dolinski, D. (2000). On inferring one's beliefs from one's attempt and consequences for subsequent compliance. *Journal of Personality and Social Psychology, 78,* 260–272.

Dolinski, D. (2016). *Techniques of social influence: The psychology of gaining compliance.* London, UK: Routledge.

Dollard, J., Miller, N. E., Doob, L. W., Mowrer, O. H., & Sears, R. R. (1939). *Frustration and aggression.* New Haven, CT: Yale University Press.

Donald, M. (2000). The central role of culture in cognitive evolution: A reflection on the myth of the "Isolated Mind." In L. P. Nucci, G. B. Saxe, & E. Turiel (Eds.), *Culture, thought, and development* (pp. 19–38). Mahwah, NJ: Lawrence Erlbaum.

Dong, P., Dai, X., & Wyer, R. S., Jr. (2015). Actors conform, observers react: The effects of behavioral synchrony on conformity. *Journal of Personality and Social Psychology, 108,* 60–75.

Dovidio, J. F. (2001). On the nature of contemporary prejudice: The third wave. *Journal of Social Issues, 57,* 829–849.

Dovidio, J. F., & Gaertner, S. L. (2010). Intergroup bias. In S. T. Fiske, D. T. Gilbert, & G. Lindzey (Eds.), *Handbook of social psychology* (Vol. 2, 5th ed., pp. 1084–1121). Hoboken, NJ: John Wiley & Sons Inc.

Dovidio, J. F., Gaertner, S. L., Shnabel, N., Saguy, T., & Johnson, J. (2010). Recategorization and prosocial behavior: Common in-group identity and a dual identity. In S. Stürmer & M. Snyder (Eds.), *The psychology of prosocial behavior: Group processes, intergroup relations, and helping* (pp. 191–207). Oxford, UK: Wiley-Blackwell.

Dovidio, J. F., Hewstone, M., Glick, P., & Esses, V. M. (Eds.). (2010). *Sage handbook of prejudice, stereotyping, and discrimination.* London, UK: Sage.

Dovidio, J. F., Kawakami, K., & Gaertner, S. L. (2002). Implicit and explicit prejudice and interracial interaction. *Journal of Personality and Social Psychology, 82,* 62–68.

Dovidio, J. F., Kawakami, K., Smoak, N., & Gaertner, S. L. (2008). The nature of contemporary racial prejudice: Insight from implicit and explicit measures of attitudes. In R. E. Petty, R. H. Fazio & P. Briñol (Eds.), *Attitudes: Insights from the new implicit measures* (pp. 165–192). New York, NY: Psychology Press.

Dovidio, J. F., Pagotto, L., & Hebl, M. R. (2011). Implicit attitudes and discrimination against people with physical disabilities. In R. L. Wiener & S. L. Willborn (Eds.), *Disability and aging discrimination: Perspectives in law and psychology* (pp. 157–183). New York, NY: Springer Science + Business Media.

Dovidio, J. F., Piliavin, J. A., Gaertner, S. L., Schroeder, D. A., & Clark, R. D., III. (1991). The arousal: Cost-reward model and the process of intervention: A review of the evidence. In M. S. Clark (Ed.), *Prosocial behavior* (pp. 86–118). Thousand Oaks, CA: Sage.

Dovidio, J. F., Piliavin, J. A., Schroeder, D. A., & Penner, L. (2006). *The social psychology of prosocial behavior.* Mahwah, NJ: Lawrence Erlbaum.

Dow, J. W. (2006). The evolution of religion: Three anthropological approaches. *Method & Theory in the Study of Religion, 18,* 67–91.

Druckman, J. N., & Bolsen, T. (2011). Framing, motivated reasoning, and opinions about emergent technologies. *Journal of Communication, 61,* 659–688.

Duckitt, J. (2001). A dual-process cognitive-motivational theory of ideology and prejudice. In M. P. Zanna (Ed.), *Advances in experimental social psychology* (Vol. 33, pp. 41–113). San Diego, CA: Academic Press.

Duckitt, J., & Mphuthing, T. (2002). Relative deprivation and intergroup attitudes: South Africa before and after the transition. In I. Walker & H. J. Smith (Eds.), *Relative deprivation: Specification, development, and integration* (pp. 69–90). New York, NY: Cambridge University Press.

Duerden, M. D., & Witt, P. A. (2010). The impact of direct and indirect experiences on the development of environmental knowledge, attitudes, and behavior. *Journal of Environmental Psychology, 30,* 379–392.

Duffy, B. (2012). Europe's anti-immigrant voters. *Wall Street Journal—Eastern Edition, 259,* A15–A15.

Duffy, S., & Kitayama, S. (2010). Cultural modes of seeing through cultural modes of being: Cultural influences on visual attention. In E. Balcetis & G. D. Lassiter (Eds.), *Social psychology of visual perception* (pp. 51–75). New York, NY: Psychology Press.

Dunbar, R. (1993). Coevolution of neocortical size, group size and language in humans. *Behavioral and Brain Sciences, 16,* 681–735.

Dunbar, R. (1998). The social brain hypothesis. *Evolutionary Anthropology, 6,* 178–190.

Dunbar, R. (2011). Evolutionary basis of the social brain. In J. Decety & J. T. Cacioppo (Eds.), *Oxford handbook of social neuroscience* (pp. 28–38). Oxford, UK: Oxford University.

Dunbar, R. I. M. (2014). The social brain: Psychological underpinnings and implications for the structure of organizations. *Current Directions in Psychological Science, 23,* 109–114.

Dunham, Y. (2013). Balanced identity in the minimal groups paradigm. *PLoS ONE, 8,* e84205-e84205.

Dunham, Y., Stepanova, E. V., Dotsch, R., & Todorov, A. (2015). The development of race-based perceptual categorization: Skin color dominates early category judgments. *Developmental Science, 18,* 469–483.

Dunn, E., Aknin, L. B., & Norton, M. I. (2014). Prosocial spending and happiness: Using money to benefit others pays off. *Current Directions in Psychological Science, 23,* 41–47.

Dunn, J., Ruedy, N. E., & Schweitzer, M. E. (2012). It hurts both ways: How social comparisons harm affective and cognitive trust. *Organizational Behavior and Human Decision Processes, 117,* 2–14.

Dunning, D. (2003). The relation of self to social perception. In M. R. Leary & J. P. Tangney (Eds.), *Handbook of self and identity* (pp. 421–441). New York, NY: Guilford Press.

Duntley, J. D., & Buss, D. M. (2008). Evolutionary psychology Is a metatheory for psychology. *Psychological Inquiry, 19,* 30–34.

Durik, A. M., & Harackiewicz, J. M. (2007). Different strokes for different folks: How individual interest moderates the effects of situational factors on task interest. *Journal of Educational Psychology, 99,* 597–610.

Durso, G. R. O., Luttrell, A., & Way, B. M. (2015). Over-the-counter relief from pains and pleasures alike: Acetaminophen blunts evaluation sensitivity to both negative and positive stimuli. *Psychological Science, 26,* 750–758.

Dursun, İ., & Tümer Kabadayi, E. (2013). Resistance to persuasion in an anti-consumption context: Biased assimilation of positive product information. *Journal of Consumer Behaviour, 12,* 93–101.

Dutton, D. G., & Aron, A. P. (1974). Some evidence for heightened sexual attraction under conditions of high anxiety. *Journal of Personality and Social Psychology, 30,* 510–517.

Dweck, C. S. (1999). *Self-theories: Their role in motivation, personality, and development.* New York, NY: Psychology Press.

Dzokoto, V., Wallace, D. S., Peters, L., & Bentsi-Enchill, E. (2014). Attention to emotion and non-Western faces: Revisiting the facial feedback hypothesis. *Journal of General Psychology, 141,* 151–168.

Eagly, A. H. (1987). *Sex differences in social behavior: A social-role interpretation.* Hillsdale, NJ: Lawrence Erlbaum Associates.

Eagly, A. H. (2009). The his and hers of prosocial behavior: An examination of the social psychology of gender. *American Psychologist, 64,* 644–658.

Eagly, A. H., & Carli, L. L. (1981). Sex of researchers and sex-typed communications as determinants of sex differences in influenceability: A meta-analysis of social influence studies. *Psychological Bulletin, 90,* 1–20.

Eagly, A. H., & Carli, L. L. (2007). *Through the labyrinth: The truth about how women become leaders.* Boston, MA: Harvard Business School Press.

Eagly, A. H., & Chaiken, S. (1993). *The psychology of attitudes.* Orlando, FL: Harcourt Brace Jovanovich College Publishers.

Eagly, A. H., & Crowley, M. (1986). Gender and helping behavior: A meta-analytic review of the social psychological literature. *Psychological Bulletin, 100,* 283–308.

Eagly, A. H., & Mladinic, A. (1989). Gender stereotypes and attitudes toward women and men. *Personality and Social Psychology Bulletin, 15,* 543–558.

Eagly, A. H., & Sczesny, S. (2009). Stereotypes about women, men, and leaders: Have times changed? In M. Barreto, M. K. Ryan, & M. T. Schmitt (Eds.), *The glass ceiling in the 21st century: Understanding barriers to gender equality* (pp. 21–47). Washington, DC: American Psychological Association.

Eagly, A. H., & Steffen, V. J. (1986). Gender and aggressive behavior: A meta-analytic review of the social psychological literature. *Psychological Bulletin, 100,* 309–330.

Eagly, A. H., & Wood, W. (1999). The origins of sex differences in human behavior: Evolved dispositions versus social roles. *American Psychologist, 54,* 408–423.

Eagly, A. H., & Wood, W. (2012). Social role theory. In P. A. M. Van Lange, A. W. Kruglanski, & E. T. Higgins (Eds.), *Handbook of theories of social psychology* (Vol. 2, pp. 458–476). Thousand Oaks, CA: Sage.

Eagly, A. H., Ashmore, R. D., Makhijani, M. G., & Longo, L. C. (1991). What is beautiful is good, but . . . : A meta-analytic review of research on the physical attractiveness stereotype. *Psychological Bulletin, 110,* 109–128.

Eagly, A. H., Johannesen-Schmidt, M. C., & van Engen, M. L. (2003). Transformational, transactional, and laissez-faire leadership styles: A meta-analysis comparing women and men. *Psychological Bulletin, 129,* 569–591.

Eagly, A. H., Wood, W., & Chaiken, S. (1978). Causal inferences about communicators and their effect on opinion change. *Journal of Personality and Social Psychology, 36,* 424–435.

Easterlin, R. A. (2010). *Happiness, growth, and the life cycle.* New York, NY: Oxford University Press.

Eastwick, P. W., & Finkel, E. J. (2008). Sex differences in mate preferences revisited: Do people know what they initially desire in a romantic partner? *Journal of Personality and Social Psychology, 94,* 245–264.

Eastwick, P. W., Eagly, A. H., Finkel, E. J., & Johnson, S. E. (2011). Implicit and explicit preferences for physical attractiveness in a romantic partner: A double dissociation in predictive validity. *Journal of Personality and Social Psychology, 101,* 993–1011.

Eastwick, P. W., Luchies, L. B., Finkel, E. J., & Hunt, L. L. (2014). The predictive validity of ideal partner preferences: A review and meta-analysis. *Psychological Bulletin, 140,* 623–665.

Eberhardt, J. L., Davies, P. G., Purdie-Vaughns, V. J., & Johnson, S. L. (2006). Looking deathworthy: Perceived stereotypicality of Black defendants predicts capital-sentencing outcomes. *Psychological Science, 17,* 383–386.

Ebster, C., & Neumayr, B. (2008). Applying the door-in-the-face compliance technique to retailing. *The International Review of Retail, Distribution and Consumer Research, 18,* 121–128.

Effron, D. A., & Knowles, E. D. (2015). Entitativity and intergroup bias: How belonging to a cohesive group allows people to express their prejudices. *Journal of Personality and Social Psychology, 108,* 234–253. [Supplemental]

Egermann, H., Kopiez, R., & Altenmüller, E. (2013). The influence of social normative and informational feedback on musically induced emotions in an online music listening setting. *Psychomusicology: Music, Mind, and Brain, 23,* 21–32. [Supplemental]

Eisenberg, N., & Miller, P. A. (1987). The relation of empathy to prosocial and related behaviors. *Psychological Bulletin, 101,* 91–119.

Ekman, P. (1972). Universals and cultural differences in facial expressions of emotion. In J. Cole (Ed.), *Nebraska symposium on motivation 1971* (Vol. 19, pp. 207–282). Lincoln, NE: University of Nebraska Press.

Ekman, P. (1999). Facial expressions. In T. Dalgleish & M. J. Power (Eds.), *Handbook of cognition and emotion* (pp. 301–320). New York, NY: John Wiley & Sons.

Ekman, P. (2004). Emotional and conversational nonverbal signals. In J. M. Larrazabal & L. A. Perez Miranda (Eds.), *Language, knowledge, and representation* (Vol. XII, pp. 39–50). Netherlands: Kluwer Academic Publishers.

Ekman, P. (2007). *Emotions revealed: Recognizing faces and feelings to improve communication and emotional life.* New York, NY: Henry Holton.

Ekman, P., & Friesen, W. V. (1971). Constants across cultures in the face and emotion. *Journal of Personality and Social Psychology, 17,* 124–129.

Ekman, P., Friesen, W. V., O'Sullivan, M., Chan, A., Diacoyanni-Tarlatzis, I., Heider, K., . . . Tzavaras, A. (1987). Universals and cultural differences in the judgments of facial expressions of emotion. *Journal of Personality and Social Psychology, 53,* 712–717.

Ekman, P., Sorenson, E. R., & Friesen, W. V. (1969). Pan-cultural elements in facial displays of emotion. *Science, 164,* 86–88.

Elfenbein, H. A., & Ambady, N. (2002). On the universality and cultural specificity of emotion recognition: A meta-analysis. *Psychological Bulletin, 128,* 203–235.

Ellemers, N., & Haslam, S. A. (2012). Social identity theory. In P. A. M. Van Lange, A. W. Kruglanski, & E. T. Higgins (Eds.), Handbook of theories of social psychology (Vol. 2, pp. 379–398). Thousand Oaks, CA: Sage.

Ellemers, N., De Gilder, D., & Haslam, S. A. (2004). Motivating individuals and groups at work: A social identity perspective on leadership and group performance. *Academy of Management Review, 29,* 459–478.

Elliot, A. J., & Fryer, J. W. (2008). The goal construct in psychology. In J. Shah & W. Gardner (Eds.), *Handbook of motivation science* (pp. 235–250). New York, NY: Guilford Press.

Elson, M., & Ferguson, C. J. (2014). Does doing media violence research make one aggressive? The ideological rigidity of social-cognitive theories of media violence and a response to Bushman and Huesmann (2013), Krahé (2013), and Warburton (2013). *European Psychologist, 19,* 68–75.

Enos, G. A. (2014). One CEO attacks bait-and-switch marketing. *Behavioral Healthcare, 34,* 16–17.

Ent, M. R., & Baumeister, R. F. (2014). Obedience, self-control, and the voice of culture. *Journal of Social Issues, 70,* 574–586.

Epley, N., & Gilovich, T. (1999). Just going along: Nonconscious priming and conformity to social pressure. *Journal of Experimental Social Psychology, 35,* 578–589.

Epley, N., & Gilovich, T. (2001). Putting adjustment back in the anchoring and adjustment heuristic: Differential processing of self-generated and experimenter-provided anchors. *Psychological Science, 12,* 391–396.

Epley, N., & Huff, C. (1998). Suspicion, affective response, and educational benefit as a result of deception in psychology research. *Personality and Social Psychology Bulletin, 24,* 759–768.

Epley, N., & Waytz, A. (2010). Mind perception. In S. T. Fiske, D. T. Gilbert & G. Lindzey (Eds.), *Handbook of social psychology* (Vol. 1, 5th ed., pp. 498–541). Hoboken, NJ: John Wiley & Sons.

Epley, N., Savitsky, K., & Gilovich, T. (2002). Empathy neglect: Reconciling the spotlight effect and the correspondence bias. *Journal of Personality and Social Psychology, 83,* 300–312.

Erickson, E. H. (1950). *Childhood and society.* New York, NY: W.W. Norton.

Eriksson, L., Garvill, J., & Nordlund, A. M. (2008). Interrupting habitual car use: The importance of car habit strength and moral motivation for personal car use reduction. *Transportation Research Part F: Traffic Psychology and Behaviour, 11,* 10–23.

Eron, L. D. (2001). Seeing is believing: How viewing violence alters attitudes and aggressive behavior. In A. C. Bohart & D. J. Stipek (Eds.), *Constructive & destructive behavior: Implications for family, school, & society* (pp. 49–60). Washington, DC: American Psychological Association.

Esser, J. K. (1998). Alive and well after 25 years: A review of groupthink research. *Organizational Behavior and Human Decision Processes, 73,* 116–141.

Esses, V. M., Dovidio, J. F., Jackson, L. M., & Armstrong, T. L. (2001). The immigration dilemma: The role of perceived group competition, ethnic prejudice, and national identity. *Journal of Social Issues, 57,* 389–412.

Esses, V. M., Jackson, L. M., Dovidio, J. F., & Hodson, G. (2005). Instrumental relations among groups: Group competition, conflict, and prejudice. In J. F. Dovidio, P. Glick, & L. A. Rudman (Eds.), *On the nature of prejudice: Fifty years after Allport* (pp. 227–243). Malden, MA: Blackwell Publishing.

Estow, S., Jamieson, J. P., & Yates, J. R. (2007). Self-monitoring and mimicry of positive and negative social behaviors. *Journal of Research in Personality, 41,* 425–433.

Evans, J. S. B. T. (2010). Intuition and reasoning: A dual-process perspective. *Psychological Inquiry, 21,* 313–326.

Evans, J. S. B. T., & Frankish, K. (2009). *In two minds: Dual processes and beyond.* New York, NY: Oxford University Press.

Evans, J. S. B. T., & Stanovich, K. E. (2013). Dual-process theories of higher cognition: Advancing the debate. *Perspectives on Psychological Science, 8,* 223–241.

Falk, C. F., & Heine, S. J. (2015). What is implicit self-esteem, and does it vary across cultures? *Personality and Social Psychology Review, 19,* 177–198.

Farley, S. D., & Stasson, M. F. (2003). Relative influences of affect and cognition on behavior: Are feelings more related to blood donation intentions? *Experimental Psychology, 50,* 55–62.

Farrelly, D., Lazarus, J., & Roberts, G. (2007). Altruists attract. *Evolutionary Psychology, 5,* 313–329.

Fazio, R. H. (1987). Self-perception theory: A current perspective. In M. P. Zanna, J. M. Olson, & C. P. Herman

(Eds.), *Social influence: The Ontario symposium* (Vol. 5, pp. 129–150). Hillsdale, NJ: Lawrence Erlbaum.

Fazio, R. H. (1995). Attitudes as object-evaluation associations: Determinants, consequences, and correlates of attitude accessibility. In R. E. Petty & J. A. Krosnick (Eds.), *Attitude strength: Antecedents and consequences* (pp. 247–282). Hillsdale, NJ: Lawrence Erlbaum.

Fazio, R. H. (2001). On the automatic activation of associated evaluations: An overview. *Cognition and Emotion, 15,* 115–141.

Fazio, R. H., & Olson, M. A. (2003). Attitudes: Foundations, functions, and consequences. In M. A. Hogg & J. Cooper (Eds.),. 139–160). Thousand Oaks, CA: Sage.

Fazio, R. H., & Zanna, M. P. (1978). On the predictive validity of attitudes: The roles of direct experience and confidence. *Journal of Personality, 46,* 228–243.

Fazio, R. H., Jackson, J. R., Dunton, B. C., & Williams, C. J. (1995). Variability in automatic activation as an unobtrusive measure of racial attitudes: A bona fide pipeline? *Journal of Personality & Social Psychology, 69,* 1013–1027.

Feagin, J. R., & Feagin, C. B. (1986). *Discrimination American style: Institutional racism and sexism.* Malabar, FL: Krieger Publishing Company.

Feeley, T. H., Anker, A. E., & Aloe, A. M. (2012). The door-in-the-face persuasive message strategy: A meta-analysis of the first 35 years. *Communication Monographs, 79,* 316–343.

Feinberg, J. M., & Aiello, J. R. (2006). Social facilitation: A test of competing theories. *Journal of Applied Social Psychology, 36,* 1087–1109.

Feinberg, M., & Willer, R. (2013). The moral roots of environmental attitudes. *Psychological Science, 24,* 56–62.

Feingold, A. (1988). Matching for attractiveness in romantic partners and same-sex friends: A meta-analysis and theoretical critique. *Psychological Bulletin, 104,* 226–235.

Feld, B. C. (2013). Real interrogation: What actually happens when cops question kids. *Law & Society Review, 47,* 1–36.

Ferguson, C. J., & Savage, J. (2012). Have recent studies addressed methodological issues raised by five decades of television violence research? A critical review. *Aggression and Violent Behavior, 17,* 129–139.

Ferrari, J. R. (2001). Procrastination as self-regulation failure of performance: Effects of cognitive load, self-awareness, and time limits on "working best under pressure." *European Journal of Personality, 15,* 391–406.

Ferreira, M. C., Fischer, R., Porto, J. B., Pilati, R., & Milfont, T. L. (2012). Unraveling the mystery of Brazilian Jeitinho: A cultural exploration of social norms. *Personality and Social Psychology Bulletin, 38,* 331–344.

Ferriere, R., & Michod, R. E. (2011). Inclusive fitness in evolution. *Nature, 471,* E6.

Festinger, L. (1954). A theory of social comparison processes. *Human Relations, 7,* 117–140.

Festinger, L. (1957). *A theory of cognitive dissonance.* Stanford, CA: Stanford University Press.

Festinger, L. (1962). *A theory of cognitive dissonance.* Stanford, CA: Stanford University Press.

Festinger, L., & Carlsmith, J. M. (1959). Cognitive consequences of forced compliance. *The Journal of Abnormal and Social Psychology, 58,* 203–210.

Festinger, L., Riecken, H. W., & Schachter, S. (1956). *When prophecy fails: A social and psychological study of a modern group that predicted the destruction of the world.* Minneapolis, MN: University of Minnesota.

Festinger, L., Schachter, S., & Back, K. (1950). *Social pressures in informal groups: A study of human factors in housing.* Oxford, UK: Harper.

Fiedler, F. E. (1978). The contingency model and the dynamics of the leadership process. *Advances in Experimental Social Psychology, 12,* 59–112.

Fiedler, K., & Hütter, M. (2014). The limits of automaticity. In J. W. Sherman, B. Gawronski, Y. Trope, J. W. Sherman, B. Gawronski, & Y. Trope (Eds.), *Dual-process theories of the social mind* (pp. 497–513). New York, NY: Guilford Press.

Fiedler, K., Brinkmann, B., Betsch, T., & Wild, B. (2000). A sampling approach to biases in conditional probability judgments: Beyond base rate neglect and statistical format. *Journal of Experimental Psychology: General, 129,* 399–418.

Figueredo, A. J., Tal, I. R., McNeil, P., & Guillén, A. (2004). Farmers, herders, and fishers: The ecology of revenge. *Evolution and Human Behavior, 25,* 336–353.

Fincham, F. D., Beach, S. R. H., & Davila, J. (2007). Longitudinal relations between forgiveness and conflict resolution in marriage. *Journal of Family Psychology, 21,* 542–545.

Fincher, C. L., Thornhill, R., Murray, D. R., & Schaller, M. (2008). Pathogen prevalence predicts human cross-cultural variability in individualism/collectivism. *Proceedings of the Royal Society B: Biological Sciences, 275,* 1279–1285.

Finkel, E. J., Eastwick, P. W., & Reis, H. T. (2015). Best research practices in psychology: Illustrating epistemological and pragmatic considerations with the case of relationship science. *Journal of Personality and Social Psychology, 108,* 275–297.

Finkel, E. J., Eastwick, P. W., Karney, B. R., Reis, H. T., & Sprecher, S. (2012). Online dating: A critical analysis from the perspective of psychological science. *Psychological Science in the Public Interest, 13,* 3–66.

Finkelstein, M. A. (2012). Individualism/collectivism and organizational citizenship behavior: An integrative framework. *Social Behavior & Personality: An International Journal, 40,* 1633–1643.

Fischer, P., Greitemeyer, T., Pollozek, F., & Frey, D. (2006). The unresponsive bystander: Are bystanders more responsive in dangerous emergencies? *European Journal of Social Psychology, 36,* 267–278.

Fischer, P., Krueger, J. I., Greitemeyer, T., Vogrincic, C., Kastenmüller, A., Frey, D., . . . Kainbacher, M. (2011). The bystander-effect: A meta-analytic review on bystander intervention in dangerous and non-dangerous emergencies. *Psychological Bulletin, 137,* 517–537.

Fischhoff, B. (1975). Hindsight is not equal to foresight: The effect of outcome knowledge on judgment under uncertainty. *Journal of Experimental Psychology: Human Perception and Performance, 1,* 288–299.

Fishbach, A., & Ferguson, M. J. (2007). The goal construct in social psychology. In A. W. Kruglanski & E. T. Higgins (Eds.), *Social psychology: Handbook of basic principles* (2nd ed., pp. 490–515). New York, NY: Guilford Press.

Fishbein, M., & Ajzen, I. (1975). *Belief, intention, and behavior: An introduction to theory and research.* Reading, MA: Addison-Wesley.

Fishbein, M., & Ajzen, I. (2010). *Predicting and changing behavior: The reasoned action approach.* New York, NY: Psychology Press.

Fisher, H. (2006). The drive to love: The neural mechanism for mate selection. In R. J. Sternberg & K. Weis (Eds.), *The new psychology of love* (pp. 87–115). New Haven, CT: Yale University Press.

Fiske, A. P., & Rai, T. S. (2015). *Virtuous violence.* Cambridge, UK: Cambridge University.

Fiske, S. T. (1998). Stereotyping, prejudice, and discrimination. In D. T. Gilbert, S. T. Fiske, & G. Lindzey (Eds.), *The handbook of social psychology* (Vols. 1 & 2, 4th ed., pp. 357–411). New York, NY: McGraw-Hill.

Fiske, S. T., & Neuberg, S. L. (1990). A continuum of impression formation, from category-based to individuating processes: Influences of information and motivation on attention and interpretation. In P. Zanna Mark (Ed.), *Advances in experimental social psychology* (Vol. 23, pp. 1–74). New York, NY: Academic Press.

Fiske, S. T., & Taylor, S. E. (1991). *Social cognition* (2nd ed.). New York, NY: Mcgraw-Hill Book Company.

Fiske, S. T., & Taylor, S. E. (2013). *Social cognition: From brains to culture* (2nd ed.). London: Sage.

Fiske, S. T., Cuddy, A. J. C., & Glick, P. (2003). Emotions up and down: Intergroup emotions result from perceived status and competition. In D. M. Mackie & E. R. Smith (Eds.), *From prejudice to intergroup emotions: Differentiated reactions to social groups* (pp. 247–264). New York, NY: Psychology Press.

Fiske, S. T., Cuddy, A. J. C., & Glick, P. (2007). Universal dimensions of social cognition: Warmth and competence. *Trends in Cognitive Sciences, 11,* 77–83.

Fiske, S. T., Harris, L. T., & Cuddy, A. J. C. (2004). Why ordinary people torture enemy prisoners. *Science, 306,* 1482–1483.

Fiske, S. T., Lin, M., & Neuberg, S. L. (1999). The continuum model: Ten years later. In S. Chaiken & Y. Trope (Eds.), *Dual-process theories in social psychology* (pp. 231–254). New York, NY: Guilford Press.

Fitzgerald, C. J., & Colarelli, S. M. (2009). Altruism and reproductive limitations. *Evolutionary Psychology, 7,* 234–252.

Fleischhauer, M., Strobel, A., & Strobel, A. (2015). Directly and indirectly assessed need for cognition differentially predict spontaneous and reflective information processing behavior. *Journal of Individual Differences, 36,* 101–109. [Supplemental]

Flere, S., & Klanjšek, R. (2009). Cross-cultural insight into the association between religiousness and authoritarianism. *Archiv für Religionspsychologie/ Archive for the Psychology of Religions, 31,* 177–190.

Foa, E. B., & Foa, U. G. (1975). *Resource theory of social exchange.* Morristown, NJ: General Learning Press.

Fointiat, V., Somat, A., & Grosbras, J. -M. (2011). Saying, but not doing: Induced hypocrisy, trivialization, and misattribution. *Social Behavior and Personality, 39,* 465–476.

Folkman, S., & Lazarus, R. S. (1988). Coping as a mediator of emotion. *Journal of Personality and Social Psychology, 54,* 466–475.

Folkman, S., Lazarus, R. S., Gruen, R. J., & DeLongis, A. (1986). Appraisal, coping, health status, and psychological symptoms. *Journal of Personality and Social Psychology, 50,* 571–579.

Ford, C. S., & Beach, F. A. (1951). *Patterns of sexual behavior.* New York, NY: Harper Row.

Ford, M. B., & Collins, N. L. (2013). Self-esteem moderates the effects of daily rejection on health and well-being. *Self and Identity, 12,* 16–38.

Forehand, M. R. (2000). Extending overjustification: The effect of perceived reward-giver intention on response to rewards. *Journal of Applied Psychology, 85,* 919–931.

Forgas, J. P. (2011). Affective influences on self-disclosure: Mood effects on the intimacy and reciprocity of disclosing personal information. *Journal of Personality and Social Psychology, 100,* 449–461.

Forgas, J. P., & Bower, G. H. (1987). Mood effects on person-perception judgments. *Journal of Personality and Social Psychology, 53,* 53–60.

Forrest-Bank, S., Jenson, J. M., & Trecartin, S. (2015). The revised 28-item racial and ethnic microaggressions scale (R28REMS): Examining the factorial structure for Black, Latino/Hispanic, and Asian young adults. *Journal of Social Service Research, 41,* 326–344

Förster, J., & Liberman, N. (2007). Knowledge activation. In A. W. Kruglanski & E. T. Higgins (Eds.), *Social psychology: Handbook of basic principles* (2nd ed., pp. 201–231). New York, NY: Guilford Press.

Forsyth, D. R., & Nye, J. L. (2008). Seeing and being a leader: The perceptual, cognitive, and interpersonal roots of conferred influence. In C. L. Hoyt, G. R. Goethals, & D. R. Forsyth (Eds.), Leadership at the crossroads (Vol. 1, pp. 116–131).

Foster, K. R., Wenseleers, T., & Ratnieks, F. L. W. (2006). Kin selection is the key to altruism. *Trends In Ecology & Evolution, 21,* 57–60.

Fowler, J. W. (1981). *Stages of faith: The psychology of human development and the quest for meaning.* San Francisco, CA: Harper & Row.

Francis, R. C. (2011). *Epigenetics: The ultimate mystery of inheritance.* New York, NY: W.W. Norton.

Frantz, C. M. (2006). I AM being fair: The bias blind spot as a stumbling block to seeing both sides. *Basic and Applied Social Psychology, 28,* 157–167.

Frederick, D. A., & Haselton, M. G. (2007). Why is muscularity sexy? Tests of the fitness indicator hypothesis. *Personality and Social Psychology Bulletin, 33,* 1167–1183.

Frederick, S., & Loewenstein, G. (1999). Hedonic adaptation. In D. Kahneman, E. Diener, & N. Schwarz (Eds.), *Well-being: The foundations of hedonic psychology* (pp. 302–329). New York, NY: Russell Sage Foundation.

Fredrickson, B. L., & Losada, M. F. (2005). Positive affect and the complex dynamics of human flourishing. *American Psychologist, 60,* 678–686.

Fredrickson, B. L., Cohn, M. A., Coffey, K. A., Pek, J., & Finkel, S. M. (2008). Open hearts build lives: Positive emotions, induced through loving-kindness meditation, build consequential personal resources. *Journal of Personality and Social Psychology, 95,* 1045–1062.

Fredrickson, B. L., Grewen, K. M., Coffey, K. A., Algoe, S. B., Firestine, A. M., Arevalo, J. M. G., . . . Cole, S.W. (2013). A functional genomic perspective on human well-being. *PNAS Proceedings of the National Academy of Sciences of the United States of America, 110,* 13684–13689.

Freedman, J. L., & Fraser, S. C. (1966). Compliance without pressure: The foot-in-the-door technique. *Journal of Personality and Social Psychology, 4,* 195–202.

Freeman, J. B., & Ambady, N. (2014). The dynamic interactive model of person construal: Coordinating sensory and social processes. In J. W. Sherman, B. Gawronski, Y. Trope, J. W. Sherman, B. Gawronski, & Y. Trope (Eds.), *Dual-process theories of the social mind* (pp. 235–248). New York, NY: Guilford Press.

Freis, S. D., & Gurung, R. A. R. (2013). A Facebook analysis of helping behavior in online bullying. *Psychology of Popular Media Culture, 2,* 11–19.

French, J. R. P., & Raven, B. (1959). The bases of social power. In D. Cartwright (Ed.), *Studies in social power* (pp. 150–167). Ann Arbor, MI: University of Michigan

Friedlander, L. J., Connolly, J. A., & Craig, W. M. (2013). Extensiveness and persistence of aggressive media exposure as longitudinal risk factors for teen dating violence. *Psychology of Violence, 3,* 310–322.

Friend, R., Rafferty, Y., & Bramel, D. (1990). A puzzling misinterpretation of the Asch "conformity" study. *European Journal of Social Psychology, 20,* 29–44.

Friese, M., Bluemke, M., & Wänke, M. (2007). Predicting voting behavior with implicit attitude measures: The 2002 German parliamentary election. *Experimental Psychology, 54,* 247–255.

Frieze, I. H., Olson, J. E., & Russell, J. (1991). Attractiveness and income for men and women in management. *Journal of Applied Social Psychology, 21,* 1039–1057.

Fu, J. H. -y., Morris, M. W., Lee, S. -1., Chao, M., Chiu, C. -y., & Hong, Y. -y. (2007). Epistemic motives and cultural conformity: Need for closure, culture, and context as determinants of conflict judgments. *Journal of Personality and Social Psychology, 92,* 191–207.

Fuglestad, P. T., & Snyder, M. (2010). Status and the motivational foundations of self-monitoring. *Social and Personality Psychology Compass, 4,* 1031–1041.

Fujita, K., & Carnevale, J. J. (2012). Transcending temptation through abstraction: The role of construal level in self-control. *Current Directions in Psychological Science, 21,* 248–252.

Fukushima, M., Sharp, S. F., & Kobayashi, E. (2009). Bond to society, collectivism, and conformity: A comparative study of Japanese and American college students. *Deviant Behavior, 30,* 434–466.

Fuller, R. A., Irvine, K. N., Devine-Wright, P., Warren, P. H., & Gaston, K. J. (2007). Psychological benefits of greenspace increase with biodiversity. *Biology Letters, 3,* 390–394.

Fulmer, C. A., Gelfand, M. J., Kruglanski, A. W., Kim-Prieto, C., Diener, E., Pierro, A., & Higgins, E. T. (2010). On "feeling right" in cultural contexts: How person-culture match affects self-esteem and subjective well-being. *Psychological Science, 21,* 1563–1569.

Gabrenya, W. K., Wang, Y. -e., & Latané, B. (1985). Social loafing on an optimizing task: Cross-cultural differences among Chinese and Americans. *Journal of Cross-Cultural Psychology, 16,* 223–242.

Gadbois, S. A., & Sturgeon, R. D. (2011). Academic self-handicapping: Relationships with learning specific and general self-perceptions and academic performance over time. *British Journal of Educational Psychology, 81,* 207–222.

Gaertner, S. L., & Dovidio, J. F. (2000). *Reducing intergroup bias: The common ingroup identity model.* New York, NY: Psychology Press.

Gaertner, S. L., & Dovidio, J. F. (2009). A common ingroup identity: A categorization-based approach for reducing intergroup bias. In T. D. Nelson (Ed.), *Handbook of prejudice, stereotyping, and discrimination* (pp. 489–505). New York, NY: Psychology Press.

Gaertner, S. L., Dovidio, J. F., & Houlette, M. A. (2010). Social categorization. In J. F. Dovidio, M. Hewstone, P. Glick, & V. M. Esses (Eds.), *SAGE handbook of prejudice, stereotyping, and discrimination* (pp. 526–543). London, UK: Sage.

Gailliot, M. T., & Baumeister, R. F. (2007). The physiology of willpower: Linking blood glucose to self-control. *Personality and Social Psychology Review, 11,* 303–327.

Galen, L. W. (2012). Does religious belief promote prosociality? A critical examination. *Psychological Bulletin, 138,* 876–906.

Galinsky, A. D., Magee, J. C., Gruenfeld, D. H., Whitson, J. A., & Liljenquist, K. A. (2008). Power reduces the press of the situation: Implications for creativity, conformity, and dissonance. *Journal of Personality and Social Psychology, 95,* 1450–1466.

Gallup, G. G., Jr., & Frederick, D. A. (2010). The science of sex appeal: An evolutionary perspective. *Review of General Psychology, 14,* 240–250.

Gamble, C., Gowlett, J., & Dunbar, R. (2014). *Thinking big: How the evolution of social life shaped the human mind.* London, UK: Thames & Hudson.

Gangestad, S. W. (1993). Sexual selection and physical attractiveness: Implications for mating dynamics. *Human Nature, 4,* 205–235.

Gangestad, S. W., & Snyder, M. (2000). Self-monitoring: Appraisal and reappraisal. *Psychological Bulletin, 126,* 530–555.

Gangestad, S. W., & Thornhill, R. (1997). Human sexual selection and developmental stability. In J. A. Simpson, & D. T. Kenrick (Eds.), *Evolutionary social psychology* (pp. 169–196). Hillsdale, NJ: Lawrence Erlbaum.

Gangestad, S. W., Haselton, M. G., & Buss, D. M. (2006). Evolutionary foundations of cultural variation: Evoked culture and mate preferences. *Psychological Inquiry, 17,* 75–95.

Ganis, G., Kosslyn, S. M., Stose, S., Thompson, W. L., & Yurgelun-Todd, D. A. (2003). Neural correlates of different types of deception: An fMRI investigation. *Cerebral Cortex, 13,* 830–836.

Gannon, T. A., Keown, K., & Polaschek, D. L. L. (2007). Increasing honest responding on cognitive distortions in child molesters: The bogus pipeline revisited. *Sexual Abuse: Journal of Research and Treatment, 19,* 5–22.

Ganzach, Y., Ellis, S., & Gotlibovski, C. (2013). On intelligence education and religious beliefs. *Intelligence, 41,* 121–128.

Garcia, J. R., Reiber, C., Massey, S. G., & Merriwether, A. M. (2012). Sexual hookup culture: A review. *Review of General Psychology, 16,* 161–176.

Garcia, P. R. J. M., Restubog, S. L. D., Kiewitz, C., Scott, K. L., & Tang, R. L. (2014). Roots run deep: Investigating psychological mechanisms between history of family aggression and abusive supervision. *Journal of Applied Psychology, 99,* 883–897.

Garcia-Marques, T., Mackie, D. M., Claypool, H. M., & Garcia-Marques, L. (2004). Positivity can cue familiarity. *Personality and Social Psychology Bulletin, 30,* 585–593.

Gardikiotis, A. (2011). Minority influence. *Social and Personality Psychology Compass, 5,* 679–693.

Garland, E. L., Fredrickson, B., Kring, A.M., Johnson, D. P., Meyer, P. S., & Penn, D. L. (2010). Upward spirals of positive emotions counter downward spirals of negativity: Insights from the broaden-and-build theory and affective neuroscience on the treatment of emotion dysfunctions and deficits in psychopathology. *Clinical Psychology Review, 30,* 849–864.

Garramone, G. M., Atkin, C. K., Pinkleton, B. E., & Cole, R. T. (1990). Effects of negative political advertising on the political process. *Journal of Broadcasting & Electronic Media, 34,* 299–311.

Gastil, J., Burkhalter, S., & Black, L. W. (2007). Do juries deliberate? A study of deliberation, individual difference, and group member satisfaction at a municipal courthouse. *Small Group Research, 38,* 337–359.

Gawronski, B. (2004). Theory-based bias correction in dispositional inference: The fundamental attribution error is dead, long live the correspondence bias. *European Review of Social Psychology, 15,* 83–217.

Gawronski, B., & Bodenhausen, G. V. (2007). Unraveling the processes underlying evaluation: Attitudes from the perspective of the APE model. *Social Cognition, 25,* 687–717.

Gawronski, B., & Strack, F. (2012). *Cognitive consistency: A fundamental principle in social cognition.* New York, NY: Guilford Press.

Gazzaniga, M. S. (2011). *Who's in charge? Free will and the science of the brain.* New York,NY: HarperCollins.

Gebauer, J. E., Nehrlich, A. D., Sedikides, C., & Neberich, W. (2013). The psychological benefits of income are contingent on individual-level and culture-level religiosity. *Social and Personality Psychology Compass, 4,* 569–578.

Geen, R. (1998). Aggression and antisocial behavior. In D. T. Gilbert, S. T. Fiske, & G. Lindzey (Eds.), *Handbook of social psychology* (4th ed., Vol. 2, pp. 317–356). Boston, MA: McGraw-Hill.

Gelfand, M. J., Chiu, C.-y., & Hong, Y.-y. (2011). *Advances in culture and psychology* (Vol. 1). New York, NY: Oxford University Press.

Gendron, M., Roberson, D., van der Vyver, J. M., & Barrett, L. F. (2014). Perceptions of emotion from facial expressions are not culturally universal: Evidence from a remote culture. *Emotion, 14,* 251–262. [Supplemental]

Gentile, D. A., & Bushman, B. J. (2012). Reassessing media violence effects using a risk and resilience approach to understanding aggression. *Psychology of Popular Media Culture, 1,* 138–151.

George, D. M., Carroll, P., Kersnick, R., & Calderon, K. (1998). Gender-related patterns of helping among friends. *Psychology of Women Quarterly, 22,* 685–704.

Gerstenfeld, P. B., Grant, D. R., & Chiang, C. -P. (2003). Hate online: A content analysis of extremist Internet sites. Analyses of Social Issues and Public Policy (ASAP), 3, 29–44.

Gervais, W. M. (2014). Religious cognition. In V. Saroglou (Ed.), *Religion, personality, and social behavior* (pp. 71–95). New York, NY: Psychology Press.

Gervais, W. M., & Norenzayan, A. (2012). Like a camera in the sky? Thinking about God increases public self-awareness and socially desirable responding. *Journal of Experimental Social Psychology, 48,* 298–302.

Gesselman, A. N., & Webster, G. D. (2012). Inclusive fitness affects both prosocial and antisocial behavior: Target gender and insult domain moderate the link between genetic telatedness and aggression. *Evolutionary Psychology, 10,* 750.

Ghang, W., & Nowak, M. A. (2015). Indirect reciprocity with optional interactions. *Journal of Theoretical Biology, 365,* 1–11.

Giancola, P. R., Duke, A. A., & Ritz, K. Z. (2011). Alcohol, violence, and the alcohol myopia model: Preliminary findings and implications for prevention. *Addictive Behaviors, 36,* 1019–1022.

Giancola, P. R., Godlaski, A. J., & Roth, R. M. (2012). Identifying component-processes of executive functioning that serve as risk factors for the alcohol-aggression relation. *Psychology of Addictive Behaviors, 26,* 201–211.

Giancola, P. R., Levinson, C. A., Corman, M. D., Godlaski, A. J., Morris, D. H., Phillips, J. P., & Holt, J. C. D. (2009). Men and women, alcohol and aggression. *Experimental and Clinical Psychopharmacology, 17,* 154–164.

Gibbons, F. X., Gerrard, M., Cleveland, M. J., Wills, T. A., & Brody, G. (2004). Perceived discrimination and substance use in African American parents and their children: A panel study. *Journal of Personality and Social Psychology, 86,* 517–529.

Gibson, J. T., & Haritos-Fatouros, M. (1986, November). The education of a torturer. *Psychology Today,* 50–58.

Gidycz, C. A., Orchowski, L. M., & Berkowitz, A. D. (2011). Preventing sexual aggression among college men: An evaluation of a social norms and bystander intervention program. *Violence Against Women, 17,* 720–742.

Giesbrecht, N. (1995). Parenting style and adolescent religious commitment. *Journal of Psychology and Christianity, 14,* 228–238.

Gifford, A., Jr. (2013). Sociality, trust, kinship and cultural evolution. *The Journal of Socio-Economics, 47,* 218–227.

Gifford, R. (2011). The dragons of inaction: Psychological barriers that limit climate change mitigation and adaptation. *American Psychologist, 66,* 290–302.

Gifford, R. (2013). Dragons, mules, and honeybees: Barriers, carriers, and unwitting enablers of climate change action. *Bulletin of the Atomic Scientists, 69,* 41–48.

Gilbert, D. T. (1991). How mental systems believe. *American Psychologist, 46,* 107–119.

Gilbert, D. T. (1998). Ordinary personology. In D. T. Gilbert, S. T. Fiske, & G. Lindzey (Eds.), *The handbook of social psychology* (Vols. 1 & 2, 4th ed., pp. 89–150). New York, NY: McGraw-Hill.

Gilbert, D. T. (2006). *Stumbling on happiness.* New York, NY: Alfred A. Knopf.

Gilbert, D. T., & Malone, P. S. (1995). The correspondence bias. *Psychological Bulletin, 117,* 21–38.

Gilbert, D. T., Lieberman, M. D., Morewedge, C. K., & Wilson, T. D. (2004). The peculiar longevity of things not so bad. *Psychological Science, 15,* 14–19.

Gilbert, D. T., Pinel, E. C., Wilson, T. D., Blumberg, S. J., & Wheatley, T. P. (1998). Immune neglect: A source of durability bias in affective forecasting. *Journal of Personality and Social Psychology, 75,* 617–638.

Gilbert, D. T., Tafarodi, R. W., & Malone, P. S. (1993). You can't not believe everything you read. *Journal of Personality and Social Psychology, 65,* 221–233.

Gilbert, S. J. (1981). Another look at the Milgram obedience studies: The role of the gradated series of shocks. *Personality and Social Psychology Bulletin, 7,* 690–695.

Gilbey, A., & Hill, S. (2012). Confirmation bias in general aviation lost procedures. *Applied Cognitive Psychology, 26,* 785–795.

Giles, H., Noels, K. A., Williams, A., Ota, H., Lim, T. -S., Sik Hung, N. G., . . . Somera, L. (2003). Intergenerational communication across cultures: Young people's perceptions of conversations with family elders, non-family elders and same-age peers. *Journal of Cross-Cultural Gerontology, 18,* 1–32.

Gilovich, T. (1991). *How we know what isn't so: The fallibility of human reason in everyday life.* New York, NY: Free Press.

Gilovich, T. D., & Griffin, D. W. (2010). Judgment and decision making. In S. T. Fiske, D. T. Gilbert & G. Lindzey (Eds.), *Handbook of social psychology* (Vol. 1, 5th ed., pp. 542–588). Hoboken, NJ: John Wiley & Sons.

Gilovich, T., & Savitsky, K. (1999). The spotlight effect and the illision of transparency: Egocentric assessments of how we are seen by others. *Current Directions in Psychological Science, 8,* 165–168.

Gilovich, T., Medvec, V. H., & Savitsky, K. (2000). The spotlight effect in social judgment: An egocentric bias in estimates of the salience of one's own actions and appearance. *Journal of Personality and Social Psychology, 78,* 211–222.

Gilovich, T., Savitsky, K., & Medvec, V. H. (1998). The illusion of transparency: Biased assessments of others' ability to read one's emotional states. *Journal of Personality and Social Psychology, 75,* 332–346.

Gilovich, T., Vallone, R., & Tversky, A. (1985). The hot hand in basketball: On the misperception of random sequences. *Cognitive Psychology, 17,* 295–314.

Gioia, D. A., & Sims, H. P. (1985). Self-serving bias and actor/observer differences in organizations: An empirical analysis. *Journal of Applied Social Psychology, 15,* 547–563.

Gladwin, T. E., & Figner, B. (2015). "Hot" cognition and dual systems: Introduction, criticisms, and ways forward. In E. A. Wilhelms, V. F. Reyna, E. A. Wilhelms, & V. F. Reyna (Eds.), *Neuroeconomics, judgment, and decision making* (pp. 157–180). New York, NY: Psychology Press.

Glasman, L. R., & Albarracín, D. (2006). Forming attitudes that predict future behavior: A meta-analysis of the attitude-behavior relation. *Psychological Bulletin, 132,* 778–822.

Glasø, L., Nielsen, M. B., & Einarsen, S. (2009). Interpersonal problems among perpetrators and targets of workplace bullying. *Journal of Applied Social Psychology, 39,* 1316–1333.

Glenn, N. D. (1980). Values, attitudes, and beliefs. In O. G. Brim Jr. & J. Kagan (Eds.), *Constancy and change in human development* (pp. 596–640). Cambridge, MA: Harvard University Press.

Glick, P., & Fiske, S. T. (1996). The ambivalent sexism inventory: Differentiating hostile and benevolent sexism. *Journal of Personality and Social Psychology, 70,* 491–512.

Glick, P., & Fiske, S. T. (2011). Ambivalent sexism revisited. *Psychology of Women Quarterly, 35,* 530–535.

Glick, P., Lameiras, M., Fiske, S. T., Eckes, T., Masser, B., Volpato, C., . . . Wells, R. (2004). Bad but Bold: Ambivalent attitudes toward men predict gender inequality in 16 nations. *Journal of Personality and Social Psychology, 86,* 713–728.

Glomb, T. M., Bhave, D. P., Miner, A. G., & Wall, M. (2011). Doing good, feeling good: Examining the role of organizational citizenship behaviors in changing mood. *Personnel Psychology, 64,* 191–223.

Göckeritz, S., Schultz, P. W., Rendón, T., Cialdini, R. B., Goldstein, N. J., & Griskevicius, V. (2010). Descriptive normative beliefs and conservation behavior: The moderating roles of personal involvement and injunctive normative beliefs. *European Journal of Social Psychology, 40,* 514–523.

Goel, S., Mason, W., & Watts, D. J. (2010). Real and perceived attitude agreement in social networks. *Journal of Personality and Social Psychology, 99,* 611–621.

Goethals, G. R. (1986). Social comparison theory: Psychology from the lost and found. *Personality and Social Psychology Bulletin, 12,* 261–278.

Goetz, A. T., & Shackelford, T. K. (2009). Sexual conflict in humans: Evolutionary consequences of asymmetric parental investment and paternity uncertainty. *Animal Biology, 59,* 449–456.

Goffman, E. (1963). *Stigma: Notes on the management of spoiled identity.* Englewood Cliffs, NJ: Prentice-Hall.

Goldstein, D. G., & Gigerenzer, G. (2011). Reasoning the fast and frugal way: Models of bounded rationality. In G. Gigerenzer, R. Hertwig, & T. Pachur (Eds.), *Heuristics: The foundations of adaptive behavior* (pp. 33–54). New York, NY: Oxford University Press.

Goldstein, N. J., Cialdini, R. B., & Griskevicius, V. (2008). A room with a viewpoint: Using social norms to motivate environmental conservation in hotels. *Journal of Consumer Research, 35,* 472–482.

Gonzalez, R., & Griffin, D. (2004). Measuring individuals in a social environment: Conceptualizing dyadic and group interaction. In C. Sansone, C. C. Morf, & A. T. Panter (Eds.), *The Sage handbook of methods in social psychology* (pp. 313–334). Thousand Oaks, CA: Sage.

Gorchoff, S. M., John, O. P., & Helson, R. (2008). Contextualizing change in marital satisfaction during middle age: An 18-year longitudinal study. *Psychological Science, 19,* 1194–1200.

Gordon, E. A., Johnson, K., Heimberg, R. G., Montesi, J. L., & Fauber, R. L. (2013). Bi-directional positive illusions in romantic relationships: Possibilities and pitfalls for the socially anxious. *Journal of Social and Clinical Psychology, 32,* 200–224.

Gore, J. S., Kiefner, A. E., & Combs, K. M. (2012). Personality traits that predict academic citizenship behavior. *Journal of Applied Social Psychology, 42,* 2433–2456.

Gosling, S. D., Augustine, A. A., Vazire, S., Holtzman, N., & Gaddis, S. (2011). Manifestations of personality in online social networks: Self-reported Facebook-related behaviors and observable profile information. *Cyberpsychology, Behavior, and Social Networking, 14,* 483–488.

Gottfredson, M. R. (2011). In pursuit of a general theory of crime. In F. T. Cullen, C. L. Jonson, A. J. Myer, & F. Adler (Eds.), *The origins of American criminology* (Vol. 16, pp. 333–346). Piscataway, NJ: Transaction Publishers.

Gottfredson, M. R., & Hirschi, T. (1990). *A general theory of crime:* Stanford University Press**:** Stanford, CA

Gottfried, M. (2008, July 18). Man gets 12 years for hallway rape captured on video, *St. Paul Pioneer Press.*

Gottman, J. M., & Levenson, R. W. (1999). Rebound from marital conflict and divorce prediction. *Family Process, 38,* 293–301.

Gottman, J. M., & Levenson, R. W. (2000). The timing of divorce: Predicting when a couple will divorce over a 14-year period. *Journal of Marriage & the Family, 62,* 737–745.

Gouldner, A. W. (1960). The norm of reciprocity: A preliminary statement. *American Sociological Review, 25,* 161–178.

Gouveia, V. V., Milfont, T. L., Martinez, M. d. C., & Paterna, C. (2011). Individualism-collectivism as predictors of prejudice toward Gypsies in Spain. *Interamerican Journal of Psychology, 45,* 223–234.

Graham, J. M., & Conoley, C. W. (2006). The role of marital attributions in the relationship between life stressors and marital quality. *Personal Relationships, 13,* 231–241.

Graña, J. L., Cruzado, J. A., Andreu, J. M., Muñoz-Rivas, M. J., Pena, M. E., & Brain, P. F. (2004). Effects of viewing videos of bullfights on Spanish children. *Aggressive Behavior, 30,* 16–28.

Granhag, P. A., & Hartwig, M. (2008). A new theoretical perspective on deception detection: On the psychology of instrumental mind-reading. *Psychology, Crime & Law, 14,* 189–200.

Granqvist, P. (2006). Religion as a by-product of evolved psychology: The case of attachment and implications for brain and religion research. In P. McNamara & P. McNamara (Eds.), *Where God and science meet: How brain and evolutionary studies alter our understanding of religion: The neurology of religious experience* (Vol. 2, pp. 105–150). Westport, CT: Praeger Publishers/Greenwood Publishing Group.

Granqvist, P. (2014). Religion and cognitive, emotional, and social development. In V. Saroglou (Ed.), *Religion, personality, and social behavior* (pp. 283–312). New York, NY: Psychology Press.

Granqvist, P., Mikulincer, M., & Shaver, P. R. (2010). Religion as attachment: Normative processes and individual differences. *Personality and Social Psychology Review, 14,* 49–59.

Graziano, W. G., Habashi, M. M., Sheese, B. E., & Tobin, R. M. (2007). Agreeableness, empathy, and helping: A person X situation perspective. *Journal of Personality and Social Psychology, 93,* 583–599.

Green, F. P., & Schneider, F. W. (1974). Age differences in the behavior of boys on three measures of altruism. *Child Development, 45,* 248–251.

Greenwald, A. G. (1968). Cognitive learning, cognitive response to persuasion, and attitude change. In A. G. Greenwald, T. C. Brock & T. Ostrom (Eds.), *Psychological foundation of attitudes* (pp. 148–170). New York: Academic Press.

Greenwald, A. G., & Banaji, M. R. (1995). Implicit social cognition: Attitudes, self-esteem, and stereotypes. *Psychological Review, 102,* 4–27.

Greenwald, A. G., Banaji, M. R., & Nosek, B. A. (2015). Statistically small effects of the implicit association test can have societally large effects. *Journal of Personality and Social Psychology, 108,* 553–561.

Greenwald, A. G., McGhee, D. E., & Schwartz, J. L. K. (1998). Implicit association test. *Measuring individual differences in implicit cognition: The implicit association test, 74,* 1464–1480.

Greenwald, A. G., Poehlman, T. A., Uhlmann, E. L., & Banaji, M. R. (2009). Understanding and using the implicit association test: III. Meta-analysis of predictive validity. *Journal of Personality and Social Psychology, 97,* 17–41.

Gregory, A. M., Light-Häusermann, J. H., Rijsdijk, F., & Eley, T. C. (2009). Behavioral genetic analyses of prosocial behavior in adolescents. *Developmental Science, 12,* 165–174.

Greitemeyer, T. (2005). Receptivity to sexual offers as a function of sex, socioeconomic status, physical attractiveness, and intimacy of the offer. *Personal Relationships, 12,* 373–386.

Greitemeyer, T., & Osswald, S. (2010). Effects of prosocial video games on prosocial behavior. *Journal of Personality and Social Psychology, 98,* 211–221.

Greitemeyer, T., Fischer, P., Frey, D., & Schulz-Hardt, S. (2009). Biased assimilation: The role of source position. *European Journal of Social Psychology, 39,* 22–39.

Grimm, S. D., & Church, A. T. (1999). A cross-cultural study of response biases in personality measures. *Journal of Research in Personality, 33,* 415–441.

Griskevicius, V., Goldstein, N. J., Mortensen, C. R., Cialdini, R. B., & Kenrick, D. T. (2006). Going along versus going alone: When fundamental motives facilitate strategic (non)conformity. *Journal of Personality and Social Psychology, 91,* 281–294.

Grossman, D. (1996). *On killing: The psychological cost of learning to kill in war and society.* New York, NY: Bay Back Books.

Grossman, D., & DeGaetano, G. (1999). *Stop teaching our kids to kill: A call to action.* New York, NY: Random House.

Grossman, R. P., & Till, B. D. (1998). The persistence of classically conditioned brand attitudes. *Journal of Advertising, 27,* 23–31.

Grossmann, T. (2015). The development of social brain functions in infancy. *Psychological Bulletin.*

Guadagno, R. E., & Cialdini, R. B. (2007). Gender differences in impression management in organizations: A qualitative review. *Sex Roles, 56,* 483–494.

Guadagno, R. E., & Cialdini, R. B. (2010). Preference for consistency and social influence: A review of current research findings. *Social Influence, 5,* 152–163.

Guadagno, R. E., & Sagarin, B. J. (2010). Sex differences in jealousy: An evolutionary perspective on online infidelity. *Journal of Applied Social Psychology, 40,* 2636–2655.

Gudjonsson, G. H., & Pearse, J. (2011). Suspect interviews and false confessions. *Current Directions in Psychological Science, 20,* 33–37.

Guéguen, N., & Pascual, A. (2014). Low-ball and compliance: Commitment even if the request is a deviant one. *Social Influence, 9,* 162–171.

Guéguen, N., Pascual, A., & Dagot, L. (2002). Low-ball and compliance to a request: An application in a field setting. *Psychological Reports, 91,* 81–84.

Guenther, C. L., & Alicke, M. D. (2010). Deconstructing the better-than-average effect. *Journal of Personality and Social Psychology, 99,* 755–770.

Guerin, B. (1986). Mere presence effects in humans: A review. *Journal of Experimental Social Psychology, 22,* 38–77.

Guerin, B. (1994). What do people think about the risks of driving? Implications for traffic safety interventions. *Journal of Applied Social Psychology, 24,* 994–1021.

Guinote, A., Brown, M., & Fiske, S. T. (2006). Minority status decreases sense of control and increases interpretive processing. Social Cognition, 24, 169–186.

Gunnell, J. J., & Ceci, S. J. (2010). When emotionality trumps reason: A study of individual processing style and juror bias. *Behavioral Sciences & the Law, 28,* 850–877.

Guo, Q., Johnson, C. A., Unger, J. B., Lee, L., Xie, B., Chou, C. -P., . . . Pentz, M. (2007). Utility of the theory of reasoned action and theory of planned behavior for predicting Chinese adolescent smoking. *Addictive Behaviors, 32,* 1066–1081.

Gupta, U., & Singh, P. (1982). An exploratory study of love and liking and type of marriages. *Indian Journal of Applied Psychology, 19,* 92–97.

Gurr, T. R. (1970). *Why men rebel.* Princeton, NJ: Princeton University.

Gustavsson, L., Johnsson, J. I., & Uller, T. (2008). Mixed support for sexual selection theories of mate preferences in the Swedish population. *Evolutionary Psychology, 6,* 575–585.

Guthrie, S. E. (2007). Anthropological theories of religion. In M. Martin (Ed.), *The Cambridge companion to atheism* (pp. 283–299). New York, NY: Cambridge University Press.

Haas, B. W., Brook, M., Remillard, L., Ishak, A., Anderson, I. W., & Filkowski, M. M. (2015). I know how you feel: The warm-altruistic personality profile and the empathic brain. *PLoS ONE, 10,* e0120639-e0120639.

Hackney, C. H., & Sanders, G. S. (2003). Religiosity and mental health: A meta-analysis of recent studies. *Journal for the Scientific Study of Religion, 42,* 43–55.

Hafer, C. L., Reynolds, K. L., & Obertynski, M. A. (1996). Message comprehensibility and persuasion: Effects of complex language in counterattitudinal appeals to laypeople. *Social Cognition, 14,* 317–337.

Hahn, U., & Harris, A. J. L. (2014). What Does It Mean to be Biased: Motivated Reasoning and Rationality. *Psychology of Learning & Motivation,* 41–102.

Haidt, J., & Keltner, D. (1999). Culture and facial expression: Open-ended methods find more expressions and a gradient of recognition. *Cognition and Emotion, 13,* 225–266.

Haidt, J., & Kesebir, S. (2010). Morality. In S. T. Fiske, D. T. Gilbert, & G. Lindzey (Eds.), *Handbook of social psychology* (Vol. 2, 5th ed., pp. 797–832). Hoboken, NJ: John Wiley & Sons.

Hajjar, L. (2009). Does torture work? A sociolegal assessment of the practice in historical and global perspective. *Annual Review of Law and Social Science, 5,* 311–345.

Hald, G. M., Malamuth, N. M., & Yuen, C. (2010). Pornography and attitudes supporting violence against women: Revisiting the relationship in nonexperimental studies. *Aggressive Behavior, 36,* 14–20.

Hall, J. A., Coats, E. J., & LeBeau, L. S. (2005). Nonverbal behavior and the vertical dimension of social relations: A meta-analysis. *Psychological Bulletin, 131,* 898–924.

Hall, J. A., Park, N., Song, H., & Cody, M. J. (2010). Strategic misrepresentation in online dating: The effects of gender, self-monitoring, and personality traits. *Journal of Social and Personal Relationships, 27,* 117–135.

Hamermesh, D. S., & Parker, A. (2005). Beauty in the classroom: Instructors' pulchritude and putative pedagogical productivity. *Economics of Education Review, 24,* 369–376.

Hamilton, D. L., & Gifford, R. K. (1976). Illusory correlation in interpersonal perception: A cognitive basis of stereotypic judgments. *Journal of Experimental Social Psychology, 12,* 392–407.

Hamilton, W. D. (1964). The genetic evolution of social behavior. I. *Journal of Theoretical Biology, 7,* 1–16.

Hancock, J. T., & Toma, C. L. (2009). Putting your best face forward: The accuracy of online dating photographs. *Journal of Communication, 59,* 367–386.

Haney, C., & Zimbardo, P. (1998). The past and future of U.S. prison policy: Twenty-five years after the Stanford Prison Experiment. *American Psychologist, 53,* 709–727.

Haney, C., Banks, C., & Zimbardo, P. (1973). Interpersonal dynamics in a simulated prison. *International Journal of Criminology & Penology, 1,* 69–97.

Hansen, C. H., & Hansen, R. D. (1988). Finding the face in the crowd: An anger superiority effect. *Journal of Personality and Social Psychology, 54,* 917–924.

Hansen, D. E., Vandenberg, B., & Patterson, M. L. (1995). The effects of religious orientation on spontaneous and nonspontaneous helping behaviors. *Personality and Individual Differences, 19,* 101–104.

Hansen, J., & Wänke, M. (2009). Liking what's familiar: The importance of unconscious familiarity in the mere-exposure effect. *Social Cognition, 27,* 161–182.

Harackiewicz, J. M., Durik, A. M., & Barron, K. E. (2005). Multiple goals, optimal motivation, and the development of interest. In J. P. Forgas, K. D. Williams, & S. M. Laham (Eds.), *Social motivation: Conscious and unconscious processes* (pp. 21–39). New York, NY: Cambridge University Press.

Hardin, E. E., & Larsen, J. T. (2014). Distinct sources of self-discrepancies: Effects of being who you want to be and wanting to be who you are on well-being. *Emotion, 14,* 214–226.

Hardin, G. (1968). The tragedy of the commons. *Science, 162,* 1243–1248.

Hareli, S., Moran-Amir, O., David, S., & Hess, U. (2013). Emotions as signals of normative conduct. *Cognition and Emotion, 27,* 1395–1404.

Haritos-Fatouros, M. (1995). The official torturer: A learning model for obedience to the authority of violence. In R. D. Crelinsten & A. P. Schmid (Eds.), *The politics of pain: Torturers and their masters* (pp. 129–146). Boulder, CO: Westview Press.

Harkins, S. G., & Petty, R. E. (1981). The multiple source effect in persuasion: The effects of distraction. *Personality and Social Psychology Bulletin, 7,* 627–635.

Harmon-Jones, E., & Allen, J. J. B. (2001). The role of affect in the mere exposure effect: Evidence from psychophysiological and individual differences approaches. *Personality and Social Psychology Bulletin, 27,* 889–898.

Harmon-Jones, E., & Mills, J. (1999). *Cognitive dissonance: Progress on a pivotal theory in social psychology.* Washington, DC: American Psychological Association.

Harmon-Jones, E., Harmon-Jones, C., Fearn, M., Sigelman, J. D., & Johnson, P. (2008). Left frontal cortical activation and spreading of alternatives: Tests of the action-based model of dissonance. *Journal of Personality and Social Psychology, 94,* 1–15.

Harmon-Jones, E., Harmon-Jones, C., Serra, R., & Gable, P.A. (2011). The effect of commitment on relative left frontal cortical activity: Tests of the action-based model of dissonance. *Personality & Social Psychology Bulletin, 37,* 395–408.

Harms, E. (1944). The development of religious experience in children. *American Journal of Sociology, 50,* 112–122.

Harris, C. R. (2003). A review of sex differences in sexual jealousy, including self-report data, psychophysiological responses, interpersonal violence, and morbid jealousy. *Personality and Social Psychology Review, 7,* 102–128.

Harris, C. R. (2005). Male and female jealousy, still more similar than different: Reply to Sagarin (2005). *Personality and Social Psychology Review, 9,* 76–86.

Harris, L. T., & Fiske, S. T. (2009). Social neuroscience evidence for dehumanised perception. *European Review of Social Psychology, 20,* 192–231.

Harris, L. T., & Fiske, S. T. (2011). Perceiving humanity or not: A social neuroscience approach to dehumanized perception. In A. Todorov, S. T. Fiske & D. A. Prentice (Eds.), *Social neuroscience: Toward understanding the underpinnings of the social mind* (pp. 123–134). New York, NY: Oxford University Press.

Hartig, T., Mang, M., & Evans, G. W. (1991). Restorative effects of natural environment experiences. *Environment and Behavior, 23,* 3–26.

Hartl, A. C., Laursen, B., & Cillessen, A. H. N. (2015). A survival analysis of adolescent friendship: The downside of dissimilarity. *Psychological Science, 26,* 1304–1315.

Harvey, P. H., Clutton-Brock, T. H., & Mace, G. A. (1980). Brain size and ecology of small mammals and primates. *PNAS, 77,* 4387–4389.

Haselton, M. G., & Buss, D. M. (2000). Error management theory: A new perspective on biases in cross-sex mind reading. *Journal of Personality and Social Psychology, 78,* 81–91.

Haselton, M. G., & Buss, D. M. (2009). Error management theory and the evolution of misbeliefs. *Behavioral and Brain Sciences, 32,* 522–523.

Haslam, N., Loughnan, S., Kashima, Y., & Bain, P. (2008). Attributing and denying humanness to others. *European Review of Social Psychology, 19,* 55–85.

Haslam, S. A. (2004). Psychology in organizations: The social identity approach. Thousand Oaks, CA: Sage.

Haslam, S. A., & Reicher, S. (2007). Beyond the banality of evil: Three dynamics of an interactionist social psychology of tyranny. *Personality and Social Psychology Bulletin, 33,* 615–622.

Haslam, S.A., & Reicher, S. D. (2012). Contesting the "nature" of conformity: What Milgram and Zimbardo's studies really show. *PLoS Biology, 10.*

Hassin, R. R., Bargh, J. A., & Zimerman, S. (2009). Automatic and flexible: The case of nonconscious goal pursuit. *Social Cognition, 27,* 20–36.

Hassin, R. R., Uleman, J. S., & Bargh, J. A. (2005). *The new unconscious.* New York, NY: Oxford University Press.

Hastie, R., & Kameda, T. (2005). The robust beauty of majority rules in group decisions. Psychological Review, 112, 494–508.

Hastorf, A. H., & Cantril, H. (1954). They saw a game; a case study. *The Journal of Abnormal and Social Psychology, 49,* 129–134.

Hastorf, A.H., & Cantril, H. (1954). They saw a game: A case study. *The Journal of Abnormal and Social Psychology, 49,* 129–134.

Hatfield, E., & Rapson, R. L. (1987). Passionate love: New directions in research. In W. H. Jones & D. Perlman (Eds.), *Advances in personal relationships* (Vol. 1, pp. 109–139). London, UK: Jessica Kingsley.

Hatfield, E., & Rapson, R. L. (1993). *Love, sex, and intimacy: Their psychology, biology, and history.* New York, NY: HarperCollins College.

Hatfield, E., & Rapson, R. L. (2012). Equity theory in close relationships. In P. A. M. Van Lange, A. W. Kruglanski, & E. T. Higgins (Eds.), *Handbook of theories of social psychology* (Vol. 2, pp. 200–217). Thousand Oaks, CA: Sage.

Hatfield, E., & Sprecher, S. (1986). Measuring passionate love in intimate relationships. *Journal of Adolescence, 9,* 383–410.

Hatfield, E., & Walster, W. G. (1978). *A new look at love.* Reading, MA: Addison-Wesley.

Hawkley, L. C., Thisted, R. A., Masi, C. M., & Cacioppo, J. T. (2010). Loneliness predicts increased blood pressure: 5-year cross-lagged analyses in middle-aged and older adults. *Psychology and Aging, 25,* 132–141.

Haxby, J. V., Hoffman, E. A., & Gobbini, M. I. (2000). The distributed human neural system for face perception. *Trends in Cognitive Sciences, 4,* 223–233.

Haxby, J. V., Hoffman, E. A., & Gobbini, M. I. (2002). Human neural systems for face recognition and social communication. *Biological Psychiatry, 51,* 59–67.

Hayward, R. D., & Krause, N. (2014). Religion, mental health, and well-being: Social aspects. In V. Saroglou (Ed.), *Religion, personality, and social behavior* (pp. 255–280). New York, NY: Psychology Press.

Hazan, C., & Shaver, P. (1987). Romantic love conceptualized as an attachment process. *Journal of Personality and Social Psychology, 52,* 511–524.

Headey, B. (2013). Set-point theory may now need replacing: Death of a paradigm? In S. A. David, I. Boniwell & A. Conley Ayers (Eds.), *The Oxford handbook of happiness* (pp. 887–900). New York, NY: Oxford University Press.

Healy, J., & Turkewitz, J. (2015a, July 17). Guilty verdict for James Holmes in Aurora attack. *New York Times, 164,* A1–A15.

Healy, J., Turkewitz, J. (2015b, August 8). Theater gunman is spared death in Aurora case. *New York Times, 164,* A1–A3.

Hearold, S. (1986). Synthesis of 1043 effects of television on social behavior. *Public Communication & Behavior, 1,* 66–133.

Heatherton, T. F., Krendl, A. C., Macrae, C. N., & Kelley, W. M. (2007). A social brain sciences approach to understanding self. In C. Sedikides & S. J. Spencer (Eds.), *The self* (pp. 3–20). New York, NY: Psychology Press.

Heberlein, T. A. (2012). *Navigating environmental attitudes.* Oxford, UK: Oxford University Press.

Hebl, M., Law, C. L., & King, E. (2010). Heterosexism. In J. F. Dovidio, M. Hewstone, P. Glick, & V. M. Esses (Eds.), *Sage handbook of prejudice, stereotyping, and discrimination* (pp. 345–360). London, UK: Sage.

Hecht, L. K., & Latzman, R. D. (2015). Revealing the nuanced associations between facets of trait impulsivity and reactive and proactive aggression. *Personality and Individual Differences, 83,* 192–197.

Hehman, E., Leitner, J. B., Deegan, M. P., & Gaertner, S. L. (2013). Facial structure is indicative of explicit support for prejudicial beliefs. *Psychological Science, 24,* 289–296.

Heider, F. (1958). *The psychology of interpersonal relations.* Hoboken, NJ: John Wiley & Sons.

Heine, S. J. (2010a). Cultural psychology. In S. T. Fiske, D. T. Gilbert, & G. Lindzey (Eds.), *Handbook of social psychology* (Vol. 2, 5th ed., pp. 1423–1464). Hoboken, NJ: John Wiley & Sons.

Heine, S. J. (2010b). Cultural psychology. In R. F. Baumeister & E. J. Finkel (Eds.), *Advanced social psychology: The state of the science* (pp. 655–696). New York, NY: Oxford University Press.

Heine, S. J., & Lehman, D. R. (1997). Culture, dissonance, and self-affirmation. *Personality and Social Psychology Bulletin, 23,* 389–400.

Heine, S. J., Lehman, D. R., Markus, H. R., & Kitayama, S. (1999). Is there a universal need for positive self-regard? *Psychological Review, 106,* 766–794.

Heine, S. J., Lehman, D. R., Peng, K., & Greenholtz, J. (2002). What's wrong with cross-cultural comparisons of subjective Likert scales?: The reference-group effect. *Journal of Personality and Social Psychology, 82,* 903–918.

Heintzelman, S. J., Trent, J., & King, L. A. (2015). Revisiting desirable response bias in well-being reports. *The Journal of Positive Psychology, 10,* 167–178.

Heiser, M., Iacoboni, M., Maeda, F., Marcus, J., & Mazziotta, J. C. (2003). The essential role of Broca's area in imitation. *European Journal of Neuroscience, 17,* 1123–1128.

Heitland, K., & Bohner, G. (2010). Reducing prejudice via cognitive dissonance: Individual differences in preference for consistency moderate the effects of counter-attitudinal advocacy. *Social Influence, 5,* 164–181.

Helmes, E., Holden, R. R., & Ziegler, M. (2015). Response bias, malingering, and impression management. In G. J. Boyle, D. H. Saklofske, G. Matthews, G. J. Boyle, D. H. Saklofske & G. Matthews (Eds.), *Measures of personality and social psychological constructs* (pp. 16–43). San Diego, CA: Elsevier Academic Press.

Henderlong, J., & Lepper, M. R. (2002). The effects of praise on children's intrinsic motivation: A review and synthesis. *Psychological Bulletin, 128,* 774–795.

Henderson, M. D., & Burgoon, E. M. (2014). Why the door-in-the-face technique can sometimes backfire: A construal-level account. *Social Psychological and Personality Science, 5,* 475–483.

Hendrick, C., & Hendrick, S. S. (2006). Styles of romantic love. In R. J. Sternberg & K. Weis (Eds.), *The new psychology of love* (pp. 149–170). New Haven, CT: Yale University Press.

Hennecke, M., & Freund, A. M. (2010). Staying on and getting back on the wagon: Age-related improvement in self-regulation during a low-calorie diet. *Psychology and Aging, 25,* 876–885.

Henningsen, D. D., & Henningsen, M. L. M. (2010). Testing error management theory: Exploring the commitment skepticism bias and the sexual overperception bias. *Human Communication Research, 36,* 618–634.

Henningsen, D. D., & Henningsen, M. L. M. (2013). Generating ideas about the uses of brainstorming: Reconsidering the losses and gains of brainstorming groups relative to nominal groups. Southern Communication Journal, 78, 42–55.

Henningsen, D. D., Henningsen, M. L. M., & Valde, K. S. (2006). Gender differences in perceptions of women's sexual interest during cross-sex interactions: An application and extension of cognitive valence theory. *Sex Roles, 54,* 821–829.

Henningsen, D. D., Henningsen, M. L. M., Eden, J., & Cruz, M. G. (2006). Examining the symptoms of groupthink and retrospective sensemaking. Small Group Research, 37, 36–64.

Henrich, J., Heine, S. J., & Norenzayan, A. (2010). Beyond WEIRD: Towards a broad-based behavioral science. *Behavioral and Brain Sciences, 33,* 111–135.

Henrich, J., Heine, S. J., & Norenzayan, A. (2010). The weirdest people in the world? *Behavioral and Brain Sciences, 33,* 61–83.

Henry, D. B., Kobus, K., & Schoeny, M. E. (2011). Accuracy and bias in adolescents' perceptions of friends' substance use. *Psychology of Addictive Behaviors, 25,* 80–89.

Henry, P. J. (2009). Low-status compensation: A theory for understanding the role of status in cultures of honor. *Journal of Personality and Social Psychology, 97,* 451–466.

Hepach, R., Vaish, A., & Tomasello, M. (2012). Young children are intrinsically motivated to see others helped. *Psychological Science, 23.*

Hepper, E. G., Gramzow, R. H., & Sedikides, C. (2010). Individual differences in self-enhancement and self-protection strategies: An integrative analysis. *Journal of Personality, 78,* 781–814.

Herdt, G. (2006). *The Sambia: Ritual, sexuality, and change in Papua New Guinea.* Belmont, CA: Thomson Wadsworth.

Herek, G. M. (2004). Beyond "homophobia": Thinking about sexual prejudice and stigma in the twenty-first century. *Sexuality Research & Social Policy: A Journal of the NSRC, 1,* 6–24.

Herek, G. M. (2009). Sexual prejudice. In T. D. Nelson (Ed.), *Handbook of prejudice, stereotyping, and discrimination* (pp. 441–467). New York, NY: Psychology Press.

Hergenhahn, B. R., & Henley, T. B. (2014). *An introduction to the history of psychology* (7th ed.). Belmont, CA: Wadsworth/Cengage.

Hergovich, A., Schott, R., & Burger, C. (2010). Biased evaluation of abstracts depending on topic and conclusion: Further evidence of a confirmation bias within scientific psychology. *Current Psychology: A Journal for Diverse Perspectives on Diverse Psychological Issues, 29,* 188–209.

Hersh, S. M. (2004a, May). Chain of Command. *New Yorker, 80,* 38–43.

Hersh, S. M. (2004b, May). Torture at Abu Ghraib. *New Yorker, 80,* 42–47.

Hertwig, R., & Hoffrage, U. (2013). *Simple heuristics in a social world.* New York, NY: Oxford University Press.

Hertwig, R., & Ortmann, A. (2008). Deception in experiments: Revisiting the arguments in its defense. *Ethics & Behavior, 18,* 59–92.

Hess, J. D., & Gerstner, E. (1998). Yes, "Bait and Switch" Really Benefits Consumers. *Marketing Science, 17,* 283–289.

Hess, U. (2009). Facial EMG. In E. Harmon-Jones & J. S. Beer (Eds.), *Methods in social neuroscience* (pp. 70–91). New York, NY: Guilford Press.

Hewstone, M. (1989). *Causal attribution: From cognitive processes to collective beliefs.* Cambridge, MA: Basil Blackwell.

Hewstone, M. (1990). The "ultimate attribution error"? A review of the literature on intergroup causal attribution. *European Journal of Social Psychology, 20,* 311–335.

Hewstone, M., & Jaspars, J. (1987). Covariation and causal attribution: A Logical Model of the intuitive analysis of variance. *Journal of Personality and Social Psychology, 53,* 663–672.

Hicks, J. A., & King, L. A. (2011). Subliminal mere exposure and explicit and implicit positive affective responses. *Cognition and Emotion, 25,* 726–729.

Higgins, E. T. (1989a). Knowledge accessibility and activation: Subjectivity and suffering from unconscious sources. In J. S. Uleman & J. A. Bargh (Eds.), *Unintended thought* (pp. 75–123). New York, NY: Guilford Press.

Higgins, E. T. (1989b). Self-discrepancy theory: What patterns of self-beliefs cause people to suffer? In L. Berkowitz (Ed.), *Advances in experimental social psychology* (Vol. 22., pp. 93–136). San Diego, CA: Academic Press.

Higgins, E. T. (1997). Beyond pleasure and pain. *American Psychologist, 52,* 1280–1300.

Higgins, R. L., & Harris, R. N. (1988). Strategic "alcohol" use: Drinking to self-handicap. *Journal of Social and Clinical Psychology, 6,* 191–202.

Highhouse, S., Beadle, D., Gallo, A., & Miller, L. (1998). Get em while they last! Effects of scarcity information in job advertisements. *Journal of Applied Social Psychology, 28,* 779–795.

Hill, C. A. (1987). Affiliation motivation: People who need people . . . but in different ways. *Journal of Personality and Social Psychology, 52,* 1008–1018.

Hill, C. A. (2009). Affiliation motivation. In M. R. Leary & R. H. Hoyle (Eds.), *Handbook of individual differences in social behavior* (pp. 410–425). New York, NY: Guilford Press.

Hill, S. E., DelPriore, D. J., & Vaughan, P. W. (2011). The cognitive consequences of envy: Attention, memory, and self-regulatory depletion. *Journal of Personality and Social Psychology, 101,* 653–666.

Hinsz, V. B., Matz, D. C., & Patience, R. A. (2001). Does women's hair signal reproductive potential? *Journal of Experimental Social Psychology, 37,* 166–172.

Hinsz, V. B., Stoesser, C. J., & Matz, D. C. (2013). The intermingling of social and evolutionary psychology influences on hair color preferences. *Current Psychology: A Journal for Diverse Perspectives on Diverse Psychological Issues, 32,* 136–149.

Hirsh, J. B., Kang, S. K., & Bodenhausen, G. V. (2012). Personalized persuasion: Tailoring persuasive appeals to recipients' personality traits. *Psychological Science, 23,* 578–581.

Hirth, F. (2010). On the origin and evolution of the tripartite brain. *Brain, Behavior, and Evolution, 76,* 3–10.

Ho, A. K., Sidanius, J., Pratto, F., Levin, S., Thomsen, L., Kteily, N., & Sheehy-Skeffington, J. (2012). Social dominance orientation: Revisiting the structure and function of a variable predicting social and political attitudes. *Personality & Social Psychology Bulletin, 38,* 583–606.

Hodges, S. D., Laurent, S. M., & Lewis, K. L. (2014). Specially motivated, feminine or just female: Do women have an empathic accuracy advantage? In J. L. Smith, W. Ickes, J. A. Hall, S. D. Hodges, J. L. Smith, W. Ickes, J. A. Hall, & S. D. Hodges (Eds.), *Managing interpersonal sensitivity: Knowing when—and when not—to understand others* (pp. 59–74). New York, NY: Novinka/Nova Science Publishers.

Hodges, S. D., Lewis, K. L., & Ickes, W. (2015). The matter of other minds: Empathic accuracy and the factors that influence it. In M. Mikulincer, P. R. Shaver, J. A. Simpson, J. F. Dovidio, M. Mikulincer, P. R. Shaver, J. A. Simpson, & J. F. Dovidio (Eds.), *APA handbook of personality and social psychology: Interpersonal relations* (Vol. 3, pp. 319–348). Washington, DC: American Psychological Association.

Hoeksema-van Orden, C. Y. D., Gaillard, A. W. K., & Buunk, B. P. (1998). Social loafing under fatigue. *Journal of Personality and Social Psychology, 75,* 1179–1190.

Hoerger, M. (2012). Coping strategies and immune neglect in affective forecasting: Direct evidence and key moderators. *Judgment and Decision Making, 7,* 86–96.

Hofer, B. K., & Pintrich, P. R. (1997). The development of epistemological theories: Beliefs about knowledge and knowing and their relation to learning. *Review of Educational Research, 67,* 88–140.

Hofer, J., Busch, H., & Schneider, C. (2015). The effect of motive-trait interaction on satisfaction of the implicit need for affiliation among German and Cameroonian adults. *Journal of Personality, 83,* 167–178.

Hoffman, C., Lau, I., & Johnson, D. R. (1986). The linguistic relativity of person cognition: An English-Chinese comparison. *Journal of Personality and Social Psychology, 51,* 1097–1105.

Hoffrage, U., Hertwig, R., & Gigerenzer, G. (2011). Hindsight bias: A by-product of knowledge updating? In R. Hertwig, G. Gigerenzer, T. Pachur, G. Gigerenzer, R. Hertwig, & T. Pachur (Eds.), *Heuristics: The foundations of adaptive behavior* (pp. 223–241). New York, NY: Oxford University Press.

Hofling, C. K., Brotzman, E., Dalrymple, S., Graves, N., & Pierce, C. M. (1966). An experimental study of nurse-physician relationships. *Journal of Nervous and Mental Disease, 143,* 171–180.

Hofmann, W., De Houwer, J., Perugini, M., Baeyens, F., & Crombez, G. (2010). Evaluative conditioning in humans: A meta-analysis. *Psychological Bulletin, 136,* 390–421.

Hofstede, G. (1986). Cultural differences in teaching and learning. *International Journal of Intercultural Relations, 10,* 301–320.

Hofstede, G., de Hilal, A. V. G., Malvezzi, S., Tanure, B., & Vinken, H. (2010). Comparing regional cultures within a country: Lessons from Brazil. *Journal of Cross-Cultural Psychology, 41,* 336–352.

Hofstede, G., Hofstede, G. J., & Minkov, M. (2010). *Cultures and organizations: Software of the mind: Intercultural cooperation and its importance for survival* (3rd ed.). New York, NY: McGraw-Hill.

Hogan, R., & Kaiser, R. B. (2005). What we know about leadership. Review of General Psychology, 9, 169–180.

Hogg, M. A. (2010). Influence and leadership. In S. T. Fiske, D. T. Gilbert, & G. Lindzey (Eds.), *Handbook of social psychology* (Vol. 2, 5th ed., pp. 1166–1207). Hoboken, NJ: John Wiley & Sons Inc.

Hogg, M. A., Adelman, J. R., & Blagg, R. D. (2010). Religion in the face of uncertainty: An uncertainty-identity theory account of religiousness. *Personality and Social Psychology Review, 14,* 72–83.

Hogue, M., Levashina, J., & Hang, H. (2013). Will I fake it? The interplay of gender, machiavellianism, and self-monitoring on strategies for honesty in job interviews. *Journal of Business Ethics, 117,* 399–411.

Høigaard, R., & Ommundsen, Y. (2007). Perceived social loafing and anticipated effort reduction among young football (soccer) players: An achievement goal perspective. Psychological Reports, 100, 857–875.

Holder, M. D., & Hawkins, C. (2007). The illusion of transparency: Assessment of sex differences in showing and hiding disgust. *Basic and Applied Social Psychology, 29,* 235–243.

Hollander, E. P. (1985). Leadership and power. In G. Lindzey & E. Aronson (Eds.), Handbook of social psychology (3rd ed., Vol. 2, pp. 485–537). New York, NY: Random House.

Hollingshead, A. B., Wittenbaum, G. M., Paulus, P. B., Hirokawa, R. Y., Ancona, D. G., Peterson, R. S., . . . Yoon, K. (2005). A look at groups from the functional perspective. In M. S. Poole & A. B. Hollingshead (Eds.), *Theories of small groups: Interdisciplinary perspectives* (pp. 21–62). Thousand Oaks, CA: Sage.

Hönekopp, J. (2006). Once more: Is beauty in the eye of the beholder? Relative contributions of private and shared taste to judgments of facial attractiveness. *Journal of Experimental Psychology: Human Perception and Performance, 32,* 199–209.

Hong, Y. -y., Wyer, R. S., Jr., & Fong, C. P. S. (2008). Chinese working in groups: Effort dispensability versus normative influence. *Asian Journal of Social Psychology, 11,* 187–195.

Hood, K. E., & Cairns, R. B. (1988). A developmental-genetic analysis of aggressive behavior in mice: II. Cross-sex inheritance. *Behavior Genetics, 18,* 605–619.

Hood, R. W., Jr., Hill, P. C., & Spilka, B. (2009). *The psychology of religion: An empirical approach* (4th ed.). New York, NY: Guilford Press.

Hoshino-Browne, E. (2012). Cultural variations in motivation for cognitive consistency: Influences of self-systems on cognitive dissonance. *Social and Personality Psychology Compass, 6,* 126–141.

Hoshino-Browne, E., Zanna, A. S., Spencer, S. J., Zanna, M. P., Kitayama, S., & Lackenbauer, S. (2005). On the cultural guises of cognitive dissonance: The case of Easterners and Westerners. *Journal of Personality and Social Psychology, 89,* 294–310.

Hosie, J., Gilbert, F., Simpson, K., & Daffern, M. (2014). An examination of the relationship between personality and aggression using the general aggression and five factor models. *Aggressive Behavior, 40,* 189–196.

Houghton, D. P. (2008). Invading and occupying Iraq: Some insights from political psychology. *Peace and Conflict: Journal of Peace Psychology, 14,* 169–192.

Hovland, C. I., & Sears, R. R. (1940). Minor studies of aggression: VI. Correlation of lynchings with economic indices. *Journal of Psychology: Interdisciplinary and Applied, 9,* 301–310.

Hovland, C. I., & Weiss, W. (1951). The influence of source credibility on communication effectiveness. *Public Opinion Quarterly, 15,* 635–650.

Hovland, C. I., Janis, I. L., & Kelley, H. H. (1953). *Communication and persuasion; psychological studies of opinion change.* New Haven, CT: Yale University Press.

Hovland, C. I., Lumsdaine, A. A., & Sheffield, F. D. (1949). *Vol 3. Studies in Social Psychology in World War II: Vol 3. Experiments on mass communication.* Princeton, NJ: Princeton University Press.

Howard, D. J., Shu, S. B., & Kerin, R. A. (2007). Reference price and scarcity appeals and the use of multiple influence strategies in retail newspaper advertising. *Social Influence, 2,* 18–28.

Howard, M. V. A., Brewer, N., & Williams, K. D. (2006). How processing resources shape the influence of stealing thunder on mock-juror verdicts. *Psychiatry, Psychology and Law, 13,* 60–66.

Howard, W., & Crano, W. D. (1974). Effects of sex, conversation, location, and size of observer group on bystander intervention in a high risk situation. *Sociometry, 37,* 491–507.

Hoyt, C. L., & Chemers, M. M. (2008). Social stigma and leadership: A long climb up a slippery ladder. In C. L. Hoyt, G. R. Goethals, & D. R. Forsyth (Eds.), *Leadership at the crossroads: Leadership and psychology* (Vol. 1, pp. 165–180). Westport, CT: Praeger.

Hřebíčková, M., & Graf, S. (2014). Accuracy of national stereotypes in central Europe: Outgroups are not better than ingroup in considering personality traits of real people. *European Journal of Personality, 28,* 60–72.

Hsiang, S. M., Burke, M., & Miguel, E. (2013). Quantifying the influence of climate on human conflict. *Science.*

Huang, F. L., & Cornell, D. G. (2015). The impact of definition and question order on the prevalence of bullying victimization using student self-reports. *Psychological Assessment.*

Huang, Y., Kendrick, K. M., & Yu, R. (2014). Conformity to the opinions of other people lasts for no more than 3 days. *Psychological Science.*

Huber, J., Kirchler, M., & Stuckl, T. (2010). The hot hand belief and the gambler's fallacy in investment decisions under risk. *Theory and Decision, 68,* 445–462.

Huesmann, L. R. (1988). An information processing model for the development of aggression. *Aggressive Behavior, 14,* 13–24.

Huesmann, L. R., & Eron, L. D. (1986). *Television and the aggressive child: A cross-national comparison.* Hillsdale, NJ: Erlbaum.

Huesmann, L. R., & Kirwil, L. (2007). Why observing violence increases the risk of violent behavior by the observer. In D. J. Flannery, A. T. Vazsonyi, & I. D. Waldman (Eds.), *The Cambridge handbook of violent behavior and aggression* (pp. 545–570). New York, NY: Cambridge University Press.

Huesmann, L. R., Dubow, E. F., & Boxer, P. (2009). Continuity of aggression from childhood to early adulthood as a predictor of life outcomes: Implications for the adolescent-limited and life-course-persistent models. *Aggressive Behavior, 35,* 136–149.

Huesmann, L. R., Dubow, E. F., & Boxer, P. (2011). The transmission of aggressiveness across generations: Biological, contextual, and social learning processes. In P. R. Shaver & M. Mikulincer (Eds.), *Human aggression and violence: Causes, manifestations, and consequences* (pp. 123–142). Washington, DC: American Psychological Association.

Huesmann, L. R., Moise-Titus, J., Podolski, C. -L., & Eron, L. D. (2003). Longitudinal relations between children's exposure to TV violence and their aggressive and violent behavior in young adulthood: 1977–1992. *Developmental Psychology, 39,* 201–221.

Hugdahl, K., & Westerhausen, R. (2010). *The two halves of the brain: Information processing in the cerebral hemispheres.* Cambridge, MA: MIT Press.

Hughes, M., & Louw, J. (2013). Playing games: The salience of social cues and group norms in eliciting aggressive behaviour. *South African Journal of Psychology, 43,* 252–262.

Huguet, P., & Régner, I. (2007). Stereotype threat among schoolgirls in quasi-ordinary classroom circumstances. *Journal of Educational Psychology, 99,* 545–560.

Huguet, P., Galvaing, M. P., Monteil, J. M., & Dumas, F. (1999). Social presence effects in the Stroop task: Further evidence for an attentional view of social facilitation. *Journal of Personality and Social Psychology, 77,* 1011–1025.

Hui, C. H., & Triandis, H. C. (1989). Effects of culture and response format on extreme response style. *Journal of Cross-Cultural Psychology, 20,* 296–309.

Hull, D. L. (1988). *Science as a process: An evolutionary account of the social and conceptual development of science.* Chicago, IL: University of Chicago Press.

Hummer, R. A., Rogers, R. G., Nam, C. B., & Ellison, C. G. (1999). Religious involvement and U.S. adult mortality. *Demography, 36,* 273–285.

Humphrey, N. (1976). The social function of intellect. In P. P. G. Bateson & R. A. Hinde (Eds.), *Growing points in ethology* (pp. 303–317). Cambridge, UK: Cambridge University.

Hung, I. W., & Labroo, A. A. (2011). From firm muscles to firm willpower: Understanding the role of embodied cognition in self-regulation. *Journal of Consumer Research, 37,* 1046–1064.

Hung, I. W., & Wyer, R. S. (2014). Effects of self-relevant perspective-taking on the impact of persuasive appeals. *Personality & Social Psychology Bulletin, 40,* 402–414.

Hunsberger, B., & Jackson, L. M. (2005). Religion, meaning, and prejudice. *Journal of Social Issues, 61,* 807–826.

Hunsberger, B., & Platonow, E. (1986). Religion and helping charitable causes. *Journal of Psychology: Interdisciplinary and Applied, 120,* 517–528.

Hunt, C. V., Kim, A., Borgida, E., & Chaiken, S. (2010). Revisiting the self-interest versus values debate: The role of temporal perspective. *Journal of Experimental Social Psychology, 46,* 1155–1158.

Hunt, M. M. (2007). *The story of psychology.* New York, NY: Anchor Books.

Hunter, B. D., & Merrill, R. M. (2013). Religious orientation and health among active older adults in the United States. *Journal of Religion and Health, 52,* 851–863.

Hunter, J. A., Stringer, M., & Watson, R. P. (1991). Intergroup violence and intergroup attributions. *British Journal of Social Psychology, 30,* 261–266.

Huntsinger, J. R. (2014). A flexible impact of affective feelings on priming effects: Assimilation and contrast. *Personality and Social Psychology Bulletin, 40,* 450–462.

Huppertz, C., Bartels, M., Jansen, I. E., Boomsma, D. I., Willemsen, G., de Moor, M. H. M., & de Geus, E. J. C. (2014). A twin-sibling study on the relationship between exercise attitudes and exercise behavior. *Behavior Genetics, 44,* 45–55.

Hurley, E. A., & Allen, B. A. (2007). Asking the how questions: Quantifying group processes behaviors. *Journal of General Psychology, 134,* 5–21.

Iacoboni, M. (2008). Mesial frontal cortex and super mirror neurons. *Behavioral and Brain Sciences, 31,* 30–30.

Iacoboni, M. (2009). Imitation, empathy, and mirror neurons. *Annual Review of Psychology, 60,* 653–670.

Ihme, T. A., & Möller, J. (2015). "He who can, does; he who cannot, teaches?": Stereotype threat and preservice teachers. *Journal of Educational Psychology, 107,* 300–308.

Ijzerman, H., van Dijk, W. W., & Gallucci, M. (2007). A bumpy train ride: A field experiment on insult, honor, and emotional reactions. *Emotion, 7,* 869–875.

Imhoff, R., & Erb, H. -P. (2009). What motivates nonconformity? Uniqueness seeking blocks majority influence. *Personality and Social Psychology Bulletin, 35,* 309–320.

Inbau, F. E., Reid, J. E., Buckley, J. P., & Jayne, B. C. (2013). *Criminal interrogations and confessions* (5th ed.). Burlington, MA: Jones & Bartlett.

Ingalls, V. (2012). Sex differences in the creation of fictional heroes with particular emphasis on female heroes and superheroes in popular culture: Insights from evolutionary psychology. *Review of General Psychology, 16,* 208–221.

Ingham, A. G., Levinger, G., Graves, J., & Peckham, V. (1974). The Ringelmann effect: Studies of group size and group performance. *Journal of Experimental Social Psychology, 10,* 371–384.

Ingold, P. V., Kleinmann, M., König, C. J., & Melchers, K. G. (2015). Shall we continue or stop disapproving of self-presentation? Evidence on impression management and faking in a selection context and their relation to job performance. *European Journal of Work and Organizational Psychology, 24,* 420–432.

Insko, C. A. (1965). Verbal reinforcement of attitude. *Journal of Personality and Social Psychology, 2,* 621–623.

Insko, C. A. (1985). Conformity and group size: The concern with being right and the concern with being liked. *Personality and Social Psychology Bulletin, 11,* 41–50.

Insko, C. A. (2012). Balance-logic theory. In P. A. M. Van Lange, A. W. Kruglanski, & E. T. Higgins (Eds.), *Handbook of theories of social psychology* (Vol. 1, pp. 178–200). Thousand Oaks, CA: Sage.

Insko, C. A., & Cialdini, R. B. (1969). A test of three interpretations of attitudinal verbal reinforcement. *Journal of Personality and Social Psychology, 12,* 333–341.

International Social Survey Programme. (1998). Religion II [Data- base]: Author. Retrieved from http://www.gesis .org/en/data_service/issp/data/1998_Religion_II.htm

Ip, G. W. -m., Chiu, C. -y., & Wan, C. (2006). Birds of a feather and birds flocking together: Physical versus behavioral cues may lead to trait-versus goal-based group perception. *Journal of Personality and Social Psychology, 90,* 368–381.

Isen, A. M., & Levin, P. F. (1972). Effect of feeling good on helping: Cookies and kindness. *Journal of Personality and Social Psychology, 21,* 384–388.

Isenberg, D. J. (1986). Group polarization: A critical review and meta-analysis. *Journal of Personality and Social Psychology, 50,* 1141–1151.

Ishii, K. (2011). Mere exposure to faces increases attention to vocal affect: A cross-cultural investigation. *Cognitive Studies: Bulletin of the Japanese Cognitive Science Society, 18,* 453–461.

Ishii, K., & Kitayama, S. (2011). Outgroup homogeneity effect in perception: An exploration with Ebbinghaus illusion. *Asian Journal of Social Psychology, 14,* 159–163.

Ito, T. A. (2011). Perceiving social category information from faces: Using ERPs to study person perception. In A. Todorov, S. T. Fiske, & D. A. Prentice (Eds.), *Social neuroscience: Toward understanding the underpinnings of the social mind* (pp. 85–100). New York, NY: Oxford University Press.

Ito, T. A., Thompson, E., & Cacioppo, J. T. (2004). Tracking the timecourse of social perception: The effects of racial cues on event-related brain potentials. *Personality and Social Psychology Bulletin, 30,* 1267–1280.

Ito, T.A., Miller, N., & Pollock, V.E. (1996). Alcohol and aggression: A meta-analysis on the moderating effects of inhibitory cues, triggering events, and self-focused attention. *Psychological Bulletin, 120,* 60–82.

Izard, C. E. (1971). *The face of emotion.* New York, NY: Appleton Century-Crofts.

Izard, C. E. (1994). Innate and universal facial expressions: Evidence from developmental and cross-cultural research. *Psychological Bulletin, 115,* 288–299.

Jack, R. E. (2013). Culture and facial expressions of emotion. *Visual Cognition, 21,* 1248–1286.

Jack, R. E., Blais, C., Scheepers, C., Schyns, P. G., & Caldara, R. (2009). Cultural confusions show that facial expressions are not universal. *Current Biology, 19,* 1543–1548.

Jackson, J. M. (1988). *Social psychology, past and present: An integrative orientation.* Hillsdale, NJ: Lawrence Erlbaum.

Jackson, L. A., Hunter, J. E., & Hodge, C. N. (1995). Physical attractiveness and intellectual competence: A meta-analytic review. *Social Psychology Quarterly, 58,* 108–122.

Jackson, M., & Moreland, R. L. (2009). Transactive memory in the classroom. *Small Group Research, 40,* 508–534.

Jackson, P. L., Brunet, E., Meltzoff, A. N., & Decety, J. (2006). Empathy examined through the neural mechanisms involved in imagining how I feel versus how you feel pain. *Neuropsychologia, 44,* 752–761.

Jacobs Bao, K., & Lyubomirsky, S. (2013). The rewards of happiness. In S. A. David, I. Boniwell, & A. Conley Ayers (Eds.), *The Oxford handbook of happiness* (pp. 119–133). New York, NY: Oxford University Press.

Jacobs, N., & Harper, B. (2013). The effects of rejection sensitivity on reactive and proactive aggression. *Aggressive Behavior, 39,* 3–12.

Jacobson, K. J. L., Hood, J. N., & Van Buren, H. J., III. (2014). Workplace bullying across cultures: A research agenda. *International Journal of Cross Cultural Management, 14,* 47–65.

Jacobson, R. P., Mortensen, C. R., Jacobson, K. J. L., & Cialdini, R. B. (2015). Self-control moderates the effectiveness of influence attempts highlighting injunctive social norms. *Social Psychological and Personality Science, 6,* 718–726.

Jahoda, G. (2007). *A history of social psychology: From the Eighteenth Century Enlightenment to the second world war.* Cambridge, UK: Cambridge University Press.

Jain, S. P., & Maheswaran, D. (2000). Motivated reasoning: A depth-of-processing perspective. *Journal of Consumer Research, 26,* 358–371.

Jang Ho, M., & Yong Jun, S. (2015). Individuality within the group: Testing the optimal distinctiveness principle through brand consumption. *Social Behavior & Personality: An International Journal, 43,* 15–26.

Janis, I. L. (1972). *Victims of groupthink: A psychological study of foreign-policy decisions and fiascoes.* Oxford, UK: Houghton Mifflin.

Janis, I. L. (1982). *Groupthink: Psychological studies of policy decisions and fiascoes* (2nd ed.). Boston, MA: Houghton Mifflin.

Janis, I. L., & Feshbach, S. (1953). Effects of fear-arousing communications. *The Journal of Abnormal and Social Psychology, 48,* 78–92.

Janiszewski, C., & Uy, D. (2008). Precision of the anchor influences the amount of adjustment. *Psychological Science, 19,* 121–127.

Jasper, F., & Ortner, T. M. (2014). The tendency to fall for distracting information while making judgments: Development and validation of the Objective Heuristic Thinking Test. *European Journal of Psychological Assessment, 30,* 193–207.

Jenkins, A. C., & Mitchell, J. P. (2011). How has cognitive neuroscience contributed to social psychological theory? In A. Todorov, S. T. Fiske, & D. A. Prentice (Eds.), *Social neuroscience: Toward understanding the underpinnings of the social mind* (pp. 3–13). New York, NY: Oxford University Press.

Job, V., Walton, G. M., Bernecker, K., & Dweck, C. S. (2015). Implicit theories about willpower predict self-regulation and grades in everyday life. *Journal of Personality and Social Psychology, 108,* 637–647.

Johnson, B. K., & Knobloch-Westerwick, S. (2014). Glancing up or down: Mood management and selective social comparisons on social networking sites. *Computers in Human Behavior, 41,* 33–39.

Johnson, B. T., Maio, G. R., & Smith-McLallen, A. (2005). Communication and Attitude Change: Causes, Processes, and Effects. In D. Albarracín, B. T. Johnson, & M. P. Zanna (Eds.), *The handbook of attitudes* (pp. 617–669). Mahwah, NJ: Lawrence Erlbaum.

Johnson, J. G., Cohen, P., Smailes, E. M., Kasen, S., & Brook, J. S. (2002). Television viewing and aggressive behavior during adolescence and adulthood. *Science, 295.*

Johnson, K. A., & Cohen, A. B. (2014). Religious and national cultures. In V. Saroglou (Ed.), *Religion, personality, and social behavior* (pp. 338–360). New York, NY: Psychology Press.

Johnson, M. K., Rowatt, W. C., & LaBouff, J. (2010). Priming Christian religious concepts increases racial prejudice. *Social Psychological and Personality Science, 1,* 119–126.

Johnson, M. K., Rowatt, W. C., & LaBouff, J. P. (2012). Religiosity and prejudice revisited: In-group favoritism, out-group derogation, or both? *Psychology of Religion and Spirituality, 4,* 154–168.

Johnson, M. K., Rowatt, W. C., Barnard-Brak, L. M., Patock-Peckham, J. A., LaBouff, J. P., & Carlisle, R. D. (2011). A mediational analysis of the role of right-wing authoritarianism and religious fundamentalism in the religiosity–prejudice link. *Personality and Individual Differences, 50,* 851–856.

Johnson, R. D., & Downing, L. L. (1979). Deindividuation and valence of cues: Effects on prosocial and antisocial behavior. *Journal of Personality and Social Psychology, 37,* 1532–1538.

Johnson, S. L. (2011). An ecological model of workplace bullying: A guide for intervention and research. *Nursing Forum, 46,* 55–63.

Johnston, L., Miles, L., & Macrae, C. N. (2010). Male or female? An investigation of factors that modulate the visual perception of another's sex. In E. Balcetis & G. D. Lassiter (Eds.), *Social psychology of visual perception* (pp. 103–122). New York, NY: Psychology Press.

Jonason, P. K., Izzo, P. L., & Webster, G. D. (2007). Helping others to find long-term and short-term mates: A test of inclusive fitness, reciprocal altruism, and parental investment theories. *Evolutionary Psychology, 5,* 716.

Jones, E. E. (1979). The rocky road from acts to dispositions. *American Psychologist, 34,* 107–117.

Jones, E. E. (1985). Major developments in social psychology during the past five decades. In G. Lindzey, & E. Aronson (Ed.), *Handbook of social psychology* (3rd ed., Vol. 1, pp. 47–107). New York, NY: Random House.

Jones, E. E. (1990). *Interpersonal perception.* New York, NY: W H Freeman/Times Books/Henry Holt & Co.

Jones, E. E., & Berglas, S. (1978). Control of attributions about the self through self-handicapping strategies: The appeal of alcohol and the role of underachievement. *Personality and Social Psychology Bulletin, 4,* 200–206.

Jones, E. E., & Harris, V.A. (1967). The attribution of attitudes. *Journal of Experimental Social Psychology, 3,* 1–24.

Jones, E. E., & Lambertus, J. D. (2014). Expecting less from groups: A new perspective on shortcomings in idea generation groups. *Group Dynamics: Theory, Research, and Practice, 18,* 237–250.

Jones, E. E., & Nisbett, R. E. (1971). The actor and the observer: Divergent perceptions of the causes of behavior. In E. E. Jones, D. E. Kanouse, H. H. Kelley, R. E. Nisbett, S. Valins, & B. Weiner (Eds.), *Attribution: Perceiving the causes of behavior* (pp. 79–94). Hillsdale, NJ: Lawrence Erlbaum.

Jones, E. E., & Pittman, T. S. (1982). Toward a general theory of strategic self-presentation. In J. Suls (Ed.), *Psychological perspectives on the self* (Vol. 1, pp. 231–262). Hillsdale, NJ: Lawrence Erlbaum.

Jones, E. E., & Sigall, H. (1971). The bogus pipeline: A new paradigm for measuring affect and attitude. *Psychological Bulletin, 76,* 349–364.

Jones, K. P., & King, E. B. (2014). Managing concealable stigmas at work: A review and multilevel model. *Journal of Management, 40,* 1466–1494.

Joshanloo, M. (2014). Eastern conceptualizations of happiness: Fundamental differences with western views. *Journal of Happiness Studies, 15,* 475–493.

Joshanloo, M., & Weijers, D. (2014). Aversion to happiness across cultures: A review of where and why people are averse to happiness. *Journal of Happiness Studies, 15,* 717–735.

Joule, R. V. (1987). Tobacco deprivation: The foot-in-the-door technique versus the low-ball technique. *European Journal of Social Psychology, 17,* 361–365.

Judd, C. M., & Park, B. (1993). Definition and assessment of accuracy in social stereotypes. *Psychological Review, 100,* 109–128.

Judge, T. A., & Piccolo, R. F. (2004). Transformational and transactional leadership: A meta-analytic test of their relative validity. *Journal of Applied Psychology, 89,* 755–768.

Judge, T. A., Colbert, A. E., & Ilies, R. (2004). Intelligence and leadership: A quantitative review and test of theoretical propositions. *Journal of Applied Psychology, 89,* 542–552.

Judge, T. A., Hurst, C., & Simon, L. S. (2009). Does it pay to be smart, attractive, or confident (or all three)? Relationships among general mental ability, physical attractiveness, core self-evaluations, and income. *The Journal of Applied Psychology, 94,* 742–755.

Jussim, L., & Harber, K. D. (2005). Teacher expectations and self-fulfilling prophecies: Knowns and unknowns, resolved and unresolved controversies. *Personality and Social Psychology Review, 9,* 131–155.

Jussim, L., Cain, T. R., Crawford, J. T., Harber, K., & Cohen, F. (2009). The unbearable accuracy of stereotypes. In T. D. Nelson (Ed.), *Handbook of prejudice, stereotyping, and discrimination* (pp. 199–227). New York, NY: Psychology Press.

Jussim, L., Robustelli, S. L., & Cain, T. R. (2009). Teacher expectations and self-fulfilling prophecies. In K. R. Wenzel & A. Wigfield (Eds.), *Handbook of motivation at school* (pp. 349–380). New York, NY: Routledge/Taylor & Francis Group.

Kafetsios, K., Andriopoulos, P., & Papachiou, A. (2014). Relationship status moderates avoidant attachment differences in positive emotion decoding accuracy. *Personal Relationships, 21,* 191–205.

Kahneman, D. (1999). Objective happiness. In D. Kahneman, E. Diener, & N. Schwarz (Eds.), *Well-being: The foundations of hedonic psychology* (pp. 3–25). New York, NY: Russell Sage Foundation.

Kahneman, D. (2011). *Thinking, fast and slow.* New York, NY: Farrar, Straus and Giroux.

Kahneman, D., & Deaton, A. (2010). High income improves evaluation of life but not emotional well-being. *Proceedings of the National Academy of Sciences of the United States of America, 107,* 16489–16493.

Kahneman, D., & Frederick, S. (2002). Representativeness revisited: Attribute substitution in intuitive judgment. In T. Gilovich, D. Griffin & D. Kahneman (Eds.), *Heuristics and biases: The psychology of intuitive judgment* (pp. 49–81). New York, NY: Cambridge University Press.

Kahneman, D., & Tversky, A. (1972). Subjective probability: A judgment of representativeness. *Cognitive Psychology, 3,* 430–454.

Kameda, T., Tsukasaki, T., Hastie, R., & Berg, N. (2011). Democracy under uncertainty: The wisdom of crowds and the free-rider problem in group decision making. *Psychological Review, 118,* 76–96.

Kammrath, L. K. (2011). What we think we do (to each other): How personality can bias behavior schemas through the projection of if-then profiles. *Journal of Personality and Social Psychology, 101,* 754–770.

Kamp Dush, C. M., & Amato, P. R. (2005). Consequences of relationship status and quality for subjective well-being. *Journal of Social and Personal Relationships, 22,* 607–627.

Kanacri, B. P. L., Pastorelli, C., Eisenberg, N., Zuffianò, A., & Caprara, G. V. (2013). The development of prosociality from adolescence to early adulthood: The role of effortful control. *Journal of Personality, 81,* 302–312.

Kang, Y., Gray, J. R., & Dovidio, J. F. (2014). The nondiscriminating heart: Lovingkindness meditation training decreases implicit intergroup bias. *Journal Of Experimental Psychology. General, 143,* 1306–1313.

Kanten, A. B. r., & Teigen, K. H. (2008). Better than average and better with time: Relative evaluations of self and others in the past, present, and future. *European Journal of Social Psychology, 38,* 343–353.

Kao, D. T. (2012). Exploring the effect of regulatory focus on ad attitudes: The moderating roles of message sidedness and argument quality. *International Journal of Psychology, 47,* 142–153.

Karau, S. J., & Williams, K. D. (1993). Social loafing: A meta-analytic review and theoretical integration. Journal of Personality and Social Psychology, 65, 681–706.

Karau, S. J., & Williams, K. D. (1997). The effects of group cohesiveness on social loafing and social compensation. *Group Dynamics: Theory, Research, and Practice, 1,* 156–168.

Karney, B. R., & Bradbury, T. N. (1997). Neuroticism, marital interaction, and the trajectory of marital satisfaction. *Journal of Personality and Social Psychology, 72,* 1075–1092.

Karraker, K. H., & Stern, M. (1990). Infant physical attractiveness and facial expression: Effects on adult perceptions. *Basic and Applied Social Psychology, 11,* 371–385.

Kärtner, J., Keller, H., & Chaudhary, N. (2010). Cognitive and social influences on early prosocial behavior in two sociocultural contexts. *Developmental Psychology, 46,* 905–914.

Kasser, T. (2004). The good life or the goods life? Positive psychology and personal well-being in the culture of consumption. In P. A. Linley & S. Joseph (Eds.), *Positive psychology in practice* (pp. 55–67). Hoboken, NJ: John Wiley & Sons.

Kassin, S. M., & Gudjonsson, G. H. (2004). The psychology of confessions: A Review of the literature and issues. *Psychological Science in the Public Interest, 5,* 33–67.

Kassin, S. M., & Kiechel, K. L. (1996). The social psychology of false confessions: Compliance, internalization, and confabulation. *Psychological Science, 7,* 125–128.

Kassin, S. M., Drizin, S. A., Grisso, T., Gudjonsson, G. H., Leo, R. A., & Redlich, A. D. (2010). Police-induced confessions, risk factors, and recommendations: looking ahead. *Law and Human Behavior, 34,* 49–52.

Kastenmüller, A., Greitemeyer, T., Zehl, S., Tattersall, A. J., George, H., Frey, D., & Fischer, P. (2014). Leadership and information processing: The influence of transformational and transactional leadership on selective information search, evaluation, and conveying. *Social Psychology (18649335), 45,* 357–370.

Katz, A. D., & Hoyt, W. T. (2014). The influence of multicultural counseling competence and anti-Black prejudice on therapists' outcome expectancies. *Journal of Counseling Psychology, 61,* 299–305.

Kauff, M., & Wagner, U. (2012). Valuable therefore not threatening: The influence of diversity beliefs on discrimination against immigrants. *Social Psychological and Personality Science, 3,* 714–721.

Kavanagh, P. S., Robins, S. C., & Ellis, B. J. (2010). The mating sociometer: A regulatory mechanism for mating aspirations. *Journal of Personality and Social Psychology, 99,* 120–132. [Supplemental]

Kawakami, K., Dion, K. L., & Dovidio, J. F. (1998). Racial prejudice and stereotype activation. *Personality and Social Psychology Bulletin, 24,* 407–416.

Keefer, L. A., Landau, M. J., Sullivan, D., & Rothschild, Z. K. (2014). Embodied metaphor and abstract problem solving: Testing a metaphoric fit hypothesis in the health domain. *Journal of Experimental Social Psychology, 55,* 12–20.

Keller, M. C., Howrigan, D. P., & Simonson, M. A. (2011). Theory and methods in evolutionary behavioral genetics. In D. M. Buss & P. H. Hawley (Eds.), *The evolution of personality and individual differences* (pp. 280–302). Oxford, UK: Oxford University Press.

Kelley, H. H. (1950). The warm-cold variable in first impressions of persons. *Journal of Personality, 18,* 431–439.

Kelley, H. H. (1967). Attribution theory in social psychology. *Nebraska Symposium on Motivation, 15,* 192–238.

Kelly, D. J., Quinn, P. C., Slater, A. M., Lee, K., Gibson, A., Smith, M., . . . Pascalis, O. (2005). Three-month-olds, but not newborns, prefer own-race faces. *Developmental Science, 8,* F31–F36.

Kelly, G. A. (1963). *A theory of personality: The psychology of personal constructs.* Oxford, UK: W. W. Norton.

Kelman, H. C. (1967). Human use of human subjects: The problem of deception in social psychological experiments. *Psychological Bulletin, 67,* 1–11.

Keltner, D. (1995). Signs of appeasement: Evidence for the distinct displays of embarrassment, amusement, and shame. *Journal of Personality and Social Psychology, 68,* 441–454.

Keltner, D., & Buswell, B. N. (1997). Embarrassment: Its distinct form and appeasement functions. *Psychological Bulletin, 122,* 250–270.

Keltner, D., & Kring, A. M. (1998). Emotion, social function, and psychopathology. *Review of General Psychology, 2,* 320–342.

Kemmelmeier, M., Jambor, E. E., & Letner, J. (2006). Individualism and good works: Cultural variation in giving and volunteering across the United States. *Journal of Cross-Cultural Psychology, 37,* 327–344.

Kemp, A. H., & Guastella, A. J. (2011). The role of oxytocin in human affect: A novel hypothesis. *Current Directions in Psychological Science, 20,* 222–231.

Kenrick, D. T., & Cohen, A. B. (2012). A history of evolutionary social psychology. In A. W. Kruglanski & W. Stroebe (Eds.), *Handbook of the history of social psychology* (pp. 101–122). New York, NY: Psychology Press.

Kenrick, D. T., & MacFarlane, S. W. (1986). Ambient temperature and horn honking: A field study of the heat/aggression relationship. *Environment and Behavior, 18,* 179–191.

Kenrick, D. T., Gabrielidis, C., Keefe, R. C., & Cornelius, J. S. (1996). Adolescents' age preferences for dating partners: Support for an evolutionary model of life-history strategies. *Child Development, 67,* 1499–1511.

Kenrick, D. T., Neuberg, S. L., & Cialdini, R. B. (2006). *Social psychology: Goals in interaction.* New York, NY: Allyn & Bacon.

Kenrick, D. T., Nieuweboer, S., & Buunk, A.P. (2010). Universal mechanisms and cultural diversity: Replacing the blank slate with a coloring book. In M. Schaller, A. Norenzayan, S. J. Heine, T. Yamagishi & T. Kameda (Eds.), *Evolution, culture, and the human mind* (pp. 257–272). New York, NY: Psychology Press.

Kenrick, D. T., Sadalla, E. K., Groth, G., & Trost, M. R. (1990). Evolution, traits, and the stages of human courtship: Qualifying the parental investment model. *Journal of Personality, 58,* 97–116.

Kernis, M. H. (2005). Measuring self-esteem in context: The importance of stability of self-esteem in psychological functioning. *Journal of Personality, 73,* 1569–1605.

Kerr, N. L. (1983). Motivation losses in small groups: A social dilemma analysis. *Journal of Personality and Social Psychology, 45,* 819–828.

Kerr, N. L., & Bruun, S. E. (1983). Dispensability of member effort and group motivation losses: Free-rider effects. *Journal of Personality and Social Psychology, 44,* 78–94.

Kervyn, N., Fiske, S. T., & Yzerbyt, V. Y. (2013). Integrating the stereotype content model (warmth and competence) and the Osgood semantic differential (evaluation, potency, and activity). *European Journal of Social Psychology, 43,* 673–681.

Kervyn, N., Fiske, S., & Yzerbyt, V. (2015). Forecasting the primary dimension of social perception. *Social Psychology (18649335), 46,* 36–45.

Keysar, B., Converse, B. A., Wang, J., & Epley, N. (2008). Reciprocity is not give and take: Asymmetric reciprocity to positive and negative acts. *Psychological Science, 19,* 1280–1286.

Kilduff, L. P., Hopp, R. N., Cook, C. J., Crewther, B. T., & Manning, J. T. (2013). Digit ratio (2D:4D), aggression, and testosterone in men exposed to an aggressive video stimulus. *Evolutionary Psychology, 11,* 953–964.

Kilic, D. (2013). The effects of jigsaw and group research techniques on democratic attitudes and academic achievements of prospective classroom teachers in educational science course. *International Journal of Academic Research, 5,* 143–150.

Kim, D., & Hommel, B. (2015). An event-based account of conformity. *Psychological Science, 26,* 484–489.

Kim, H., & Markus, H. R. (1999). Deviance or uniqueness, harmony or conformity? A cultural analysis. *Journal of Personality and Social Psychology, 77,* 785–800.

Kim, P., & Lee, J. -H. (2012). The influence of collectivism and rater error on organizational citizenship and impression management behaviors. *Social Behavior & Personality: An international journal, 40,* 545–555.

Kimel, S. Y., Grossmann, I., & Kitayama, S. (2012). When gift-giving produces dissonance: Effects of subliminal affiliation priming on choices for one's self versus close others. *Journal of Experimental Social Psychology, 48,* 1221–1224.

Kimmel, A. J. (2004). Ethical issues in social psychology research. In C. Sansone, C. C. Morf, & A. T. Panter (Eds.), *The SAGE handbook of methods in social psychology* (pp. 45–70). Thousand Oaks, CA: Sage.

Kimmel, A. J. (2011). Deception in psychological research—a necessary evil? *The Psychologist, 24,* 580–585.

Kinder, D. R., & Sears, D. O. (1985). Public opinion and political action. In G. Lindzey & E. Aronson (Eds.), *The handbook of social psychology* (3rd ed., pp. 659–742). New York, NY: Random House.

King, E. B., Dunleavy, D. G., Dunleavy, E. M., Jaffer, S., Morgan, W. B., Elder, K., & Graebner, R. (2011). Discrimination in the 21st century: Are science and the law aligned? *Psychology, Public Policy, and Law, 17,* 54–75.

King, L. A., & Napa, C. K. (1998). What makes a life good? *Journal of Personality and Social Psychology, 75,* 156–165.

Kingston, D. A., Malamuth, N. M., Fedoroff, P., & Marshall, W. L. (2009). The importance of individual differences in pornography use: Theoretical perspectives and implications for treating sexual offenders. *Journal of Sex Research, 46,* 216–232.

Kirkpatrick, L. A. (1997). A longitudinal study of changes in religious belief and behavior as a function of individual differences in adult attachment style. *Journal for the Scientific Study of Religion, 36,* 207–217.

Kirkpatrick, L. A. (2005). *Attachment, evolution, and the psychology of religion.* New York, NY: Guilford Press.

Kirkpatrick, L. A. (2012). Attachment theory and the evolutionary psychology of religion. *International Journal for the Psychology of Religion, 22,* 231–241.

Kitayama, S., & Markus, H. R. (2000). The pursuit of happiness and the realization of sympathy: Cultural patterns of self, social relations, and well-being. In E. Diener & E. M. Suh (Eds.), *Culture and subjective well-being* (pp. 113–161). Cambridge, MA: The MIT Press.

Klehe, U. -C., & Anderson, N. (2007). The moderating influence of personality and culture on social loafing in typical versus maximum performance situations. *International Journal of Selection and Assessment, 15,* 250–262.

Kleinke, C. L., Peterson, T. R., & Rutledge, T. R. (1998). Effects of self-generated facial expressions on mood. *Journal of Personality and Social Psychology, 74,* 272–279.

Kliger, D., & Kudryavtsev, A. (2010). The availability heuristic and investors' reaction to company-specific events. *Journal of Behavioral Finance, 11,* 50–65.

Kling, K. C., Hyde, J. S., Showers, C. J., & Buswell, B. N. (1999). Gender differences in self-esteem: A meta-analysis. *Psychological Bulletin, 125,* 470–500.

Klinger, M. R., & Greenwald, A. G. (1994). Preferences need no inferences?: The cognitive basis of unconscious mere exposure effects. In P. M. Niedenthal & S. Kitayama (Eds.), *The heart's eye: Emotional influences in perception and attention* (pp. 67–85). San Diego, CA: Academic Press.

Knafo, A., & Israel, S. (2010). Genetic and environmental influences on prosocial behavior. In M. Mikulincer, P. R. Shaver, M. Mikulincer, & P. R. Shaver (Eds.), *Prosocial motives, emotions, and behavior: The better angels of our nature* (pp. 149–167). Washington, DC: American Psychological Association.

Knafo, A., Schwartz, S. H., & Levine, R. V. (2009). Helping strangers is lower in embedded cultures. *Journal of Cross-Cultural Psychology, 40,* 875–879.

Knapton, H. M., Bäck, H., & Bäck, E. A. (2015). The social activist: Conformity to the ingroup following rejection as a predictor of political participation. *Social Influence, 10,* 97–108.

Kniffin, K. M., & Wilson, D. S. (2004). The effect of nonphysical traits on the perception of physical attractiveness: Three naturalistic studies. *Evolution and Human Behavior, 25,* 88–101.

Knowles, E. S., & Linn, J. A. (2004). *Resistance and persuasion*. Mahwah, NJ: Lawrence Erlbaum.

Knox, R. E., & Inkster, J. A. (1968). Postdecision dissonance at post time. *Journal of Personality and Social Psychology, 8,* 319–323.

Koenig, H. G., McCullough, M. E., & Larson, D. B. (2001). *Handbook of religion and health.* New York, NY: Oxford University Press.

Koenig, L. B., McGue, M., & Iacono, W. G. (2008). Stability and change in religiousness during emerging adulthood. *Developmental Psychology, 44,* 532–543.

Kohl, C., & Robertson, J. (2014). The sexual overperception bias: An exploration of the relationship between mate value and perception of sexual interest. *Evolutionary Behavioral Sciences, 8,* 31–43.

Kokkoris, M. D., & Kühnen, U. (2013). Choice and dissonance in a European cultural context: The case of Western and Eastern Europeans. *International Journal of Psychology, 48,* 1260–1266.

Konrath, S., Bushman, B. J., & Campbell, W. K. (2006). Attenuating the link between threatened egotism and aggression. *Psychological Science, 17,* 995–1001.

Koole, S. L., Dijksterhuis, A., & van Knippenberg, A. (2001). What's in a name: Implicit self-esteem and the automatic self. *Journal of Personality and Social Psychology, 80,* 669–685.

Kopko, K. C., Bryner, S. M., Budziak, J., Devine, C. J., & Nawara, S. P. (2011). In the eye of the beholder? Motivated reasoning in disputed elections. *Political Behavior, 33,* 271–290.

Kors, D. J., Linden, W., & Gerin, W. (1997). Evaluation interferes with social support: Effects on cardiovascular stress reactivity in women. *Journal of Social and Clinical Psychology, 16,* 1–23.

Koster, E. H. W., Soetens, B., Braet, C., & De Raedt, R. (2008). How to control a white bear? Individual differences involved in self-perceived and actual thought-suppression ability. *Cognition and Emotion, 22,* 1068–1080.

Krahé, B., & Busching, R. (2014). Breaking the vicious cycle of media violence use and aggression: A test of intervention effects over 30 months. *Psychology of Violence, 5,* 217–226.

Krahé, B., Möller, I., Huesmann, L. R., Kirwil, L., Felber, J., & Berger, A. (2011). Desensitization to media violence: Links with habitual media violence exposure, aggressive cognitions, and aggressive behavior. *Journal of Personality and Social Psychology, 100,* 630–646.

Kramer, R. M. (1998). Revisiting the Bay of Pigs and Vietnam decisions 25 years later: How well has the groupthink hypothesis stood the test of time? *Organizational Behavior and Human Decision Processes, 73,* 236–271.

Kramer, R. M. (2011). Cooperation and the commons: Laboratory and field investigations of a persistent dilemma. In R. M. Kramer, G. J. Leonardelli, & R. W. Livingston (Eds.), *Social cognition, social identity, and intergroup relations: A Festschrift in honor of Marilynn B. Brewer* (pp. 297–317). New York, NY: Psychology Press.

Kraus, S. J. (1995). Attitudes and the prediction of behavior: A meta-analysis of the empirical literature. *Personality and Social Psychology Bulletin, 21,* 58–75.

Krebs, D. L. (2011). *The origins of morality: An evolutionary account.* New York, NY: Oxford University Press.

Krizan, Z., & Baron, R. S. (2007). Group polarization and choice-dilemmas: How important is self-categorization? *European Journal of Social Psychology, 37,* 191–201.

Krosnick, J. A., Judd, C. M., & Wittenbrink, B. (2005). The Measurement of Attitudes. In D. Albarracin, B. T. Johnson, & M. P. Zanna (Eds.), *The handbook of attitudes* (pp. 21–76). Mahwah, NJ: Lawrence Erlbaum.

Krosnick, J. A., Lavarakas, P. J., & Kim, N. (2014). Survey research. In H. T. Reis & C. M. Judd (Eds.), *Handbook of research methods in social and personality psychology* (2 ed., pp. 404–442). New York: Cambridge University.

Kruglanski, A. W. (1989). *Lay epistemics and human knowledge: Cognitive and motivational bases.* New York, NY: Plenum Press.

Krull, D. S., Loy, M. H. -M., Lin, J., Wang, C. -F., Chen, S., & Zhao, X. (1999). The fundamental fundamental attribution error: Correspondence bias in individualist and collectivist cultures. *Personality and Social Psychology Bulletin, 25,* 1208–1219.

Kubota, J. T., & Ito, T.A. (2009). You were always on my mind: How event-related potentials inform impression formation research. In T. D. Nelson (Ed.), *Handbook of prejudice, stereotyping, and discrimination* (pp. 333–345). New York, NY: Psychology Press.

Kukucka, J., & Kassin, S. M. (2014). Do confessions taint perceptions of handwriting evidence? An empirical test of the forensic confirmation bias. *Law and Human Behavior, 38,* 256–270.

Kumru, A., Carlo, G., Mestre, M. V., & Samper, P. (2012). Prosocial moral reasoning and prosocial behavior among Turkish and Spanish adolescents. *Social Behavior and Personality, 40,* 205–214.

Kunda, Z. (1990). The case for motivated reasoning. *Psychological Bulletin, 108,* 480–498.

Kunda, Z. (1999). *Social cognition: Making sense of people.* Cambridge, MA: The MIT Press.

Kunda, Z., & Sinclair, L. (1999). Motivated reasoning with stereotypes: Activation, application, and inhibition. *Psychological Inquiry, 10,* 12–22.

Kunimi, M., & Kojima, H. (2014). The effects of processing speed and memory span on working memory.

GeroPsych: The Journal of Gerontopsychology and Geriatric Psychiatry, 27, 109–114.

Kunstman, J. W., & Maner, J. K. (2011). Sexual overperception: Power, mating motives, and biases in social judgment. *Journal of Personality and Social Psychology, 100,* 282–294.

Kunstman, J. W., & Plant, E. A. (2008). Racing to help: Racial bias in high emergency helping situations. *Journal of Personality and Social Psychology, 95,* 1499–1510.

Kunz, P. R., & Woolcott, M. (1976). Season's greetings: From my status to yours. *Social Science Research, 5,* 269–278.

Kurdek, L. A. (1999). The nature and predictors of the trajectory of change in marital quality for husbands and wives over the first 10 years of marriage. *Developmental Psychology, 35,* 1283–1296.

Kurdek, L. A. (2008). Change in relationship quality for partners from lesbian, gay male, and heterosexual couples. *Journal of Family Psychology, 22,* 701–711.

Kurina, L. M., Knutson, K. L., Hawkley, L. C., Cacioppo, J. T., Lauderdale, D. S., & Ober, C. (2011). Loneliness is associated with sleep fragmentation in a communal society. *Sleep, 34,* 1519–1526.

Kurland, J. A., & Gaulin, S. J. C. (2005). Cooperation and conflict among kin. In D. M. Buss & D. M. Buss (Eds.), *The handbook of evolutionary psychology* (pp. 447–482). Hoboken, NJ: John Wiley & Sons Inc.

Kurt, D. D., Inman, J. J., & Argo, J. J. (2011). The influence of friends on consumer spending: The role of agency-communion orientation and self-monitoring. *Journal of Marketing Research, 48,* 741–754.

Kutzner, F. L., & Fiedler, K. (2015). No correlation, no evidence for attention shift in category learning: Different mechanisms behind illusory correlations and the inverse base-rate effect. *Journal of Experimental Psychology: General, 144,* 58–75.

Kutzner, F. L., & Fiedler, K. (2015). No correlation, no evidence for attention shift in category learning: Different mechanisms behind illusory correlations and the inverse base-rate effect. *Journal of Experimental Psychology: General, 144,* 58–75.

Kwan, V. S. Y., & Mandisodza, A. N. (2007). Self-esteem: On the relation between conceptualization and measurement. In C. Sedikides & S. J. Spencer (Eds.), *The self* (pp. 259–282). New York, NY: Psychology Press.

Kwang, T., & Swann, W. B. (2010). Do people embrace praise even when they feel unworthy? A review of critical tests of self-enhancement versus self-verification. *Personality and Social Psychology Review, 14,* 263–280.

La France, B. H., Henningsen, D. D., Oates, A., & Shaw, C. M. (2009). Social-sexual interactions? Meta-analyses of sex differences in perceptions of flirtatiousness, seductiveness, and promiscuousness. *Communication Monographs, 76,* 263–285.

LaBouff, J. P., Rowatt, W. C., Johnson, M. K., & Finkle, C. (2012). Differences in attitudes toward outgroups in religious and nonreligious contexts in a multinational sample: A situational context priming study. *International Journal for the Psychology of Religion, 22,* 1–9.

Lagerspetz, K. M. J. (1979). Modification of aggressiveness in mice. In S. Feshbach & S. Fraczek (Eds.), *Aggression and behaviour change* (pp. 66–82). New York, NY: Praeger.

Lagerspetz, K. M. J., Björkqvist, K., & Peltonen, T. (1988). Is indirect aggression typical of females? *Aggressive Behavior, 14,* 403–414.

Lakey, B. (2013). Perceived social support and happiness: The role of personality and relational processes. In S. A. David, I. Boniwell, & A. C. Ayers (Eds.), *The Oxford handbook of happiness* (pp. 847–859). Oxford, UK: Oxford University.

Lakoff, G., & Johnson, M. (1999). *Philosophy in the flesh: The embodied mind and its challenge to Western thought.* New York: Basic Books.

Lalancette, M. -F., & Standing, L. G. (1990). Asch fails again. *Social Behavior and Personality, 18,* 7–12.

Landau, M. J., Solomon, S., Greenberg, J., Cohen, F., Pyszczynski, T., Arndt, J., . . . Cook, A. (2004). Deliver us from evil: The effects of mortality salience and reminders of 9/11 on support for President George W. Bush. *Personality and Social Psychology Bulletin, 30,* 1136–1150.

Langer, E. J. (1975). The illusion of control. *Journal of Personality and Social Psychology, 32,* 311–328.

Langer, E. J. (1977). The psychology of chance. *Journal for the Theory of Social Behaviour, 7,* 185–207.

Langleben, D. D., & Moriarty, J. C. (2013). Using brain imaging for lie detection: Where science, law, and policy collide. *Psychology, Public Policy, and Law, 19,* 222–234.

Langlois, J. H., & Roggman, L. A. (1990). Attractive faces are only average. *Psychological Science, 1,* 115–121.

Langlois, J. H., Kalakanis, L., Rubenstein, A. J., Larson, A., Hallam, M., & Smoot, M. (2000). Maxims or myths of beauty? A meta-analytic and theoretical review. *Psychological Bulletin, 126,* 390–423.

LaPiere, R. T. (1934). Attitudes vs. actions. *Social Forces, 13,* 230–237.

Larsen, J. T., & Green, J. D. (2013). Evidence for mixed feelings of happiness and sadness from brief moments in time. *Cognition and Emotion, 27,* 1469–1477.

Larson, J. R., Jr. (2010). In search of synergy in small group performance. New York, NY: Psychology Press.

Lasswell, H. D. (1948). *Power and personality.* New York, NY: W W Norton.

Latané, B., & Dabbs, J. M. (1975). Sex, group size and helping in three cities. *Sociometry, 38,* 180–194.

Latané, B., & Darley, J. M. (1968). Group inhibition of bystander intervention in emergencies. *Journal of Personality and Social Psychology, 10,* 215–221.

Latané, B., & Darley, J. M. (1969). Bystanders "apathy." *American Scientist, 57,* 244–268.

Latané, B., & Nida, S. (1981). Ten years of research on group size and helping. *Psychological Bulletin, 89,* 308–324.

Latané, B., Williams, K., & Harkins, S. (1979). Many hands make light the work: The causes and consequences of social loafing. *Journal of Personality and Social Psychology, 37,* 822–832.

Lau, R. R., Sigelman, L., & Rovner, I. B. (2007). The effects of negative political campaigns: A meta-analytic reassessment. *The Journal of Politics, 69,* 1176–1209.

Laumann, K., Gärling, T., & Stormark, K. M. (2003). Selective attention and heart rate responses to natural and urban environments. *Journal of Environmental Psychology, 23,* 125–134.

Laurencelle, R. M., Abell, S. C., & Schwartz, D. J. (2002). The relation between intrinsic religious faith and psychological well-being. *International Journal for the Psychology of Religion, 12,* 109–123.

Lavine, R. A. (2009). Personality traits across cultures and research on obedience. *American Psychologist, 64,* 620–620.

Lawrence, C., & Hutchinson, L. (2014). The impact of non-aggressive behaviour early in aggressive interactions: Sex differences in direct and indirect aggression in response to provocation. *British Journal of Psychology, 105,* 127–144.

Lawrence, N. K. (2015). Highlighting the injunctive norm to reduce phone-related distracted driving. *Social Influence, 10,* 109–118.

Lawson, T. J. (2010). The Social Spotlight Increases Blindness to Change Blindness. *Basic & Applied Social Psychology, 32,* 360–368.

Layous, K., Nelson, S. K., & Lyubomirsky, S. (2013). What is the optimal way to deliver a positive activity intervention? The case of writing about one's best possible selves. *Journal of Happiness Studies, 14,* 635–654.

Lazarus, R. S. (2006). *Stress and emotion.* New York, NY: Springer.

Lazarus, R. S. (2012). Evolution of a model of stress, coping, and discrete emotions. In V. H. Rice & V. H. Rice (Eds.), *Handbook of stress, coping, and health: Implications for nursing research, theory, and practice* (2nd ed., pp. 199–223). Thousand Oaks, CA: Sage.

Lazarus, R. S., & Folkman, S. (1984). *Stress, appraisal, and coping.* New York, NY: Springer.

Le Hénaff, B., Michinov, N., Le Bohec, O., & Delaval, M. (2015). Social gaming is inSIDE: Impact of anonymity and group identity on performance in a team game-based learning environment. *Computers & Education, 82,* 84–95.

Le Pelley, M. E., Reimers, S. J., Calvini, G., Spears, R., Beesley, T., & Murphy, R. A. (2010). Stereotype formation: Biased by association. *Journal of Experimental Psychology: General, 139,* 138–161.

Leak, G. K., & Finken, L. L. (2011). The relationship between the constructs of religiousness and prejudice: A structural equation model analysis. *International Journal for the Psychology of Religion, 21,* 43–62.

Leander, N. P., Chartrand, T. L., & Wood, W. (2011). Mind your mannerisms: Behavioral mimicry elicits stereotype conformity. *Journal of Experimental Social Psychology, 47,* 195–201.

Leaper, C., & Ayres, M. M. (2007). A meta-analytic review of gender variations in adults' language use: Talkativeness, affiliative speech, and assertive speech. *Personality and Social Psychology Review, 11,* 328–363.

Leary, M. R. (1999). The social and psychological importance of self-esteem. In R. M. Kowalski & M. R. Leary (Eds.), *The social psychology of emotional and behavioral problems: Interfaces of social and clinical psychology* (pp. 197–221). Washington, DC: American Psychological Association.

Leary, M. R. (2005). Interpersonal cognition and the quest for social acceptance: Inside the sociometer. In M. W. Baldwin (Ed.), *Interpersonal cognition* (pp. 85–102). New York, NY: Guilford Press.

Leary, M. R. (2010). Affiliation, acceptance, and belonging: The pursuit of interpersonal connection. In S. T. Fiske, D. T. Gilbert, & G. Lindzey (Eds.), *Handbook of social psychology* (Vol. 2, 5th ed., pp. 864–897). Hoboken, NJ: John Wiley & Sons.

Leary, M. R., & Allen, A. B. (2011). Self-presentational persona: Simultaneous management of multiple impressions. *Journal of Personality and Social Psychology, 101,* 1033–1049.

Leary, M. R., & Tangney, J. P. (2003). *Handbook of self and identity.* New York, NY: Guilford Press.

Leary, M. R., & Toner, K. (2015). Self-processes in the construction and maintenance of personality. In M. Mikulincer, P. R. Shaver, M. L. Cooper, R. J. Larsen, M. Mikulincer, P. R. Shaver, M. L. Cooper & R. J. Larsen (Eds.), *APA handbook of personality and social psychology, Volume 4: Personality processes and individual differences* (pp. 447–467). Washington, DC: American Psychological Association.

Lecat, B., Hilton, D. J., & Crano, W. D. (2009). Group status and reciprocity norms: Can the door-in-the-face effect be obtained in an out-group context? *Group Dynamics: Theory, Research, and Practice, 13,* 178–189.

Lee, H. I., Leung, A.K.y., & Kim, Y. H. (2014). Unpacking East–West differences in the extent of self-enhancement from the perspective of face versus dignity culture. *Social and Personality Psychology Compass, 8,* 314–327.

Lee, K., Ogunfowora, B., & Ashton, M. C. (2005). Personality traits beyond the big five: Are they within the HEXACO space? *Journal of Personality, 73,* 1437–1463.

Lee, M. K. O., Shi, N., Cheung, C. M. K., Lim, K. H., & Sia, C. L. (2011). Consumer's decision to shop online: The moderating role of positive informational social influence. *Information & Management, 48,* 185–191.

Lee, S. Y., Oh, S., & Jung, S. (2014). The effects of scarcity appeal on product evaluation: Consumers' cognitive resources and company reputation. *Social Behavior and Personality, 42,* 743–756.

Lee, T. L., & Fiske, S. T. (2006). Not an outgroup, not yet an ingroup: Immigrants in the Stereotype Content Model. *International Journal of Intercultural Relations, 30,* 751–768.

Legault, L., & Green-Demers, I. (2012). The protective role of self-determined prejudice regulation in the relationship between intergroup threat and prejudice. *Motivation and Emotion, 36,* 143–158.

Leippe, M. R., & Eisenstadt, D. (2010). Self-persuasion when it matters to self: Attitude importance and dissonance reduction after counterattitudinal advocacy. In M. H. Gonzales, C. Tavris, & J. Aronson (Eds.), *The scientist and the humanist: A festschrift in honor of Elliot Aronson* (pp. 175–199). New York, NY: Psychology Press.

Lemay, E. P., Jr., Clark, M. S., & Greenberg, A. (2010). What is beautiful is good because what is beautiful is desired: Physical attractiveness stereotyping as projection of interpersonal goals. *Personality and Social Psychology Bulletin, 36,* 339–353.

Lemmon, G., & Wayne, S. J. (2015). Underlying motives of organizational citizenship behavior: Comparing egoistic and altruistic motivations. *Journal of Leadership & Organizational Studies, 22,* 129–148.

Lench, H. C., Safer, M. A., & Levine, L. J. (2011). Focalism and the underestimation of future emotion: When it's worse than imagined. *Emotion, 11,* 278–285.

Lepper, M. R., Greene, D., & Nisbett, R. E. (1973). Undermining children's intrinsic interest with extrinsic reward: A test of the "overjustification" hypothesis. *Journal of Personality and Social Psychology, 28,* 129–137.

Lepper, M. R., Henderlong, J., & Gingras, I. (1999). Understanding the effects of extrinsic rewards on intrinsic motivation: Uses and abuses of meta-anlysis: Comment on Deci, Koestner, and Ryan (1999) *Psychological Bulletin, 125,* 669–676.

Lerner, M. J. (1980). *The belief in a just world: A fundamental delusion.* New York, NY: Plenum.

Leshner, G., Bolls, P., & Wise, K. (2011). Motivated processing of fear appeal and disgust images in televised anti-tobacco ads. *Journal of Media Psychology: Theories, Methods, and Applications, 23,* 77–89.

Leung, A. K. Y., & Cohen, D. (2011). Within- and between-culture variation: Individual differences and the cultural logics of honor, face, and dignity cultures. *Journal of Personality and Social Psychology, 100,* 507–526.

Levashina, J., & Campion, M. A. (2007). Measuring faking in the employment interview: Development and validation of an interview faking behavior scale. *Journal of Applied Psychology, 92,* 1638–1656.

Levashina, J., Weekley, J. A., Roulin, N., & Hauck, E. (2014). Using blatant extreme responding for detecting faking in high-stakes selection: Construct validity, relationship with general mental ability, and subgroup differences. *International Journal of Selection and Assessment, 22,* 371–383.

LeVay, S. (1991). A difference in hypothalamic structure between heterosexual and homosexual men. *Science, 253,* 1034–1037.

LeVay, S. (2011). *Gay, straight, and the reason why: The science of sexual orientation.* New York, NY: Oxford University Press.

Levenson, R. W., & Gottman, J. M. (1983). Marital interaction: Physiological linkage and affective exchange. *Journal of Personality and Social Psychology, 45,* 587–597.

Levine, J. M. (1999). Solomon Asch's legacy for group research. *Personality and Social Psychology Review, 3,* 358–364.

Levine, J. M. (2007). Conformity. In R. F. Baumeister & K. D. Vohs (Eds.), *Encyclopedia of social psychology* (pp. 167–171). Los Angeles, CA: Sage.

Levine, J. M. (2013). *Group processes.* New York, NY: Psychology Press.

Levine, J. M., & Prislin, R. (2013). Majority and minority influence. In J. M. Levine (Ed.), *Group processes* (pp. 135–163). New York, NY: Psychology Press.

Levine, J. M., & Russo, E. M. (1987). Majority and minority influence. In C. Hendrick (Ed.), *Group processes* (pp. 13–54). Thousand Oaks, CA: Sage.

Levine, M. (2012). Helping in emergencies: Revisiting Latané and Darley's bystander studies. In J. R. Smith & S. A. Haslam (Eds.), *Social psychology: Revisiting the classic studies* (pp. 192–208). Los Angeles, CA: Sage.

Levine, M., & Cassidy, C. (2010). Groups, identities, and bystander behavior: How group processes can be used to promote helping. In S. Stürmer & M. Snyder (Eds.), *The psychology of prosocial behavior: Group processes, intergroup relations, and helping* (pp. 209–222). Malden, MA: Wiley-Blackwell.

Levine, M., & Crowther, S. (2008). The responsive bystander: How social group membership and group size can encourage as well as inhibit bystander intervention. *Journal of Personality and Social Psychology, 95,* 1429–1439.

Levine, M., Cassidy, C., & Jentzsch, I. (2010). The implicit identity effect: Identity primes, group size, and helping. *British Journal of Social Psychology, 49,* 785–802.

Levine, M., Prosser, A., Evans, D., & Reicher, S. (2005). Identity and emergency intervention: How social group membership and inclusiveness of group boundaries shape helping behavior. *Personality and Social Psychology Bulletin, 31,* 443–453.

Levine, R. V. (2015). Keeping time. In M. Stolarski, N. Fieulaine, W. van Beek, M. Stolarski, N. Fieulaine, & W. van Beek (Eds.), *Time perspective theory; Review, research and application: Essays in honor of Philip G. Zimbardo* (pp. 189–196). Cham, Switzerland: Springer International Publishing.

Levine, R. V., Martinez, T. S., Brase, G., & Sorenson, K. (1994). Helping in 36 U.S. cities. *Journal of Personality and Social Psychology, 67,* 69–82.

Levine, R. V., Reysen, S., & Ganz, E. (2008). The kindness of strangers revisited: A comparison of 24 U.S. cities. *Social Indicators Research, 85,* 461–481.

Levine, R. V., West, L. J., & Reis, H. T. (1980). Perceptions of time and punctuality in the United States and Brazil. *Journal of Personality and Social Psychology, 38,* 541–550.

Levine, R., Sato, S., Hashimoto, T., & Verma, J. (1995). Love and marriage in eleven cultures. *Journal of Cross-Cultural Psychology, 26,* 554–571.

Lewandowsky, S., Stritzke, W. G. K., Oberauer, K., & Morales, M. (2005). Memory for fact, fiction, and misinformation: The Iraq War 2003. *Psychological Science, 16,* 190–195.

Lewin, K. (1946). Behavior and development as a function of the total situation. In L. Carmichael (Ed.), *Manual of child psychology* (pp. 791–844). Hoboken, NJ: John Wiley & Sons.

Lewin, K. (1946). Behavior and development as a function of the total situation. In L. Carmichael (Ed.), *Manual of child psychology* (pp. 791–844). Hoboken, NJ: John Wiley & Sons.

Lewis, D. M. G., Russell, E. M., Al-Shawaf, L., & Buss, D. M. (2015). Lumbar curvature: A previously undiscovered standard of attractiveness. *Evolution and Human Behavior.*

Lewis, G. J., Ritchie, S. J., & Bates, T. C. (2011). The relationship between intelligence and multiple domains of religious belief: Evidence from a large adult US sample. *Intelligence, 39,* 468–472.

Lewis, M., & Lyall, S. (2012, August 24) Norway mass killer gets the maximum: 21 years, *New York Times.* Retrieved from http://www.nytimes.com

Li, N. P., & Kenrick, D. T. (2006). Sex similarities and differences in preferences for short-term mates: What, whether, and why. *Journal of Personality and Social Psychology, 90,* 468–489.

Li, N. P., Bailey, J. M., Kenrick, D. T., & Linsenmeier, J. A. W. (2002). The necessities and luxuries of mate preferences: Testing the tradeoffs. *Journal of Personality and Social Psychology, 82,* 947–955.

Li, N., Kirkman, B. L., & Porter, C. O. L. H. (2014). Toward a model of work team altruism. *The Academy of Management Review, 39,* 541–565.

Li, Y. J., Johnson, K. A., Cohen, A. B., Williams, M. J., Knowles, E. D., & Chen, Z. (2012). Fundamental(ist) attribution error: Protestants are dispositionally focused. *Journal of Personality and Social Psychology, 102,* 281–290.

Lickel, B., Hamilton, D. L., Wieczorkowska, G., Lewis, A., Sherman, S. J., & Uhles, A. N. (2000). Varieties of groups and the perception of group entitativity. *Journal of Personality and Social Psychology, 78,* 223–246.

Liddle, J. R., Shackelford, T. K., & Weekes-Shackelford, V. A. (2012). Why can't we all just get along? Evolutionary perspectives on violence, homicide, and war. *Review of General Psychology, 16,* 24–36.

Lieberman, D., & Hatfield, E. (2006). Passionate love: Cross-cultural and evolutionary perspectives. In R. J. Sternberg & K. Weis (Eds.), *The new psychology of love* (pp. 274–297). New Haven, CT: Yale University Press.

Lieberman, J. D. (2011). The utility of scientific jury selection: Still murky after 30 years. *Current Directions in Psychological Science, 20,* 48–52.

Lieberman, M. D. (2007). The X- and C-systems: The neural basis of automatic and controlled social Cognition. In E. Harmon-Jones & P. Winkielman (Eds.), *Social neuroscience: Integrating biological and psychological explanations of social behavior* (pp. 290–315). New York, NY: Guilford Press.

Lieberman, M. D. (2007a). Social cognitive neuroscience: A review of core processes. *Annual Review of Psychology, 58,* 259–289.

Lieberman, M. D. (2007b). The X- and C-systems: The neural basis of automatic and controlled social cognition. In E. Harmon-Jones & P. Winkielman (Eds.), *Social neuroscience: Integrating biological and psychological explanations of social behavior* (pp. 290–315). New York, NY: Guilford Press.

Lieberman, M. D. (2010). Social cognitive neuroscience. In S. T. Fiske, D. T. Gilbert, & G. Lindzey (Eds.), *Handbook of social psychology* (Vol. 1, 5th ed., pp. 143–193). Hoboken, NJ: John Wiley & Sons.

Lieberman, M. D. (2013). *Social: Why our brains are wired to connect.* New York, NY: Crown Publishers.

Lieberman, M. D., Gaunt, R., Gilbert, D. T., & Trope, Y. (2002). Reflexion and reflection: A social cognitive neuroscience approach to attributional inference. In M. P. Zanna (Ed.), *Advances in experimental social psychology* (Vol. 34., pp. 199–249). San Diego, CA: Academic Press.

Lieberman, M., & Peskin, H. (1992). Adult life crises. In J. Birren, R. Sloane, & G. Cohen (Eds.), *Handbook of mental health and aging* (2nd ed., pp. 119–143). San Diego, CA: Academic Press.

Likert, R. (1932). A technique for the measurement of attitudes. *Archives of Psychology, 22,* 1–55.

Liljenquist, K., Zhong, C.-B., & Galinsky, A. D. (2010). The smell of virtue: Clean scents promote reciprocity and charity. *Psychological Science, 21,* 381–383.

Lim, B. -C., & Klein, K. J. (2006). Team mental models and team performance: A field study of the effects of team mental model similarity and accuracy. Journal of Organizational Behavior, 27, 403–418.

Lin, K. -H., & Lundquist, J. (2013). Mate selection in cyberspace: The intersection of race, gender, and education. *American Journal of Sociology, 119,* 183–215.

Liu, J. H., Campbell, S. M., & Condie, H. (1995). Ethnocentrism in dating preferences for an American sample: The ingroup bias in social context. *European Journal of Social Psychology, 25,* 95–115.

Liu, J., Harris, A., & Kanwisher, N. (2002). Stages of processing in face perception: An MEG study. *Nature Neuroscience, 5,* 910–916.

Locke, E. A. (2009). It's time we brought introspection out of the closet. *Perspectives on Psychological Science, 4,* 24–25.

Locke, K. D. (2009). Aggression, narcissism, self-esteem, and the attribution of desirable and humanizing traits to self versus others. *Journal of Research in Personality, 43,* 99–102.

Locksley, A., Ortiz, V., & Hepburn, C. (1980). Social categorization and discriminatory behavior: Extinguishing the minimal intergroup discrimination effect. *Journal of Personality and Social Psychology, 39,* 773–783.

Lockwood, P., & Matthews, J. (2007). The self as a social comparer. In C. Sedikides & S. J. Spencer (Eds.), *The self* (pp. 95–113). New York, NY: Psychology Press.

Loeber, R., & Hay, D. (1997). Key issues in the development of aggression and violence from childhood to early adulthood. *Annual Review of Psychology, 48,* 371–410.

Lomas, T., Cartwright, T., Edginton, T., & Ridge, D. (2014). A religion of wellbeing? The appeal of Buddhism to men in London, United Kingdom. *Psychology of Religion and Spirituality, 6,* 198–207.

Lönnqvist, J. -E., Konstabel, K., Lönnqvist, N., & Verkasalo, M. (2014). Accuracy, consensus, in-group bias, and cultural frame shifting in the context of national character stereotypes. *The Journal of Social Psychology, 154,* 40–58.

Lord, C. G., & Saenz, D. S. (1985). Memory deficits and memory surfeits: Differential cognitive consequences of tokenism for tokens and observers. *Journal of Personality and Social Psychology, 49,* 918–926.

Lord, C. G., Ross, L., & Lepper, M. R. (1979). Biased assimilation and attitude polarization: The effects of prior theories on subsequently considered evidence. *Journal of Personality and Social Psychology, 37,* 2098–2109.

Lovett, F. (1997). Thinking about values (Report of December 13, 1996 *Wall Street Journal* national survey). *The Responsive Community, 7,* 63.

Lu, H., While, A. E., & Barriball, K. L. (2008). Role perceptions and reported actual role content of hospital nurses in Mainland China. Journal of Clinical Nursing, 17, 1011–1022.

Lucas, R. E. (2005). Time does not heal all wounds: A longitudinal study of reaction and adaptation to divorce. *Psychological Science, 16,* 945–950.

Lucas, R. E. (2008). Personality and subjective well-being. In M. Eid & R. J. Larsen (Eds.), *The science of subjective well-being* (pp. 171–194). New York, NY: Guilford Press.

Lucas, R. E., Clark, A. E., Georgellis, Y., & Diener, E. (2003). Reexamining adaptation and the set point model of happiness: Reactions to changes in marital status. *Journal of Personality and Social Psychology, 84,* 527–539.

Luhmann, M., Hofmann, W., Eid, M., & Lucas, R. E. (2012). Subjective well-being and adaptation to life events: A meta-analysis. *Journal of Personality and Social Psychology, 102,* 592–615.

Luhrmann, T. M. (2013, August 3). Addicted to prayer. *New York Times, 162,* 11–11.

Luo, S., & Klohnen, E. C. (2005). Assortative mating and marital quality in newlyweds: A couple-centered approach. *Journal of Personality and Social Psychology, 88,* 304–326.

Luo, Y., Hawkley, L. C., Waite, L. J., & Cacioppo, J. T. (2012). Loneliness, health, and mortality in old age: a national longitudinal study. *Social Science & Medicine (1982), 74,* 907–914.

Lynn, M. (1992). The psychology of unavailability: Explaining scarcity and cost effects on value. *Basic and Applied Social Psychology, 13,* 3–7.

Lyons, A., & Kashima, Y. (2001). The reproduction of culture: Communication processes tend to maintain cultural stereotypes. *Social Cognition, 19,* 372–394.

Lyubomirsky, S. (2013). *The myths of happiness: What should make you happy, but doesn't, what shouldn't make you happy, but does.* New York, NY: The Penguin Press.

Lyubomirsky, S., King, L., & Diener, E. (2005). The benefits of frequent positive affect: Does happiness lead to success? *Psychological Bulletin, 131,* 803–855.

Lyubomirsky, S., Sheldon, K. M., & Schkade, D. (2005). Pursuing happiness: The architecture of sustainable change. *Review of General Psychology, 9,* 111–131.

Ma, Q., & Hu, Y. (2015). Beauty matters: Social preferences in a three-person ultimatum game. *PLoS ONE, 10.*

Maass, A., & Clark, R. D. (1984). Hidden impact of minorities: Fifteen years of minority influence research. *Psychological Bulletin, 95,* 428–450.

Macaulay, J. R., & Berkowitz, L. (1970). *Altruism and helping behavior.* New York, NY: Academic Press.

MacBrayer, E. K., Milich, R., & Hundley, M. (2003). Attributional biases in aggressive children and their mothers. *Journal of Abnormal Psychology, 112,* 698–708.

MacDonald, G. (2007). Self-esteem: A human elaboration of prehuman belongingness motivation. In C. Sedikides & S. J. Spencer (Eds.), *The self* (pp. 235–257). New York, NY: Psychology Press.

MacGeorge, E. L. (2003). Gender differences in attributions and emotions in helping contexts. *Sex Roles, 48,* 175–182.

MacInnis, C. C., Mackinnon, S. P., & MacIntyre, P. D. (2010). The illusion of transparency and normative beliefs about anxiety during public speaking. *Current Research in Social Psychology, 15.*

Mackie, D. M. (1986). Social identification effects in group polarization. *Journal of Personality and Social Psychology, 50,* 720–728.

Mackinnon, S. P., Jordan, C. H., & Wilson, A. E. (2011). Birds of a feather sit together: Physical similarity predicts seating choice. *Personality and Social Psychology Bulletin, 37,* 879–892.

MacLean, P. D. (1973). *A triune concept of the brain and behavior.* Toronto, Canada: University of Toronto.

Macmillan, M. (2008). Phineas Gage: Unravelling the myth. *The Psychologist, 21,* 828–831.

Macmillan, M., & Lena, M. L. (2010). Rehabilitating Phineas Gage. *Neuropsychological Rehabilitation, 20,* 641–658.

Madden, M., & Lenhart, A. (2006). Online dating. *Pew Internet & American Life Project.* http://www.pewinternet.org/~/media//Files/Reports/2006/PIP_Online_Dating.pdf.

Madey, S. F., & Rodgers, L. (2009). The effect of attachment and Sternberg's triangular theory of love on relationship satisfaction. *Individual Differences Research, 7,* 76.

Madon, S., Guyll, M., Buller, A. A., Scherr, K. C., Willard, J., & Spoth, R. (2008). The mediation of mothers' self-fulfilling effects on their children's alcohol use: Self-verification, informational conformity, and modeling processes. *Journal of Personality and Social Psychology, 95,* 369–384.

Madon, S., Guyll, M., Scherr, K. C., Willard, J., Spoth, R., & Vogel, D. L. (2013). The role of the self-fulfilling prophecy in young adolescents' responsiveness to a substance use prevention program. *Journal of Applied Social Psychology, 43,* 1784–1798.

Madon, S., Willard, J., Guyll, M., & Scherr, K. C. (2011). Self-fulfilling prophecies: Mechanisms, power, and links to social problems. *Social and Personality Psychology Compass, 5,* 578–590.

Madsen, E. A., Tunney, R. J., Fieldman, G., Plotkin, H. C., Dunbar, R. I. M., Richardson, J. -M., & McFarland, D. (2007). Kinship and altruism: A cross-cultural experimental study. *British Journal of Psychology, 98,* 339–359.

Magoo, G., & Khanna, R. (1991). Altruism and willingness to donate blood. *Journal of Personality and Clinical Studies, 7,* 21–24.

Maguire, E. A., & Gadian, D. G. (2000). Navigation-related structural change in the hippocampi of taxi drivers. *Proceedings of the National Academy of Sciences of the United States of America, 97,* 4398–4398.

Major, B., Barr, L., Zubek, J., & Babey, S.H. (1999). Gender and self-esteem: A meta-analysis. In W. B. Swann, J. H. Langlois, & L. A. Gilbert (Eds.), *Sexism and stereotypes in modern society: The gender science of Janet Taylor Spence* (pp. 223–253). Washington, DC: American Psychological Association.

Major, B., Eliezer, D., & Rieck, H. (2012). The psychological weight of weight stigma. *Social Psychological and Personality Science, 3,* 651–658.

Malamuth, N. M., Hald, G. M., & Koss, M. (2012). Pornography, individual differences in risk and men's acceptance of violence against women in a representative sample. *Sex Roles, 66,* 427–439.

Malinowski, P. (2013). Flourishing through meditation and mindfulness. In S. A. David, I. Boniwell, & A. Conley Ayers (Eds.), *The Oxford handbook of happiness* (pp. 384–396). New York, NY: Oxford University Press.

Malle, B. F. (2004). *How the mind explains behavior: Folk explanations, meaning, and social interaction.* Cambridge, MA: MIT Press.

Malle, B. F. (2006). The actor-observer asymmetry in attribution: A (surprising) meta-analysis. *Psychological Bulletin, 132,* 895–919.

Malle, B. F. (2011). Attribution theories: How people make sense of behavior. In D. Chadee (Ed.), *Theories in social psychology* (pp. 72–95). Hoboken, NJ: Wiley-Blackwell.

Malle, B. F., Knobe, J. M., & Nelson, S. E. (2007). Actor-observer asymmetries in explanations of behavior: New answers to an old question. *Journal of Personality and Social Psychology, 93,* 491–514.

Maltby, J., & Day, L. (2003). Religious orientation, religious coping and appraisals of stress: Assessing primary appraisal factors in the relationship between religiosity and psychological well-being. *Personality and Individual Differences, 34,* 1209–1224.

Mancini, A. D., Bonanno, G. A., & Clark, A. E. (2011). Stepping off the hedonic treadmill: Individual differences in response to major life events. *Journal of Individual Differences, 32,* 144–152.

Mandler, G. (2013). The limit of mental structures. *Journal of General Psychology, 140,* 243–250.

Maner, J. K., Luce, C. L., Neuberg, S. L., Cialdini, R. B., Brown, S., & Sagarin, B. J. (2002). The effects of perspective taking on motivations for helping: Still no evidence for altruism. *Personality and Social Psychology Bulletin, 28,* 1601–1610.

Mann, L. (1981). The baiting crowd in episodes of threatened suicide. Journal of Personality and Social Psychology, 41, 703–709.

Manning, R., Levine, M., & Collins, A. (2007). The Kitty Genovese murder and the social psychology of helping: The parable of the 38 witnesses. *American Psychologist, 62,* 555–562.

Mares, M. -L., & Woodard, E. (2005). Positive effects of television on children's social interactions: A Meta-Analysis. *Media Psychology, 7,* 301–322.

Markey, P. M. (2000). Bystander intervention in computer-mediated communication. *Computers in Human Behavior, 16,* 183–188.

Marks, E., Manning, M., & Ajzen, I. (2012). The impact of negative campaign ads. *Journal of Applied Social Psychology, 42,* 1280–1292.

Marks, G. (1984). Thinking one's abilities are unique and one's opinions are common. *Personality and Social Psychology Bulletin, 10,* 203–208.

Marks, G., & Miller, N. (1987). Ten years of research on the false-consensus effect: An empirical and theoretical review. *Psychological Bulletin, 102,* 72–90.

Marks, M. J., & Fraley, R. C. (2006). Confirmation Bias and the Sexual Double Standard. *Sex Roles, 54,* 19–26.

Markus, H. (1977). Self-schemata and processing information about the self. *Journal of Personality and Social Psychology, 35,* 63–78.

Markus, H. R., & Kitayama, S. (1991). Culture and the self: Implications for cognition, emotion, and motivation. *Psychological Review, 98,* 224–253.

Markus, H., & Wurf, E. (1987). The dynamic self-concept: A social psychological perspective. *Annual Review of Psychology, 38,* 299–337.

Marroquín, B., & Nolen-Hoeksema, S. (2015). Event prediction and affective forecasting in depressive cognition: Using emotion as information about the future. *Journal of Social and Clinical Psychology, 34,* 117–134.

Marroquín, B., Nolen-Hoeksema, S., & Miranda, R. (2013). Escaping the future: Affective forecasting in escapist fantasy and attempted suicide. *Journal of Social and Clinical Psychology, 32,* 446–463.

Martin, M. P., Miller, R. B., Kubricht, B., Yorgason, J. B., & Carroll, J. S. (2015). Relational aggression and self-reported spousal health: A longitudinal analysis. *Contemporary Family Therapy: An International Journal.*

Maruna, S., & Mann, R. E. (2006). A fundamental attribution error? Rethinking cognitive distortions. *Legal and Criminological Psychology, 11,* 155–177.

Maruna, S., & Mann, R. E. (2006). A fundamental attribution error? Rethinking cognitive distortions. Legal and Criminological Psychology, 11, 155–177.

Masuda, T., Gonzalez, R., Kwan, L., & Nisbett, R. E. (2008). Culture and aesthetic preference: Comparing the attention to context of East Asians and Americans. *Personality and Social Psychology Bulletin, 34,* 1260–1275.

Matejkowski, J., McCarthy, K. S., & Draine, J. (2011). The personal norm of reciprocity among mental health service users: Conceptual development and measurement. *Psychiatric Rehabilitation Journal, 34,* 202–213.

Mathews, T., & Meyer, M. (1992, May 10). The siege of L.A. (Cover story). *Newsweek, 119,* 30–30.

Matsumoto, D. (1993). Ethnic differences in affect intensity, emotion judgments, display rule attitudes, and self-reported emotional expression in an American sample. *Motivation and Emotion, 17,* 107–123.

Matsumoto, D., & Juang, L. (2004). *Culture and psychology* (3rd ed.). Belmont, CA: Wadsworth/Thomson Learning.

Matsumoto, D., & Willingham, B. (2009). Spontaneous facial expressions of emotion of congenitally and noncongenitally blind individuals. *Journal of Personality and Social Psychology, 96,* 1–10.

Matsumoto, D., Keltner, D., Shiota, M. N., O'Sullivan, M., & Frank, M. (2008). Facial expressions of emotion. In M. Lewis, J. M. Haviland-Jones, & L. F. Barrett (Eds.), *Handbook of emotions* (3rd ed., pp. 211–234). New York, NY: Guilford Press.

Matthews, K. A., Batson, C. D., Horn, J., & Rosenman, R. H. (1981). "Principles in his nature which interest him in the fortune of others . . .": The heritability of empathic concern for others. *Journal of Personality, 49,* 237–247.

Matthews, L. J. (2012). The recognition signal hypothesis for the adaptive evolution of religion: A phylogenetic test with Christian denominations. *Human Nature, 23,* 218–249.

Matthies, S., Rüsch, N., Weber, M., Lieb, K., Philipsen, A., Tuescher, O., . . . van Elst, L. T. (2012). Small amygdala—High aggression? The role of the amygdala in modulating aggression in healthy subjects. *The World Journal of Biological Psychiatry, 13,* 75–81.

Mattis, J. S., Jagers, R. J., Hatcher, C. A., Lawhon, G. D., Murphy, E. J., & Murray, Y. F. (2000). Religiosity, volunteerism, and community involvement among African American men: An exploratory analysis. *Journal of Community Psychology, 28,* 391–406.

Matusall, S., Kaufmann, I. M., & Christen, M. (2011). The emergence of social neuroscience as an academic discipline. In J. Decety & J. T. Cacioppo (Eds.), *The Oxford handbook of social neuroscience* (pp. 9–27). Oxford, UK: Oxford University.

Mayseless, O., & Scharf, M. (2011). Respecting others and being respected can reduce aggression in parent–child relations and in schools. In P. R. Shaver & M. Mikulincer (Eds.), *Human aggression and violence: Causes,* manifestations, and consequences (pp. 277–294). Washington, DC: American Psychological Association.

Mazar, N., & Zhong, C.-B. (2010). Do green products make us better people? *Psychological Science, 21,* 494–498.

McAndrew, F. T. (2002). New evolutionary perspectives on altruism: Multilevel-selection and costly-signaling theories. *Current Directions in Psychological Science, 11,* 79–82.

McAndrew, F. T., & De Jonge, C. R. (2011). Electronic person perception: What do we infer about people from the style of their e-mail messages? *Social Psychological and Personality Science, 2,* 403–407.

McAuliff, B. D., Kovera, M. B., & Nunez, G. (2009). Can jurors recognize missing control groups, confounds, and experimenter bias in psychological science? *Law and Human Behavior, 33,* 247–257.

McCabe, D. P., & Castel, A. D. (2008). Seeing is believing: The effect of brain images on judgments of scientific reasoning. *Cognition, 107,* 343–352.

McCauley, C. (2007). Psychological issues in understanding terrorism and the response to terrorism. In B. Bongar, L. M. Brown, L. E. Beutler, J. N. Breckenridge, & P. G. Zimbardo (Eds.), *Psychology of terrorism* (pp. 13–31). New York, NY: Oxford University Press.

McConahay, J. B. (1986). Modern racism, ambivalence, and the modern racism scale. In J. F. Dovidio & S. L. Gaertner (Eds.), *Prejudice, discrimination, and racism* (pp. 91–125). San Diego, CA: Academic Press.

McConnell, A. R., & Leibold, J. M. (2001). Relations among the implicit association test, discriminatory behavior, and explicit measures of racial attitudes. *Journal of Experimental Social Psychology, 37,* 435–442.

McConnell, A. R., & Rydell, R. J. (2014). The systems of evaluation model: A Dual-systems approach to attitudes. In J. W. Sherman, B. Gawronski, Y. Trope, J. W. Sherman, B. Gawronski, & Y. Trope (Eds.), *Dual-process theories of the social mind* (pp. 204–218). New York, NY: Guilford Press.

McConnell, A.R., & Strain, L.M. (2007). Content and structure of the self-concept. In C. Sedikides & S. J. Spencer (Eds.), *The self.* (pp. 51–73). New York, NY US: Psychology Press.

McCrae, R. R., & Costa, P. T. (1991). Adding Liebe und Arbeit: The full five-factor model and well-being. *Personality and Social Psychology Bulletin, 17,* 227–232.

McCrea, S. M., & Hirt, E. R. (2001). The role of ability judgments in self-handicapping. *Personality and Social Psychology Bulletin, 27,* 1378–1389.

McDonald, M. M., Navarrete, C. D., & Van Vugt, M. (2012). Evolution and the psychology of intergroup conflict: the male warrior hypothesis. *Philosophical Transactions Of The Royal Society Of London. Series B, Biological Sciences, 367,* 670–679.

McDougall, W. (1960). *An introduction to social psychology.* Oxford England: Barnes & Noble. (Original work published 1908)

McGuire, W. J. (1964). Inducing resistance to persuasion: Some contemporary approaches. In L. Berkowitz (Ed.), *Advances in Experimental Social Psychology* (Vol. 1, pp. 191–229). New York, NY: Academic Press.

McGuire, W. J. (1968). Personality and susceptibility to social influence. In E. F. Borgatta & W. W. Lambert (Eds.), *Handbook of personality theory and research* (pp. 1130–1187). Chicago, IL: Rand McNally.

McKay, R., & Efferson, C. (2010). The subtleties of error management. *Evolution and Human Behavior, 31,* 309–319.

McKenzie-Mohr, D. (2011). *Fostering sustainable behavior: An introduction to community-based social marketing* (2nd ed.). Gabriola Island, BC, Canada: New Society.

McKenzie-Mohr, D., Lee, N. R., Schultz, W., & Kotler, P. (2012). *Social marketing to protect the environment: What works.* Thousand Oaks, CA: Sage.

McKown, C. (2013). Social equity theory and racial-ethnic achievement gaps. *Child Development, 84,* 1120–1136.

McMillen, D. L., & Austin, J. B. (1971). Effect of positive feedback on compliance following transgression. *Psychonomic Science, 24,* 59–61.

McPherson, M., Smith-Lovin, L., & Cook, J. M. (2001). Birds of a feather: Homophily in social networks. *Annual Review of Sociology, 27,* 415–444.

Medin, D. L., & Atran, S. (2004). The Native Mind: Biological categorization and reasoning in development and across cultures. *Psychological Review, 111,* 960–983.

Medin, D. L., Unsworth, S. J., & Hirschfeld, L. (2007). Culture, categorization, and reasoning. In S. Kitayama & D. Cohen (Eds.), *Handbook of cultural psychology* (pp. 615–644). New York, NY: Guilford Press.

Medler-Liraz, H., & Yagil, D. (2013). Customer emotion regulation in the service interactions: Its relationship to employee ingratiation, satisfaction and loyalty intentions. *The Journal of Social Psychology, 153,* 261–278.

Medvec, V. H., Madey, S. F., & Gilovich, T. (1995). When less is more: Counterfactual thinking and satisfaction among Olympic medalists. *Journal of Personality and Social Psychology, 69,* 603–610.

Mehl, M. R., Gosling, S. D., & Pennebaker, J. W. (2006). Personality in its natural habitat: Manifestations and implicit folk theories of personality in daily life. *Journal of Personality and Social Psychology, 90,* 862–877.

Meier, B. P., Robinson, M. D., Carter, M. S., & Hinsz, V. B. (2010). Are sociable people more beautiful? A zero-acquaintance analysis of agreeableness, extraversion, and attractiveness. *Journal of Research in Personality, 44,* 293–296.

Meisel, M. K., & Goodie, A. S. (2014). Descriptive and injunctive social norms' interactive role in gambling behavior. *Psychology of Addictive Behaviors, 28,* 592–598.

Meiser, T., & Hewstone, M. (2006). Illusory and spurious correlations: Distinct phenomena or joint outcomes of exemplar-based category learning? *European Journal of Social Psychology, 36,* 315–336.

Mendel, R., Traut-Mattausch, E., Jonas, E., Leucht, S., Kane, J. M., Maino, K., . . . Hamann, J. (2011). Confirmation bias: Why psychiatrists stick to wrong preliminary diagnoses. *Psychological Medicine: A Journal of Research in Psychiatry and the Allied Sciences, 41,* 2651–2659.

Mendes, W. B. (2009). Assessing autonomic nervous system activity. In E. Harmon-Jones & J. S. Beer (Eds.), *Methods in social neuroscience* (pp. 118–147). New York, NY: Guilford Press.

Mercer, N. (2013). The social brain, language, and goal-directed collective thinking: A social conception of cognition and its implications for understanding how we think, teach, and learn. *Educational Psychologist, 48,* 148–168.

Merton, R. K. (1948). The self-fulfilling prophecy. *Antioch Review, 8,* 193–210.

Mesmer-Magnus, J. R., & DeChurch, L. A. (2009). Information sharing and team performance: A meta-analysis. Journal of Applied Psychology, 94, 535–546.

Messick, D. M. (2005). On the psychological exchange between leaders and followers. In D. M. Messick & R. M. Kramer (Eds.), *The psychology of leadership: New perspectives and research* (pp. 81–96). Mahwah, NJ: Lawrence Erlbaum.

Mezulis, A. H., Abramson, L. Y., Hyde, J. S., & Hankin, B. L. (2004). Is there a universal positivity bias in attributions? A meta-analytic review of individual, sevelopmental, and cultural differences in the self-serving attributional bias. *Psychological Bulletin, 130,* 711–747.

Mezzacappa, E. S., Katkin, E. S., & Palmer, S. N. (1999). Epinephrine, arousal, and emotion: A new look at two-factor theory. *Cognition and Emotion, 13,* 181–199.

Michaels, J. W., Blommel, J. M., Brocato, R. M., Linkous, R. A., & Rowe, J. S. (1982). Social facilitation and inhibition in a natural setting. *Replications in Social Psychology, 2,* 21–24.

Michinov, N., Jamet, E., Métayer, N., & Le Hénaff, B. (2015). The eyes of creativity: Impact of social comparison and individual creativity on performance and attention to others' ideas during electronic brainstorming. *Computers in Human Behavior, 42,* 57–67.

Middlemist, R. D., Knowles, E. S., & Matter, C. F. (1976). Personal space invasions in the lavatory: Suggestive evidence for arousal. *Journal of Personality and Social Psychology, 33,* 541–546.

Midlarsky, E., Jones, S. F., & Corley, R. P. (2005). Personality correlates of heroic rescue during the Holocaust. *Journal of Personality, 73,* 907–934.

Miklowitz, D. J., Alatiq, Y., Geddes, J. R., Goodwin, G. M., & Williams, J. M. G. (2010). Thought suppression in patients with bipolar disorder. *Journal of Abnormal Psychology, 119,* 355–365.

Mikulincer, M., & Shaver, P. R. (2007). *Attachment in adulthood: Structure, dynamics, and change.* New York, NY: Guilford Press.

Miles, J. A., & Greenberg, J. (1993). Using punishment threats to attenuate social loafing effects among swimmers. Organizational Behavior and Human Decision Processes, 56, 246–265.

Milgram, S. (1963). Behavioral study of obedience. *The Journal of Abnormal and Social Psychology, 67,* 371–378.

Milgram, S. (1965). Some conditions of obedience and disobedience to authority. *Human Relations, 18,* 57–76.

Milgram, S. (1969). The lost-letter technique. *Psychology Today, 3,* 30–33, 66, 68.

Milgram, S. (1970). The experience of living in cities: A psychological analysis. In F. F. Korten, S. W. Cook, & J. I. Lacey (Eds.), *Psychology and the problems of society* (pp. 152–173). Washington, DC: American Psychological Association.

Milgram, S. (1974). *Obedience to authority: An experimental view.* New York, NY: Harper & Row.

Milgram, S., Mann, L., Harter, S., & Kass, B. (1965). The lost-letter technique: A tool of social research. *Public Opinion Quarterly, 29,* 437–437.

Miller, A. G. (2004a). *The social psychology of good and evil.* New York, NY: Guilford Press.

Miller, A. G. (2004b). What can the Milgram obedience experiments tell us about the Holocaust?: Generalizing from the social psychology laboratory. In A. G. Miller (Ed.), *The social psychology of good and evil* (pp. 193–239). New York, NY: Guilford Press.

Miller, D. T., & Prentice, D. A. (1996). The construction of social norms and standards. In E. T. Higgins & A. W. Kruglanski (Eds.), *Social psychology: Handbook of basic principles* (pp. 799–829). New York, NY: Guilford Press.

Miller, E. K., & Cohen, J. D. (2001). An integrative theory of prefrontal cortex function. *Annual Review of Neuroscience, 24,* 167–202.

Miller, G. (2000). *The mating mind: How sexual choice shaped the evolution of human nature.* New York, NY: Doubleday.

Miller, J. G. (1984). Culture and the development of everyday social explanation. *Journal of Personality and Social Psychology, 46,* 961–978.

Miller, J. G. (2004). Culturally sensitive research questions and methods in social psychology. In

C. Sansone, C. C. Morf, & A. T. Panter (Eds.), *The SAGE handbook of methods in social psychology* (pp. 93–116). Thousand Oaks, CA: Sage.

Miller, J. G., Bersoff, D. M., & Harwood, R. L. (1990). Perceptions of social responsibilities in India and in the United States: Moral imperatives or personal decisions? *Journal of Personality and Social Psychology, 58,* 33–47.

Miller, N. E. (1941). I. The frustration-aggression hypothesis. *Psychological Review, 48,* 337–342.

Miller, P. A., Kozu, J., & Davis, A.C. (2001). Social influence, empathy, and prosocial behavior in cross-cultural perspective. In W. Wosinska, R. B. Cialdini, D. W. Barrett, & J. Reykowski (Eds.), *The practice of social influence in multiple cultures* (pp. 63–77). Mahwah, NJ: Lawrence Erlbaum.

Miller, P. J. E., & Rempel, J. K. (2004). Trust and partner-enhancing attributions in close relationships. *Personality and Social Psychology Bulletin, 30,* 695–705.

Miller, P. J., Wang, S. -h., Sandel, T., & Cho, G. E. (2002). Self-esteem as folk theory: A comparison of European American and Taiwanese mothers' beliefs. *Parenting: Science and Practice, 2,* 209–239.

Miller, S. L., & Maner, J. K. (2011). Ovulation as a male mating prime: Subtle signs of women's fertility influence men's mating cognition and behavior. *Journal of Personality and Social Psychology, 100,* 295–308.

Millett, C., Gray, J., Bottle, A., & Majeed, A. (2008). Ethnic disparities in blood pressure management in patients with hypertension after the introduction of pay for performance. *Annals of Family Medicine, 6,* 490–496.

Mills, R. S., & Grusec, J. E. (1989). Cognitive, affective, and behavioral consequences of praising altruism. *Merrill-Palmer Quarterly, 35,* 299–326.

Mims, P. R., Hartnett, J. J., & Nay, W. R. (1975). Interpersonal attraction and help volunteering as a function of physical attractiveness. *Journal of Psychology: Interdisciplinary and Applied, 89,* 125–131.

Mischel, W., & Ayduk, O. (2011). Willpower in a cognitive affect processing system: The dynamics of delay of gratification. In K. D. Vohs & R. F. Baumeister (Eds.), *Handbook of self-regulation: Research, theory, and applications* (2nd ed., pp. 83–105). New York, NY: Guilford Press.

Mita, T. H., Dermer, M., & Knight, J. (1977). Reversed facial images and the mere-exposure hypothesis. *Journal of Personality and Social Psychology, 35,* 597–601.

Mitchell, J. P., Heatherton, T. F., & Macrae, C. N. (2002). Distinct neural systems subserve person and object knowledge. *Proceedings of the National Academy of Sciences of the United States of America, 99,* 15238–15238.

Mitchell, J. P., Heatherton, T. F., & Macrae, C. N. (2005). Distinct neural systems subserve person and object knowledge. In J. T. Cacioppo & G. G. Berntson (Eds.), *Social neuroscience: Key readings* (pp. 53–62). New York, NY: Psychology Press.

Mitchell, T. L., Haw, R. M., Pfeifer, J. E., & Meissner, C. A. (2005). Racial bias in mock juror decision-making: A meta-analytic review of defendant treatment. *Law and Human Behavior, 29,* 621–637.

Mittone, L., & Savadori, L. (2009). The scarcity bias. *Applied Psychology: An International Review, 58,* 453–468.

Moghaddam, F. M. (2005). Psychological processes and "the staircase to terrorism." *American Psychologist, 60,* 1039–1041.

Mohanty, M. S. (2014). What determines happiness? Income or attitude: Evidence from the U.S. longitudinal data. *Journal of Neuroscience, Psychology, and Economics, 7,* 80–102.

Mojzisch, A., Grouneva, L., & Schulz-Hardt, S. (2010). Biased evaluation of information during discussion: Disentangling the effects of preference consistency, social validation, and ownership of information. *European Journal of Social Psychology, 40,* 946–956.

Molden, D. C. (2014). *Understanding priming effects in social psychology.* New York, NY: Guilford Press.

Mongeau, P. (2013). Fear appeals. In J. P. Dillard & L. Shen (Eds.), *The Sage handbook of persuasion: Developments in theory and practice* (2nd ed., pp. 184–199). Thousand Oaks, CA: Sage.

Monin, B. (2007). Normative influence. In R. F. Baumeister & K. D. Vohs (Eds.), *Encyclopedia of social psychology* (Vol. 2, pp. 627–629). Los Angeles, CA: Sage.

Monin, B., & Norton, M. I. (2003). Perceptions of a fluid consensus: Uniqueness bias, false consensus, false polarization, and pluralistic ignorance in a water conservation crisis. *Personality and Social Psychology Bulletin, 29,* 559–567.

Montoya, E. R., Terburg, D., Bos, P. A., & van Honk, J. (2012). Testosterone, cortisol, and serotonin as key regulators of social aggression: A review and theoretical perspective. *Motivation and Emotion, 36,* 65–73.

Montoya, R. M. (2008). I'm hot, so I'd say you're not: The influence of objective physical attractiveness on mate selection. *Personality and Social Psychology Bulletin, 34,* 1315–1331.

Montoya, R. M., & Horton, R. S. (2012). The reciprocity of liking effect. In M. A. Paludi (Ed.), *The psychology of love* (Vols. 1–4, pp. 39–57). Santa Barbara, CA: Praeger/ABC-CLIO.

Moors, A. (2013). On the causal role of appraisal in emotion. *Emotion Review, 5,* 132–140.

Morales, A. C., Wu, E. C., & Fitzsimons, G. J. (2012). How Disgust Enhances the Effectiveness of Fear Appeals. *Journal of Marketing Research (JMR), 49,* 383–393.

Moran, C. M., Diefendorff, J. M., & Greguras, G. J. (2013). Understanding emotional display rules at work and outside of work: The effects of country and gender. *Motivation and Emotion, 37,* 323–334.

Moran, J. M., Jolly, E., & Mitchell, J. P. (2014). Spontaneous mentalizing predicts the fundamental attribution error. *Journal of Cognitive Neuroscience, 26,* 569–576.

Moreland, R. L. (1987). The formation of small groups. In C. Hendrick (Ed.), *Group processes* (pp. 80–110). Thousand Oaks, CA: Sage.

Moreland, R. L. (1999). Transactive memory: Learning who knows what in work groups and organizations. In L. L. Thompson, J. M. Levine, & D. M. Messick (Eds.), *Shared cognition in organizations: The management of knowledge* (pp. 3–31). Mahwah, NJ: Lawrence Erlbaum.

Morewedge, C. K., & Todorov, A. (2012). The least likely act: Overweighting atypical past behavior in behavioral predictions. *Social Psychological and Personality Science, 3,* 760–766.

Mori, K., & Arai, M. (2010). No need to fake it: Reproduction of the Asch experiment without confederates. *International Journal of Psychology, 45,* 390–397.

Morris, M. W., & Peng, K. (1994). Culture and cause: American and Chinese attributions for social and physical events. *Journal of Personality and Social Psychology, 67,* 949–971.

Morrongiello, B. A., & Mark, L. (2008). "Practice what you preach": Induced hypocrisy as an intervention strategy to reduce children's intentions to risk take on playgrounds. *Journal of Pediatric Psychology, 33,* 1117–1128.

Morrow, J. (2002). Demonstrating the anchoring-adjustment heuristic and the power of the situation. *Teaching of Psychology, 29,* 129–132.

Moscovici, S. (1976). Social influence and social change. London, UK: Academic Press.

Moscovici, S. (1994). Three concepts: Minority, conflict, and behavioral style. In S. Moscovici, A. Mucchi-Faina, & A. Maass (Eds.), *Minority influence* (pp. 233–251). Chicago, IL: Nelson-Hall.

Moscovici, S., & Faucheux, C. (1972). Social influence, conformity bias, and the study of active minorities. In L. Berkowitz (Ed.), *Advances in Experimental Social Psychology* (Vol. 6, pp. 149–202). New York, NY: Academic Press.

Moscovici, S., & Markova, I. (2006). *The making of modern social psychology: The hidden story of how an international social science was created.* Cambridge, UK: Polity.

Moscovici, S., & Nemeth, C. (1974). Social influence: II. Minority influence. *Social psychology: Classic and contemporary integrations.* Oxford, UK: Rand Mcnally.

Moscovici, S., & Zavalloni, M. (1969). The group as a polarizer of attitudes. Journal of Personality and Social Psychology, 12, 125–135.

Moscovici, S., Lage, E., & Naffrechoux, M. (1969). Influence of a consistent minority on the responses of a majority in a color perception task. *Sociometry, 32,* 365–380.

Moskowitz, G. B. (2005). *Social cognition: Understanding self and others.* New York, NY: Guilford Press.

Moss, M. K., & Page, R. A. (1972). Reinforcement and helping behavior. *Journal of Applied Social Psychology, 2,* 360–371.

Moss-Racusin, C. A., & Rudman, L. A. (2010). Disruptions in women's self-promotion: The backlash avoidance model. *Psychology of Women Quarterly, 34,* 186–202.

Moyer, K. E. (1976). *The psychobiology of aggression.* New York, NY: Harper & Row.

Mucchi-Faina, A., Pacilli, M. G., & Pagliaro, S. (2010). Minority influence, social change, and social stability. Social and Personality Psychology Compass, 4, 1111–1123.

Mullen, B. (1985). The false consensus effect: A meta-analysis of 115 hypothesis tests. *Journal of Experimental Social Psychology, 21,* 262–283.

Mullen, B. (1986). Atrocity as a function of lynch mob composition: A self-attention perspective. Personality and Social Psychology Bulletin, 12, 187–197.

Mullen, B., Johnson, C., & Salas, E. (1991). Productivity loss in brainstorming groups: A meta-analytic integration. Basic and Applied Social Psychology, 12, 3–23.

Mullen, E., & Skitka, L. J. (2006). Exploring the psychological underpinnings of the moral mandate effect: Motivated reasoning, group differentiation, or anger? *Journal of Personality and Social Psychology, 90,* 629–643.

Mummendey, A., Kessler, T., Klink, A., & Mielke, R. (1999). Strategies to cope with negative social identity: Predictions by social identity theory and relative deprivation theory. *Journal of Personality and Social Psychology, 76,* 229–245.

Muraven, M., & Baumeister, R. F. (2000). Self-regulation and depletion of limited resources: Does self-control resemble a muscle? *Psychological Bulletin, 126,* 247–259.

Murdoch, D., Pihl, R. O., & Ross, D. (1990). Alcohol and crimes of violence: Present issues. *International Journal of the Addictions, 25,* 1065–1081.

Murray, D. R., Trudeau, R., & Schaller, M. (2011). On the origins of cultural differences in conformity: Four tests of the pathogen prevalence hypothesis. *Personality and Social Psychology Bulletin, 37,* 318–329.

Murray, S. L., & Holmes, J. G. (1994). Storytelling in close relationships: The construction of confidence. *Personality and Social Psychology Bulletin, 20,* 650–663.

Murray, S. L., Griffin, D. W., Derrick, J. L., Harris, B., Aloni, M., & Leder, S. (2011). Tempting fate or inviting happiness?: Unrealistic idealization prevents the decline of marital satisfaction. *Psychological Science, 22,* 619–626.

Murray, S. L., Holmes, J. G., & Griffin, D. W. (1996). The benefits of positive illusions: Idealization and the construction of satisfaction in close relationships. *Journal of Personality and Social Psychology, 70,* 79–98.

Muscanell, N. L., Guadagno, R. E., Rice, L., & Murphy, S. (2013). Don't it make my brown eyes green? An analysis of Facebook use and romantic jealousy. *Cyberpsychology, Behavior, and Social Networking, 16,* 237–242.

Mussweiler, T., Rüter, K., & Epstude, K. (2006). The why, who, and how of social comparison: A social-cognition perspective. In S. Guimond (Ed.), *Social comparison and social psychology: Understanding cognition, intergroup relations, and culture* (pp. 33–54). New York, NY: Cambridge University Press.

Myers, D. G. (2013). Religious engagement and well-being. In S. A. David, I. Boniwell, & A. Conley Ayers (Eds.), *The Oxford handbook of happiness* (pp. 88–100). New York, NY: Oxford University Press.

Myers, D. G., & Bishop, G. D. (1971). Enhancement of dominant attitudes in group discussion. Journal of Personality and Social Psychology, 20, 386–391.

Myers, D. G., & Bishop, G. D. (1971). Enhancement of dominant attitudes in group discussion. *Journal of Personality and Social Psychology, 20,* 386–391.

Na, J., Kosinski, M., & Stillwell, D. J. (2015). When a new tool is introduced in different cultural contexts: Individualism–collectivism and social network on Facebook. *Journal of Cross-Cultural Psychology, 46,* 355–370.

Nadal, K. L. (2011). The racial and ethnic microaggressions scale (REMS): Construction, reliability, and validity. *Journal of Counseling Psychology, 58,* 470–480.

Nahemow, L., & Lawton, M. P. (1975). Similarity and propinquity in friendship formation. *Journal of Personality and Social Psychology, 32,* 205–213.

Nahmias, E., Shepard, J., & Reuter, S. (2014). It's OK if "my brain made me do it": People's intuitions about free will and neuroscientific prediction. *Cognition, 133,* 502–516.

Nakamura, M., & Masuda, N. (2011). Indirect reciprocity under incomplete observation. *Plos Computational Biology, 7,* e1002113-e1002113.

Namie, G. (2014). 2014 WBI U.S. workplace bullying survey. WBI: Bellingham, WA.

Namie, G., & Namie, R. (2009). U.S. workplace bullying: Some basic considerations and consultation interventions. *Consulting Psychology Journal: Special Issue: Workplace bullying and mobbing, 61,* 202–219.

Narchet, F. M., Meissner, C. A., & Russano, M. B. (2011). Modeling the influence of investigator bias on the elicitation of true and false confessions. *Law and Human Behavior, 35,* 452–465.

NASA. (2013). Global climate change: Vital signs of the planet. Retrieved from http://climate.nasa.gov/evidence

National Center for Health Statistics. (2006). *Health, United States, 2006 with chartbook on trends in the health of Americans.* Hyattsville, MD: Government Printing Office.

Navarro, A. D., & Fantino, E. (2009). The sunk-time effect: An exploration. *Journal of Behavioral Decision Making, 22,* 252–270.

Neal, D. T., Wood, W., Wu, M., & Kurlander, D. (2011). The pull of the past: When do habits persist despite conflict with motives? *Personality and Social Psychology Bulletin, 37,* 1428–1437.

Needleman, S. (2007, November 6). Speed interviewing grows as skills shortage looms; Strategy may help lock in top picks; some drawbacks, *The Wall Street Journal.*

Negy, C., Ferguson, C. J., Galvanovskis, A., & Smither, R. (2013). Predicting violence: A cross-national study of United States and Mexican young adults. *Journal of Social & Clinical Psychology, 32,* 54–70.

Neiss, M. B., Sedikides, C., & Stevenson, J. (2006). Genetic influences on level and stability of self-esteem. *Self and Identity, 5,* 247–266.

Nelson, S. K., Kushlev, K., English, T., Dunn, E. W., & Lyubomirsky, S. (2013). In defense of parenthood: Children are associated with more joy than misery. *Psychological Science, 24,* 3–10.

Nelson, T. D. (2009). Ageism. In T. D. Nelson (Ed.), *Handbook of prejudice, stereotyping, and discrimination* (pp. 431–440). New York, NY: Psychology Press.

Nelson, T. D. (2009). Ageism. In T. D. Nelson (Ed.), *Handbook of prejudice, stereotyping, and discrimination* (pp. 431–440). New York, NY: Psychology Press.

Nestler, S. (2010). Belief perseverance: The role of accessible content and accessibility experiences. *Social Psychology, 41,* 35–41.

Neuberg, S. L., & Cottrell, C. A. (2006). Evolutionary bases of prejudices. In M. Schaller, J. A. Simpson, & D. T. Kenrick (Eds.), *Evolution and social psychology* (pp. 163–187). Madison, CT: Psychosocial Press.

Neuberg, S. L., Kenrick, D. T., & Schaller, M. (2010). Evolutionary social psychology. In S. T. Fiske, D. T. Gilbert & G. Lindzey (Eds.), *Handbook of social psychology* (Vol. 2, 5th ed., pp. 761–796). Hoboken, NJ: John Wiley & Sons.

Neumark-Sztainer, D., & Eisenberg, M. (2005). Weight bias in a teen's world. In K. D. Brownell, R. M. Puhl, M. B. Schwartz, & L. Rudd (Eds.), *Weight bias: Nature, consequences, and remedies* (pp. 68–79). New York, NY: Guilford Publications.

Newcomb, T. M. (1961). The acquaintance process as a prototype of human interaction. In *The acquaintance process* (pp. 259–261). New York, NY: Holt, Rinehart & Winston.

Newell, B. R., & Shanks, D. R. (2014). Prime numbers: Anchoring and its implications for theories of behavior priming. In D. C. Molden & D. C. Molden (Eds.), *Understanding priming effects in social psychology* (pp. 93–113). New York, NY: Guilford Press.

Newman, G. E., & Cain, D. M. (2014). Tainted altruism: When doing some good is evaluated as worse than doing no good at all. *Psychological Science, 25,* 648–655.

Nezlek, J. B. (1993). The stability of social interaction. *Journal of Personality and Social Psychology, 65,* 930–941.

Nicholls, E., & Stukas, A. A. (2011). Narcissism and the self-evaluation maintenance model: Effects of social comparison threats on relationship closeness. *The Journal of Social Psychology, 151,* 201–212.

Nichols, A. L., & Webster, G. D. (2014). The single-item Need for Consistency Scale. *Individual Differences Research, 12,* 50–58.

Nicholson, I. (2011). "Torture at Yale": Experimental subjects, laboratory torment and the "rehabilitation" of Milgram's "Obedience to Authority." *Theory & Psychology, 21,* 737–761.

Nickerson, R. S. (1998). Confirmation bias: A ubiquitous phenomenon in many guises. *Review of General Psychology, 2,* 175–220.

Nielsen, M. B., & Einarsen, S. (2012). Outcomes of exposure to workplace bullying: A meta-analytic review. *Work & Stress, 26,* 309–332.

Nielsen, M. B., Matthiesen, S. B., & Einarsen, S. (2010). The impact of methodological moderators on prevalence rates of workplace bullying. A meta-analysis. *Journal of Occupational and Organizational Psychology, 83,* 955–979.

Nijstad, B. A. (2013). Performance. In J. M. Levine (Ed.), Group processes (pp. 193–213). New York, NY: Psychology Press.

Nijstad, B. A., & Stroebe, W. (2006). How the group affects the mind: A cognitive model of idea generation in groups. *Personality and Social Psychology Review, 10,* 186–213.

Nisbett, R. E. (2003). *The geography of thought: How Asians and Westerners think differently . . . and why.* New York, NY: Free Press.

Nisbett, R. E., & Cohen, D. (1996). *Culture of honor: The psychology of violence in the South.* Boulder, CO: Westview Press.

Nisbett, R. E., & Wilson, T. D. (1977). Telling more than we can know: Verbal reports on mental processes. *Psychological Review, 84,* 231–259.

Nisbett, R. E., Peng, K., Choi, I., & Norenzayan, A. (2001). Culture and systems of thought: Holistic versus analytic cognition. *Psychological Review, 108,* 291–310.

Nolan, J., & Nail, P. (2014). Further evidence that individuals with a high preference for consistency are more susceptible to cognitive dissonance. *Psi Chi Journal of Psychological Research, 19,* 214–219.

Norenzayan, A., & Schwarz, N. (1999). Telling what they want to know: Participants tailor causal attributions to researchers' interests. *European Journal of Social Psychology, 29,* 1011–1020.

Norenzayan, A., Choi, I., & Nisbett, R.E. (2002). Cultural similarities and differences in social inference: Evidence from behavioral predictions and lay theories of behavior. *Personality and Social Psychology Bulletin, 28,* 109–120.

Norenzayan, A., Choi, I., & Peng, K. (2007). Perception and cognition. In S. Kitayama & D. Cohen (Eds.), *Handbook of cultural psychology* (pp. 569–594). New York, NY: Guilford Press.

Norenzayan, A., Smith, E. E., Kim, B. J., & Nisbett, R. E. (2002). Cultural preferences for formal versus intuitive reasoning. *Cognitive Science: A Multidisciplinary Journal, 26,* 653–684.

North, M. S., & Fiske, S. T. (2012). A history of social cognition. In A. W. Kruglanski & W. Stroebe (Eds.), *Handbook of the history of social psychology* (pp. 81–99). New York, NY: Psychology Press.

North, R. J., & Swann, W. B. (2009a). Self-verification 360°: Illuminating the light and dark sides. *Self and Identity, 8,* 131–146.

North, R. J., & Swann, W. B. (2009b). What's positive about self-verification? In S. J. Lopez & C. R. Snyder (Eds.), *Oxford handbook of positive psychology* (2nd ed., pp. 464–474). New York, NY: Oxford University Press.

Northcraft, G. B., & Neale, M. A. (1987). Experts, amateurs, and real estate: An anchoring-and-adjustment perspective on property pricing decisions. *Organizational Behavior and Human Decision Processes, 39,* 84–97.

Norton, M. I., Sommers, S. R., & Brauner, S. (2007). Bias in jury selection: Justifying prohibited peremptory challenges. *Journal of Behavioral Decision Making, 20,* 467–479.

Nosek, B. A., Banaji, M. R., & Greenwald, A. G. (2002). Math = male, me = female, therefore math ≠ me. *Journal of Personality and Social Psychology, 83,* 44–59.

Nosek, B. A., Greenwald, A. G., & Banaji, M. R. (2007). The implicit association test at age 7: A methodological and conceptual review. In J. A. Bargh (Ed.), *Social psychology and the unconscious: The automaticity of higher mental processes* (pp. 265–292). New York, NY: Psychology Press.

Nouvion, S. O., Cherek, D. R., Lane, S. D., Tcheremissine, O. V., & Lieving, L. M. (2007). Human proactive aggression: Association with personality disorders and psychopathy. *Aggressive Behavior, 33,* 552–562.

Novaco, R. W. (2011). Anger dysregulation: Driver of violent offending. *Journal of Forensic Psychiatry & Psychology, 22,* 650–668.

Nowak, M. A., & Sigmund, K. (2005). Evolution of indirect reciprocity. *Nature, 437,* 1291–1298.

Nudelman, G. (2013). The belief in a just world and personality: A meta-analysis. *Social Justice Research, 26,* 105–119.

Nudelman, G., & Shiloh, S. (2011). Who deserves to be sick? An exploration of the relationships between belief in a just world, illness causal attributions and their fairness judgements. *Psychology, Health & Medicine, 16,* 675–685.

Nyborg, H. (2009). The intelligence-religiosity nexus: A representative study of white adolescent Americans. *Intelligence, 37,* 81–93.

O'Connell, M. S., Kung, M. C., & Tristan, E. (2011). Beyond impression management: Evaluating three measures of response distortion and their relationship to job performance. *International Journal of Selection and Assessment, 19,* 340–351.

O'Hara, R. E., Armeli, S., Boynton, M. H., & Tennen, H. (2014). Emotional stress-reactivity and positive affect among college students: The role of depression history. *Emotion, 14,* 193–202.

O'Keefe, D. J., & Figgé, M. (1999). Guilt and expected guilt in the door-in-the-face technique. *Communication Monographs, 66,* 312–324.

Ochsner, K. N. (2007). Social cognitive neuroscience: Historical development, core principles, and future promise. In A. W. Kruglanski & E. T. Higgins (Eds.), *Social psychology: Handbook of basic priinciples* (pp. 39–66). New York, NY: The Guilford Press.

Ochsner, K. N. (2007). Social cognitive neuroscience: Historical development, core principles, and future promise. In A. W. Kruglanski & E. T. Higgins (Eds.), *Social psychology: Handbook of basic priinciples* (pp. 39–66). New York, NY: The Guilford Press.

Ogawa, S., Lee, T. M., Kay, A. R., & Tank, D. W. (1990). Brain magnetic resonance imaging with contrast dependent on blood oxygenation. *PNAS, 87,* 9686–9872.

Ogunfowora, B., Bourdage, J. S., & Nguyen, B. (2013). An exploration of the dishonest side of self-monitoring: Links to moral disengagement and unethical business decision making. *European Journal of Personality, 27,* 532–544.

Oh, S. H. (2013). Do collectivists conform more than individualists? Cross-cultural differences in compliance and internalization. *Social Behavior and Personality, 41,* 981–994.

Oishi, S. (2012). *The psychological wealth of nations: Do happy people make a happy society?* Walden, MA: Wiley-Blackwell.

Oishi, S., Rothman, A. J., Snyder, M., Su, J., Zehm, K., Hertel, A. W., . . . Sherman, G. D. (2007). The socioecological model of procommunity action: The benefits of residential stability. *Journal of Personality and Social Psychology, 93,* 831–844.

O'Keefe, D.J. (1999). How to handle opposing arguments in persuasive messages: A meta-analytic review of the effects of one-sided and two-sided messages. *Communication Yearbook, 22,* 209–249.

Oliner, S. P. (2003). *Do unto others: Extraordinary acts of ordinary people. How altruism inspires true acts of courage.* Cambridge, MA: Westview Press.

Oliner, S. P. (2008). *Altruism, intergroup apology, forgiveness, and reconciliation.* St. Paul, MN: Paragon House.

Oliner, S. P., & Oliner, P. M. (1988). *The altruistic personality: Rescuers of Jews in Nazi Europe.* New York, NY: Free Press.

Olson, J. M., & Stone, J. (2005). The influence of behavior on attitudes. In D. Albarracín, B. T. Johnson, & M. P. Zanna (Eds.), *The handbook of attitudes* (pp. 223–271). Mahwah, NJ: Lawrence Erlbaum.

Olson, J. M., Vernon, P. A., Harris, J. A., & Jang, K. L. (2001). The heritability of attitudes: A study of twins. *Journal of Personality and Social Psychology, 80,* 845–860.

Olson, M. A., & Kendrick, R. V. (2008). Origins of attitudes. In W. D. Crano & R. Prislin (Eds.), *Attitudes and attitude change* (pp. 111–130). New York, NY: Psychology Press.

Olson, M. L., Jr. (1965). *The logic of collective action: Public goods and the theory of groups.* Cambridge, MA: Harvard University Press.

Olsson, A., & Phelps, E. A. (2004). Learned fear of "unseen" faces after Pavlovian, observational, and instructed fear. *Psychological Science, 15,* 822–828.

Oman, D., & Thoresen, C. E. (2005). Do religion and spirituality influence health? In R. F. Paloutzian & C. L. Park (Eds.), *Handbook of the psychology of religion and spirituality* (pp. 435–459). New York, NY: Guilford Press.

Oppezzo, M., & Schwartz, D. L. (2014). Give your ideas some legs: The positive effect of walking on creative thinking. *Journal of Experimental Psychology: Learning, Memory, and Cognition, 40,* 1142–1152.

Organ, D. W., Podsakoff, P. M., & MacKenzie, S. B. (2006). *Organizational citizenship behavior: Its nature, antecedents, and consequences.* Thousand Oaks, CA: Sage.

Orobio de Castro, B., Veerman, J. W., Koops, W., Bosch, J. D., & Monshouwer, H. J. (2002). Hostile attribution of intent and aggressive behavior: A meta-analysis. *Child Development, 73,* 916–934.

Orue, I., Bushman, B. J., Calvete, E., Thomaes, S., de Castro, B. O., & Hutteman, R. (2011). Monkey see, monkey do, monkey hurt: Longitudinal effects of exposure to violence on children's aggressive behavior. *Social Psychological and Personality Science, 2,* 432–437.

Osborn, A. F. (1953). *Applied imagination: Principles and procedures of creative thinking.* New York, NY: Scribners.

Osborn, A. F. (1957). Applied imagination: Principles and procedures of creative thinking (Rev. ed.). New York, NY: Scribners.

Osborne, D., Smith, H. J., & Huo, Y. J. (2012). More than a feeling: Discrete emotions mediate the relationship between relative deprivation and reactions to workplace furloughs. *Personality and Social Psychology Bulletin, 38,* 628–641.

Oskamp, S. (2000). A sustainable future for humanity? How can psychology help? *American Psychologist, 55,* 496–508.

Owen, J., Quirk, K., & Fincham, F. (2014). Toward a more complete understanding of reactions to hooking up among college women. *Journal of Sex & Marital Therapy, 40,* 396–409.

Packer, D. J. (2008). Identifying systematic disobedience in Milgram's obedience experiments: A meta-analytic review. *Perspectives on Psychological Science, 3,* 301–304.

Panadero, S., Guillén, A. I., & Vázquez, J. J. (2015). Happiness on the street: Overall happiness among homeless people in Madrid (Spain). *American Journal of Orthopsychiatry, 85,* 324–330.

Park, C. L. (2007). Religiousness/spirituality and health: A meaning systems perspective. *Journal of Behavioral Medicine, 30,* 319–328.

Park, C. L. (2011). Meaning and growth within positive psychology: Toward a more complete understanding. In K. M. Sheldon, T. B. Kashdan, & M. F. Steger (Eds.), *Designing positive psychology: Taking stock and moving forward* (pp. 324–334). New York, NY: Oxford University Press.

Park, C. L. (2012). Meaning, spirituality, and growth: Protective and resilience factors in health and illness. In A. Baum, T. A. Revenson, & J. Singer (Eds.), *Handbook of health psychology* (2nd ed., pp. 405–429). New York, NY: Psychology Press.

Park, C. L. (2013). Spirituality and meaning making in cancer survivorship. In K. D. Markman, T. Proulx, & M. J. Lindberg (Eds.), *The psychology of meaning* (pp. 257–277). Washington, DC: American Psychological Association.

Park, C. L., Edmondson, D., & Hale-Smith, A. (2013). Why religion? Meaning as motivation. In K. I. Pargament, J. J. Exline, & J. W. Jones (Eds.), *APA handbook of psychology, religion, and spirituality: Context, theory, and research* (Vol. 1, pp. 157–171). Washington, DC: American Psychological Association.

Park, H. S. (2012). Culture, need for uniqueness, and the false consensus effect. *Journal of Social, Evolutionary, and Cultural Psychology, 6,* 82–92.

Park, J. H., & Schaller, M. (2005). Does attitude similarity serve as a heuristic cue for kinship? Evidence of an implicit cognitive association. *Evolution and Human Behavior, 26,* 158–170.

Park, L. E., & Maner, J. K. (2009). Does self-threat promote social connection? The role of self-esteem and contingencies of self-worth. *Journal of Personality and Social Psychology, 96,* 203–217.

Park, S. W., & Brown, C. M. (2014). Different perceptions of self-handicapping across college and work contexts. *Journal of Applied Social Psychology, 44,* 124–132.

Park, S., & Catrambone, R. (2007). Social facilitation effects of virtual humans. *Human Factors, 49,* 1054–1060.

Parker, D. R., & Rogers, R. W. (1981). Observation and performance of aggression: Effects of multiple models and frustration. *Personality and Social Psychology Bulletin, 7,* 302–308.

Parker, S. T., & Gibson, K. R. (1977). Object manipulation, tool use and sensorimotor intelligence as feeding adaptations in great apes and cebus monkeys. *Journal of Human Evolution, 6,* 623–641.

Parkinson, C., & Wheatley, T. (2015). The repurposed social brain. *Trends in Cognitive Sciences, 19,* 133–141.

Pascarella, E. T., & Terenzini, P. T. (1991). *How college affects students: Findings and insights from twenty years of research.* San Francisco, CA: Jossey-Bass.

Pashler, H., Coburn, N., & Harris, C. R. (2012). Priming of social distance? Failure to replicate effects on social and food judgments. *PLoS ONE, 7.*

Pashler, H., Rohrer, D., & Harris, C. R. (2013). Can the goal of honesty be primed? *Journal of Experimental Social Psychology, 49,* 959–964.

Patrick, C. J., & Verona, E. (2007). The psychophysiology of aggression: Autonomic, electrocortical, and neuro-imaging findings. In D. J. Flannery, A. T. Vazsonyi, & I. D. Waldman (Eds.), *The Cambridge handbook of violent behavior and aggression* (pp. 111–150). New York, NY: Cambridge University Press.

Pauker, K., Weisbuch, M., Ambady, N., Sommers, S. R., Adams, R. B., Jr., & Ivcevic, Z. (2009). Not so black and white: Memory for ambiguous group members. *Journal of Personality and Social Psychology, 96,* 795–810.

Paul, E. L., & Hayes, K. A. (2002). The causalities of "casual" sex: A qualitative exploration of the phenomenology of college students' hookups. *Journal of Social and Personal Relationships, 19,* 639–661.

Paulhus, D. L., & Carey, J. M. (2011). The FAD-Plus: Measuring lay beliefs regarding free will and related constructs. *Journal of Personality Assessment, 93,* 96–104.

Paulus, P. B., & Brown, V. R. (2007). Toward more creative and innovative group idea generation: A cognitive-social-motivational perspective of brainstorming. *Social and Personality Psychology Compass, 1,* 248–265.

Paulus, P. B., & Coskun, H. (2013). Creativity. In J. M. Levine (Ed.), *Group processes* (pp. 215–239). New York, NY: Psychology Press.

Paulus, P. B., Dzindolet, M. T., Poletes, G., & Camacho, L. M. (1993). Perception of performance in group brainstorming: The illusion of group productivity. *Personality and Social Psychology Bulletin, 19,* 78–89.

Paustian-Underdahl, S. C., Walker, L. S., & Woehr, D. J. (2014). Gender and perceptions of leadership effectiveness: A meta-analysis of contextual moderators. Journal of Applied Psychology, 99, 1129–1145. [Supplemental]

Pavitt, C. (2003). Colloquy: Do interacting groups perform better than aggregates of individuals? Why we have to be reductionists about group memory. Human Communication Research, 29, 592–599.

Pavlov, I. (1906). The scientific investigation of psychical faculties or processes in higher animals. *Science, 24,* 613–619.

Pavot, W., & Diener, E. (1993). Review of the Satisfaction With Life Scale. *Psychological Assessment, 5,* 164–172.

Pavot, W., & Diener, E. (2013). Happiness experienced: The science of subjective well-being. In S. A. David, I. Boniwell, & A. Conley Ayers (Eds.), *The Oxford handbook of happiness* (pp. 134–151). New York, NY: Oxford University Press.

Pearson, A. R., Dovidio, J. F., & Gaertner, S. L. (2009). Teaching & learning guide for: The nature of contemporary prejudice: Insights from aversive racism. *Social and Personality Psychology Compass, 3,* 1120–1128.

Pedersen, E. J., Forster, D. E., & McCullough, M. E. (2014). Life history, code of honor, and emotional responses to inequality in an economic game. *Emotion, 14,* 920–929.

Pedersen, W. C., Miller, L. C., Putcha-Bhagavatula, A. D., & Yang, Y. (2002). Evolved sex differences in the number of partners desired? The long and short of it. *Psychological Science, 13,* 157–161.

Pedersen, W. C., Vasquez, E. A., Bartholow, B. D., Grosvenor, M., & Truong, A. (2014). Are you insulting me? Exposure to alcohol primes increases aggression following ambiguous provocation. *Personality & Social Psychology Bulletin, 40,* 1–13.

Pehrson, S., Gheorghiu, M. A., & Ireland, T. (2012). Cultural threat and anti-immigrant prejudice: The case of Protestants in Northern Ireland. *Journal of Community & Applied Social Psychology, 22,* 111–124.

Pelham, B. W., Koole, S. L., Hardin, C. D., Hetts, J. J., Seah, E., & DeHart, T. (2005). Gender moderates the relation between implicit and explicit self-esteem. *Journal of Experimental Social Psychology, 41,* 84–89.

Peltokorpi, V. (2008). Transactive memory systems. *Review of General Psychology, 12,* 378–394.

Pendry, L., & Carrick, R. (2001). Doing what the mob do: Priming effects on conformity. *European Journal of Social Psychology, 31,* 83–92.

Peng, K., & Nisbett, R. E. (1999). Culture, dialectics, and reasoning about contradiction. *American Psychologist, 54,* 741–754.

Penner, L., Albrecht, T. L., Orom, H., Coleman, D. K., & Underwood III, W. (2010). Health and health care disparities. In J. F. Dovidio, M. Hewstone, P. Glick, & V. M. Esses (Eds.), *SAGE handbook of prejudice, stereotyping, and discrimination* (pp. 472–489). London, UK: Sage.

Peplau, L. A., Garnets, L. D., Spalding, L. R., Conley, T. D., & Veniegas, R. C. (1998). A critique of Bem's "exotic becomes erotic" theory of sexual orientation. *Psychological Review, 105,* 387–394.

Perkins, D. V., & Tagler, M. J. (2011). Jigsaw classroom. In R. L. Miller, E. Amsel, B. Marsteller Kowalewski, B. C. Beins, K. D. Keith, & B. F. Peden (Eds.), *Promoting student engagement (Vol 1): Programs, techniques and opportunities* (pp. 195–197). Washington, DC: Society for the Teaching of Psychology.

Perrett, D. I. (2012). *In your face: The new science of human attraction.* Hampshire, UK: Palgrave.

Perrett, D. I., Lee, K. J., Penton-Voak, I., Rowland, D., Yoshikawa, S., Burt, D. M., . . . Akamatsu, S. (1998). Effects of sexual dimorphism on facial attractiveness. *Nature, 394,* 884–887.

Perrett, D. I., May, K. A., & Yoshikawa, S. (1994). Facial shape and judgements of female attractiveness. *Nature, 368,* 239–242.

Perry, G. (2012). *Beyond the shock machine: The untold story of the notorious Milgram psychology experiments.* New York, NY: The New Press.

Perry, S. P., Dovidio, J. F., Murphy, M. C., & van Ryn, M. (2015). The joint effect of bias awareness and self-reported prejudice on intergroup anxiety and intentions for intergroup contact. *Cultural Diversity & Ethnic Minority Psychology, 21,* 89–96.

Petersen, M. B., Skov, M., Serritzlew, S., & Ramsøy, T. (2013). Motivated reasoning and political parties: Evidence for increased processing in the face of party cues. *Political Behavior, 35,* 831–854.

Peterson, A. A., Haynes, G. A., & Olson, J. M. (2008). Self-esteem differences in the effects of hypocrisy induction on behavioral intentions in the health domain. *Journal of Personality, 76,* 305–322.

Peterson, C., Park, N., & Seligman, M. E. P. (2005). Orientations to happiness and life satisfaction: The full life versus the empty life. *Journal of Happiness Studies, 6,* 25–41.

Petrocelli, J. V., Percy, E. J., Sherman, S. J., & Tormala, Z. L. (2011). Counterfactual potency. *Journal of Personality and Social Psychology, 100,* 30–46.

Petrocelli, J. V., Tormala, Z. L., & Rucker, D. D. (2007). Unpacking attitude certainty: Attitude clarity and attitude correctness. *Journal of Personality and Social Psychology, 92,* 30–41.

Pettigrew, T. F., & Tropp, L. R. (2006). A meta-analytic test of intergroup contact theory. *Journal of Personality and Social Psychology, 90,* 751–783.

Pettigrew, T. F., & Tropp, L. R. (2008). How does intergroup contact reduce prejudice? Meta-analytic tests of three mediators. *European Journal of Social Psychology, 38,* 922–934.

Pettit, G. S., & Mize, J. (2007). Social-cognitive processes in the development of antisocial and violent behavior. In D. J. Flannery, A. T. Vazsonyi, & I. D. Waldman (Eds.), *The Cambridge handbook of violent behavior and aggression* (pp. 322–343). New York, NY: Cambridge University Press.

Petty, R. E., & Briñol, P. (2012). The elaboration likelihood model. In P. A. M. Van Lange, A. W. Kruglanski, & E. T. Higgins (Eds.), *Handbook of theories of social psychology* (Vol. 1, pp. 224–245). Thousand Oaks, CA: Sage.

Petty, R. E., & Briñol, P. (2014). The elaboration likelihood and metacognitive models of attitudes: Implications for prejudice, the self, and beyond. In J. W. Sherman, B. Gawronski, Y. Trope, J. W. Sherman, B. Gawronski, & Y. Trope (Eds.), *Dual-process theories of the social mind* (pp. 172–187). New York, NY: Guilford Press.

Petty, R. E., & Cacioppo, J. T. (1981). *Attitudes and persuasion: Classic and contemporary approaches.* Dubuque, IA: Wm. C. Brown.

Petty, R. E., & Krosnick, J. A. (1995). *Attitude strength: Antecedents and consequences.* Hillsdale, NJ: Lawrence Erlbaum.

Petty, R. E., & Wegener, D. T. (1998). Attitude change: Multiple roles for persuasion variables. In D. T. Gilbert, S. T. Fiske, & G. Lindzey (Eds.), *The handbook of social psychology* (Vols. 1 & 2, 4th ed., pp. 323–390). New York, NY: McGraw-Hill.

Petty, R. E., & Wegener, D. T. (1999). The elaboration likelihood model: Current status and controversies. In S. Chaiken & Y. Trope (Eds.), *Dual-process theories in social psychology* (pp. 37–72). New York, NY: Guilford Press.

Petty, R. E., Cacioppo, J. T., & Goldman, R. (1981). Personal involvement as a determinant of argument-based persuasion. *Journal of Personality and Social Psychology, 41,* 847–855.

Petty, R. E., Cacioppo, J. T., Strathman, A. J., & Priester, J. R. (2005). To think or not to think: Exploring two routes to persuasion. In T. C. Brock & M. C. Green (Eds.), *Persuasion: Psychological insights and perspectives* (2nd ed., pp. 81–116). Thousand Oaks, CA: Sage.

Petty, R. E., Fazio, R. H., & Briñol, P. (2008). *Attitudes: Insights from the new implicit measures.* New York, NY: Psychology Press.

Petty, R. E., Wheeler, S. C., & Tormala, Z. L. (2013). Persuasion and attitude change. In H. Tennen, J. Suls, I. B. Weiner, H. Tennen, J. Suls, & I. B. Weiner (Eds.), *Handbook of psychology, Vol. 5: Personality and social psychology* (2nd ed., pp. 369–389). Hoboken, NJ: John Wiley & Sons.

Pew Religion and Public Life Project. (2012). The global religious landscape (Vol. 2013).

Pew Research Center (2015). Global publics back U.S. on fghting ISIS, but are Critical of Post-9/11 Torture. Retrieved from Pew Research website http://www .pewglobal.org/2015/06/23/global-publics-back-u-s-on-fighting-isis-but-are-critical-of-post-911-torture/

Pew Research Center. (2012). *Trends in American Values, 1978–2012.* Retrieved from http://www.people-press .org/files/legacy-pdf/06–04–12 Values Release.pdf.

Pfeffer, J., Fong, C. T., Cialdini, R. B., & Portnoy, R. R. (2006). Overcoming the self-promotion dilemma: Interpersonal attraction and extra help as a consequence of who sings one's praises. *Personality and Social Psychology Bulletin, 32,* 1362–1374.

Pfeifer, J. H., & Dapretto, M. (2009). "Mirror, mirror, in my mind": Empathy, interpersonal competence, and the mirror neuron system. In J. Decety & W. Ickes (Eds.), *The social neuroscience of empathy* (pp. 183–197). Cambridge, MA: MIT Press.

Phelan, S. M., Dovidio, J. F., Puhl, R. M., Burgess, D. J., Nelson, D. B., Yeazel, M. W., . . . van Ryn, M. (2014). Implicit and explicit weight bias in a national sample of 4,732 medical students: The medical student CHANGES study. *Obesity (19307381), 22,* 1201–1208.

Phillips, D. P. (1979). Suicide, motor vehicle fatalities, and the mass media: Evidence toward a theory of suggestion. *American Journal of Sociology, 84,* 1150–1174.

Phillips, M. L., Young, A. W., Senior, C., Brammer, M., Andrew, C., Calder, A. J., . . . David, A. S. (1997). A specific neural substrate for perceiving facial expressions of disgust. *Nature, 389,* 495–498.

Pilch, I., & Turska, E. (2015). Relationships between Machiavellianism, organizational culture, and workplace bullying: Emotional abuse from the target's and the perpetrator's perspective. *Journal of Business Ethics, 128,* 83–93).

Piliavin, J. A. (2005). Feeling good by doing good: Health consequences of social service. In A. M. Omoto (Ed.), *Processes of community change and social action* (pp. 29–50). Mahwah, NJ: Lawrence Erlbaum.

Piliavin, J. A., & Charng, H. -w. (1990). Altruism: A review of recent theory and research. *Annual Review of Sociology, 16,* 27–65.

Piliavin, J. A., Dovidio, J. F., Gaertner, S. L., & Clark, R. D. I. (1981). *Emergency intervention.* New York, NY: Academic Press.

Pinel, E. C., & Long, A. E. (2012). When I's meet: Sharing subjective experience with someone from the outgroup. *Personality and Social Psychology Bulletin, 38,* 296–307.

Pinel, E. C., Long, A. E., & Crimin, L. A. (2010). I-sharing and a classic conformity paradigm. *Social Cognition, 28,* 277–289.

Pinker, S. (2007). *The stuff of thought: Language as a window into human nature.* New York, NY: Viking.

Pinker, S. (2011). *The better angels of our nature: Why violence has declined.* New York, NY: Viking.

Pipher, M. (1994). *Reviving Ophelia: Saving the selves of adolescent girls.* New York, NY: Ballantine Books.

Pipher, M. (2013). *The green boat: Reviving ourselves in our capsized culture.* New York, NY: Riverhead Books.

Pittinsky, T. L., & Diamante, N. (2015). Global bystander nonintervention. *Peace and Conflict: Journal of Peace Psychology, 21,* 226–247.

Pitts, S., Wilson, J. P., & Hugenberg, K. (2013). When one is ostracized, others loom: Social rejection makes other people appear closer. *Social Psychological and Personality Science, 5,* 550–557.

Platania, J., & Moran, G. P. (2001). Social facilitation as a function of mere presence of others. *The Journal of Social Psychology, 141,* 190–197.

Platje, E., Popma, A., Vermeiren, R. R. J. M., Doreleijers, T. A. H., Meeus, W. H. J., van Lier, P. A. C., . . . Jansen, L. M. C. (2015). Testosterone and cortisol in relation to aggression in a non-clinical sample of boys and girls. *Aggressive Behavior.*

Platow, M. J., & Hunter, J. E. (2012). Integroup relations and conflict: Revisting Sherif's boys' camp studies. In J. R. Smith & S. A. Haslam (Eds.), *Social psychology: Revisiting the classic studies* (pp. 142–159). Thousand Oaks, CA: Sage.

Platt, J. (1973). Social traps. *American Psychologist, 28,* 641–651.

Polgreen, L. (2007, Feb. 11). In Niger, trees and crops turn back the desert. (Cover story). *New York Times, 156,* 1–6.

Pomery, E. A., Gibbons, F. X., Reis-Bergan, M., & Gerrard, M. (2009). From willingness to intention: Experience moderates the shift from reactive to reasoned behavior. *Personality and Social Psychology Bulletin, 35,* 894–908.

Poole, D. A., Bruck, M., & Pipe, M. -E. (2011). Forensic Interviewing aids: Do props help children answer questions about touching? *Current Directions in Psychological Science, 20,* 11–15.

Porath, C. L., & Bateman, T. S. (2006). Self-regulation: From goal orientation to job performance. *Journal of Applied Psychology, 91,* 185–192.

Pornpitakpan, C. (2003). The effect of celebrity endorsers' perceived credibility on product purchase intention: The case of Singaporeans. *Journal of International Consumer Marketing, 16,* 55–74.

Porter, R. H., Cernoch, J. M., & Balogh, R. D. (1984). Recognition of neonates by facial-visual characteristics. *Pediatrics, 74,* 501–501.

Porter, R. H., Cernoch, J. M., & McLaughlin, F. J. (1983). Maternal recognition of neonates through olfactory cues. *Physiology & Behavior, 30,* 151–154.

Portin, P. (2015). A comparison of biological and cultural evolution. *Journal of Genetics, 94,* 155–168.

Post, J. M. (2011). Crimes of obedience: "Groupthink"' at Abu Ghraib. *International Journal of Group Psychotherapy, 61,* 49–66.

Poulin, M. J., Holman, E. A., & Buffone, A. (2012). The neurogenetics of nice: Receptor genes for oxytocin and vasopressin interact with threat to predict prosocial behavior. *Psychological Science, 23,* 446–452.

Pratkanis, A. R. (2007a). *The science of social influence: Advances and future progress.* New York, NY: Psychology Press.

Pratkanis, A. R. (2007b). Social influence analysis: An index of tactics. In A. R. Pratkanis (Ed.), *The science of social influence: Advances and future progress* (pp. 17–82). New York, NY: Psychology Press.

Pratto, F., Çidam, A., Stewart, A. L., Zeineddine, F. B., Aranda, M., Aiello, A., . . . Henkel, K. E. (2013). Social dominance in context and in individuals: Contextual moderation of robust effects of social dominance orientation in 15 languages and 20 countries. *Social Psychological and Personality Science, 4,* 587–599.

Pratto, F., Sidanius, J., Stallworth, L. M., & Malle, B. F. (1994). Social dominance orientation: A personality variable predicting social and political attitudes. *Journal of Personality and Social Psychology, 67,* 741–763.

Prentice, D. A., Miller, D. T., & Lightdale, J. R. (1994). Asymmetries in attachments to groups and to their members: Distinguishing between common-identity and common-bond groups. Personality and Social Psychology Bulletin, 20, 484–493.

Prentice-Dunn, S., & Rogers, R. W. (1982). Effects of public and private self-awareness on deindividuation and aggression. *Journal of Personality and Social Psychology, 43,* 503–513.

Pressman, S. D., Cohen, S., Miller, G. E., Barkin, A., Rabin, B. S., & Treanor, J. J. (2005). Loneliness, social network size, and immune response to influenza vaccination in college freshmen. *Health Psychology, 24,* 297–306.

Preston, J. L., Ritter, R. S., & Hernandez, J. I. (2010). Principles of religious prosociality: A review and reformulation. *Social and Personality Psychology Compass, 4,* 574–590.

Preston, S. D., & de Waal, F. B. M. (2002). Empathy: Its ultimate and proximate bases. *Behavioral and Brain Sciences, 25,* 1–20.

Prislin, R., & Crano, W. D. (2008). Attitudes and attitude change: The fourth peak. In W. D. Crano & R. Prislin (Eds.), *Attitudes and attitude change* (pp. 3–15). New York, NY: Psychology Press.

Prislin, R., & Crano, W. D. (2012). A history of social influence research. In A. W. Kruglanski & W. Stroebe (Eds.), *Handbook of the history of social psychology* (pp. 321–339). New York, NY: Psychology Press.

Prochaska, J. O., DiClemente, C. C., & Norcross, J. C. (1992). In search of how people change: Applications to addictive behaviors. *American Psychologist, 47,* 1102–1114.

Programme, I. S. S. (1998). Religion II [Database]. Retrieved from http://www.gesis.org/en/data_service/issp/data/1998_Religion_II.htm

Pronin, E., Lin, D. Y., & Ross, L. (2002). The bias blind spot: Perceptions of bias in self versus others. *Personality and Social Psychology Bulletin, 28,* 369–381.

Proost, K., Schreurs, B., De Witte, K., & Derous, E. (2010). Ingratiation and self-promotion in the selection interview: The effects of using single tactics or a combination of tactics on interviewer judgments. *Journal of Applied Social Psychology, 40,* 2155–2169.

Proulx, C. M., Helms, H. M., & Buehler, C. (2007). Marital quality and personal well-being: A meta-analysis. *Journal of Marriage and Family, 69,* 576–593.

Puce, A., & Perrett, D. I. (2005). Electrophysiology and brain imaging of biological motion. In J. T. Cacioppo & G. G. Berntson (Eds.), *Social neuroscience: Key readings* (pp. 115–129). New York, NY: Psychology Press.

Quan, L., Zhen, R., Yao, B., & Zhou, X. (2014). The effects of loneliness and coping style on academic adjustment among college freshmen. *Social Behavior and Personality, 42,* 969–978.

Quattrone, G. A., & Jones, E. E. (1980). The perception of variability within in-groups and out-groups: Implications for the law of small numbers. *Journal of Personality and Social Psychology, 38,* 141–152.

Quigley-Fernandez, B., & Tedeschi, J. T. (1978). The bogus pipeline as lie detector: Two validity studies. *Journal of Personality and Social Psychology, 36,* 247–256.

Quirk, K., Owen, J., & Fincham, F. (2014). Perceptions of partner's deception in friends with benefits relationships. *Journal of Sex & Marital Therapy, 40,* 43–57.

Raab, M., Gula, B., & Gigerenzer, G. (2011). The hot hand exists in volleyball and is used for allocation decisions. *Journal of Experimental Psychology: Applied.*

Rabow, J., Newcomb, M. D., Monto, M. A., & Hernandez, A. C. (1990). Altruism in drunk driving situations: Personal and situational factors in intervention. *Social Psychology Quarterly, 53,* 199–213.

Räikkönen, K., Katainen, S., Keskivaara, P., & Kelikangas-Järvinen, L. (2000). Temperament, mothering, and hostile attitudes: A 12-year longitudinal study. *Personality and Social Psychology Bulletin, 26,* 3–12.

Ralston, D. A., Egri, C. P., Furrer, O., Kuo, M. -H., Li, Y., Wangenheim, F., . . . Weber, M. (2014). Societal-level versus individual-level predictions of ethical behavior: A 48-society study of collectivism and individualism. *Journal of Business Ethics, 122,* 283–306.

Ramsay, J. E., Pang, J. S., Shen, M. J., & Rowatt, W. C. (2014). Rethinking value violation: Priming religion increases prejudice in Singaporean Christians and Buddhists. *International Journal for the Psychology of Religion, 24,* 1–15.

Ramsey, R. D. (2006). Speed interviewing: Hiring the right people when you don't have the time to do it right. *Supervision, 67,* 7–9.

Rankin, L. E., & Eagly, A. H. (2008). Is his heroism hailed and hers hidden? Women, men, and the social construction of heroism. *Psychology of Women Quarterly, 32,* 414–422.

Rassin, E., Eerland, A., & Kuijpers, I. (2010). Let's find the evidence: An analogue study of confirmation bias in criminal investigations. *Journal of Investigative Psychology and Offender Profiling, 7,* 231–246.

Ratelle, C. F., Carbonneau, N., Vallerand, R. J., & Mageau, G. (2013). Passion in the romantic sphere: A look at relational outcomes. *Motivation and Emotion, 37,* 106–120.

Ratneshwar, S., & Chaiken, S. (1991). Comprehension's role in persuasion: The case of its moderating effect on the persuasive impact of source cues. *Journal of Consumer Research, 18,* 52–62.

Redelmeier, D. A., & Tversky, A. (2004). On the belief that arthritis pain is related to the weather. In E. Shafir (Ed.), *Preference, belief, and similarity: Selected writings by Amos Tversky* (pp. 377–381). Cambridge, MA: MIT Press.

Reed, L. I., DeScioli, P., & Pinker, S. (2014). The commitment function of angry facial expressions. *Psychological Science.*

Regan, D. T. (1971). Effects of a favor and liking on compliance. *Journal of Experimental Social Psychology, 7,* 627–639.

Regan, D. T., & Fazio, R. (1977). On the consistency between attitudes and behavior: Look to the method of attitude formation. *Journal of Experimental Social Psychology, 13*(1), 28–45.

Regan, D. T., & Kilduff, M. (1988). Optimism about elections: Dissonance reduction at the ballot box. *Political Psychology, 9,* 101–107.

Regan, P. C. (1996). Sexual outcasts: The perceived impact of body weight and gender on sexuality. *Journal of Applied Social Psychology, 26,* 1803–1815.

Reiber, C., & Garcia, J. R. (2010). Hooking up: Gender differences, evolution, and pluralistic ignorance. *Evolutionary Psychology, 8,* 390–404.

Reicher, S., Spears, R., & Postmes, T. (1995). A social identity model of deindividuated phenomena. In W. Stroebe & M. Hewstone (Eds.), European Review of Social Psychology (Vol. 6, pp. 161–198). Chichester, UK: Wiley.

Reifman, A. S., Larrick, R. P., & Fein, S. (1991). Temper and temperature on the diamond: The heat-aggression relationship in major league baseball. *Personality and Social Psychology Bulletin, 17,* 580–585.

Reimann, M., & Zimbardo, P. G. (2011). The dark side of social encounters: Prospects for a neuroscience of human evil. *Journal of Neuroscience, Psychology, and Economics, 4,* 174–180.

Reinhard, M. -A., Greifeneder, R., & Scharmach, M. (2013). Unconscious processes improve lie detection. *Journal of Personality and Social Psychology, 105,* 721–739.

Reis, H. T., Aron, A., Clark, M. S., & Finkel, E. J. (2013). Ellen Berscheid, Elaine Hatfield, and the emergence of relationship science. *Perspectives on Psychological Science, 8,* 558–572.

Reisenzein, R. (1983). The Schachter theory of emotion: Two decades later. *Psychological Bulletin, 94,* 239–264.

Renfrew, J. W. (1997). *Aggression and its causes: A biopsychosocial approach.* New York, NY: Oxford University Press.

Reysen, S., & Ganz, E. (2006). Gender differences in helping in six U.S. cities. *North American Journal of Psychology, 8,* 63–67.

Rhee, S. H., & Waldman, I. D. (2011). Genetic and environmental influences on aggression. In P. R. Shaver & M. Mikulincer (Eds.), *Human aggression and violence: Causes, manifestations, and consequences* (pp. 143–163). Washington, DC: American Psychological Association.

Rheingold, H. (2003). Smart mobs: The next social revolution. New York, NY: Basic Books.

Rhodes, G., & Tremewan, T. (1996). Averageness, exaggeration, and facial attractiveness. *Psychological Science, 7,* 105–110.

Rhodes, G., Halberstadt, J., Jeffery, L., & Palermo, R. (2005). The attractiveness of average faces is not a generalized mere exposure effect. *Social Cognition, 23,* 205–217.

Rhodes, G., Yoshikawa, S., Palermo, R., Simmons, L. W., Peters, M., Lee, K., . . . Crawford, J. R. (2007). Perceived health contributes to the attractiveness of facial symmetry, averageness, and sexual dimorphism. *Perception, 36,* 1244–1252.

Rhodes, N., & Wood, W. (1992). Self-esteem and intelligence affect influenceability: The mediating role of message reception. *Psychological Bulletin, 111,* 156–171.

Rhodewalt, F. (1990). Self-handicappers: Individual differences in the preference for anticipatory, self-protective acts. In R. L. Higgins (Ed.), *Self-handicapping: The paradox that isn't* (pp. 69–106). New York, NY: Plenum Press.

Rhodewalt, F., Saltzman, A. T., & Wittmer, J. (1984). Self-handicapping among competitive athletes: The role of practice in self-esteem protection. *Basic and Applied Social Psychology, 5,* 197–209.

Rice, D. H., Kelting, K., & Lutz, R. J. (2012). Multiple endorsers and multiple endorsements: The influence of message repetition, source congruence and involvement on brand attitudes. *Journal of Consumer Psychology, 22,* 249–259.

Richards, Z., & Hewstone, M. (2001). Subtyping and subgrouping: Processes for the prevention and promotion of stereotype change. *Personality & Social Psychology Review, 5,* 52–73.

Richardson, D. S. (2014). Everyday aggression takes many forms. *Current Directions in Psychological Science, 23,* 220–224.

Richardson, D. S., & Hammock, G. S. (2007). Social context of human aggression: Are we paying too much attention to gender? *Aggression and Violent Behavior, 12,* 417–426.

Richardson, R. C. (2015). Evolutionary psychology, altruism, and kin selection. In T. Breyer & T. Breyer (Eds.), *Epistemological dimensions of evolutionary psychology* (pp. 103–115). New York, NY,: Springer Science + Business Media.

Richerson, P. J., & Boyd, R. (2005). *Not by genes alone: How culture transformed human evolution.* Chicago, IL: University of Chicago Press.

Richerson, P. J., Boyd, R., & Henrich, J. (2010). Colloquium paper: Gene-culture coevolution in the age of genomics. *Proceedings of the National Academy of Sciences of the United* States of America, 107 Suppl 2, 8985–8992.

Ridley, M. (1996). *The origins of virtue: Human instincts and the evolution of cooperation.* New York, NY: Penguin Books.

Riemer, H., & Shavitt, S. (2011). Impression management in survey responding: Easier for collectivists or individualists? *Journal of Consumer Psychology, 21,* 157–168.

Rilling, J. K. (2011). The social brain in interactive games. In A. Todorov, S. T. Fiske, & D. A. Prentice (Eds.), *Social neuroscience: Toward understanding the underpinnings of the social mind* (pp. 217–228). New York, NY: Oxford University Press.

Ringelmann, M. (1913). Research on animate sources of power: The work of man. *Annales de l'Institute National Agrnomique, 2e sene—tome XII,* 1–40.

Risen, J. L., Gilovich, T., & Dunning, D. (2007). One-shot illusory correlations and stereotype formation. *Personality and Social Psychology Bulletin, 33,* 1492–1502.

Rivera-Maestre, R. (2015). Relational aggression narratives of African American and Latina young women. *Clinical Social Work Journal, 43,* 11–24.

Roberts, G. (2015). Partner choice drives the evolution of cooperation via indirect reciprocity. *PLoS ONE, 10*(6), e0129442-e0129442.

Roberts, G. (2015). Partner choice drives the evolution of cooperation via indirect reciprocity. *PLoS ONE, 10,* e0129442-e0129442.

Roberts, L. M., Cha, S. E., & Kim, S. S. (2014). Strategies for managing impressions of racial identity in the workplace. *Cultural Diversity and Ethnic Minority Psychology, 20,* 529–540.

Rodenborg, N. A., & Boisen, L. A. (2013). Aversive racism and intergroup contact theories: Cultural competence in a segregated world. *Journal of Social Work Education, 49,* 564–579.

Rodrigues, A., Assmar, E. M. L., & Jablonski, B. (2005). Social-psychology and the invasion of Iraq. *Revista de Psicología Social, 20,* 387–398.

Roese, N. J., & Jamieson, D. W. (1993). Twenty years of bogus pipeline research: A critical review and meta-analysis. *Psychological Bulletin, 114,* 363–375.

Roese, N. J., & Vohs, K. D. (2012). Hindsight bias. *Perspectives on Psychological Science, 7,* 411–426.

Rohan, M. J., & Zanna, M. P. (1996). Value transmission in families. In C. Seligman, J. M. Olson, & M. P. Zanna (Eds.), *The psychology of values: The Ontario symposium* (Vol. 8., pp. 253–276). Hillsdale, NJ: Lawrence Erlbaum.

Romero-Canyas, R., Downey, G., Reddy, K. S., Rodriguez, S., Cavanaugh, T. J., & Pelayo, R. (2010). Paying to belong: When does rejection trigger ingratiation? *Journal of Personality and Social Psychology, 99,* 802–823.

Rosar, U., Klein, M., & Beckers, T. (2012). Magic mayors: Predicting electoral success from candidates' physical attractiveness under the conditions of a presidential electoral system. *German Politics, 21,* 372–391.

Rosenbaum, J. E., & Johnson, B. K. (2015). Who's afraid of spoilers? Need for cognition, need for affect, and narrative selection and enjoyment. *Psychology of Popular Media Culture.*

Rosenberg, M. (1965). *Society and the adolescent self-image.* Princeton, NJ: Princeton University Press.

Rosenberg, M. (1989). *Society and the adolescent self-image* (Rev. ed.). Middletown, CT: Wesleyan University Press.

Rosenberg, M. J., Hovland, C. I., McGuire, W. J., Abelson, R. P., & Brehm, J. W. (1960). Attitude organization and change: An analysis of consistency among attitude components. *Yales studies in attitude and communication* (Vol. 3). Oxford, UK: Yale Univer. Press.

Rosenbloom, T., Shahar, A., Perlman, A., Estreich, D., & Kirzner, E. (2007). Success on a practical driver's license test with and without the presence of another testee. *Accident Analysis and Prevention, 39,* 1296–1301.

Rosenthal, L., Levy, S. R., & Earnshaw, V. A. (2012). Social dominance orientation relates to believing men should dominate sexually, sexual self-efficacy, and taking free female condoms among undergraduate women and men. *Sex Roles, 67,* 659–669.

Rosenthal, R., & Fode, K. L. (1963). The effect of experimenter bias on the performance of the albino rat. *Behavioral Science, 8,* 183–189.

Rosenthal, R., & Jacobson, L. (1968). *Pygmalion in the classroom: Teacher expectation and pupils' intellectual development.* New York, NY: Holt, Rinehart & Winston.

Rosnow, R. L., & Rosenthal, R. (1997). *People studying people: Artifacts and ethics in behavioral health research.* New York, NY: W.H. Freeman.

Rosnow, R. L., & Rosenthal, R. (1999). *Beginning behavioral research: A conceptual primer* (3rd ed.). Englewood Cliffs, NJ: Prentice-Hall.

Ross, E. A. (1908). *Social psychology: An outline and source book.* New York, NY: MacMillan Co.

Ross, L. (1977). The intuitive psychologist and his shortcomings: Distortions in the attribution process. In L. Berkowitz (Ed.), *Advances in Experimental Social Psychology* (Vol. 10, pp. 173–200). New York, NY: Academic Press.

Ross, L. L., & Bowen, A. M. (2010). Sexual decision making for the "better than average" college student. *Journal of American College Health, 59,* 211–216.

Ross, L., & Nisbett, R. E. (1991). *The person and the situation: Perspectives of social psychology.* New York, NY: McGraw-Hill.

Ross, L., Greene, D., & House, P. (1977). The false consensus effect: An egocentric bias in social perception and attribution processes. *Journal of Experimental Social Psychology, 13,* 279–301.

Ross, L., Lepper, M. R., & Hubbard, M. (1975). Perseverance in self-perception and social perception: Biased attributional processes in the debriefing paradigm. *Journal of Personality and Social Psychology, 32,* 880–892.

Ross, L., Lepper, M. R., & Hubbard, M. (1975). Perseverance in self-perception and social perception: Biased attributional processes in the debriefing paradigm. *Journal of Personality and Social Psychology, 32,* 880–892.

Ross, L., Lepper, M., & Ward, A. (2010). History of social psychology: Insights, challenges, and contributions to theory and application. In S. T. Fiske, D. T. Gilbert & G. Lindzey (Eds.), *Handbook of social psychology* (Vol. 1, 5th ed., pp. 3–50). Hoboken, NJ: John Wiley & Sons.

Rotella, K. N., & Richeson, J. A. (2013). Body of guilt: Using embodied cognition to mitigate backlash to reminders of personal & ingroup wrongdoing. *Journal of Experimental Social Psychology, 49,* 643–650.

Roulin, N., Bangerter, A., & Levashina, J. (2015). Honest and deceptive impression management in the employment interview: Can it be detected and how does it impact evaluations? *Personnel Psychology, 68,* 395–444.

Rowatt, W. C., Carpenter, T., & Haggard, M. C. (2014). Religion, prejudice, and intergroup relations. In V. Saroglou (Ed.), *Religion, personality, and social behavior* (pp. 170–192). New York, NY: Psychology Press.

Rowatt, W. C., Cunningham, M. R., & Druen, P. B. (1998). Deception to get a date. *Personality and Social Psychology Bulletin, 24,* 1228–1242.

Rozin, P., & Fallon, A. E. (1987). A perspective on disgust. *Psychological Review, 94,* 23–41.

Ruby, P., & Decety, J. (2004). How would you feel versus how do you think she would feel? A neuroimaging study of perspective-taking with social emotions. *Journal of Cognitive Neuroscience, 16,* 988–999.

Rudman, L. A. (1998). Self-promotion as a risk factor for women: The costs and benefits of counterstereotypical impression management. *Journal of Personality and Social Psychology, 74,* 629–645.

Rudolph, U., Roesch, S. C., Greitemeyer, T., & Weiner, B. (2004). A meta-analytic review of help giving and aggression from an attributional perspective: Contributions to a general theory of motivation. *Cognition and Emotion, 18,* 815–848.

Ruiz-Pamies, M., Lorenzo-Seva, U., Morales-Vives, F., Cosi, S., & Vigil-Colet, A. (2014). I-DAQ: A new test to assess direct and indirect aggression free of response bias. *The Spanish Journal of Psychology, 17.*

Rule, N. O., & Ambady, N. (2008). Brief exposures: Male sexual orientation is accurately perceived at 50ms. *Journal of Experimental Social Psychology, 44,* 1100–1105.

Rushton, J. P. (1975). Generosity in children: Immediate and long-term effects of modeling, preaching, and moral judgment. *Journal of Personality and Social Psychology, 31,* 459–466.

Russano, M. B., Meissner, C. A., Narchet, F. M., & Kassin, S. M. (2005). Investigating true and false confessions within a novel experimental paradigm. *Psychological Science, 16,* 481–486.

Russell, K. C. (2012). Therapeutic uses of nature. In S. Clayton (Ed.), *The Oxford handbook of environmental and conservation psychology* (pp. 428–444). Oxford, UK: Oxford University Press.

Ruys, K. I., Aarts, H., Papies, E. K., Oikawa, M., & Oikawa, H. (2012). Perceiving an exclusive cause of affect prevents misattribution. *Consciousness and Cognition: An International Journal, 21,* 1009–1015.

Saam, N. J. (2010). Interventions in workplace bullying: A multilevel approach. *European Journal of Work and Organizational Psychology, 19,* 51–75.

Sagarin, B. J., & Wood, S. E. (2007). Resistance to influence. In A. R. Pratkanis (Ed.), *The science of social influence: Advances and future progress* (pp. 321–340). New York, NY: Psychology Press.

Sagarin, B. J., Cialdini, R. B., Rice, W. E., & Serna, S. B. (2002). Dispelling the illusion of invulnerability: The motivations and mechanisms of resistance to persuasion. *Journal of Personality and Social Psychology, 83,* 526–541.

Said, C. P., & Todorov, A. (2011). A statistical model of facial attractiveness. *Psychological Science, 22,* 1183–1190.

Sakalli-Uğurlu, N., & Glick, P. (2003). Ambivalent sexism and attitudes toward women who engage in premarital sex in Turkey. *Journal of Sex Research, 40,* 296–302.

Salmoirago-Blotcher, E., Fitchett, G., Ockene, J. K., Schnall, E., Crawford, S., Granek, I., . . . Rapp, S. (2011). Religion and healthy lifestyle behaviors among postmenopausal women: The Women's Health Initiative. *Journal of Behavioral Medicine, 34,* 360–371.

Sanders, G. S., & Baron, R. S. (1977). Is social comparison irrelevant for producing choice shifts? Journal of Experimental Social Psychology, 13, 303–314.

Sansom-Daly, U. M., & Forgas, J. P. (2010). Do blurred faces magnify priming effects? The interactive effects of perceptual fluency and priming on impression formation. *Social Cognition, 28,* 630–640.

Sansone, C., Morf, C. C., & Panter, A. T. (2004). *The Sage handbook of methods in social psychology.* Thousand Oaks, CA: Sage.

Sansone, R. A., & Sansone, L. A. (2015). Workplace bullying: A tale of adverse consequences. *Innovations in Clinical Neuroscience, 12,* 32–37.

Saphire-Bernstein, S., & Taylor, S. E. (2013). Close relationships and happiness. In S. A. David, I. Boniwell, & A. Conley Ayers (Eds.), *The Oxford handbook of happiness* (pp. 821–833). New York, NY: Oxford University Press.

Sapolsky, R. M. (1998). *The trouble with testosterone: And other essays on the biology of the human predicament.* New York, NY: Scribner.

Sarnoff, I., & Zimbardo, P. G. (1961). Anxiety, fear, and social isolation. The Journal of Abnormal and Social Psychology, 62, 356–363.

Saroglou, V. (2010). Religiousness as a cultural adaptation of basic traits: A five-factor model perspective. *Personality and Social Psychology Review, 14,* 108–125.

Saroglou, V. (2011). Believing, bonding, behaving, and belonging: The Big Four religious dimensions and cultural variation. *Journal of Cross-Cultural Psychology, 42,* 1320–1340.

Saroglou, V. (2012). Is religion not prosocial at all? Comment on Galen (2012). *Psychological Bulletin, 138,* 907–912.

Saroglou, V. (2014a). Introduction: Studying religion in personality and social psychology. In V. Saroglou (Ed.), *Religion, personality, and social behavior* (pp. 1–28). New York, NY: Psychology Press.

Saroglou, V. (Ed.). (2014b). *Religion, personality, and social behavior*. New York, NY: Psychology Press.

Sasaki, J. Y., Kim, H. S., & Xu, J. (2011). Religion and well-being: The moderating role of culture and the oxytocin receptor (OXTR) gene. *Journal of Cross-Cultural Psychology, 42,* 1394–1405.

Satel, S., & Lilienfeld, S. O. (2013). *Brainwashed: The seductive appeal of mindless neuroscience.* New York, NY: Basic Books.

Savalei, V., & Falk, C. F. (2014). Recovering substantive factor loadings in the presence of acquiescence bias: A comparison of three approaches. *Multivariate Behavioral Research, 49,* 407–424.

Schachner, D. A., & Shaver, P. R. (2004). Attachment dimensions and sexual motives. *Personal Relationships, 11,* 179–195.

Schachter, S. (1964). The interaction of cognitive and physiological determinants of emotional state. In L. Berkowitz (Ed.), *Advances in Experimental Social Psychology* (Vol. 1, pp. 49–80). New York, NY: Academic Press.

Schachter, S., & Singer, J. (1962). Cognitive, social, and physiological determinants of emotional state. *Psychological Review, 69,* 379–399.

Schaefer, C. A., & Gorsuch, R. L. (1991). Psychological adjustment and religiousness: The multivariate belief-motivation theory of religiousness. *Journal for the Scientific Study of Religion, 30,* 448–461.

Schaller, M., & Cialdini, R. B. (1990). Happiness, sadness, and helping: A motivational integration. In E. T. Higgins & R. M. Sorrentino (Eds.), *Handbook of motivation and cognition: Foundations of social behavior* (Vol. 2, pp. 265–296). New York, NY: Guilford Press.

Schaller, M., & Murray, D. R. (2011). Infectious disease and the creation of culture. In M. J. Gelfand, C.-y. Chiu & Y.-y. Hong (Eds.), *Advances in culture and psychology* (Vol. 1, pp. 99–151). New York, NY: Oxford University Press.

Schaller, M., Conway, L. G., III, & Peavy, K. M. (2010). Evolutionary processes. In J. F. Dovidio, M. Hewstone, P. Glick, & V. M. Esses (Eds.), *SAGE handbook of prejudice, stereotyping, and discrimination* (pp. 81–96). Thousand Oaks, CA: Sage.

Scheepers, D., Spears, R., Doosje, B., & Manstead, A. S. R. (2006). The social functions of ingroup bias: Creating, confirming, or changing social reality. *European Review of Social Psychology, 17,* 359–396.

Scheibehenne, B., Wilke, A., & Todd, P.M. (2011). Expectations of clumpy resources influence predictions of sequential events. *Evolution and Human Behavior, 32,* 326–333.

Schiffman, L. G., Kanuk, L. L., & Das, M. (2006). *Consumer behavior*. Toronto, Ontario, Canada: Pearson Education.

Schimmack, U., Oishi, S., Furr, R. M., & Funder, D. C. (2004). Personality and life satisfaction: A facet-level analysis. *Personality and Social Psychology Bulletin, 30,* 1062–1075.

Schlenker, B. R. (2000). Impression management. In A. E. Kazdin (Ed.), *Encyclopedia of psychology* (Vol. 4., pp. 236–237). Washington, DC & New York, NY: Oxford University Press.

Schmader, T., & Johns, M. (2003). Converging evidence that stereotype threat reduces working memory capacity. *Journal of Personality and Social Psychology, 85,* 440–452.

Schmidt, G., & Weiner, B. (1988). An attribution-affect-action theory of behavior: Replications of judgments of help-giving. *Personality and Social Psychology Bulletin, 14,* 610–621.

Schmidt, P. (2015). Campaigns against microaggressions prompt big concerns about free speech. Available from EBSCOhost nmr. Retrieved from http://search.ebscohost.com/login.aspx?direct=true&db=nmr&AN=WBNC148B9468EC9F378B00A2C3F1E347BFCB50CF75F&login.asp&site=ehost-live&scope=site

Schmidt-Daffy, M. (2011). Modeling automatic threat detection: Development of a face-in-the-crowd task. *Emotion, 11,* 153–168.

Schmitt, D. P. (2003). Universal sex differences in the desire for sexual variety: Tests from 52 nations, 6 continents, and 13 islands. *Journal of Personality and Social Psychology, 85,* 85–104.

Schmitt, D. P. (2006). Sexual strategies across sexual orientations: How personality traits and culture relate to sociosexuality among gays, lesbians, bisexuals, and heterosexuals. *Journal of Psychology & Human Sexuality, 18,* 183–214.

Schmitt, D. P., & Allik, J. (2005). Simultaneous administration of the Rosenberg Self-Esteem Scale in 53 nations: Exploring the universal and culture-specific features of global self-esteem. *Journal of Personality and Social Psychology, 89,* 623–642.

Schnall, E., Wassertheil-Smoller, S., Swencionis, C., Zemon, V., Tinker, L., O'Sullivan, M.J., . . . Goodwin, M. (2010). The relationship between religion and cardiovascular outcomes and all-cause mortality in the women's health initiative observational study. *Psychology & Health, 25,* 249–263.

Schneiderman, R. M. (2008, October 30). Do Americans still hate welfare, *The New York Times.*

Schnuerch, R., & Gibbons, H. (2014). A review of neurocognitive mechanisms of social conformity. *Social Psychology* (18649335), *45,* 466–478.

Schriesheim, C. A., Tepper, B. J., & Tetrault, L. A. (1994). Least preferred co-worker score, situational control, and leadership effectiveness: A meta-analysis of contingency model performance predictions. *Journal of Applied Psychology, 79,* 561–573.

Schultz, P. W., Nolan, J. M., Cialdini, R. B., Goldstein, N. J., & Griskevicius, V. (2007). The constructive, destructive, and reconstructive power of social norms. *Psychological Science, 18,* 429–434.

Schultz, P. W., Tabanico, J. J., & Rendón, T. (2008). Normative beliefs as agents of influence: Basic processes and real-world applications. In W. D. Crano & R. Prislin (Eds.), *Attitudes and attitude change* (pp. 385–409). New York, NY: Psychology Press.

Schützwohl, A. (2004). Which infidelity type makes you more jealous? Decision strategies in a forced-choice between sexual and emotional infidelity. *Evolutionary Psychology, 2,* 121–128.

Schützwohl, A., Fuchs, A., McKibbin, W. F., & Shackelford, T. K. (2009). How willing are you to accept sexual requests from slightly unattractive to exceptionally attractive imagined requestors? *Human Nature, 20,* 282–293.

Schwartz, S. (1977). Normative influences on altruism. In L. Berkowitz (Ed.), *Advances in Experimental Social Psychology* (Vol. 10, pp. 222–280). New York, NY: Academic Press.

Schwartz, S. H., & Howard, J. A. (1980). Explanations of the moderating effect of responsibility denial on the personal norm behavior relationship. *Social Psychology Quarterly, 43,* 441–446.

Schwarz, N. (1999). Self-reports: How the questions shape the answers. *American Psychologist, 54,* 93–105.

Schwarz, N. (2007a). Cognitive aspects of survey methodology. *Applied Cognitive Psychology, 21,* 277–287.

Schwarz, N. (2007b). Evaluating surveys and questionnaires. In R. J. Sternberg, H. L. Roediger, & D. F. Halpern (Eds.), *Critical thinking in psychology* (pp. 54–74). New York, NY: Cambridge University Press.

Schwarz, N., Strack, F., Hilton, D. J., & Naderer, G. (1991). Base rates, representativeness, and the logic of conversation: The contextual relevance of "irrelevant" information. *Social Cognition, 9,* 67–84.

Schwarz, S., & Hassebrauck, M. (2012). Sex and age differences in mate-selection preferences. *Human Nature, 23,* 447–466.

Scopelliti, M., Carrus, G., & Bonnes, M. (2012). Natural landscapes. In S. Clayton (Ed.), *The Oxford handbook of environmental and conservation psychology* (pp. 332–347). Oxford, UK: Oxford University Press.

Scott, I. M., Clark, A. P., Josephson, S. C., Boyette, A. H., Cuthill, I. C., Fried, R. L., . . . Penton-Voak, I. S. (2014). Human preferences for sexually dimorphic faces may be evolutionarily novel. *PNAS Proceedings of the National Academy of Sciences of the United States of America, 111,* 14388–14393.

Sears, D. O. (1986). College sophomores in the laboratory: Influences of a narrow data base on social psychology's view of human nature. *Journal of Personality and Social Psychology, 51,* 515–530.

Sechrist, J., Suitor, J. J., Howard, A. R., & Pillemer, K. (2014). Perceptions of equity, balance of support exchange, and mother–adult child relations. *Journal of Marriage and Family, 76,* 285–299.

Sedikides, C. (1993). Assessment, enhancement, and verification determinants of the self-evaluation process. *Journal of Personality and Social Psychology, 65,* 317–338.

Sedikides, C., & Anderson, C. A. (1994). Causal perceptions of intertrait relations: The glue that holds person types together. *Personality and Social Psychology Bulletin, 20,* 294–302.

Sedikides, C., & Gregg, A. P. (2003). Portraits of the self. In M. A. Hogg & J. Cooper (Eds.), *The Sage handbook of social psychology* (pp. 110–138). Thousand Oaks, CA: Sage.

Sedikides, C., & Spencer, S. J. (2007). *The self.* New York, NY: Psychology Press.

Seery, M. D., Blascovich, J., Weisbuch, M., & Vick, S. B. (2004). The relationship between self-esteem level, self-esteem stability, and cardiovascular reactions to performance feedback. *Journal of Personality and Social Psychology, 87,* 133–145.

Segal, M. W. (1974). Alphabet and attraction: An unobtrusive measure of the effect of propinquity in a field setting. *Journal of Personality and Social Psychology, 30,* 654–657.

Segal, N. L. (1984). Cooperation, competition, and altruism within twin sets: A reappraisal. *Ethology & Sociobiology, 5,* 163–177.

Segall, M. H., Campbell, D. T., & Herskovits, M. J. (1963). Cultural differences in the perception of geometric illusions. *Science, 139,* 769–771.

Segall, M. H., Dasen, P. R., Berry, J. W., & Poortinga, Y. H. (1999). *Human behavior in global perspective: An introduction to cross-cultural psychology* (2nd ed.). Needham Heights, MA: Allyn & Bacon.

Séguin, J. R., Sylvers, P., & Lilienfeld, S. O. (2007). The neuropsychology of violence. In D. J. Flannery, A. T. Vazsonyi, & I. D. Waldman (Eds.), *The Cambridge handbook of violent behavior and aggression* (pp. 187–214). New York, NY: Cambridge University Press.

Seiffge-Krenke, I., & Burk, W. J. (2015). "Bad Romance": Links between psychological and physical aggression and relationship functioning in adolescent couples. *Behavioral Sciences (Basel, Switzerland), 5,* 305–323.

Seirmarco, G., Neria, Y., Insel, B., Kiper, D., Doruk, A., Gross, R., & Litz, B. (2012). Religiosity and mental health: Changes in religious beliefs, complicated grief, posttraumatic stress disorder, and major depression following the September 11, 2001, attacks. *Psychology of Religion and Spirituality, 4,* 10–18.

Seiter, J. S. (2007). Ingratiation and gratuity: The effect of complimenting customers on tipping behavior in restaurants. *Journal of Applied Social Psychology, 37,* 478–485.

Seligman, M. E. P., & Csikszentmihalyi, M. (2000). Positive psychology: An introduction. *American Psychologist, 55,* 5–14.

Semin, G. R., & Echterhoff, G. (2011). *Grounding sociality: Neurons, mind, and culture.* New York, NY: Psychology Press.

Sénémeaud, C., Georget, P., Guéguen, N., Callé, N., Plainfossé, C., Touati, C., & Mange, J. (2014). Labeling of previous donation to encourage subsequent donation among experienced blood donors. *Health Psychology, 33,* 656–659.

Seta, J. J., Crisson, J. E., Seta, C. E., & Wang, M. A. (1989). Task performance and perceptions of anxiety: Averaging and summation in an evaluative setting. Journal of Personality and Social Psychology, 56, 387–396.

Shackelford, T. K., Goetz, A. T., LaMunyon, C. W., Quintus, B. J., & Weekes-Shackelford, V. A. (2004). Sex differences in sexual psychology produce sex-similar preferences for a short-term mate. *Archives of Sexual Behavior, 33,* 405–412.

Shackelford, T. K., Voracek, M., Schmitt, D. P., Buss, D. M., Weekes-Shackelford, V. A., & Michalski, R. L. (2004). Romantic jealousy in early adulthood and in later life. *Human Nature, 15,* 283–300.

Shadish, W. R., Cook, T. D., & Campbell, D. T. (2002). *Experimental and quasi-experimental designs for generalized causal inference.* Boston, MA: Houghton Mifflin.

Sharif, A. F., Greene, J. D., Karremans, J. C., Luguri, J. B., Clark, C. J., Schooler, J. W., . . . Vohs, K. D. (2014). Free will and punishment: A mechanistic view of human nature reduces retribution. *Psychological Science.*

Shariff, A. F., Norenzayan, A., & Henrich, J. (2010). The birth of the high gods: How the cultural evolution of supernatural policing influenced the emergence of complex, cooperative human societies, paving the way for civilization. In M. Schaller, A. Norenzayan, S. J. Heine, T. Yamagishi, & T. Kameda (Eds.), *Evolution, culture, and the human mind* (pp. 119–136). New York, NY: Psychology Press.

Sharma, S., & Agarwala, S. (2014). Self-esteem and collective self-esteem as predictors of depression. *Journal of Behavioural Sciences, 24,* 21–28.

Shaver, P. R., & Mikulincer, M. (2012a). Attachment anxiety and motivational patterns in close relationships.

In L. Campbell, J. G. La Guardia, J. M. Olson, & M. P. Zanna (Eds.), *The science of the couple* (Vol. 12, pp. 17–39). New York, NY: Psychology Press.

Shaver, P. R., & Mikulincer, M. (2012b). Attachment theory. In P. A. M. Van Lange, A. W. Kruglanski, & E. T. Higgins (Eds.), *Handbook of theories of social psychology* (Vol. 2, pp. 160–179). Thousand Oaks, CA: Sage.

Shaw, J. D., Duffy, M. K., & Stark, E. M. (2000). Interdependence and preference for group work: Main and congruence effects on the satisfaction and performance of group members. Journal of Management, 26, 259–279.

Shedlosky-Shoemaker, R., Costabile, K. A., DeLuca, H. K., & Arkin, R. M. (2011). The social experience of entertainment media: Effects of others' evaluations on our experience. *Journal of Media Psychology: Theories, Methods, and Applications, 23,* 111–121.

Sheldon, K. M., & Lyubomirsky, S. (2006a). Achieving sustainable gains in happiness: Change your actions, not your circumstances. *Journal of Happiness Studies, 7,* 55–86.

Sheldon, K. M., & Lyubomirsky, S. (2006b). How to increase and sustain positive emotion: The effects of expressing gratitude and visualizing best possible selves. *The Journal of Positive Psychology, 1,* 73–82.

Shen, H., Wan, F., & Wyer, R. S., Jr. (2011). Cross-cultural differences in the refusal to accept a small gift: The differential influence of reciprocity norms on Asians and North Americans. *Journal of Personality and Social Psychology, 100,* 271–281.

Shepperd, J. A., & Taylor, K. M. (1999). Social loafing and expectancy-value theory. *Personality and Social Psychology Bulletin, 25,* 1147–1158.

Shepperd, J. A., Waters, E. A., Weinstein, N. D., & Klein, W. M. P. (2015). A primer on unrealistic optimism. *Current Directions in Psychological Science, 24,* 232–237.

Shepperd, J., Klein, W. M. P., Waters, E. A., & Weinstein, N. D. (2013). Taking stock of unrealistic optimism. *Perspectives on Psychological Science, 8,* 395–411.

Shepperd, J., Malone, W., & Sweeny, K. (2008). Exploring causes of the self-serving bias. *Social and Personality Psychology Compass, 2,* 895–908.

Sherif, M. (1956). Experiments in group conflict. *Scientific American, 195,* 54–58.

Sherif, M. (1966). *The psychology of social norms.* Oxford, UK: Harper Torchbooks.

Sherif, M., Harvey, O. J., White, B. J., Hood, W. R., & Sherif, C. W. (1988). *The Robbers Cave experiment: Integroup conflict and cooperation.* Middletown, CT: Wesleyan University. (Original work published 1961)

Sherman, D. K., & Hartson, K. A. (2011). Reconciling self-protection with self-improvement: Self-affirmation theory. In M. D. Alicke & C. Sedikides (Eds.),

Handbook of self-enhancement and self-protection (pp. 128–151). New York, NY: Guilford Press.

Sherman, J. W., Gawronski, B., & Trope, Y. (Eds.). (2014). *Dual-process theories of the social mind*. New York, NY: Guilford Press.

Shinoura, N., Yamada, R., Tabei, Y., Otani, R., Itoi, C., Saito, S., & Midorikawa, A. (2011). Left or right temporal lesion might induce aggression or escape during awake surgery, respectively: Role of the amygdala. *Acta Neuropsychiatrica, 23,* 119–124.

Shotland, R. L., & Heinold, W. D. (1985). Bystander response to arterial bleeding: Helping skills, the decision-making process, and differentiating the helping response. *Journal of Personality and Social Psychology, 49,* 347–356.

Shotland, R. L., & Straw, M. K. (1976). Bystander response to an assault: When a man attacks a woman. *Journal of Personality and Social Psychology, 34,* 990–999.

Sidanius, J., & Pratto, F. (1999). *Social dominance: An intergroup theory of social hierarchy and oppression.* New York, NY: Cambridge University Press.

Sidanius, J., & Pratto, F. (2012). Social dominance theory. In P. A. M. Van Lange, A. W. Kruglanski, & E. T. Higgins (Eds.), *Handbook of theories of social psychology* (Vol. 2, pp. 418–438). Thousand Oaks, CA: Sage.

Sidanius, J., Kteily, N., Sheehy-Skeffington, J., Ho, A.K., Sibley, C., & Duriez, B. (2013). You're inferior and not worth our concern: The interface between empathy and social dominance orientation. *Journal of Personality, 81,* 313–323.

Siegel Christian, J., Pearsall, M. J., Christian, M. S., & Ellis, A. P. J. (2014). Exploring the benefits and boundaries of transactive memory systems in adapting to team member loss. *Group Dynamics: Theory, Research, and Practice, 18,* 69–86.

Sigall, H., & Page, R. (1971). Current stereotypes: A little fading, a little faking. *Journal of Personality and Social Psychology, 18,* 247–255.

Sim, J. J., Goyle, A., McKedy, W., Eidelman, S., & Correll, J. (2014). How social identity shapes the working self-concept. *Journal of Experimental Social Psychology, 55,* 271–277.

Simmons, V. N., & Brandon, T. H. (2007). Secondary smoking prevention in a university setting: A randomized comparison of an experiential, theory-based intervention and a standard didactic intervention for increasing cessation motivation. *Health Psychology, 26,* 268–277.

Singer, T., Snozzi, R., Bird, G., Petrovic, P., Silani, G., Heinrichs, M., & Dolan, R. J. (2008). Effects of oxytocin and prosocial behavior on brain responses to direct and vicariously experienced pain. *Emotion, 8,* 781–791.

Singh, D. (1995). Female judgment of male attractiveness and desirability for relationships: Role of waist-to-hip ratio and financial status. *Journal of Personality and Social Psychology, 69,* 1089–1101.

Sistrunk, F., & McDavid, J. W. (1971). Sex variable in conforming behavior. *Journal of Personality and Social Psychology, 17,* 200–207.

Skewes, J. C., Skewes, L., Roepstorff, A., & Frith, C. D. (2013). Doing what others see: Visuomotor conversion to informational social influence. *Journal of Experimental Psychology: Human Perception and Performance, 39,* 1291–1303.

Slavin, R. E., & Cooper, R. (1999). Improving intergroup relations: Lessons learned from cooperative learning programs. *Journal of Social Issues, 55,* 647–663.

Sloman, S. (2014). Two systems of reasoning: An update. In J. W. Sherman, B. Gawronski, Y. Trope, J. W. Sherman, B. Gawronski & Y. Trope (Eds.), *Dual-process theories of the social mind* (pp. 69–79). New York, NY: Guilford Press.

Slothuus, R., & de Vreese, C.H. (2010). Political parties, motivated reasoning, and issue framing effects. *The Journal of Politics, 72,* 630–645.

Slotter, E. B., Duffy, C. W., & Gardner, W. L. (2014). Balancing the need to be "me" with the need to be "we": Applying optimal distinctiveness rheory to the understanding of multiple motives within romantic relationships. *Journal of Experimental Social Psychology, 52,* 71–81.

Slotter, E. B., Winger, L., & Soto, N. (2015). Lost without each other: The influence of group identity loss on the self-concept. *Group Dynamics: Theory, Research, and Practice, 19,* 15–30.

Slovic, P., & Fischhoff, B. (1977). On the psychology of experimental surprises. *Journal of Experimental Psychology: Human Perception and Performance, 3,* 544–551.

Smith, E. R., & Collins, E. C. (2009). Contextualizing person perception: Distributed social cognition. *Psychological Review, 116,* 343–364.

Smith, H. J., Pettigrew, T. F., Pippin, G. M., & Bialosiewicz, S. (2012). Relative deprivation: A theoretical and meta-analytic review. *Personality and Social Psychology Review, 16,* 203–232.

Smith, T. B., McCullough, M. E., & Poll, J. (2003). Religiousness and depression: Evidence for a main effect and the moderating influence of stressful life events. *Psychological Bulletin, 129,* 614–636.

Snyder, C. R., Lopez, S. J., & Pedrotti, J. T. (2011). *Positive psychology: The scientific and practical explorations of human strengths (2nd ed.).* Thousand Oaks, CA: Sage.

Snyder, M. (1974). Self-monitoring of expressive behavior. *Journal of Personality and Social Psychology, 30,* 526–537.

Snyder, M., & Cantor, N. (1998). Understanding personality and social behavior: A functionalist strategy. In

D. T. Gilbert, S. T. Fiske, & G. Lindzey (Eds.), *The handbook of social psychology* (Vols. 1 & 2, 4th ed., pp. 635–679). New York, NY: McGraw-Hill.

Snyder, M., & DeBono, K. G. (1985). Appeals to image and claims about quality: Understanding the psychology of advertising. *Journal of Personality and Social Psychology, 49,* 586–597.

Snyder, M., & Swann, W.B. (1978a). Behavioral confirmation in social interaction: From social perception to social reality. *Journal of Experimental Social Psychology, 14,* 148–162.

Snyder, M., & Swann, W.B. (1978b). Hypothesis-testing processes in social interaction. *Journal of Personality and Social Psychology, 36,* 1202–1212.

Snyder, M., Tanke, E. D., & Berscheid, E. (1977). Social perception and interpersonal behavior: On the self-fulfilling nature of social stereotypes. *Journal of Personality and Social Psychology, 35,* 656–666.

Sober, E., & Wilson, D. S. (1998). *Unto others: The evolution and psychology of unselfish behavior.* Cambridge, MA: Harvard University Press.

Sober, E., & Wilson, D. S. (1998). *Unto others: The evolution and psychology of unselfish behavior.* Cambridge, MA: Harvard University Press.

Sommers, S. R. (2008). Determinants and consequences of jury racial diversity: Empirical findings, implications, and directions for future research. *Social Issues and Policy Review, 2,* 65–102.

Sommers, S. R. (2010). What we do (and don't) know about race and jurors. Jury Expert, 22, 1–9.

Sommers, S. R., & Ellsworth, P. C. (2009). "Race salience" in juror decision-making: Misconceptions, clarifications, and unanswered questions. *Behavioral Sciences & the Law, 27,* 599–609.

Sommers, S. R., & Norton, M. I. (2008). Race and jury selection: Psychological perspectives on the peremptory challenge debate. *American Psychologist, 63,* 527–539.

Sorrentino, R. M., & Field, N. (1986). Emergent leadership over time: The functional value of positive motivation. *Journal of Personality and Social Psychology, 50,* 1091–1099.

Sosis, R. (2009). The adaptationist-byproduct debate on the evolution of religion: Five misunderstandings of the adaptationist program. *Journal of Cognition and Culture, 9,* 315–332.

Souchet, L., & Girandola, F. (2013). Double foot-in-the-door, social representations, and environment: Application for energy savings. *Journal of Applied Social Psychology, 43,* 306–315.

Spencer, S. J., Fein, S., Wolfe, C. T., Fong, C., & Dunn, M. A. (1998). Automatic activation of stereotypes: The role of self-image threat. *Personality and Social Psychology Bulletin, 24,* 1139–1152.

Spencer-Rodgers, J., Williams, M. J., Hamilton, D. L., Peng, K., & Wang, L. (2007). Culture and group perception: Dispositional and stereotypic inferences about novel and national groups. *Journal of Personality and Social Psychology, 93,* 525–543.

Sperry, R. W. (1961). Cerebral organization and behavior. *Science, 133,* 1749–1757.

Sprecher, S. (1999). "I love you more today than yesterday": Romantic partners' perceptions of changes in love and related affect over time. *Journal of Personality and Social Psychology, 76,* 46–53.

Sprecher, S., Aron, A., Hatfield, E., Cortese, A., Potapova, E., & Levitskaya, A. (1994). Love: American style, Russian style and Japanese style. *Personal Relationships, 1,* 349–369.

Spunt, R. P., & Lieberman, M. D. (2013). The busy social brain: Evidence for automaticity and control in the neural systems supporting social cognition and action understanding. *Psychological Science, 24,* 80–86.

Spunt, R. P., Meyer, M. L., & Lieberman, M. D. (2015). The default mode of human brain function primes the intentional stance. *Journal of Cognitive Neuroscience, 27,* 1116–1124.

St. Jacques, P. L., Conway, M. A., Lowder, M. W., & Cabeza, R. (2011). Watching my mind unfold versus yours: An fMRI study using a novel camera technology to examine neural differences in self-projection of self versus other perspectives. *Journal of Cognitive Neuroscience, 23,* 1275–1284.

Staats, A. W., Staats, C. K., & Crawford, H. L. (1962). First-order conditioning of meaning and the parallel conditioning of a GSR. *Journal of General Psychology, 67,* 159–167.

Stanca, L. (2009). Measuring indirect reciprocity: Whose back do we scratch? *Journal of Economic Psychology, 30,* 190–202.

Stanley, M., & Burrow, A. L. (2015). The distance between selves: The influence of self-discrepancy on purpose in life. *Self and Identity, 14,* 441–452.

Stanovich, K. E., & West, R. F. (2002). Individual differences in reasoning: Implications for the rationality debate? In T. Gilovich, D. Griffin & D. Kahneman (Eds.), *Heuristics and biases: The psychology of intuitive judgment* (pp. 421–440). New York, NY: Cambridge University Press.

Stark, E. M., Shaw, J. D., & Duffy, M. K. (2007). Preference for group work, winning orientation, and social loafing behavior in groups. *Group & Organization Management, 32,* 699–723.

Stasser, G. (1999). The uncertain role of unshared information in collective choice. In L. L. Thompson, J. M. Levine, & D. M. Messick (Eds.), *Shared cognition in organizations: The management of knowledge* (pp. 49–69). Mahwah, NJ: Lawrence Erlbaum.

Stasser, G., & Titus, W. (1985). Pooling of unshared information in group decision making: Biased information sampling during discussion. *Journal of Personality and Social Psychology, 48,* 1467–1478.

Statistics, N. C. f. H. (2006). Health United States 2006 with chartbook on trends in the health of Americans. Hyattsville, MD: US Government Printing Office.

Staub, E. (1989). *The roots of evil: The origins of genocide and other group violence.* New York, NY: Cambridge University Press.

Staub, E. (2003). *The psychology of good and evil: Why children, adults, and groups help and harm others.* New York, NY: Cambridge University Press.

Staub, E. (2003). The psychology of good and evil: Why children, adults, and groups help and harm others. New York, NY: Cambridge University Press.

Staub, E. (2003). *The psychology of good and evil: Why children, adults, and groups help and harm others.* New York, NY: Cambridge University Press.

Steblay, N. M. (1987). Helping behavior in rural and urban environments: A meta-analysis. *Psychological Bulletin, 102,* 346–356.

Steele, C. M. (1988). The psychology of self-affirmation: Sustaining the integrity of the self. In L. Berkowitz (Ed.), *Advances in experimental social psychology, Vol. 21: Social psychological studies of the self: Perspectives and programs* (pp. 261–302). San Diego, CA: Academic Press.

Steele, C. M. (2010). *Whistling Vivaldi: And how other clues to stereotypes affect us.* New York, NY: W.W. Norton.

Steele, C. M., & Aronson, J. (1995). Stereotype threat and the intellectual test performance of African Americans. *Journal of Personality and Social Psychology, 69,* 797–811.

Steele, C. M., & Liu, T. J. (1981). Making the dissonant act unreflective of self: Dissonance avoidance and the expectancy of a value-affirming response. *Personality and Social Psychology Bulletin, 7,* 393–397.

Steele, L. G., & Lynch, S. M. (2013). The pursuit of happiness in China: Individualism, collectivism, and subjective well-being during China's economic and social transformation. *Social Indicators Research, 114,* 441–451.

Steers, M. N., Wickham, R. E., & Acitelli, L. K. (2014). Seeing everyone else's highlight reels: How Facebook usage is linked to depressive symptoms. *Journal of Social & Clinical Psychology, 33,* 701–731.

Steg, L., & Vlek, C. (2009). Encouraging pro-environmental behaviour: An integrative review and research agenda. *Journal of Environmental Psychology, 29,* 309–317.

Steiner, I. D. (1972). Group process and productivity. New York, NY: Academic Press.

Stepanova, E. V., Strube, M. J., & Hetts, J. J. (2009). They saw a triple Lutz: Bias and its perception in American and Russian newspaper coverage of the 2002 Olympic figure skating scandal. *Journal of Applied Social Psychology, 39,* 1763–1784.

Stephan, W. G., & Renfro, C. L. (2003). The role of threat in intergroup relations. In D. M. Mackie & E. R. Smith (Eds.), *From prejudice to intergroup emotions: Differentiated reactions to social groups* (pp. 191–207). New York, NY: Psychology Press.

Stephan, W. G., & Stephan, C. W. (2000). An integrated threat theory of prejudice. In S. Oskamp (Ed.), *Reducing prejudice and discrimination* (pp. 23–45). Mahwah, NJ: Lawrence Erlbaum.

Stephan, W. G., Boniecki, K. A., Ybarra, O., Bettencourt, A., Ervin, K. S., Jackson, L.A., . . . Renfro, C.L. (2002). The role of threats in the racial attitudes of Blacks and White. *Personality and Social Psychology Bulletin, 28,* 1242–1254.

Stephan, W. G., Stephan, C. W., & de Vargas, M. C. (1996). Emotional expression in Costa Rica and the United States. *Journal of Cross-Cultural Psychology, 27,* 147–160.

Stephan, W. G., Ybarra, O., & Morrison, K. R. (2009). Intergroup threat theory. In T. D. Nelson (Ed.), *Handbook of prejudice, stereotyping, and discrimination* (pp. 43–59). New York, NY: Psychology Press.

Sternberg, R. J. (1986). A triangular theory of love. *Psychological Review, 93,* 119–135.

Stevens, C. K., & Kristof, A. L. (1995). Making the right impression: A field study of applicant impression management during job interviews. *Journal of Applied Psychology, 80,* 587–606.

Stevens, J. R., & King, A. J. (2013). The lives of others: Social rationality in animals. In R. Hertwig, U. Hoffrage, R. Hertwig, & U. Hoffrage (Eds.), *Simple heuristics in a social world* (pp. 409–431). New York, NY: Oxford University Press.

Stewart, D. D., & Stasser, G. (1995). Expert role assignment and information sampling during collective recall and decision making. *Journal of Personality and Social Psychology, 69,* 619–628.

Stice, E., Rohde, P., Gau, J., & Shaw, H. (2009). An effectiveness trial of a dissonance-based eating disorder prevention program for high-risk adolescent girls. *Journal of Consulting and Clinical Psychology, 77,* 825–834.

Stickley, A., Koyanagi, A., Leinsalu, M., Ferlander, S., Sabawoon, W., & McKee, M. (2015). Loneliness and health in Eastern Europe: Findings from Moscow, Russia. *Public Health, 129,* 403–410.

Stogdill, R. M. (1948). Personal factors associated with leadership; a survey of the literature. Journal of Psychology: Interdisciplinary and Applied, 25, 35–71.

Stok, F. M., de Ridder, D. T. D., de Vet, E., & de Wit, J. B. F. (2014). Don't tell me what I should do, but what others do: The influence of descriptive and injunctive peer norms on fruit consumption in adolescents. *British Journal of Health Psychology, 19,* 52–64.

Stoliker, B. E., & Lafreniere, K. D. (2015). The influence of perceived stress, loneliness, and learning burnout on university students' educational experience. *College Student Journal, 49,* 146–160.

Stoliker, B. E., & Lafreniere, K. D. (2015). The influence of perceived stress, loneliness, and learning burnout on university students' educational experience. *College Student Journal, 49,* 146–160.

Stone, J. (2012). Consistency as a basis for behavioral interventions: Using hypocrisy and cognitive dissonance to motivate behavior change. In B. Gawronski & F. Strack (Eds.), *Cognitive consistency: A fundamental principle in social cognition* (pp. 326–347). New York, NY: Guilford Press.

Stone, J., & Focella, E. (2011). Hypocrisy, dissonance and the self-regulation processes that improve health. *Self and Identity, 10,* 295–303.

Stone, J., Aronson, E., Crain, A. L., Winslow, M. P., & Fried, C. B. (2003). Inducing hypocrisy as a means of encouraging young adults to use condoms. In P. Salovey & A. J. Rothman (Eds.), *Social psychology of health* (pp. 272–285). New York, NY: Psychology Press.

Stouffer, S. A., Suchman, E. A., Devinney, L. C., Star, S. A., & Williams, R. M., Jr. (1949). *The American soldier: Adjustment during army life. (Studies in social psychology in World War II, Vol. 1.).* Oxford, UK: Princeton Univ. Press.

Strack, F., & Mussweiler, T. (1997). Explaining the enigmatic anchoring effect: Mechanisms of selective accessibility. *Journal of Personality and Social Psychology, 73,* 437–446.

Strack, F., Martin, L. L., & Stepper, S. (1988). Inhibiting and facilitating conditions of the human smile: A nonobtrusive test of the facial feedback hypothesis. *Journal of Personality and Social Psychology, 54,* 768–777.

Strack, J., & Esteves, F. (2015). Exams? Why worry? Interpreting anxiety as facilitative and stress appraisals. *Anxiety, Stress & Coping: An International Journal, 28,* 205–214.

Stricker, L. J. (1967). The true deceiver. *Psychological Bulletin, 68,* 13–20.

Strickhouser, J. E., & Zell, E. (2015). Self-evaluative effects of dimensional and social comparison. *Journal of Experimental Social Psychology, 59,* 60–66.

Stroebe, W. (2012). The truth about Triplett (1898), but nobody seems to care. Perspectives on Psychological Science, 7, 54–57.

Stroebe, W. (2012). The truth about Triplett (1898), but nobody seems to care. *Perspectives on Psychological Science, 7,* 54–57.

Stroebe, W., Diehl, M., & Abakoumkin, G. (1992). The illusion of group effectivity. Personality and Social Psychology Bulletin, 18, 643–650.

Strube, M. J. (2005). What did Triplett really find? A contemporary analysis of the first experiment in social psychology. *American Journal of Psychology, 118,* 271–286.

Strube, M. J., & Garcia, J. E. (1981). A meta-analytic investigation of Fiedler's contingency model of leadership effectiveness. *Psychological Bulletin, 90,* 307–321.

Stukas, A. A., Snyder, M., & Clary, E. G. (2008). The social marketing of volunteerism: A functional approach. In C. P. Haugtvedt, P. M. Herr, & F. R. Kardes (Eds.), *Handbook of consumer psychology.* (Vol. 4, pp. 959–979). New York, NY: Taylor & Francis Group/Lawrence Erlbaum.

Sturman, E. D. (2011). Involuntary subordination and its relation to personality, mood, and submissive behavior. *Psychological Assessment, 23,* 262–276.

Stürmer, S., & Snyder, M. (2010). *The psychology of prosocial behavior: Group processes, intergroup relations, and helping.* Oxford, UK: Wiley-Blackwell.

Sue, D. W. (2010). *Microaggressions in everday life: Race, gender, and sexual orientation.* New York, NY: Wiley.

Sue, D. W., Capodilupo, C. M., Torino, G. C., Bucceri, J. M., Holder, A., Nadal, K. L., & Esquilin, M. (2007). Racial microaggressions in everyday life: Implications for clinical practice. *American Psychologist, 62,* 271–286.

Suedfeld, P. (2007). Torture, interrogation, security, and psychology: Absolutistic versus complex thinking. *Analyses of Social Issues and Public Policy (ASAP), 7,* 55–63.

Suh, E. M., & Koo, J. (2008). Comparing subjective well-being across cultures and nations: The "what" and "why" questions. In M. Eid & R. J. Larsen (Eds.), *The science of subjective well-being* (pp. 414–427). New York, NY: Guilford Press.

Sundali, J., & Croson, R. (2006). Biases in casino betting: The hot hand and the gambler's fallacy. *Judgment and Decision Making, 1,* 1–12.

Surowiecki, J. (2004). The wisdom of crowds: Why the many are smarter than the few and how collective wisdom shapes business, economies, societies, and nations. New York, NY: Doubleday & Co.

Swami, V., Frederick, D. A., Aavik, T., Alcalay, L., Allik, J., Anderson, D., . . . Zivcic-Becirevic, I. (2010). The attractive female body weight and female body dissatisfaction in 26 countries across 10 world regions: Results of the international body project I. *Personality and Social Psychology Bulletin, 36,* 309–325.

Swann, W. B. (1990). To be adored or to be known? The interplay of self-enhancement and self-verification.

In E. T. Higgins & R. M. Sorrentino (Eds.), *Handbook of motivation and cognition: Foundations of social behavior* (Vol. 2., pp. 408–448). New York, NY: Guilford Press.

Swann, W. B., & Bosson, J. K. (2010). Self and identity. In S. T. Fiske, D. T. Gilbert, & G. Lindzey (Eds.), *Handbook of social psychology* (Vol. 1, 5th ed., pp. 589–628). Hoboken, NJ: John Wiley & Sons.

Swann, W. B., Chang-Schneider, C., & Angulo, S. (2008). Self-verification in relationships as an adaptive process. In J. V. Wood, A. Tesser & J. G. Holmes (Eds.), *The self and social relationships* (pp. 49–72). New York, NY: Psychology Press.

Swann, W. B., Pelham, B. W., & Krull, D. S. (1989). Agreeable fancy or disagreeable truth? Reconciling self-enhancement and self-verification. *Journal of Personality and Social Psychology, 57,* 782–791.

Swaray, R. (2012). An evaluation of a group project designed to reduce free-riding and promote active learning. *Assessment & Evaluation in Higher Education, 37,* 285–292

Swim, J. K. (1994). Perceived versus meta-analytic effect sizes: An assessment of the accuracy of gender stereotypes. *Journal of Personality and Social Psychology, 66,* 21–36.

Swim, J. K., & Hyers, L. L. (2009). Sexism. In T. D. Nelson (Ed.), *Handbook of prejudice, stereotyping, and discrimination* (pp. 407–430). New York, NY: Psychology Press.

Tagler, M. J. (2010). Sex differences in jealousy: Comparing the influence of previous infidelity among college students and adults. *Social Psychological and Personality Science, 1,* 353–360.

Tajfel, H., & Billig, M. (1974). Familiarity and categorization in intergroup behavior. *Journal of Experimental Social Psychology, 10,* 159–170.

Tajfel, H., & Turner, J. C. (1979). An integrative theory of intergroup conflict. In W. G. Austin & S. Worchel (Eds.), *The social psychology of intergroup relations* (pp. 33–47). Monterey, CA: Brooks/Cole.

Tajfel, H., & Turner, J. C. (1986). The social identity theory of intergroup behavior. In S. Worchel & W. G. Austin (Eds.), Psychology of intergroup relations (pp. 7–24). Chicago, IL: Nelson Hall.

Tajfel, H., & Turner, J. C. (2010). An integrative theory of intergroup conflict. In T. Postmes & N. R. Branscombe (Eds.), Rediscovering social identity (pp. 173–190). New York, NY: Psychology Press.

Tajfel, H., Billig, M. G., Bundy, R. P., & Flament, C. (1971). Social categorization and intergroup behaviour. *European Journal of Social Psychology, 1,* 149–178.

Takahashi, A., Quadros, I. M., de Almeida, R. M. M., & Miczek, K. A. (2011). Brain serotonin receptors and transporters: Initiation vs. termination of escalated aggression. *Psychopharmacology, 213,* 183–212.

Takano, Y., & Sogon, S. (2008). Are Japanese more collectivistic than Americans? Examining conformity in in-groups and the reference-group effect. *Journal of Cross-Cultural Psychology, 39,* 237–250.

Tal, A., & Wansink, B. (2014). Blinded with science: Trivial graphs and formulas increase ad persuasiveness and belief in product efficacy. *Public Understanding Of Science.* http://pus .sagepub.com/content/early/2014/ 09/23/0963662514549688.abstract

Talley, A. E., Kocum, L., Schlegel, R. J., Molix, L., & Bettencourt, B. A. (2012). Social roles, basic need satisfaction, and psychological health: The central role of competence. Personality and Social Psychology Bulletin, 38, 155–173.

Tal-Or, N. (2010a). Direct and indirect self-promotion in the eyes of the perceivers. *Social Influence, 5,* 87–100.

Tal-Or, N. (2010b). Indirect ingratiation: Pleasing people by associating them with successful others and by praising their associates. *Human Communication Research, 36,* 163–189.

Tal-Or, N., & Papirman, Y. (2007). The fundamental attribution error in attributing fictional figures' characteristics to the actors. *Media Psychology, 9,* 331–345.

Tangney, J. P., Baumeister, R. F., & Boone, A. L. (2004). High self-control predicts good adjustment, less pathology, better grades, and interpersonal success. *Journal of Personality, 72,* 271–322.

Taras, V., Sarala, R., Muchinsky, P., Kemmelmeier, M., Singelis, T. M., Avsec, A., . . . Sinclair, H. C. (2014). Opposite ends of the same stick? Multi-method test of the dimensionality of individualism and collectivism. *Journal of Cross-Cultural Psychology, 45,* 213–245.

Tate, C. C., Youssef, C. P., & Bettergarcia, J. N. (2014). Integrating the study of transgender spectrum and cisgender experiences of self-categorization from a personality perspective. *Review of General Psychology, 18,* 302–312.

Tay, L., Morrison, M., & Diener, E. (2014). Living among the affluent: Boon or bane? *Psychological Science, 25,* 1235–1241.

Taylor, S. E., & Thompson, S. C. (1982). Stalking the elusive "vividness" effect. *Psychological Review, 89,* 155–181.

Taylor, S. E., Crocker, J., Fiske, S. T., Sprinzen, M., & Winkler, J. D. (1979). The generalizability of salience effects. *Journal of Personality and Social Psychology, 37,* 357–368.

Taylor, S. P., & Chermack, S. T. (1993). Alcohol, drugs and human physical aggression. *Journal of Studies on Alcohol, SUPPL 11,* 78–88.

Tekleab, A. G., Quigley, N. R., & Tesluk, P. E. (2009). A longitudinal study of team conflict, conflict management, cohesion, and team effectiveness. *Group & Organization Management, 34,* 170–205.

Tesser, A. (1988). Toward a self-evaluation maintenance model of social behavior. In L. Berkowitz (Ed.), *Advances in experimental social psychology: Social psychological studies of the self: Perspectives and programs* (Vol. 21, pp. 181–227). San Diego, CA: Academic Press.

Tesser, A. (1993). The importance of heritability in psychological research: The case of attitudes. *Psychological Review, 100,* 129–142.

Tesser, A. (2003). Self-evaluation. In M. R. Leary & J. P. Tangney (Eds.), *Handbook of self and identity* (pp. 275–290). New York, NY: Guilford Press.

Teven, J. J., & McCroskey, J. C. (1997). The relationship of perceived teacher caring with student learning and teacher evaluation. *Communication Education, 46,* 1–9.

The Innocence Project. (2015a). The causes of wrongful conviction. Retrieved from http://www.innocence project.org/causes-wrongful-conviction

The Innocence Project. (2015b). False confessions or admissions. Retrieved from http://www.innocence project.org/causes-wrongful-conviction/false-confessions-or-admissions

Thibaut, J. W., & Kelley, H. H. (1959). *The social psychology of groups.* Oxford, UK: John Wiley.

Thomaes, S., & Bushman, B. J. (2011). Mirror, mirror, on the wall, who's the most aggressive of them all? Narcissism, self-esteem, and aggression. In P. R. Shaver & M. Mikulincer (Eds.), *Human aggression and violence: Causes, manifestations, and consequences* (pp. 203–219). Washington, DC: American Psychological Association.

Thompson, S. C., & Schlehofer, M. M. (2008). The many sides of control motivation: Motives for high, low, and illusory control. In J. Y. Shah & W. L. Gardner (Eds.), *Handbook of motivation science* (pp. 41–56). New York, NY: Guilford Press.

Thompson, S. C., Armstrong, W., & Thomas, C. (1998). Illusions of control, underestimations, and accuracy: A control heuristic explanation. *Psychological Bulletin, 123,* 143–161.

Thompson, S., Marks, N., & Jackson, T. (2013). Well-being and sustainable development. In S. A. David, I. Boniwell, & A. Conley Ayers (Eds.), *The Oxford handbook of happiness* (pp. 498–516). New York, NY: Oxford University Press.

Thompson, W. C., Kaasa, S. O., & Peterson, T. (2013). Do jurors give appropriate weight to forensic identification evidence? Journal of Empirical Legal Studies, 10, 359–397.

Tiggemann, M., & Polivy, J. (2010). Upward and downward: Social comparison processing of thin idealized media images. *Psychology of Women Quarterly, 34,* 356–364.

Timmers, R., & van der Wijst, P. (2007). Images as anti-smoking fear appeals: The effect of emotion on the persuasion process. *Information Design Journal, 15,* 21–36.

Tindale, R. S., Talbot, M., & Martinez, R. (2013). Decision making. In J. M. Levine (Ed.), *Group processes* (pp. 165–192). New York, NY: Psychology Press.

Todorov, A., & Porter, J. M. (2014). Misleading first impressions: Different for different facial images of the same person. *Psychological Science.*

Todorov, A., Fiske, S. T., & Prentice, D. A. (2011). *Social neuroscience: Toward understanding the underpinnings of the social mind.* New York, NY: Oxford University Press.

Todorov, A., Fiske, S. T., & Prentice, D. A. (2011). *Social neuroscience: Toward understanding the underpinnings of the social mind.* New York, NY: Oxford University Press.

Todorov, A., Mandisodza, A. N., Goren, A., & Hall, C. C. (2005). Inferences of competence from faces predict election outcomes. *Science, 308,* 1623–1626.

Toepoel, V., & Couper, M. P. (2011). Can verbal instructions counteract visual context effects in web surveys? *Public Opinion Quarterly, 75,* 1–18.

Tohidian, I. (2009). Examining linguistic relativity hypothesis as one of the main views on the relationship between language and thought. *Journal of Psycholinguistic Research, 38,* 65–74.

Toma, C. L., & Hancock, J. T. (2010). Looks and lies: The role of physical attractiveness in online dating self-presentation and deception. *Communication Research, 37,* 335–351.

Tormala, Z. L. (2008). A new framework for resistance to persuasion: The resistance appraisals hypothesis. In W. D. Crano & R. Prislin (Eds.), *Attitudes and attitude change* (pp. 213–234). New York, NY: Psychology Press.

Tormala, Z. L., Falces, C., Briñol, P., & Petty, R. E. (2007). Ease of retrieval effects in social judgment: The role of unrequested cognitions. *Journal of Personality and Social Psychology, 93,* 143–157.

Torres, L., & Taknint, J. T. (2015). Ethnic microaggressions, traumatic stress symptoms, and Latino depression: A moderated mediational model. *Journal of Counseling Psychology.*

Torres-Harding, S. R., Andrade, A. L., Jr., & Romero Diaz, C. E. (2012). The racial microaggressions scale (RMAS): A new scale to measure experiences of racial microaggressions in people of color. *Cultural Diversity and Ethnic Minority Psychology, 18,* 153–164.

Tourangeau, R., Rips, L. J., & Rasinski, K. (2000). *The psychology of survey response.* New York, NY: Cambridge University Press.

Tov, W., & Au, E. W. M. (2013). Comparing well-being across nations: Conceptual and empirical issues. In S. A. David, I. Boniwell, & A. Conley Ayers (Eds.), *The Oxford handbook of happiness* (pp. 449–464). New York, NY: Oxford University Press.

Tracy, J. L., & Matsumoto, D. (2008). The spontaneous expression of pride and shame: Evidence for biologically innate verbal displays. *Proceedings of the National Academy of Sciences, 105,* 11655–11660.

Tracy, J. L., & Robins, R. W. (2007). Emerging insights into the nature and function of pride. *Current Directions in Psychological Science, 16,* 147–150.

Tracy, J. L., Shariff, A. F., Zhao, W., & Henrich, J. (2013). Cross-cultural evidence that the nonverbal expression of pride is an automatic status signal. *Journal of Experimental Psychology: General, 142,* 163–180.

Trafimow, D., & Clayton, K. D. (2006). The self in its cultural context: Effects on content and processes. In A. P. Prescott (Ed.), *The concept of self in psychology* (pp. 113–127). Hauppauge, NY: Nova Science Publishers.

Traupmann, J., & Hatfield, E. (1981). Love and its effect on mental and physical health. In R. Fogel, E. Hatfield, S. Kiesler, & E. Shanas (Eds.), *Aging: Stability and change in the family* (pp. 253–274). New York, NY: Academic Press.

Traut-Mattausch, E., Jonas, E., Frey, D., & Zanna, M.P. (2011). Are there "his" and "her" types of decisions? Exploring gender differences in the confirmation bias. *Sex Roles, 65,* 223–233.

Triandis, H. C. (1993). Collectivism and individualism as cultural syndromes. *Cross-Cultural Research: The Journal of Comparative Social Science, 27,* 155–180.

Triandis, H. C. (1995). *Individualism & collectivism.* Boulder, CO: Westview Press.

Triandis, H. C., & Gelfand, M. J. (2012). A theory of individualism and collectivism. In P. A. M. Van Lange, A. W. Kruglanski, E. T. Higgins (Eds.), *Handbook of theories of social psychology* (Vol. 2, pp. 498–520). Thousand Oaks, CA: Sage.

Triandis, H. C., & Singelis, T. M. (1998). Training to recognize individual differences in collectivism and individualism within culture. *International Journal of Intercultural Relations, 22,* 35–47.

Triplett, N. (1897). The dynamogenic factors in pacemaking and competition. *American Journal of Psychology, 9,* 507–533.

Trivers, R. (1971). The evolution of reciprocal altruism. *Quarterly Review of Biology, 46,* 35–57.

Trivers, R. (1972). Parental investment and sexual selection. In B. G. Campbell (Ed.), *Sexual selection and the descent of man* (pp. 136–179). Chicago, IL: Aldine.

Trope, Y., & Liberman, A. (1993). The use of trait conceptions to identify other people's behavior and to draw inferences about their personalities. *Personality and Social Psychology Bulletin, 19,* 553–562.

Trope, Y., & Liberman, A. (1996). Social hypothesis testing: Cognitive and motivational mechanisms. In E. T. Higgins & A. W. Kruglanski (Eds.), *Social psychology: Handbook of basic principles* (pp. 239–270). New York, NY: Guilford Press.

Trope, Y., & Liberman, N. (2012). Construal level theory. In P. A. M. Van Lange, A. W. Kruglanski, E. T. Higgins, P. A. M. Van Lange, A. W. Kruglanski & E. T. Higgins (Eds.), *Handbook of theories of social psychology (Vol 1).* (pp. 118–134). Thousand Oaks, CA: Sage Publications Ltd.

Trotter, R. J. (1985). Muzafer Sherif: A life of conflict and goals. *Psychology Today, 19.*

Tsai, W. -C., Huang, T. -C., & Yu, H. -H. (2012). Investigating the unique predictability and boundary conditions of applicant physical attractiveness and non-verbal behaviours on interviewer evaluations in job interviews. *Journal of Occupational and Organizational Psychology, 85,* 60–79.

Tsai, W. -C., Huang, T. -C., Wu, C. -Y., & Lo, I. H. (2010). Disentangling the effects of applicant defensive impression management tactics in job interviews. *International Journal of Selection and Assessment, 18,* 131–140.

Tsui, K. M., Desai, M., Yanco, H. A., Cramer, H., & Kemper, N. (2010). Measuring attitudes toward telepresence robots. *International Journal of Intelligent Control and Systems,* 1–11.

Tubre, T. C., & Collins, J. M. (2000). Jackson and Schuler (1985) revisited: A meta-analysis of the relationships between role ambiguity, role conflict, and job performance. *Journal of Management, 26,* 155–169.

Tuckey, M. R., & Neall, A. M. (2014). Workplace bullying erodes job and personal resources: Between- and within-person perspectives. *Journal of Occupational Health Psychology, 19,* 413–424.

Turchin, P., Whitehouse, H., François, P., Slingerland, E., & Collard, M. (2012). A historical database of sociocultural evolution. Cliodynamics: The Journal of Theoretical & Mathematical History, 3, 271–293.

Turner, C. W., Layton, J. F., & Simons, L. S. (1975). Naturalistic studies of aggressive behavior: Aggressive stimuli, victim visibility, and horn honking. *Journal of Personality and Social Psychology, 31,* 1098–1107.

Turner, J. C. (1991). *Social influence.* Belmont, CA: Thomson Brooks/Cole Publishing.

Turner, J. C., & Reynolds, K J. (2012). Self-categorization theory. In P. A. M. Van Lange, A. W. Kruglanski, & E. T. Higgins (Eds.), *Handbook of theories of social psychology* (Vol. 2, pp. 399–417). Thousand Oaks, CA: Sage.

Turner, J. C., Hogg, M. A., Oakes, P. J., Reicher, S. D., & Wetherell, M. S. (1987). *Rediscovering the social group: A self-categorization theory*. Cambridge, MA: Basil Blackwell.

Turner, M. E., Pratkanis, A. R., & Struckman, C. K. (2007). Groupthink as social identity maintenance. In A. R. Pratkanis (Ed.), The science of social influence: Advances and future progress (pp. 223–246). New York, NY: Psychology Press.

Turner, M. M., Tamborini, R., Limon, M. S., & Zuckerman-Hyman, C. (2007). The moderators and mediators of door-in-the-face requests: Is it a negotiation or a helping experience? *Communication Monographs, 74,* 333–356.

Tversky, A., & Kahneman, D. (1973). Availability: A heuristic for judging frequency and probability. *Cognitive Psychology, 5,* 207–232.

Tversky, A., & Kahneman, D. (1974). Judgment under uncertainty: Heuristics and biases. *Science, 185,* 1124–1131.

Twenge, J. M. (2006). *Generation me: Why today's young Americans are more confident, assertive, entitled—and more miserable than ever before*. New York, NY: Free Press.

Twenge, J. M. (2007). The socially excluded self. In C. Sedikides & S. J. Spencer (Eds.), *The self* (pp. 311–323). New York, NY: Psychology Press.

Twenge, J. M. (2009). Change over time in obedience: The jury's still out, but it might be decreasing. *American Psychologist, 64,* 28–31.

Twenge, J. M., & Campbell, W. K. (2009). *The narcissism epidemic: Living in the age of enlightenment*. New York, NY: Free Press.

Twenge, J. M., & Crocker, J. (2002). Race and self-esteem: Meta-analyses comparing Whites, Blacks, Hispanics, Asians, and American Indians and comment on Gray-Little and Hafdahl (2000). *Psychological Bulletin, 128,* 371–408.

Twenge, J. M., Baumeister, R. F., DeWall, C. N., Ciarocco, N. J., & Bartels, J. M. (2007). Social exclusion decreases prosocial behavior. *Journal of Personality and Social Psychology, 92,* 56–66.

Twenge, J. M., Baumeister, R. F., Tice, D. M., & Stucke, T. S. (2001). If you can't join them, beat them: Effects of social exclusion on aggressive behavior. *Journal of Personality and Social Psychology, 81,* 1058–1069.

Tybout, A. M., & Talch, R. F. (1980). The effect of experience: A matter of salience? *Journal of Consumer Research, 6,* 406–413.

Tybur, J. M., Lieberman, D., Kurzban, R., & DeScioli, P. (2013). Disgust: Evolved function and structure. *Psychological Review, 120,* 65–84.

Tykocinski, O. E., & Ortmann, A. (2011). The lingering effects of our past experiences: The sunk-cost fallacy and the inaction-inertia effect. *Social and Personality Psychology Compass, 5,* 653–664.

Ufkes, E. G., Otten, S., Van der Zee, K. I., Giebels, E., & Dovidio, J. F. (2012). Urban district identity as a common ingroup identity: The different role of ingroup prototypicality for minority and majority groups. European Journal of Social Psychology, 42, 706–716.

Ulrich, R. S., Simons, R. F., Losito, B. D., Fiorito, E., Miles, M. A., & Zelson, M. (1991). Stress recovery during exposure to natural and urban environments. *Journal of Environmental Psychology, 11,* 201–230.

Underation, C. (2009). Political rhetoric that strikes a responsive chord: Why some negative ads hit the mark while others miss it. *Ohio Communication Journal, 47,* 247–263.

Underwood, M. K., Beron, K. J., Gentsch, J. K., Galperin, M. B., & Risser, S. D. (2008). Family correlates of children's social and physical aggression with peers: Negative interparental conflict strategies and parenting styles. *International Journal of Behavioral Development, 32,* 549–562.

Unzueta, M. M., Everly, B. A., & Gutiérrez, A. S. (2014). Social dominance orientation moderates reactions to Black and White discrimination claimants. *Journal of Experimental Social Psychology, 54,* 81–88.

Usborne, E., & Taylor, D. M. (2010). The role of cultural identity clarity for self-concept clarity, self-esteem, and subjective well-being. *Personality and Social Psychology Bulletin, 36,* 883–897.

Uziel, L. (2010). Look at me, I'm happy and creative: The effect of impression management on behavior in social presence. *Personality and Social Psychology Bulletin, 36,* 1591–1602.

Valentiner, D. P., Hiraoka, R., & Skowronski, J. J. (2014). Borderline personality disorder features, self-verification, and committed relationships. *Journal of Social & Clinical Psychology, 33,* 463–480.

Valentiner, D. P., Skowronski, J. J., McGrath, P. B., Smith, S. A., & Renner, K. A. (2011). Self-verification and social anxiety: Preference for negative social feedback and low social self-esteem. *Behavioural and Cognitive Psychotherapy, 39,* 601–617.

Valentino, N. A., & Brader, T. (2011). The sword's other edge: Perceptions of discrimination and racial policy opinion after Obama. *Public Opinion Quarterly, 75,* 201–226.

Vallerand, R. J., Blanchard, C., Mageau, G. A., Koestner, R., Ratelle, C., Leonard, M., . . . Marsolais, J. (2003). Les passions de l'âme: On obsessive and harmonious passion. *Journal of Personality and Social Psychology, 85,* 756–767.

Vallone, R. P., Ross, L., & Lepper, M. R. (1985). The hostile media phenomenon: Biased perception and perceptions of media bias in coverage of the Beirut massacre. *Journal of Personality and Social Psychology, 49,* 577–585.

Valsiner, J. (Ed.). (2012). *The Oxford handbook of culture and psychology.* Oxford, UK: Oxford University Press.

van Bommel, M., van Prooijen, J. -W., Elffers, H., & Van Lange, P. A. M. (2012). Be aware to care: Public self-awareness leads to a reversal of the bystander effect. *Journal of Experimental Social Psychology, 48,* 926–930.

van Bommel, M., van Prooijen, J. -W., Elffers, H., & Van Lange, P. A. M. (2014). Intervene to be seen: The power of a camera in attenuating the bystander effect. *Social Psychological and Personality Science, 5,* 459–466.

Van Dyne, L., Graham, J. W., & Dienesch, R. M. (1994). Organizational citizenship behavior: Construct redefinition, measurement, and validation. *Academy of Management Journal, 37,* 765–802.

van Ginkel, W.P., & van Knippenberg, D. (2009). Knowledge about the distribution of information and group decision making: When and why does it work? *Organizational Behavior and Human Decision Processes, 108,* 218–229.

van Hoorn, A. (2015). Individualist–collectivist culture and trust radius: A multilevel approach. *Journal of Cross-Cultural Psychology, 46,* 269–276.

van Horn, J. D., Irimia, A., Torgerson, C. M., Chambers, M. C., Kikinis, R., & Toga, A. W. (2012). Mapping connectivity damage in the case of Phineas Gage. *PLoS ONE, 7*(5).

Van Knippenberg, A., & Wilke, H. (1988). Social categorization and attitude change. *European Journal of Social Psychology, 18,* 395–406.

Van Lange, P. A. M., Joireman, J., Parks, C. D., & Van Dijk, E. (2013). The psychology of social dilemmas: A review. *Organizational Behavior and Human Decision Processes, 120,* 125–141.

van Veelen, R., Otten, S., & Hansen, N. (2013). Social identification when an in-group identity is unclear: The role of self-anchoring and self-stereotyping. *British Journal of Social Psychology, 52,* 543–562.

Van Vugt, M., & Kameda, T. (2013). Evolution and groups. In J. M. Levine (Ed.), Group processes. (pp. 297–322). New York, NY: Psychology Press.

van Woerkom, M., & Sanders, K. (2010). The romance of learning from disagreement. The effect of cohesiveness and disagreement on knowledge sharing behavior and individual performance within teams. Journal of Business and Psychology, 25, 139–149.

Vandello, J. A., Cohen, D., & Ransom, S. (2008). U.S. Southern and Northern differences in perceptions of norms about aggression: Mechanisms for the perpetuation of a culture of honor. *Journal of Cross-Cultural Psychology, 39,* 162–177.

Vandello, J. A., Cohen, D., Grandon, R., & Franiuk, R. (2009). Stand by your man: Indirect prescriptions for honorable violence and feminine loyalty in Canada, Chile, and the United States. *Journal of Cross-Cultural Psychology, 40,* 81–104.

VanderWeele, T. J., Hawkley, L. C., & Cacioppo, J. T. (2012). On the reciprocal association between loneliness and subjective well-being. *American Journal Of Epidemiology, 176,* 777–784.

Vangelisti, A. L., Pennebaker, J. W., Brody, N., & Guinn, T. D. (2014). Reducing social pain: Sex differences in the impact of physical pain relievers. *Personal Relationships, 21,* 349–363.

Vanhove, A., & Gordon, R. A. (2014). Weight discrimination in the workplace: A meta-analytic examination of the relationship between weight and work-related outcomes. *Journal of Applied Social Psychology, 44,* 12–22.

Vanman, E. J., Saltz, J. L., Nathan, L. R., & Warren, J. A. (2004). Racial discrimination by low-prejudiced Whites facial movements as implicit measures of attitudes related to behavior. *Psychological Science, 15,* 711–714.

Varela, F. J., Thompson, E., & Rosch, E. (1991). *The embodied mind: Cognitive science and human experience.* Cambridge, MA: The MIT Press.

Varma, A., Toh, S. M., & Pichler, S. (2006). Ingratiation in job applications: Impact on selection decisions. *Journal of Managerial Psychology, 21,* 200–210.

Vasey, P. L., & VanderLaan, D. P. (2010). An adaptive cognitive dissociation between willingness to help kin and nonkin in Samoan Fa'afafine. *Psychological Science, 21,* 292–297.

Vasey, P. L., & VanderLaan, D. P. (2012). Sexual orientation in men and avuncularity in Japan: Implications for the kin selection hypothesis. *Archives of Sexual Behavior, 41,* 209–215.

Vasey, P. L., & VanderLaan, D. P. (2014). Evolving research on the evolution of male androphilia. *Canadian Journal of Human Sexuality, 23,* 137–147.

Vassos, E., Collier, D. A., & Fazel, S. (2014). Systematic meta-analyses and field synopsis of genetic association studies of violence and aggression. *Molecular Psychiatry, 19,* 471–477.

Vauclair, C. -M., Fischer, R., Ferreira, M. C., Guerra, V., Hößler, U., Karabati, S., . . . Spieß, E. (2015). What kinds of value motives guide people in their moral attitudes? The role of personal and prescriptive values at the culture level and individual level. *Journal of Cross-Cultural Psychology, 46,* 211–228.

Vaughn, D. (1986). *Uncoupling: Turning points in intimate relationships.* New York, NY: Oxford University Press.

Veenhoven, R. (1999). Quality-of-life in individualistic society: A comparison of 43 nations in the early 1990's. *Social Indicators Research, 48,* 157–186.

Verweij, K. J. H., Shekar, S. N., Zietsch, B. P., Eaves, L. J., Bailey, M., Boomsma, D. I., & Martin, N. G. (2008). Genetic and environmental influences on individual differences in attitudes toward homosexuality: An Australian twin study. *Behavior Genetics, 38,* 257–265.

Viggiano, M. P., & Marzi, T. (2010). Context and social effects on face recognition. In E. Balcetis & G. D. Lassiter (Eds.), *Social psychology of visual perception* (pp. 171–200). New York, NY: Psychology Press.

Villepoux, A., Vermeulen, N., Niedenthal, P., & Mermillod, M. (2015). Evidence of fast and automatic gender bias in affective priming. *Journal of Cognitive Psychology, 27,* 301–309.

Visser, P. S., & Holbrook, A. L. (2012). Metacognitive determinants of attitude strength. In P. Briñol, K. DeMarree, P. Briñol & K. DeMarree (Eds.), *Social metacognition* (pp. 21–41). New York, NY: Psychology Press.

Visser, P. S., & Krosnick, J. A. (1998). Development of attitude strength over the life cycle: Surge and decline. *Journal of Personality and Social Psychology, 75,* 1389–1410.

Vogel, E. A., Rose, J. P., Roberts, L. R., & Eckles, K. (2014). Social comparison, social media, and self-esteem. *Psychology of Popular Media Culture, 3,* 206–222.

Vogel, T., Kutzner, F., Fiedler, K., & Freytag, P. (2013). How majority members become associated with rare attributes: Ecological correlations in stereotype formation. *Social Cognition, 31,* 427–442.

Vohs, K. D., & Schmeichel, B. J. (2007). Self-regulation: How and why people reach (and fail to reach) their goals. In C. Sedikides & S. J. Spencer (Eds.), *The self* (pp. 139–162). New York, NY: Psychology Press.

Vohs, K. D., & Schooler, J. W. (2008). The value of believing in free will: Encouraging a belief in determinism increases cheating. *Psychological Science, 19,* 49–54.

Volk, A. A., Camilleri, J. A., Dane, A. V., & Marini, Z. A. (2012). Is adolescent bullying an evolutionary adaptation? *Aggressive Behavior, 38,* 222–238.

Vrangalova, Z., & Savin-Williams, R. C. (2012). Mostly heterosexual and mostly gay/lesbian: Evidence for new sexual orientation identities. *Archives of Sexual Behavior, 41,* 85–101.

Vrij, A., Edward, K., Roberts, K. P., & Bull, R. (2000). Detecting deceit via analysis of verbal and nonverbal behavior. *Journal of Nonverbal Behavior, 24,* 239–263.

Vrij, A., Fisher, R. P., Mann, S., & Leal, S. (2010). Lie detection: Pitfalls and opportunities. In G. D. Lassiter & C. A. Meissner (Eds.), *Police interrogations and false confessions: Current research, practice, and policy recommendations* (pp. 97–110). Washington, DC: American Psychological Association.

Vrij, A., Granhag, P. A., Mann, S., & Leal, S. (2011). Outsmarting the liars: Toward a cognitive lie detection approach. *Current Directions in Psychological Science, 20,* 28–32.

Vrij, A., Leal, S., Granhag, P. A., Mann, S., Fisher, R. P., Hillman, J., & Sperry, K. (2009). Outsmarting the liars: The benefit of asking unanticipated questions. *Law and Human Behavior, 33,* 159–166.

Vrij, A., Mann, S., Jundi, S., Hillman, J., & Hope, L. (2014). Detection of concealment in an information-gathering interview. *Applied Cognitive Psychology.*

Vroom, V. H., & Jago, A. G. (2007). The role of the situation in leadership. *American Psychologist, 62,* 17–24.

Vugt, M. v., & Kameda, T. (2014). Evolution of the social brain: Psychological adaptations for group living. In M. Mikulincer, P. R. Shaver, M. Mikulincer, & P. R. Shaver (Eds.), *Mechanisms of social connection: From brain to group* (pp. 335–355). Washington, DC: American Psychological Association.

Wager, T. D., & Lindquist, M. A. (2011). Essentials of functional magnetic resonance imaging. In J. Decety & J. T. Cacioppo (Eds.), *Oxford handbook of social neuroscience* (pp. 69–96). Oxford, UK: Oxford University.

Wagner, J., Hoppmann, C., Ram, N., & Gerstorf, D. (2015). Self-esteem is relatively stable late in life: The role of resources in the health, self-regulation, and social domains. *Developmental Psychology, 51,* 136–149.

Wagner, J.A. (1995). Studies of individualism-collectivism: Effects on cooperation in groups. *Academy of Management Journal, 38,* 152–172.

Wagner, U., Christ, O., & Heitmeyer, W. (2010). Anti-immigration bias. In J. F. Dovidio, M. Hewstone, P. Glick & V. M. Esses (Eds.), *The SAGE handbook of prejudice, stereotyping, and discrimination* (pp. 361–276). London, UK: Sage.

Walker, M. B., & Andrade, M. G. (1996). Conformity in the Asch task as a function of age. *The Journal of Social Psychology, 136,* 367–372.

Walker, R., Burger, O., Wagner, J., & Von Rueden, C. R. (2006). Evolution of brain size and juvenile periods in primates. *Journal of Human Evolution, 51,* 480–489.

Walker, S., Richardson, D. S., & Green, L. R. (2000). Aggression among older adults: The relationship of interaction networks and gender role to direct and indirect responses. *Aggressive Behavior, 26,* 145–154.

Wallach, M. A., Kogan, N., & Bem, D. J. (1962). Group influence on individual risk taking. *The Journal of Abnormal and Social Psychology, 65,* 75–86.

Waller, N. G., Kojetin, B.A., Bouchard, T. J., Lykken, D. T., & Tellegen, A. (1990). Genetic and environmental influences on religious interests, attitudes, and values: A study of twins reared apart and together. *Psychological Science, 1,* 138–142.

Wals, A. E., & Dillon, J. (2012). Conventional and emerging learning theories: Implications and choices for educational researchers with a planetary consciousness. In R. Stevenson, M. Brody, J. Dillon, & A. E. Wals (Eds.), *International handbook of environmental education* (pp. 253–261). Washington, DC: AERA/Routledge.

Walther, E., & Weil, R. (2012). Balance principles in attitude formation and change: The desire to maintain consistent cognitions about people. In B. Gawronski & F. Strack (Eds.), *Cognitive consistency: A fundamental principle in social cognition* (pp. 351–368). New York, NY: Guilford Press.

Wang, J., Leu, J., & Shoda, Y. (2011). When the seemingly innocuous "stings": Racial microaggressions and their emotional consequences. *Personality and Social Psychology Bulletin, 37,* 1666–1678.

Wang, R. Y., & Ng, C. N. (2015). Can centralized sanctioning promote trust in social dilemmas? A two-level trust game with incomplete information. *PLoS ONE, 10,* e0124513-e0124513

Wang, S. S., Moon, S. -I., Kwon, K. H., Evans, C. A., & Stefanone, M. A. (2010). Face off: Implications of visual cues on initiating friendship on Facebook. *Computers in Human Behavior, 26,* 226–234.

Ward, J., & Voracek, M. (2004). Evolutionary and social cognitive explanations of sex differences in romantic jealousy. *Australian Journal of Psychology, 56,* 165–171.

Watson, J. B. (1925/1998). *Behaviorism.* Piscataway, NJ: Transaction Publishers.

Waytz, A., & Epley, N. (2012). Social connection enables dehumanization. *Journal of Experimental Social Psychology, 48,* 70–76.

Webb, E. J., Campbell, D. T., Schwartz, R. D., & Sechrest, L. (1966). *Unobtrusive measures: Nonreactive research in the social sciences.* Oxford, UK: Rand Mcnally.

Webster, G. D., DeWall, C. N., Pond, R. S., Jr., Deckman, T., Jonason, P. K., Le, B. M., . . . Bator, R. J. (2014). The brief aggression questionnaire: Psychometric and behavioral evidence for an efficient measure of trait aggression. *Aggressive Behavior, 40,* 120–139.

Webster, G. D., DeWall, C. N., Pond, R. S., Jr., Deckman, T., Jonason, P. K., Le, B. M., . . . Bator, R. J. (2015). The brief aggression questionnaire: Structure, validity, reliability, and generalizability. *Journal of Personality Assessment,* 1–12.

Wegner, D. M. (1987). Transactive memory: A contemporary analysis of the group mind. In B. Mullen & G. R. Goethals (Eds.), *Theories of group behavior* (pp. 185–205). New York, NY: Springer-Verlag.

Wegner, D. M. (2002). *The illusion of conscious will.* Cambridge, MA: MIT Press.

Wegner, D. M., & Crano, W. D. (1975). Racial factors in helping behavior: An unobtrusive field experiment. *Journal of Personality and Social Psychology, 32,* 901–905.

Wegner, D. M., Schneider, D. J., Carter, S. R., & White, T. L. (1987). Paradoxical effects of thought suppression. *Journal of Personality and Social Psychology, 53,* 5–13.

Weijters, B., Geuens, M., & Baumgartner, H. (2013). The effect of familiarity with the response category labels on item response to Likert scales. *Journal of Consumer Research, 40,* 368–381.

Weiner, B. (1995). *Judgments of responsibility: A foundation for a theory of social conduct.* New York, NY: Guilford Press.

Weiner, B. (2010). The development of an attribution-based theory of motivation: A history of ideas. *Educational Psychologist, 45,* 28–36.

Weisberg, D. S., Keil, F. C., Goodstein, J., Rawson, E., & Gray, J. R. (2008). The seductive allure of neuroscience explanations. *Journal of Cognitive Neuroscience, 20,* 470–477.

Weisbuch, M., Seery, M. D., Ambady, N., & Blascovich, J. (2009). On the correspondence between physiological and nonverbal responses: Nonverbal behavior accompanying challenge and threat. *Journal of Nonverbal Behavior, 33,* 141–148.

Weiss, B., & Feldman R. S. (2006). Looking good and lying to do it: Deception as an impression management strategy in job interviews. *Journal of Applied Social Psychology, 36,* 1070–1086.

Weiss, S. J. (2014). Instrumental and classical conditioning: Intersections, interactions and stimulus control. In F. K. McSweeney, E. S. Murphy (Eds.), *The Wiley Blackwell handbook of operant and classical conditioning* (pp. 417–451). Hobeken, NJ: Wiley-Blackwell.

Wells, G. L., & Petty, R. E. (1980). The effects of overt head movements on persuasion: Compatibility and incompatibility of responses. *Basic and Applied Social Psychology, 1,* 219–230.

Welsh, D. T., & Ordóñez, L. D. (2014). Conscience without cognition: The effects of subconscious priming on ethical behavior. *Academy of Management Journal, 57,* 723–742.

Wemm, S., Fanean, A., Baker, A., Blough, E. R., Mewaldt, S., & Bardi, M. (2013). Problematic drinking and physiological responses among female college students. *Alcohol, 47,* 149–157.

West, R. F., Meserve, R. J., & Stanovich, K. E. (2012). Cognitive sophistication does not attenuate the bias blind spot. *Journal of Personality and Social Psychology, 103,* 506–519.

Westen, D. (2007). *The political brain: The role of emotion in deciding the fate of the nation.* New York, NY: Public Affairs Books.

Westphal, J. D., & Stern, I. (2007). Flattery will get you everywhere (especially if you are a male Caucasian): How ingratiation, boardroom behavior, and demographic minority status affect additional board appointments at U.S. Companies. *Academy of Management Journal, 50,* 267–288.

Whatley, M. A., Webster, J. M., Smith, R. H., & Rhodes, A. (1999). The effect of a favor on public and private compliance: How internalized is the norm of reciprocity? *Basic and Applied Social Psychology, 21,* 251–259.

Wheeler, L., & Kim, Y. (1997). What is beautiful is culturally good: The physical attractiveness stereotype has different content in collectivistic cultures. *Personality and Social Psychology Bulletin, 23,* 795–800.

White, B. A., Gordon, H., & Guerra, R. C. (2015). Callous–unemotional traits and empathy in proactive and reactive relational aggression in young women. *Personality and Individual Differences, 75,* 185–189.

Whitley, B. E. (1998). False consensus on sexual behavior among college women: Comparison of four theoretical explanations. *Journal of Sex Research, 35,* 206–214.

Whitley, B. E., Jr. (2009). Religiosity and attitudes toward lesbians and gay men: A meta-analysis. *International Journal for the Psychology of Religion, 19,* 21–38.

Whitman, W. (1993). *Leaves of grass.* New York, NY: Barnes & Noble. (Original work published 1892)

Whitmarsh, L. (2009). Behavioural responses to climate change: Asymmetry of intentions and impacts. *Journal of Environmental Psychology, 29,* 13–23.

Whorf, B. L. (1956). *Language, thought, and reality: Selected writing.* Cambridge, MA: Technology Press of Massachusetts Institute of Technology.

Wicker, A. W. (1969). Attitudes versus actions: The relationship of verbal and overt behavioral responses to attitude objects. *Journal of Social Issues, 25,* 41–78.

Wicker, A. W. (1971). An examination of the "other variables" explanation of attitude-behavior inconsistency. *Journal of Personality and Social Psychology, 19,* 18–30.

Widmeyer, W. N., & Loy, J. W. (1988). When you're hot, you're hot! Warm-cold effects in first impressions of persons and teaching effectiveness. *Journal of Educational Psychology, 80,* 118–121.

Wilkie, W. L., Mela, C. F., & Gundlach, G. T. (1998). Does "bait and switch" really benefit consumers? *Marketing Science, 17,* 273–282.

Williams, D. (2004). Improving race relations in higher education: The jigsaw classroom as a missing piece to the puzzle. *Urban Education, 39,* 316–344.

Williams, J. C., & Jovanovic, J. (2015). Third wave feminism and emerging adult sexuality: Friends with benefits relationships. *Sexuality & Culture: An Interdisciplinary Quarterly, 19,* 157–171.

Williams, J. E., & Best, D. L. (1990). *Sex and psyche: Gender and self viewed cross-culturally.* Thousand Oaks, CA: Sage.

Williams, J. E., & Morland, J. K. (1976). *Race, color and the young child.* Chapel Hill, NC: University of North Carolina Press.

Williams, K., Harkins, S. G., & Latané, B. (1981). Identifiability as a deterrent to social loafing: Two cheering experiments. Journal of Personality and Social Psychology, 40, 303–311.

Williams, M. J., & Spencer-Rodgers, J. (2010). Culture and stereotyping processes: Integration and new directions. *Social and Personality Psychology Compass, 4,* 591–604.

Williamson, P., Weber, N., & Robertson, M. T. (2013). The effect of expertise on memory conformity: A test of informational influence. *Behavioral Sciences & the Law, 31,* 607–623.

Willis, J., & Todorov, A. (2006). First impressions: Making up your mind after a 100-ms exposure to a face. *Psychological Science, 17,* 592–598.

Wilson, B. J., Petaja, H. S., Stevens, A. D., Mitchell, M. F., & Peterson, K. M. (2011). Children's responses to entry failure: Attention deployment patterns and self-regulation skills. *The Journal of Genetic Psychology: Research and Theory on Human Development, 172,* 376–400.

Wilson, D. S. (2007). The role of group selection in human psychological evolution. In S. W. Gangestad & J. A. Simpson (Eds.), *The evolution of mind: Fundamental questions and controversies* (pp. 213–220). New York, NY: Guilford Press.

Wilson, D. S., Van Vugt, M., & O'Gorman, R. (2008). Multilevel selection theory and major evolutionary transitions: Implications for psychological science. *Current Directions in Psychological Science, 17,* 6–9.

Wilson, M., & Daly, M. (1985). Competitiveness, risk taking, and violence: The young male syndrome. *Ethology & Sociobiology, 6,* 59–73.

Wilson, R. E., Gosling, S. D., & Graham, L. T. (2012). A review of Facebook research in the social sciences. *Perspectives on Psychological Science, 7,* 203–220.

Wilson, S. J., & Lipsey, M. W. (2000). Wilderness challenge programs for delinquent youth: A metaanalysis of outcome evaluations. *Evaluation and Program Planning, 23,* 1–12.

Wilson, T. D. (2002). *Strangers to ourselves: Discovering the adaptive unconscious.* Cambridge, MA: Belknap Press/Harvard University Press.

Wilson, T. D., & Gilbert, D. T. (2005). Affective forecasting: Knowing what to want. *Current Directions in Psychological Science, 14,* 131–134.

Wilson, T. D., & Kraft, D. (1993). Why do I love thee?: Effects of repeated introspections about a dating relationship on attitudes toward the relationship. *Personality and Social Psychology Bulletin, 19,* 409–418.

Wilson, T. D., Aronson, E., & Carlsmith, K. (2010). The art of laboratory experimentation. In S. T. Fiske, D. T. Gilbert, & G. Lindzey (Eds.), *Handbook of social psychology* (Vol. 1, 5th ed., pp. 51–81). Hoboken, NJ: John Wiley & Sons.

Wilson, T. D., Lindsey, S., & Schooler, T. Y. (2000). A model of dual attitudes. *Psychological Review, 107*, 101–126.

Wilson, T. D., Lisle, D. J., Schooler, J. W., Hodges, S. D., Klaaren, K. J., & LaFleur, S. J. (1993). Introspecting about reasons can reduce post-choice satisfaction. *Personality and Social Psychology Bulletin, 19*, 331–339.

Wilson, T. D., Wheatley, T., Meyers, J. M., Gilbert, D. T., & Axsom, D. (2000). Focalism: A source of durability bias in affective forecasting. *Journal of Personality and Social Psychology, 78*, 821–836.

Wines, M., Saul, S., & Bhaskar, S. (2015, July 5). Supremacists extend reach through web. (Cover story). *New York Times, 164*, A1-A3.

Winkler, J. D., & Taylor, S. E. (1979). Preference, expectations, and attributional bias: Two field studies. *Journal of Applied Social Psychology, 9*, 183–197.

Witte, K. (1998). Fear as motivator, fear as inhibitor: Using the extended parallel process model to explain fear appeal successes and failures. In P. A. Andersen & L. K. Guerrero (Eds.), *Handbook of communication and emotion: Research, theory, applications, and contexts* (pp. 423–450). San Diego, CA: Academic Press.

Witte, K., & Allen, M. (2000). A meta-analysis of fear appeals: Implications for effective public health campaigns. *Health Education & Behaviors,* (5), 591–615.

Wittenbaum, G. M., Hollingshead, A. B., & Botero, I. C. (2004). From cooperative to motivated information sharing in groups: Moving beyond the hidden profile paradigm. *Communication Monographs, 71*, 286–310.

Witts, B. N., Loudermilk, K., & Kosel, D. (2014). Adult samples suggest slot machine and Casino characteristics are possible sources for investigating the illusion of control. *Analysis of Gambling Behavior, 8*, 79–85.

Wohl, M. J. A., & Branscombe, N. R. (2005). Forgiveness and collective guilt assignment to historical perpetrator groups depend on level of social category inclusiveness. *Journal of Personality and Social Psychology, 88*, 288–303.

Wood, D., & Brumbaugh, C. C. (2009). Using revealed mate preferences to evaluate market force and differential preference explanations for mate selection. *Journal of Personality and Social Psychology, 96*, 1226–1244.

Wood, J. V. (1996). What is social comparison and how should we study it? *Personality and Social Psychology Bulletin, 22*, 520–537.

Wood, J. V., Michela, J. L., & Giordano, C. (2000). Downward comparison in everyday life: Reconciling self-enhancement models with the mood-cognition priming model. *Journal of Personality and Social Psychology, 79*, 563–579.

Wood, J. V., Taylor, S. E., & Lichtman, R. R. (1985). Social comparison in adjustment to breast cancer. *Journal of Personality and Social Psychology, 49*, 1169–1183.

Wood, S. L., & Bettman, J. R. (2007). Predicting happiness: How normative feeling rules influence (and even reverse) durability bias. *Journal of Consumer Psychology, 17*, 188–201.

Wood, W. (1982). Retrieval of attitude-relevant information from memory: Effects on susceptibility to persuasion and on intrinsic motivation. *Journal of Personality and Social Psychology, 42*, 798–810.

Wood, W., Lundgren, S., Ouellette, J. A., Busceme, S., & Blackstone, T. (1994). Minority influence: A meta-analytic review of social influence processes. *Psychological Bulletin, 115*, 323–345.

Word, C. O., Zanna, M. P., & Cooper, J. (1974). The nonverbal mediation of self-fulfilling prophecies in interracial interaction. *Journal of Experimental Social Psychology, 10*, 109–120.

Worldwatch Institute. (2013). *State of the world, 2013: Is sustainability possible?* Washington, DC: Island Press.

Wrangham, R. W., & Peterson, D. (1996). *Demonic males: Apes and the origins of human violence.* Boston, MA: Houghton, Mifflin and Company.

Wu, L. -Z., Zhang, H., Chiu, R., Kwan, H., & He, X. (2014). Hostile attribution bias and negative reciprocity beliefs exacerbate incivility's effects on interpersonal deviance. *Journal of Business Ethics, 120*, 189.

Wurm, S., Warner, L. M., Ziegelmann, J. P., Wolff, J. K., & Schüz, B. (2013). How do negative self-perceptions of aging become a self-fulfilling prophecy? *Psychology and Aging, 28*, 1088–1097.

Wyer, R. S., Jr., & Albarracín, D. (2005). Belief formation, organization, and change: Cognitive and motivational influences. In D. Albarracín, B. T. Johnson, & M. P. Zanna (Eds.), *The handbook of attitudes* (pp. 273–322). Mahwah, NJ: Lawrence Erlbaum.

Yamada, D. (2009). Understanding and responding to bullying and related behaviors in healthcare workplaces. *Frontiers of Health Services Management, 25*, 33.

Yanagida, T., Strohmeier, D., Toda, Y., & Spiel, C. (2014). The self group distinction scale: A new approach to measure individualism and collectivism in adolescents. *Psychological Test and Assessment Modeling, 56*, 304–313.

Yang, J., Shi, Y., Luo, Y.L.L., Shi, J., & Cai, H. (2014). The brief implicit association test is valid: Experimental evidence. *Social Cognition, 32*, 449–465.

Yarritu, I., Matute, H., & Vadillo, M. A. (2014). Illusion of control: The role of personal involvement. *Experimental Psychology, 61*, 38–47.

Yeager, D. S., Johnson, R., Spitzer, B. J., Trzesniewski, K. H., Powers, J., & Dweck, C. S. (2014). The far-reaching effects of believing people can change: Implicit theories of personality shape stress, health, and achievement during adolescence. *Journal of Personality & Social Psychology, 106*, 867–884.

Yee, N., & Bailenson, J. N. (2009). The difference between being and seeing: The relative contribution of self-perception and priming to behavioral changes via digital self-representation. *Media Psychology, 12,* 195–209.

Yeung, V. W. L., & Kashima, Y. (2012). Culture and stereotype communication: Are people from Eastern cultures more stereotypical in communication? *Journal of Cross-Cultural Psychology, 43,* 446–463.

Ying, X., Li, H., Jiang, S., Peng, F., & Lin, Z. (2014). Group laziness: The effect of social loafing on group performance. *Social Behavior and Personality, 42,* 465–472.

Yousaf, O., & Gobet, F. (2013). The emotional and attitudinal consequences of religious hypocrisy: Experimental evidence using a cognitive dissonance paradigm. *The Journal of Social Psychology, 153,* 667–686.

Yuki, G. A. (2013). *Leadership in organizations* (8th ed.). Boston, MA: Pearson.

Zajonc, R. B. (1965). Social facilitation. *Science, 149,* 269–274.

Zajonc, R. B. (1968). Attitudinal effects of mere exposure. *Journal of Personality and Social Psychology, 9,* 1–27.

Zajonc, R. B. (1980a). Compresence. In P. B. Paulus (Ed.), Psychology of group influence (pp. 35–60). Mahwah, NJ: Erlbaum.

Zajonc, R. B. (1980b). Feeling and thinking: Preferences need no inferences. *American Psychologist, 35,* 151–175.

Zajonc, R. B. (2001). Mere exposure: A gateway to the subliminal. *Current Directions in Psychological Science, 10,* 224–228.

Zajonc, R. B., Heingartner, A., & Herman, E. M. (1969). Social enhancement and impairment of performance in the cockroach. *Journal of Personality and Social Psychology, 13,* 83–92.

Zak, P. J., Kurzban, R., & Matzner, W. T. (2005). Oxytocin is associated with human trustworthiness. *Hormones and Behavior, 48,* 522–527.

Zak, P. J., Stanton, A. A., & Ahmadi, S. (2007). Oxytocin increases generosity in humans. *PLoS ONE, 2,* e1128.

Zaki, J. (2014). Empathy: A motivated account. *Psychological Bulletin, 140,* 1608–1647.

Zanna, M. P., & Pack, S. J. (1975). On the self-fulfilling nature of apparent sex differences in behavior. *Journal of Experimental Social Psychology, 11,* 583–591.

Zanna, M. P., & Pack, S. J. (1975). On the self-fulfilling nature of apparent sex differences in behavior. *Journal of Experimental Social Psychology, 11,* 583–591.

Zanna, M. P., & Rempel, J. K. (1988). Attitudes: A new look at an old concept. In D. Bar-Tal & A. W. Kruglanski (Eds.), *The social psychology of knowledge* (pp. 315–334). New York, NY/Paris, France: Editions de la Maison des Sciences de l'Homme.

Zarate, M. A., & Smith, E. R. (1990). Person categorization and stereotyping. *Social Cognition, 8,* 161–185.

Zaroff, C., D'Amato, R. C., & Bender, H. A. (2014). Understanding differences in cognition across the lifespan: Comparing Eastern and Western cultures. In J. M. Davis, R. C. D'Amato, J. M. Davis, & R. C. D'Amato (Eds.), *Neuropsychology of Asians and Asian Americans: Practical and theoretical considerations.* (pp. 91–116). New York, NY: Springer Science + Business Media.

Zelenski, J. M., Whelan, D. C., Nealis, L. J., Besner, C. M., Santoro, M. S., & Wynn, J. E. (2013). Personality and affective forecasting: Trait introverts underpredict the hedonic benefits of acting extraverted. *Journal of Personality and Social Psychology, 104,* 1092–1108.

Zemanek, J. E., Jr., McIntyre, R. P., & Zemanek, A. (1998). Salespersons' weight and ratings of characteristics related to effectiveness of selling. *Psychological Reports, 82,* 947–952.

Zengel, B., Edlund, J. E., & Sagarin, B. J. (2013). Sex differences in jealousy in response to infidelity: Evaluation of demographic moderators in a national random sample. *Personality and Individual Differences, 54,* 47–51.

Zentner, M., & Mitura, K. (2012). Stepping out of the caveman's shadow: Nations' gender gap predicts degree of sex differentiation in mate preferences. *Psychological Science, 23,* 1176–1185.

Zhang, Y., & Epley, N. (2009). Self-centered social exchange: Differential use of costs versus benefits in prosocial reciprocity. *Journal of Personality and Social Psychology, 97,* 796–810.

Zhang, Y., & Risen, J. L. (2014). Embodied motivation: Using a goal systems framework to understand the preference for social and physical warmth. *Journal of Personality and Social Psychology, 107,* 965–977.

Zillmann, D. (2003). Theory of affective dynamics: Emotions and moods. In J. Bryant, D. Roskos-Ewoldsen & J. Cantor (Eds.), *Communication and emotion: Essays in honor of Dolf Zillmann* (pp. 533–567). Mahwah, NJ: Lawrence Erlbaum.

Zillmann, D., Katcher, A. H., & Milavsky, B. (1972). Excitation transfer from physical exercise to subsequent aggressive behavior. *Journal of Experimental Social Psychology, 8,* 247–259.

Zimbardo, P. (2007). *The Lucifer effect: Understanding how good people turn evil.* New York, NY: Random House.

Zimbardo, P. G. (1969). The human choice: Individuation, reason, and order versus deindividuation, impulse, and chaos. In W. J. Arnold & D. Levine (Eds.), *Nebraska Symposium on Motivation* (Vol. 17th, pp. 237–307). Lincoln, NE: University of Nebraska Press.

Zuckerman, M., Silberman, J., & Hall, J. A. (2013). The relation between intelligence and religiosity: A meta-analysis and some proposed explanations. *Personality and Social Psychology Review, 17*(4), 325–354.

Author Index

Subject Index